Using 1-2-3

Special Edition

Developed by
 Corporation

QUE™ Corporation
Carmel, Indiana

Dedication

To the one million readers who *already* have made this book special.

Product Director
David P. Ewing

Editorial Director
David F. Noble, Ph.D.

Acquisitions Editor
Pegg Kennedy

Editors
Gail S. Burlakoff
Katherine Murray
Lloyd J. Short
Rebecca Whitney

Technical Editors
Stephen L. Nelson
Timothy S. Stanley
David P. Gobel
Bill Nolan
Robert Quinn

Book Design and Production
Dan Armstrong
Jennifer Matthews
Joe Ramon
Dennis Sheehan
Ann K. Taylor
Peter J. Tocco
Carrie L. Torres

Screen reproductions in this book were created by means of the INSET program of Inset Systems, Inc.

Using 1-2-3, Special Edition, is based on *Using 1-2-3*, 2nd Edition, 1-2-3 Release 2.01, and the earlier 1-2-3 Releases 1, 1A, and 2.

Acknowledgments

First and foremost, we must thank Lloyd Short for his clear vision, calm leadership, and extraordinary effort in ensuring that this book is indeed a "special" edition.

Second, we thank the many staff members at Lotus Development Corporation who have helped us stay in touch with their products and customers over the past five years.

Our thanks to Ron Person for much of the material that is now the Command Reference section.

Last but not least—many thanks to all members of the team listed on the opposite page, who made this book possible.

About the Authors

The team of authors who worked on this title is nearly as large and diverse as the book itself.

David P. Ewing, Director of Product Development for Que Corporation, is the author of Que's *1-2-3 Macro Library* and coauthor of *Using Symphony*, *Using Q&A*, and *Using Javelin*, also published by Que.

Marianne B. Fox teaches in the School of Business at Indiana University-Purdue University at Indianapolis. Fox is a partner in A & M Services, Inc., which provides computer consulting and training.

Timothy Hock, president of Software Systems, consults and trains with Lotus products.

David Maguiness, Business Applications Specialist for Que Corporation, is the revision author of Que's *1-2-3 for Business*, Second Edition.

Lawrence C. Metzelaar, who teaches in the School of Continuing Education at Indiana University-Purdue University at Indianapolis, is also a partner in A & M Services, Inc.

Patty Stonesifer, former Editor-in-Chief and Publisher of Que's journals *Absolute Reference* and *IBM PC Update*, is Director of Marketing for Que Corporation.

Bill Weil works extensively with 1-2-3 and Symphony, and contributed also to Que's *1-2-3 Tips, Tricks, and Traps*. Weil, who has 20 years of experience with computers of all sizes, formed Pacific Micro Group in 1987 to provide consulting services to large businesses.

Contents at a Glance

Table of Contents

Part I Building the 1-2-3 Spreadsheet

2 Getting Started 37

3 Learning Spreadsheet Basics 57

4 Learning Fundamental 1-2-3 Commands 77

6 Using Functions in the Spreadsheet 167

Part II Creating 1-2-3 Reports and Graphs

10 Creating and Displaying Graphs 355

Part III Customizing 1-2-3: Databases, Macros, and the Command Language

14 Using Macros To Customize Your Spreadsheet 533

15 Introduction to the Command Language 561

Part IV Quick Reference Guide to 1-2-3

Troubleshooting Section 621

Troubleshooting Index 691

1-2-3 Command Reference 701

xxiv

Trademark Acknowledgments

Que Corporation has made every attempt to supply trademark information about company names, products, and services mentioned in this book. Trademarks indicated below were derived from various sources. Que Corporation cannot attest to the accuracy of this information.

1-2-3, DIF, Freelance, Freelance Plus, Jazz, Lotus, Symphony, and Visicalc are registered trademarks of Lotus Development Corporation. Lotus HAL and Metro are trademarks of Lotus Development Corporation. Lotus HAL is distinguished from HAL, which is a trademark of Qantel for its Hotel And Leisure software.

4WORD, SQZ!, The Cambridge Spreadsheet Analyst, and Turner Hall are trademarks of Turner Hall Publishing.

Above Board is a trademark of Intel Corporation. Intel is a registered trademark of Intel Corporation.

Apple, Apple II, and Apple III are registered trademarks of Apple Computer, Inc.

Ashton-Tate, dBASE, dBASE II, dBASE III, dBASE III Plus, and Framework are registered trademarks of Ashton-Tate Company.

AT&T is a registered trademark of AT&T.

BYTE is a registered trademark of McGraw-Hill, Inc.

Cell Noter and Macro Analyzer are trademarks of Computer Associates International, Inc. Spreadsheet AUDITOR, SuperCalc, and SuperCalc² are registered trademarks of Computer Associates International, Inc.

Commodore PET is a registered trademark of Commodore Electronics Ltd.

COMPAQ, COMPAQ Deskpro, COMPAQ Portable Computer, and COMPAQ PLUS are registered trademarks of COMPAQ Computer Corporation.

Context MBA is a trademark of Context Management Systems, Inc. and LeMain, Inc.

CP/M is a registered trademark of Digital Research Inc.

EPSON is a registered trademark of EPSON Corporation. Epson FX-80, and Epson FX-100, and MX-100 are trademarks of Epson America, Inc.

Hercules Graphics Card is a trademark of Hercules Computer Technology.

IBM is a registered trademark of International Business Machines Corp. IBM PC XT, OS/2, and Personal System/2 are trademarks of International Business Machines Corp.

Micropro and WordStar are registered trademarks of Micropro International Corporation.

Microrim and R:BASE are registered trademarks of Microrim, Inc.

Microsoft and Multiplan are registered trademarks of Microsoft Corporation.

MOS Technologies and 6502 are trademarks of MOS Technologies.

NEC APC Advanced Personal Computer is a registered trademark of NEC Corporation.

PFS:FILE is a registered trademark of Software Publishing Corporation.

Radio Shack and TRS-80 are registered trademarks of Radio Shack, Division of Tandy Corporation.

Rainbow is a registered trademark of Digital Equipment Corporation.

Rampage is a registered trademark of AST Research, Inc.

Sideways is a registered trademark of Funk Software, Inc.

VisiPlot is a trademark of Paladin Software Corporation.

WordPerfect is a registered trademark of WordPerfect Corporation.

Z80 is a registered trademark of Zilog, Inc.

Zenith is a registered trademark of Zenith Electronics Corporation.

Conventions Used In This Book

A number of conventions are used in *Using 1-2-3* to help you learn the program. One example is provided of each convention to help you distinguish among the different elements in 1-2-3.

References to keys are as they appear on the keyboard of the IBM Personal Computer. Direct quotations of words that appear on the screen are spelled as they appear on the screen and are printed in a `special typeface`. Information you are asked to type is printed in italic; if the context indicates clearly what is to be typed, no special typeface is used.

The first letter of each command from 1-2-3's menu system appears in **boldface**: **/R**ange **F**ormat **C**urrency. Abbreviated commands appear as in the following example: /RFC. **/R**ange **F**ormat **C**urrency indicates that you type /rfc to select this command if you are entering it manually. The first letter of menu choices also appears in boldface: **C**opy.

Words printed in uppercase include range names (SALES), functions (@PMT), modes (READY), and cell references (A1..G5).

Conventions that pertain to macros deserve special mention here:

1. Macro names (Alt-character combinations) appear with the backslash (\) and single-character name in lowercase: \a. In this example, the \ indicates that you press the Alt key and hold it down while you also press the A key.

2. All /x macro commands, such as /xm or /xn, appear in lowercase, but commands from 1-2-3's command language within braces appear in uppercase: {WAIT}.

3. 1-2-3 menu keystrokes in a macro line appear in lowercase: /rnc.

4. Range names within macros appear in uppercase: /rncTEST.

5. In macros, representations of cursor-movement keys, such as {DOWN}; function keys, such as {CALC}; and editing keys, such as {DEL}, appear in uppercase letters and are surrounded by braces.

6. Enter is represented by the tilde (~). (Note that throughout the text, Enter is used instead of Return.)

The function keys, F1 through F10, are used for special situations in 1-2-3. In the text, the function key number is usually followed by the name in parentheses: F10 (Graph).

Ctrl-Break indicates that you press the Ctrl key and hold it down while you press also the Break key. Other hyphenated key combinations, such as Alt-F10, are performed in the same manner.

Introduction

In October 1986, two of us from Que Corporation stood outside Lotus® Development's Cambridge, Massachusetts headquarters, staring up at the giant three-story diskette that had been erected that day to celebrate the sale of the two-millionth copy of 1-2-3®. The sounds of the nearby river, the darkness of the night, and the position of the floodlights heightened the impact of this Paul Bunyanesque creation.

Our awe was not related to the structure itself, however, or even to the enormous business success it represented. The message we received was the importance of our obligation at Que to provide excellent tutorial and reference books for those two million users. So as we stood there looking up, we wondered, "How do you get your arms around an audience that big?"

Que and 1-2-3

The answer for us at Que is not unlike the famous admonition used by countless mothers in years past: You listen, and you listen hard. We make it our business to listen to personal computer users. They write to us, they talk to us, they call us; and we listen. We try to respond to their needs through the books and journals we publish.

We have learned from all this communication that 1-2-3 is being purchased, pushed, and programmed for purposes and in ways the eight original employees who started Lotus Development Corporation in 1982 never dreamed possible. We also learned that the book *Using 1-2-3* is being used in equally diverse ways.

Users of 1-2-3 tell us they use this package for a vast number of applications, including project management, inventory control, general ledger maintenance, statistical analysis, engineering applications, cashflow analysis, storing and updating mailing lists, forecasting, servicing accounts receivable and bills of materials, portfolio management, and maintaining personnel records. The list of 1-2-3 applications is nearly as long, and as diverse, as the audience.

Using 1-2-3, Special Edition: How Did We Get Here?

The first edition of *Using 1-2-3,* published in the fall of 1983, was a relatively slim tutorial, aimed at teaching spreadsheet basics to a presumed audience of accountants, analysts, and number crunchers. We envisioned that our audience would use 1-2-3 to automate their existing financial applications. The authors of that book were two Que employees who actually were far more representative of our prospective readers than of a typical authoring team.

Geoffrey T. LeBlond was an MBA graduate student at Indiana University who took on the task of co-authoring the first edition of *Using 1-2-3* with Douglas Ford Cobb. Doug, armed with his M.S. in accounting from New York University, came to Que from his previous position as president of his own computer consulting firm. The enthusiasm these two men brought to the new software and the corresponding book project was reflected in the text, which quickly became the industry's best-selling book—a position it has held ever since.

Both Geoff and Doug moved on to more entrepreneurial activities in 1984 and now own and operate their own businesses. Geoff has become one of the most respected software developers in our industry, creating add-in software for Lotus products. His most recent product, 4WORD™, is a powerful add-in word processor that can be activated from within 1-2-3. Doug returned home to head his own firm, Cobb & Associates, which is located in Louisville, Kentucky.

The second edition of *Using 1-2-3,* which was published in 1985, was thoroughly rewritten by another financial analyst, Tom Carlton. This edition included the new and advanced features of 1-2-3, Release 2, that made the product even more versatile and useful for our same perceived audience.

In both of these editions, the book retained the special magic that helped it maintain its place as *the* book on 1-2-3. Readers recommended it to fellow users, who passed their copies on to still more readers. *Using 1-2-3,* 2nd Edition, became the industry standard for users wanting a targeted, yet friendly tutorial on 1-2-3.

Why the Special Edition?

In the meantime, we were collecting more and more information indicating that both the 1-2-3 audience and the use of this book were changing. Although the majority of 1-2-3 users are still automating and analyzing number-oriented applications, their diversity is far wider than we had originally presumed.

We came to realize that people were using *Using 1-2-3*, 2nd Edition, as a reference book as much as an entry-level tutorial. Through the continually increasing amount of reader research going on at Que, we learned that our readers had two distinct needs: some readers were more interested in learning to use the software quickly with a step-by-step tutorial, without spending a large amount of time learning the program; others wanted to "jump in" to the program and use our book as a reference to get them out of troublesome jams and to explain seldom-used concepts and commands.

At the end of 1986, we started a "wish list" of features that would enhance this already number one text. We placed great importance on preserving the excellent tutorial of the early editions, while addressing the growing user need for ready-reference materials. As we approached the sale of our one-millionth copy of *Using 1-2-3*, we decided to celebrate by producing a text that reflected our enthusiasm for our audience and its diversity as well as the wealth of ideas and suggestions we had accumulated. It was this goal, this attempt to "get our arms around our audience," that compelled us to create this special edition of *Using 1-2-3*.

What Is the Special Edition?

Using 1-2-3, Special Edition, is a unique book. After rewriting and expanding the text by more than 400 pages, we are bringing into the microcomputer book publishing market a book that is actually two complete books in one. In this book, you'll find 15 chapters of targeted, easy-to-follow tutorial text combined with an all-new Quick Reference section.

The detailed tutorial section has been expanded to include hands-on practice exercises for readers eager to apply the information provided. We've included new information on the IBM Personal System/2™, the Lotus Command Language, database management, Lotus HAL™, and other popular add-in and add-on programs.

The all-new Quick Reference Guide to 1-2-3 combines two types of information. The comprehensive Troubleshooting Section cites 70 of the most common pitfalls encountered by 1-2-3 users and offers solutions for fast recovery. The 165-page Command Reference lists 110 1-2-3 commands and combinations and provides quick instructions, comments, and cautions to give users rapid access to the information they need when using 1-2-3.

How Did We Do It?

In order to create a book for such a diverse audience, we used a large team of experts to provide critiques, write specific sections, and verify technical accuracy.

A team of university instructors developed the hands-on exercises, based on their extensive experience with adults learning 1-2-3. An experienced West Coast consultant developed the Troubleshooting Section based on the everyday 1-2-3 problems he has solved while advising his clients. Our staff at Que added information about Lotus HAL and other add-in and add-on programs from experience gained developing materials and applications on 1-2-3 for *Absolute Reference*, our monthly journal for 1-2-3 and Symphony users.

The list of contributors goes on, but the message is clear: No one person could possibly represent—or attempt to fill—the needs of two million 1-2-3 users. For that reason, we sought out a variety of people who *could* represent the diversity of that audience. This book is, in large part, a tribute to that diversity.

Who Should Read This Book?

If you own 1-2-3 or are considering purchasing the program, you should own this book. In its new form, *Using 1-2-3,* Special Edition, has something for everyone.

If you are new to 1-2-3, the detailed tutorial information will complement the Lotus instructional material by providing easy-to-read, easy-to-follow instructions written in a style designed to give you maximum information in the quickest form possible.

If you have been using 1-2-3 for a while, the Troubleshooting Section will get you out of costly jams and provide quick solutions to common stumbling blocks.

If you have mastered the fundamentals of 1-2-3, the 1-2-3 Command Reference, with its easy-to-find format, will become a constant companion, giving you immediate access to command syntax and information.

The Details of This Book

Flip through the book to get a better sense of the organization and layout. We have purposefully organized the book to follow the natural flow of learning and using 1-2-3.

Part I—Building the 1-2-3 Spreadsheet

Chapter 1, "An Overview of 1-2-3," introduces you to electronic spreadsheets, describes the basic features of 1-2-3, and also describes many of the popular 1-2-3 add-in and add-on programs.

Chapter 2, "Getting Started," shows you how to start up and exit 1-2-3, describes how to use the keyboard and screen display with 1-2-3, and tells you how to access the program's Help systems.

Chapter 3, "Learning Spreadsheet Basics," shows you how to move the cell pointer around the worksheet, and starts you building a spreadsheet by entering and editing data and formulas.

Chapter 4, "Learning Fundamental 1-2-3 Commands," teaches you how to use the command menus and how to use and name "ranges" (blocks of cells) in the worksheet. This chapter provides a comprehensive tutorial and reference for the **Worksheet, Range, Copy, Move, System,** and **Quit** commands.

Chapter 5, "Formatting Cell Contents," shows you how to change the way data is displayed in the worksheet (for example, as currency, percentages, dates, or in scientific notation).

Chapter 6, "Using Functions in the Spreadsheet," provides an extensive tutorial and complete reference for 1-2-3's built-in formulas, the @functions. The functions can be learned and referenced according to the following groups: mathematical, statistical, financial, data-management, logical, special, date and time, and string.

Chapter 7, "Managing Files in 1-2-3," teaches you the basics of saving, retrieving, listing, and protecting your 1-2-3 files, and how to extract and combine data from portions of files. The chapter also shows you how to use DOS subdirectories with 1-2-3, and how to use the Translate utility program to transfer files between different Releases of 1-2-3 and between 1-2-3 and other programs.

Chapter 8, "Building a Model Spreadsheet: Hands-On Practice," provides a "quick-start" opportunity to use your newly acquired skills to build a model spreadsheet in a realistic practice session.

Part II—Creating 1-2-3 Reports and Graphs

Chapter 9, "Printing Reports," shows you how to print basic draft-quality reports from your 1-2-3 spreadsheets, and how to use a variety of print options to enhance the appearance of your printed reports. The chapter also shows you how to tailor 1-2-3 to your specific hardware and printing needs.

Chapter 10, "Creating and Displaying Graphs," shows you how to take advantage of 1-2-3's considerable graphics capabilities by creating basic line, bar, stacked-bar, XY, and pie graphs. The chapter shows you how to enhance basic graphs in a variety of ways including adding legends and titles, changing scale, and displaying graphs in color.

Chapter 11, "Printing Graphs," teaches you how to use the PrintGraph utility program to print your graphs, and how to improve the appearance of printed graphs. The chapter also shows you how to tailor PrintGraph to your particular hardware setup.

Chapter 12, "Creating Output: Hands-On Practice," provides another quick-start opportunity to test your printing and graphing skills in a realistic practice session.

Part III—Customizing 1-2-3: Databases, Macros, and the Command Language

Chapter 13, "Managing Databases with 1-2-3," shows you how the 1-2-3 spreadsheet can give you many of the same capabilities of specialized database-management programs, by allowing you to create and maintain large lists of data. The chapter shows you how to create, modify, and sort the database, and search for individual records from the database. You will also learn how to load and use data from other programs, and how to use specialized statistical functions to extract meaningful information from the database.

Chapter 14, "Using Macros To Customize Your Spreadsheet," teaches you how to create and use 1-2-3 macros to reduce keyboard activity by automating repetitive tasks. The chapter also shows you how to debug the macros you create, and gives numerous examples of frequently used macros.

Chapter 15, "Introduction to the Command Language," presents the powerful Lotus Command Language in a step-by-step, simple-to-complex tutorial that will get you started developing your own Command Language programs. The chapter includes a complete reference for all the LCL commands, with numerous examples of their use.

Part IV—Quick Reference Guide to 1-2-3

"Troubleshooting Section"—an easy-to-use problem-solving section that can help everyone from the novice user to the most advanced "power user." You can use the section both as a reference when you have problems and as a source of sage and practical advice and tips during "browsing sessions."

"1-2-3 Command Reference"—a quick, easy-to-use, and comprehensive guide to the procedures for using almost every command on the command menus and in the PrintGraph program. The section also gives numerous Reminders, Important Cues, Cautions, and Warnings that will greatly simplify and expedite your day-to-day use of 1-2-3.

The book also includes an appendix to show you how to install 1-2-3 on a hard disk or a floppy disk system for the IBM PC, PC-compatible machines, or the IBM PS/2 family of computers.

Other Titles To Enhance Your Personal Computing

Although *Using 1-2-3,* Special Edition, is the largest and most comprehensive book Que has ever published, no single book can fill all your information needs for increasing your effectiveness with personal computers and 1-2-3.

Que Corporation publishes a full line of microcomputer books with the same philosophy that underlies this best-seller: Provide readers with concise, practical information that will enhance their use of computers and software.

Using PC DOS, 2nd Edition, (or its DOS-compatible counterpart, *MS-DOS User's Guide,* 2nd Edition) provides the same type of strong tutorial and complete Command Reference that you will find in *Using 1-2-3,* Special Edition. Either of these books will enhance your control of your system and provide valuable tips on better ways to organize your approach to DOS.

Our research has shown us that most 1-2-3 users today use hard disk systems. For that reason, *Using 1-2-3,* Special Edition, was expanded to include significant details on how to install and use 1-2-3 on a hard disk. If you want to know more about getting the most from your hard disk, streamlining your use of directories, creating batch files, and reaping the maximum overall benefit from your hard disk investment, Que's *Managing Your Hard Disk* will be an invaluable addition to your library.

Learning More about 1-2-3

If *Using 1-2-3,* Special Edition, doesn't satisfy your appetite for information about 1-2-3, you're in good company: Hundreds of thousands of *Using 1-2-3* readers have gone on to purchase one or more additional Que books about 1-2-3.

1-2-3 for Business, 2nd Edition, provides ready-to-run (or ready-to-modify, depending on your application) models for 1-2-3 Release 2.01. These applications reflect the list of business models most frequently mentioned by our readers, including a General Ledger, an Accounts Receivable system, and a Loan Amortization model.

1-2-3 Tips, Tricks, and Traps, 2nd Edition, offers hundreds of concise, hard-hitting tips and tricks to keep you moving quickly in your expanded use of 1-2-3. Similarly, by avoiding the traps discussed in this book, you can save valuable time that you might otherwise spend getting around trouble spots or recovering lost or damaged data.

1-2-3 Command Language is for 1-2-3 users who want to learn how to implement programs and macros, using the more sophisticated Command Language provided in 1-2-3, Release 2.

Using Lotus HAL is a new title from Que, designed to help 1-2-3 users get the most from Lotus Development's powerful new natural-language processor.

1-2-3 QueCards are an all-new reference-product concept from Que, incorporating quick-access information on 1-2-3 commands and functions in an index-card format that is easy to use. Even if you are an experienced 1-2-3 user, the concise information presented on these cards can solve the frustration of searching through the user's manual when you simply need to find a particular command syntax and a few pointers.

1-2-3 Macro Library, 2nd Edition, contains dozens of ready-to-run macros popular with 1-2-3 users who want to streamline their work by automating often-repeated procedures.

Absolute Reference, now entering its fifth year in publication, is Que's monthly journal read by thousands of 1-2-3 and Symphony users eager to get new information, applications, and tips every month.

Summary

Using 1-2-3 has become our all-time best-seller largely because of Que's philosophy of providing quality text that is targeted appropriately for the real-life 1-2-3 user. Because of our dedication to this goal, we ultimately have only one way of getting better: We need to hear from you. Let us know how you feel about this book or any other Que title. We want to keep improving our books, and you are our best source of direction.

And, finally, let us know how you are *Using 1-2-3*!

Part I

Building the
1-2-3 Spreadsheet

Includes

An Overview of 1-2-3

Getting Started

Learning Spreadsheet Basics

Learning Fundamental 1-2-3 Commands

Formatting Cell Contents

Using Functions in the Spreadsheet

Managing Files in 1-2-3

Building a Model Spreadsheet:
Hands-On Practice

1

An Overview of 1-2-3

Introduced in 1983, 1-2-3 was hailed immediately as the most significant new software product since VisiCalc®, which appeared in 1978. In 1987, four years after it was introduced to computer users, 1-2-3 continues to dominate the business software market as the most impressive business tool available today. It is firmly entrenched as the best-selling software program for the IBM® PC and compatible computers, and for IBM Personal System/2 computers.

The excitement over 1-2-3 comes primarily from the program's tremendous power. One of the first integrated office-management software programs, 1-2-3 means 3 programs in 1. It combines three of the most popular business applications programs (electronic spreadsheet, business graphics, and data management) into one sophisticated program.

When 1-2-3 was introduced, it was one of the first members of a new generation of microcomputer software programs designed specifically for 16-bit computers like the IBM Personal Computer. Designed to take full advantage of the computer's speed and memory capacity, 1-2-3, Releases 1 and 1A, quickly became the standard for judging all other software programs with similar capabilities. As computer hardware advanced, providing power far beyond the original IBM PC, 1-2-3 kept in step by taking advantage of the newer machines' expanded capabilities. With the availability (and lower costs) of more memory, faster speed, and hard disk drives, Lotus developed Release 2, adding a host of exciting features and capabilities that significantly increase the power originally available in Release 1A.

This chapter introduces you to the power in Release 2. You'll learn about the basic features that classify 1-2-3 as a traditional spreadsheet software program, and about the special features that make it an outstanding program.

This overview of 1-2-3 will help you understand 1-2-3's design and prepare you for applying 1-2-3 to your business tasks.

What is 1-2-3?

1-2-3 integrates graphics and data management with a first-rate spreadsheet. What makes 1-2-3 such an impressive spreadsheet program? 1-2-3's overall design, built-in functions, and commands are based on the conventions used by such early spreadsheet programs as VisiCalc and SuperCalc®. Those conventions are still part of 1-2-3; but today they are greatly improved, making 1-2-3 the most popular business software ever developed.

What are the conventions that make 1-2-3 an excellent spreadsheet program? First, 1-2-3 is designed as an "electronic" replacement for the accountant's columnar pad, pencil, and calculator. Second, 1-2-3 understands relationships among all of the numbers and formulas in a single application, and automatically updates values whenever a change occurs. Third, 1-2-3's commands simplify and automate all the procedures related to creating, changing, updating, printing, and graphing spreadsheet data.

The 1-2-3 "Electronic" Spreadsheet

Basically, 1-2-3 is an electronic spreadsheet—an electronic replacement for the traditional financial modeling tools: the accountant's columnar pad, pencil, and calculator. In some ways, spreadsheet programs are to those tools what word processors are to typewriters. Spreadsheets offer dramatic improvements in ease of creating, editing, and using financial models.

The electronic spreadsheet is the foundation of the 1-2-3 program. The framework of this spreadsheet contains the graphics and data-management elements of the program. Graphics are produced through the use of spreadsheet commands. Data management occurs in the standard row-column spreadsheet layout.

The importance of the spreadsheet as the basis for the whole product cannot be overemphasized. All the commands for the related features are initiated from the same main command menu as the spreadsheet commands, and all the commands are in the same style. (For a complete listing of all of 1-2-3's commands, see the Command Menu Map included at the back of the book.) All of 1-2-3's special features originate from the spreadsheet. For instance, in data management, the database is composed of records that are cell entries in a spreadsheet. Similarly, macros and Command Language programs are statements placed in adjacent cells in out-of-the-way sections of a spreadsheet. And all the commands for displaying graphs refer to entries in the spreadsheet and use these entries to draw graphs on the screen.

The typical electronic spreadsheet configures a computer's memory to resemble an accountant's columnar pad. Because this "pad" exists in the dynamic world of the computer's memory, the pad is different from paper pads in some important ways. For one thing, electronic spreadsheets are much larger than their paper counterparts. 1-2-3 has 8,192 rows and 256 columns!

Each row in 1-2-3 is assigned a number, and each column a letter. The intersections of the rows and columns are called *cells*. Cells are identified by their row-column coordinates. For example, the cell located at the intersection of column A and row 15 is called A15. The cell at the intersection of column X and row 55 is called X55. Cells can be filled with three kinds of information: numbers; mathematical formulas, including special spreadsheet functions; and text (or labels).

A *cell pointer* allows you to write information into the cells much as a pencil lets you write on a piece of paper. In 1-2-3, as in most spreadsheets, the cell pointer looks like a bright rectangle on the computer's screen. The cell pointer typically is one row high and one column wide.

With 8,192 rows and 256 columns, the 1-2-3 worksheet contains more than 2,000,000 cells. Each column is assigned a letter value ranging from A for the first column to IV for the last. A good way to visualize the worksheet is as one giant sheet of grid paper that is about 21 feet wide and 171 feet high!

Although the 1-2-3 spreadsheet contains 256 columns and 8,192 rows, there are some limitations to using the entire sheet. If you imagine storing just one character in each of the 2,097,152 cells that are available, you end up with a worksheet that is far larger than the 640K maximum random-access memory (RAM) of an IBM PC.

For Release 2, the program alone requires 215K of RAM. 1-2-3 needs this amount of RAM because the program remembers cell formats, worksheet and command ranges, print options, and graph settings. (See table 1.1 for a complete list of 1-2-3 specifications.) Although some information is saved automatically by 1-2-3, some information must be saved by the user. (For more information, see "1-2-3's Use of Memory" later in the chapter.)

Because the 1-2-3 grid is so large, the entire spreadsheet cannot be viewed on the screen at one time. The screen thus serves as a window onto the worksheet. To view other parts of the sheet, you *scroll* the cell pointer across and down (or up) the worksheet with the arrow keys (and other *cursor-movement keys*; see Chapter 3). When the cell pointer reaches the edge of the current window, the window begins to shift to follow the cell pointer across and down (or up) the sheet.

Table 1.1
1-2-3 Release 2 at a Glance

Published by:
  Lotus Development Corporation
  55 Cambridge Parkway
  Cambridge, Massachusetts 02142

System requirements:
  IBM PC or compatible
  Display: color or monochrome
  Disk capacity: two 360K double-sided disk drives
  Memory size: 256K
  Maximum usable memory size: 640K
  Operating system: PC DOS V2.0 or above
  Other hardware: color/graphics adapter, printer, plotter, expanded
      memory (to 4 megabytes), 8087 coprocessor, hard disk

Price: $495.00

Also available for:
  IBM Personal Computer AT
  IBM PS/2 Computers
  IBM 3270 PC
  COMPAQ Portable Computer
  COMPAQ Deskpro
  COMPAQ 286
  AT&T PC 6300
  1-2-3 certified compatibles

To illustrate the window concept, imagine cutting a hole one inch square in a piece of cardboard. If you placed the cardboard over this page, you would be able to see only a one-inch square piece of text. Naturally, the rest of the text is still on the page; it is simply hidden from view. When you move the cardboard around the page (in much the same way that the window moves when the cursor-movement keys are used), different parts of the page become visible.

Figure 1.1 gives you an idea of the vast scope of the 1-2-3 spreadsheet. If you apply the window concept to an imaginary 1-2-3 worksheet in which the default column width of 9 characters is used, you can readily understand that only 20 rows and 8 columns can be seen on-screen at one time.

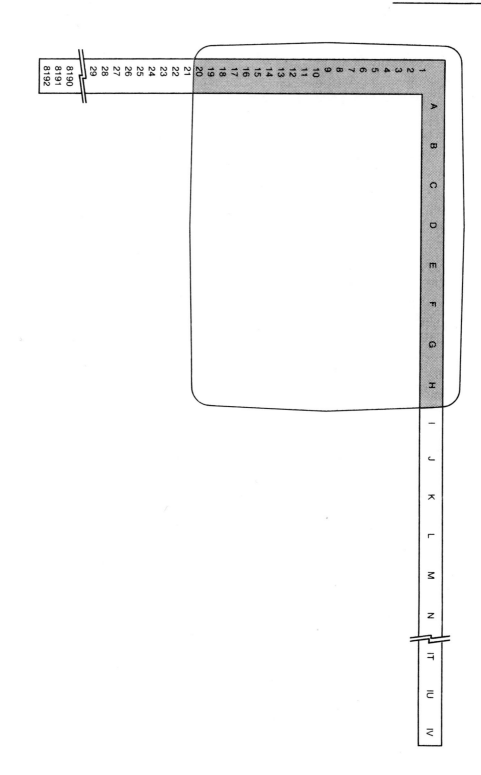

Fig. 1.1
The 1-2-3 Spreadsheet, showing the on-screen portion.

Formulas

Electronic spreadsheets allow mathematical relationships to be created between cells. For example, if the cell named C1 contains the formula

+A1+B1

then C1 will display the sum of the contents of cells A1 and B1. (The + sign before A1 tells 1-2-3 that this is a formula, not text.) The cell references serve as variables in the equation. No matter what numbers are entered in A1 and B1, cell C1 will always return their sum. For example, if cell A1 contains the number 5 and cell B1 contains the number 10, the formula in cell C1 returns the value 15. If you change the number in cell A1 to 4, C1 will also change to 14. Of course, spreadsheet formulas can be much more complex than this simple example. A cell can be added to, subtracted from, multiplied by, or divided by any other cell.

Playing "What If"

Through formulas, 1-2-3 maintains the relationships between cells. Until you decide to change the relationships, every sum, product, division, subtraction, average, and net present value will remain the same. Each time you enter data into the model, computations will be calculated at your command with no effort on your part. All of these computations will be calculated correctly; spreadsheets don't make math errors. And next month, when you decide to use the same model again, the formulas will still be set, ready to calculate at your command.

Even more important, spreadsheet software allows you to play "what if" with your model. After a set of mathematical relationships has been built into the worksheet, the worksheet can be recalculated with amazing speed, using different sets of assumptions. If you use only paper, a pencil, and a calculator to build your models, every change to the model will require recalculating every relationship in the model. If the model has 100 formulas and you change the first one, you must make 100 calculations by hand so that the change flows through the entire model. If, on the other hand, you use a spreadsheet, the same change requires the press of only a few keys; the program does the rest. This capability permits extensive "what if" analysis.

For example, suppose that you build a financial projection for your business for the years 1987 through 1992. In building this forecast, you assume that your sales will grow at an annual rate of 10 percent. But what happens to your projections if the rate of growth is only 3 percent? What if the rate is 15 percent? If you were using a pencil and a calculator to do this analysis, it might take hours to compute the effects of these changes. With 1-2-3 or other electronic spreadsheets, all that is required is to change the growth rate you entered in the sheet and strike one key to recompute. The entire process takes just seconds.

As your models become more complex, this capability becomes more and more valuable.

Functions

As explained previously, you can create simple formulas involving only a few cells by entering cell addresses with the appropriate operator (+, -, /, *). 1-2-3 functions are the tools for creating complex formulas. Spreadsheet functions are shortcuts that help the user perform common mathematical computations with a minimum of typing. Functions are like abbreviations for otherwise long and cumbersome formulas. You use an @ symbol to signal 1-2-3 that an expression is a function. For instance, the SUM function in 1-2-3 is written as @SUM(A1..C1).

1-2-3 offers all the spreadsheet functions you would expect to find in a powerful spreadsheet program—and then some. The functions available in 1-2-3 have become a standard that has been matched eventually by every competing spreadsheet and integrated package. The complete set of functions in 1-2-3 cover a wide range of application needs from financial to statistical to string functions. As illustrated in Chapter 15, combining 1-2-3's set of functions with the program's Command Language provides the capabilities available in high-level programming languages.

Mathematical Functions

1-2-3 offers a complete set of mathematical functions, not only for use in business, but also for engineering and scientific use. 1-2-3 includes such common mathematical functions as @LOG, @EXP, @SQRT, @INT, and @ABS; a complete set of common trigonometric functions; a random-number-generator function; and functions for rounding and determining remainders.

Financial Functions

1-2-3 has a wealth of financial functions. In addition to the basic financial functions for net present value and internal rate of return calculations, the program includes a complete set of functions for annuity and compound growth rate calculations. 1-2-3 even has functions for calculating depreciation by several common methods—straight line, sum of the years digits, and double declining balance.

Statistical Functions

1-2-3 offers basic statistical functions to calculate the sum, average, minimum, maximum, count, variance, and standard deviation of a range of values. These functions provide the worksheet's basic statistical capabilities. Corresponding database statistical functions perform the same calculations on those rows of a 1-2-3 database that meet specified selection criteria.

For those who need greater statistical capabilities, 1-2-3 also includes a multiple regression command (not a function) that can perform a regression with up to 16 independent variables.

String Functions

1-2-3's string functions give you the power to manipulate strings in much the same way that you manipulate numbers in the spreadsheet. The @FIND function, for example, allows you to locate the starting position of one string within another string. With the @MID, @LEFT, and @RIGHT functions, you can extract one string from another. 1-2-3 includes several other string functions that provide a complete capability for manipulating alphanumeric data. These functions significantly enhance the integration of 1-2-3's spreadsheet and database capabilities.

Date and Time Functions

The 1-2-3 date and time functions give you tremendous flexibility for manipulating dates and times in your worksheets. With the basic @NOW function, you can capture the current date and time from your system clock. The @DATE and @DATEVALUE functions allow you to enter dates in numeric or string formats, whereas @TIME and @TIMEVALUE give you the same capability for times.

Once dates and times are stored as date serial numbers in the worksheet, you can use ordinary mathematical commands to perform date and time arithmetic. A complete set of functions lets you extract the second, minute, hour, day, month, and year from a date serial number. 1-2-3 also has a variety of formats for displaying date serial numbers as dates and times in the worksheet.

Special Functions

Special 1-2-3 functions include those to change numeric entries to strings (and vice versa), and others that help you manage the use of both numbers and strings in your worksheets. Also included are such special functions as @@, the indirect addressing function, and @CELL.

@CELL provides information about the contents of spreadsheet cells. If, for example, you enter @CELL("width",b12..b12), 1-2-3 returns the width of column B as viewed in the current window. In addition to indicating width, the @CELL function can indicate a cell's address, data type, label prefix, format, or row and column number.

Spreadsheet Commands

1-2-3 includes several important commands that manipulate the worksheet in various ways. For example, all electronic spreadsheets include a command (or commands) that can be used to format the appearance of the contents of cells in the sheet. These commands can alter the display to make numbers appear in a variety of forms. Commands are activated by pressing the slash (/) key. After the slash is typed, a menu of commands appears on the screen. The user then selects the command to be implemented.

Spreadsheet commands can be used at every phase of building and using a model. Because a spreadsheet holds in the computer's memory a model while you build it, you are not bound by the physical limitations of the printed page. Are some of your formulas repeated in different sections of your model? Use the spreadsheet's copy feature to quickly project your assumptions from one cell to another. Did you forget a row or a column? Simply insert the row or column at the appropriate point. Is one of your assumptions or formulas incorrect, or is there a typographical error in one of your headings? Correct the error instantly with 1-2-3's editing capabilities.

1-2-3 has many commands that allow the user to perform a number of tasks in the spreadsheet. Commands are available to format the worksheet, name ranges, erase and copy data, perform calculations, store files, protect worksheet cells, protect files with passwords, and print your spreadsheets.

Formatting the Worksheet

1-2-3 offers a wide variety of formats for numeric entries. These formats include the ability to display or print numbers with embedded commas, dollar signs, parentheses, or percent signs, and to specify the exact number of digits that will be displayed to the right of the decimal. For example, 1-2-3 can format the number 12345 to look like $12,345.00, 12,345, 1.2345+4E, or 12345; the number -12345 to look like ($12,345.00) or -12,345; and the number .45 to look like 45% or $.45. (The details of all of 1-2-3's cell formats are covered in Chapter 5.)

These formatting features allow users to create finished reports and financial statements directly from analyses. Numbers can appear as you would expect them to in a formal document, and eye-pleasing spacing can be achieved by varying column widths.

In 1-2-3, formats are always assigned to a range of cells. In fact, the format command is an option of a higher level command called /**R**ange. A range in 1-2-3 can be as small as a single cell or as large as the entire worksheet. When you assign a format, the program prompts you to provide the appropriate range for that format by pointing to its limits with the cell pointer.

International Formats

International formats and an international character set became available with Release 2. Through the /**W**orksheet **G**lobal **D**efault command, you have the options of changing **C**urrency, **D**ate, and **T**ime formats to International formats. The **C**urrency option, for example, enables you to change the default dollar sign ($) to a foreign currency sign like that for the British pound (£) if you plan to use that format regularly throughout your worksheet. The international character set, referred to as the Lotus International Character Set (LICS), provides characters from many languages. In the 1-2-3 manual, you will find a complete list of the international and special characters available in LICS.

Naming Ranges

1-2-3 also allows a name to be assigned to a range. This feature lets you label an area for use in formulas or as the range for a command. For example, if a part of your worksheet has been named SUMMARY, you can tell 1-2-3 to print the section of the sheet called SUMMARY (see fig. 1.2). Only the cells contained in that region will be printed. Similarly, if you have created a temporary area called SCRATCH, you can use that name with 1-2-3's /RE (for /**R**ange **E**rase) command to blank that part of the screen. (This exciting feature is discussed in Chapter 4.)

Copying Cell Entries

1-2-3 uses a /**C**opy command to make replicas of values, labels, or formulas in other cells. This replication allows the user to develop a model quickly by

Fig. 1.2

Using range names in 1-2-3.

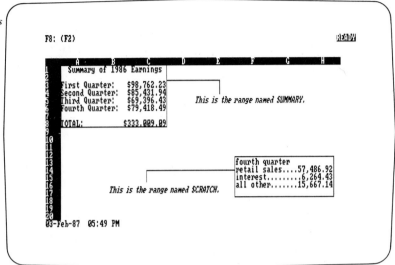

building a few key relationships, then replicating them over the entire workspace.

1-2-3 allows cell references to be defined as relative or absolute at the time the cell is defined. Relative cell references are entered in the normal way. Absolute references are entered with a dollar sign ($) preceding the reference. For example, in the formula

+A1+$A2+A$3+$A$4

the reference to cell A1 is relative. The references to cells A2 and A3 are mixed (relative in one direction and absolute in the other). The reference to A4 is absolute in both directions.

This method of determining absolute and relative references has some interesting advantages. For example, you can /Copy a single cell into a block of cells without making complicated formula adjustments. (See Chapter 4 for complete details of this important feature.)

Recalculating the Worksheet

1-2-3 offers a *natural* order of recalculation. Natural recalculation begins by discerning the most fundamental cell in the worksheet (that is, the cell on which most other cells are based). This cell is evaluated first. Next, the program searches for the second most basic formula in the worksheet and evaluates that cell. This process continues until the entire worksheet is recomputed.

Accompanying natural recalculation is the capability to perform iterative calculations. In 1-2-3, the user can specify the number of passes the program should make through the same worksheet each time the worksheet is recalculated. Iterative calculation helps to relieve the problem of circular references.

The addition of these two features simplifies the design and use of complex spreadsheets. With 1-2-3, the user does not have to be as careful about planning the locations of the various model sections. Instead, the computer can manage the order of recalculation. (More details on recalculation are provided in Chapter 4.)

1-2-3 File Commands

1-2-3 offers the basic loading and saving commands found in other electronic spreadsheets. Three types of files can be created: normal spreadsheet files (.WK1), text files (.PRN), and graph files (.PIC). In addition, the program has the capacity to load a text file created by another program, including WordStar®, WordPerfect®, Microsoft® Word, and other word-processing files. This feature allows you to load information from other sources into 1-2-3.

1-2-3 can import files created by dBASE II®, dBASE III®, dBASE III® Plus, Jazz®, and VisiCalc. The program also has a utility that translates a dBASE® file into a .WK1 file. The file will appear in standard 1-2-3 database format, with each row representing a record and each column representing a field. (Chapter 7, "File Operations," covers in detail the use of 1-2-3's storage commands.)

Finally, 1-2-3 Release 2 has the capability to read directly both Release 1A and Symphony® worksheets. Release 2 also has utilities to write worksheets that those two programs can read.

Protecting Cells and Files

1-2-3 allows you to protect cells in a worksheet so that changes cannot be made, for example, in cells that contain important formulas. You can also hide ranges of cells and use passwords to protect your worksheets when you save them on disk.

Whenever you protect an area of your worksheet, you use two commands: the /Worksheet Global Protection command and the /Range Protect command. These commands prevent someone from erasing, moving, or changing the cells even though the cell contents are displayed on the screen. If you also want to prevent the display of cell contents, you can use the /Range Format Hidden command.

1-2-3 also lets you password protect your worksheet files when you save them. A password-protected file is encrypted and cannot be examined or retrieved without the password. Your confidential or sensitive data is protected from use by anyone who does not have the correct password.

Printing the Worksheet

1-2-3 has more printing flexibility than any other spreadsheet. The user has the choice of printing the entire worksheet or any part of the worksheet. In addition, the user can alter the left, right, top, and bottom margins on the page; change the page length and width; insert page headers and footers, which can even contain the date and page number; and send setup codes to the printer to alter the size and style of type used to print. (For more information on printing, see Chapter 9.)

1-2-3 Graphics

The spreadsheet alone makes 1-2-3 a powerful program with all the capabilities needed by many users. Graphics added to 1-2-3's spreadsheet extend 1-2-3 as a tool for presenting data and conducting "what if" analysis. As originally conceived by Mitch Kapor, the creator of 1-2-3, graphics capability was planned as a significant feature of 1-2-3. Mitch Kapor's background in graphics software design is evident in the graphics portion of 1-2-3.

The capability of converting spreadsheet data into graphs is not unique to 1-2-3. Kapor's own program, VisiPlot™, made graphics available to VisiCalc users. However, 1-2-3 ties the graphics capability directly into the spreadsheet so that there is no need to use a DIF® (VisiCalc), SDI (SuperCalc), SYLK (Multiplan®), or other communications file. 1-2-3's graphics capability is also remarkably versatile, easy to use, and even allows you to do "what if" analysis with the graphs.

1-2-3 has five basic graph types: bar, stacked bar, line, scatter, and pie. Up to six ranges of data can be represented on a single graph (except for pie graphs and scatter diagrams). This means, for example, that a line graph with six different lines can be created.

Graphs are created with 1-2-3's /Graph command. Although the program has a number of options, the user need specify only a graph type and a single data range. After providing the required information, the user simply types v, for View. This will plot the graph to the screen. If the computer has both a color and a monochrome display, the graph will appear on the color screen while the spreadsheet remains on the monochrome monitor. If there is only a color monitor, the graph will replace the spreadsheet on the display until a key is pressed.

1-2-3 gives the user an exceptional amount of flexibility in formatting graphs. Up to three different colors can be used to represent graphs on a color monitor. On a black-and-white monitor, the user can choose different shading patterns. The *color legend*, which defines the color or pattern for each data range, can also be displayed on the screen.

Labels can be inserted in graphs by referencing a list in the worksheet. Although 1-2-3 automatically scales the x- and y-axes to fit the data being plotted, users are free to adjust the scaling to suit their tastes. A grid can be placed over the worksheet. The user can specify a title and a subtitle for each graph, as well as labels for both the vertical and horizontal axes. In line and scatter graphs, the user has the option of selecting the type of symbol that will represent the data on the graph and connecting the data points with a line.

Because 1-2-3 lets the user name graphs after they are created, these graphs can be replotted by typing /gnu (for /**G**raph **N**ame **U**se) and supplying the graphs' names. With this feature, you can create a slide show of graphs that are recalled, one after another, and plotted.

"What If" with Graphics

The most exciting thing about 1-2-3's graphics is not the variety of graphs, but the degree to which the graphics and spreadsheet elements are interrelated. With 1-2-3, graphs can be quickly designed and altered as worksheet data changes. This means that graphs may be changed almost as fast as the data is recalculated.

True graphics "what if" analysis can be performed with 1-2-3. In fact, the F10 function key on the IBM PC and PS/2 computers allows the user to replot a graph after making changes to the worksheet, without having to redefine the graph with the /G command. This replotting immediately shows the effects of changes on the current graph.

Printing Graphics

Because the basic 1-2-3 program is not capable of producing printed graphics, the program is accompanied by a second program, called PrintGraph, which is used to create printed or plotted copies of graphs. After a graph is created by 1-2-3, the graph can be saved in a file on a disk. These files, called .PIC files, are created with the /GS (for /**G**raph **S**ave) command. The graph files can then be read into the PrintGraph program for additional formatting and printing.

The PrintGraph program offers a number of options for further formatting before the graphs are printed. The Color option allows parts of the graph to be assigned different colors. The Font option allows the labels and titles in the graph to be printed in one or several of eight different fonts, including a script face and a block face. The Size option allows the user to specify the size of the printed graph. A graph can be printed full size to occupy an entire printed page, or half size to fill half a page; or a manual option can be chosen. After the options have been selected, the PrintGraph program will print the graph to the specified graphics device.

The professional results that can be obtained from the PrintGraph program are another indication of the overall high quality of the 1-2-3 program. The user friendliness of 1-2-3's graphics capability is also important.

With previous graphics software, the time and trouble involved in creating and changing graphs often outweighed the benefits. 1-2-3 graphs, however, can be quickly and easily created and changed. With 1-2-3, managers will use graphs more frequently both to increase their own understanding and to communicate their analyses to others.

1-2-3 Database Management

The column-row structure used to store data in a spreadsheet program is similar to the structure of a relational database. The similarity between a database and a spreadsheet is demonstrated by the expanded Lookup capabilities of the spreadsheet programs developed before and at the same time as 1-2-3. 1-2-3 provides true database-management commands and functions so that you can sort, query, extract, and perform statistical analysis on data. One important advantage of 1-2-3's database manager over independent database programs is that its commands are similar to the other commands used in the 1-2-3 program. The user can, therefore, learn how to use the 1-2-3 database manager along with the rest of the 1-2-3 program.

Database Commands and Functions

Once a database has been built in 1-2-3 (which is no different from building any other spreadsheet table), a variety of functions can be performed on the database. Some of the tasks you will want to perform on a 1-2-3 database can be accomplished with standard 1-2-3 commands. For example, records can be added to a database with the /WIR (/Worksheet Insert Row) command. Fields can be added with the /WIC (/Worksheet Insert Column) command. Editing the contents of a database cell is as easy as editing any other cell; you simply move the cursor to that location, press F2 to call up the editor, and start typing.

Data can also be sorted. Sorts can be done with both a primary and a secondary key, in ascending or descending order, using alphabetic or numeric keys. In addition, various kinds of mathematical analyses can be performed on a field of data over a specified range of records. For example, you can count the number of items in a database that match a set of criteria; compute a mean, variance, or standard deviation; and find the maximum or minimum value in the range. The capacity to perform statistical analysis on a database is an advanced feature for database management systems on any microcomputer.

Other database operations require database commands, such as /DQU (/**Data Query Unique**) and /DQF (/**Data Query Find**). A 1-2-3 database can be queried in several ways. After specifying the criteria on which you are basing your search, you can ask the program to point to each selected record in turn, or to extract the selected records to a separate area of the spreadsheet. You can also ask the program to delete records that fit your specified criteria.

Several commands help the user make inquiries and clean the data of duplications. All of these commands are subcommands of the /DQ (/**Data Query**) command. These commands require that the user specify one or more criteria for searching the database. The criteria refer to a field in the database and set the conditions that data must meet in order to be selected.

1-2-3 allows a great deal of latitude in defining criteria. As many as 32 cells across, each containing multiple criteria, can be included in the criteria range. Criteria can include complex formulas as well as simple numbers and text entries. Two or more criteria in the same row are considered to be joined with an *and*. Criteria in different rows are assumed to be combined with an *or*. Criteria can also include "wildcard" characters that stand for other characters.

1-2-3 also has a special set of statistical functions that operate only on information stored in the database. Like the query commands, the statistical functions use criteria to determine which records they will operate on.

The following database functions are supported: @DCOUNT, @DSUM, @DAVG, @DVAR, @DSTD, @DMAX, and @DMIN. These functions perform essentially the same tasks as their spreadsheet counterparts. For example, @DMIN finds the minimum number in a given range. @DCOUNT counts all of the nonblank entries in a range. @DSTD computes the standard deviation of the items in the range.

The combination of these functions and 1-2-3's database commands makes this program a capable data manager. 1-2-3's data management capabilities, however, do not put the program in competition with more sophisticated database languages such as dBASE III Plus or R:BASE® System V. Both of these programs use a database language to translate the user's requests to the computer. By comparison, 1-2-3's data management is fairly simple.

When compared to less powerful data managers, however, such as PFS®:FILE, 1-2-3 looks good. 1-2-3 is fast and has adequate capacity (at 8,192 records) for most data management tasks. Because 1-2-3's data management uses the same basic command structure as the rest of 1-2-3, the program is easy to learn. In summary, the database function of 1-2-3 is valuable and sets 1-2-3 apart from the generic spreadsheet. (1-2-3's data management capabilities are covered in detail in Chapter 13.)

Using the /Data Table Command

One of the most useful, but most misunderstood, commands in 1-2-3's menu of /**Data** commands is /**Data Table**. A data table is simply a way to look at all the outcomes of a set of conditions without having to enter manually each condition into the equation. The command simply allows you to build a table that defines the formula you wish to evaluate and contains all the values you want to test. A data table is very similar to the X-Y decision grids you probably built as a math student in high school.

The /**Data Table** command can be used to structure a variety of "what if" problems. It can also be combined with 1-2-3's database and statistical functions to solve far more complex problems. (Chapter 13 explains in detail the /**Data Table** command and gives examples that will help you master this powerful tool.)

Multiple Regression and Simultaneous Equations

1-2-3's multiple regression command significantly expands the program's capabilities for statistical analysis. If you use regression analysis, the regression command could save you the cost of a stand-alone statistical package. For business applications, the /**Data Regression** command probably will meet all your regression analysis needs.

A /**Data Matrix** command can be used to solve systems of simultaneous equations. This capability, although likely to be of more interest to scientific and engineering users, is available to all.

Keyboard Macros and the Lotus Command Language

One of 1-2-3's most exciting features is its macro and Command Language capability, which allows you to automate and customize 1-2-3 for your special applications. 1-2-3's macro and Command Language capability allow you to create, inside the 1-2-3 spreadsheet, user-defined programs that can be used for a variety of purposes. At the simplest level, these programs are typing alternative programs that reduce, from many to two, the number of keystrokes for a 1-2-3 operation. At a more complex level, 1-2-3's Command Language gives the user a full-featured programming capability.

Whether you use 1-2-3's programming capability as a typing alternative or as a programming language, you'll find that it can simplify and automate many of your 1-2-3 applications. When you create typing-alternative macros, you group together and name a series of normal 1-2-3 commands, text, or numbers. Once you have named a macro or Command Language program, you can activate its series of commands and input data by pressing two keys—the Alt key and a letter key.

The implications for such typing-alternative macros are limited only by 1-2-3's capabilities. For example, typing the names of months as column headings is a task frequently performed in budget building. This task can be easily turned into a 1-2-3 macro, thereby reducing multiple keystrokes to a two-keystroke combination—the Alt key and a letter key. An Alt sequence in 1-2-3 can be structured to make decisions when the sequence is executed. These decisions can be based either on values found in the spreadsheet or on input from the user at the time the sequence is executed. By combining the typing-alternative features of 1-2-3's macro capability with the Command Language, you can cause the program to pause and wait for user input.

When you begin to use 1-2-3's sophisticated Command Language, you'll discover the power available for your special applications of 1-2-3. For the application developer, the Command Language is much like a programming language (such as BASIC), but the programming process is simplified significantly by all the powerful features of 1-2-3's spreadsheet, database, and graphics commands. Whether you want to use 1-2-3 to create typing alternative macros or to program, Chapters 14 and 15 give you the information you need to get started.

1-2-3 Software and Hardware Requirements and Options

Understanding the operation of the 1-2-3 spreadsheet, the types of commands and functions, and the program's advanced features is the first step to becoming a proficient 1-2-3 user. But learning how to benefit most from 1-2-3's capabilities also involves understanding 1-2-3's capabilities in reference to specific software and hardware capabilities. How much memory does

1-2-3 require to run? How much memory is used by 1-2-3 worksheet applications? What additional software or hardware can be used with 1-2-3 beyond what's minimally required? How do additional software and hardware expand 1-2-3's capabilities? The following sections answer these questions and discuss the specific software and hardware requirements and options available with 1-2-3.

The 1-2-3 Disks

It is obvious that 1-2-3 is a formidable product from the moment you open the package. The program is so large that it is distributed on six disks in the 5 1/4-inch floppy version for IBM PC and compatible systems (System disk, Backup System disk, Install Library disk, Utility disk, PrintGraph disk, and A View of 1-2-3 disk). 1-2-3 is distributed on four disks in the 3 1/2-inch micro-floppy version for the IBM PS/2 computers (System Disk with PrintGraph, Backup System Disk with PrintGraph, Install Disk, and A View of 1-2-3 with Translate).

1-2-3 on the IBM PC and PS/2

The IBM PC and PS/2 computers, with their memory capabilities and video displays, enable 1-2-3 to be a true business tool, capable of performing tasks that at one time were possible only on mini- and mainframe computers. Many corporations and individuals have found the IBM-plus-spreadsheet combination to be a terrific investment, saving time and effort while improving analysis.

For the first six months of its life, 1-2-3 was available only for the IBM Personal Computer. 1-2-3 was one of the first programs specifically designed for the IBM PC. 1-2-3 uses virtually every key on the PC's keyboard, including all the function keys, the Scroll Lock key, the delete (Del) key, and the alternate (Alt) key. The function keys serve several purposes. The F1 key activates 1-2-3's on-line help facility. F2 activates the program's editor. The F10 key replots graphics. The PgUp key jumps the cell pointer up one screen, and the PgDn key moves the cell pointer down one screen. The Home key returns the cell pointer to cell A1.

The PC keyboard layout poses one problem, however. Because the numeric keypad doubles as a cursor-movement keypad, using these keys both for entering numbers and for moving the cell pointer can be quite cumbersome.

The enhanced keyboard provided with all IBM PS/2 computers solves this numeric keypad problem. Because the enhanced keyboard has a separate cursor-movement keypad as well as a numeric keypad, users no longer need to press the Num Lock key to switch from one function to the other on the numeric keypad. (See Chapter 2 for more information on how 1-2-3 uses keys on IBM keyboards.)

Hardware Requirements and Extras

At one time, a considerable investment in hardware was required to make full use of 1-2-3's capabilities. Today, with the availability (and lower costs) of computers equipped with at least 512K of memory, that investment is smaller. In fact, many new 1-2-3 users and businesses are able to purchase computer equipment that is more powerful than the minimum equipment required to run 1-2-3. To run 1-2-3, you must have at least 256K of random-access memory (RAM) and at least one double-sided disk drive. However, because of the disk swapping that is required on a one-drive system, we recommend running 1-2-3 with two double-sided disk drives. And for users who will need to store, keep organized, and frequently use many 1-2-3 files, we highly recommend a computer with a hard disk drive.

A color monitor is required if you want to view 1-2-3's color graphics. If you have only a monochrome monitor, you will be able to see the spreadsheet and database parts of 1-2-3 and produce printed graphs. If you use a Hercules Graphics Card™ (or another 1-2-3-compatible monochrome graphics adapter) or have a PS/2 computer with a monochrome monitor, you will be able to view your graphs in black and white on your monochrome monitor.

For maximum use of 1-2-3's capabilities, you need appropriate hardware. If you are just getting started, you may want to consider investing in a Model 50, 60, or 80 IBM PS/2 computer. If you currently have an IBM PC or compatible, you may want to invest in the following additional hardware:

- Additional RAM memory, up to 640K

- Four megabytes of expanded memory

- An 8087 or 80287 coprocessor chip

These hardware extras greatly expand the practical size of 1-2-3's spreadsheet, and speed up calculations. If you are considering investing in new equipment, investigate the IBM PS/2 Model 50, 60, or 80 to determine which is best suited for your business needs—today and in the future. With any of the four PS/2 models, all of which allow you to add an 80287 math coprocessor and come with support for graphics, you can take immediate advantage of 1-2-3's speed, memory, and graphics capabilities.

You will also need a printer with graphics capabilities (like an EPSON® FX or LQ series printer) or a plotter to produce printed graphs. For professional-quality graphs and reports, 1-2-3 supports a number of laser printers.

1-2-3's Use of Memory

1-2-3 offers 256 columns by 8,192 rows, or more than 2,000,000 cells. To take advantage of all of that space, you'll need much more than the 256K required to run the program. 1-2-3 can accommodate up to 640K of RAM memory plus up to 4 megabytes of extended memory.

There is no simple way to equate the number of active cells in a worksheet to its RAM requirements because the contents of cells can vary greatly. Perhaps the best way to get a realistic notion of the potential size of a worksheet is to conduct two simple tests. In the first, we'll relate the size of the worksheet to the number of standard 8 1/2-inch-by-11-inch pages that can fit into it. In the second, we'll experiment—using 1-2-3's /Copy command to fill cells in the worksheet to see when we run out of main memory. From these two tests, we can draw conclusions about realistic worksheet size.

To begin the first test, we will use 640K of RAM—the maximum configuration possible for 1-2-3 without an extended memory card. After subtracting the 215K required for the 1-2-3 program, 425K of usable memory remains. If we divide this amount by the number of pica type characters on a standard 8 1/2-inch-by-11-inch page (66 lines by 80 characters = 5,280 total characters), we get approximately 86 pages. Although this is a rough measure, it points out the tremendous capacity of the 1-2-3 worksheet.

For the second test, we again use a system with 640K of main memory. This time we make various types of entries in cell A1 and copy the entries to other cells until the worksheet is full. Table 1.2 shows the result.

Table 1.2
Spreadsheet Capacity To Hold Various Types of Entries

Type of Entry	Maximum Number of Cells
Integer (the number 1)	109,580
Real Number (the number 1.1)	36,526
10-Character Label (ABCDEFGHIJ)	27,394
Small Formula (+B1+B2)	10,690
50-Character Label (ABCDEFGHIJKLMNOPQRSTUVWXYZabcdefghijklmnopqrstuvwx)	7,827

As the table shows, the maximum number of nonblank cells in the 1-2-3 spreadsheet depends on the kinds of entries made in those cells. Integer numbers require the least memory per entry; therefore, a spreadsheet containing integer numbers can have substantially more entries than a spreadsheet containing formulas or long labels. In practice, a worksheet for a business application will contain entries of different types, and the maximum number of nonblank cells will be somewhere between the value for all integers and the value for formulas or long labels.

There are few situations in which the size of your worksheet will exceed main memory, unless your system is configured at substantially less than 640K. If you do have an application that exceeds the capacity of your system's main memory, 1-2-3 has the capacity to use such special expanded memory boards as Intel's Above Board™ or the AST Rampage® board, to add up to four megabytes of spreadsheet memory to the 640K maximum main memory.

1-2-3 uses the expanded memory to store real numbers, formulas, and labels in the worksheet. Integer numbers are still stored in the main memory, and a pointer is stored in the main memory for each item stored in expanded memory. This expanded memory increases the spreadsheet capacity for any type of entry to the number of integers that can be stored in your system's main memory—approximately 109,000 entries for a system with 640K.

One application that may require large amounts of memory is database management. A computer with 640K of main memory can store about 1,000 four-hundred byte records, or 8,000 fifty-byte records. To handle even larger databases, you will need to invest in an expanded memory card. A database of 8,000 five-hundred byte records requires the maximum four megabytes of expanded memory.

All other things being equal, too much memory is better than too little memory. Because RAM is relatively inexpensive (and is getting even more so) and is important to increasing your productivity with 1-2-3, it makes sense to buy as much RAM as you can.

Remember, though, that an application which requires four megabytes of expanded memory will also require about the same amount of storage on disk. Large spreadsheets or databases that require expanded memory are practical only if you have a hard disk installed in your computer.

1-2-3 Release 2 has an advanced memory management scheme that allots main or expanded memory space only to cells with entries. Blank, unformatted cells use no memory space. Earlier spreadsheet programs, including earlier releases of 1-2-3, use memory space for every cell in the active worksheet area (defined as the smallest rectangle that contains all cells with entries). For example, in 1-2-3 Release 2 an entry in cell IV8192, the cell in the lower right corner of the worksheet, takes up no more space than an entry in cell A1. In 1-2-3 Release 1A, however, an attempt to enter a value in cell IV2048 (the lower right corner of 1A's worksheet) results in the error message Memory Full.

When you delete part of a worksheet, 1-2-3 reclaims some of the main memory; you can reuse that memory immediately. This capability is in contrast to earlier spreadsheet programs. After you deleted part of the worksheet in earlier versions of 1-2-3, you had to save and retrieve the worksheet to reclaim memory.

Operating Speed of 1-2-3

Given the staggering size of the 1-2-3 spreadsheet, it is reasonable to expect the program to be a bit slow. This is not the case. 1-2-3's spreadsheet is one of the fastest spreadsheet programs available today—particularly when used with computers containing an 80286 or 80386 microprocessor and 80287 or 80387 coprocessor chip.

1-2-3 is written in assembly language, the closest language to the hexadecimal numbers the computer uses. The program is well designed, and 1-2-3 retains its advantage in speed over competing spreadsheets and integrated packages.

Using 1-2-3 with Add-In and Add-On Software

As 1-2-3 users have become more experienced, so too has the need to provide them with additional features not available within the 1-2-3 program. Recognizing this need, Lotus Corporation has responded by supporting (and developing its own) supplementary software programs that can be used with or in addition to 1-2-3. These programs fall into two groups: 1-2-3 *add-in* programs and 1-2-3 *add-on* programs.

1-2-3 add-in programs become a part of 1-2-3; loaded into your computer's memory along with 1-2-3, these programs remain in memory as you use 1-2-3. Whenever you want to use the add-in, simply press a key or a two-key combination to access the feature. Some add-ins operate while the worksheet remains in view; others allow you to leave the worksheet momentarily and then return as soon as you have completed an operation. You can, for example, purchase add-in programs to access "note pad" windows as you work in the 1-2-3 worksheet. You can store text notes or document a spreadsheet application while the worksheet remains in view. Unlike 1-2-3, such "note pad" add-ins provide basic word-processing features for entering and editing text.

1-2-3 add-on programs, on the other hand, run outside of 1-2-3; loaded into memory separately, these programs use 1-2-3 files to perform operations that either are not available in 1-2-3 or expand 1-2-3's capabilities. Software for enhancing 1-2-3's print and graph output are examples of two types of popular add-on programs. With these add-ons, you can print 1-2-3 worksheets sideways or produce and customize presentation-quality graphs. Because such programs read 1-2-3 files directly and have command menus and functions keys similar to 1-2-3's, learning and using them is easy.

Although hundreds of add-in and add-on programs are available for 1-2-3, this book introduces you to seven of the most popular: Lotus HAL™, SQZ!™, 4WORD™, Freelance® Plus, The Spreadsheet Auditor®, the Cambridge Spreadsheet Analyst™, and Sideways®. The first three, Lotus HAL, SQZ, and 4WORD, are add-in programs that run with 1-2-3 and can be accessed from the worksheet. Although Freelance, the Spreadsheet Auditor, the Cambridge Spreadsheet Analyst, and Sideways run separately from 1-2-3, these programs use 1-2-3 files to perform special graph, print, and auditing operations on 1-2-3 files.

The three add-in programs covered in this book enhance 1-2-3 in quite diverse ways. Lotus HAL is a popular add-in program from Lotus Corporation that enables you to perform both routine and complex 1-2-3 tasks by entering simple English requests instead of using the 1-2-3 commands. For example, instead of having to select a series of six or more graph commands to create a bar graph of sales data in your worksheet, you can simply access HAL's special prompt box and type *Graph SALES as bar*. HAL is a valuable tool for both beginning and experienced 1-2-3 users. By bypassing some of the complicated and confusing sequences of 1-2-3 commands, beginners can more easily and quickly create 1-2-3 applications. Experienced users can benefit from HAL features that are not available in 1-2-3, such as the ability to undo changes to a worksheet and return to original data.

SQZ!, the Turner Hall™ add-in program, enables users to compact 1-2-3 files and thus fit more files on a disk. Whether you are saving files on a floppy or hard disk, SQZ! lets you store four or five times the number of 1-2-3 files you can normally store. In addition to its file-compression capability, SQZ! provides a special password-protection feature, allowing you to limit others' access to your files.

The third add-in program covered in this book—4WORD—is a sophisticated word processor that you use right in the 1-2-3 worksheet. Similar to the word-processing module in Symphony, 4WORD uses the worksheet's column and row format; text is stored as long labels in column A. The 4WORD and 1-2-3 command menus are similar; commands are selected by typing the first letter of the command or moving the menu pointer to the command.

The four add-on programs provide enhanced capabilities for creating graphs, auditing and debugging worksheets, and printing reports. Freelance Plus, the graphics program from 1-2-3, lets you dress up and customize 1-2-3 graphs.

With Freelance Plus, for example, you can improve the presentation quality of 1-2-3 graphs and include custom logos or special symbols in your graphs. Although some 1-2-3 features help you with basic worksheet auditing, 1-2-3 has limited capacity to find errors. Two add-on programs, the Spreadsheet Auditor and the Cambridge Spreadsheet Analyst, provide more sophisticated auditing capabilities. With these programs, you can easily search for and view formula relationships, check for circular references, and test for overlapping ranges. If you have worksheets with so many columns that they won't print horizontally, you can use Funk Software's Sideways program to solve the problem. With Sideways, you can rotate worksheets ninety degrees and print them.

At the end of many chapters, you will find a summary of the advantages of using each of these packages. These summaries point out how the programs work and how they enhance features in 1-2-3. For example, if you're looking for an easier way to debug your worksheet formulas, turn to the end of Chapter 4 for an overview of the two most popular 1-2-3 auditing programs. If you would like to have basic word-processing capabilities without having to leave the 1-2-3 worksheet and load a separate program, review the introduction to 4WORD in Chapter 5. And if you want to know more about HAL and the benefits of using HAL, read the sections in Chapters 3-14.

Chapter Summary

1-2-3 has become an extraordinarily popular program for many reasons. First, it combines several sought-after functions into one program. Second, and more important, the program is "done right." 1-2-3 is one of the first microcomputer programs ever released that is not filled with compromises. Third, the program is fun to use, especially for those who have used VisiCalc.

Although 1-2-3 should not be mistaken for a full-featured office automation system, the program does represent a bridge between traditional spreadsheets and integrated programs such as Symphony and Framework®. Each element of the program is a full-fledged application program in its own right. Together, these elements offer unprecedented power and flexibility.

Getting Started

This chapter will help you get started using 1-2-3. Before you begin, be sure that 1-2-3 is installed for your computer system. Follow the instructions in Appendix A to complete installation for your system. Even if you have already installed 1-2-3, you may want to check the appendix to make sure that you haven't overlooked any important details.

The information contained here will be useful if you have little familiarity with computers or with 1-2-3. If you find this introductory material too basic and want to begin using the 1-2-3 spreadsheet immediately, skip to Chapter 3.

The last section in this chapter shows you how to use the various learning aids that Lotus includes in the 1-2-3 package. Many first-time users find these aids a helpful introduction to 1-2-3. You may want to use them with this book during the early stages of learning the program.

The following topics are covered:

- Starting up and exiting from 1-2-3
- Using the 1-2-3 Access System
- How 1-2-3 uses the computer keyboard
- How 1-2-3 uses the screen display
- Using the 1-2-3 learning aids

Starting Up and Exiting 1-2-3

You can start up 1-2-3 in two different ways: from within the 1-2-3 Access System, or directly from DOS. Most users start directly from DOS because this method is easier, faster, and uses less memory.

Starting up 1-2-3 from DOS requires three steps. If you have installed 1-2-3 on your hard disk according to the directions in Appendix A, the 1-2-3 program will be on your hard disk in a subdirectory named *123*.

Start up 1-2-3 on a hard disk system as follows:

1. Place the 1-2-3 System disk in drive A. For the IBM Personal System/2 (PS/2), the System disk is called the *System Disk with PrintGraph*. If you installed 1-2-3 with the COPYHARD procedure, as described in Appendix A, this step is not necessary.

2. Change to directory 123 by typing *CD \123* and pressing Enter

3. Start 1-2-3 by typing *123* and pressing Enter

If you have a two floppy or a two microfloppy disk system, the startup procedure is slightly different. Note that in this book we use the term *microfloppy* to designate the 3 1/2-inch disks enclosed in a hard-plastic case that are used by the IBM PC Convertible and the IBM PS/2 family of computers

Start up 1-2-3 on a two floppy or two microfloppy disk system as follows:

1. Place the 1-2-3 System disk (the System disk with PrintGraph for PS/2) into drive A

2. If the A> prompt is not displayed, type *a:* and press Enter

3. Start 1-2-3 by typing *123* at the A> system prompt and pressing Enter

After a few seconds, the 1-2-3 logo appears. The logo remains on the screen for a few seconds; then the worksheet appears and you're ready to start using 1-2-3.

The other method of starting 1-2-3 uses the 1-2-3 Access System, which is explained in the next section.

To exit 1-2-3, you must use the 1-2-3 main command menu. 1-2-3 commands and their menus are explained extensively throughout the book. At this point, however, you need to know only how to access the main menu and to use one of two easy commands.

To access the command menu, press the slash (/) key. A menu containing 10 options appears across the top of the worksheet (see fig. 2.1). Select either **System** or **Quit** to exit the worksheet in one of two ways.

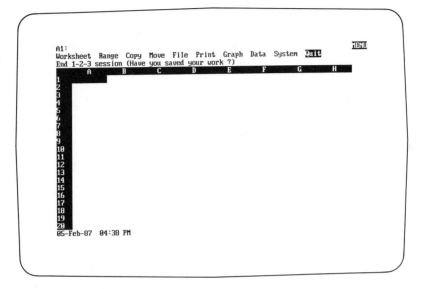

Fig. 2.1

The 1-2-3 main command menu.

/**System** returns you to the DOS system prompt, but does not exit the 1-2-3 program. You can perform system operations at the DOS level, including changing directories and drives, and then return to the 1-2-3 spreadsheet by typing *exit*. To select the /**System** option, type *s*; or use the right- and left-arrow keys to move the pointer (the highlighter) to the option, and then press Enter. Remember that 1-2-3 stays in memory with your current worksheet. If you have not saved your file, you will lose your work if you shut down your computer or reboot. (For additional information about saving files, see Chapter 7 and the section "Saving Your File before You /Quit" of this chapter.)

Caution:
Save your file before you leave the worksheet.

/**Quit** exits the worksheet and the 1-2-3 program. Type *q* or use the pointer to select this option. You are asked to verify this choice before you exit 1-2-3 because your data will be lost if you **Quit** 1-2-3 without saving your file. To verify that you want to exit, type *y* to select **Yes**, or move the pointer to **Yes** and then press Enter.

Using the 1-2-3 Access System

Lotus devised the 1-2-3 Access System as a way to tie together in one unit all of 1-2-3's different functions (see fig. 2.2). The system is useful if you need to move quickly and frequently from 1-2-3 to other programs in the 1-2-3 package. The Access System provides a series of menus that enable you to move back and forth between 1-2-3 and other Lotus programs for printing graphs; to transfer files between 1-2-3 and other outside programs, such as dBASE, Symphony, and VisiCalc; and to access the Install and A View of 1-2-3 programs within 1-2-3.

Fig. 2.2

The 1-2-3 Access System.

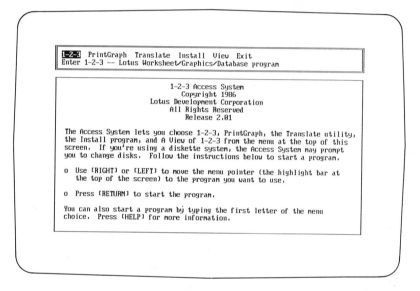

To start up the 1-2-3 Access System if you have a hard disk system and have not created your own driver, as described in Appendix A, proceed as follows:

1. Change to your 123 subdirectory by typing *CD \123* and pressing Enter

2. Type *lotus* at the DOS C> prompt and press Enter

If you have a two floppy or a two microfloppy disk system:

1. Place the 1-2-3 System disk (the System disk with PrintGraph for PS/2) into drive A

2. If the A> prompt is not displayed, type *a:* and press Enter

3. Type *lotus* at the A> system prompt and press Enter

Notice that you type *lotus*, not *1-2-3*. (You may find it convenient to think of the 1-2-3 Access System as the "Lotus Access System.")

The 1-2-3 Access System command menu appears after a few seconds. Six functions are available in the command menu:

    1-2-3   PrintGraph   Translate   Install   View   Exit

These options should not intimidate you. Taken individually, they are easy to understand and use. If you have any questions when you are in the Access System, you can always get help by pressing F1. The help screen lists the Access System options and their use. If you have questions about a particular option, you can press F1 to get information.

Cue:
Press the F1 (Help) key to see each option explained.

Starting Up and Exiting 1-2-3 from the 1-2-3 Access System

The first option in the 1-2-3 Access System menu is to start up 1-2-3. Before you select this option, however, be sure that you have loaded the System disk (for PS/2, the System disk with PrintGraph) into drive A. This step is not necessary if you have a hard disk and have used the COPYHARD procedure.

When the menu appears, the pointer is on the first option; to select the option, press Enter. If you have moved the pointer to another option, you can start up 1-2-3 by using the right- and left-arrow keys to return to the first option and then pressing Enter; or you can start up 1-2-3 by typing *1*. After several seconds, the 1-2-3 logo will appear on the screen. The 1-2-3 logo will remain on the screen for a few seconds, after which the worksheet will appear.

To exit the 1-2-3 program, press the slash (/) key to access the 1-2-3 main command menu and then choose **Quit** from that menu. The **Quit** command is used by all the programs in the 1-2-3 Access system.

If you look at the 1-2-3 command menu, you will see the **Quit** option at the end of the list of menu items. If you started up 1-2-3 from the 1-2-3 Access System, **/Quit** will return you to it. Before 1-2-3 exits, you will be asked to verify this choice, because if you **Quit** 1-2-3 without saving your file, your data will be lost. To verify that you want to exit, type *y* to select **Yes**, or move the pointer to **Yes** and then press Enter.

If you choose **/System** from the main command menu, you get the same result as if you were not using the Access system: you return to the DOS system prompt, but you do not exit the 1-2-3 program. You can perform system operations at the DOS level, including changing directories and drives, and then return to the 1-2-3 spreadsheet by typing *exit*. To select the **System** option, type *s* or use the pointer.

Exit is the final option in the 1-2-3 Access System menu. You must choose Exit to end the 1-2-3 Access System program. When you do so, the DOS prompt C> (or A> for a two floppy or a two microfloppy system) will appear.

If you exit the 1-2-3 Access System prematurely, you can easily restart it by typing *lotus* at the DOS prompt.

Choosing the Other Options in the 1-2-3 Access System

The Access System allows you to call several other programs in the 1-2-3 package, not just the 1-2-3 spreadsheet. The options available include programs for printing graphs, translating data files from other programs, installing drivers, and viewing the basics of 1-2-3. The successive options on the Access menu load these programs and make them available for your use. Select the options in the same way you select the *1-2-3* option: by highlighting the menu entry and pressing Enter, or by typing the first letter of the menu entry.

The PrintGraph option on the Access System menu initiates the PrintGraph program for printing graph files. Select this option by using the right- and left-arrow keys to move the pointer to **PrintGraph** and pressing Enter; or type *p*. If you have a two floppy disk system, the PrintGraph disk must be placed in drive A to run the program (see Chapter 11). For a two microfloppy system (the PS/2 Model 30), the System Disk with PrintGraph must be placed in drive A.

You also can go directly to the PrintGraph program without going through the 1-2-3 Access System. To do this, type *pgraph* at the DOS prompt. If you have installed 1-2-3 on your hard disk, you must first change directories to the directory that holds 1-2-3. If you have a two floppy disk system, the PrintGraph disk must be in drive A when you enter the word *pgraph* at the A> prompt. For a two microfloppy system, the System disk with PrintGraph must be in the drive.

The Translate option accesses the Translate Utility. This utility provides a link between Release 1A and Release 2 of 1-2-3 and between 1-2-3 and outside programs, including dBASE II, dBASE III, dBASE III Plus, Symphony, Jazz, and VisiCalc (see Chapter 7). If you have a two floppy disk system, the Utility disk must be placed in drive A to run the program. For a two microfloppy system (the PS/2 Model 30), the View of 1-2-3 with Translate disk must be placed in drive A.

You can go directly to the Translate program by typing *trans* at the DOS prompt and pressing Enter. If you have installed 1-2-3 on your hard disk, you must first change directories to the directory that holds 1-2-3. For a two floppy system, the Utility disk must be in drive A when you type *trans* at the A> prompt. For a two microfloppy system, the View of 1-2-3 with Translate disk must be in the drive.

The Install option accesses the Install program, which you can use to change the options that you set during initial installation, or to create new driver sets for using 1-2-3 on a different system. One option you may want to change is the sort order, which is specified in the Advanced Options section of the Install program. If you have a two floppy disk system, the Utility disk must be placed in drive A to run the program, and the Install Library disk must be used to complete installation of drivers. For a two microfloppy system (the PS/2 Model 30), the Install disk must be placed in drive A; the PS/2 Install disk includes a library of drivers. See Appendix A for complete instructions on installation.

Cue:
*Appendix A contains
complete installation
instructions.*

You can go directly to the Install program by typing *install* at the DOS prompt and pressing Enter. If you have already copied the 1-2-3 programs to your hard disk, you must first change directories to the directory that holds 1-2-3. For a two floppy system, the Utility disk must be in drive A when you type *install* at the A> prompt. For a two microfloppy system, the Install disk must be in the drive.

The View option simply accesses the disk containing A View of 1-2-3. The disk contains an overview of 1-2-3. (See the "A View of 1-2-3" section of this chapter.) If you have a two floppy disk system, the A View of 1-2-3 disk must be placed in drive A to run the program. For a two microfloppy system (the PS/2 Model 30), the View of 1-2-3 with Translate disk must be placed in drive A.

You can also go directly to the View program by typing *view* at the DOS prompt and pressing Enter. If you have installed 1-2-3 on your hard disk, you must first change directories to the directory that holds 1-2-3. For a two floppy system, the A View of 1-2-3 disk must be in drive A when you type *view* at the A> prompt. For a two microfloppy system, the View of 1-2-3 with Translate disk must be in the drive.

Learning the 1-2-3 Keyboard

The three most commonly used keyboards on IBM and IBM compatible personal computers are shown in figures 2.3, 2.4, and 2.5. The keyboards are divided into three sections: the alphanumeric keyboard in the center, the numeric keypad on the right, and the function key section on the left or across the top. The enhanced keyboard, which is used by the IBM Personal System/2 family of computers, also has a separate grouping of cursor-movement keys.

Fig. 2.3

The keyboard of the IBM PC.

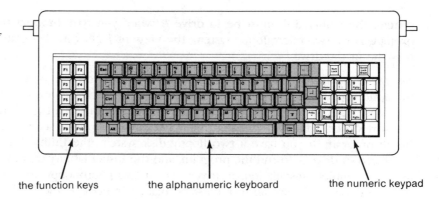

the function keys   the alphanumeric keyboard   the numeric keypad

Fig. 2.4

The keyboard of the IBM Personal Computer AT.

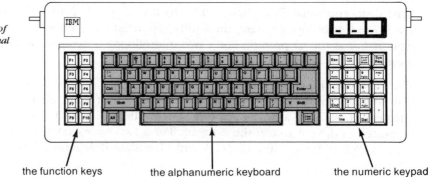

the function keys   the alphanumeric keyboard   the numeric keypad

the function keys

Fig. 2.5

The keyboard of the IBM PS/2 (the enhanced keyboard).

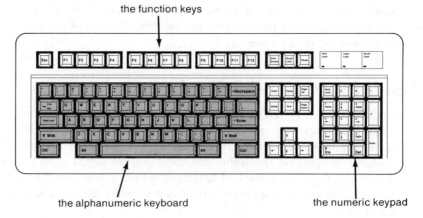

the alphanumeric keyboard   the numeric keypad

Most of the keys in the alphanumeric section at the center of the keyboard are found on a typewriter, and most of these keys maintain their normal functions in 1-2-3. Several keys, however, take on new and unique functions or are not found on typewriter keyboards: Esc, Tab, Shift, and Alt.

The numeric keypad on the right-hand side of the keyboard is normally used for entering numbers in most programs on IBM personal computers. The main purpose of the numeric keypad in 1-2-3, however, is cursor movement, except on the enhanced keyboard. The IBM PS/2 enhanced keyboard has separate cursor keys; the numeric keypad of this keyboard can also be used for cursor movement, but ordinarily is used only for entering numbers.

The function keys are designed for special situations ranging from getting help to drawing graphs. These keys are located across the top of the enhanced keyboard and on the left-hand side of the other two keyboards.

The Alphanumeric Keyboard

Although most of the alphanumeric keys shown in figures 2.3, 2.4, and 2.5 have the same functions as on a typewriter, several keys have special functions in 1-2-3. These keys and their functions are listed in table 2.1. If some of the functions do not make much sense the first time through, don't worry. Their meaning will become clearer as you read this book.

Table 2.1
Alphanumeric Key Operation

Key	Function
⇤⇥ (Tab)	Moves cursor one screen to the right when used alone, and one screen to the left when used with the Shift key
Alt	When used simultaneously with other individual alpha keys, invokes keyboard macros and Command Language programs. (See Chapters 14 and 15.)
⇧ (Shift)	Changes the central section of the keyboard to uppercase letters and characters. It also allows you to key in numbers, using the numeric keypad on the right (equivalent of a temporary Num Lock).
← (Backspace)	During cell definition, erases the previous character in a cell

Key	Function
/ (Slash)	Starts a command. It is also used in its normal function as a division sign.
. (Period)	Separates cell addresses when ranges of cells are defined and, in a different manner, anchors cell addresses during the pointing procedure. (For more on ranges, see Chapter 4.) It is also used as a decimal point.

The Numeric Keypad and the Cursor-Movement Keys

The keys in the numeric keypad on the right-hand side of the IBM PC- and AT-style keyboards are used mainly for cursor movement (refer to figs. 2.3 and 2.4). The IBM PS/2 enhanced keyboard has separate keys for cursor movement (see fig. 2.5). The functions of the cursor-movement keys are explained in Chapter 3; the other keys on the numeric keypad are listed in table 2.2.

Table 2.2
Numeric Key Operation

Keys	Function
Num Lock	Activates the numeric character of the keys in the numeric keypad
Esc	Escapes from a command menu and moves to the previous menu, erases current entry when specifying a command line or range, or returns from a help screen
Del	Deletes the character above the cursor during the process of editing command lines (for more about editing, see Chapter 3)
Scroll Lock/ Break	In Scroll Lock position, scrolls the entire screen one row or column in any direction each time the cell pointer is moved. In the Break position, this key is used with Ctrl to return 1-2-3 to READY mode or to halt execution of a macro.

When you want to use the numeric keypad to enter numbers rather than to position the cursor (on the PC- or AT-style keyboard), you can do one of two things. First, you can press the Num Lock key before entering the numbers, and press the key again when you are done. (This is the method used in most IBM personal computer software.) The second way is to hold down the Shift key while pressing the number keys.

Neither way is ideal, because you have to worry about switching back and forth between using the keypad for entering numbers and using it for cursor movement. This worry is removed if you have a PS/2 computer or a PC AT that uses an enhanced keyboard. Because you have a separate set of cursor-movement keys, you can reserve the numeric keypad for entering numbers.

If you don't have an enhanced keyboard, you can solve the problem by using a macro. You can create a macro to enter numbers down a column of cells without having to press the Num Lock key or hold down the Shift key. You can easily apply the macro to entering numbers in any direction.

Cue:
Macros can solve numeric-keypad problems.

The Function Keys

The function keys, F1 through F10 (refer to figs. 2.3, 2.4, and 2.5), are used for special situations in 1-2-3. Notice the difference in location of the function keys on the two types of keyboard; the keys are on the far left of the PC and AT keyboards, but across the top of the enhanced keyboard.

Lotus provides a plastic function-key template that fits over the function keys of the IBM PC. A special version of this template is available also for COMPAQ owners. Unfortunately, the template does not give you adequate information when you are first starting out. To help you in early sessions until you have memorized the functions, we have provided table 2.3, which lists the function keys, an explanation of what each key does, and a reference to subsequent discussion.

Learning the 1-2-3 Screen Display

The main 1-2-3 display is divided into two parts: the control panel at the top of the screen, and the worksheet area itself (see fig. 2.6). A reverse-video border separates the two areas. This border contains the letters and numbers that mark columns and rows.

Other important areas of the screen are the mode indicators (upper right corner), the lock key indicators (lower right corner), and the message area

Table 2.3
Function Key Operation

Key	Function	Chapter and Section
Alt-F1 (Compose)	Used with other keys to make International Characters	Appendix B
Alt-F2 (Step)	Shifts 1-2-3 into single-step mode for debugging macros	Chapter 14, "Debugging a Macro"
F1 (Help)	Accesses 1-2-3's on-line help facility	Chapter 2, "Finding On-Screen Help"
F2 (Edit)	Shifts 1-2-3 into EDIT mode. Allows contents of cells to be altered without retyping the entire cell.	Chapter 3, "Editing Data in the Worksheet"
F3 (Name)	In POINT mode, displays a list of the range names in the current worksheet. Pressing F3 a second time switches to a full screen display of range names.	Chapter 4, "Getting a List of Range Names"
F4 (Abs)	During cell definition, changes a relative cell address into an absolute or mixed address	Chapter 4, "Using the F4 (Abs) Key To Set Absolute and Relative References"
F5 (GoTo)	Moves the cursor to the cell coordinates (or range name) provided	Chapter 3, "Moving Around the Spreadsheet"
F6 (Window)	Moves the cursor to the other side of a split screen	Chapter 4, "Splitting the Screen"
F7 (Query)	Repeats the most recent Data Query operation	Chapter 13, "Output Range"
F8 (Table)	Repeats the most recent Data Table operation	Chapter 13, "Table-Building"

Key	Function	Chapter and Section
F9 (Calc)	Recalculates the worksheet	Chapter 4, "Iterative Recalculation"
F10 (Graph)	Redraws the graph defined by the current graph settings	Chapter 11, "Previewing a Graph"

Fig. 2.6.

The 1-2-3 display showing the control panel at the top of the screen.

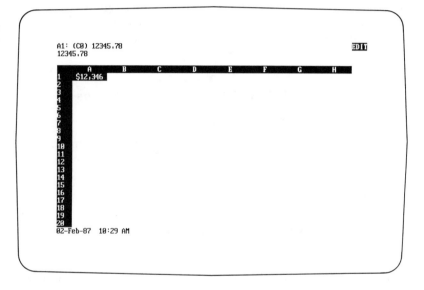

in the lower left corner. The message area normally shows the date and time but will show an error message when certain kinds of errors are made.

The Control Panel

The control panel is the area above the reverse-video border. This area has three lines, each with a special purpose. As figure 2.6 indicates, the first line contains all the information about the *current cell*. A current cell is the cell where the cell pointer is currently located. The first item in the line is the address of the cell. The second item is the display format, which is always displayed in parentheses. (Display formats are covered in detail in Chapter 5.) The last item in the first line is the actual contents of the current cell. The first line may also contain items explaining protection status (PR or U) and column width ([Wxx]). Both column width and protection status are explained in Chapter 4.

The second line in the control panel contains the characters that are being entered or edited. The third line contains explanations of the current command menu item. As you move the pointer from one item to the next in a command menu, the explanation on the third line of the control panel will change. If a command menu is not in effect, this line will be blank.

The Mode Indicators

One of 1-2-3's different modes is always in effect, depending on what you are doing. The mode indicator, located in the upper right corner of the screen, always shows which mode 1-2-3 is in. The mode indicators and descriptions of the functions are listed in table 2.4.

Table 2.4
Mode Indicators and Descriptions

Mode	Description
READY	1-2-3 is waiting for you to enter a command or make a cell entry.
VALUE	A number or formula is being entered.
LABEL	A label is being entered.
EDIT	A cell entry is being edited.
POINT	A range is being pointed to.
FILES	1-2-3 is waiting for you to select a file name from the list of file names.
NAMES	1-2-3 is waiting for you to select a range name from the list of range names.
MENU	A menu item is being selected.
HELP	1-2-3 is displaying a help screen.
ERROR	An error has occurred, and 1-2-3 is waiting for you to press Esc or Enter to acknowledge the error.
WAIT	1-2-3 is in the middle of a command and cannot respond to other commands. Flashes on and off.
FIND	1-2-3 is in the middle of a /**Data Query** operation and cannot respond to commands.
STAT	1-2-3 is displaying the status of your worksheet.

The Lock Key Indicators

IBM personal computers have three "lock" keys: Num Lock, Caps Lock, and Scroll Lock. In 1-2-3, you always know the status of these keys because a special area of the screen has been set aside to show that information. Each key has its own reverse-video indicator that appears in the lower right corner of the screen when the key has been activated (see fig. 2.7).

Fig. 2.7.

The 1-2-3 display showing the lock key indicators in the lower right corner of the screen.

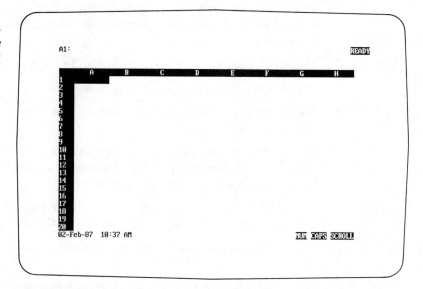

Other Indicators

Other indicators in 1-2-3 also appear at the bottom of the screen. These indicators, which display the status of certain keys and special situations, are listed in table 2.5.

The Error Messages Area

When an error occurs in 1-2-3, a message appears in the lower left corner of the screen. Errors may occur for many reasons: the disk to which you are trying to save a file is full, there are no files on disk of the type you are looking for, etc.

To clear the error and get back to READY mode, you must press Esc or Enter. If you do not press one of these keys, the message will not clear.

Table 2.5
Status Indicators and Descriptions

Indicator	Description
NUM	The Num Lock key has been pressed; pressing the number keys on the numeric keypad will produce numbers.
CAPS	The Caps Lock key has been pressed; pressing the letter keys on the alphanumeric keyboard will produce capital letters.
SCROLL	The Scroll Lock key has been pressed and is now active.
END	The End key has been pressed and is now active.
OVR	The Insert key has been pressed, and 1-2-3 is now in typeover mode.
CALC	The worksheet has not been recalculated since the last change to cell contents (see the "Automatic versus Manual Recalculation" section of Chapter 4).
CIRC	A circular reference has been found in the worksheet (see the "Iterative Recalculation" section of Chapter 4).
MEM	Random-access memory is almost exhausted. Flashes on and off.
HAL \	HAL, a Lotus add-in that provides a natural-language interface for 1-2-3, is active in your computer's random-access memory and can be accessed by pressing the backslash key (\ ).
CMD	A keyboard macro or Command Language program is in the process of execution (see Chapters 14 and 15).
SST	A keyboard macro or Command Language program is in single-step execution.
STEP	Alt-F2 has been pressed, and you are currently stepping through a macro or Command Language program one cell at a time (see Chapters 14 and 15).

Using the 1-2-3 Help Features

One of the biggest selling points of 1-2-3 is its user friendliness. Lotus obviously went to a great deal of trouble to ensure that the spreadsheet is easy to learn and use.

The most conspicuous user-friendly feature of 1-2-3 is the support Lotus provides for new users who are learning 1-2-3. Lotus provides *A View of 1-2-3* as an on-line introduction to the features and business applications of 1-2-3, and also provides context-sensitive help screens. The printed Tutorial is a self-paced instructional manual that leads you through a series of actual 1-2-3 worksheets that use important features of the program.

A View of 1-2-3

A View of 1-2-3, as shown in figure 2.8, has three sections: an introductory section that presents an overview of 1-2-3 for the new user, a sample business analysis session that shows how 1-2-3 can be used to evaluate alternative business strategies, and for the experienced Release 1 or 1A user, a section that describes the differences between Release 2 and Release 1A.

Fig. 2.8.

A sample screen display from the A View of 1-2-3 disk.

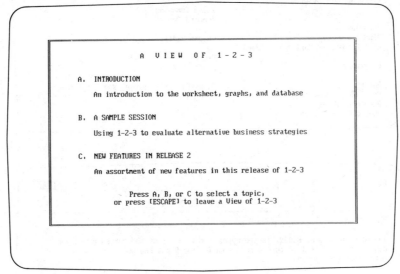

```
              A  V I E W  O F  1 - 2 - 3

     A.  INTRODUCTION
         An introduction to the worksheet, graphs, and database


     B.  A SAMPLE SESSION
         Using 1-2-3 to evaluate alternative business strategies


     C.  NEW FEATURES IN RELEASE 2
         An assortment of new features in this release of 1-2-3


              Press A, B, or C to select a topic,
           or press [ESCAPE] to leave a View of 1-2-3
```

If you are a new 1-2-3 user, we recommend that you work through the introductory section and the sample business analysis section of A View of 1-2-3. Each section takes from a half hour to a couple of hours to complete, and you gain a good overview of how 1-2-3 operates and what its capabilities are.

Finding On-Screen Help

One user-friendly feature of 1-2-3 is its extensive series of interconnected help screens. By pressing the Help (F1) key, you can gain access to the Help Index screen, shown in figure 2.9. This screen has headings that can connect you to more than 200 Help screens (see fig. 2.10).

Fig. 2.9

The Help Index screen.

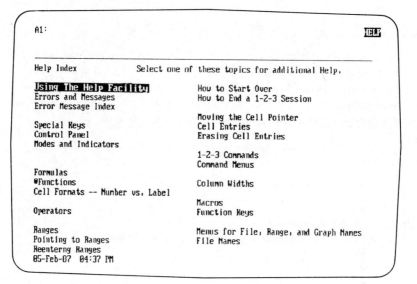

Fig. 2.10

The screen that appears when you press Help (F1).

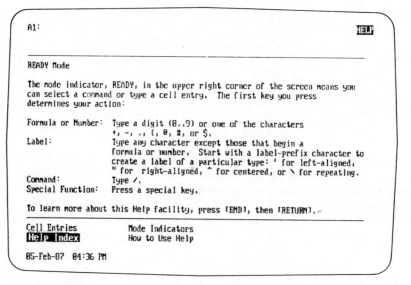

Each Help screen contains information about a single topic as well as names of other topics; these names are positioned at the foot of the screen. To move to another topic, use the cursor-movement keys to move the cursor to the name of that topic, and then press Enter. To return to the Help Index screen, move the cursor to Help Index and press Enter.

One of the best features of the on-screen help facility is that you can press the F1 key at any time during a 1-2-3 session, even while issuing a command or defining a cell. The F1 key is context-sensitive; if you are using a particular command when you press F1, 1-2-3 gives you a screenful of help on that command. Once you have the information, you return to 1-2-3 by pressing the Esc key.

Reminder:
The F1 (Help) key is context-sensitive.

Other good features of this help facility are that many of the screens refer to pages in the 1-2-3 manual so that you can get more explanation if you need it. Also, by pressing the Backspace key, you can again view previous help screens.

Taking the 1-2-3 Tutorial

Another learning resource from Lotus is the Tutorial manual, a book that comes with the documentation; the Tutorial provides a self-paced guide to learning 1-2-3. The Tutorial goes through a series of lessons on 1-2-3 in a step-by-step fashion. The lessons are arranged in order of increasing difficulty and build on each other. The Tutorial does not cover all of 1-2-3's functions and commands but covers enough to give you a basic understanding of the program.

The Tutorial assumes that you have successfully installed your 1-2-3 disks and have worked through A View of 1-2-3. The Tutorial begins by providing complete instructions for starting up your computer with 1-2-3, moving the cursor around the worksheet, and accessing the 1-2-3 command menu.

The Tutorial then progresses through lessons on basic worksheet skills, more advanced worksheet skills, printing reports from the worksheet, printing graphs with PrintGraph, using the database functions, and using 1-2-3 macros to simplify and automate your 1-2-3 applications.

Lotus designed the Tutorial to take as little of your time as possible, but you won't be able to complete it in one sitting. The Tutorial is divided into six chapters with several lessons in each chapter. We recommend that you do one or two lessons at a time. You can go back later to different lessons to refresh your memory.

If you are comfortable with basic spreadsheet skills and want to learn about a more specialized topic such as database skills or macros, the lessons in the

Tutorial are organized so that you can work through only those lessons that cover the topic of interest.

For further detail on 1-2-3 functions and commands, you can refer to the *Reference Manual*, to the appropriate sections of this book, and to the Command Reference Section and Command Menu Map at the back of this book.

Chapter Summary

In this chapter, you learned how to get started using 1-2-3. You learned how to use the 1-2-3 Access System to start up the program, and to choose other options available in the 1-2-3 package. The chapter also explains how the computer keyboard is adapted for use with 1-2-3, and how 1-2-3 uses the screen display to convey important status information to the user. And you have been introduced to the 1-2-3 overview (A View of 1-2-3) and the 1-2-3 Tutorial.

The next step in learning 1-2-3 is to start working with the 1-2-3 spreadsheet. Chapter 3 shows you how to enter and edit data in the worksheet, how to move the cursor around the worksheet, and how to start using the power of 1-2-3 by entering and using formulas.

3

Learning Spreadsheet Basics

If you are new to spreadsheet software, this chapter will introduce you to the features that make an electronic spreadsheet a powerful tool of data analysis. If you are familiar with spreadsheets but new to 1-2-3, you will learn the conventions and features that are unique to this program.

The fundamental power of the 1-2-3 spreadsheet is its ability to store and manipulate large amounts of information. The first step in accessing that power is to enter data into the cells of the worksheet. This chapter will show you how to enter data and how to modify, or edit, that data.

If you are like most people, you're using 1-2-3 because you work with quantifiable information, such as inventories, schedules, budgets, financial analyses, work plans, or production forecasts. Whatever kind of data you work with, you will want to know how to enter numbers and how to start manipulating them. The sections on using formulas, operators, and functions will get you started using 1-2-3 to meet your needs.

Computers love numbers, but the human mind needs a mixture of numbers and language. To organize and keep track of the numeric data in the worksheet, you will need titles, headings, names, comments, descriptions, and a variety of other English-language entries. 1-2-3 calls all these entries *labels*, and handles them in a slightly different way than numbers. The section on entering labels will show you how to use labels in the worksheet.

Because of the size of the worksheet, you will need to learn quick, easy ways to move around in it. Moving the cell pointer is a skill and an art, learned mostly by practice. This chapter will show you the available tools and how to use them.

You will learn how to

- Enter data in the worksheet

- Enter formulas, operators, and functions

- Enter labels

- Edit data in the worksheet

- Move the cell pointer around the worksheet

Entering Data into the Worksheet

You enter data into a cell simply by highlighting the cell with the cell pointer and then typing the entry. To complete the entry, press Enter or any of the cursor-movement keys discussed later in this chapter.

If you enter data into a cell that already contains information, the new data replaces the earlier entry. This is one way to change information in a cell; the other way, which involves the F2 (Edit) key, is explained in this chapter's "Editing Data in the Worksheet" section.

There are two types of cell entries: values and labels. Values can be either numbers or formulas (including functions, which 1-2-3 treats as built-in formulas). 1-2-3 determines which type of cell entry you are making from the first character that you enter. If you start with one of the following characters,

0 1 2 3 4 5 6 7 8 9 + - . (@ # $

1-2-3 treats your entry as a value (a number or a formula). If you begin by entering a character other than one of the above, 1-2-3 treats your entry as a label.

Entering Numbers

The rules for entering numbers are simple.

1. A number cannot begin with any character except 0 through 9, a decimal point, a minus sign (-), or a dollar sign ($). Numbers can also begin with a plus sign (+), or be entered in parentheses, but the + and the ( ) will not appear in the cell.

2. You can end a number with a percent sign (%), which tells 1-2-3 to divide by 100 the number that precedes the sign.

3. A number cannot have more than one decimal point.

4. You can enter a number in scientific notation—what 1-2-3 calls the Scientific format (for example, 1.234E+06).

If you do not follow these rules, 1-2-3 will beep when you press Enter while trying to enter the number into the spreadsheet, and 1-2-3 will automatically shift to EDIT mode just as though you had pressed F2. (The "Editing" section later in this chapter explains how to respond.)

Entering Formulas

In addition to simple numbers, formulas also can be entered into cells. You can enter formulas by either typing the formula into the cell or combining typing with moving the cell pointer.

Suppose that you want to create a formula that adds a row of numbers. For example, suppose that you want to add the amounts in cells B1, C1, D1, and E1, and place the result in cell F1 (see fig. 3.1).

Fig. 3.1

A simple addition formula.

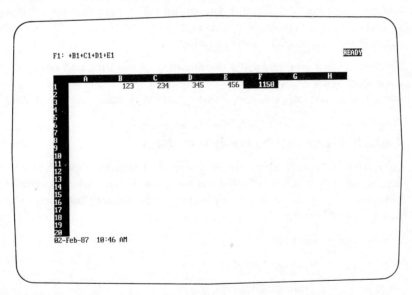

One formula that will perform the addition is +B1+C1+D1+E1. You can place the result of the addition into cell F1 simply by typing this formula into cell F1. Notice the + sign at the beginning of the formula. For 1-2-3 to recognize the formula as a formula and not a label, the formula must begin with one of the following characters:

0 1 2 3 4 5 6 7 8 9 . + - (@ # $

Because we started with +, 1-2-3 recognizes our entry as a formula and switches to VALUE mode, the appropriate mode for entering numbers and formulas.

Remember that two methods can be used to enter a formula that contains a cell address: typing and pointing. Both methods accomplish the same result, and you can mix and match the two techniques within the same formula. Pointing to cell addresses requires some explanation.

Cue:
The pointing method can be an easier way to enter formulas.

For example, to enter the formula in figure 3.1 by pointing, you begin with the cell pointer highlighting cell F1 and you enter the first plus sign into F1; then you move the cell pointer to B1. The mode indicator in the upper right corner of the screen shifts from VALUE to POINT mode as you move the cell pointer to cell B1. Notice that the address for the cell appears after the plus sign in the second line of the control panel—that is, +B1.

To continue to the next address in the formula, keep the cell pointer in cell B1 and type another plus sign. The cursor moves immediately from cell B1 to the cell at which it was located when you began entering the formula—in this case, cell F1. Also, the mode indicator shifts back to VALUE. Now move the cell pointer to cell C1 and type another plus sign. Continue this sequence of pointing and entering plus signs until you have the formula you want. Then press Enter to complete the operation.

Remember that you may use a combination of pointing and typing. Use whatever works best for you. Usually, the easiest method is to point at cells that are close to the cell you are defining, and type references to distant cells.

Using Operators in Formulas

Operators indicate arithmetic operations in formulas. Operators can be separated into two types: mathematical and logical. The logical operators will be covered in Chapter 6, in connection with the logical functions. The mathematical operators are

Operator	Meaning
^	Exponentiation
+, -	Positive, Negative
*, /	Multiplication, Division
+, -	Addition, Subtraction

An important part of understanding operators is knowing their order of precedence. The list of mathematical operators is arranged in order of precedence. Operators higher on the list are evaluated before operators that are lower. Operators with equal precedence are on the same line; in these cases, the operators are evaluated from left to right.

The first operator that is evaluated in a formula is exponentiation—the power of a number. In the formula 8+2^3, for example, 2^3 (2 to the power of 3) is evaluated before the addition. The answer is 16 (8+8), not 1000 (10 to the power of 3).

The next set of operators to be evaluated indicates the sign of a value (whether the value is positive or negative). Notice that 1-2-3 knows the difference between a + or - sign that indicates positive or negative value and a + or - sign that indicates addition or subtraction. Used as a sign, these operators are evaluated before multiplication and division; used as indicators of addition and subtraction, the operators are evaluated after multiplication and division. For example, 5+4/-2 is evaluated as 5+(-2), giving 3 as the answer. Notice that 1-2-3 first recognizes that the - sign indicates that 2 is negative, then divides 4 by -2, and finally adds 5 to -2, giving the answer of 3.

You can always use parentheses to override the order of precedence. Consider the order of precedence in the following formulas, where B3=2, C3=3, and D3=4, and see if you get the same answers. In the first two formulas, notice particularly how parentheses affect the order of precedence and, ultimately, the answer.

Formula	Evaluation	Answer
+C3-D3/B3	3-(4/2)	1
(C3-D3)/B3	(3-4)/2	-0.5
+D3*C3-B3^C3	(4*3)-(2^3)	4
+D3*C3*B3/B3^C3-25/5	((4*3*2)/(2^3)-(25/5))	-2

Correcting Errors in Formulas

It is easy to make errors entering formulas. The more complex the formula you are trying to use, the more likely you are to confirm the saying "Whatever can go wrong, will." 1-2-3 provides ways to help you discover and correct the inevitable errors.

If you attempt to enter a formula that contains a logical or mathematical error, the program will beep, change to EDIT mode, and move the cursor to the section of the formula where the problem most likely exists. You can then correct the problem and continue.

Cue:
You can debug a formula by temporarily converting it to a label and moving it to another part of the worksheet.

If you don't know what the problem is, you can buy yourself some think time by converting the formula to a label. Do this by pressing the Home key and then entering an apostrophe (') at the beginning of the formula. Then use the /Copy command (discussed in Chapter 4) to copy the label-formula to another section of the worksheet for debugging and testing. When you have discovered the problem, correct the original formula and remove the apostrophe.

If your formula is long and complex, try breaking it into logical segments and testing each segment separately. Using smaller segments is not only an aid in debugging, but may also be necessary in order for the program to accept the formula. 1-2-3 limits cell entries to 240 characters. If your formula exceeds the length limit, you will have to use smaller segments.

Some common errors are open parentheses and commas missing from built-in formulas (functions, covered in Chapter 6). What appears to be a logical error may be only a missing punctuation mark. When 1-2-3 beeps to indicate a formula error, check the formula for a missing parenthesis or comma at the place where the cursor is positioned.

Cue:
Use special commands to see all your formulas at once.

The program also provides two commands to help you examine and analyze your formulas. If you are not yet familiar with the use of commands, keep these debugging methods in mind until you are. Commands are discussed extensively in the next chapter.

The /**Print P**rinter **O**ptions **O**ther **C**ell-Formulas command will print a list of all the formulas in your worksheet. The /**W**orksheet **G**lobal **F**ormat **T**ext command produces a screen display that shows all your formulas in their spreadsheet locations. To make analysis easier, use both commands to get a complete view of your formulas.

Using Functions

Like most electronic spreadsheets, 1-2-3 includes built-in functions. These functions are of three basic types: (1) simple abbreviations for long or complex mathematical formulas—these functions are considered formulas by 1-2-3; (2) non-mathematical, "string" functions that work with alphanumeric data—these functions manipulate labels; and (3) special functions that provide information or perform other specialized spreadsheet tasks. All three types of functions are considered values by 1-2-3, and all three are entered in the same way.

Functions consist of three parts: the @ sign, a function name, and an argument or range. The @ sign signals to 1-2-3 that a function is coming. The name indicates which function is being used. The argument or range is the data required by 1-2-3 to perform the function; the argument is always placed within parentheses.

Before we cover functions in detail (in Chapter 6), we need to cover several other topics, such as the concept of ranges. The following example, however, will help you begin to understand 1-2-3 functions.

In figure 3.1, we needed to refer individually to four cells to create the desired formula. We could, however, use the @SUM function to sum the numbers in the example. The concept of ranges is important to the @SUM function. (Ranges are covered in detail in Chapter 4.) For now, simply think of a range as a rectangular block of cells.

The equivalent to the +B1+C1+D1+E1 formula, using the @SUM function, is @SUM(B1..E1). The only difference between the two formulas is one of convenience. If we had several other entries extending down the row, the @SUM function would change only slightly to use the address of the last cell to be summed. For example, @SUM(B1..Z1) would sum the contents of the first row all the way from B to Z.

To make full use of formulas you need to understand relative, absolute, and mixed addressing. These concepts are covered extensively in the "Copying the Contents of Cells" section of Chapter 4.

Entering Labels

The third type of data that can be entered in a cell consists of labels. Labels, commonly used for row and column headings and a variety of other purposes, can be up to 240 characters long and may contain any string of characters and numbers. A label that is too long for the width of a cell continues (for display purposes) across the cells to the right, as long as the neighboring cells contain no other entries (see fig. 3.2).

When you make an entry into a cell and the first character is not a number or an indicator for entering numbers and formulas, 1-2-3 assumes that you are entering a label. As you type the first character, 1-2-3 shifts to LABEL mode.

One of the advantages of 1-2-3 is that you can left-justify, center, or right-justify labels when you display them (see fig. 3.3). To determine a label's position, you must begin the label with one of the following label-prefix characters:

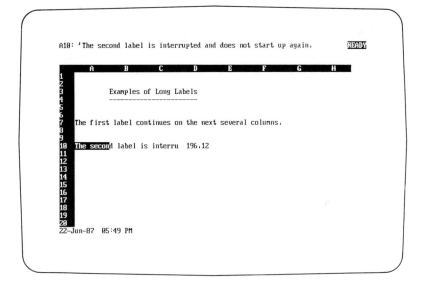

```
A10: 'The second label is interrupted and does not start up again.          READY
        A       B       C       D       E       F       G       H
1
2
3             Examples of Long Labels
4             -----------------------
5
6
7  The first label continues on the next several columns.
8
9
10 The second label is interru   196.12
11
12
13
14
15
16
17
18
19
20
22-Jun-87  05:49 PM
```

Label Prefix	Action
'	Left-justifies
^	Centers
"	Right-justifies
\	Repeats

The default for displaying labels is left-justification. You don't have to enter the label prefix in this case because 1-2-3 automatically supplies the prefix for you. If you want to, however, you can enter the ' label prefix just as you can enter any of the other label prefixes.

What You Enter	What 1-2-3 Stores
Net Income	`'Net Income`

The one exception for all types of alignment occurs when the first character of the label is a number or an indicator of a number or formula (see the list in the "Entering Formulas" section of this chapter). For example, suppose that you want to enter the number 1987 as a label. If you type *1987*, 1-2-3 assumes that you are entering a value. You need some way to signal that you intend this numeric entry to be treated as text. You can indicate this by using one of the label-prefix characters. In this case, you could enter 1987 as a centered label by typing *^1987*.

Fig. 3.3

Examples of left-justified, centered, right-justified, and repeated labels.

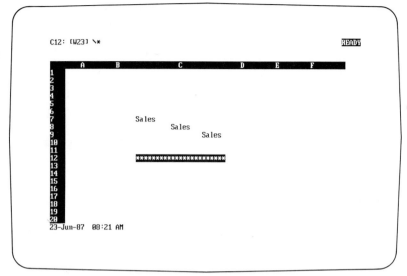

The most unusual label prefix is the backslash (\ ), which is used for repetition. One of the most frequent uses of this prefix is to create a separator line.

The first step in creating the separator line is to enter * into the first cell (in fig. 3.3, cell C12). This entry causes asterisks to appear across the entire cell. Once you have set up the first cell, you can use the /Copy command to replicate the cell across the page. (For additional information about the /Copy command and replication in general, see Chapter 4.)

There are several ways to control label prefixes. For example, suppose that you have entered a series of labels, using the standard default of left-justification, but you decide that you would rather have the labels centered. You could manually change all the label prefixes or, using the /Range Label command, you could change the prefixes all at once.

From this point on in the book, you will need to know how to use the 1-2-3 command menus. Remember from Chapter 2 that you access the main command menu by pressing the slash (/) key. When the main command menu appears, you can choose any item on the menu, either by using the right- and left-arrow keys to point to the item and then pressing Enter or by typing the first letter of the item.

For example, **R**ange is an option on the main command menu. Either highlight this word and then press Enter, or simply type *r*. When you make this selection, the main menu disappears and the Range menu appears in its place. **L**abel is an option on the Range menu; you choose this option as you would choose an option from the main menu. As you work with 1-2-3, you probably will find that typing the initial letter is easier than using the pointing method.

This book uses the following convention when giving a command:

/**O**ption1 **O**ption2 **O**ption3 . . .

Notice that the first letter of the option is in boldface. This is the letter to type to select the option. To help you follow the sometimes bewildering sequence of 1-2-3 commands, we have included a command reference chart at the back of this book. You may want to tear out the chart and keep it near your computer as you use 1-2-3.

Now, using whatever method you prefer, select the /**R**ange **L**abel command. When you select this command, you are given the following choices:

Left   Right   Center

Each choice gives you the appropriate label prefix.

If you select **C**enter, 1-2-3 asks you to designate a range of cells to change. When you specify a range and press Enter, the cells are displayed as centered.

Another option for changing label prefixes is to change the default setting for text justification. The command to do this is /**W**orksheet **G**lobal **L**abel-Prefix. This command gives you the same options as the /**R**ange **L**abel command. Previously entered cells, however, are not affected by the /**W**orksheet **G**lobal **L**abel-Prefix command. Only subsequent entries will show the change. In addition, cells that have been previously set, using /**R**ange **L**abel, will maintain the alignment set by that command.

Editing Data in the Worksheet

When you start using 1-2-3, one of the first things you will want to do is modify the contents of cells without retyping the complete entry. This modification is quite easy to do in 1-2-3. You begin by moving the cursor to the appropriate cell and pressing the F2 (Edit) key. An alternative is to press F2 when you are entering cell contents.

When you press F2, 1-2-3 enters EDIT mode. Normally, 1-2-3 is in READY mode. The main difference between the two modes is that some keys take on different meanings. Table 3.1 shows the function of keys that are used differently in EDIT mode.

After you press F2, the mode indicator in the upper right corner of the screen changes to EDIT. The contents of the cell are then duplicated in the second line of the control panel (the edit line) and are ready for editing.

Table 3.1.
Key Action in EDIT Mode

Key	Action
←	Moves the cursor one position to the left
→	Moves the cursor one position to the right
Tab or Ctrl→	Moves the cursor five characters to the right
Shift-Tab or Ctrl←	Moves the cursor five characters to the left.
Home	Moves the cursor to the first character in the entry
End	Moves the cursor to the last character in the entry
Backspace	Deletes the character just to the left of the cursor
Ins	Toggles between INSERT and OVERTYPE modes
Del	Deletes the character above the cursor
Esc	Clears the edit line but does not take you out of EDIT mode

To show how the various keys are used, let's consider two examples. First, suppose that you want to edit in cell E4 an entry that reads Sales Comparisson. After you highlight cell E4 with the cell pointer, correct the misspelling of Comparisson by pressing the following keys:

Keys	Edit Line	Explanation
F2	'Sales Comparisson_	The cursor always appears at the end of the edit line when you press F2.
←	'Sales Comparisson	
←	'Sales Comparisson	
←	'Sales Comparisson	The cursor now appears below the errant s.
Del	'Sales Comparison	The Del key deletes the character above the cursor.
Enter		You press Enter to update the entry in the spreadsheet and return to READY mode.

Now suppose that you want to modify a formula in cell G6 from +D4/H3*(Y5+4000) to +C4/H3*(Y5+4000). After you highlight cell G6 with the cell pointer, press the following keys to change the formula:

Keys	Edit Line	Explanation
F2	+D4/H3*(Y5+4000)_	Again, the cursor always appears at the end of the edit line when you first press F2.
Home	+D4/H3*(Y5+4000)	The Home key takes you to the first position in the edit line.
→	+D4/H3*(Y5+4000)	The → key moves the cursor one position to the right.
C	+CD4/H3*(Y5+4000)	When you enter a character in EDIT mode, the character normally is inserted to the left of the cursor. Entering a character will never cause you to write over another, unless you have pressed the Ins key to toggle into OVERTYPE mode. Unwanted characters can be eliminated with the Del and Backspace keys.
Del	+C4/H3*(Y5+4000)	Use the Del key to delete the character above the cursor.
Enter		Again, you press Enter to update the entry in the spreadsheet and return to READY mode.

Reminder:
*For convenience,
use EDIT mode
when you enter data.*

One thing to remember about using EDIT mode is that you can use it also when you enter data into a cell for the first time. If you make a mistake when you are in EDIT mode, you do not have to retype the entire entry.

Moving Around the Spreadsheet

Soon after you start entering data in your worksheet, you will find that you need some easy ways to move the cell pointer quickly and accurately. Remember that the 1-2-3 spreadsheet is immense—8,192 rows and 256 columns, or more than 2,000,000 cells. As your use of 1-2-3 becomes more extensive, you may have blocks of data of various sizes in widely separated parts of the worksheet. The program provides several ways to move the cell pointer quickly anywhere in the worksheet.

Remember that the cell pointer is not the same as the cursor. The cell pointer is the bright rectangle that highlights an entire cell. The cursor is the blinking line that is sometimes inside the cell pointer and sometimes in the control panel. The cursor indicates the position on the screen where your keyboard activity takes effect; the cell pointer indicates the cell that is affected. Whenever you move the cell pointer, the cursor is inside the pointer and moves also. That is why we sometimes talk about cursor-movement keys when we really mean keys that move the cell pointer.

When 1-2-3 is in READY mode, the cursor-movement keys are used to move the cell pointer; when 1-2-3 is in POINT mode, these keys are used to point out a range. The cursor-movement keys either cannot be used at all or have a different action when you are in EDIT mode, making a cell entry, or in the process of entering a 1-2-3 command.

Using the Basic Cursor-Movement Keys

The arrow keys on the numeric keypad, or on a separate pad of the enhanced keyboard, are the basic keys for moving the cell pointer. The cell pointer moves in the direction of the arrow on the key as long as you hold down the key. When you reach the edge of the screen, the worksheet scrolls in the direction of the arrow.

If you press the Scroll Lock key to activate the scroll function, the worksheet scrolls in the direction of whatever arrow key you press no matter where the cell pointer is positioned on the screen. Leaving the scroll function off is usually easier and less confusing.

You can scroll the worksheet one screenful at a time to the left or right by holding down the Ctrl key and pressing the left- or right-arrow key. You also can scroll the worksheet to the right with the Tab key, and to the left with Shift-Tab (hold down the Shift key while you press Tab). These four keys and key combinations provide quick ways of "paging through" the worksheet.

To get the same effect up or down, don't use the up- and down-arrow keys—use the PgUp and PgDn keys.

The Home key provides a quick way to return to the beginning of the worksheet. From anywhere in the worksheet, pressing Home causes the cell pointer to return to cell A1. Table 3.2 summarizes the action of the cursor-movement keys. Remember from the "Editing Data" section earlier in this chapter that some keys, such as Home and End, have different actions in EDIT mode.

Reminder:
The Home key returns the cell pointer to cell A1.

Using the End Key for Cursor Movement

1-2-3 uses the End key in a unique way. When you press an arrow key after you have pressed and released the End key, the cell pointer moves in the direction of the arrow key to the next boundary between a blank cell and a

Table 3.2
Cursor-Movement Key Operation

Keys	Function
→	Positions the cell pointer one column right
←	Positions the cell pointer one column left
↑	Positions the cell pointer one row up
↓	Positions the cell pointer one row down
Ctrl→ or Tab	Moves the cell pointer one screen to the right
Ctrl ← or Shift-Tab	Moves the cell pointer one screen to the left
PgUp	Moves the cell pointer up an entire screen
PgDn	Moves the cell pointer down an entire screen
Home	Returns the cell pointer to cell A1 from any location in the worksheet. Also used after the End key to position the cell pointer at the end of the active worksheet.
End	When entered prior to any of the arrow keys, positions the cell pointer in the direction of the arrow key to the cell on the boundary of an empty and filled space.
F5 (GoTo)	Moves the cell pointer to the cell coordinates (or range name) provided

cell that contains data. For example, the indicator in the lower right corner of the screen in figure 3.4 shows that the End key has been pressed. If you now press the right-arrow key, the cell pointer will jump to the first boundary, as shown in figure 3.5.

If you again press the End key followed by the right-arrow key, the cell pointer will jump to the next boundary, cell E7 containing the value 1500. If you repeat the process one more time, the cell pointer will jump all the way to the right boundary of the spreadsheet, cell IV7. The End key works in similar fashion for the other arrow keys.

You can also use the End key, followed by the Home key, to move the cell pointer from any position on the spreadsheet to the lower right corner of your active worksheet. In figure 3.4, this corner is cell E9 containing the value 2500. In a sense, the End-Home combination has the opposite effect of the

Fig. 3.4

*Using the End key
to move the cell
pointer.*

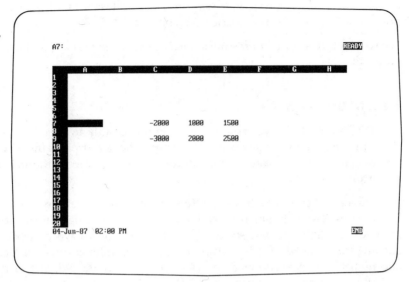

Fig. 3.5

*Using the right-
arrow key after
pressing the End
key.*

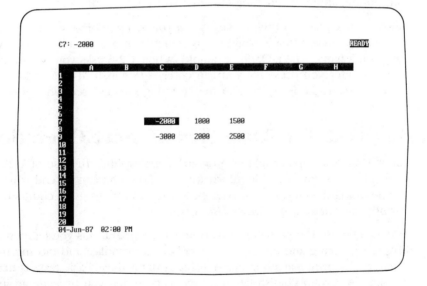

Home key used alone, because the Home key always moves the cell pointer
to cell A1, the upper left corner of every spreadsheet.

Although using the End key for cursor movement may sound complex, in
practice it is an easy and quick way to find the boundaries of blocks of data
in your worksheet. Remember, however, that if there are gaps in the blocks

of data, the End key procedure will probably be less useful because the cell pointer will go to the boundaries of each gap.

We will look at several interesting applications for the End key in the following chapters.

Jumping to a Cell

The F5 (GoTo) key gives you a way to jump directly to a cell location. To move the cell pointer to any cell on the spreadsheet, just press the F5 function key. When 1-2-3 asks you for the address to go to, type in the cell address you want.

Remember that every cell has an address, defined by the cell's row and column coordinates. The columns have alphabetic names, starting with A through Z, then AA through AZ, and so on up to IV. The rows have numeric names, running from 1 to 8192. The cell addresses are a combination of the alphabetic and numeric names, running from A1 through IV8192. When you press F5 and then type any one of the 2,097,152 addresses on the spreadsheet, the cell pointer immediately jumps to that address.

Cue:
You can use range names with the F5 (GoTo) key.

Another nice feature of the F5 key is that you can combine the key with range names. Remember that a range is a rectangular block of cells; this block can be given a name—RATIOS for example. When 1-2-3 asks you for the address to go to after you press F5, you can enter *ratios* instead of an address such as *A94*. This topic is covered in the "Naming Ranges" section of Chapter 4.

Using HAL for Basic Spreadsheet Operations

Lotus HAL is a popular add-in program that simplifies the use of 1-2-3. This book provides considerable information on how you can extend your use of 1-2-3 with HAL, but does not attempt to explain the program completely. For further information, see Que's *Using Lotus HAL*.

HAL can be used to perform many of the 1-2-3 operations you learned in this chapter: entering and editing data, labels, and formulas; and moving the cell pointer. The principal advantage of using HAL for these basic tasks is that HAL recognizes certain English language requests. When you precede an instruction with one of the words HAL recognizes, HAL performs the task for you. HAL also gives you the option of performing the same tasks in the normal 1-2-3 manner.

Entering Data with HAL

HAL recognizes the verbs *Enter*, *Put*, and *Type* as valid requests for entering data. To enter data with one of these verbs, you enter the verb in HAL's request box, followed by the data (see fig. 3.6). In the example in the figure, the request *put 10,25,15,18 across in c11* will enter *10* in cell C11, *25* in cell D11, *15* in cell E11, and *18* in cell F11.

Figure 3.6

Using a HAL request to enter data into the worksheet.

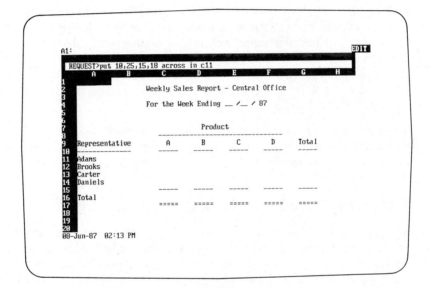

```
A1:                                                              EDIT
REQUEST>put 10,25,15,18 across in c11
        A        B       C        D       E       F       G       H
1
2                         Weekly Sales Report - Central Office
3
4                         For the Week Ending __ /__ / 87
5
6
7                                   Product
8                         --------------------------------
9  Representative         A        B       C       D       Total
10 ----------------       ------   ------  ------  ------  ------
11 Adams
12 Brooks
13 Carter
14 Daniels
15                        ------   ------  ------  ------  ------
16 Total
17                        ======   ======  ======  ======  ======
18
19
20
08-Jun-87  02:13 PM
```

HAL always enters data in the current cell unless you specify another location; in figure 3.6, A1 is the current cell but C11 is specified in the request. HAL enters multiple data vertically unless the request includes the word "across," as in the example in the figure.

Because the backslash (\) cues 1-2-3 that you are about to make a HAL request, you must precede each request by a backslash. If you have used HAL's *Stay* command, you don't need to press the backslash key to enter a request.

You also can enter data using HAL by typing the value into HAL's request box and then pressing the Insert key. The value will be placed in the current cell.

Entering Formulas and Functions with HAL

Make and *Put* are two general HAL requests you can use to enter formulas and functions in the worksheet. In addition, you can make specific HAL requests to find the sum, average, maximum, minimum, standard deviation, and variance of a range of values. For example, if you make the request *sum col* *g,* the values in Column G are added up, a dashed line is entered below the last value in the column, and the sum is entered below the dashed line.

HAL makes use of a concept called a *table,* somewhat similar to the concept of a range. More specifically, a *table* is any continuous rectangular block of data; the *current table* is the table at which the cursor is located. For example, if you make the simple request *average,* HAL takes the average of the current table and enters the result below the table.

HAL accepts range names in requests. Suppose, for example, that you wanted to calculate the net income in a worksheet that included gross income and taxes, and you had the values entered in appropriately named ranges. You could instruct HAL to *make net_income=gross_income-taxes.* The values in the range named TAXES would then be subtracted from the values in the range named GROSS_INCOME, and the result entered in the range named NET_INCOME.

You also can enter any formula or 1-2-3 @function into the current cell in the worksheet by entering the formula or function into HAL's request box and then pressing the Insert key.

Entering Labels with HAL

You enter labels with HAL the same way you enter numeric data, by using the requests *Enter, Put,* or *Type,* or by entering the label into the request box and pressing the Insert key. The HAL verbs can provide many shortcuts in entering labels. You could, for example, tell HAL to *put Jan thru Dec across in b3.* The months of the year would then be entered across the worksheet, beginning in cell B3.

Be careful when you use HAL to repeat a label. The key that 1-2-3 uses to repeat a label is the backslash key—the same key you use to invoke HAL. To repeat a label with HAL, first use the backslash key to invoke HAL; then press the backslash key and type the label you want to repeat.

To repeat a label in the 1-2-3 worksheet without using HAL, press the Ctrl key and backslash key simultaneously; then type the characters you want to repeat, and press Enter.

HAL can also be used to align labels in the worksheet. The appropriate HAL requests are *Center, Left align,* and *Right align.* For example, you can center all the labels in a worksheet by using the simple request *center all.* Or, you can right-justify all the labels in column D by using the request *right align column d.* As you can see, HAL can significantly speed up the process of centering and justifying labels.

Editing Cell Contents with HAL

You can make a HAL editing request by typing *Edit*, *Alter*, or *Fix*, followed by the cell address; if the address is not the current address, HAL moves the cell pointer to the specified cell. You can also make the editing request (if HAL's request box is active) by positioning the cell pointer on the cell that contains the data you want to change, and pressing the F2 key. In either case, the cell's contents will be displayed in HAL's request box and 1-2-3 will shift to EDIT mode.

The capacity to edit a cell you are not currently pointing to can be convenient. You simply make the request, for example, to *fix a1*, and the contents of cell A1 appear in the request box; 1-2-3 also shifts to EDIT mode, ready for you to make your changes.

The UNDO key is another convenient HAL editing feature. Suppose that you change a data or formula entry and then discover that you've made an error. UNDO returns the previous entry to the cell, allowing you to change your mind.

The special actions of certain keys in 1-2-3 EDIT mode are the same when using HAL (see table 3.1). You must be careful using the Backspace key, however, because HAL uses the Backspace key as the UNDO key. If you are using the Backspace key to erase cell contents and you inadvertently press the key one more time than necessary, HAL brings up your last spreadsheet (the one preceding the last cell entry). You must press the UNDO (Backspace) key once more to return to your current spreadsheet.

Moving the Cell Pointer with HAL

To use HAL to move the cell pointer, simply type *go to* and the cell address in HAL's request box, and then press Enter. Or press F5, and then respond to HAL's Go to prompt by entering the cell address or range name and then pressing Enter. In both cases, HAL moves the cell pointer for you.

HAL provides no significant advantage over the use of F5 within 1-2-3, except that you don't have to remember that F5 is the correct function key for cursor movement. You have to remember only that you want to "go to" someplace in the worksheet, and enter that phrase into the request box.

Chapter Summary

This chapter showed you the basics of entering and editing data in the worksheet. You learned how to enter and use formulas, as well as operators within formulas. You also learned that functions are built-in formulas that can be used for rapid, easy manipulation of data. And you learned how to move the cell pointer quickly and easily to any part of the worksheet.

Chapter 4 takes you the next step into mastery of the 1-2-3 spreadsheet—using commands. You had a brief introduction to commands in Chapter 2, where you learned to start up and exit 1-2-3, but in Chapter 4 you will start using the program's extensive command structure to accomplish a wide variety of spreadsheet tasks.

4

Learning Fundamental 1-2-3 Commands

U sing 1-2-3 means using 1-2-3 commands. Commands are the tools the program provides for performing its tasks. If you want to rearrange the data on your worksheet, save the worksheet or access a different one, print reports or create graphs based on the worksheet, or accomplish a wide variety of other tasks, you need to use commands.

This chapter will teach you the principles of using commands and how to use some of the fundamental 1-2-3 commands. If you have read Chapter 2, you've already been given a brief introduction to commands, but, because you will need to use them regularly from this point on, you now should learn thoroughly how to use them.

To make sense of the command structure, you need to understand one preliminary concept: the concept of ranges. Some commands affect the entire worksheet but others affect only certain cells or groups of cells. 1-2-3 uses the term *range* for a rectangular block of cells, and builds many highly useful actions around the concept of ranges. This chapter explains ranges and the group of commands that are designated specifically as range commands.

The chapter also explains the commands that affect the entire worksheet. Commands that accomplish several other important spreadsheet tasks are also covered.

This chapter shows you how to

- Use ranges in a worksheet

- Use /**R**ange commands

- Use /**W**orksheet commands

- /**C**opy and /**M**ove data within a worksheet

- Reference cells with relative and absolute addressing

- Save your worksheet before you /**Q**uit 1-2-3

- Use the /**S**ystem command to access DOS

Selecting Commands from Command Menus

If commands are the tools for performing 1-2-3 tasks, command menus are
the toolboxes. The menus display the commands that are available for use.
In 1-2-3, the command menus are especially helpful for several reasons. First,
1-2-3 lists the full command words (see fig. 4.1).

Fig. 4.1

*The 1-2-3 Main
Menu.*

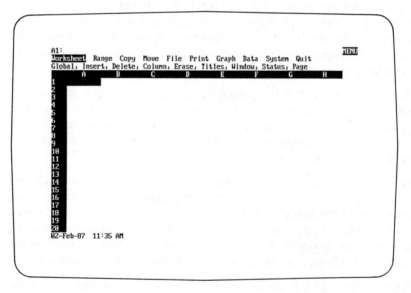

To display the main command menu shown in the figure, press the slash
(/) key. Remember to press the slash key while in READY mode whenever
you want to activate a command.

A second feature of the command menus is illustrated on the third line of
the display in figure 4.1. This line contains an explanation of the **W**orksheet

menu item on which the command cursor is positioned. In fact, as you point to the different items in the command menu by moving the cursor across the list, a new explanation appears in the third line for each command-menu item. This happens in every command menu.

A third friendly aspect of command menus relates to how a command is initiated. You can either point to the option you want, or you can enter the first letter of the command name.

To point to the command-menu item, use the left- and right-arrow keys on the right-hand side of the keyboard. When the cursor is positioned at the proper item, press Enter. If you move the cursor to the last item in the list and then press the → again, the cursor will "round the horn" and reappear on the first item in the list. Similarly, if the cursor is on the first item in the menu, press the ← to move the cursor to the last option. Note that you can move the cursor to the end of the command line also by pressing the End key, and to the beginning of the line by pressing the Home key.

Entering the first letter of the command-menu item is the other way to select a command. For example, to select the /Worksheet Status command, which informs you of the status of several of 1-2-3's global parameters, you type / to select the main command menu, followed by *w* to select **W**orksheet. At this point, another menu appears:

  Global   Insert   Delete   Column   Erase   Titles   Window   Status   Page

From this line, select **S**tatus by pressing the S key. A display similar to the one shown in figure 4.2 will appear.

Fig. 4.2

A spreadsheet status report.

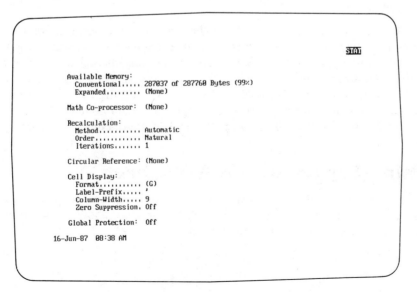

```
                                                              STAT

          Available Memory:
             Conventional..... 287037 of 287760 Bytes (99%)
             Expanded......... (None)

          Math Co-processor: (None)

          Recalculation:
             Method........... Automatic
             Order............ Natural
             Iterations....... 1

          Circular Reference: (None)

          Cell Display:
             Format........... (G)
             Label-Prefix..... '
             Column-Width..... 9
             Zero Suppression. Off

          Global Protection: Off

      16-Jun-87  08:38 AM
```

Reminder:
Press Esc to return
to the previous
command menu.
Press Ctrl-Break to
cancel the
command.

If you make the wrong command selection, you can press Esc at any time to return to the previous command menu. For instance, if you realize that you should have entered **Delete**, not **Insert**, press Esc to return to the **Worksheet** menu. You can press Esc as many times as necessary to return to whatever point you want in the series of command menus, even out of MENU mode altogether. One alternative to pressing Esc repeatedly is to hold down the Ctrl (Control) key and then press the Break key. Doing so cancels the entire command and returns you to READY mode.

Setting up two alternatives for command selection is just one of the ways that 1-2-3 has oriented itself successfully to both the novice and the experienced user. The novice can point to the different commands and get a full explanation of each one, and the experienced user can enter at high speed a long series of commands, using the first-letter convention without reading the explanations.

If you look at 1-2-3's main command menu, shown in figure 4.1, you can see the wide range of commands offered by 1-2-3. For a complete picture of the complexity of the command structure, look at the Command Reference chart at the back of the book (or next to your computer, if you have already torn out the chart and are keeping it close by as a reference).

This book also offers a complete Command Reference section in Part IV. The Command Reference lists all the 1-2-3 commands in alphabetical order, with basic instructions for their use, as well as some tips and warnings. After you have learned how to use 1-2-3, the Command Reference section will become an invaluable guide when you need to check quickly how to use a particular command.

As you read this book, you'll see that we have grouped the commands into several logical divisions instead of addressing each command in the order in which it appears in the menu. For example, this chapter covers **Copy**, **Move**, the **Worksheet** and **Range** commands (except **Worksheet Format** and **Range Format**, which are discussed in Chapter 5), and the **System** command. The **Graph** commands are covered in Chapter 10. **Data** commands are explained in Chapter 13, **Print** in Chapter 9, and **File** management in Chapter 7.

Using Ranges in the Worksheet

1-2-3's commands and functions often require that you deal with a *range*, a group of cells in aggregate. Before learning more about 1-2-3's commands, you need to learn a bit about ranges.

1-2-3's definition of a range is one or more cells in a rectangular group. With this definition, one cell is the smallest possible range, and the largest range is the entire worksheet.

The use of ranges offers many advantages, making your work less tedious and more efficient. Giving names to ranges allows you to process blocks of cells in commands and formulas at the same time, by using the range name instead of cell addresses.

When to use ranges in 1-2-3 depends to some degree on your personal preference. In many cases, such as in a formula or macro, you decide whether to provide ranges. In other cases, however, 1-2-3 will prompt you for ranges.

Ranges are rectangular in shape, as illustrated in figure 4.3. The expanding cell pointer allows you to see the shape of ranges in 1-2-3. When you are using a 1-2-3 command and you're asked to designate a range, you can do so in one of three ways. You can enter the addresses of the cells in the range, use the cell pointer to point to the cells in the range, or simply enter a name you have assigned to the range.

Fig. 4.3

A sample of 1-2-3 ranges.

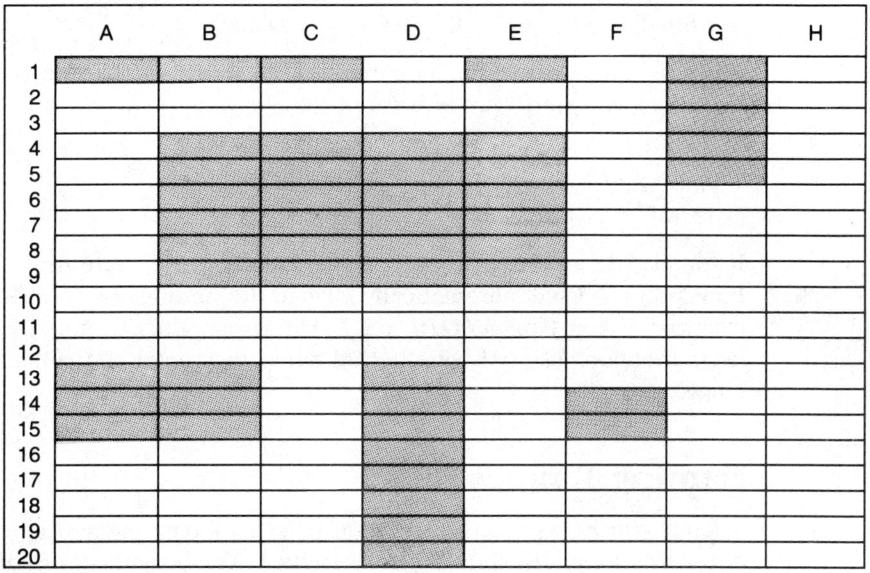

When a range has been designated, the cells of the range show up in reverse video. Reverse video makes pointing an easy way to designate ranges, because the reverse-video rectangle expands as the cell pointer moves (see fig. 4.4).

Ranges are specified by diagonally opposite corners, usually the upper left and lower right cells. The other set of corners, however, may also be used

Fig. 4.4

A range highlighted by the expanding cursor.

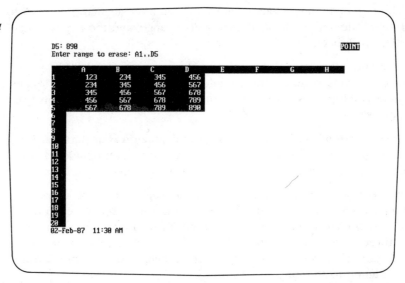

to identify the range. For example, the range shown in figure 4.4 could be identified as A1..D5, A5..D1, D5..A1, or D1..A5.

The usual custom is to separate the two cell addresses that specify the corners by one or two periods. For example,

A7..D10
AA1.AB20
J2..K4

Cue:
When you enter a range, you can type one or more periods between the cell addresses.

If you choose anything other than two periods to separate the cell addresses, however, 1-2-3 will automatically change the number of periods to two. For example, if you type *A7.D10*, 1-2-3 will display the range as A7..D10. Many users therefore use only one period when they enter the cell addresses of a range.

Naming Ranges

A name can be assigned to a range of cells. Range names can be up to 15 characters long and should be descriptive. The advantage of naming ranges is that range names are easier to understand than cell addresses and allow you to work more naturally. For example, the phrase *SALES_MODEL25* is a more understandable way of describing the sales for Model #25 than *A7..D10*.

Range names are created with the **/R**ange Name Create and **/R**ange Name Labels commands. Once names are established, they can be applied easily in both commands and formulas.

The /**R**ange Name **C**reate command allows you to specify a name for any range, even one cell. To access this command, first type a slash (/) from READY mode. At the main command menu, type an *r* to access the following **R**ange command menu:

Format   Label   Erase   Name   Justify   Protect   Unprotect   Input   Value   Transpose

This menu presents the set of commands that affect ranges. Select **N**ame by typing *n*. Then type *c* to select **C**reate. When the program asks you to Enter name:, type whatever range name you want and then press Enter. Don't use a name, however, that could be confused with a cell address. For example, don't name a range *EX87*, even though 1-2-3 allows the use of such a name. When you try to use this name in a command or formula, or with the F5 (GoTo) key, 1-2-3 will use the cell address EX87 instead of the range address.

When you are asked to Enter range:, you can do so by one of two methods: typing the cell addresses or pointing. If you choose the pointing method, the cell pointer will expand as you use the arrow keys to designate the range.

/**R**ange Name **C**reate can be used also to respecify a range if its location has changed. If minor changes occur to the range, such as a column or row of numbers being deleted from the range, 1-2-3 will handle these changes internally without any respecification. If you delete a column or row that contains a corner of the range, however, the range will be corrupted.

Caution:
Deleting a corner of a range will corrupt the range.

The /**R**ange Name **L**abels command is similar to /**R**ange Name **C**reate except that the names for ranges are taken directly from adjacent label entries. The adjacent entry must be a label; numeric entries and blank cells are ignored. Figure 4.5 illustrates one example of using the /RNL command to name a range.

If you use the /**R**ange Name **L**abels command and specify that the appropriate name for cell B1 is to the left in cell A1, you can assign the name CASH to the range B1. In this example, place the cell pointer on cell A1, type /rnlr, and press Enter; the name CASH will be assigned to the one-cell range to the right—cell B1.

If you also use the /**R**ange Name **L**abels command for ACCOUNTS RECEIV-ABLE, remember that a range name can be only 15 characters long. The resulting range name will be ACCOUNTS RECEIV. Another alternative would be to use the /**R**ange Name **C**reate command to give cell B2 an appropriate name.

The /**R**ange Name **C**reate and /**R**ange Name **L**abels commands do not have quite the same effect. When you **C**reate a name, you assign a name to a group of cells, perhaps as few as one cell but probably more. When you assign a **L**abel, you pick up a label from the spreadsheet and make that label the range

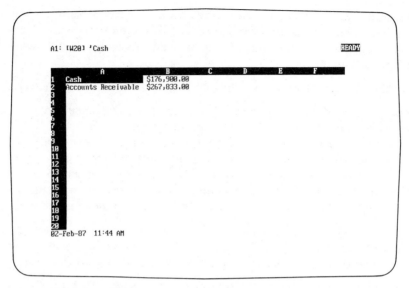

name of a one-cell range above, below, to the left, or to the right of the label. You can assign more than one label at a time, but each label applies only to one adjacent cell.

The advantage of using **/R**ange Name Create is that you can give a name to a multi-cell range. This is important if you are using range names in functions and formulas, or in move and copy operations. On the other hand, if you have a series of one-cell entries with adjacent labels, or a series of columns or rows with headings, the **/R**ange Name **L**abels command is a quick way to assign appropriate range names to the one-cell ranges or to the first entry of the column or row. The label at least provides an easy way to find the column or row: you press F5 (GoTo), enter the label (range name) and press Enter, and the cell pointer jumps to the head of the column or row.

Range names are used also for naming macros. Although macros are covered in detail in Chapter 14, we should note here that macros are named with the same commands that name a range. You will learn that when you access a macro you are jumping to the first entry in a range, because a macro name is actually a range name.

Using Range Names To Streamline Your Work

Cue:
Range names, rather than cell addresses, can be used in formulas.

Range names can be useful tools for processing commands and generating formulas. In both cases, whenever a range must be designated, you can respond with a name instead of entering cell addresses or pointing to cell locations. For example, suppose that you had designated the range name SALES for the range A5..J5 in one of your worksheets. The simplest way to compute the sum of this range would be to use the function @SUM(SALES). Similarly, to determine the maximum value in the range, you could use the function @MAX(SALES). In functions and formulas, range names always can be used in place of cell addresses.

Notice that 1-2-3 allows you to use multiple names for the same range. For example, a cell can be given the range names SALES_1987 and SALES_PREV_YR in the same worksheet. (Note that the underlines are part of the range names.) We'll see an application for this trick in Chapter 14, which discusses keyboard macros.

Still another advantage is that once a range name has been established, 1-2-3 automatically uses that name throughout the worksheet in place of cell addresses. The following list shows the effect of assigning the name REVENUES to the range A5..J5.

Before Creating Range Name	*After Creating Range Name*
@SUM(A5..J5)	@SUM(REVENUES)
@MAX(A5..J5)	@MAX(REVENUES)

Figure 4.6 shows an example of a simple case of summing a range of values.

Fig. 4.6

Using range names in @SUM functions.

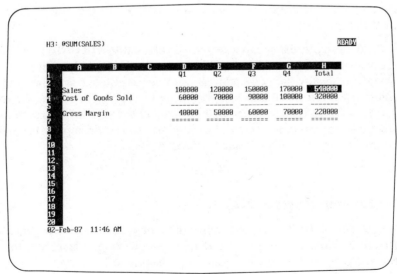

If the range name SALES is assigned to the range D3..G3 and the name CGS to range D4..G4, cell H3 can be defined with the formula

@SUM(SALES)

Similarly, cell H4 can be assigned the formula

@SUM(CGS)

Finally, cell H6 can contain the formula

@SUM(SALES)-@SUM(CGS)

The formulas in cells D6, E6, F6, and G6 cannot be defined in terms of the two ranges SALES and CGS, however, because these ranges refer to the two groups of cells that contain the values for all four quarters, not to the individual cells that contain the values for each quarter.

Another example uses names to designate the ranges of cells to be printed or extracted and saved to another worksheet. Suppose that you set up special names corresponding to different areas, and then you want to print, or extract and save to another worksheet, the corresponding portions of the current worksheet.

Cue:
Use range names to streamline entering print ranges.

When 1-2-3 prompts you for a range, you can enter a predefined name rather than actual cell addresses. For example, suppose that you were using the /**Print Printer Range** command to print a portion of a worksheet. In response to the Enter Print range: prompt, you could enter the range name PAGE_1 or the name PAGE_5.

A third example using range names involves the F5 (GoTo) key. You may recall that the F5 key allows you to move the cell pointer directly to a cell when you specify the cell's address. Another alternative is to provide a range name instead of a cell address. For example, suppose that you use the range name INSTRUCT for a set of cells that includes a set of instructions. When you press F5 and enter *Instruct* in response to the prompt Enter address to go to, you could get the results shown in figure 4.7.

Deleting Range Names

Caution:
The /Range Name Reset command deletes all range names.

Range names can be deleted individually or all at once. The /**Range Name Delete** command allows you to delete a single range name, and the /**Range Name Reset** command causes all range names to be deleted. Because of its power, the latter command should be used with caution.

If a range name is deleted, 1-2-3 no longer uses that name and reverts to cell addresses; for example, @SUM(REVENUES) returns to @SUM(A5..J5). The

Fig. 4.7

A screen display of instructions.

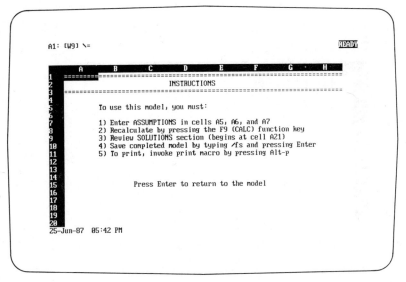

```
A1: [W9] \=                                                    READY

        A       B       C       D       E       F       G       H
1  ==================================================================
2                            INSTRUCTIONS
3  ==================================================================
4
5        To use this model, you must:
6
7        1) Enter ASSUMPTIONS in cells A5, A6, and A7
8        2) Recalculate by pressing the F9 (CALC) function key
9        3) Review SOLUTIONS section (begins at cell A21)
10       4) Save completed model by typing /fs and pressing Enter
11       5) To print, invoke print macro by pressing Alt-p
12
13
14
15                  Press Enter to return to the model
16
17
18
19
20
25-Jun-87  05:42 PM
```

contents of the cells within the range, however, remain intact. To erase the contents of ranges, you use the **/R**ange Erase command, which is explained next.

Erasing Ranges

The **/R**ange Erase command allows you to erase sections of the worksheet. This command can operate on a range as small as a single cell or as large as the entire worksheet.

For an example of this command, suppose that you created the simple worksheet shown in figure 4.8. Now suppose that you want to erase the range from A1 to C3. To remove this range, issue the **/R**ange Erase command. 1-2-3 prompts you to supply a range to delete. Either by pointing or by entering the coordinates from the keyboard, you instruct 1-2-3 to erase the range A1..C3. After you press Enter, 1-2-3 immediately erases the range.

After you erase a range, it cannot be recovered. You have to reenter all the data to restore the range.

Warning! Data cannot be recovered from an erased range.

You can erase ranges more easily if you have already assigned names to them. Using the example in figure 4.6 again, suppose that you have assigned the name CGS to the range D4..G4. You can erase this portion of the worksheet by typing **/R**ange Erase and entering the range name *CGS* rather than the cell coordinates D4..G4.

Fig. 4.8

A simple worksheet with values in cells A1..C3.

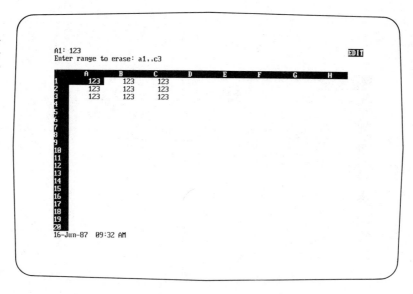

Getting a List of Range Names

Using figure 4.6 again, suppose that you type the /**Range Erase** command and then can't remember the name of the range you want to erase. You could press the F3 (Names) key to produce a list of the range names in the current worksheet. Figure 4.9 shows the screen at that point.

Fig. 4.9

The effect of using the F3 (Names) key during a /Range Erase command.

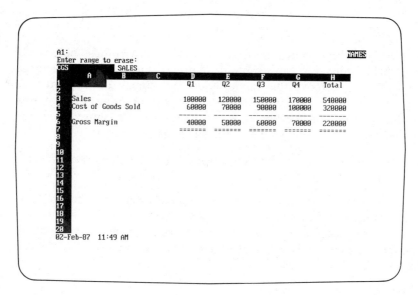

After the list appears, you can use the cursor to point to the first alternative, CGS, and then select CGS by pressing Enter. If there are more names than can be displayed at once on the command line, press F3 again to get a full screen display of the range names.

The Names key can be used whenever the worksheet is in POINT mode. You can print a copy of this list by holding down the Shift key and pressing the PrtSc (PrintScreen) key. (Using Shift-PrtSc while your printer is turned on and on-line will print whatever is on the screen.)

You can use the Names key with the F5 (GoTo) key to select the name of a range to which you want to move the cell pointer. If you press F5 and then press F3, an alphabetical list of the range names in your spreadsheet appears in the control panel. To designate the range you want to jump to, select a name from the list by using the right- and left-arrow keys or the space bar. When you press Enter, the list disappears and the cell pointer is positioned at the beginning of the selected range.

If you have more range names than will fit on the control panel, you can use the arrow keys or the space bar to "wrap around" to the rest of the names, or you can press F3 again. After you press F3 a second time, the worksheet disappears and the entire list (or as much of it as the screen can hold) is displayed. Use the space bar or the arrow keys, including the up- and down-arrow keys, or the Home and End keys to select the name of the range you want to jump to. When you press Enter, the list disappears and the worksheet reappears with the cell pointer at the beginning of the selected range.

Creating a Table of Range Names

If you are using range names in a worksheet and have created several range names, you may want to document the names in a table in the worksheet. To perform this task, 1-2-3 provides the /**R**ange **N**ame **T**able command. Creating a range name table is simple, but you must exercise care in your placement of the table. Make certain that your placement will not write the table over an important part of the worksheet.

Reminder:
The /RNT command gives you a record of all range names (with cell references) in the worksheet.

To create the range name table, you select the /**R**ange **N**ame **T**able command. When 1-2-3 asks for the location for the table, indicate the cell where you want the upper left corner of the table to appear, and then press Enter.

1-2-3 writes a table that consists of all your range names in a column, with the referenced ranges in the cells to the immediate right of each range name. Figure 4.10 shows a range name table containing several names and referenced ranges.

Fig. 4.10

*A range name
table created with
the /RNT
command.*

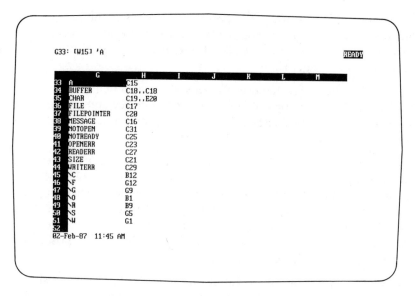

```
G33: [W15] 'A                                                    READY

              G              H          I       J       K       L       M
33  A                  C15
34  BUFFER             C18..C18
35  CHAR               C19..E20
36  FILE               C17
37  FILEPOINTER        C20
38  MESSAGE            C16
39  NOTOPEN            C31
40  NOTREADY           C25
41  OPENERR            C23
42  READERR            C27
43  SIZE               C21
44  WRITERR            C29
45  \C                 B12
46  \F                 G12
47  \G                 G9
48  \O                 B1
49  \R                 B9
50  \S                 G5
51  \W                 G1
52
02-Feb-87  11:45 AM
```

Using Worksheet Commands

1-2-3 offers a group of commands that are similar to the **Range** commands but affect the entire worksheet or preset segments of it. With **Range** commands, you define the range of cells that is affected by the commands; you do not have the same liberty with **Worksheet** commands—they affect the entire worksheet or entire rows or columns.

When you issue the /**Worksheet** command, the following menu appears:

> Global Insert Delete Column Erase Titles Window Status Page

These commands are used for a variety of tasks, including erasing the entire worksheet, setting column widths, splitting the screen into two sections, freezing titles so that they remain on the screen as you move around the worksheet, and setting the method of recalculating all the formulas in a worksheet.

Erasing the Worksheet

The /**Worksheet** Erase command clears the entire spreadsheet. This command not only erases all the contents of the worksheet but also restores all global settings to their default condition, destroys any range names or graph names in the worksheet, and clears any title lock or window split in the worksheet.

Be sure that you understand the difference between the /**Worksheet** Erase command and the /**Range** Erase A1..IV8192 command. The /**Range** Erase command will remove the contents of every cell in the worksheet, except those that are protected. It will not, however, alter any of the global settings, including column widths or print settings. /Worksheet Erase, however, literally restores the 1-2-3 worksheet to its default configuration. After the /WE command is issued, the worksheet is exactly as it was when loaded.

Obviously, the /Worksheet Erase command is a powerful and potentially destructive command. For this reason, 1-2-3 will always force you either to type a *y*, for "Yes, I want to erase the entire worksheet," or to point to Yes and press Enter, before this command will be executed.

Once a worksheet has been erased in this way, it cannot be recovered. Always save your worksheets before you erase them. To learn how to save your worksheet, see Chapter 7 or this chapter's "Saving Your Worksheet before You /Quit" section.

Warning!
/Worksheet Erase
clears all the data
and settings from the
entire worksheet.
The data and
settings cannot be
recovered.

Setting Column Widths

You can control the width of columns in the worksheet to accommodate data entries that are too wide for the default column width of 9 characters. You also can reduce column widths, perhaps to give the worksheet a better appearance when a column contains narrow entries. In 1-2-3, you can set the width of all the columns in the worksheet at once or separately control the width of each column.

Suppose that you are setting up a projection of expenses for the next five years and want to display the full descriptions of the expense items (some of them 20 characters wide). You can set the first column of your projection of expenses to be 20 characters wide (to accommodate the descriptions) and then set the other columns to whatever width you want.

The command used to set individual column widths is /Worksheet Column Set-Width. You can set one column width at a time either by entering a number or by using the left- and right-arrow keys followed by Enter. The advantage of the left- and right-arrow keys is that the column width expands and contracts each time you press a key. To get a good idea of what the width requirements are, experiment when you enter the command.

There are two things to remember about this command. First, you must position the pointer in the proper column before you initiate the command. Otherwise, you will have to start over. Second, to reset the column width to the standard setting, you must use the /Worksheet Column Reset-Width command.

Reminder:
Position the cell
pointer in the correct
column before
initiating the "Set-
Width command."

You can also control all the column widths in the worksheet at once. The command to do this in 1-2-3 is /Worksheet Global Column-Width. This is one of the Global commands—commands that affect the entire worksheet. Many of the Global commands have corresponding **Range** commands to affect only certain areas of the worksheet, although in this case the corresponding command is the /Worksheet Column Set-Width command, as explained previously.

/**Range** commands typically take precedence over /Worksheet commands. In this case, the /Worksheet Column Set-Width command takes precedence over the /Worksheet Global Column-Width command. That is, any column width previously set by the /Worksheet Column Set-Width command will not be affected by a change in the global setting.

For example, if you set the width of column A to 12 using the /Worksheet Column Set-Width command, and then change all the columns in the worksheet to a width of 5 using the /Worksheet Global Column-Width command, every column except column A will change to 5. Column A will remain at a width of 12 and will have to be reset to 5 with the /Worksheet Column Reset-Width command.

Splitting the Screen

You can split the 1-2-3 screen display into two parts, either horizontally or vertically. This feature helps you to overcome some of the inconvenience of not being able to see the entire spreadsheet at one time.

Suppose, for example, that you are working on a large model which spans several columns and that you are having trouble keeping track of how the changes made in one area of the worksheet are affecting another area. By splitting the screen, you can make the changes in one area and immediately see their effect in the other.

The command for splitting the screen is /Worksheet Window. When you enter this command, the following menu choices appear:

> Horizontal   Vertical   Sync   Unsync   Clear

Reminder:
Before using /WW, move the cell pointer to where you want the split to appear.

Horizontal and Vertical split the screen in the manner indicated by their names. The screen will split at the point at which the cell pointer is positioned when you enter Horizontal or Vertical. In other words, you don't have to split the screen exactly in half. Remember that the dividing line will require either one row or one column, depending on how you split the screen.

After you split the screen using Horizontal, the cell pointer appears in the top window. When you create a Vertical division, the cell pointer appears in the left window (see fig. 4.11). To jump the division between the windows, use the F6 (Window) key.

Fig. 4.11

A vertically split screen.

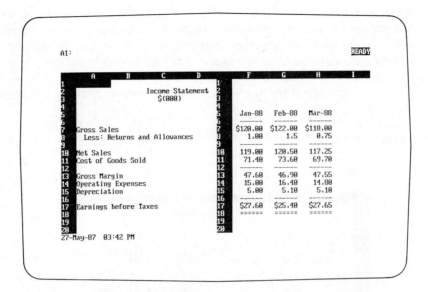

The **S**ync and **U**nsync options work as a pair. In **S**ync screen mode, when you scroll one screen, the other screen automatically scrolls with it. Horizontally split screens always keep the same columns in view, and vertically split screens always keep the same rows. **S**ync is the standard default for 1-2-3.

Unsync screens allow you to control one screen independently of the other in all directions. In fact, you can even show the same cells in the two different windows.

The **C**lear option removes the split-window option and reverts the screen to a single window. When you use this option, the single window takes on the settings of the top or left-hand window, depending on how the screen was split.

Freezing Titles on the Screen

The /**W**orksheet **T**itles command is similar to the /**W**orksheet **W**indow command. Both commands allow you to see one area of a worksheet while you work on another. The unique function of the /**W**orksheet **T**itles command, however, is that it freezes all the cells to the left or above (or both to the left and above) the cell pointer's current position so that those cells cannot move off the screen.

A classic example of the advantage of this command occurs when you enter the items on a pro forma Balance Sheet and Income Statement. Suppose that you are trying to set up a budget to project the level of the financial statement items month by month for the next year. Because the normal screen, without any special column widths, shows 20 rows by 7 columns, you undoubtedly will have to shift the screen so that cell A1 is no longer in the upper left corner. In fact, if you enter the month headings across row 1 and the Balance Sheet and Income Statement headings down column A, as shown in figure 4.12, you must scroll the screen several different times in order to enter all the items.

Fig. 4.12

A balance-sheet worksheet.

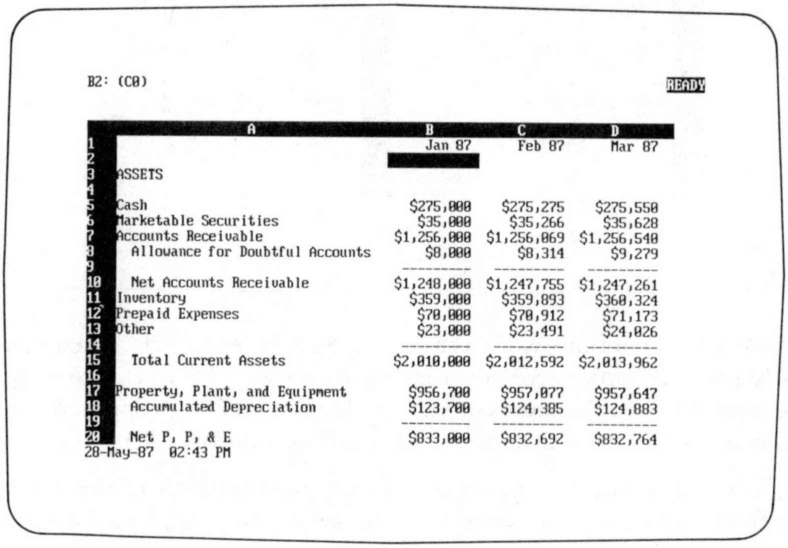

```
B2: (C0)                                                              READY

              A                      B           C           D
 1                                 Jan 87      Feb 87      Mar 87
 2
 3  ASSETS
 4
 5  Cash                          $275,000    $275,275    $275,550
 6  Marketable Securities          $35,000     $35,266     $35,628
 7  Accounts Receivable         $1,256,000  $1,256,069  $1,256,540
 8     Allowance for Doubtful Accounts  $8,000   $8,314      $9,279
 9                               ----------  ----------  ----------
10     Net Accounts Receivable   $1,248,000  $1,247,755  $1,247,261
11  Inventory                     $359,000    $359,893    $360,324
12  Prepaid Expenses               $70,000     $70,912     $71,173
13  Other                         $23,000     $23,491     $24,026
14                               ----------  ----------  ----------
15     Total Current Assets     $2,010,000  $2,012,592  $2,013,962
16
17  Property, Plant, and Equipment  $956,700    $957,077    $957,647
18  Accumulated Depreciation      $123,700    $124,385    $124,883
19                               ----------  ----------  ----------
20     Net P, P, & E             $833,000    $832,692    $832,764
28-May-87  02:43 PM
```

To keep the headings in view on the screen, even when you scroll the screen, enter /wt when the cell pointer is highlighting cell B2. When you enter the /WT command, the following menu items appear:

    Both   Horizontal   Vertical   Clear

Reminder:

Move the cell pointer to the appropriate position before executing the /WT command.

If you select **H**orizontal, the rows on the screen above the cell pointer become frozen. That is, they don't move off the screen when you scroll up and down. If you select **V**ertical, the columns to the left of the cell pointer are frozen and move only when you scroll up and down (but not when you move left and right). The **B**oth option freezes the rows above and the columns to the left of the cell pointer. Remember to move the cell pointer to the desired location before executing the /WT command. Clear unlocks the worksheet titles.

In our pro forma example, we have selected the **B**oth option. In this case, when you scroll right and left as well as up and down, the headings always remain in view. Figures 4.13 and 4.14 show two examples of how this works. In figure 4.13, we scrolled across the spreadsheet to display columns F, G, and H, while keeping the headings in Column A on the screen. In figure 4.14, we scrolled down the spreadsheet to display rows 21 through 39, while keeping the headings in row 1 on the screen.

Fig. 4.13

Moving to the right in the worksheet after setting titles.

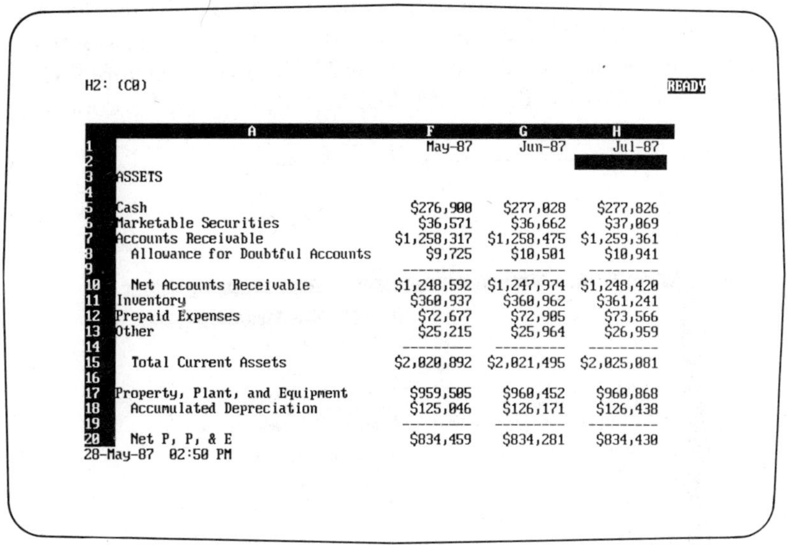

```
H2: (C0)                                                    READY

                   A              F          G          H
1                               May-87     Jun-87     Jul-87
2
3         ASSETS
4
5         Cash                  $276,900   $277,028   $277,826
6         Marketable Securities  $36,571    $36,662    $37,069
7         Accounts Receivable  $1,258,317 $1,258,475 $1,259,361
8           Allowance for Doubtful Accounts  $9,725  $10,501  $10,941
9                               ---------  ---------  ---------
10          Net Accounts Receivable $1,248,592 $1,247,974 $1,248,420
11        Inventory             $360,937   $360,962   $361,241
12        Prepaid Expenses       $72,677    $72,905    $73,566
13        Other                  $25,215    $25,964    $26,959
14                              ---------  ---------  ---------
15          Total Current Assets $2,020,892 $2,021,495 $2,025,081
16
17        Property, Plant, and Equipment $959,505 $960,452 $960,868
18          Accumulated Depreciation $125,046 $126,171 $126,438
19                              ---------  ---------  ---------
20          Net P, P, & E        $834,459   $834,281   $834,430
20-May-87  02:50 PM
```

Fig. 4.14

Moving down in the worksheet after setting titles.

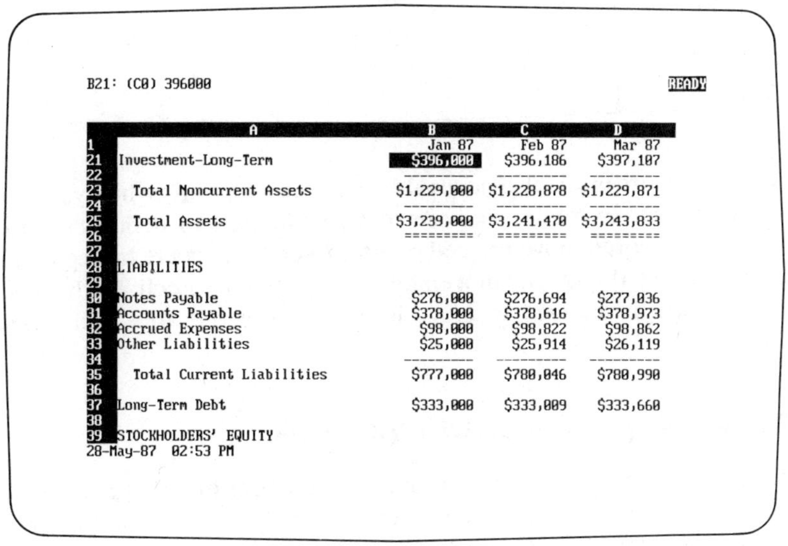

```
B21: (C0) 396000                                            READY

                   A              B          C          D
1                               Jan 87     Feb 87     Mar 87
21        Investment-Long-Term  $396,000   $396,186   $397,187
22                              ---------  ---------  ---------
23          Total Noncurrent Assets $1,229,000 $1,228,878 $1,229,871
24                              ---------  ---------  ---------
25          Total Assets       $3,239,000 $3,241,470 $3,243,833
26                              =========  =========  =========
27
28        LIABILITIES
29
30        Notes Payable         $276,000   $276,694   $277,036
31        Accounts Payable      $378,000   $378,616   $378,973
32        Accrued Expenses       $98,000    $98,822    $98,862
33        Other Liabilities      $25,000    $25,914    $26,119
34                              ---------  ---------  ---------
35          Total Current Liabilities $777,000 $780,046 $780,990
36
37        Long-Term Debt        $333,000   $333,009   $333,660
38
39        STOCKHOLDERS' EQUITY
20-May-87  02:53 PM
```

When you freeze rows or columns, you cannot move the cell pointer into the frozen area. In our example, if you try to move the cell pointer into cell A2 from cell B2, 1-2-3 will beep and not allow the cell pointer to move into the protected area. Similarly, using the Home key will move the cell pointer only to the upper left cell in the unlocked area. In our example, this is cell B2. Normally, the Home function moves the cell pointer to cell A1.

Cue:

The F5 key will jump the cell pointer into the frozen area.

One exception to this restriction occurs when you use the F5 (GoTo) key. If you use the GoTo function to jump to cell A1, you will see two copies of the title rows and/or columns. Figure 4.15 shows our example when you use the F5 key to go to cell A1. The dual set of titles can be confusing.

Fig. 4.15

The display after using the F5 (GoTo) key to move to cell A1.

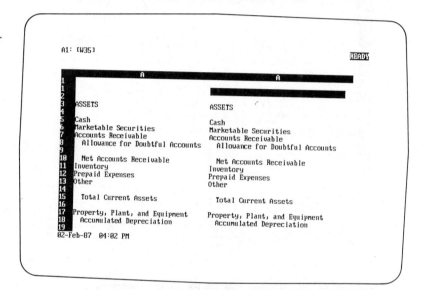

The frozen areas are also accessible in other situations when you're in POINT mode. In our example, suppose that you wanted to define cell B6 as equal to A1. You would move the cell pointer to cell B6, type + to begin the formula, and then use the cursor-movement keys to point to cell A1. In this case, the cell pointer is allowed to move into the protected area, and 1-2-3 will not beep.

Inserting Rows and Columns

Suppose that you have finished building a model in a worksheet but want to dress up its general appearance before you show the model to anyone. One of the techniques for improving a worksheet's appearance is to insert blank rows and columns in strategic places to highlight headings and other important items.

The command for inserting rows and columns in 1-2-3 is /Worksheet Insert. You can insert multiple rows and columns each time you invoke this command. After you select /Worksheet Insert, you are asked for the method of insertion, Column or Row. After you have selected one or the other, you are asked for an insert range. Depending on how you set up this range, one or more columns or rows will be inserted.

Inserted columns appear to the left of the specified range, and inserted rows appear above the specified range. For example, suppose that you created the worksheet shown in figure 4.16. If you issue the /Worksheet Insert Column command and specify an insert range of A10..A10, a single blank column is inserted at column A, as shown in figure 4.17. 1-2-3 automatically shifts all the values over one column and modifies all the cell formulas for the change. If you then repeat the command, but specify the Row option and a range of A10..A10, 1-2-3 inserts one blank row at row 10; the values that were contained in row 10 move to row 11. Figure 4.18 illustrates the results of that operation.

1-2-3 does not have the capability of inserting or deleting partial rows and columns.

Fig. 4.16

The worksheet before using insert commands.

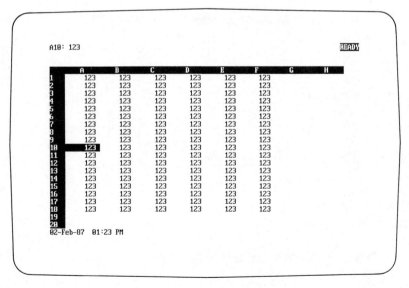

Fig. 4.17

The worksheet
after inserting a
column.

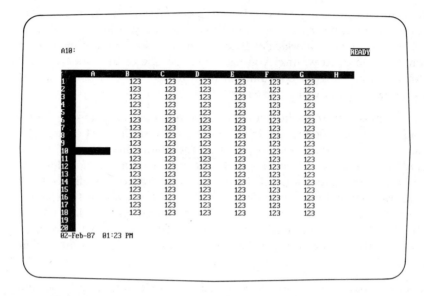

Fig. 4.18

The worksheet
after inserting a
row.

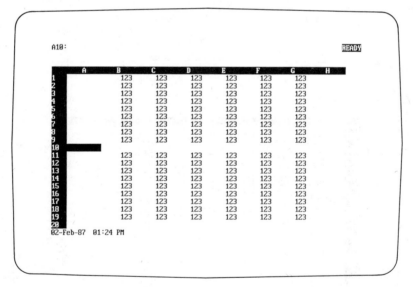

Deleting Rows and Columns

Deleting rows and columns is the opposite of inserting them. 1-2-3 allows
you to delete multiple rows or columns at the same time with the /Worksheet
Delete command. After you choose this command, you then choose Column
or Row from the submenu that appears on the screen. If you choose Row,
1-2-3 asks you to specify a range of cells to be deleted. Just as for the

/**W**orksheet **I**nsert command, the range you specify includes one cell from a given row.

For example, to delete rows 2 and 3 in the worksheet in figure 4.19, you should specify A2..A3. Other acceptable range designations are B2..B3, C2..C3, C2..G3, etc. The results of the deletion are shown in figure 4.20.

Fig. 4.19

The worksheet before deleting rows.

A1: 1 READY

	A	B	C	D	E	F	G	H
1	1	1	1	1	1	1	1	1
2	2	2	2	2	2	2	2	2
3	3	3	3	3	3	3	3	3
4	4	4	4	4	4	4	4	4
5	5	5	5	5	5	5	5	5
6	6	6	6	6	6	6	6	6
7	7	7	7	7	7	7	7	7
8	8	8	8	8	8	8	8	8
9	9	9	9	9	9	9	9	9
10	10	10	10	10	10	10	10	10
11	11	11	11	11	11	11	11	11
12	12	12	12	12	12	12	12	12
13	13	13	13	13	13	13	13	13
14	14	14	14	14	14	14	14	14
15	15	15	15	15	15	15	15	15
16	16	16	16	16	16	16	16	16
17	17	17	17	17	17	17	17	17
18	18	18	18	18	18	18	18	18
19	19	19	19	19	19	19	19	19
20	20	20	20	20	20	20	20	20

02-Feb-87 01:25 PM

Fig. 4.20

The worksheet after deleting rows.

A2: 4 READY

	A	B	C	D	E	F	G	H
1	1	1	1	1	1	1	1	1
2	4	4	4	4	4	4	4	4
3	5	5	5	5	5	5	5	5
4	6	6	6	6	6	6	6	6
5	ERR	ERR	ERR	ERR	ERR	ERR	ERR	ERR
6	8	8	8	8	8	8	8	8
7	9	9	9	9	9	9	9	9
8	10	10	10	10	10	10	10	10
9	11	11	11	11	11	11	11	11
10	12	12	12	12	12	12	12	12
11	13	13	13	13	13	13	13	13
12	14	14	14	14	14	14	14	14
13	15	15	15	15	15	15	15	15
14	16	16	16	16	16	16	16	16
15	17	17	17	17	17	17	17	17
16	18	18	18	18	18	18	18	18
17	19	19	19	19	19	19	19	19
18	20	20	20	20	20	20	20	20
19								
20								

02-Feb-87 01:26 PM

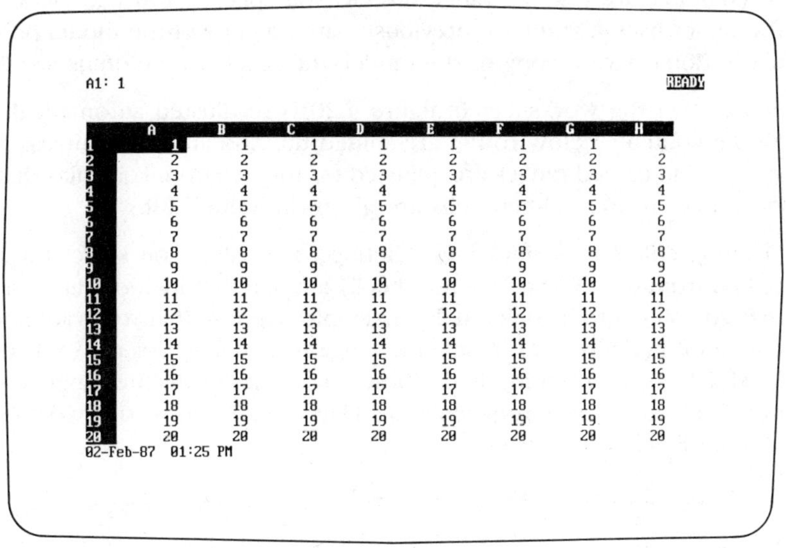

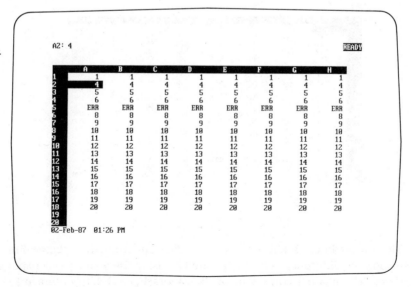

The easiest way to designate the range to be deleted is to point to the appropriate cells. You also can enter the cell addresses from the keyboard. Pointing to cells, however, helps you to avoid inadvertently choosing the wrong range.

Warning!
The /WD command destroys all the data in a row or column. The data cannot be recovered.

Remember that when you use the /**W**orksheet **D**elete command, the rows or columns you delete are gone forever. This includes all the cells in the rows or columns, not just the range of cells you specify. You may be able to get the values back if you have previously saved a copy of the model on disk. But if you don't have a copy of the model, the rows and columns are lost.

Notice that the worksheet in figure 4.20 is readjusted automatically so that all the contents below row 3 are shifted up. And all the formulas, command ranges, and named ranges are adjusted for the deletion. Formulas that contain references to the deleted cells are given the value ERR.

Cue:
The pointing method helps you avoid deleting the wrong column or row.

Deleting columns is similar to deleting rows. After you select the **C**olumns option from the /WD submenu, specify a range that includes at least one cell in each column to be deleted. For example, suppose that you wanted to delete column B in figure 4.21. A suitable range to designate for the /WD command is B1..B1. Again, pointing is the best way to designate the range so that you avoid selecting the wrong column. Figure 4.22 shows the worksheet after column B has been deleted.

Fig. 4.21
The worksheet before deleting a column.

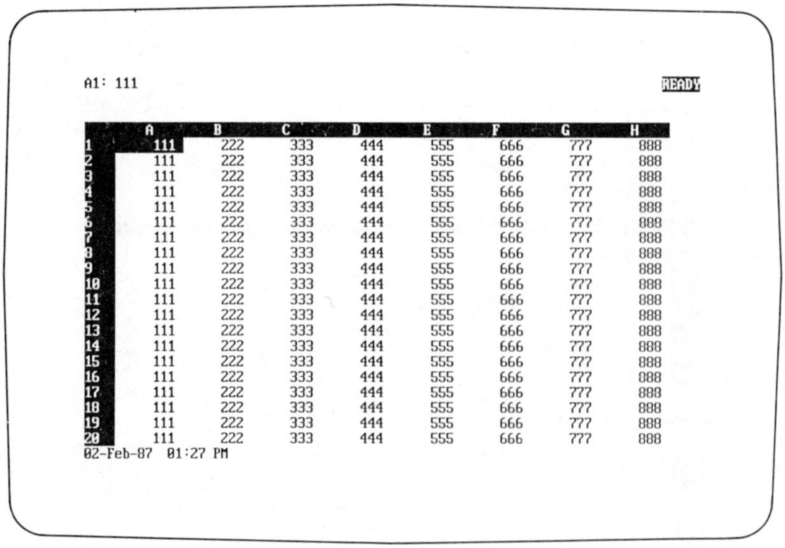

A1: 111 READY

	A	B	C	D	E	F	G	H
1	111	222	333	444	555	666	777	888
2	111	222	333	444	555	666	777	888
3	111	222	333	444	555	666	777	888
4	111	222	333	444	555	666	777	888
5	111	222	333	444	555	666	777	888
6	111	222	333	444	555	666	777	888
7	111	222	333	444	555	666	777	888
8	111	222	333	444	555	666	777	888
9	111	222	333	444	555	666	777	888
10	111	222	333	444	555	666	777	888
11	111	222	333	444	555	666	777	888
12	111	222	333	444	555	666	777	888
13	111	222	333	444	555	666	777	888
14	111	222	333	444	555	666	777	888
15	111	222	333	444	555	666	777	888
16	111	222	333	444	555	666	777	888
17	111	222	333	444	555	666	777	888
18	111	222	333	444	555	666	777	888
19	111	222	333	444	555	666	777	888
20	111	222	333	444	555	666	777	888

02-Feb-87 01:27 PM

The /**W**orksheet **D**elete command is different from the /**R**ange **E**rase command. The difference is best explained by using the analogy of a paper spreadsheet. The manual equivalent of the /**W**orksheet **D**elete command is to cut

Fig. 4.22

The worksheet after deleting a column.

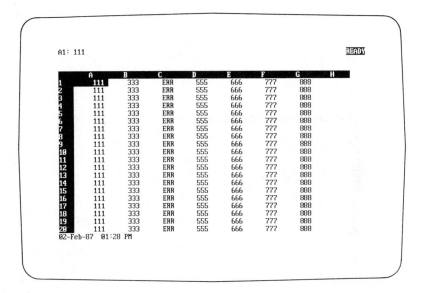

apart the columnar sheet (using a pair of scissors), remove the unwanted columns and/or rows, and then paste the pieces of the sheet back together. The /Range Erase command, on the other hand, is like using an eraser to erase ranges of cells from the sheet. Do not forget the difference between these powerful commands.

In native 1-2-3 terms, there are two differences between deleting cells using /Worksheet Delete and erasing cells using /Range Erase. First, /Worksheet Delete deletes entire columns and rows within a worksheet, whereas /Range Erase erases particular ranges of cells, which may be as small or as large as you wish. Second, the worksheet is readjusted automatically to fill in the gaps created by the deleted columns or rows when you use the /Worksheet Delete command. This is not the case, however, for the /Range Erase command. The cells in the range that has been erased are merely blanked.

Hiding Columns

The /Worksheet Column Hide command allows you to suppress the display of any columns in the worksheet. One important use for this command is to suppress display of unwanted columns when printing reports. When intervening columns are hidden, a report can display on a single page data from two or more separated columns.

Figures 4.23 and 4.24 show an example of the process of hiding columns. In the worksheet shown in figure 4.23, columns A through G are filled with numbers. Figure 4.24 shows the same worksheet after the /Worksheet Column Hide command has been used to hide columns C, D, and E.

Fig. 4.23.

The worksheet with numbers in columns A through G.

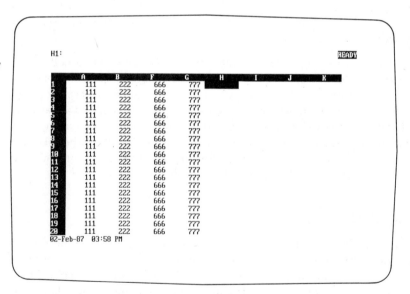

Fig. 4.24.

The same worksheet with columns C, D, and E hidden.

Numbers and formulas in hidden columns are still present, and cell references to cells in hidden columns continue to work properly. But the hidden columns do not appear on the display. You can tell which columns are missing only by noting the break in the column letters at the top of the display. The hidden columns are temporarily redisplayed, however, when you use certain commands, such as /Copy or /Move; the hidden columns are marked with an asterisk (e.g., H*) during this temporary display.

When you select the /Worksheet Column Hide command, 1-2-3 prompts you for the range of columns to hide. You must invoke the command once for each range of adjacent columns that you hide.

To redisplay hidden columns, use /Worksheet Column Display. When you select this command, all hidden columns are redisplayed with asterisks by the column letters at the top of the display. You are prompted for a range of columns to "unhide."

If the screen has been split, certain 1-2-3 commands affect only the current window. For example, the /Worksheet Column Hide command can be used to hide a column in the current window without affecting the display in the other window.

Suppressing the Display of Zeros

The /Worksheet Global Zero command allows you to suppress the display of all the cells in the worksheet that have a numeric value of zero. This is often useful for preparing reports for presentation. You can enter formulas and values for all the items in the report, including the zero items, and then display the results with all the zeros removed. The /Worksheet Global Zero command also has an option to reinstate the display of zero values. If you use /WGZ, save the file, and then retrieve the file, /WGZ will be disabled and the display of zeros will no longer be suppressed.

Recalculating the Worksheet

One of the primary functions of a spreadsheet program is to recalculate all the cells in a worksheet when a value or a formula in one of the cells changes. This is the feature that makes it possible to build a model—of sales projections, for example—and predict the results when you change various elements of the model. To see the effects of each change or set of changes, you need to recalculate the worksheet. You use another Global command, the /Worksheet Global Recalculation command, to choose the method and order of recalculation.

1-2-3 provides two basic recalculation methods: *automatic recalculation* and *manual recalculation*. Using automatic recalculation, which is the default, 1-2-3 recalculates the worksheet whenever any cell in the worksheet changes. In manual recalculation, the worksheet is recalculated only when the user requests it, either from the keyboard or from a macro.

1-2-3 also provides three orders of recalculation: the *natural order* and two linear orders, either *columnwise* or *rowwise*. *Natural order* is the default, but you can choose any of the three orders.

You also can choose the number of times the spreadsheet is recalculated; because of circular references, which are explained in this section, the spreadsheet may need to be recalculated several times whenever you request recalculation.

You select all the recalculation options by using the /Worksheet Global Recalculation command.

Choosing a Recalculation Method: Automatic or Manual

When you are working on a large worksheet that involves many formulas, worksheet recalculation may take some time. Recalculation occurs each time a value is changed or a new entry is made, even if the entry is only a label. One way to get around this problem is to change from the standard automatic to manual recalculation. This is done easily by executing /Worksheet Global Recalculation, and then choosing Manual.

With manual recalculation, you can control 1-2-3 so that it recalculates only when you press the F9 (Calc) key or when a macro forces a recalculation. Manual recalculation is an advantage only with large worksheets in which you are changing many values, or if you have a slow computer. Otherwise, 1-2-3's speed is enough for recalculation to occur almost instantly.

The Edit and F9 (Calc) functions can be used together to convert a formula stored in a cell to a simple number. F9 is normally used for recalculating when /Worksheet Global Recalculation is set to Manual. When you are in EDIT mode, however, pressing F9 will cause a formula to be converted to a number, its current value.

For example, suppose that you want to use F9 to convert the formula +C4/H3*(Y5+4000) to its current value (which we'll assume is 64,000), and store the result. Position the cell pointer on the cell containing the formula and proceed as follows:

Keys	Edit Line	Explanation
F2	+C4/H3*(Y5+4000)	F2 puts 1-2-3 in EDIT mode.
F9	64000	F9 converts the formula to its current value. We picked 64,000 at random.
Enter		Stores the entry in the current cell and shifts back to READY mode.

Be careful when you use this technique. Converting the formula to a value in this way destroys the formula.

This trick will also cause a cell address that references a label to convert to a label. For example, suppose that you have the label *'Monthly Contributions* entered in cell B2, and then you want to enter the same label elsewhere in your worksheet, say in cell AA25. You could enter *+b2* into cell AA25 to cause *Monthly Contributions* to appear on the display in cell location AA25.

The problem is that cell AA25 still contains the entry *+B2*; if you ever decide to copy the contents of the cell, relative addressing will cause the B2 to change to something else (see the "Relative Addressing" section of this chapter). Solve the problem by using the F2 (Edit) and the F9 (Calc) keys. *+B2* will convert to the label *'Monthly Contributions.*

Choosing the Order of Recalculation: Columnwise or Rowwise

Although 1-2-3 normally uses the *natural order* of recalculation, explaining this order is difficult without having first explained the two linear orders: Columnwise and **Rowwise**.

In the **Columnwise** procedure, recalculation begins at the entry in cell A1 and proceeds down column A, then continues at cell B1 and moves down column B, and so on. In contrast, **Rowwise** recalculation starts at cell A1 and proceeds across row 1, then moves down to cell A2 and across row 2, and so on.

These orders of recalculation can often lead to the wrong answer unless you are careful about how you set up the worksheet. Forward and circular references are among the errors that can occur with linear recalculation.

A forward reference occurs when a cell refers to another cell that is lower in the worksheet. For example, imagine that you have created a worksheet with four cells: A1, C1, C2, and C3. Suppose that those cells had the following contents:

    A1 = +C3
    C1 = 100
    C2 = 200
    C3 = +C1+C2

Both A1 and C3 would have the value 300. Now, suppose that the number in cell C2 is changed to 100. Let's step through the recalculative process. Because the recalculation begins at the upper left corner of the worksheet, cell A1 would be evaluated first. Because the prior value of C3, 300, has not changed, A1 retains the value 300. The recalculation then proceeds either column by column or row by row across the worksheet until it comes to cell C3. Because the value of cell C2 has changed, the value in C3 changes to 200.

Clearly, it does not make sense to have A1 and C3 contain different values when cell A1 is defined to be equal to C3. Although recalculating the worksheet again would eliminate the inequality, it would not remove the basic problem. In large and complex models, you often intentionally build in forward references, but you also can easily build in undetected, and unwanted, forward references.

If you want 1-2-3 to recalculate in a linear fashion, override the default natural order setting by using /Worksheet Global Recalculation <Columnwise or Rowwise>.

Cue:
Reasons for overriding the natural order of recalculation.

There are at least three situations in which you would select Columnwise or Rowwise recalculation: (1) if you are importing a file that is built around the linear recalculation order; (2) if you are solving intentional circular references (for example, to reflect the true algebraic relationship among the variables); or (3) if the same number of iterations is needed under both natural and linear orders (in this case, one of the linear orders can be a bit faster than the natural order). (For an explanation of iterations and circular references, see the "Iterative Recalculation" section of this chapter.)

Recalculating the Worksheet in the Natural Order

1-2-3 normally recalculates in what Lotus calls a *natural order*. Because this order is the default, you do not have to issue a command for this option. If you have changed the default and want to change back to natural order, use the /Worksheet Global Recalculation Natural command.

Natural order means that all the active cells in a worksheet are interrelated, and 1-2-3 does not recalculate any given cell until after the cells that it depends on have been recalculated. Recalculation occurs in a topological fashion, starting at the lowest level and working up.

C3

B1　B3　B4

A1　A2　A4　A7　A9

With natural recalculation, you do not have to worry about the order of recalculation or the problem of forward references. If we were to re-create our forward reference example in 1-2-3 and use natural recalculation, cell C3—the most fundamental cell in the worksheet—would be evaluated before cell A1, eliminating the forward reference.

Iterative Recalculation

In most cases, recalculating a worksheet takes only one pass. This is not possible, however, when a worksheet contains a circular reference, and may be impossible also when **Columnwise** or **Rowwise** recalculation is used even if there is no circular reference.

A classic example of a circular reference is the problem of trying to determine the amount of a bonus to be paid to the executive of a corporation. Consider the following steps in the process of making the calculation:

1. The bonus is set at 10% of the after-tax profits of the corporation.

2. The bonus is a tax-deductible expense of the corporation, and therefore must be known in order to calculate the after-tax profits.

3. The after-tax profits must be known in order to calculate the bonus.

You can see the circular pattern. When this kind of circular reference occurs, 1-2-3 displays a CIRC indicator in the lower right corner of the screen. When you recalculate this type of worksheet using regular natural calculation, 1-2-3 will not accurately recompute all the values. Because each value in the circular set depends, directly or indirectly, on all the others, 1-2-3 cannot find a "toehold"; that is, 1-2-3 cannot find the most fundamental cell in the worksheet because there is no such cell.

Iterative recalculation allows 1-2-3 to overcome this problem. You choose iterative recalculation with the **/W**orksheet **G**lobal **R**ecalculation **I**teration command. The command allows you to choose as many as 50 iterations.

When 1-2-3 is in ITERATIVE mode, the worksheet will recalculate a specified number of times for each time you change cell contents for automatic recalculation, or for each time you press the F9 (Calc) key for manual recalculation. Normally, the worksheet will recalculate only once for each F9 keystroke. The default number of iterations under ITERATION mode is 1, but you can alter this number as you see fit up to the maximum of 50.

If your worksheet contains circular references, we suggest that you keep the number of recalculation passes high. Because 1-2-3 does not recognize the iteration parameter when you're using natural order and the worksheet has no circular references, keeping the number of iterations high does not waste recalculation time.

Cue:
To overcome circular-reference problems, keep the number of iterations high.

Iterative recalculation overcomes a circular reference because each recalculative pass through the worksheet causes the actual values of the cells to approach more closely their correct values. For example, suppose that you built a worksheet with the following set of relationships:

A3 = .05*A5
A4 = 100
A5 = +A3+A4

When you first enter this formula, A3 has a value of 0, A4 equals 100, and A5 equals 100. Suppose that you recalculate the worksheet five times. Table 4.1 shows the values of each cell after each recalculative pass.

Table 4.1
Changing Values of Cells during Five Recalculations

Pass	Cell A3	Cell A4	Cell A5
1	5	100	105
2	5.25	100	105.25
3	5.2625	100	105.2625
4	5.263125	100	105.263125
5	5.26315625	100	105.26315625

Notice that on each pass, the difference between the prior and the current value of cells A3 and A5 becomes smaller. After only five passes, the difference is too small to be significant. After nine passes, in fact, the difference becomes too small for 1-2-3 to recognize. At that point, the problem with the circular reference is eliminated, although the circular reference remains (and the CIRC indicator remains on the screen). The most efficient number of recalculations depends on the application; the only way to be sure is to experiment.

Cue:
Even with a high number of iterations, you may need to recalculate the worksheet twice.

Four things should be noted about iterative recalculation. First, suppose that you have the number of iterations set to a high figure (say 20) but 1-2-3 encounters a set of circular references that is still too complicated to sort out. If this happens with one of your models, simply recalculate the worksheet *twice*. If, for example, the number of iterations is set to 20, recalculating the worksheet twice is identical to setting the iteration count to 40.

Second, remember that recalculating a large worksheet as many as 20 times can take a long time. Be patient; control over 1-2-3 will be returned to you.

Third, note that it is possible to enter circular references that cannot be solved using this iterative approach, for example, when a formula references the cell that contains the formula. One symptom of this problem is that values quickly grow larger after each iteration. Another symptom is that the output variables do not converge on the correct answer, but instead bounce around.

Finally, some circular references are correct; that is, they describe true algebraic, modeling relationships. You would ordinarily plan to build these references into your model. If you get unplanned circular references, chances are good that they are incorrect.

You can use the /Worksheet Status command to check on the recalculation status of your worksheet. This command delivers, among other information, the current recalculation method and order, the number of iterations in effect, and the number of circular references. Figure 4.2, early in this chapter, shows a typical report from the /Worksheet Status command.

Cue:
Check recalculation status with the /WS command.

Protecting Cell Contents and Areas of the Worksheet

1-2-3 has special features that protect areas of a worksheet from possible destruction. With a series of commands, you can set up ranges of cells that cannot be changed without special effort. In fact, rows and columns containing protected cells cannot be deleted from the worksheet. These commands are particularly beneficial when you are setting up worksheets in which data will be entered by people who are not familiar with 1-2-3.

Cue:
Protect your worksheet against unintentional destruction by inexperienced users.

When a worksheet is first created, every cell is protected. The global protection command is disabled, however. This means that each cell has the potential of being protected, but is not protected at the moment.

This protection system may be thought of as a series of electric fences that are set up around all of the cells in the worksheet. The "juice" to these fences is turned off when the sheet is first loaded. This means that all the cells in the worksheet can be modified, which is appropriate because you will want to have access to everything in the worksheet at this time. After you have finished making all your entries in the worksheet, however, there may be areas that you do not want modified, or you may want to set up special form-entry areas and not allow the cell pointer to move anywhere else.

To accomplish either of these tasks, you must first enable protection. This is accomplished with the /Worksheet Global Protection Enable command. After this command has been issued, all of the cells in the worksheet are protected. To continue the analogy, this command is like the switch that activates all of the electric fences in the worksheet.

Now you can selectively unprotect certain ranges with the /Range Unprotect command. To use the analogy once again, you tear down the fences that surround these cells. You can, of course, reprotect these cells at any time by issuing the /Range Protect command.

Suppose that you create a worksheet which includes a number of long and important formulas. You may want to protect these formulas against accidental deletion by using 1-2-3's protection capability. But what if you need to make a change in several of these formulas? You could move around the worksheet, unprotecting cells, changing the formulas, and then protecting the cells again. Or you could use the /Worksheet Global Protection Disable command to lower the fences around all the cells. After making the necessary changes, you could restore protection to all of the cells by using the /Worksheet Global Protection Enable command.

For even more protection, you can limit the movement of the cell pointer by using the /Range Input command. This command, which allows movement to only /Range Unprotected cells, must be used when you set up the special form-entry areas mentioned previously.

For example, suppose that you created the simple worksheet shown in figure 4.25. Every cell in the worksheet is protected except E5, E7, and E9. Note that unprotected cells are indicated in the control panel by the U prefix.

Fig. 4.25

An example of protected and unprotected cells.

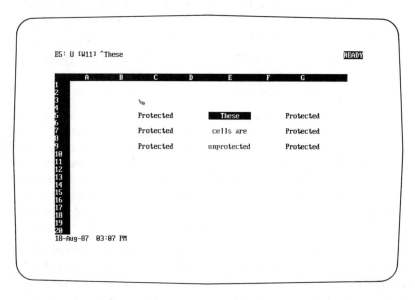

Now suppose that you issue the /Range Input command. 1-2-3 will prompt you to supply a data input range. In our example, this could be the range A1..F20 or the range E1..E9. The exact size of the range doesn't matter, as long as the range includes all of the unprotected cells. After the range has been specified, the cell pointer will jump immediately to cell E5 and wait for you to enter a number or label. Also, the upper left corner of the input range is positioned at the upper left corner of the screen.

Don't press Enter to terminate the input; use one of the arrow keys. In the example, you might use the down arrow. Notice that the cell pointer jumps to cell E7. Once again, you will want to make a cell entry and use an arrow key to move on.

The /RI command will remain in effect until you press either the Enter key or the Esc key. When you press either key, the cell pointer will return to the upper left corner of the input range, and the worksheet will return to the same position on the screen as before the /RI command was issued.

The /Range Input command can be used to automate the process of entering data in the worksheet. This command can be included in a keyboard macro that will execute automatically when a model is loaded into the worksheet. Such a macro would allow a 1-2-3 novice to enter information into the worksheet with no risk of erasing or overwriting important information. (See Chapters 14 and 15 to learn how to create a macro.)

Cue:
To completely protect against accidental erasure during data input, include the /RI command in an automatically executing macro.

Checking the Status of Global Settings

The /Worksheet Status command allows you to check the status of all the global settings for the worksheet. Figure 4.26 shows an example of what is displayed. This command gives you an easy way to check the settings without having to experiment to find out what the settings are.

Fig. 4.26

Global settings in the worksheet.

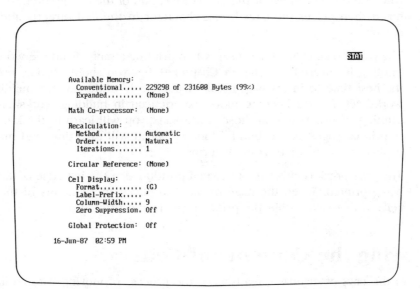

The information in figure 4.26 indicates that the following worksheet global settings are active:

1. Recalculation is **Automatic**, with **Natural** order and **1** iteration. This is the normal default setting (covered in this chapter).

2. The Global **Format** is **General**. Again, this is the default setting (covered in Chapter 5).

3. The Global **Label-Prefix** is (') for left-justification (covered in Chapter 3).

4. The Global **Column-Width** is nine characters (covered in this chapter).

5. **Zero** suppression is off (covered in this chapter).

6. Global **Protection** is off (covered in this chapter).

Entering a Page-Break Character

The /Worksheet **Page** command inserts a blank row, and then a page-break character in the cell at which the cursor was originally positioned. This command is similar to the /Worksheet **Insert Row** command that inserts a row at the row(s) specified by the cell pointer. /Worksheet **Page** inserts a new row into the worksheet at the current location of the cell pointer. The command then places the page-break character in the cell directly above the cursor.

Cue:
Enter page-breaks while you are building your worksheet.

The page-break character is used when printing a range from the worksheet. Printing is covered in detail in Chapter 9, but you should realize now that the best time to insert page-break characters is while you are building the worksheet. As you become more experienced in building worksheets and printing reports based on those worksheets, you will learn to think in terms of printed pages as you build. Thinking ahead will save time and minimize confusion when you're ready to print.

The page break is effective only when positioned at the left edge of the range being printed. When the page break is in effect, the contents of the other cells in that row within the print range are not printed.

Moving the Contents of Cells

In the days of manual spreadsheets, the process of moving data around on the page was called *cutting and pasting* because scissors and glue were used to move sections of the spreadsheet. 1-2-3 lets you cut and paste automatically.

The /**W**orksheet **I**nsert and the /**W**orksheet **D**elete commands, covered previously in this chapter, allow you to enter and delete rows and columns in the worksheet. The /**M**ove and /**C**opy commands allow you to move and copy the contents of cells and ranges of cells from one part of the worksheet to another. The difference between moving and copying is that data which is *moved* from one cell to another disappears from the first cell; data that is *copied* appears in both cells.

For an example of moving data, suppose that you created the sample worksheet shown in figure 4.27. Suppose further that you want to move the contents of range C1..D3 to the range E1..F3. After you enter /**M**ove, 1-2-3 will respond with the message Enter range to move FROM. You will notice that a range is already specified after this message. If the cell pointer was at cell D7 when you started, the range specified is D7..D7. 1-2-3 always tries to stay one step ahead in helping you designate ranges.

Fig. 4.27

The worksheet before using the /Move command.

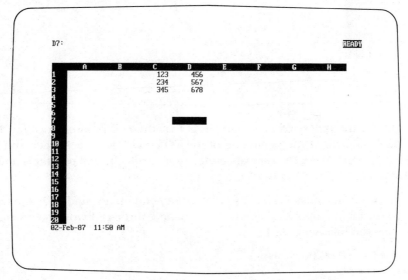

To enter the appropriate range, start typing. The D7..D7 will disappear immediately. As you type, the characters will appear where the D7..D7 was. To designate the proper FROM range for our example, enter *C1..D3*. Then press Enter.

1-2-3 then will ask you to Enter the range to move TO. Again, a range is already specified for you. The range is just a one-cell range this time but, as before, the cell address is the address of the cell at which the pointer was located when you initiated the command. To enter your own range, start typing again. For the TO range, you can specify just the single cell E1. 1-2-3 is smart enough to know that E1..F3 is implied and will use that range. As soon as you finish designating the TO range and pressing Enter, the pointer will return immediately to where it was when you initiated the command. Figure 4.28 shows the results of the /Move operation.

Fig. 4.28

The result of the /Move operation.

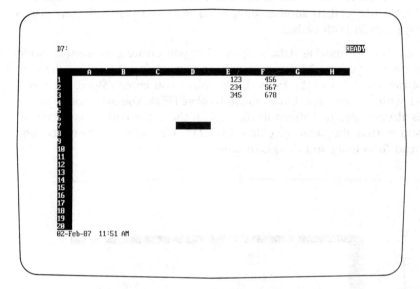

One of the points of this example is that the cell pointer does not have to be positioned at the beginning of the TO or FROM ranges when you initiate a command. You can designate either range while the cell pointer is positioned anywhere on the worksheet.

All of the formulas involved in a /Move operation are updated automatically. For example, suppose that you have a simple three-cell worksheet which contains the following data:

    A1 = +D1*100
    C1 = 15
    D1 = +C1

Now, suppose that you /Move the contents of cell D1 to cell E1. The formulas would be altered to the following:

    A1 = +E1*100
    C1 = 15
    E1 = +C1

You must be careful about the finality of the /Move command. When you move a range of cells, the TO range is completely overwritten by the FROM range, and the previous contents of those cells are lost forever. If there are other cells whose formulas depend on the cell addresses of the lost cells, the other cells will be given the value ERR instead of the cell address. For example, if you add one more cell to the preceding example,

   E2 = +E1

and repeat the move operation (/Move D1 E1), the value of cell E2 will change from 0 to ERR, and the contents of that cell will become +ERR. The cell to which E2 once referred, E1, has been removed and replaced as a result of the /Move operation.

Warning!
The /Move command overwrites and destroys any data currently in the TO range.

Using the Expanding Cell Pointer for Pointing to Ranges

As previously mentioned, 1-2-3's unique pointing capabilities can be used to specify a range. This method is somewhat similar to menu pointing, but you will find that pointing to specify a range has a character all its own.

Suppose that you want to shift the contents of the range C1..D3 to E1..F3, but you don't want to enter the cell addresses from the keyboard. We will assume that the cell pointer was highlighting cell D7 before you initiated the command. When 1-2-3 asks for the FROM range, press Esc.

Esc is used because cell D7 has been automatically "anchored" for you by 1-2-3. This means that 1-2-3 has automatically designated D7 as one corner of the FROM range. If you do not press Esc but move the cell pointer, you will see the reverse-video field begin to expand starting at cell D7. Because you do not want cell D7 to be one corner of the range, press Esc. (You can anchor cells yourself by entering a period [.] when you enter a range; and you can tell whether a cell has been anchored by how it is designated in the control panel—for example, D7..D7 shows that the cell is anchored, D7 shows that it is not.)

Because you want C1 to be one corner of the FROM range, move the cell pointer up to this cell. You will see the address designation in the command field change as you move the cell pointer upward from cell to cell. When you arrive at cell C1, press the period (.) to anchor the cell.

From this point on, cell C1 is referred to as the anchor cell, and the cell diagonally opposite the anchored cell is the free cell. A blinking underscore character is in the middle of the free cell. At this point, cell C1 is both the anchor cell and the free cell. As you move the cell pointer over and down to cell D3 to point to the other corner of the range, however, you will see the reverse-video field expand as you shift the free cell. You also will see the second part of the range designation change as you move from cell to cell. For example, C1..D1 will appear when you move the cell pointer to cell D1.

When you reach cell D1, start moving down to cell D3. Now you will see the reverse-video field expand in a columnar fashion. When you reach cell D3, lock in the range by pressing Enter. The designation of the FROM range will appear, as though you had entered the range from the keyboard (see fig. 4.29).

Fig. 4.29

Using the expanding cell pointer to point to a range.

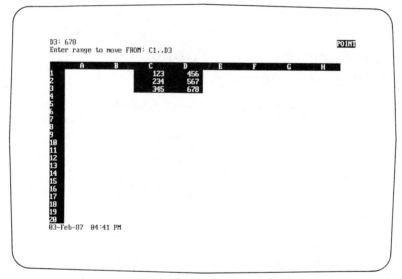

The process is similar for designating the TO range. After you have specified the FROM range, the cell pointer will return automatically to cell D7. You then move the cell pointer over to E1 and press Enter. You can designate the TO range by pointing to the entire range, but remember that 1-2-3 knows what you are implying when you enter just E1.

The Esc key can be used also when you are using a command, but no cell has been anchored. Pressing Esc will return you to the previous command step. If you are in the middle of a formula, pressing the Esc key will erase the cell address from the end of the formula and return the cell pointer to the current cell. In other words, with numbers already in cells A1..A3, if you type @*SUM(* at cell A4, and then point with the cell pointer to cell A1, your formula so far is @SUM(A1. If you press Esc, the formula again becomes @SUM(, and the cell pointer goes to cell A4.

The Backspace key also can be used for pointing to ranges. Pressing Backspace cancels the range specification, whether or not a cell has been anchored, and returns the cell pointer to the location at which you began the command or formula. The Backspace key is slightly more powerful than the Esc key for returning you to this location.

Cue:
The Backspace key can be helpful when pointing to ranges.

Using the End Key for Pointing to Ranges

1-2-3's use of the End key makes pointing to large ranges easy. For example, suppose that you want to move the contents of the range A1..C5 to the range that begins at cell A7. By now, you should be familiar with the /**M**ove command. But you're not familiar with using the End key to point to a range. When the range prompt A1..A1 appears, press the End key and then the down-arrow key. The cell pointer jumps to cell A5, and the prompt reads A1..A5. Now move the cell pointer by pressing the End key and then the right-arrow key. The prompt now reads A1..C5.

The End key can accelerate the process of pointing to ranges. Using the End key, we were able to define the range in our example with only four key-strokes. The process would have taken seven keystrokes if we had used only the two arrow keys. The difference is dramatic when you work with larger ranges.

You can use the End key even in situations in which it seems to be of little value. For example, figure 4.30 shows a worksheet consisting of two rows of information. One row is continuous; the other is broken. Suppose that you want to erase the contents of the broken row. To do this, issue the /**R**ange **E**rase command. 1-2-3 then prompts you for a range to delete. You can enter the range either by typing the coordinates or by pointing with the cell pointer. If you point, you may want to try using the End key; but because the range is not continuous, the End key will not move the pointer easily from one end of the range to the other.

Try this trick. When you specify the range, first move the cell pointer *up* one row to cell A2; use the End key and the right-arrow key to move the cell pointer to the end of the range; then move the cell pointer down one row. Presto! The correct range has been specified. Figures 4.31, 4.32, and 4.33 illustrate this process. Use this technique as often as possible when you designate ranges—it is more convenient than simply using the right-arrow key to point.

Fig. 4.30

A broken row next to a complete row.

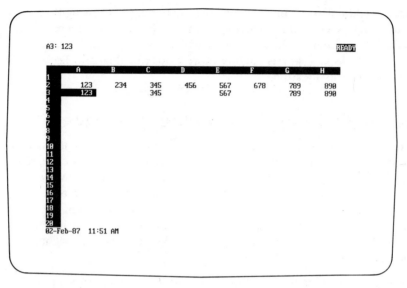

Fig. 4.31

The first step in using the End key on a broken row.

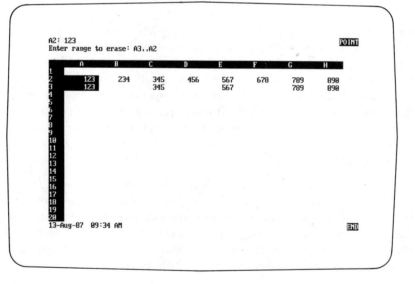

Fig. 4.32

The second step in using the End key on a broken row.

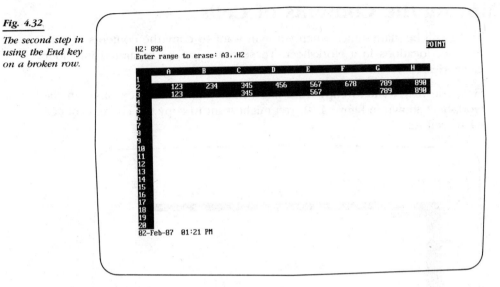

Fig. 4.33

The final step in using the End key on a broken row.

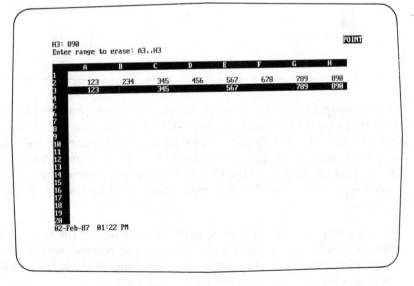

Copying the Contents of Cells

There will be many times when you will want to copy the contents of cells to other locations in a worksheet. These times can be separated into four categories.

First, you may want to copy from one cell to another. For example, in the worksheet shown in figure 4.34, you might want to copy the contents of cell A1 to cell A2.

Fig. 4.34.

The worksheet before using the /Copy command.

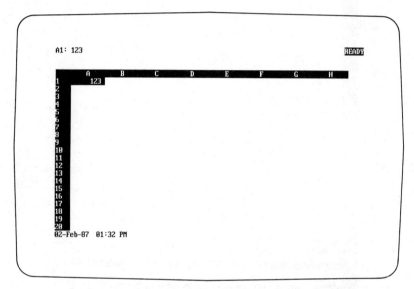

```
A1: 123                                                    READY

        A        B       C       D       E       F       G       H
1       123
2
3
4
5
6
7
8
9
10
11
12
13
14
15
16
17
18
19
20
02-Feb-87  01:32 PM
```

To do this, you issue the command /Copy. 1-2-3 then prompts you to supply a FROM range: Enter range to copy FROM:. Because you want to copy from cell A1, enter *A1* in response to this message. (Because the cell pointer is on cell A1, you can simply press Enter.) Next, 1-2-3 prompts for a TO range: Enter range to copy TO:. Because you want to copy the contents of cell A1 to cell A2, enter *A2* as the TO range. Figure 4.35 shows the results of this operation.

The steps required for all copy operations are basically the same as for this simple example: first, issue the /Copy command; second, specify the FROM range; third, specify the TO range. The only things that change are the size, shape, and locations of the FROM and TO ranges.

Reminder:
Two methods are available for designating the TO range.

In the second type of copy operation, you copy from one cell to a range of cells. Suppose that you want to copy the contents of cell A1 (in the worksheet shown in fig. 4.34) into the range A1..H1. To do this, issue the /Copy command, specify A1 as the FROM range, and then specify A1..H1 as the TO range.

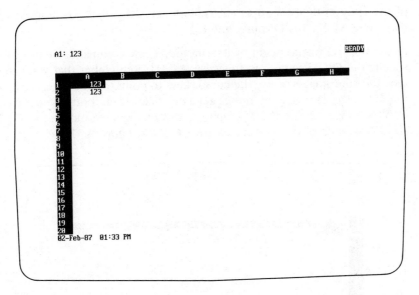

Fig. 4.35

The worksheet after using the /Copy command.

Remember that you can either type the coordinates of the TO range from the keyboard or point to the range, using POINT mode. The results of this copy are shown in figure 4.36.

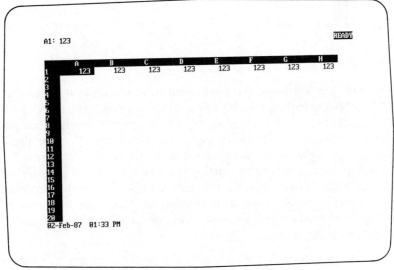

Fig. 4.36

The result of copying from a cell to a range.

The third type of copy operation is a little more complicated. You may want to copy a range of cells to another place in the worksheet. Using the results of the copy in figure 4.36 as an example, suppose that you wanted to copy the range A1..H1 to the range A2..H2.

As always, you would begin by issuing the /Copy command. Next, you would specify the FROM range—in this case, A1..H1. Remember that you can either type the coordinates or use the cursor keys to point to the range. Next, specify the TO range. At this point, things get a bit tricky. Even though you are copying into the range A2..H2, the TO range in this example would be the single cell A2. The results of this command are shown in figure 4.37.

Fig. 4.37

The result of copying the partial row A1..H1 to A2.

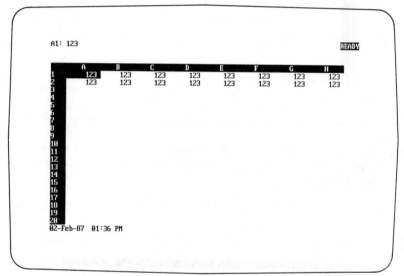

Although this TO range does not seem to make sense, it is perfectly logical. Think about selecting the TO range this way. You want to /Copy the eight-cell partial row A1..H1. Because the FROM range is an eight-cell partial row, the TO range also must be an eight-cell partial row. Because the TO range must be an eight-cell partial row, the first cell in that partial row is sufficient to define the range. Given a starting point of A2, the only possible destination for the copy is the range A2..H2. Similarly, specifying the single cell H3 as the TO range would imply a destination of H3..O3. In other words, 1-2-3 is smart enough to deduce the rest of the destination from the single cell provided as the TO range.

The same principle applies to copies of partial columns. For example, look back at figure 4.35, which shows the results of our first copy example, and suppose that you want to copy the range A1..A2 to the range B1..B2. The first two steps should be familiar by now: issue the /Copy command and specify the FROM range A1..A2. What would the TO range be? Because you want to copy the two-cell partial column A1..A2 into the two-cell partial column B1..B2, you need supply only the starting point (B1) of the TO range to create figure 4.38.

Fig. 4.38

The result of copying the partial column A1..A2 to B1.

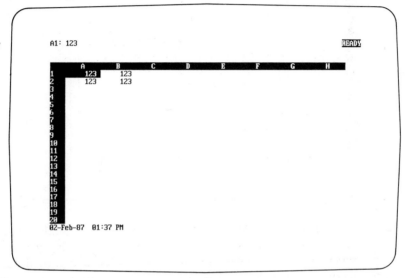

Finally, you may want to copy a range of cells to an even larger range of cells somewhere else in the worksheet. Using figure 4.36 once again as an example, suppose that you want to copy the range A1..H1 into the rectangular block A2..H20. As before, you issue the /Copy command and define the FROM range as A1..H1. The TO range is A2..A20. Figure 4.39 shows the results of this copy.

You can think of this type of copy as an extension of the previous type. In essence, the copy we made in figure 4.39 could have been created also by repeating the copy command 19 times and specifying 19 different single-row TO ranges. The first TO range would be A2, the second would be A3, the third A4, and so on. The results are the same for either method, but you can save a great deal of time by using the A2..A20 range as shown.

The concept of TO ranges is tricky. The best way to learn about the effects of using different TO and FROM ranges is to experiment on your own. After a while, the rules of copying will be second nature to you.

Addressing Cells

Two different methods of addressing cells can be used in replication: *relative* and *absolute*. These two methods of referencing cells are important for build-

Fig. 4.39

The result of copying the range A1..H1 to the range A2..A20.

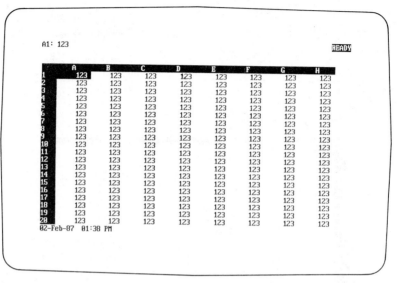

ing formulas. In fact, it is difficult to talk about the two methods of addressing without treating both topics at once. The type of addressing you use when you reference cells in formulas can affect the results yielded by the formulas when you copy or move those formulas to different positions in the worksheet.

Referencing Cells with Relative Addressing

1-2-3's default is relative addressing. This means that when you copy or move a formula, unless you specify otherwise, the addresses of the cells in the formula will be adjusted automatically to fit the new location.

As an example of relative addressing, suppose that you want to sum the contents of several columns of cells, but you don't want to enter the @SUM function over and over again. Figure 4.40 shows a sample worksheet with five columns of numbers. Only column C has been summed, using the formula @SUM(C5..C8) in cell C10.

You want to add the contents of the cells in columns D, E, F, and G in the same manner that the contents of the cells in column C were added. To do this, use the /Copy command, the command for replicating cells in 1-2-3.

To initiate the command, choose /Copy from the main command menu. 1-2-3 then asks for a range of cells to copy FROM. You enter *C10*, and press Enter. Next, 1-2-3 asks for a range of cells to copy TO. You enter *D10..G10* by pointing or by entering the cell addresses. When you press Enter, 1-2-3 will replicate the @SUM formula in cell C10 to the other cells, as shown in figure 4.41.

Fig. 4.40

A sample worksheet with one column summed.

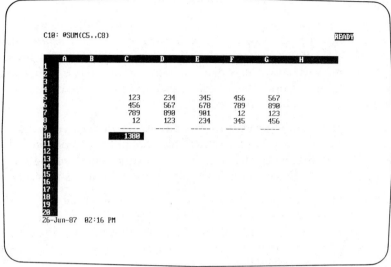

Fig. 4.41

Copied @SUM formulas with relative addressing.

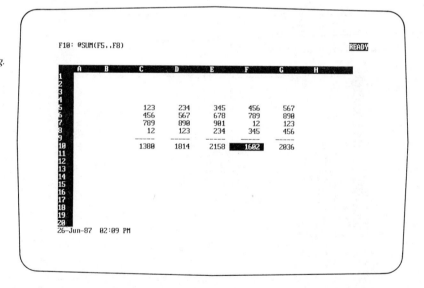

Notice that the formula in the first line of the control panel contains the proper cell addresses for adding the cells in column F—not column C. 1-2-3 was smart enough to know that you meant the relative addresses of the cells in column F, not their absolute addresses.

Mixing Relative and Absolute Addressing

In some cases, a formula has an important address that cannot be changed as the formula is copied. In 1-2-3, you can create an *absolute address*, an address that will not change at all as the address is copied. You also can create a *mixed address*, an address that will sometimes change, depending on the direction of the /Copy. The following examples will help clarify the concepts of absolute and mixed addresses.

Mixed cell-addressing refers to a combination of relative and absolute addressing. Because a cell address has two components—a column and a row—it is possible to fix (make absolute) either portion while leaving the other unfixed (relative). The best way to explain this capability is to use an example.

Suppose that you want to create a projection of monthly sales in dollars for Product 1. In the first pass, you want to use a specific retail price, average discount rate, and unit volume for the projection. But later you will want to change these parameters to see what happens. Figure 4.42 shows how you might set up the projection.

Fig. 4.42

A single formula using mixed addressing.

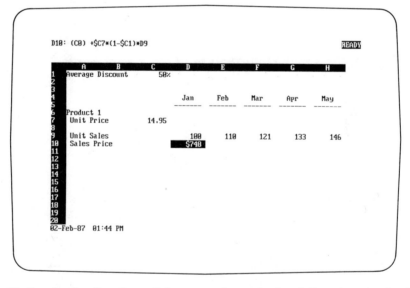

Notice, in the first line of the control panel, the dollar signs in the formula for cell D10. These dollar signs signal 1-2-3 to use absolute addressing on the column portion of the addresses. Because there are no dollar signs in front of the row portion of the addresses, 1-2-3 will use relative addressing there.

To see the importance of this type of referencing, /Copy the contents of cell D10 into the range E10..H10. As before, you first issue the /Copy command and then designate the FROM range (D10) and the TO range (E10..H10). Figure 4.43 shows the results of the command.

Fig. 4.43

The result of copying the mixed address formula.

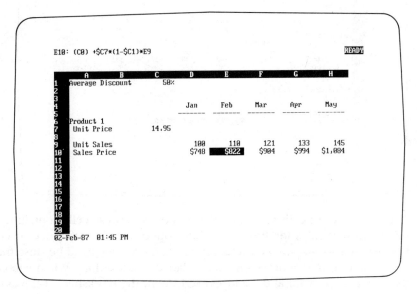

Compare the formula in cell E10 with the original formula in cell D10:

    E10 = +$C7*(1-$C1)*E9
    D10 = +$C7*(1-$C1)*D9

Notice that the formulas are identical except for the last term. 1-2-3 has held constant the addresses for C7 and C1. Only the reference to cell D9 has been altered. In essence, this formula says, "Using a constant price (C7) and a constant discount (C1), compute the dollar sales for Product 1 at each month's sales volume (D9..H9)."

Now suppose that you want to create a projection for a second product. You can do this by duplicating the labels in column A and changing the product name to Product 2. Finally, you copy the contents of the range C7..H10 to the range C14..H17. Figure 4.44 shows the results of the copy operation.

Notice that the numbers in row 17 are not correct. Although you assigned the same price and unit sales volumes to Product 2, that product shows monthly dollar sales double those for Product 1. To figure out why, look at the formula in cell D17:

    +$C14*(1-$C8)*D16

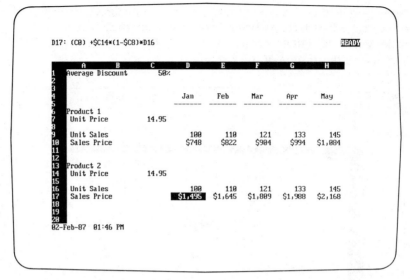

The references to cells C14 and D16 are correct. These cells contain the unit price and unit sales for Product 2. But notice that the reference to cell C1 has changed so that the cell refers to cell C8. This occurred because the row designation in that address—8—was relative, not absolute. When you copied the formulas containing the address $C1 down the worksheet, 1-2-3 assumed that you wanted to adjust the row component of the address.

You can correct the problem by changing the reference to cell C1 from a mixed reference to an absolute reference. Going back to the model in figure 4.42, edit cell D10 and change the formula to

    +$C7*(1-$C$1)*D9

The only difference between this formula and its predecessor is the addition of a $ in front of the 1 in the address $C$1. This added $ changes the address from mixed to absolute.

Now you must copy the new formula in cell D10 to the range E10..H10 so that all of the formulas in the row are the same. Then you can recopy the areas D10..H10 into the range D17..H17. Figure 4.45 illustrates the adjusted worksheet.

Notice that the numbers in cells D17..H17 are now correct. Look at the formula in cell D17:

    +$C14*(1-$C$1)*D16

The reference to cell C1 remained fixed during the copy.

Fig. 4.45.

*A copied formula
using an absolute
address.*

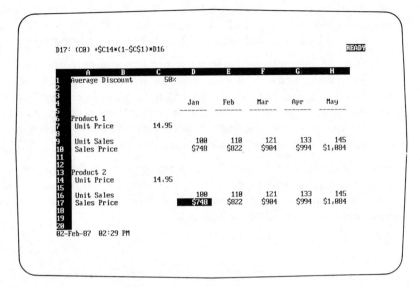

Fig. 4.45.

*A copied formula
using an absolute
address.*

Remember that when you copy cells using absolute addressing, you must prepare the cell to be copied before initiating the command. That is, you must enter dollar signs in the appropriate column and row designations when the cell is defined. If you forget to prepare the cell, you may get results you neither expected nor wanted.

*Reminder:
To use absolute
addressing, enter the
dollar signs **before**
you initiate the
/Copy command.*

Using the F4 (Abs) Key To Set Absolute and Relative References

There are two ways to enter dollar signs in the formula for cell D10 in the example. You can type the dollar signs as you enter the formula, or you can use the F4 (Abs) key to have 1-2-3 automatically enter the dollar signs for you.

Here is what happens to a cell address when you press F4 after typing the address (but before pressing Enter or a cursor-movement key) or while in EDIT mode. (Note that, for F4 to work, the cursor must be pointing to the proper address.)

First time	$C$7
Second	C$7
Third	$C7
Fourth	C7

Suppose that your typing or pointing (or both) results in C7, the first portion of the formula shown in the control panel of figure 4.42. To change this to an absolute address, you press the F4 key. The formula in the control panel changes to $C$7. Pressing the F4 key again shifts the address to C$7. A third press of F4 changes the address to $C7, which is the desired result.

Notice that we did not use range names in this example; the F4 key loses much of its power when used with range names. Most important, you cannot use F4 with a range name to set a mixed address. You can change from relative to absolute addresses using F4, and from absolute to relative addresses, but not within the same edit operation. You cannot toggle back and forth without first ending the edit operation and starting a new one.

A second example of mixed cell-addressing appears in figure 4.46. Here we have created a table to explore the effect of different interest rates and years-to-maturity on the monthly payment for a $100,000 mortgage. The general format of the built-in @PMT function is

@PMT(principal,interest,term)

Fig. 4.46

Using a @PMT formula with mixed addresses.

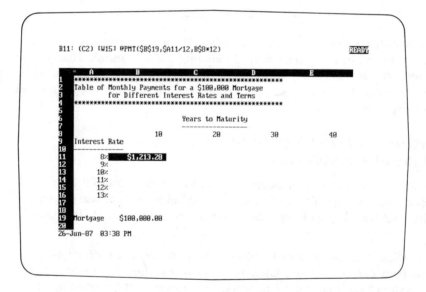

The object of this example is to use a single formula for the entire model, and then copy the formula using mixed cell-addressing, as shown in figure 4.46.

Once again, if you look at the command line, you will see the special places at which dollar signs appear. The idea in this example is to use absolute addressing on the column portion of the interest rate address and relative addressing on the row portion ($A15). Conversely, we want to use relative addressing on the column portion of the years-to-maturity address and absolute addressing on the row portion (B$8).

Compare the formula for cell B11 in the control panel in figure 4.46 with the one for cell D15 in figure 4.47. Notice that column A for the interest rate and row 8 for the years-to-maturity have not changed, but the other portions of the addresses have.

Fig. 4.47

The result of copying the @PMT formula.

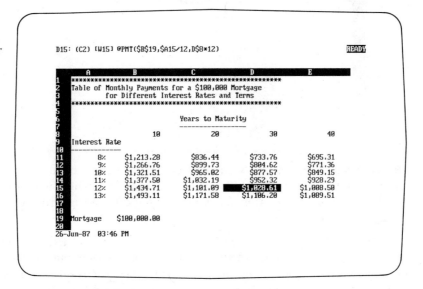

A third way mixed cell-addressing can be used is to accumulate a running total across a row of numbers. In this example, we will use the formula @SUM($C$5..C5) in cell C7 and copy the formula across cells D7 through G7. In figure 4.48, notice in the first line of the control panel that the formula for cell E7 has changed to @SUM($C$5..E5); the relative address in the formula changed when we copied cell C7 to cell E7.

The best way to become comfortable with mixed cell-addressing is to experiment with it. Try several different examples and see what you come up with.

Transposing Rows and Columns with the /Range Transpose Command (/RT)

For copy operations that are difficult to perform with 1-2-3's normal copy commands, 1-2-3 has two specialized copy commands: /**R**ange **T**ranspose and

Fig. 4.48

*Using absolute
addressing to
create a running
total.*

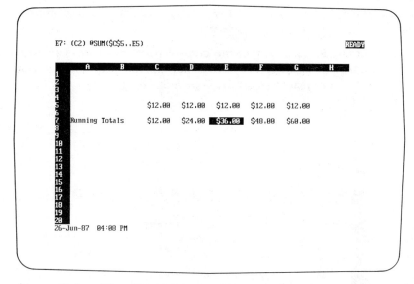

```
E7: (C2) @SUM($C$5..E5)                                          READY

      A      B        C       D       E       F       G       H
1
2
3
4
5                  $12.00  $12.00  $12.00  $12.00  $12.00
6
7     Running Totals  $12.00  $24.00  $36.00  $48.00  $60.00
8
9
10
11
12
13
14
15
16
17
18
19
20
26-Jun-87  04:00 PM
```

/Range Value. The /**R**ange **T**ranspose command copies columns into rows and rows into columns. The /**R**ange **V**alue command, which is explained in the next section, copies the values (but not the formulas) from one range to another.

The /**R**ange **T**ranspose command copies each row of the FROM range into the corresponding column of the TO range, or each column of the FROM range into the corresponding row of the TO range. The result is a transposed copy of the FROM range. Figure 4.49 shows the result of using the /**R**ange **T**ranspose command to transpose the range A1..D2 to the range A5..B8, and then the range A5..B8 to the range A11..D12.

When copying formulas, the /**R**ange **T**ranspose command behaves just like the /**C**opy command. When a range is transposed, cell references in the transposed range are adjusted, just as references are adjusted in a normal /**C**opy command.

Caution:
*The /RT command
can garble the
addresses in
formulas.*

This adjustment of cell references can lead to serious trouble when you use the /**R**ange **T**ranspose command to transpose a range containing formulas. The transposed formulas will be incorrect; the values, however, will remain in the same order. Because the cell references are not transposed, the relative and mixed cell references in the transposed range will refer to unintended locations after the transposition.

Cue:
*Solve addressing
problems by using
/RV before using
/RT.*

You can avoid the problem of incorrect cell references in transposed ranges by converting the formulas in the FROM range to values before transposing. The /**R**ange **V**alue command is a convenient way to convert a range of formulas to values.

Fig. 4.49

Transposing ranges.

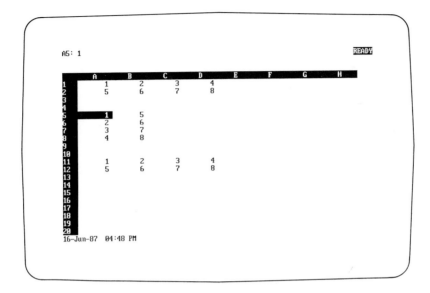

Converting Formulas to Values with the /Range Value Command (/RV)

The /Range Value command lets you copy the values of the cells in one range to another range. This command is useful whenever you want to preserve the current values of a range of cells instead of having only the changed values after the worksheet has been updated. What is particularly important about the /Range Value command is that it converts formulas to values. You don't have to worry, therefore, about formulas that depend on cell references (when using /Range Transpose, for example).

Figure 4.50 shows a worksheet with a monthly income statement and a year-to-date total column. As you change the worksheet every month, the year-to-date (Y-T-D) totals will also change. If, however, you want to save the Y-T-D totals to compare them with previous years or quarters, the /Range Value command enables you to do so. When you use the command, the program asks for a range to copy from and a range to copy to, just as it does with the /Copy command. In the example in figure 4.51, the Y-T-D totals in column G are being saved in column N.

Fig. 4.50

The worksheet with a monthly and a year-to-date income column.

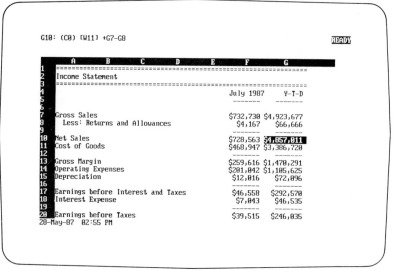

```
G10: (C0) [W11] +G7-G8                                          READY

        A      B      C      D    E      F          G
1  ==================================================================
2  Income Statement
3  ==================================================================
4                                         July 1987    Y-T-D
5                                         --------    --------
6
7  Gross Sales                             $732,730 $4,923,677
8    Less: Returns and Allowances            $4,167    $66,666
9                                         --------    --------
10 Net Sales                               $728,563 $4,857,011
11 Cost of Goods                           $468,947 $3,386,720
12                                         --------    --------
13 Gross Margin                            $259,616 $1,470,291
14 Operating Expenses                      $201,042 $1,105,625
15 Depreciation                             $12,016    $72,096
16                                         --------    --------
17 Earnings before Interest and Taxes       $46,558   $292,570
18 Interest Expense                          $7,043    $46,535
19                                         --------    --------
20 Earnings before Taxes                    $39,515   $246,035
28-May-87  02:55 PM
```

Fig. 4.51.

Saving the year-to-date values with /Range Value.

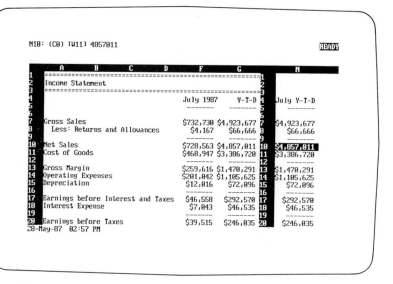

```
N10: (C0) [W11] 4857011                                        READY

        A      B      C      D        F          G          N
1  ==============================================  1  ================
2  Income Statement                                2
3  ==============================================  3  ================
4                               July 1987   Y-T-D  4  July Y-T-D
5                               --------  --------  5  --------
6                                                  6
7  Gross Sales                  $732,730 $4,923,677 7  $4,923,677
8    Less: Returns and Allowances $4,167   $66,666  8     $66,666
9                               --------  --------  9  --------
10 Net Sales                    $728,563 $4,857,011 10 $4,857,011
11 Cost of Goods                $468,947 $3,386,720 11 $3,386,720
12                              --------  --------  12 --------
13 Gross Margin                 $259,616 $1,470,291 13 $1,470,291
14 Operating Expenses           $201,042 $1,105,625 14 $1,105,625
15 Depreciation                  $12,016   $72,096  15    $72,096
16                              --------  --------  16 --------
17 Earnings before Interest and Taxes $46,558 $292,570 17 $292,570
18 Interest Expense               $7,043   $46,535  18    $46,535
19                              --------  --------  19 --------
20 Earnings before Taxes         $39,515  $246,035  20   $246,035
28-May-87  02:57 PM
```

Miscellaneous Comments on Copying

Remember the following points whenever you intend to copy data within the worksheet:

- When you copy a cell, 1-2-3 automatically copies the format of the cell with it. (See Chapter 5 for more information on formats.) This automatic format-copying feature saves you from having to preset the format for an entire range of cells before copying to them.

- Sometimes the TO and FROM ranges will overlap when you copy. The general rule is that if you do not overlap the end points of the FROM and TO ranges, there will be no problems in the copy. If you do overlap them, however, you may get mixed results. You can overlap ranges legitimately when the FROM and TO ranges have the same upper left boundary.

- Note particularly the finality of the /Copy command. If you copy over the contents of a cell, there is no way to retrieve them. Make sure that your ranges have been designated properly before you press Enter.

Reminder:
Cell formats are copied with cell contents.

Warning!
Overlapping TO and FROM ranges can destroy data.

Warning!
Copying destroys data currently in the TO range.

Saving Your File before You /Quit

You may remember from Chapter 2, or have already discovered on your own, that 1-2-3 provides two ways to exit the spreadsheet: the /Quit command and the /System command. Both commands are options on 1-2-3's main command menu. The /Quit command exits the program as well as the spreadsheet, but the /System command exits the spreadsheet only, giving you access to the DOS operating system, and therefore to other programs, without leaving 1-2-3.

When you exit the spreadsheet by using the /System command, you do not lose the information that you have entered, unless you shut the computer off. By typing *exit* (for "exit the system") at the system prompt and then pressing Enter, you return to your worksheet with all the information intact.

When you use the /Quit command, however, you exit 1-2-3 entirely, and all newly entered information is lost. To keep from losing the information, you need to save your file before you /Quit. File operations are explained in detail in Chapter 7, but you should learn as early as possible the basic operation of saving a file, and you should get in the habit of saving your file frequently.

Cue:
To avoid data loss, save your file regularly and frequently.

The /File Save command allows you to save an entire worksheet to a file on disk. This command makes an exact copy of the current worksheet, including all the formats, range names, and settings you have specified.

To save your current worksheet, type /fs and then respond to the `Enter save file name:` prompt by typing the name you have chosen for your file. Then press Enter. Your file is saved to disk—it's as easy as that.

Don't use a name you have used before unless you want your current worksheet to replace the one with the same name on disk. If you do type in a name that's already in use, 1-2-3 asks whether you really do want to replace the existing file. Select **R**eplace if you do; otherwise, select **C**ancel and then type in a different name.

Whenever you have to choose a file name for a file command, 1-2-3 helps you by displaying a list of the 1-2-3 files on the current drive and directory. If the file name you want is in the list, you can select it by pointing. If you want to replace an existing file, you can point to one of the entries on the list and then press Enter. Otherwise, you can type in the file name you want. Some characters are not allowed in file names; if the program does not accept the name you enter, check Chapter 7 for the rules for file names. Whatever name you use, 1-2-3 automatically supplies a .WK1 extension.

When a worksheet is saved, the date and time are saved with all other data. This can be helpful if you want to see the last time a file was accessed. If you want to see the date and time information, use the /File List command and highlight the name of the file you are interested in.

Cue:
For precise file documentation, keep the system date and time accurate.

To be certain you have accurate dates and times, make sure that the date and time have been entered correctly with the DOS DATE and TIME commands. If your system has an internal clock, you won't have to worry about entering the time and date.

To call a file back into main memory from disk, use the /File **R**etrieve command. Again, 1-2-3 will display a list of all the file names currently on disk.

For information on using other than the current drive and directory to store your files, see Chapter 7.

Accessing DOS from 1-2-3

The /System command suspends the operation of 1-2-3 and returns you to the system prompt (C⟩ for hard disk systems, A⟩ for floppy and microfloppy disk systems). Once at the system prompt, you can execute other programs and DOS commands. To return to 1-2-3, you type *exit* at the system prompt.

The /System command is particularly useful for giving you access to your system's native file-handling commands. For example, if you want to save your worksheet but your data disk is full, you can use the /System command to suspend 1-2-3 processing while you initialize a new data disk, using the DOS

FORMAT command. After you return to 1-2-3 by typing *exit*, you can save your worksheet to the new data disk with /File Save.

You should be aware of a few warnings about using the /System command. First, if you have a large spreadsheet that takes up almost all of main memory, the /System command may fail because of insufficient memory to run another program. If the /System command fails, 1-2-3 displays the error message Cannot Invoke DOS and turns on the ERROR indicator.

The second warning is that certain programs which are run from 1-2-3 using the /System command may cause 1-2-3 to abort when you try to return by typing *exit*. The DOS file-management commands, such as FORMAT, COPY, DELETE, DIRECTORY, and DISKCOPY, can be invoked safely from 1-2-3, as can most business application programs. Calling one of the many so-called resident utility programs, however, will cause 1-2-3 to abort when you type *exit*. Take a few minutes to experiment with the programs you may want to use with the /System command before attempting to use this command during an important 1-2-3 session.

Caution: As an extra precaution, save your file before using the /System command.

Using HAL To Issue Commands

1-2-3's /Worksheet, /Range, /Copy, and /Move commands can all be invoked from HAL's request box. This section includes a few examples of how you can use Lotus HAL as an easier, more natural way to issue some of the commands discussed in this chapter. Remember, however, that HAL's capabilities extend far beyond these examples, which should serve only as a suggestion of how HAL can be used. For a complete discussion of HAL, see Que's book, *Using Lotus HAL*.

You can execute a /Copy command from HAL by typing the verbs *Copy*, *Duplicate*, or *Dup* into the request box. This approach can be much easier than using the /Copy command from within 1-2-3. For example, you can copy the contents of an entire row of cells by issuing the request *duplicate row 10 to row 20*. You can also copy one range to another with a request such as *dup depreciation1 to depreciation2*.

Move operations can be performed just as easily, using the following verbs: *Move, Relocate, Reloc, Displace,* and *Drag*. Asking HAL to *relocate*, for example, can be a natural way of rearranging data on your worksheet. You could request HAL to *relocate this col right 2*, and the contents of the current column will be moved two columns to the right.

HAL has several verbs for inserting and deleting rows and columns. The insert verbs are *Insert, Ins,* and *Put in*; the delete verbs are *Delete, Drop, Omit,* and *Remove*. To delete rows 5 to 8, for example, you simply ask HAL to *remove *rows 5 to 8*. It's easy to become comfortable with HAL's natural-language approach, rather than trying to remember "Do I use **/W**orksheet **D**elete or **/R**ange **E**rase? And should I give addresses or point to rows? Did I forget something?"

Another significant HAL benefit is its capacity to audit your spreadsheet, checking for circular references and analyzing formulas. The audit is a powerful tool of formula analysis because it provides the following information:

- a list of formulas

- a list of dependent cells. A dependent cell depends on the current cell for its value; dependent cells contain formulas or cell references.

- a list of precedent cells. The current cell depends on precedent cells for its value.

- a list of cell relations, as shown in figure 4.52

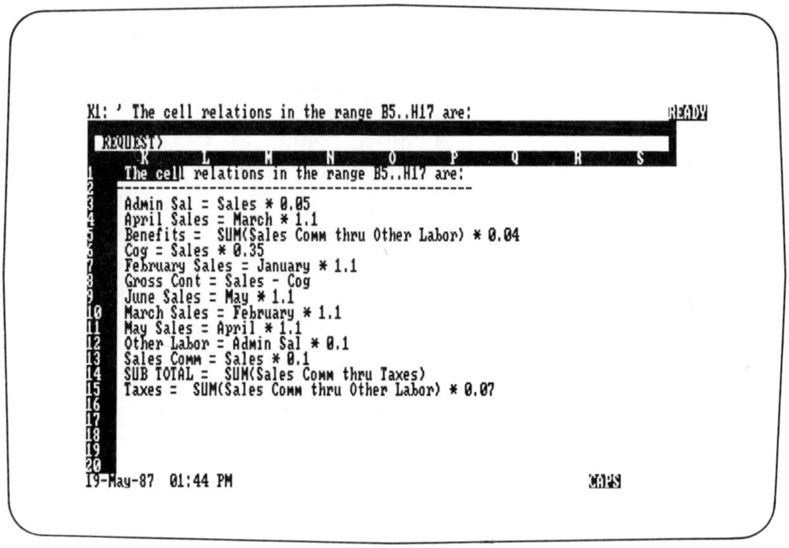

Fig. 4.52

Auditing your spreadsheet with HAL.

HAL's auditing tools are fairly basic; for many users, however, these tools are enough of an aid to successfully analyze and debug formulas and cell-reference problems. If your auditing needs are more complex, read the next section.

The Spreadsheet Auditor and the Cambridge Spreadsheet Analyst

The Spreadsheet Auditor and The Cambridge Spreadsheet Analyst (CSCAN) are two programs that provide a much more sophisticated and powerful way to audit your spreadsheet than HAL provides. You can use these add-on products to search for and identify spreadsheet errors such as circular references and overlapping ranges. The auditing capacity of these add-ons is most useful when you have created a complex worksheet or need to modify an application created by someone else. Table 4.2 compares the system characteristics of these two programs. You can see from the table that the significant difference is the minimum RAM needed.

Table 4.2
System Characteristics of Auditing Add-ons

	The Spreadsheet Auditor, Version 3.0	**The Cambridge Spreadsheet Analyst**
Publisher	Computer Associates	Turner Hall
Price	$99.00	$99.95
Hardware	IBM PC, XT, AT, or compatible; minimum two disk drives or one floppy and one hard disk drive; minimum 256K RAM	IBM PC, XT, AT, or compatible; minimum two disk drives or one floppy and one hard disk drive; minimum 192K RAM
Software Requirements	PC DOS 2.0 or higher, 1-2-3	PC DOS 2.0 or higher, 1-2-3

The Spreadsheet Auditor uses a 1-2-3 type display and menu command system, as shown in figure 4.53.

The Auditor's main menu offers eight commands for examining your spreadsheets:

View allows you to study your spreadsheet three different ways: (1) Map View summarizes your spreadsheet's cell contents with an appropriate character; (2) Formula View displays all spreadsheet formulas; and (3) Sheet View returns you to the familiar 1-2-3 spreadsheet display.

Figure 4.54 shows the result of choosing Formula View; the address of every cell containing a formula is displayed, and the formula of the cell you select

Fig. 4.53

The main menu of The Spreadsheet Auditor.

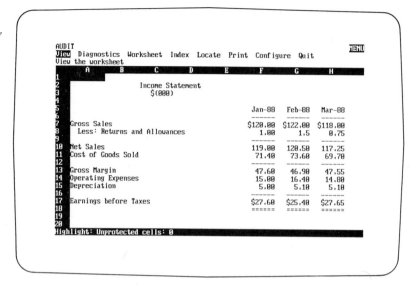

is displayed also. While in any of the three display modes, you can perform a wide variety of tests of the relationships of cells by using your computer's function keys. For example, F7 (Clone) tests for a copied cell, F8 (Ref) checks cell references, and F10 (Detail) furnishes information on all aspects of a specific cell.

Fig. 4.54

Examining formulas with The Spreadsheet Auditor.

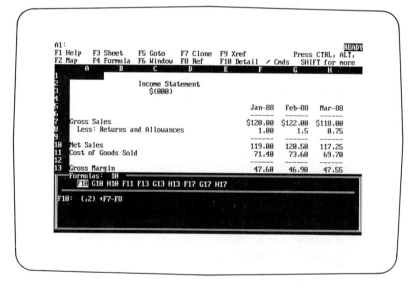

Diagnostics enables you to examine the cells, formulas, and ranges in your spreadsheet. For example, you can test for overlapping ranges with this command.

Worksheet allows you to define how the Auditor's test results will be displayed. For example, you can change column widths, create screen windows, and choose the display characters for the Map View.

Index provides a summary of the spreadsheet's formula relationships.

Locate helps you quickly find selected ranges, formulas, macros, circular references, etc., by highlighting the requested spreadsheet area.

Print generates a screen, file, or hard copy report of your spreadsheet or audit examination.

Configure allows you to change default screen and printer settings, and then save the settings to disk.

Quit returns you to the Auditor's main menu.

The Auditor also is available with a Macro Analyzer™ module that helps you locate, document, and analyze any macros contained in your spreadsheet. A companion product to the Auditor, Cell Noter™, can also be purchased. Cell Noter is a memory-resident "pop-up" program that you can use for attaching notes to individual cells for documentation purposes.

The structure of the Cambridge Spreadsheet Analyst is similar to that of the Auditor. The CSCAN main menu offers a choice of ten commands, including the command to quit the program (see fig. 4.55).

The following commands from CSCAN's main menu illustrate some of the program's capabilities:

SCAN automatically searches your entire spreadsheet for formula and range errors.

CIRC searches the entire spreadsheet for circular reference errors. In contrast, 1-2-3's /Worksheet Status command will identify only one cell with a circular reference error.

XREF (cross reference) identifies how a selected cell, range, or function is used throughout your spreadsheet.

PROBE enables you to trace, or walk through, the cells on which a selected formula is dependent.

REPORTS provides a variety of report options for documenting your auditing analysis and spreadsheet formulas. You can document your spreadsheet formulas within 1-2-3 by using /**Print Printer Options Other Cell-Formulas** to

Fig. 4.55

CSCAN's main command menu.

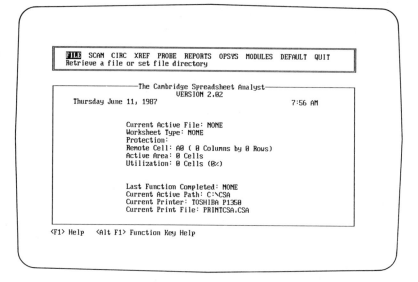

```
┌─────────────────────────────────────────────────────────────────┐
│ FILE SCAN CIRC XREF PROBE REPORTS OPSYS MODULES DEFAULT QUIT      │
│ Retrieve a file or set file directory                            │
└─────────────────────────────────────────────────────────────────┘

              ┌──────────The Cambridge Spreadsheet Analyst──────────┐
              │                    VERSION 2.02                     │
          Thursday June 11, 1987                          7:56 AM

                    Current Active File: NONE
                    Worksheet Type: NONE
                    Protection:
                    Remote Cell: A0 ( 0 Columns by 0 Rows)
                    Active Area: 0 Cells
                    Utilization: 0 Cells (0%)


                    Last Function Completed: NONE
                    Current Active Path: C:\CSA
                    Current Printer: TOSHIBA P1350
                    Current Print File: PRINTCSA.CSA

          <F1> Help    <Alt F1> Function Key Help
```

print the formulas for all the cells in the worksheet, but CSCAN performs the task much more efficiently.

MODULES allows you to use CSCAN add-in products, such as the Macro Analysis Module.

In addition to the main commands, CSCAN offers three optional views for examining your spreadsheet. The Citation View presents two boxes on the screen; the top box lists cells that meet your search criteria (such as circular references). The lower box displays more detailed information about the highlighted cell in the top box: the cell's formula, format, and current screen display, for example.

The Worksheet View shows a simulation of your spreadsheet. The actual spreadsheet is not active in 1-2-3 while you have this view; you get only a screen display. This technique permits you to view your spreadsheet without damaging the integrity of your 1-2-3 files.

Finally, the Map View displays a normal 1-2-3 view of the spreadsheet, except that columns are one space wide. Each active cell displays one of the following letters, indicating the contents of the cell:

A (Aggregate cell)—cells that contain several types of entries

B—Blank formatted cell

F—Numeric formula

M—Macro statements

N—Numeric data

S—String formula

Map View is helpful when you need to understand the organization and logic of a spreadsheet that was developed by someone else.

CSCAN comes with a Macro Analyzer module as part of the basic package.

You can see from the comparison that the capabilities offered by the two programs are similar but arranged differently. Choosing between the programs may be as much a matter of taste as anything else. If your spreadsheets are relatively simple and small, you may not even need an auditing program, or you may find HAL's limited auditing capability sufficient. However, if you frequently develop and use spreadsheets that contain multiproduct or organizational data, an auditing program may be a necessity. Either The Spreadsheet Auditor or The Cambridge Spreadsheet Analyst should meet your needs.

Chapter Summary

This chapter laid the foundation for your mastery of 1-2-3. You learned about several of 1-2-3's most important, basic commands, including the commands that affect the entire worksheet and those that affect only certain designated ranges of cells. A wide variety of other fundamentals were covered: setting column widths, inserting rows and columns, hiding columns, protecting cells, erasing the worksheet, recalculating the worksheet, splitting the screen, and freezing titles on the screen.

You learned also how to move and copy data from one part of the worksheet to another, and how to make formulas that are copied or moved end up the way you want them, by using relative and absolute addressing. Finally, you learned to save your file before quitting 1-2-3 and how to access DOS and return to your worksheet without quitting the program.

Now that you know the fundamentals of building a spreadsheet and manipulating the data on that spreadsheet, you're ready to dress up your work—to make it look the way you want it to look. The next chapter shows you how to use 1-2-3's format commands to control the appearance of your worksheet.

Formatting Cell
Contents

You may have already discovered that 1-2-3 expects you to enter data in a certain way. If, for example, you try to enter *1,234*, the program beeps, switches to EDIT mode, and waits for you to remove the comma. You get the same result if you try to enter *10:08 AM*—the colon and the AM are the offenders. If you try to enter *$9.23*, the program accepts the entry, but without the *$*. If you could not change the way data is displayed on the screen, 1-2-3 would have limited usefulness.

But you can control data display, not only for commas, currency, and time, but also for a variety of other purposes. *Formats* control how cell contents are displayed. You change formats with one of the /**R**ange Format or the /**W**orksheet Global Format commands.

1-2-3 offers ten cell formats:

Fixed

Scientific

Currency

, (Comma)

General

+/- (Horizontal Bar Graph)

Percent

Date (includes Time format)

Text

Hidden

These formats primarily affect the way numeric values are displayed in a worksheet. Text format causes a formula to appear in a cell as a formula rather than a value. Hidden format affects the display of every kind of entry.

For a complete listing of all format commands, see the 1-2-3 Command Menu Map and the Command Reference section at the back of this book.

This chapter shows you how to

- Use all ten formats
- Control international formats
- Use /Range Justify for text formatting techniques
- Handle some format problems

Setting Range and Worksheet Global Formats

The commands for controlling formats are /Worksheet Global Format and /Range Format. The former controls the format of all the cells in the worksheet, and the latter controls specific ranges within the worksheet.

Reminder:
Before you enter data, format your worksheet with the /WGF command.

Generally, you use the /Worksheet Global Format command when you are just starting to enter data in a worksheet. You will want to choose a format that the majority of cells will take. Once you have set all the cells to that format, you can use the /Range Format command to override the global format setting for specific cell ranges.

The /Range Format command takes precedence over the /Worksheet Global Format command. This means that whenever you change the global format, all the numbers and formulas affected will change automatically unless they were previously formatted with the /Range Format command. In turn, when you format a range, the format for that range will override any already set by /Worksheet Global Format.

When you enter either format command, the menu that appears contains the following entries:

Fixed   Scientific   Currency ,   General +/-   Percent   Date   Text   Hidden

General Format

Although General format is not the first item on the menu, it is discussed first because it is the default format for all new worksheets.

When numbers are displayed in General format, insignificant zeros to the right of the decimal point are suppressed. If numbers are too large or too small to be displayed normally, scientific notation is used. Some examples of numbers displayed in General format are

123.456
5.63E+14
-22.1
1.9E-09

General format does not control how labels are displayed. When you are using General format, labels are displayed as left-justified, right-justified, or centered, depending on the setting you have made with the /Worksheet Global Label-Prefix or the /Range Label command. Left-justification is the default.

General is the default setting for the /Worksheet Global Format. You can check the default setting by entering /Worksheet Status. (This command is explained in Chapter 4.)

Reminder:
General is the default setting for the /WGF command.

All formats specified with /Range Format show format indicators in the command line. You do not have to enter these indicators; 1-2-3 automatically provides them. When you use /Range Format and specify General format for a range, the number on the command line is preceded by the indicator (G) whenever the cell pointer is within the formatted range.

Fixed Format

1-2-3's Fixed format is similar to General format in that it does not display commas or dollar signs. The difference is that Fixed format lets you control the number of places to the right of the decimal point. When you select Fixed format, 1-2-3 prompts you for the number of decimal places you want displayed. When you subsequently enter a whole number into a formatted cell, 1-2-3 enters a decimal point and, to the right of the decimal, the number of zeros corresponding to the number you selected when you set the fixed format. Conversely, if the number of decimal places you selected is fewer than the number of decimal places in the numbers entered into the formatted cells, 1-2-3 rounds the numbers as displayed in the worksheet to the selected number of decimal places.

Reminder:
Fixed format allows you to control the number of decimal places; General does not.

Notice that only the numbers as displayed are rounded; the numbers that 1-2-3 actually stores in the cells are not. For example, if cell F33 contains the value 1.26, and the cell is formatted Fixed with 1 decimal place, you see 1.3 on screen. But cell F33 still contains the value 1.26.

The following are examples of numbers in Fixed format.

In the Command Line	In the Cell	Displayed in the Worksheet
(F0)15.5	15.5	16
(F2)1000.2145	1000.2415	1000.21
(F3)-21.405	-21.405	-21.405
(F4)93.1	93.1	93.1000

You do not have to enter the format indicator (for example, F0) in the command line. 1-2-3 enters the indicator automatically. The indicator for the default format, however, will not appear in the command line. For example, if you have not used the /Worksheet Global Format command to change the default from F2, (F2) will not appear in the command line.

Cue:
You can enter decimal numbers using the percent sign.

You can enter decimal numbers in two ways: with the decimal point (.12) or with the percent sign (%). In F2 format, for example, if you enter either .12 or 12% the worksheet will contain 0.12.

This format can be useful when you want to control the number of places to the right of the decimal point without the automatic removal of insignificant digits that occurs in General format. Fixed format is particularly appealing when you want all the numbers in your columns to show the same number of decimal places.

Scientific Format

Scientific format causes 1-2-3 to display numbers in exponential scientific notation. You will recall that this notation is used in General format when numbers are too large or too small to be displayed any other way. By choosing Scientific format instead of General format, however, you can control the number of decimal places and so determine the amount of precision that will be displayed. 1-2-3's General format controls the number of decimal places by default. Numbers that are rounded for display in the worksheet keep their value in the cell to the same precision as they were entered. Some examples follow:

In the Command Line	In the Cell	Displayed in the Worksheet
(S2)27.1	27.1	2.71E+01
(S4)453.235	453.235	4.5324E+02
(S1)-21	-21	-2.1E+01
(S0)-1	-1	-1E+00

Currency Format

Currency format displays numbers in cells with a currency indicator before each entry, and with commas separating hundreds from thousands, hundreds of thousands from millions, etc. Negative values appear in parentheses ( ). The dollar sign is the default for the currency indicator.

Currency format also gives you the option of controlling the number of places to the right of the decimal point. This feature is helpful if you are having trouble displaying values that are too large for the column width. One solution is to override the default of two places to the right of the decimal point.

If the value you want to display in Currency format is too large for the column width, a series of asterisks instead of the value will appear across the cell. This is true for all formats. The problem of space is particularly acute with this format, however, because the dollar sign, commas, and parentheses take up space. The best way to handle this situation is to experiment with the formatting parameters and the column width until you get the appearance you want.

Reminder:
Asterisks are displayed in a cell when the value is too long for the column width.

You will recall that column width is controlled through either the /Worksheet Column Set-Width or /Worksheet Global Column-Width command. The former controls specific columns in the worksheet, and the latter controls all the columns at the same time.

Numbers that appear in the command line are preceded by the indicator (C) for Currency. This format indicator is followed by an integer to indicate the number of decimal places you have chosen, all in parentheses. The following examples show how numbers appear in the command line after you have entered them, how they are stored in the cell, and how they are displayed in the worksheet with Currency format. Notice that numbers that are rounded with the Format command are not stored in the cell as rounded numbers; the full value is still available for all calculation purposes.

In the Command Line	In the Cell	Displayed in the Worksheet
(C2)45	45	$45.00
(C2)1612.3	1612.3	$1,612.30
(C3)22.805	22.805	$22.805
(C1)105.56	105.56	$105.6
(C2)-210.99	-210.99	($210.99)

Depending on how cell-specific you want the control to be, cell formats are controlled with the /Worksheet Global Format or the /Range Format command followed (in this case) by Currency.

Comma Format

Cue:
In financial statements, use a combination of comma and currency formats.

The , (comma) format resembles Currency format, except that no dollar signs appear when the numbers are displayed. Commas separate hundreds from thousands, hundreds of thousands from millions, etc. Parentheses ( ) identify negative numbers. After the , (comma) format has been chosen, you can specify the number of decimal places you want.

This format can be particularly useful in financial statements for displaying all the numbers, except those at the top and bottom of columns, with commas but without dollar signs. For example, a portion of a balance sheet follows:

Cash	$1,750
Receivables	3,735
Inventories	9,200
Current Assets	$14,685

The numbers corresponding to Receivables and Inventories are displayed with , (comma) format, and those corresponding to Cash and Current Assets are displayed with Currency format.

The +/- Format

The +/- format creates a horizontal bar graph of plus or minus signs, depending on the value of the number you enter in the cell. Asterisks are displayed if the size of the bar graph exceeds the column width. If zero is entered in a cell, a period (.) is displayed on the graph and left-justified in the cell.

In the Command Line	*In the Worksheet*
(+)6	++++++
(+)-4	----
(+)0	

Some applications use this format to mark a value in a long column of numbers. As you scan the column, the +'s and -'s stand out and are easy to locate (fig. 5.1)

Fig. 5.1

*Using the +/-
format to identify
values of numbers.*

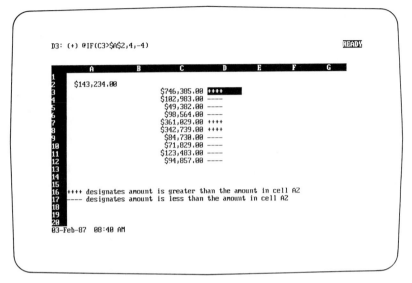

Percent Format

The **P**ercent format is used to display percentages; when you select this format you also select the number of decimal places. The values displayed in the worksheet are the values you enter, multiplied by 100 and followed by a percent sign. Notice that numbers which are rounded for display purposes are not altered in the cell.

In the Command Line	In the Cell	Displayed in the Worksheet
(P0).12	.12	12%
(P4)12.134	12.134	1213.4000%
(P2).5675	.5675	56.75%

One of the difficulties with this format is that it seems natural to want to enter integers instead of decimals (for example, 12 instead of .12 in the first example). But 1-2-3 persists in its method of storing cell contents in only one way and allowing you to control only the display of the output.

*Caution:
To have the proper percent displayed, you must enter numbers with the correct decimal point.*

Date and Time Formats

1-2-3 represents any given date internally as an integer equal to the number of days from December 31, 1899, to the given date. For example, January 1, 1900, is represented by the number 1; December 31, 2099 (which is the last date in 1-2-3's calendar), is represented by 73050. To enter a date into the worksheet, you use one of the date functions: @DATE, @DATEVALUE, or @NOW.

1-2-3 calculates a period of hours as a fraction expressed in decimals. The calculations are based on a 24-hour clock, so-called military time. Use one of the time functions: @TIME, @TIMEVALUE, or @NOW to enter a time into the worksheet.

To display a date or time in its proper format, use either the /**R**ange **F**ormat **D**ate or /**W**orksheet **G**lobal **F**ormat **D**ate commands; to format for time, use /RFDT or /WGFDT. When you use the /**R**ange **F**ormat **D**ate command, any range that you have set using the Date format will appear in one of nine date and time formats. When you use the /**W**orksheet **G**lobal **F**ormat **D**ate command, dates or times (as well as all other numbers entered in any cell in the worksheet) will be displayed in the selected date and time format.

The nine date and time formats that you can specify with the /**R**ange **F**ormat **D**ate and /**W**orksheet **G**lobal **F**ormat **D**ate commands are shown in tables 5.1 and 5.2.

Table 5.1
Date Formats

Number	Description	Example
1	Day-Month-Year DD-MMM-YY	19-Jul-87
2	Day-Month DD-MMM	19-Jul
3	Month-Year MMM-YY	Jul-87
4	Long International MM/DD/YY or DD/MM/YY or DD.MM.YY or YY-MM-DD	07/19/87 19/07/87 19.07.87 87-07-19
5	Short International MM/DD or DD/MM or DD.MM or MM-DD	07/19 19/07 19.07 07-19

Table 5.2
Time Formats

Number	Description	Example
1	Hour:Minute:Second	
	HH:MM:SS AM/PM	11:37:43 PM
2	Hour:Minute	
	HH:MM AM/PM	11:37 PM
3	Long International	
	HH:MM:SS	23:37:43
	or HH.MM.SS	23.37.43
	or HH,MM,SS	23,37,43
	or HHhMMmSSs	23h37m43s
4	Short International	
	HH:MM	23:37
	or HH.MM	23.37
	or HH,MM	23,37
	or HHhMMm	23h37m

For more information on date and time functions and formats, see Chapter 6.

Text Format

Text format displays formulas as they are entered in the command line, not the computed values that 1-2-3 normally displays. Numbers entered using this format are displayed in the same manner used in **General** format.

Probably the most important application of this format is setting up Table Ranges for /**D**ata **T**able commands, but another important application is debugging. Because you can display all the formulas on the screen with the **Text** format, finding and correcting problems is a relatively easy task. If the characters in your formulas exceed the cell width, you will see one less character than the column-width setting. When you use this technique for debugging your model, you may have to widen the cell width to see your complete formulas.

Cue:
As a debugging aid, Text format can be used to display all formulas in the worksheet.

Some examples of Text format follow:

In the Command Line	*In the Worksheet*
(T)+C4/B12	+C4/B12
(T)(A21*B4)	(A21*B4)
(T)567.6	567.6

Hidden Format

Hidden format will suppress the display of cell contents for any range that you indicate after you invoke the **/Range Format Hidden** command. If, instead, you want to hide all the cells in a column or range of columns, use the **/Worksheet Column Hide** command, discussed in Chapter 4.

Although a cell with Hidden format will appear as a blank cell on the screen, its contents will be displayed in the control panel when you place the cursor over the cell. The hidden cell will be a part of calculations as if it weren't hidden. All formulas and values can be calculated and readjusted when values are changed.

Reminder:
Long labels will not overwrite nonblank cells that are hidden with the /RFH command.

You might think that you could disguise macros in cells by allowing long labels of alphanumeric characters to overwrite hidden cells. For example, suppose that you put a macro in cell F5, hid the macro using the **/Range Format Hidden** command, and then put a long label in cell E5 in an attempt to overwrite the apparently blank cell F5. 1-2-3 will not let cell F5 be overwritten; if you use **/RFH** to hide a cell that contains data, the cell will still block out long labels.

Reset Format

The **/Range Format Reset** command resets the format of the indicated range to the global default setting. When the format of a range is reset, the format indicator for any cell within the range disappears from the control panel.

When you issue the **/Range Format Reset** command, hidden columns are displayed temporarily, with an asterisk next to the column letter (see fig. 5.2). After you reset the format for the range you select, the hidden columns again disappear.

Fig. 5.2

Showing hidden columns while resetting formats.

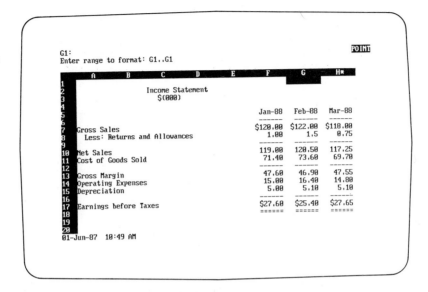

Controlling the International Formats

1-2-3 allows you to control the punctuation and currency sign displayed by Comma and Currency formats, and to control the way the date and time are displayed when you use the special international Date and Time formats. To control these settings globally for the worksheet, use the /Worksheet Global Default Other International command.

The Punctuation option of the /Worksheet Global Default Other International command gives you a choice of eight ways to punctuate numbers and to delimit function arguments. The default is the standard American convention of a period between an integer and its fractional component, commas to delimit thousands, and commas to delimit function arguments. Should you need to change the default, however, seven other combinations are available for punctuating numbers.

The Currency option allows you to change the currency symbol displayed by Currency format and to specify whether that symbol is a prefix or suffix. You can enter any character in the Lotus International Character Set (LICS) or a string of characters (such as *$US* or *$CAN*) to be displayed. (For more on LICS characters, see Chapter 6 and Appendix B.)

The Date and Time options allow you to set the International Date and Time formats. You have four choices each for date and time format. The default format for dates is MM/DD/YY (01/16/88) and, for times, HH:MM:SS in 24-hour time (19:25:33).

Using the /Range Justify Command
for Text Formatting (/RJ)

1-2-3's /Range Justify command is something of an orphan. This command provides 1-2-3 with the first hint of word-processing capabilities but is completely unsupported by other text-processing tools. For this reason, we think of the /Range Justify command as an advanced formatting tool rather than a simple word processor.

As you have seen, 1-2-3 allows text entries to be wider than the width of the column in which they are entered. The labels will overwrite adjoining cells, unless a cell already contains text. After the text has been entered, a /Range Justify command will block the text into the space you indicate. For example, suppose that you typed the line of text shown on the 1-2-3 worksheet in figure 5.3.

Fig. 5.3

A long label overwrites adjoining cells.

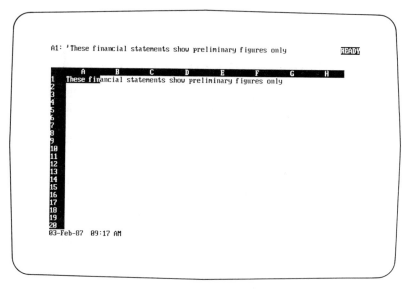

Notice that this label, which was entered in cell A1, extends across the cells from A1 through F1. Using the /Range Justify command, you can ask 1-2-3 to justify this text into columns A and B; A, B, and C; or A, B, C, and D. By issuing the command /rjA1..C1, for example, you could specify that the text be blocked into three 9-character columns (A, B, and C). Figure 5.4 shows the results of this command.

Fig. 5.4

Using /Range Justify to block a label into three columns.

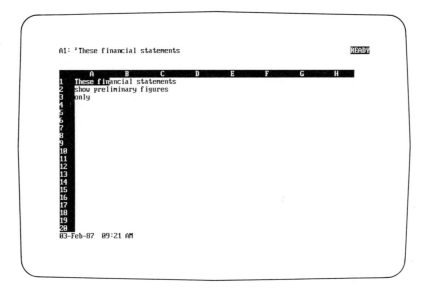

This function can be used to fine-tune the captions and notes that are commonly attached to financial documents. But /Range Justify has some limitations. The worst of these is that the command pushes down any entries in cells below the cell being justified. Normally this effect is not a problem, but in some cases the rearrangement can mess up a carefully constructed worksheet.

Caution:
/Range Justify pushes down any entries in the cells below the cell being justified.

For example, figure 5.5 shows a sample worksheet. Figure 5.6 shows the same sheet after the /RJ command has been used on cell A1. Notice that the labels which were aligned in the first figure are no longer aligned in the second. Be careful when you use /Range Justify—its results are sometimes difficult to predict.

Dealing with Format Problems

Despite the ease with which you can ordinarily use 1-2-3's formats, you may encounter some problems in using them. First, there is no provision to left-justify or center numbers. Unlike labels, numbers can be only right-justified.

Reminder:
Numbers can be only right-justified.

Having only right-justified numbers can create an unsightly appearance when you need to display different-size numbers in the same column (see fig. 5.7). Because of this problem, using the /Data Fill command for numbers used as column headers is less than convenient. (The /Data Fill command is discussed in Chapter 13.)

Fig. 5.5

*The worksheet
before using
/Range Justify.*

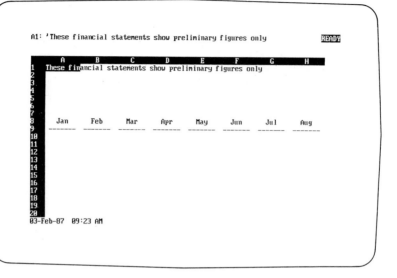

Fig. 5.6

*The worksheet
after using /Range
Justify.*

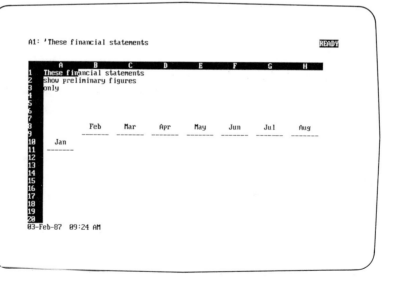

Fig. 5.7

Headings with numbers right-justified.

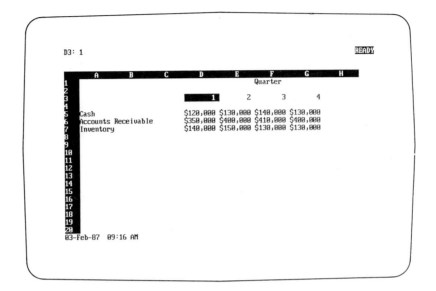

The only way around this particular problem is to make the Quarter numbers labels; then you can control the alignment.

Another problem with appearance occurs when, in the same column, you center labels that are an odd number of characters long and those that are an even number of characters. The results may appear to be slightly out of kilter. If the column is an even number of characters wide, labels that are an even number of characters will center exactly, but labels that are an odd number of characters will not. If the column is an odd number of characters wide, the reverse is true. The following example illustrates this problem.

Reminder:
Column width affects how labels are centered.

Column Even Number	*Column Odd Number*
of Characters Wide	*of Characters Wide*
1234567890	123456789
RALPHS	RALPHS
SOFT	SOFT
SHOES	SHOES

There is really no way around this problem except to try different alignments by inserting blanks or extra characters wherever possible. The problem of alignment is one that you will have to learn to live with and do your best to work around.

Because the /**R**ange Format and /**W**orksheet **G**lobal **F**ormat commands punctuate numeric values, 1-2-3 may display asterisks in the cell (see fig. 5.8). This occurs when the requested format exceeds the number of character places available, as determined by the column width. The solution is to widen the column to accommodate the punctuation. Additional information on this procedure can be found in Chapter 4 of this book.

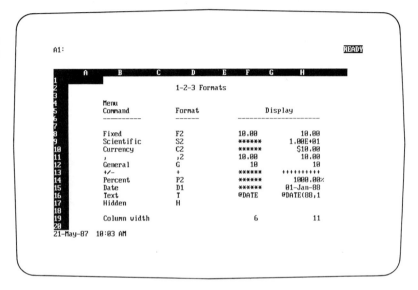

Using HAL To Format the Spreadsheet

Lotus HAL recognizes all the 1-2-3 formatting commands except the /**Range Format Hidden** command, and **Date** commands two through five. To format data with HAL, you begin your request with the verbs *Display*, *Format*, or *Show*.

HAL can be used to format data in two different ways: (1) by requesting a specific 1-2-3 format; and (2) by requesting that a range be formatted like another preformatted range.

The first method is simply an easy and natural way to ask for a format. For example, the request *format row 20 as $* will format row 20 in currency format with two decimal places. HAL assumes a default of two decimal places; you can stipulate a different number of places by adding the phrase *with x places* to your HAL requests, where *x* is the number of decimal places.

As with other HAL requests, you can use range names in this method. For example, the request *display net_income ,* will format the range NET_INCOME in comma format with 2 decimal places. Notice that you have to type only the , symbol, not the word *comma*.

The second method of formatting with HAL is even more convenient, because you don't have to remember the exact format you used elsewhere in the worksheet; you only have to tell HAL to use the same format. The requests *format row 20 like row 3* and *show net-income like gross-sales* are shortcut ways to get the format you need.

Adding Word-Processing Capabilities to 1-2-3—4WORD

As we noted in the discussion of the /Range Justify command in this chapter, 1-2-3 contains only a faint hint of genuine word-processing capabilities. 4WORD, published by Turner Hall, can fill this large gap by providing what is, in effect, a built-in word processor. The two major advantages of 4WORD over other word-processors are (1) you don't have to leave 1-2-3 to use 4WORD; and (2) you can establish a link between a 4WORD document and a 1-2-3 spreadsheet.

Because 4WORD uses the new Lotus Add-In Manager, you can access and use 4WORD from within 1-2-3. The Add-In Manager lets you access as many as eight add-in programs from within 1-2-3, three of which can be accessed by using only two keystrokes. To use 4WORD from the spreadsheet, if you have made 4WORD one of the three easily accessed add-ins, you need only hold down the Alt key and press the F7, F8, or F9 function key, depending on which key you have selected.

When you access 4WORD, a 1-2-3 type command-menu structure appears, from which you can choose a variety of word-processing tools (see fig. 5.9). 4WORD provides a substantially easier environment for dealing with text than does the 1-2-3 spreadsheet. You can format a document with margins to fit an 8 1/2-by-11-inch page, and justify the margins to be even or ragged. You can then type the document and enter a variety of print enhancements, such as boldface, underline, italics, superscript, and subscript. Figure 5.10 shows a 4WORD document containing print-enhancement characters (the boldface indicators enclosing the headings).

Fig. 5.9

The 4WORD main command menu.

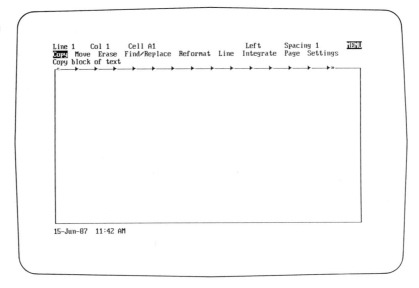

Fig. 5.9

The 4WORD main command menu.

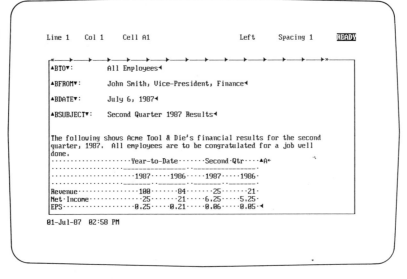

Fig. 5.10

A 4WORD document showing print enhancements.

The figure shows how your document appears on-screen. The print-enhancement characters disappear if you press the F2 function key to get a preview of the printed report. To print a 4WORD document, you use the normal 1-2-3 /**Print Printer** command.

4WORD adapts many 1-2-3 capabilities and key operations to a text environment. The cursor-movement keys and key combinations are used to move line by line or word by word, for example. Tab stops can be set at various intervals. Words and blocks of text can be moved or copied to other parts of the document. Inserting and deleting characters and blocks of text is done in context (rather than in a command line on a cell-by-cell basis). If you have worked with a word processor, you will recognize that 4WORD supplies the capabilities you would expect from a word processor.

The second major advantage of 4WORD is that it provides an active link with the 1-2-3 spreadsheet, so that any changes in the spreadsheet are automatically reflected in the document. This capability makes it almost ridiculously easy to generate form reports based on the changing values on your working spreadsheet.

Figure 5.10 displays a 4WORD document that is linked to the 1-2-3 spreadsheet shown in figure 5.11. Suppose that you want to change the values in the 1987 Quarterly Report column. When you make the change in the spreadsheet (see fig. 5.12), the 4WORD document also changes automatically (see fig. 5.13). When the document is finished, you can print it from within 1-2-3. Notice the bold headings in the printed memorandum shown in figure 5.14.

Fig. 5.11

A 1-2-3 spreadsheet linked to a 4WORD document.

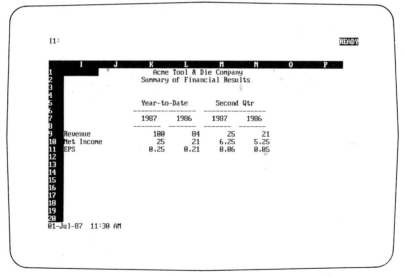

Fig. 5.12

Changing the entries in the spreadsheet.

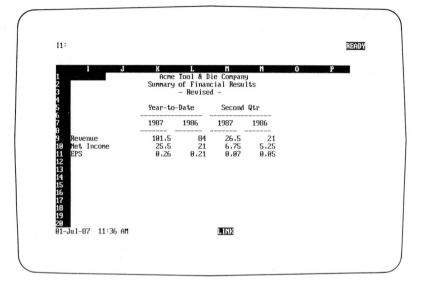

Fig. 5.13

The 4WORD document is updated automatically.

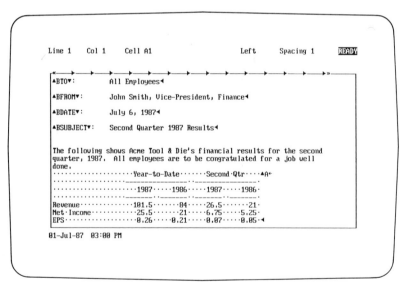

Fig. 5.14

*The printed
4WORD document.*

```
TO:        All Employees

FROM:      John Smith, Vice-President, Finance

DATE:      July 6, 1987

SUBJECT:   Second Quarter 1987 Results


The following shows Acme Tool & Die's financial results for the second
quarter, 1987.  All employees are to be congratulated for a job well
done.
                Year-to-Date    Second Qtr
                ---------------- ----------------
                1987    1986    1987    1986
                ------- ------- ------- -------
Revenue         101.5    84     26.5     21
Net Income       25.5    21     6.75     5.25
EPS              0.26    0.21    0.07     0.05
```

1-2-3 spreadsheets can also be linked manually to 4WORD documents, with a cut and paste operation. Essentially, a range can be marked in the spreadsheet and copied to a specified location in the 4WORD document. Because more than one 4WORD document may be created for each spreadsheet, manual linking allows you to update some documents but not others. Text can also be copied from one document to another.

Automatic and manual linking capabilities by themselves would make 4WORD an impressive companion to 1-2-3, but 4WORD offers additional benefits.

Like many stand-alone word-processors, 4WORD has mailmerge capabilities. Mailmerge allows you to make a series of printouts of the same document, with selected changes made to each printout. The classic example is the merge of a mailing list with a form letter. The attractive feature of 4WORD's mailmerge function is its capacity to merge records from a 1-2-3 database with a form document created with 4WORD.

4WORD also allows you to use macros that are created in 1-2-3. This advanced feature will not be needed by everyone, but it could be extraordinarily useful for anyone with extensive word-processing needs.

Finally, because the print enhancements provided by 4WORD can be used in the 1-2-3 spreadsheet without going through 4WORD at all, you can use bold or italic text in your spreadsheet, or use superscript or subscript numbers or text. Depending on your printer's capabilities, you may or may not be able to print these enhancements, whether they were entered in the spreadsheet or a 4WORD document.

Because 4WORD is a genuine 1-2-3 add-in, which works as a part of 1-2-3, you can save your 4WORD document as part of your spreadsheet, by using 1-2-3's /**F**ile **S**ave command.

4WORD is an easy program to learn and use. If you are a Symphony user, the process will be even easier, because of the similarity between 4WORD and Symphony. As an added bonus, 4WORD is not a memory hog—using at most 60K of RAM.

Chapter Summary

In this chapter, you learned how to display your data as currency, dates and times, with commas and percent signs, in scientific notation, and in several other ways. You learned also how to hide a range of cells for purposes of appearance and secrecy, and how to control international formats. And you learned how to use the /Range Justify command for advanced formatting techniques.

Now that you have learned formatting, you know most of the basics of building a spreadsheet and you probably are already a competent user of 1-2-3. The next chapter takes you a long step further into mastery. In Chapters 3 and 4, you learned to use formulas and a few simple functions, which are built-in formulas, but Chapter 6 will show you how 1-2-3's extensive library of functions make the program a powerful and easy-to-use tool for data analysis and manipulation.

6

Using Functions in the Spreadsheet

1-2-3's functions are, in effect, built-in subroutines—mini-programs that perform well-defined tasks and return the results of those tasks to the spreadsheet. This capability greatly extends the power of 1-2-3; with functions, you can perform tasks that would take much longer or could not be done at all with only such basic 1-2-3 tools as commands and operators.

Functions can help you solve an endless variety of problems. Perhaps their most basic use is to substitute for long, cumbersome, and mistake-prone mathematical formulas. In previous chapters you have already encountered the simple @SUM formula as a substitute for a formula such as +B3+B4+B5+B6+B7+B8+B9+B10. Using a function with a range name, you could instead enter something like @SUM(SALES87)—an easier-to-use and more intelligible statement.

The 1-2-3 functions do not solve only mathematical problems. Financial and statistical operations constitute another major class of tasks performed by functions. If you are a financial or statistical analyst with regular and extensive budgetary, investment, or market-research responsibilities, you will find these functions invaluable. Otherwise, your need of the financial and statistical functions may be only occasional, and you will need to refer to these sections of the chapter only as need demands.

Dates and times can be incorporated into the worksheet in a variety of ways by using functions. 1-2-3 also offers other specialized functions to further expand the capabilities of the spreadsheet. You may want to scan the section

167

on special, logical, error-trapping, and data-management functions to learn what is available, and then return to that section to experiment as possibilities arise in your worksheet. One special capability that can be of particular use when managing a 1-2-3 database is the sophisticated lookup table. (Further information on database management can be found in Chapter 13.)

A major capability of 1-2-3 often neglected by beginning users is its capacity to manipulate alphanumeric data. String functions provide tools to search and replace, make logical comparisons based on alphanumeric data, convert labels to values and vice versa, and a variety of other tasks. We strongly recommend that you take some time to learn how string functions can help you streamline your spreadsheet.

The dramatic power of all the 1-2-3 functions can be even further increased by incorporating them into macros and Command Language programs. The more competent and confident you become in using 1-2-3, the more you will want to join functions with macros to reach the full versatility and power of the program. (See Chapters 14 and 15 to learn how to build and use macros and Command Language programs.)

This chapter fills a double role: (1) it introduces you to and teaches you to use functions; and (2) it provides you with a reference section in which you can quickly find and review a function's use. Within each section, the functions are presented in a logical way, either from simple to complex or in another natural learning order. Thus, if you are trying to learn the capabilities of a certain class of functions, you can easily work through the section.

The following classes of function are covered in this chapter:

- mathematical
- statistical
- financial
- logical
- error-trapping
- data management
- string
- date and time

How To Enter a 1-2-3 Function

A 1-2-3 function is always identified by the @ symbol preceding the function's name in capital letters. So identified, functions can be distinguished easily from all other entries.

The function's *arguments*, written in parentheses, specify the cell or cells on which the function will act. For example, the following function, which we will assume lies in cell B21, computes the total of a range of the eight cells from B12 to B19:

   B21: @SUM(B12..B19)

In this function, @ signals that the entry is a function, SUM is the name of the function being used, and the statement (B12..B19) is the argument (in this case, a range). This function tells 1-2-3 to compute the sum of the numbers located in cells B12, B13, B14, B15, B16, B17, B18, and B19 and display the result in cell B21.

A few functions, like @ERR and @NA, do not take an argument. These functions are discussed in detail later.

Some functions can be quite complex. For example, several functions can be combined in a single cell by having one function use other functions as its arguments. The length of an argument, however, is limited; like formulas, functions can contain a maximum of 240 characters per cell.

Reminder:
Because functions cannot contain more than 240 characters per cell, the length of an argument is limited.

Mathematical Functions

1-2-3 contains 17 functions that perform mathematical, logarithmic, and trigonometric operations. These functions are built-in mathematical formulas that perform tasks which would take much longer or could not be done at all with mathematical operators alone, such as *, /, +, or -.

General Mathematical Functions

At least a few of the six functions that perform general mathematical operations will be useful to almost everyone who works with 1-2-3. These functions are summarized in table 6.1.

Table 6.1
General Mathematical Functions

Function	Description
@ABS(number or cell reference)	Computes absolute value
@INT(number or cell reference)	Computes the integer portion of a specified number
@MOD(number,divisor)	Computes the remainder (the modulus) in division
@ROUND(number or cell reference, number)	Rounds numbers to a specified precision
@SQRT(number or cell reference)	Computes the square root
@RAND	Generates random numbers

@ABS—Computing Absolute Value

The @ABS function computes the absolute value of a number. Use this function when you need to convert a value from negative to positive. The form of this function is

@ABS(number or cell reference)

The @ABS function is particularly useful when a calculation in one area of your spreadsheet results in a negative value that you need to use as a positive value in another area of your spreadsheet. For example, you can use @ABS to reference a depreciation calculation for use in the expense portion of an income statement. Figure 6.1 shows how the @ABS function can be used for this purpose. Cell B8 contains the formula @ABS(B15); this formula returns to cell B8 the absolute value of the value contained in cell B15. Although B15 contains negative 33, the formula in B8 returns positive 33. The other cells in row 8 contain similar formulas.

@INT—Computing the Integer

The @INT function computes the integer portion of a number by eliminating all digits to the right of the decimal point. The form of this function is

@INT(number or cell reference)

Using the @INT function is not the same as formatting the cell to display zero decimal places. @INT differs from a zero decimal point format in two

Fig. 6.1

Using the @ABS function to convert a negative value to positive.

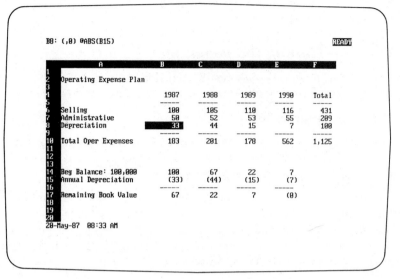

ways: (1) formatting changes only the display, but continues to store the value to its full precision; computations based on the cell containing the value will use the full value. @INT, on the other hand, actually eliminates the decimal portion of the number and stores only the integer portion. (2) The formatted display shows rounded numbers; @INT does not round, but simply eliminates the decimal portion. With @INT, 4.99999 is changed to 4, not to 5.

Use the @INT function when you need to know the whole-number equivalent of the outcome of a computation. In the example in figure 6.2, we want to know the number of products that can be completed with the inventory in stock; a fraction of a number is of no use. What we need, then, is the integer portion of the quotient of 50,000 divided by 64. The function in cell G8 returns the correct number.

Reminder:
@INT eliminates the decimal portion of a number, and stores only the integer portion.

Fig. 6.2

Using the @INT function to find the whole-number portion of a computation.

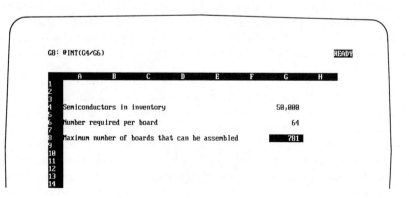

If you need the other portion of a division calculation (the remainder), use the @MOD function.

@MOD—Finding the Remainder

The @MOD function computes the remainder, or modulus, that results from the division of one numbers by another. The form of this function is

@MOD(dividend,divisor)

Both the dividend (the number to be divided) and the divisor (the number to divide by) can be either a number or a cell reference. As you would expect, the divisor in the @MOD argument cannot be zero.

Use @MOD when you need the remainder of a division calculation. Extending the example of figure 6.2, figure 6.3 shows how the @MOD function computes the number of semiconductors remaining after the largest possible number of computers have been assembled from the available inventory. The function in cell G10 divides 50,000 by 64 and then returns the remainder to cell G10.

Fig. 6.3

Using the @MOD function to return the remainder from a division.

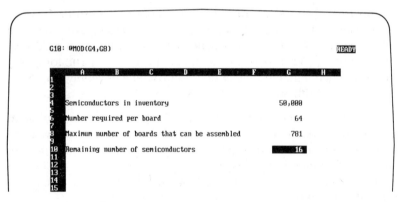

Cue:

Use @MOD with @DATE to compute days of the week.

@MOD is frequently used in calculations involving dates. You can use @MOD, for example, to determine the day of the week. The @MOD functions in figure 6.4 use the @DATE function as one of the arguments (the dividend). (For more on the @DATE function, see this chapter's "Date and Time Functions" section.)

The @DATE function returns a serial number that is a sum of the year (starting at 0 for the year 1900), the month, and the day. Saturday equals zero, Sunday, one, and so on, for the remaining days of the week. When you divide the @DATE serial number by 7, the remainder will be a number between 0 and 6. If the remainder is 0, the day is Saturday, 1, Sunday, and so on. You can use this information in a string formula to develop a date that includes the day of the week. (See the section on "String Functions" in this chapter.)

Fig. 6.4

Using @MOD to determine the day of the week.

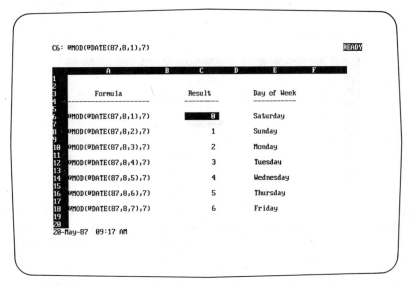

```
C6: @MOD(@DATE(87,8,1),7)                                          READY

          A              B      C          D      E        F
1
2
3          Formula              Result          Day of Week
4         ─────────            ──────          ───────────
5
6    @MOD(@DATE(87,8,1),7)        0             Saturday
7
8    @MOD(@DATE(87,8,2),7)        1             Sunday
9
10   @MOD(@DATE(87,8,3),7)        2             Monday
11
12   @MOD(@DATE(87,8,4),7)        3             Tuesday
13
14   @MOD(@DATE(87,8,5),7)        4             Wednesday
15
16   @MOD(@DATE(87,8,6),7)        5             Thursday
17
18   @MOD(@DATE(87,8,7),7)        6             Friday
19
20
20-May-87  09:17 AM
```

@ROUND—Rounding Numbers

The @ROUND function is used to round numbers to a specified precision between negative fifteen and positive fifteen. @ROUND helps you avoid potential problems caused by 1-2-3's floating-point arithmetic. The general form of the @ROUND function is

@ROUND(number or cell reference, number)

The first argument is the number to be rounded. The second argument specifies the number of decimal places.

@ROUND differs both from a formatting change and from the @INT function. Formatting changes simply change the way values are displayed, not the way they are stored. @INT changes the way values are displayed and how they are stored, but does not round the values. @ROUND changes the way values are displayed and how they're stored but, instead of just deleting the decimal part of the value (as @INT does), rounds the numbers to a specified precision.

Reminder:
@ROUND changes the way numbers are stored; formatting changes only the display.

Figure 6.5 shows the different results of using formatting changes and the @INT and @ROUND functions. Column A contains the original values; in column B, the values have been formatted using the /Range Format Fixed 2 command; column C's values have been rounded to two decimal places; and finally, column D's total has been truncated by using 1-2-3's @INT function.

Notice that column B appears to have the wrong total. Remember that changing the format affects only the way values are displayed; it does not affect

Fig. 6.5

*Comparing
@ROUND with
@INT and /Range
Format Fixed 2.*

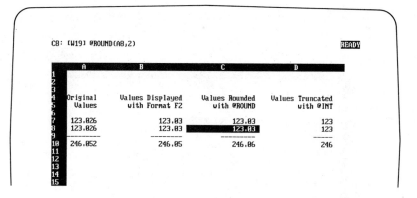

how 1-2-3 stores the values. The total shown in cell B10 (246.05) is therefore correct, even though it appears incorrect. Because the @ROUND function changes how values are stored, the total shown in cell C10 (246.06) is correct and appears correct.

Choosing when to @ROUND and when to format can be a precarious matter. For example, if we use @ROUND(@SUM(B7..B8),2) to round the sum in column B while leaving the two values formatted F2, the sum will still appear to be incorrect. In financial statements, where the totals must both be and appear to be correct, you should look carefully for instances in which you must use @ROUND to round the values in a list before you calculate totals.

@SQRT—Finding the Square Root

The @SQRT function computes the square root of a positive number. The form of the function is

@SQRT(number or cell reference)

@SQRT is a simple but useful function with few restrictions. If you try to take the square root of a negative number or of a number divided by zero, the function returns an ERR. Results are accurate to 15 decimal places. To see the full 15 places, you may need to adjust the column width and the formatted number of decimal places. Figure 6.6 shows a few examples of the @SQRT function.

@RAND—Generating Random Numbers

The @RAND built-in function generates random numbers between 0 and 1 with up to 15 decimal places. Cells containing the @RAND function display a different value between 0 and 1 each time the worksheet is recalculated. Figures 6.7 and 6.8 show worksheets with columns B, D, F, and H filled with @RAND functions. Notice that, because the second worksheet has been re-

Fig. 6.6

Calculating square roots with the @SQRT function.

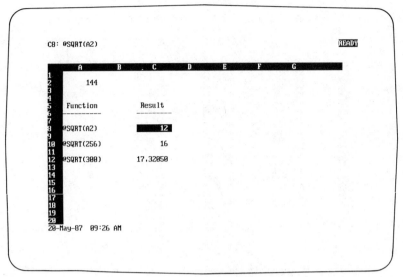

calculated, the value in each cell in those columns in the second worksheet is different from that in the first worksheet. Notice also that the numbers are displayed to six decimal places in the default column-width setting of 9 and the default **G**eneral format. To see the full 15 decimal places, you must expand the column width to 18 and change the format to F15.

Fig. 6.7

Table of values generated by the @RAND function.

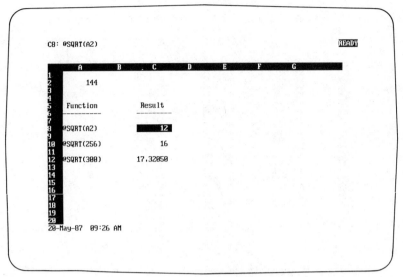

Fig. 6.8

A second table generated by the @RAND function.

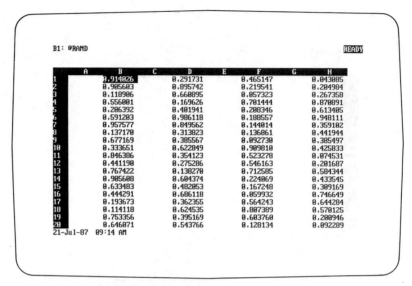

```
B1: @RAND                                                              READY

         A          B         C         D         E         F         G         H
1                0.914026        0.291731            0.465147            0.043885
2                0.905603        0.895742            0.219541            0.204984
3                0.118906        0.660095            0.057323            0.267358
4                0.556001        0.169626            0.701444            0.870891
5                0.206392        0.401941            0.208346            0.613405
6                0.591203        0.986118            0.188557            0.948111
7                0.957577        0.849562            0.144014            0.359102
8                0.137170        0.313823            0.136861            0.441944
9                0.677169        0.385567            0.092730            0.385497
10               0.333651        0.622049            0.909810            0.425833
11               0.846306        0.354123            0.523278            0.074531
12               0.441190        0.275286            0.546163            0.201687
13               0.767422        0.138270            0.712585            0.584344
14               0.905608        0.604374            0.224069            0.433545
15               0.633483        0.402053            0.167248            0.309169
16               0.444291        0.686118            0.059932            0.746649
17               0.193673        0.362355            0.564243            0.644284
18               0.114118        0.624535            0.807389            0.570125
19               0.753356        0.395169            0.603760            0.200946
20               0.646071        0.543766            0.128134            0.092209
21-Jul-87  09:14 AM
```

Trigonometric Functions

1-2-3 also has a complete set of trigonometric functions. If you normally use the program only for financial calculations, you probably will never need these functions. Trigonometric functions will be invaluable, however, if you are developing engineering and scientific applications. Table 6.2 summarizes the trigonometric functions available in 1-2-3.

Table 6.2
Trigonometric Functions

Function	Description
@PI	Computes the value of the constant *pi*
@SIN(number or cell reference)	Computes the sine
@COS(number or cell reference)	Computes the cosine
@TAN(number or cell reference)	Computes the tangent
@ASIN(number or cell reference)	Computes the arcsine
@ACOS(number or cell reference)	Computes the arccosine
@ATAN(number or cell reference)	Computes the arctangent
@ATAN2(number,number)	Computes the four-quadrant arctangent

@PI—Computing Pi

The @PI function simply computes the value of pi, accurate to 15 decimal places, or 3.141592653589794. @PI is one of the functions that take no arguments. The form of @PI is

@PI

Remember that whenever @PI is used in the worksheet, the full 15-place value is returned, even though the column width or the formatted number of decimal places may be too small to display the entire value.

@PI is useful in a variety of trigonometric equations, such as converting the degrees of an angle to radians. Figure 6.9 shows how to compute the radians of an angle using the following formula:

Radians = @PI $*$ Degrees/180

Cue:
*Use @PI to change
angle measurement
to radians.*

Fig. 6.9

*Using the @PI
function to convert
angles from
degrees to radians.*

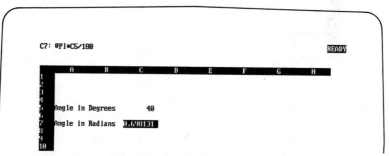

@SIN, @COS, and @TAN—Computing Trigonometric Functions

The @SIN, @COS, and @TAN functions calculate the sine, cosine, and tangent, respectively, of an angle in radians. These functions take the following form:

@SIN(angle in radians or cell reference)

@COS(angle in radians or cell reference)

@TAN(angle in radians or cell reference)

If you know the degrees of an angle, you can compute the radians by using the formula shown in the section on the @PI function:

Radians = @PI $*$ Degrees/180

Figure 6.9 shows an example of converting degrees to radians. Figure 6.10 shows examples of using the @SIN, @COS, and @TAN functions to compute the respective trigonometric ratios of an angle measured in radians. Because cell C4 contains the formula @PI*C2/180, the functions referencing C4 use the radians measurement of a 45-degree angle. Notice (in cell C17) that you can get the same results by using the conversion formula as the argument of the trigonometric functions.

Fig. 6.10

Using the @SIN, @COS, and @TAN functions.

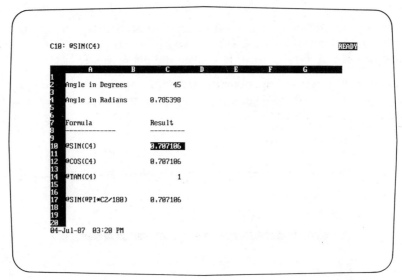

Generating a table of trigonometric values is easy in 1-2-3. Figure 6.11 shows a table of sines that was created by the following steps:

1. Enter *1* into cell A4

2. Enter *+A4+1* into cell A5

3. Copy cell A5 to A6..A93 (for angles 1 through 90 degrees)

4. Enter *@PI*A4/180* into cell C4

5. Copy cell C4 to C5..C93

6. Enter *@SIN(C4)* into cell E4

7. Copy cell E4 to E5..E93

The highlighted cell (E9) shows that relative addressing adjusts the formula as it is copied. If you do not want to display the angle in radians, you can omit steps 4 and 5. Instead, use the formula @SIN(@PI*A4/180) in the sine column and copy this formula the length of the column. And you can substitute the /Data Fill command, which is explained in Chapter 13, for steps 1 through 3.

Fig. 6.11

Using the @SIN function to create a table of sine values.

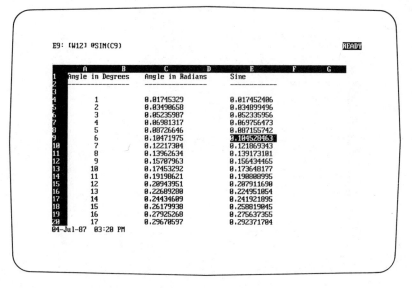

```
E9: [W12] @SIN(C9)                                              READY

          A         B          C         D          E        F        G
1    Angle in Degrees    Angle in Radians     Sine
2    ──────────────      ──────────────       ──────
3
4         1            0.01745329          0.017452406
5         2            0.03490658          0.034899496
6         3            0.05235987          0.052335956
7         4            0.06981317          0.069756473
8         5            0.08726646          0.087155742
9         6            0.10471975          0.104528463
10        7            0.12217304          0.121869343
11        8            0.13962634          0.139173181
12        9            0.15707963          0.156434465
13        10           0.17453292          0.173648177
14        11           0.19198621          0.190808995
15        12           0.20943951          0.207911690
16        13           0.22689280          0.224951054
17        14           0.24434609          0.241921895
18        15           0.26179938          0.258819045
19        16           0.27925268          0.275637355
20        17           0.29670597          0.292371704
04-Jul-87  03:20 PM
```

@ASIN, @ACOS, @ATAN, and @ATAN2—Inverse Trigonometric Functions

The @ASIN, @ACOS, @ATAN, and @ATAN2 functions compute the arcsine, arccosine, arctangent, and four-quadrant arctangent respectively. The @ASIN, @ACOS, and @ATAN functions are the reciprocals of the @SIN, @COS, and @TAN functions. @ATAN2 is similar to @ATAN, except that @ATAN2 computes the four-quadrant arctangent of the ratio of its two arguments (*number2/number1*). The general form of these functions is

@ASIN(number or cell reference)

@ACOS(angle in radians or cell reference)

@ATAN(angle in radians or cell reference)

@ATAN2(number1,number2)

The *A* at the beginning of each function is interpreted as "the angle whose." Therefore, the function @ASIN(1) returns "the angle whose" sine is one, or 1.570796 in radians. Figure 6.12 shows that @ASIN, @ACOS, and @ATAN, are reciprocals of @SIN, @COS, and @TAN.

Notice in the figure that cells C2, C4, and C6 contain the sine, cosine, and tangent, respectively, of a 45 degree angle. The arc functions in cells C12, C14, and C16 therefore all return the value .785398, which is the radian equivalent of a 45 degree angle. Formulas in cells E12, E14, and E16 convert

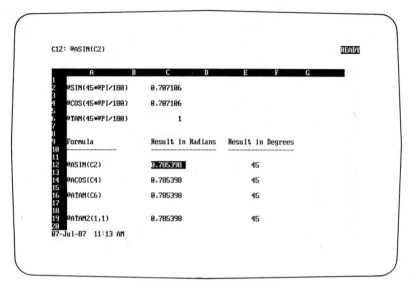

Fig. 6.12

Examples of the arc trigonometric functions.

the radians to degrees. Cell E12, for example, contains the formula 180*C12/@PI. The formula to convert radians to degrees is the reciprocal of the formula that converts degrees to radians.

Cell C19 contains the function @ATAN2(1,1), which is the "angle whose tangent equals 1/1." The value of this function is also .785928 radians, or 45 degrees.

When using the arc trigonometric functions, keep in mind the following points:

- The argument of the @ASIN and @ACOS functions must have a value of between 1 and -1, or the function will return ERR, indicating error

- The value of the @ASIN function is always between -pi/2 and +pi/2. The value of the @ACOS function is always between 0 and pi/2.

- The argument of the @ATAN function can be any value. The value of the function lies between -pi/2 and +pi/2.

- The arguments of the @ATAN2 function can be any combination of positive and negative values, but both arguments cannot be 0. The value of the function lies between -pi and +pi.

Logarithmic Functions

Lotus provides three logarithmic functions primarily for use in engineering, scientific, and other complex equations. Table 6.3 lists the logarithmic functions with descriptions of their use.

Table 6.3
Logarithmic Functions

Functions	Description
@LOG(number or cell reference)	Computes the (base 10) logarithm
@EXP(number or cell reference)	Computes the value of the constant *e* raised to a specified power
@LN(number or cell reference)	Computes the natural logarithm

@LOG—Computing Logarithms

As its name implies, the @LOG function calculates the logarithm (base 10) of a positive number. The form of the function is

@LOG(number or cell reference)

If the argument of the @LOG function is a negative value or is zero, an ERR will be returned. Figure 6.13 shows several examples of @LOG.

Reminder:
The argument of @LOG should be positive.

Fig. 6.13

Using the @LOG function to calculate base 10 logarithms.

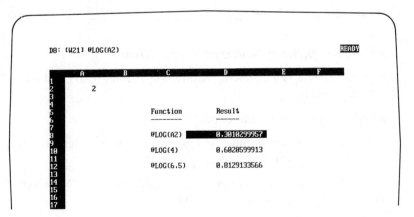

@EXP—Finding Powers of e

The @EXP function calculates the value of the constant e raised to a power specified by the argument, where e equals approximately 2.7182818. The form of @EXP is

@EXP(number or cell reference)

If the argument is greater than 230, 1-2-3 cannot display the value, no matter how wide you set the column; instead, asterisks (*) are displayed in the cell. 1-2-3 stores the value, however, which can be used in calculations; the results of the calculations will be useful if they are small enough to fit in the cell.

Figure 6.14 shows some results of using the @EXP function.

Fig. 6.14

Finding the powers of the constant e with @EXP.

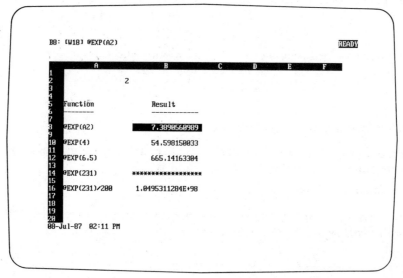

@LN—Computing Natural Logarithms

The @LN function calculates the natural logarithm (base e) of the argument. The form of @LN is

@LN(number or cell reference)

Reminder:
The argument of @LN should be positive.

The value of the argument must be a positive number; otherwise, the function will calculate an error and display ERR in the cell.

Figure 6.15 shows some examples of the @LN function. Note that the @LN function is the reciprocal of the @EXP function.

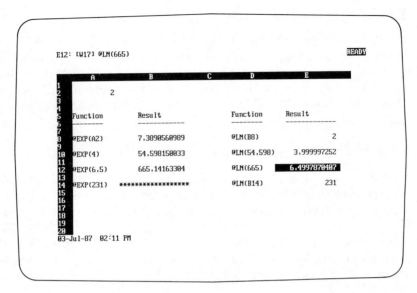

Fig. 6.15

Using the @LN function to calculate natural logarithms.

Statistical Functions

1-2-3 contains a set of functions that can perform simple statistical analyses. These functions are used typically with an argument consisting of a range of cells. A range is a rectangular block of one or more cells.

Table 6.4 summarizes the statistical functions available in 1-2-3.

Table 6.4
Statistical Functions

Function	Calculates
@AVG(range)	Average of nonblank cells in the range
@COUNT(range)	Number of nonblank entries in the range
@MAX(range)	Maximum value in the range
@MIN(range)	Minimum value in the range
@SUM(range)	Total of values in the range
@VAR(range)	Population variance of values in the range
@STD(range)	Population standard deviation of values in the range

Basic Statistical Functions

1-2-3's simpler statistical functions are @SUM, @MAX, @MIN, @COUNT, and @AVG. The most basic of these (@SUM) has many uses outside as well as within a statistical context. We have consistently used @SUM throughout the book for a variety of examples, and you will undoubtedly find it useful in many applications. The other basic statistical functions are used less widely but are still handy tools.

@SUM—Calculating Sums

@SUM(range) computes the sum of a range of entries. The range is typically a partial row or a column, but a range can also be a named area or a block defined by cell coordinates. For example, in the simple worksheet in figure 6.16, the function @SUM(A1..A2) returns the value 1110, or 345 + 765. The function @SUM(A1..C1) returns the value 1368, or 345 + 456 + 567. The function @SUM(SALES) returns the value 3330, the total of all the numbers in the six-cell range. Notice that the range in this case consists of two partial rows.

Fig. 6.16

Comparing the @SUM function to a formula.

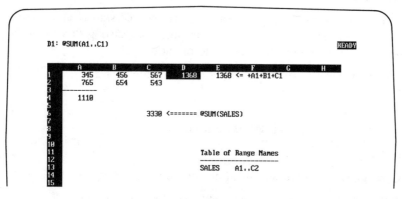

Cue:

You can use @SUM to total the values in a discontinuous set of cells.

You can also define the range of the @SUM function as a discontinuous set of cells. For example, the function @SUM(A1,B2,C1) returns the value 1566. This function is equivalent to the formula +A1+B2+C1. A more useful hybrid is the function @SUM(A1..B2,C1), which computes the total of the range A1 to B2 plus the value in C1, or 2787.

In figure 6.16, using @SUM is only slightly faster than using the longhand arithmetic +A1+B1+C1. But in cases where the range is long, this function can save time.

Another advantage of the @SUM function (and other range functions as well) is that @SUM is more adaptable than a formula to changes made in the worksheet with cut-and-paste commands. For example, in figure 6.16, the function @SUM(A1..C1) in cell D1 is equivalent to the formula +A1+B1+C1 in cell E1. But if we use /WDC (for /Worksheet Delete Column) to delete column B, the worksheet changes to look like figure 6.17.

Fig. 6.17

@SUM and the formula after deleting column B.

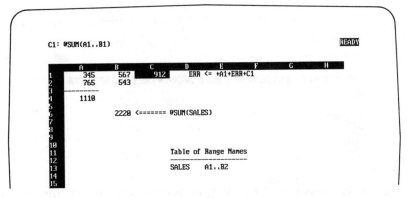

The formula has changed to +A1+ERR+B1, which returns the message ERR. The function, on the other hand, has changed to @SUM(A1..B1) and returns the correct answer, 912. Notice also that the SALES range has adjusted so that the function @SUM(SALES) continues to return the correct total.

If we go the other way and use /WIC to insert a column, what happens? The resulting worksheet looks like figure 6.18.

Fig. 6.18

@SUM and the formula after inserting a column.

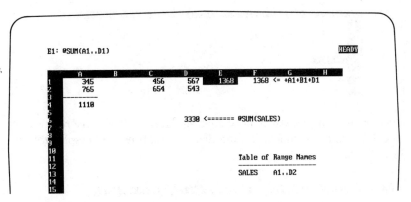

The formula is +A1+C1+D1 and still has the value 1368. The function is now @SUM(A1..D1). If we insert a number in the new cell B1, the function includes that number in the new total; but the formula does not. Again, @SUM(SALES) has also adjusted and will return correct totals if numbers are inserted in cells B1 and B2.

This insert feature has a practical application. Whenever possible, we define a sum range to include one extra cell at the end of the range. Frequently, this can be done by including the cell that contains the underline to mark the addition in the range. For example, in the sheet shown in figure 6.19, we can enter the formula @SUM(A1..A4) in cell A5.

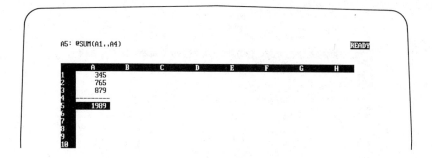

Fig. 6.19

Use of @SUM including the underline in the range.

Because the label in cell A4 has a mathematical value of 0, the cell does not affect our sum. But because we include the cell in the formula, we can add an extra item in the list simply by inserting a row at row 4. The worksheet will then look like figure 6.20.

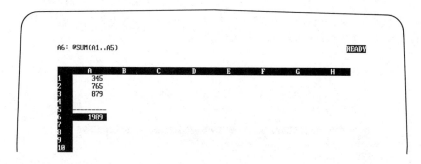

Fig. 6.20

The @SUM function after inserting a row.

The formula in cell A6 is now @SUM(A1..A5). If we insert the number 111 in cell A4, the formula will immediately pick it up and display the value 2,100 in cell A6.

@MAX and @MIN—Computing Maximum and Minimum Values

The @MAX and @MIN functions return the maximum and minimum values in a range. As with the @SUM function, the range can be a partial row or column, a block of several partial rows and columns, a named area, or a discontinuous group of cells joined by commas.

Both of these functions assign a value of 0 to labels but completely ignore empty cells. For example, in the simple worksheet in figure 6.21, the function @MAX(B6..E8) returns the value 750, and the function @MIN(B6..E8) returns the value 95. The function @MIN(B5..E8) also would return 95 because cells B5..E5 are blank. But the function @MIN(B6..E9) would return the value 0 because of the label "-----" in cells B9..E9. Labels are evaluated as 0, and 0 is the minimum value in the range B6..E9.

Fig. 6.21

Finding the minimum and maximum sales in a sales report.

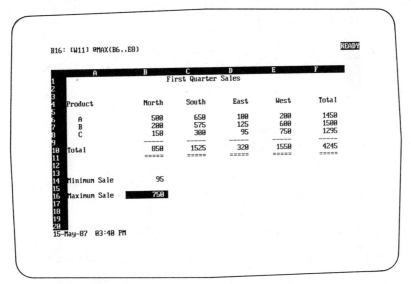

@COUNT—Counting Entries in a Range

The @COUNT function is similar to the @MAX, @MIN, and @SUM functions. @COUNT returns the count of the number of nonblank entries in a range. In figure 6.22, the function @COUNT(A6..A9) returns the value 3. The value of the function @COUNT(B6..B9) would be 4 because of the label in cell B9.

The @COUNT function works properly only when its argument is a range, even when the range is a single cell like the range A1..A1. When the argument is a single cell reference like A1, @COUNT always returns 1, even if the cell is blank.

Caution: With a single-cell reference, @COUNT counts a blank cell as 1.

To return a zero for a blank cell, you must use @COUNT with the @@ function discussed later in this chapter. To return a zero for the blank cell A1, for example, you would use @COUNT with @@ in the following way: enter the label A1..A1 in cell A2; then, in cell A3, enter the formula

@COUNT(@@(A2))

Fig. 6.22

Counting the number of products in a sales report.

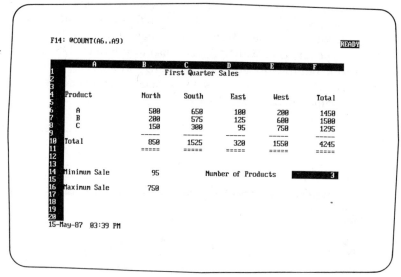

Because of the @@ function, 1-2-3 interprets the A2 in the formula as A1..A1. The outcome of the formula will be 0.

@AVG—Computing the Average (Mean)

The final function in this group is @AVG. This function computes the mean, or average, of all the cells in the range. In figure 6.23, the function @AVG(B6..E8) returns the value 353.75, which is the average of all the sales in the report.

The @AVG function returns the same value as the @SUM function divided by the @COUNT function, but the @AVG function is more straightforward and easier to use. Be careful, however, not to use this function with a range of all blank cells. Because blank cells are ignored by the function, an @AVG function that refers to a range with all blank cells will return the value ERR.

Be careful also not to use @AVG with a range that includes cells which contain labels. Because 1-2-3 evaluates labels as zero, those cells will be included in the computation and will skew the result.

Caution:
Cells that contain labels will be included in the average if those cells are in the range specified for @AVG.

Advanced Statistical Functions

Although you are probably familiar with statistics if you are interested in using advanced statistical functions, we will provide a brief review here as a foundation for the explanation of 1-2-3's functions.

Fig. 6.23

Computing the average sales.

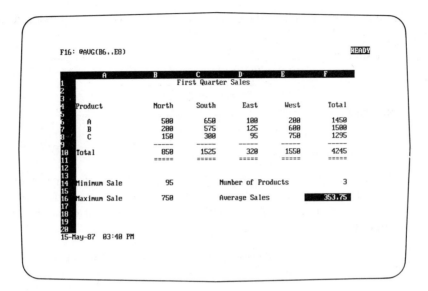

```
F16: @AVG(B6..E8)                                                        READY

             A          B        C         D         E         F
1                               First Quarter Sales
2
3
4    Product            North    South     East      West      Total
5
6         A              500      650       100       200      1450
7         B              200      575       125       600      1500
8         C              150      300        95       750      1295
9                       ------   ------    ------    ------    ------
10   Total               850     1525       320      1550      4245
11                      ======   ======    ======    ======    ======
12
13
14   Minimum Sale         95              Number of Products         3
15
16   Maximum Sale        750              Average Sales          353.75
17
18
19
20
     15-May-87  03:40 PM
```

One basic statistic is the *mean*, often called the arithmetic average, which is commonly used to mark the average of a group of data values. The mean is calculated by adding the values and dividing the sum by the number of values. The mean is not to be confused with the *median* or the *mode*, which are also measures of central tendency. The median is the value midway between the highest and lowest values in the group, in terms of probability. Half of the values in the group are above the median, and half are below it. The mode is the most probable value in a group of items (that is, the value that occurs most often).

Variance and *standard deviation* are related dispersion statistics. The variance is the amount of deviation from the mean. The standard deviation, closely related to the variance, is the degree of deviation from the mean.

To calculate the variance, you subtract the mean of the numbers from each number in the group and square each result. You then add the squares and divide the total by the number of items in the group. To compute the standard deviation, you take the square root of the variance.

1-2-3 has two functions that automatically perform these calculations for you. These advanced statistical functions are

@VAR(list)	Computes the population variance
@STD(list)	Computes the standard deviation of a population

The two functions make their calculations based on the following formulas:

$$\text{Variance} = \frac{\Sigma(i - @AVG(list))^2}{@COUNT(list)}$$

$$\text{Standard Deviation} = \sqrt{\frac{\Sigma(i - @AVG(list))^2}{@COUNT(list)}}$$

where i = item value

A simple example that uses both @VAR and @STD is shown in figure 6.24. This example uses a list of salesmen and the number of items they sold during a given period. The list of the number of items sold is used as the range for the functions.

Fig. 6.24

Using the @VAR and @STD functions to compute variance and standard deviation.

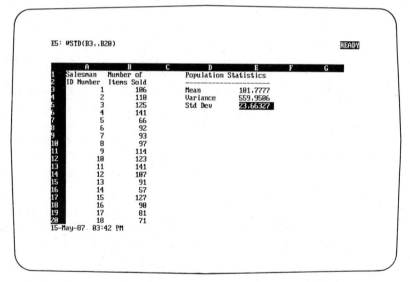

The mean of the number of items sold (about 101) is computed using the @AVG function. The standard deviation is about 24.

What does the standard deviation tell you? As a general rule, about 67 percent of the items in a normally distributed population will fall within a range that is plus or minus one standard deviation of the mean. In the example, that means that roughly 67 percent of the salesmen sold between 77 and 125 items. About 95 percent of the items in a normally distributed population fall within plus or minus two standard deviations of the mean.

To make further use of the statistical functions, you should know the difference between *population* and *sample* statistics. Population statistics are used when you know the value of all the items in a population. But when the number of items is large and you don't know them all (which is usually the case), you are unable to compute the population statistics. Instead, you must rely on sample statistics as estimates of the population statistics.

In the sales example, if we realistically assume that we had only a small portion of the entire population of sales figures, we can compute the *sample* statistics. This is even more realistic if we examine only one month's sales out of the total population of all the monthly sales for a year. When we move into the realm of sample statistics, we start dealing with much more sophisticated statistical concepts.

To calculate the sample variance for the previous sales data, you multiply the population variance by *n/n-1* (degrees of freedom), where *n* equals the number of items in the sample. The degrees of freedom tell you how much freedom you have in calculating a variance.

We use the @COUNT function to determine the degrees of freedom:

degrees of freedom = @COUNT(list)/(@COUNT(list)-1)

To compute the sample variance, we use the formula:

Sample Variance = @COUNT(list)/(@COUNT(list)-1)*@VAR(list)

To compute the standard deviation of the sample, we take the square root of the sample variance. A convenient way to do this is to use the @SQRT function (see fig. 6.25):

Sample Standard Deviation = @SQRT(Sample Variance) =

@SQRT(@COUNT(list)/(@COUNT(list)-1)*@VAR(list))

Because standard deviation is the square root of the variance, we can also compute the sample standard deviation using the following formula (see fig. 6.26):

Sample Standard Deviation = @SQRT(degrees of freedom)*@STD(list) =

@SQRT(@COUNT(list)/(@COUNT(list)-1))*@STD(list)

Cue:
You can compute the sample standard deviation two different ways with 1-2-3 functions.

Analyzing Investments and Calculating Depreciation

1-2-3 has eight financial functions that perform a variety of investment calculations, and three functions that calculate book depreciation. The basic

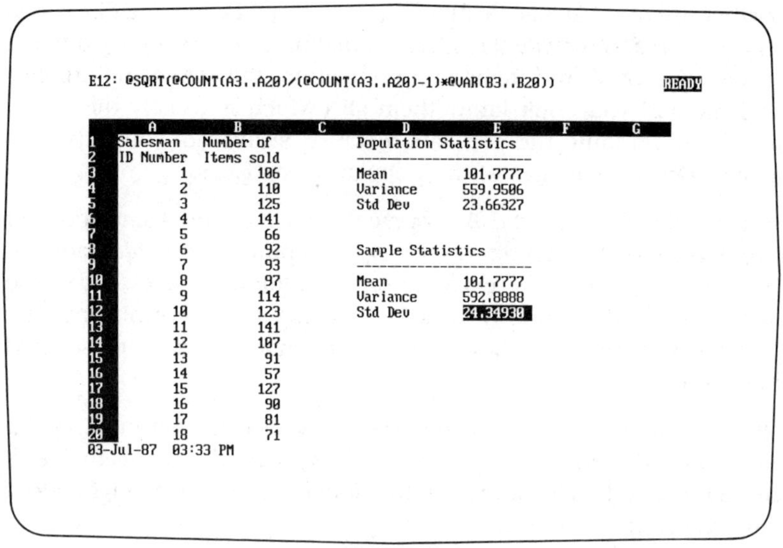

Fig. 6.25

Computing the sample standard deviation based on the sample variance.

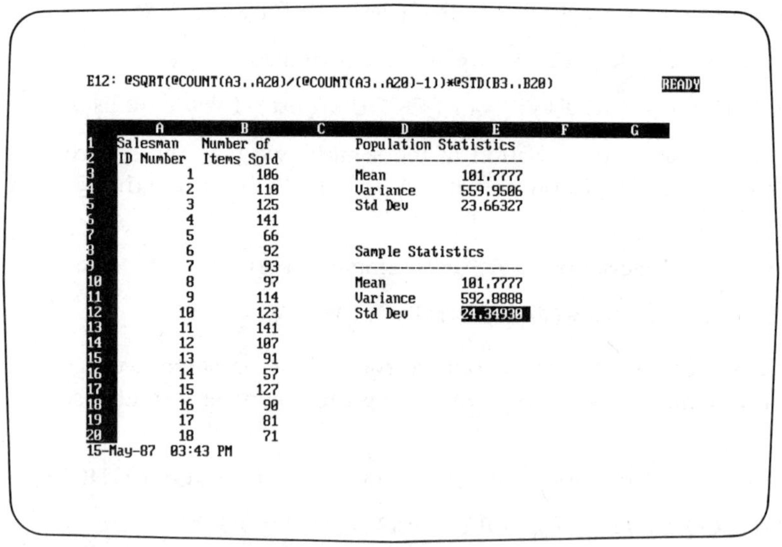

```
E12: @SQRT(@COUNT(A3..A20)/(@COUNT(A3..A20)-1)*@VAR(B3..B20))          READY

        A         B          C         D           E        F        G
1  Salesman  Number of              Population Statistics
2  ID Number Items sold             ---------------------
3      1        106               Mean       101.7777
4      2        110               Variance   559.9506
5      3        125               Std Dev     23.66327
6      4        141
7      5         66
8      6         92               Sample Statistics
9      7         93               ---------------------
10     8         97               Mean       101.7777
11     9        114               Variance   592.8888
12    10        123               Std Dev     24.34930
13    11        141
14    12        107
15    13         91
16    14         57
17    15        127
18    16         90
19    17         81
20    18         71
03-Jul-87  03:33 PM
```

Fig. 6.26

Computing the sample standard deviation based on the standard deviation.

```
E12: @SQRT(@COUNT(A3..A20)/(@COUNT(A3..A20)-1))*@STD(B3..B20)          READY

        A         B          C         D           E        F        G
1  Salesman  Number of              Population Statistics
2  ID Number Items Sold             ---------------------
3      1        106               Mean       101.7777
4      2        110               Variance   559.9506
5      3        125               Std Dev     23.66327
6      4        141
7      5         66
8      6         92               Sample Statistics
9      7         93               ---------------------
10     8         97               Mean       101.7777
11     9        114               Variance   592.8888
12    10        123               Std Dev     24.34930
13    11        141
14    12        107
15    13         91
16    14         57
17    15        127
18    16         90
19    17         81
20    18         71
15-May-87  03:43 PM
```

financial functions, @NPV and @IRR, calculate the return on an investment; @PV, @FV, and @PMT perform loan and annuity calculations. The @RATE, @TERM, and @CTERM functions perform compound-growth calculations, and @SLN, @DDB, and @SYD calculate depreciation by three commonly used methods. Table 6.5 reviews the financial functions available in 1-2-3.

Table 6.5
Financial Functions

Investment Function	Calculates
@NPV(int, range)	Present value of an investment and a series of periodic cash flows
@IRR(guess,range)	Internal rate-of-return of a series of periodic cash flows
@PV(pmt,int,term)	Present value of a series of periodic, equal cash flows
@FV(pmt,int,term)	Future value of a series of equal payments
@PMT(prin,int,term)	Periodic payment amount
@RATE(fv,pv,term)	Return on an investment
@TERM(pmt,int,fv)	Number of payment periods of an investment
@CTERM(int,fv,pv)	Number of compounding periods an investment must grow for a desired return

Depreciation Function	Calculates
@DDB(cost,salvage, life,period)	Double-declining-balance depreciation
@SLN(cost,salvage, life)	Straight-line depreciation
@SYD(cost,salvage, life,period)	Sum-of-the-years' digits depreciation

Definition of terms

int	=	periodic interest rate	cost	=	cost of asset
prin	=	principal amount	salvage	=	asset salvage value
pv	=	present value	life	=	asset life
fv	=	future value	period	=	specific year
term	=	number of periods			

@NPV—Net Present Value

The @NPV function computes the net present value of a stream of cash flows. The form of this function is

@NPV(Discount Rate,Range)

The equation for calculating net present value is

$$NPV = \sum \frac{payment_n}{(1+\text{interest rate})^n} \quad \begin{array}{l}(\text{or substitute} \\ \text{cash flow for} \\ \text{payment})\end{array}$$

where n = time period

Discount Rate is the interest rate that 1-2-3 uses to compute the net present value. *Range* is the stream of cash flows to be discounted. The interval between the cash flows must be constant and must agree with the period of the discount rate. For example, an annual discount rate should be used for cash flows occurring a year apart. If the cash flows occur every month, a monthly rate should be used (dividing the annual discount rate by 12).

The @NPV function can be used to evaluate a variety of investment opportunities. For example, suppose that you had an opportunity to invest in a share of real estate which would create the following cash flows over the next five years:

End of Yr	Cash Flow
1	(2,000)
2	1,000
3	1,500
4	1,500
5	1,500

You can create a simple worksheet to evaluate this investment, as illustrated in figure 6.27. The function @NPV(B1,C7..G7) returns the value 2202.63, the net present value of that stream at a discount rate of 9 percent if the investment is made at the end of year 1. The function @NPV(B1,D9..G9)+C9 returns a value of 2400.86 at a discount rate of 9 percent if the investment is made at the beginning of year 1.

If 9 percent represents the rate you need to earn on the investment, and could earn on other investments with a similar degree of risk, and the NPV of the investment is greater than or equal to $2,000, you can conclude that the real estate share probably offers a good investment opportunity. Note that the difference in the two calculated NPVs shows that the timing of the investment is important; you can earn an extra $198.23 if you make the investment at the beginning of year 1.

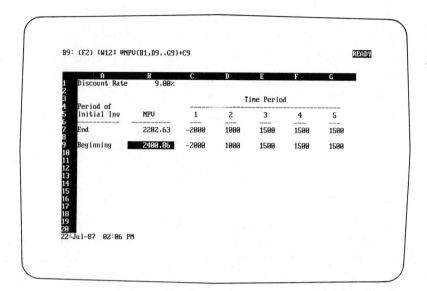

Fig. 6.27

Using @NPV to compute net present value.

We use a cell reference, B1, to enter the discount rate into the function. Because it would be just as easy to enter the formula @NPV(.09,D9..G9), you might wonder why we took the approach we did. In fact, there is no advantage to using either method until you decide to change the rate.

Cue:
To make updating easier, use a cell reference to enter the discount rate.

For example, assume that in figure 6.27 you wanted to evaluate the investment using a rate of 14 percent. With the method we used, all you need to do is enter the number .14 in cell B1 and recalculate the worksheet. If the rate had been embedded in the formula, we would have to edit the cell, replace the .09 with .14, close the cell, and then recalculate. If several changes were required, this operation would waste valuable time. Using a cell reference, however, we can quickly update the analysis as interest rates change or new investment opportunities arise.

@IRR—Internal Rate of Return

Internal rate of return (IRR) is the discount rate that equates the present value of expected cash outflows with the present value of expected inflows. In simpler terms, IRR is the rate of return, or profit, that an investment is expected to earn. Like net present value, internal rate of return determines the attractiveness of an investment opportunity.

The @IRR function is built on an iterative process in which you provide an initial estimated discount rate (anything between 0 and 1 will do); 1-2-3 then calculates the actual discount rate, equating the present value of the series of cash outflows with the present value of the series of inflows. 1-2-3 uses the same method you would use to calculate IRR manually.

Given the format of the equation, all the inflows and outflows must be in the same range. The general form of the @IRR function is

@IRR(estimate,range)

The equation for calculating internal rate of return is

$$IRR = \sum \frac{payment_n}{(1+interest\ rate)^n}$$
(or substitute *cash flow* for *payment*)

where n = time period

1-2-3 should reach convergence on a discount rate within .0000001 after a maximum of 20 iterations; if 20 iterations aren't enough, ERR is returned. Figure 6.28 shows an example of how the @IRR built-in function is used.

Fig. 6.28

Internal rate of return of a stream of cash flows.

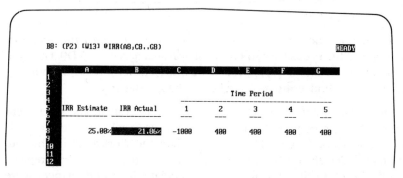

The internal rate of return, or profit, for the project illustrated in figure 6.28 is about 22 percent.

You may encounter some problems with the @IRR function. As indicated earlier, 1-2-3 may not converge on a value based on your initial estimate. Either the stream of cash flows does not have an internal rate of return, or your initial estimate is too far from the actual internal rate of return for 1-2-3 to converge within 20 iterations.

An extreme example of the stream of cash flows without an internal rate of return is a stream of all outflows with no inflows. Without income to cover the expenditures, no interest rate will yield a net present value of 0, and @IRR will return an ERR message.

Cue:
Use different initial estimates if @IRR returns strange values.

If you get an ERR message or an unreasonable value from the @IRR function, try different initial estimates and then double-check the result.

The investment opportunity itself may present IRR problems. If the stream of cash flows changes signs more than once, the investment may have multiple IRRs. For example, the cash flows in figures 6.29 and 6.30 start out negative, then become positive, and are negative once again at the end of the stream. If the initial estimate is 0, the @IRR function converges on the value of 0. On the other hand, if the initial estimate is 58%, @IRR converges on the value of approximately 58 percent. When the IRR calculation is based on cash flows with more than one change of sign, interpret the results with caution, or use @NPV to evaluate investments.

Fig. 6.29

Example of a stream of cash flows with two internal rates of return.

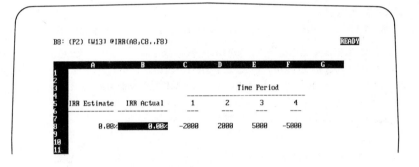

Fig. 6.30

Changing the estimated internal rate of return changes the result of @IRR.

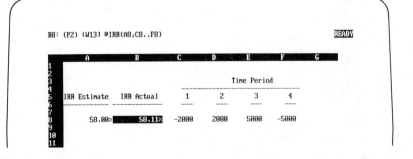

@PV—Present Value

The @PV function is used to calculate the present value of an ordinary annuity for a given number of periods and interest rate. An *ordinary annuity* is a series of payments made at the end of equally spaced intervals, and *present value* is the value today of the payments to be made or received later, discounted at a given interest or discount rate.

Calculating the present value of an ordinary annuity gives you a way to compare different investment opportunities or potential obligations while taking into account the time value of money.

The general form of the @PV function is

@PV(payment,interest,term)

The equation for calculating the present value of an ordinary annuity is

$$PV = payment * \frac{1-(1+interest)^{-n}}{interest}$$

You can use the @PV function in a formula to calculate the present value of an annuity due, or annuity in arrears. That formula is

Present Value of
an Annuity Due = @PV(payment,interest,term)*(1+interest)

Like an ordinary annuity, an annuity due is a series of payments, but made at the beginning of equally spaced time intervals. Figure 6.31 shows the results of calculating the present value of an ordinary annuity and an annuity due.

Fig. 6.31

Using @PV to calculate the present value of an ordinary annuity and an annuity due.

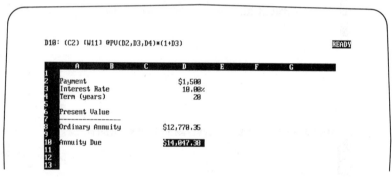

Reminder:
Use @NPV to compute the present value of a stream of unequal cash flows.

The difference between @NPV, the function for net present value, and @PV stems from the difference in cash flows and how the cash flow values are arranged in the worksheet. @NPV calculates the net present value of a series of flows that may or may not be equal, but that are all contained in a range of cells in the worksheet. The cash flows in the @PV function must all be equal, and the amount of the flows must be contained in a single cell or entered as a value in the @PV function. Remember to use the @NPV function to calculate the present value of a stream of unequal cash flows.

@FV—Future Value

The @FV function is similar in form to the @PV function, but is used to calculate the future value of an ordinary annuity. *Future value* is the value at a given day in the future of a series of payments or receipts, compounded at a given interest or discount rate. Calculating the future value of an ordinary annuity allows you to compare different investment alternatives or potential obligations. The @FV function looks like this:

@FV(payment,interest,term)

The equation for calculating the future value of an ordinary annuity is

$$FV = payment * \frac{(1+interest)^n - 1}{interest}$$

You can calculate the future value of an annuity due with a formula similar to the one that calculates present value of an annuity due. The formula is

Future Value of
an Annuity Due = @FV(payment,interest,term)*(1+interest)

Figure 6.32 shows the results of calculating the future value of an ordinary annuity and an annuity due.

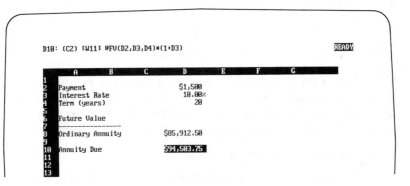

Fig. 6.32

Using @FV to calculate the future value of an ordinary annuity and an annuity due.

@PMT—Calculating Payment Amounts

The @PMT function calculates the payment required for a given principal, interest rate, and number of periods. This function is often used to calculate mortgage payments. The format of the @PMT function with n equalling the number of periods is

@PMT(principal,interest,n)

The formula that the function represents calculates the period payment by rearranging the formula which calculates the present value of an ordinary annuity. The formula for payment is

$$PMT = principal * \frac{interest}{1-(1+interest)^{-n}}$$

This function is a variation of the @PV function discussed earlier. The @PMT function can help you build a table of mortgage payments as shown in figure 6.33.

```
C4: (C2) [W11] @PMT(C1,C2/12,C3*12)                                    READY

         A      B        C        D      E      F      G
1  Loan Amount       $20,000.00
2  Interest Rate         10.00%
3  Term (years)             20
4  Payment Amount      $193.00
5
6
7
8  Month  Principal Interest    Balance
9  -----  --------- --------    -------
10 Jan-88    26.34    166.67    19,973.66
11 Feb-88    26.56    166.45    19,947.11
12 Mar-88    26.78    166.23    19,920.33
13 Apr-88    27.00    166.00    19,893.33
14 May-88    27.23    165.78    19,866.10
15 Jun-88    27.45    165.55    19,838.65
16 Jul-88    27.68    165.32    19,810.96
17 Aug-88    27.91    165.09    19,783.05
18 Sep-88    28.15    164.86    19,754.90
19 Oct-88    28.38    164.62    19,726.52
20 Nov-88    28.62    164.39    19,697.91
08-May-87  08:48 AM
```

To construct the table in the figure, first enter the headings in cells A1..A4 and the appropriate amounts in cells C1..C3. Then calculate the payment amount by inserting the function @PMT(C1,C2/12,C3*12) in cell C4. This form of the function gives the payment amount as a monthly figure.

Construct the table using the following steps:

1. Enter *@DATE(88,1,1)* in cell A10 (see the @DATE section of this chapter for an explanation)

2. Enter *+A10+31* in cell A11 (use relative addressing). This formula advances the date one month.

3. Enter *+C4-C10* in cell B10. This formula calculates the Principal portion of the monthly payment as the difference between the Payment Amount and the Interest portion.

4. Enter *+$C$4-C11* in cell B11 (use mixed addressing). This formula updates the calculation of the Principal portion.

5. Enter *+C1/12*C2* in cell C10. This is a simple formula to calculate the Interest portion of the first monthly payment.

6. Enter *+D10*$C$2/12* in cell C11 (use mixed addressing). This formula updates the Interest formula based on the remaining Principal Balance.

7. Enter *+C1-B10* in cell D10, and *+D10-B11* in cell D11 (use relative addressing). These simple formulas calculate the new Principal Balance by subtracting the Principal portion of the monthly payment from the current Principal Balance.

8. Use the **/R**ange Format Date **3** command to format the range A10..A11. Format B10..D11 with the comma 2 format and adjust the column widths.

9. Use the **/C**opy command to copy A11..D11 to A12..A249 (for the 20-year life of the mortgage). Notice how the mixed and relative addressing of the formulas in row 11 adjust the formulas to their new location. You will need to make a few adjustments in the date column; after several years the formula is inexact because not every month contains 31 days.

You can use these steps to construct a monthly mortgage payment schedule for any loan amount, interest, or term.

You can also use the @PMT function in a formula to compute the payment of an annuity due. The form of the equation is

Annuity Due PMT = @PMT(principal,interest,term)/(1+interest)

Cue:
Use @PMT in a formula to calculate the payment of an annuity due.

Figure 6.34 shows a monthly schedule of annuity due payments. Compare the table in figures 6.34 and 6.33; note the impact that timing has on the payment amount—a difference of $1.59 per month.

@RATE—Compound Growth Rate

The @RATE function calculates the compound growth rate for an initial investment that grows to a specified future value over a specified number of periods. The rate is the periodic interest rate and not necessarily an annual rate. The format of this function, where *n* equals the number of periods, is

@RATE(future value,present value,n)

The @FV function's basic formula calculates the future value of an initial investment given the interest rate and the number of periods. For the @RATE calculation, the formula is rearranged to compute the interest rate in terms of the initial investment, the future value, and the number of periods.

Interest Rate = (future value/present value)$^{1/n}$ - 1

Fig. 6.34

*A table of annuity
due payments.*

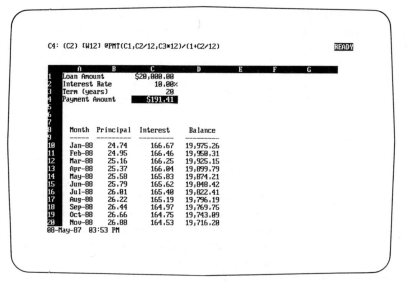

```
C4: (C2) [W12] @PMT(C1,C2/12,C3*12)/(1+C2/12)                    READY

        A         B          C          D        E       F       G
1  Loan Amount        $20,000.00
2  Interest Rate          10.00%
3  Term (years)            20
4  Payment Amount       $191.41
5
6
7
8  Month  Principal  Interest   Balance
9  ------ ---------  --------   --------
10  Jan-88    24.74    166.67   19,975.26
11  Feb-88    24.95    166.46   19,950.31
12  Mar-88    25.16    166.25   19,925.15
13  Apr-88    25.37    166.04   19,899.79
14  May-88    25.58    165.83   19,874.21
15  Jun-88    25.79    165.62   19,848.42
16  Jul-88    26.01    165.40   19,822.41
17  Aug-88    26.22    165.19   19,796.19
18  Sep-88    26.44    164.97   19,769.75
19  Oct-88    26.66    164.75   19,743.09
20  Nov-88    26.88    164.53   19,716.20
08-May-87  03:53 PM
```

Cue:
*Use @RATE to
calculate the yield
of a zero-coupon
bond.*

As an example, you could use the @RATE function to determine the yield of a zero-coupon bond that is sold at a discount of its face value. Suppose that for $350 you can purchase a zero-coupon bond with a $1,000 face value maturing in 10 years. What is the implied annual interest rate? The answer is 11.07 percent, as shown in figure 6.35.

Fig. 6.35

*Using the @RATE
function to
compute the yield
of a bond.*

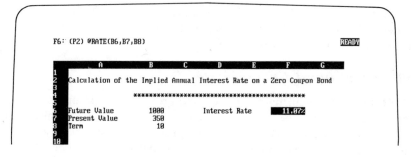

```
F6: (P2) @RATE(B6,B7,B8)                                         READY

        A         B        C        D        E        F        G
1
2  Calculation of the Implied Annual Interest Rate on a Zero Coupon Bond
3
4  ********************************************************
5
6  Future Value      1000         Interest Rate      11.07%
7  Present Value       350
8  Term                10
9
10
```

The @RATE function is also useful in forecasting compound growth rate between current and projected future revenues, earnings, and so on.

@TERM—Term of an Investment

The @TERM function calculates the number of periods required to accumulate a specified future value by making equal payments into an interest-bearing account at the end of each period. The form of the @TERM function is

@TERM(payment,interest,future value)

The @TERM function is similar to the @FV function except that instead of finding the future value of a stream of payments over a specified period, the @TERM function finds the number of periods required to reach the given future value. The actual equation for calculating the number of periods is

$$n = \frac{@LN(1+(interest*future\ value)/payment)}{@LN(1+interest)}$$

Suppose that you want to determine the number of months required to accumulate $5,000 by making a monthly payment of $50 into an account paying 6 percent annual interest compounded monthly (.5 percent per month). Figure 6.36 shows how @TERM can help you get the answer, which is slightly more than 81 months (6 years and 9 months) for an ordinary annuity, but slightly less than 81 months for an annuity due. For this account, making the deposit at the beginning of the month makes only a little difference.

Fig. 6.36

Using @TERM to compute time needed to accumulate $5,000 in an account.

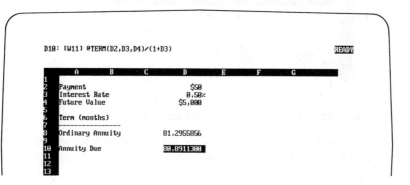

To calculate the TERM for an annuity due, use the equation

TERM for an
Annuity Due = @TERM(payment,interest,future value)/(1+interest)

@CTERM—Compound Term of an Investment

The @CTERM function calculates the number of periods required for an initial investment earning a specified interest rate to grow to a specified future value. Whereas @TERM calculates the number of periods needed for a series of payments to grow to a future value at a specified interest rate, the @CTERM function specifies the present value, the future value, and the interest rate, and finds the required number of periods. The form of the @CTERM function is

@CTERM(interest,future value,present value)

The equation used to calculate @CTERM is

$$\text{TERM} = \frac{\text{@LN(future value/present value)}}{\text{@LN(1+interest)}}$$

Cue:
Use @CTERM to find out how long an IRA will take to grow to a certain amount.

The @CTERM function is useful for determining the term of an investment necessary to achieve a specific future value. For example, suppose that you want to determine how many years it will take for $2,000 invested in an IRA account at 10 percent interest to grow to $10,000. Figure 6.37 shows how to use the @CTERM function to determine the answer, which is just over 16 years and 10 months.

Fig. 6.37

Using @CTERM to compute time needed for an IRA to accumulate $10,000.

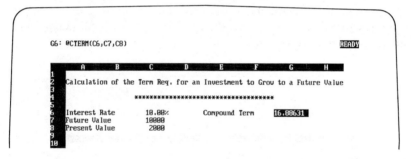

@SLN—Straight-Line Depreciation

The @SLN function calculates straight-line depreciation given the asset's cost, salvage value, and depreciable life. The form of the function is

@SLN(cost,salvage value,life)

The formula used to calculate @SLN is

SLN = (cost-salvage value)/life

The @SLN function conveniently calculates straight-line depreciation for an asset. For example, suppose that you have purchased a machine for $1,000 that has a useful life of three years and a salvage value estimated to be 10 percent of the purchase price ($100) at the end of its useful life. Figure 6.38 shows how to use the @SLN function to determine the straight-line depreciation for the machine, $300 per year.

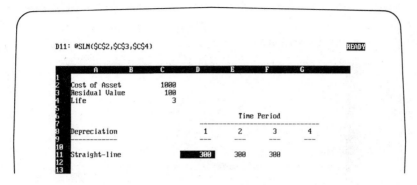

@DDB—Double-Declining-Balance Depreciation

The @DDB function calculates depreciation using the double-declining-balance method, with depreciation ceasing when the book value reaches the salvage value. Double-declining-balance depreciation is a method of accelerating depreciation so that greater depreciation expense occurs in the earlier periods rather than the later ones. Book value in any period is the purchase price less the total depreciation in all prior periods.

The form of the @DDB function is

@DDB(cost,salvage value,life,period)

In general, the double-declining-balance depreciation in any period is

book value*2/n

in which *book value* is the book value in the period, and *n* is the depreciable life of the asset. 1-2-3, however, adjusts the results of this formula in later periods to ensure that total depreciation does not exceed the purchase price less the salvage value.

Figure 6.39 shows how the @DDB function can calculate depreciation on an asset purchased for $1,000, with a depreciable life of three years and an estimated salvage value of $100. The figure also shows a comparison of the results of the @DDB and the @SLN functions.

Keep in mind that when you use the double-declining-balance depreciation method for an asset with a small salvage value, the asset will not be fully depreciated in the final year. If this is the case with one of your assets, you'll need to calculate the remaining depreciation for one additional year. For example, if the asset in figure 6.39 has a salvage value of $10 rather than $100, you can use the formula (C2-C3)-@SUM(D13..F13) in cell G13 to calculate the remaining depreciation.

Reminder:
For an asset with a small salvage value, use a formula to calculate an additional year of depreciation.

Fig. 6.39

Using @SLN and @DDB to compare straight-line and double-declining-balance depreciation.

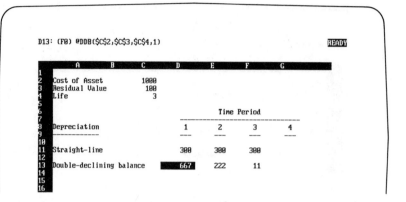

```
D13: (F0) @DDB($C$2,$C$3,$C$4,1)                                        READY

          A        B       C         D       E       F       G
 1
 2  Cost of Asset           1000
 3  Residual Value           100
 4  Life                       3
 5
 6                                         Time Period
 7                                   -------------------------------
 8  Depreciation                     1       2       3       4
 9                                   ---     ---     ---     ---
10
11  Straight-line                    300     300     300
12
13  Double-declining balance         667     222      11
14
15
16
```

@SYD—Sum-of-the-Years'-Digits Depreciation

The @SYD function calculates depreciation by the sum-of-the-years'-digits method. This method also accelerates depreciation so that the earlier life of the item reflects greater depreciation than later periods.

The form of the function is

> @SYD(cost,salvage value,life,period)

in which the cost is the purchase cost of the asset, the salvage value is the estimated value of the asset at the end of the depreciable life, life is the depreciable life of the asset, and period is the period for which depreciation is to be computed.

@SYD calculates depreciation with the following formula:

$$SYD = \frac{(\text{cost-salvage value})*(\text{life period}+1)}{(\text{life}*(\text{life}+1)/2)}$$

The expression *life period+1* in the numerator shows the life of the depreciation in the first period, decreased by 1 in each subsequent period. This reflects the declining pattern of depreciation over time. The expression in the denominator, *life*(life+1)/2*, is equal to the sum of the digits *1 + 2 + . . . + life*. This is the origin of the name *sum-of-the-years' digits*.

Figure 6.40 shows how the @SYD function can calculate depreciation for an asset costing $1,000 with a depreciable life of three years and an estimated salvage value of $100.

Cue:
Develop formulas to calculate modified ACRS depreciation.

Figure 6.41 shows a complete comparison of the different methods of depreciation, including a modified ACRS method under the regulations of the Tax Reform Act of 1986. In general, the modified ACRS method lengthens

Fig. 6.40

Calculating sum-of-the-years'-digits depreciation using @SYD.

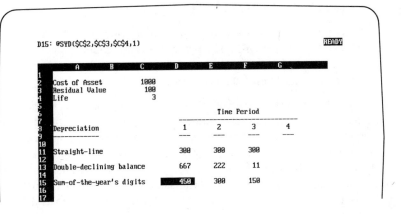

the depreciable life of an asset, and does not take residual value into account. Although 1-2-3 does not yet include functions to calculate modified ACRS depreciation, you can develop formulas to make the computations, as shown in the control panel in figure 6.41.

Fig. 6.41

Comparing depreciation using four different methods.

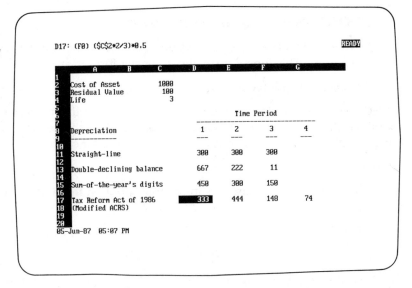

In the ACRS example in figure 6.41, the cost of the asset in cell C2 is multiplied by 2/3, which is the proper fraction for 200% double declining balance for a three year asset (200%/3). The result is multiplied by 0.5 to comply with the half-year convention.

Data Management Functions

1-2-3 has four simple data management functions: @CHOOSE, @VLOOKUP, @HLOOKUP, and @INDEX. These functions are called "special" functions by Lotus, but we prefer the term data management functions, because the functions retrieve data from lists and tables.

Reminder:
A string is a label or a portion of a label. A string is never a value, even if all the characters are numeric.

Because of the purpose of these functions, they need to work with textual data as well as with numeric values. 1-2-3 uses a concept called *strings*. A string is simply a unit of data consisting of one or more connected characters (alphabetic, numeric, blank, or special). A string can be an entire label or only a portion of a label but is never a value, even if all the characters are numeric. The string "123" is not the same as the value 123, just as the label '123 is not the same as the value 123. Strings are designated by quotation marks (" "). 1-2-3 has a separate set of functions called *string functions*, discussed elsewhere in this chapter, that perform a variety of tasks with strings.

The data management functions discussed in this section should not be confused with 1-2-3's database statistical functions, which operate only on databases. Those functions are explained in Chapter 13.

@CHOOSE—Selecting an Entry from a List

The @CHOOSE function uses a key value provided by the user to select an entry from a list. This function has the following form:

@CHOOSE(Key,Argument,Argument, . . . ,Argument)

@CHOOSE displays the argument whose position in the list matches the key (with the first position corresponding to a key of 0, the second position corresponding to a key of 1, etc.). For example, the function

@CHOOSE(2,3,4,5)

returns the number 5 because 5 is in the third position in the list. If the key is changed to 0, as in

@CHOOSE(0,3,4,5)

the function will return the value 3.

The first argument (the key) in the @CHOOSE function can be a number, a cell reference, a formula, or a function with numeric value. The remaining arguments can have either numeric or alphanumeric (string) values.

Cue:
The @CHOOSE function can simplify the computation of modified ACRS depreciation.

The @CHOOSE function can be used also to select formulas that will vary in different situations. For example, the percentage rate used to compute depreciation under the modified ACRS depreciation system varies with the useful life of the asset. Thus, an asset with a three-year life would be depreciated at a different rate in the first year of its life from that of an asset with a five-year life. The @CHOOSE function shown in figure 6.42 dramatically simplifies the computation.

Fig. 6.42

Using the @CHOOSE function to determine the correct modified ACRS depreciation calculation.

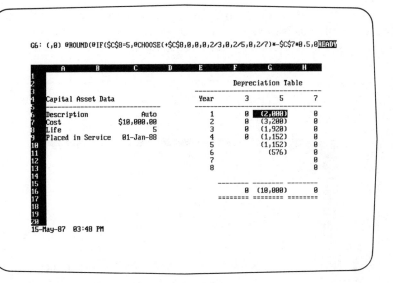

@HLOOKUP and @VLOOKUP— Finding Values from a Table

@HLOOKUP and @VLOOKUP are two functions that "look up" a value from a table based on the value of a test variable. The forms of these functions are

@HLOOKUP (test variable, range, row offset number)

@VLOOKUP (test variable, range, column offset number)

The first argument, the test variable, can have either a numeric value or a string value. The test variable may be any valid 1-2-3 numeric or string expression (number or string formula). The test variable may also be a cell or range reference to a single cell containing the value.

The second argument is a range containing at least one partial row or column. This range includes the entire lookup table from the top left corner of the comparison column to the bottom right corner of the last data column. A range name can be used in place of actual cell references.

The third argument, called the offset number, determines which data column or row should supply the data to the function. In every case, the comparison column or row has an offset number of 0, the first column to the right of, or row below the comparison column has an offset number of 1, and so on. The offset number must be between 0 and the maximum number of columns or rows in the lookup table. You will receive an ERR message if you try to include negative or excessive offset numbers.

To use the lookup functions, you need a lookup table in your worksheet. This table will usually consist of two or more adjacent partial rows or columns. An example of a numeric vertical lookup table is illustrated in figure 6.43.

Fig. 6.43

Using @VLOOKUP to perform a numeric lookup from a vertical lookup table.

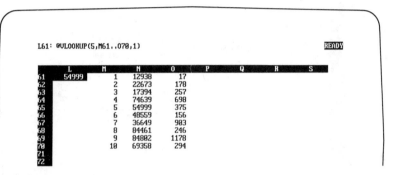

What differentiates this table from a string vertical lookup table is the contents of M, the first column. (The first column in a vertical lookup table is called the comparison column.) In a numeric vertical lookup table, the comparison column must contain numbers arranged in ascending order. In a string vertical lookup table, the comparison column can contain labels in any order.

In figure 6.43 the comparison column contains the values that will be used to look up the data shown in the second and third columns (N and O). To access this columnar table, use the @VLOOKUP or vertical lookup function.

In this table, the function

@VLOOKUP(5,M61..O70,1)

returns the value 54999. To get this result, 1-2-3 searches the comparison column for the largest value that is not greater than the key and returns the value in the data column with an offset number of 1 (in this case, column N). Remember that the comparison column has an offset number of 0. Column N, therefore, has an offset number of 1, and column O has an offset number of 2.

Because the lookup table searches for the largest entry in the comparison column that is not greater than the search variable or is an exact match, the function @VLOOKUP(5.5,M61..O70,1) would also return the value 54999. Similarly, a key of 100 would return 69358, the number that corresponds to the largest key in the list. If 0 is used as the key, an ERR message will appear because no key in the table is less than or equal to 0.

The data in column O also can be looked up with @VLOOKUP. For example, the function @VLOOKUP(10,M61..O70,2) would return the value 294.

Lookup tables must follow specific rules. As mentioned earlier, the comparison column values for numeric lookups must be arranged in ascending order. (In other words, a comparison value cannot be listed out of sequence or repeated.) For example,

Reminder:
The comparison column values for numeric lookups must be arranged in ascending order.

@VLOOKUP(2,M61..O70,1)

in figure 6.44 returns 12938 instead of the correct value 22673 because the comparison values in column M are not in ascending order. At the same time,

@VLOOKUP(5,M61..O70,1)

in figure 6.45 returns 74639 instead of the correct value 54999 because the key 5 is repeated.

Fig. 6.44

Numeric @VLOOKUP with keys out of sequence.

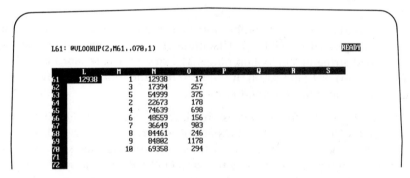

Fig. 6.45

Numeric @VLOOKUP with duplicate keys.

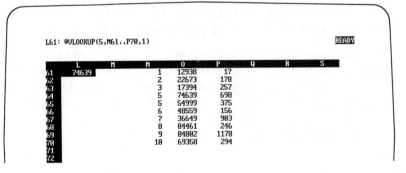

Besides numeric-table lookups, 1-2-3 can also perform string-table lookups. In a string-table lookup, 1-2-3 looks for a perfect match between a entry in the comparison column and the test variable. For example, in figure 6.46, 1-2-3 uses the function

@VLOOKUP("rakes",M101..O110,1)

to search for the entry in column N corresponding to *rakes*. Notice that the string argument is enclosed in double quotation marks.

Fig. 6.46

Example of string @VLOOKUP.

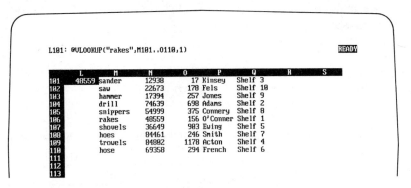

```
L101: @VLOOKUP("rakes",M101,.O110,1)                                    READY

       L      M        N       O      P        Q        R      S
101  48559 sander    12938        17 Kinsey  Shelf 3
102        saw       22673       178 Fels    Shelf 10
103        hammer    17394       257 Jones   Shelf 9
104        drill     74639       698 Adams   Shelf 2
105        snippers  54999       375 Connery Shelf 8
106        rakes     48559       156 O'Conner Shelf 1
107        shovels   36649       983 Ewing   Shelf 5
108        hoes      84461       246 Smith   Shelf 7
109        trowels   84802      1178 Acton   Shelf 4
110        hose      69358       294 French  Shelf 6
111
112
113
```

If 0 is used as the offset number for the @VLOOKUP statement in figure 6.46, the value returned will be 5. This number corresponds to the position of the matched string in the lookup range. The first entry (sander) is 0, the second entry (saw) is 1, and so on. If the search of the lookup table fails to produce a match, the value returned is ERR.

The @HLOOKUP function is essentially the same as @VLOOKUP, except that @HLOOKUP operates on tables arranged across rows instead of in columns. The rules here are the same as those for vertical tables. Now look at the example in figure 6.47 of how the @HLOOKUP function works for a numeric lookup. (Again, the same rules apply for a string lookup). The function @HLOOKUP(5,L123..S125,1) returns the value 567. The function @HLOOKUP(8,L123..S125,1) would return the value 890, and the function @HLOOKUP(3,L123..S125,2) would return the value 765.

Cue:

Use the lookup functions for automatic retrieval of tax rates from tables.

A useful application for the @VLOOKUP and @HLOOKUP functions is creating tax tables that automatically retrieve the appropriate rate based on income. In fact, this application is the one for which the function was originally developed. These functions can also be used for simple data management, such as handling inventory and employee lists, although in 1-2-3 these functions can be performed better with the database commands.

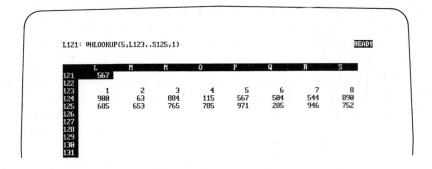

Fig. 6.47

Example of numeric @HLOOKUP.

@INDEX—Retrieving Data from Specified Locations

The last data management function, @INDEX, is similar to the table-lookup functions described earlier; however, @INDEX has some unique features. The general form of the function is

@INDEX(range,column-number,row-number)

Like the table-lookup functions, the @INDEX function works with a table of numbers. But unlike the table-lookup functions, the @INDEX function does not use a test variable and a comparison column (or row). Instead, the @INDEX function requires you to indicate the row-number and column-number of the range from which you wish to retrieve data. For example, the function

@INDEX(L142..S145,3,2)

in figure 6.48 returns the value 2625.

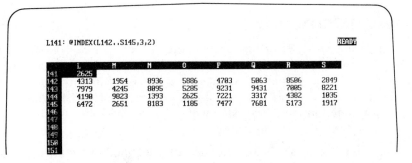

Fig. 6.48

Example of @INDEX function.

Notice that the number 0 corresponds to the first column, 1 corresponds to the second column, and so on. The same numbering scheme applies to rows. Using 3 for the column-number and 2 for the row-number indicates that you want an item from the fourth column, third row.

With the @INDEX function, you cannot use column and row numbers that fall outside the relevant range. Using either negative numbers or numbers too large for the range will cause 1-2-3 to return the ERR message.

The @INDEX function is useful when you know the exact position of a data item in a range of cells and wish to locate the item quickly. For instance, the @INDEX function works well for rate quotation systems. Figure 6.49 shows an example of a system for quoting full-page magazine advertising rates.

Fig. 6.49

Use of @INDEX for advertising rate quotations.

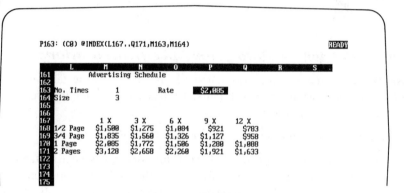

In this example, the function

@INDEX(L167..Q171,M163,M164)

returns a value of $2,085. This value corresponds to the amount in the first column and the third row of the index range. If a 6 is entered for the frequency, the ERR message will appear instead of a valid dollar amount.

Logical Functions

1-2-3 includes a set of logical functions, which can be considered a subset of the mathematical functions. 1-2-3 evaluates logical functions as either true or false. A logical function evaluated as true has a numeric value of 1; a logical function evaluated as false has a numeric value of 0. The importance of a logical function's numeric value will be made clear shortly. The logical functions are summarized in table 6.6.

Logical functions are helpful because they let you build conditional tests into cells. These tests return different values, depending on whether they are true (1) or false (0). 1-2-3's primary conditional function is @IF. Several additional logical functions, however, are included to further increase the power of the program.

Table 6.6
Logical Functions

Function	Description
@IF(cond,a,b)	If cond is TRUE, then a; if cond is FALSE, then b
@ISERR(cell reference)	If a is ERR, then TRUE; otherwise, FALSE
@ISNA(cell reference)	If a is NA, then TRUE; otherwise, FALSE
@ISNUMBER(cell reference)	If a is a numeric value, then TRUE; otherwise, FALSE
@ISSTRING(cell reference)	If a is a string value, then TRUE; otherwise, FALSE
@TRUE	Returns a value of 1
@FALSE	Returns a value of 0

@IF—Creating Conditional Tests

The @IF function allows you to test one or more conditions in your worksheet and perform appropriate tasks based on the outcome of the test. You could, for example, have a worksheet that functions as a job-application data-entry form that you want to make sensitive to the age of the applicant. You could construct a formula using the @IF function that would make certain automatic cell displays if the age is less than 21, and other automatic displays if the age is greater than or equal to 21.

The basic form of the @IF function is

@IF(condition,vtrue,vfalse)

where the first argument (*condition*) is tested for true or false. If the result of the test is true (1), the function will take the value (including string values) of the second argument (*vtrue*). If the value of the first argument is false (0), the function will take the value (including string values) of the third argument (*vfalse*).

Using Logical Operators in Conditional Tests

Logical operators are used with the @IF function and other conditional functions to perform conditional tests. These operators help determine the relationship between two or more numbers or strings.

Logical operators can be grouped, according to their order of precedence, into *simple operators* and *complex operators*. The simple logical operators have lower precedence than any mathematical operator but higher precedence than any complex operator. All the simple operators have equal precedence within their group. Table 6.7 lists the simple logical operators and their meanings.

Table 6.7
Simple Logical Operators

Operator	Meaning
=	Equal
<	Less than
<=	Less than or equal to
>	Greater than
>=	Greater than or equal to
<>	Not equal

The logical operators build conditional statements that are either true (1) or false (0). For example, the statement 5<3 has the value false (0), whereas the statement 16<27 has the value true (1). 1-2-3's @IF function tests the conditional statement as either true (1) or false (0) and returns a value based on the results of the test.

The following are examples of logical statements that use the @IF function and simple logical operators:

@IF(B4>=450,B5,C7)
    If the value in cell B4 is greater than or equal to 450, then use the value in cell B5. Otherwise, use the value in cell C7.

@IF(A3<A2,5,6)
    If the value in cell A3 is less than the value in cell A2, then assign the number 5. Otherwise, assign the number 6.

@IF(G9<>B7,G5/9,G7)
    If the value in cell G9 is not equal to the value in cell B7, then use the value in cell G5 divided by 9. Otherwise, use the value in cell G7.

Things get more complicated when complex logical operators are introduced. Table 6.8 lists the complex operators.

Table 6.8
Complex Logical Operators

Operator	Meaning
#NOT#	NOT (logical)
#AND#	AND (logical)
#OR#	OR (logical)

The complex logical operators have lower precedence than the simple logical operators. #AND# and #OR# have equal precedence in this group; #NOT# has a precedence greater than #AND# and #OR#, but less than the simple logical operators.

Now that we have a complete set of logical operators, we can combine simple and complex operators to create the following @IF functions:

@IF(A1<>1#AND#G5="yes",E7,E6)
>   If the numeric value in cell A1 is not equal to 1 and
>   the string value in cell G5 is yes, use the value in
>   cell E7. Otherwise, use the value in cell E6.

@IF(#NOT#(Cost=50)#AND#A1=1,L10,K10)
>   If the amount stored in the cell named Cost is not $50
>   and the value in cell A1 is equal to 1, then use the
>   value in cell L10. Otherwise, use the value in cell K10.

1-2-3's conditional functions are quite sophisticated and can be complicated. The @IF statement can be used in a wide variety of situations to allow 1-2-3 to make decisions. Figure 6.50 is a simple example of how the @IF function can be used.

The figure shows a simple worksheet that summarizes a company's expenditures for the month of July, 1987. Column A contains the date of each expenditure, and column B contains the amounts of the disbursements. Notice that column C has been labeled "Code" and that row 4 contains a sequence of numbers, beginning with 1 in column D and ending with 5 in column H. We'll call these numbers Accounts. Now suppose that the following formula were entered in cell E6:

@IF($C6=E$4,$B6,0)

```
D6: (C2) @IF($C6=D$4,$B6,0)                                           READY

         A        B       C        D       E       F       G       H
1    ========================================================================
2    ABC Company July 1987 Expense Report
3    ========================================================================
4    DATE     Amount   Code        1       2       3       4       5
5    -------  ------   ----     ------  ------  ------  ------  ------
6    01-Jul   $678.00           $0.00   $0.00   $0.00   $0.00   $0.00
7    01-Jul    $52.00           $0.00   $0.00   $0.00   $0.00   $0.00
8    01-Jul   $265.00           $0.00   $0.00   $0.00   $0.00   $0.00
9    02-Jul   $347.00           $0.00   $0.00   $0.00   $0.00   $0.00
10   02-Jul    $13.00           $0.00   $0.00   $0.00   $0.00   $0.00
11   02-Jul    $86.00           $0.00   $0.00   $0.00   $0.00   $0.00
12   02-Jul    $90.00           $0.00   $0.00   $0.00   $0.00   $0.00
13   03-Jul   $341.00           $0.00   $0.00   $0.00   $0.00   $0.00
14   03-Jul   $255.00           $0.00   $0.00   $0.00   $0.00   $0.00
15   03-Jul   $754.00           $0.00   $0.00   $0.00   $0.00   $0.00
16   03-Jul   $324.00           $0.00   $0.00   $0.00   $0.00   $0.00
17   04-Jul   $462.00           $0.00   $0.00   $0.00   $0.00   $0.00
18   04-Jul   $142.00           $0.00   $0.00   $0.00   $0.00   $0.00
19   04-Jul   $876.00           $0.00   $0.00   $0.00   $0.00   $0.00
20   04-Jul   $354.00           $0.00   $0.00   $0.00   $0.00   $0.00
     03-Jul-87  04:17 PM
```

Similarly, suppose that the formula

@IF($C6=F$4,$B6,0)

were entered in cell F6. These formulas can be translated as: If the number in cell C6 (the code) equals the number in cell E4 or cell F4 (the account), then enter the value in cell B6 here; otherwise, enter 0 here.

Suppose that similar formulas exist in all the cells in range D6..H20. Now suppose that we enter a code for each check recorded in column A. The code for each disbursement should be a number less than six. Now, imagine that you recalculate the worksheet. The result would look like figure 6.51.

Notice that in each cell, 1-2-3 has compared each code to the account numbers located in row 4. In the cells where the code and account match, 1-2-3 has recorded the amount of the disbursement. In all the other cells, 1-2-3 has entered a zero. This is exactly what we would expect from the conditional tests we used in these cells.

Multiple @IF functions can be used in combination to perform conditional tests. Figure 6.52 contains the following formula in cell F74:

+F72*@IF(@SUM($E$72..F72)>335000,0.34,
  @IF(@SUM($E$72..F72)>100000,0.39,
  @IF(@SUM($E$72..F72)>75000,0.34,
  @IF(@SUM($E$72..F72)>50000,0.25,0.15))))

Fig. 6.51

*Account
distribution
worksheet after
recalculation.*

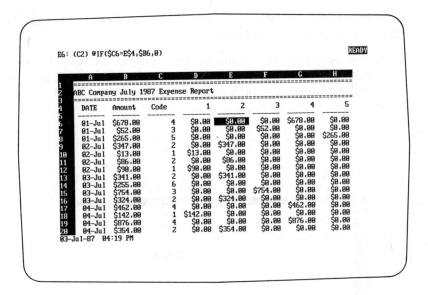

The @IF functions in the formula select the appropriate federal corporate
income tax rate based on the corporation's cumulative income.

Fig. 6.52

*Using multiple @IF
functions to
calculate corporate
income tax.*

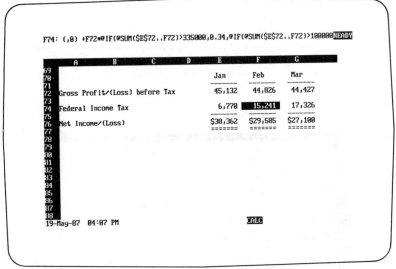

Using strings with logical operators in the @IF function further increases the
power and flexibility of conditional statements. Strings are connected alphanumeric characters (including blanks and special characters) that are

marked by quotation marks (" "). Strings are the opposite of values; they are either labels or portions of labels.

When you use strings in conditional functions, notice how 1-2-3 reacts to your entering numbers or leaving cells blank. The results can be quite different from similar numeric conditional tests. Figures 6.53A, 6.53B, and 6.53C illustrate some of the differences.

Fig. 6.53A

Simple numeric conditional tests.

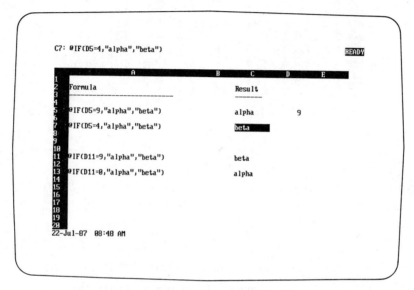

Fig. 6.53B

Comparing numeric and string conditional tests.

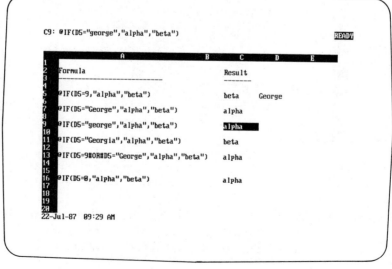

Fig. 6.53C

Numeric and string conditional tests involving a blank cell.

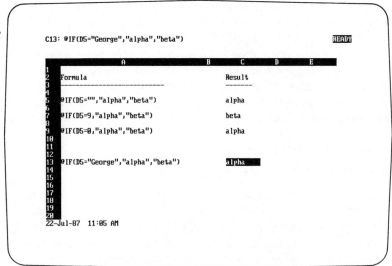

```
C13: @IF(D5="George","alpha","beta")                              READY

               A                         B    C      D      E
1
2   Formula                                   Result
3   ─────────────────────                     ──────
4
5   @IF(D5="","alpha","beta")                 alpha
6
7   @IF(D5=9,"alpha","beta")                  beta
8
9   @IF(D5=0,"alpha","beta")                  alpha
10
11
12
13  @IF(D5="George","alpha","beta")           alpha
14
15
16
17
18
19
20
    22-Jul-87  11:05 AM
```

The first two results in figure 6.53A are what you would expect, because cell D5 contains the value 9. The third result is also expected because cell D11 is blank, but the fourth result may surprise you. This result can be explained by the way 1-2-3 handles blank cells. Because blank cells actually contain invisible zeros, the statement D11=0 is true if cell D11 is blank.

Figure 6.53B uses the @IF function to test for string values. Notice in the third example (row 9) that case is irrelevant in this test ("george" is the same as "George"). The fifth example (row 13) uses the logical operator #OR# in the test. The surprising result in this figure is the final one (row 16). Because 1-2-3 equates a cell that contains a label to zero, you will get a true result ("alpha") if you test for the value zero in such a cell (D5=0).

The real surprise when you use strings with @IF functions comes when you compare a string value to a blank cell. The first three results in figure 6.53C are expected; the first function tests for a blank string (true), the second for the value 9 (false), and the third for the value 0 (true). The fourth result, however, is unexpected; testing for the string "George" should return a true result only if cell D5 contains the string "George" (or "george" or some other combination of upper- and lowercase). Although it's true that cell D5 equates to the value 0 because the cell contains a string, testing for a string is not equivalent to testing for the value 0; otherwise, the fourth example in figure 6.53B would return a true, not a false, result. Be careful of this inconsistency in 1-2-3 when you test blank cells for strings.

Caution: 1-2-3 can give inconsistent results when you test blank cells for strings.

For more information on performing logical tests involving strings, see the discussion on the @ISSTRING, @ISNUMBER, @CELL, and @CELLPOINTER functions later in this chapter. For more information on logical functions in general and for more examples of how these functions are used, see the second editions of *1-2-3 for Business* and *1-2-3 Tips, Tricks, and Traps*, as well as *Absolute Reference: The Journal for 1-2-3 and Symphony Users*, all published by Que Corporation. These publications contain a number of practical business models that demonstrate a variety of valuable 1-2-3 techniques.

Using @ISERR and @ISNA in Conditional Tests To Trap Errors

@ISERR and @ISNA are usually used with the @IF function to test the value in a cell for the value ERR or NA. 1-2-3 may automatically place the value ERR in the worksheet when an error is made. And by using the @ERR and @NA functions, explained later in the chapter, you can manually set both ERR and NA in the worksheet for error-trapping purposes.

The @ISERR and @ISNA functions are like the logical operators; they are always either true or false. The function @ISERR(A1) is false if cell A1 does not contain the value ERR, and true if cell A1 equals ERR (A1 "is ERR"). Similarly, the @ISNA function is true if the cell referred to contains the value NA, and false if the cell does not.

Cue:
@ISERR can keep your worksheet clear of ERR messages that result from division by zero.

The @ISERR function is frequently used to keep ERR messages resulting from division by 0 from appearing in the worksheet. For example, at one time or another as you use 1-2-3, you will create a formula that divides a number by a cell reference, as in the formula 23/A4.

If A4 contains a value, the function will simply return the value of the division. But if A4 contains a label, a 0, or is blank, the function will return the value ERR. The ERR will be passed along to other cells in the worksheet, creating an unnecessary mess.

Using the formula

@IF(@ISERR(23/A4),0,23/A4)

will eliminate the ERR result. This function says: If the value of 23/A4 is ERR, then enter a 0 in this cell; otherwise, enter the value of the division 23/A4. The function essentially traps the ERR message and keeps the message off the worksheet.

@ISNA works in much the same way. For example, the formula

@IF(@ISNA(A4),0,A4)

tests cell A4 for the value of NA. If the value of A4 is NA, the formula returns a 0. Otherwise, the formula returns the value in A4. This type of formula can be used to keep an NA message from spreading throughout a worksheet.

@TRUE and @FALSE—Checking for Errors

@TRUE and @FALSE are logical functions that can be used to check for errors. Neither one of these functions requires an argument. The numeric value of @TRUE is 1, and the numeric value of @FALSE is 0.

Typically, these functions are used with @IF and @CHOOSE, mainly for documentation. For example, the first two @IF functions in figure 6.54 are the exact equivalents of the second two @IF functions. Using @TRUE instead of 1, and @FALSE instead of 0, makes the function easier to understand, and therefore provides better documentation.

Cue:
@TRUE and
@FALSE provide
documentation for
your conditional
tests.

Fig. 6.54

Using the @TRUE and @FALSE functions to improve readability of conditional function arguments.

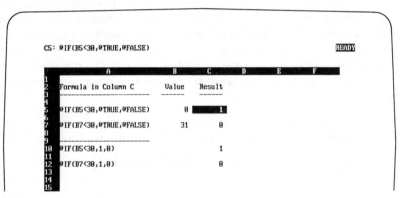

@ISSTRING and @ISNUMBER—Checking the Cell's Aspect

Before using the contents of a cell, you may want to use functions to test the cell's aspect. You may want to look at the type of cell—whether contained data is a number or a label, or whether the cell is empty. A cell's aspect also concerns the cell's address, the row and column the cell resides in, the cell's label prefix (if any), the width of the cell, and the cell's format. Depending on the characteristics of a cell's aspect, you may need to use different cell-processing methods.

Two functions that help you determine the type of value stored in a cell are @ISSTRING and @ISNUMBER. Both of these functions are most often used with the @IF function, but they can be used with other types of functions as well.

The @ISNUMBER function helps to verify whether a cell entry is a number. The general format of the function is

@ISNUMBER(argument)

If the argument is a number, the numeric value of the function is 1 (*true*—that is, the argument is a number). If the argument is a string, including the null string "", the numeric value of the function is 0 (*false*—that is, the argument is not a number).

As a simple example, suppose that you want to test whether the value entered in cell B3 is a number. If the value is a number, you want to show the label "number" in the current cell; otherwise, you want to show the label "string". The function you can use is

@IF(@ISNUMBER(B3),"number","string")

With this function, you can be fairly certain that the appropriate label will appear in the current cell. The @ISNUMBER function, however, gives the numeric value of 1 to blank cells as well as to numbers, because blank cells actually contain invisible zeros. Obviously, the function itself is incomplete because the function will assign the label "number" to the current cell if cell B3 is empty. For complete reliability, the function must be modified to handle blank cells.

Cue:
The @COUNT function can be combined with @ISNUMBER and @ISSTRING to test for blank cells.

You can distinguish between a number and an empty cell by using the following formula (note that cell AA3 must contain the label B3..B3):

@IF(@ISNUMBER(B3),@IF(@COUNT(@@(AA3)),"number", "blank"),"string")

The first step this function performs is to test whether the cell contains a number or a blank. If so, then the function uses the @COUNT function to test whether the range B3..B3 contains an entry. (Recall that @COUNT assigns a value of 0 to blank cells and a value of 1 to cells with an entry when the argument used is a range rather than a cell reference. See the discussion of the @COUNT function earlier in this chapter for more explanation.) If the cell contains an entry, the label "number" is displayed. Otherwise, the label "blank" is displayed. If the cell does not contain a number or a blank, the cell must contain a string with the "string" label displayed.

As an alternative, you may consider using the @ISSTRING function. @ISSTRING works in nearly the same way as the @ISNUMBER function. @ISSTRING, however, determines whether a cell entry is a string value. The general format of the command is

@ISSTRING(argument)

If the argument for the @ISSTRING function is a string, then the value of the function is 1 (*true*—the argument is a string). If the argument is a number or blank, however, the value of the function is 0 (*false*—the argument is not a string). One nice feature of @ISSTRING is that you can use this function to stop what Lotus calls the "ripple-through" effect of NA and ERR in cells that should have a string value. 1-2-3 considers both NA and ERR as numeric values.

Returning to the earlier example about discriminating between a number and an empty cell, you can also complete the function with the help of @ISSTRING by using the following formula (note that cell AA3 must contain the label B3..B3):

@IF(@ISSTRING(B3),"string",@IF(@COUNT(@@(AA3))>0, "number","blank"))

The first step that this function performs is to test whether string data is present. If string data is present, then the function assigns the label "string". Otherwise, the @COUNT function is used to determine whether the range B3..B3 contains a number or is empty. If the data is a number, then the label "number" is assigned. Otherwise, the label "blank" is assigned.

@ISNUMBER provides the capability to test for a number, although the function's inability to distinguish between numbers and blank cells is its principal weakness. In many applications, however, @ISNUMBER provides sufficient testing of values, especially when you are certain that a cell is not blank. @ISSTRING provides the capability to test for a string. With the @COUNT function, @ISSTRING can distinguish blank cells from strings. The @COUNT function combined with both @ISNUMBER and @ISSTRING can help you distinguish between blank cells and numbers.

Special Functions

The following functions are listed together in a separate category because they provide information about cell or range content or spreadsheet location. @CELL and @CELLPOINTER are two of 1-2-3's most powerful special functions with many different capabilities. @NA and @ERR allow you to trap errors that might appear in your worksheet. @ROWS and @COLS let you determine the size of a range. The function @@ lets you indirectly reference one cell with another cell within the spreadsheet.

Table 6.9 lists 1-2-3's special functions.

Table 6.9
Special Functions

Function	Description
@CELL(string,range)	Returns the attribute designated by the string for the cell in the upper left corner of the range
@CELLPOINTER(string)	Returns the attribute designated by the string for the current cell
@ERR	Displays ERR in the cell
@NA	Displays NA in the cell
@COLS(range)	Computes the number of columns in the range
@ROWS(range)	Computes the number of rows in the range
@@(cell address)	Returns the contents of the cell referenced by the cell address in the argument

@CELL and @CELLPOINTER—Checking Cell Attributes

The @CELL and @CELLPOINTER functions provide an efficient way to determine the nature of a cell because these functions return up to nine different characteristics of a cell. The @CELL and @CELLPOINTER functions are used primarily in macros and Lotus Command Language (LCL) programs (see Chapters 14 and 15).

The general form of the @CELL and @CELLPOINTER functions is

@CELL(string,range)

@CELLPOINTER(string)

Both functions have a string argument, which is the aspect of a cell you wish to examine. The @CELL function, however, requires the specification of a range; the @CELLPOINTER function works with the current cell.

The following examples illustrate how the @CELL function can be used to examine some cell attributes:

@CELL("address",SALES)
>   If the range named SALES is C187..E187, 1-2-3 returns
>   the absolute address $C$187. This is a convenient way
>   of listing the upper left corner of a range's address

in the worksheet. To list all the range names and their addresses, see the /**R**ange **N**ame **T**able command.

@CELL("prefix",C195..C195)

If the cell C195 contains the label 'Chicago, 1-2-3 will return ' (indicating left alignment). If, however, cell C195 is blank, 1-2-3 will return nothing; in other words, the current cell will appear blank.

@CELL("format",A10)

1-2-3 changes the second argument to range format (A10..A10) and returns the format of cell A10.

@CELL("width",B12..B12)

1-2-3 will return the width of column B as viewed in the current window regardless of whether that width was set using the /**W**orksheet **C**olumn **S**et-Width command (for the individual column) or the /**W**orksheet **G**lobal **C**olumn-Width command (for the default column width).

The other attributes that can be examined with either the @CELL or the @CELLPOINTER function are "row", "col", "contents", "type", and "protect".

The difference between @CELL and @CELLPOINTER is important. The @CELL function examines the string attribute of a cell that you designate in a range format, such as A1..A1; if you use a single range format, such as A1, 1-2-3 changes to the range format (A1..A1) and returns the attribute of the single-cell range. If you define a range larger than a single cell, 1-2-3 evaluates the cell in the upper left corner of the range.

On the other hand, the @CELLPOINTER function operates on the current cell—the cell where the cell pointer was positioned when the spreadsheet was last recalculated. The result will remain the same until you enter a value or press the F9 (Calc) key if your worksheet is in automatic recalculation mode, or until you press F9 in manual calculation mode.

Reminder: @CELLPOINTER operates on the cell where the cell pointer was positioned when the spreadsheet was last recalculated.

For example, to determine the address of the current cell, you can enter @CELLPOINTER("address") in cell B22. If recalculation is set to automatic, the value displayed in that cell will be the absolute address $B$22. This same address will remain displayed until you recalculate the worksheet by making an entry elsewhere in the worksheet or by pressing the F9 (Calc) key. The address that appears in cell B22 will change to reflect the position of the cell pointer when the worksheet was recalculated. If recalculation is manual, you can change only the address by pressing the F9 (Calc) key. Figure 6.55 illustrates the use of the @CELLPOINTER function with all the attributes that can be examined by both the @CELLPOINTER and @CELL functions.

Fig. 6.55

Using the @CELLPOINTER function to examine cell attributes.

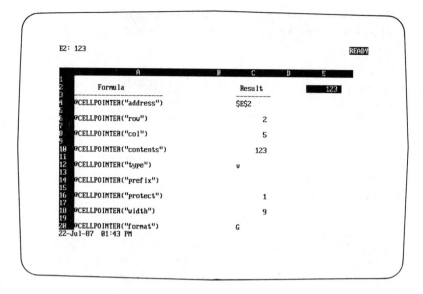

```
E2: 123                                                        READY

              A              B      C      D      E
1
2      Formula                    Result            123
3     ────────────────────────   ──────
4    @CELLPOINTER("address")      $E$2
5
6    @CELLPOINTER("row")               2
7
8    @CELLPOINTER("col")               5
9
10   @CELLPOINTER("contents")        123
11
12   @CELLPOINTER("type")          v
13
14   @CELLPOINTER("prefix")
15
16   @CELLPOINTER("protect")           1
17
18   @CELLPOINTER("width")             9
19
20   @CELLPOINTER("format")        G
22-Jul-87  01:43 PM
```

@NA and @ERR—Trapping Errors

If you find yourself in a situation in which you simply don't know what number to enter for a value, but you don't want to leave the cell blank, you can enter NA (for "Not Available"). 1-2-3 will then display NA in that cell and in any other cell that depends on that cell.

Cue:
Use @ERR when setting up data-entry templates for use by other people.

Another condition that you may encounter, particularly when you are setting up templates for other people, is that of screening out unacceptable values for cells. For example, suppose that you are developing a checkbook-balancing macro in which checks with values less than or equal to zero are unacceptable. One way to indicate the unacceptability of these checks is to use ERR to signal that fact. You might use the following version of the @IF function:

@IF(B9<=0,@ERR,B9)

In simple English, this statement says: If the amount in cell B9 is less than or equal to zero, then display ERR on the screen; otherwise, use the amount. Notice that we have used the @ERR function to control the display in almost the same way that we used @NA in the previous example.

1-2-3 also uses ERR as a signal for unacceptable numbers—for example, a division by zero or mistakenly deleted cells. ERR often will show up temporarily when you are reorganizing the cells in a worksheet. If the ERR message persists, however, you may have to do some careful analysis to figure out why.

As it does for NA, 1-2-3 displays ERR in any cells that depend on a cell with an ERR value. Sometimes many cells will display ERR after only one or two small changes have been made to a worksheet. To correct the errors, you must trace back through the chain of references to find the root of the problem.

@ROWS and @COLS—Finding the Dimensions of Ranges

Both @ROWS and @COLS are used to describe the dimensions of ranges. The general form of these functions is

@ROWS(range)

@COLS(range)

Suppose that you want to determine the number of columns in a range called RANDOM and to display that value in the current cell. The function you enter is @COLS(RANDOM). Similarly, you can enter @ROWS(RANDOM) to display the number of rows in the range. Figure 6.56 shows the results of entering @ROWS(RANDOM) in cell C5 and @COLS(RANDOM) in cell C7.

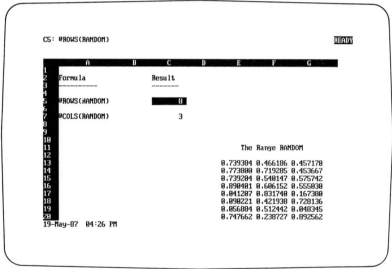

Fig. 6.56

Using @ROWS and @COLS to count the number of rows and columns in a range.

If you specify a single cell (C3 for example) as the argument for the @ROWS or @COLS function, 1-2-3 changes the argument to range format (C3..C3) and returns the value 1 for both functions.

@@—Referencing Cells Indirectly

The @@(cell reference) function provides a way of indirectly referencing one cell by way of another cell. A simple example shows what the @@ function does. If cell A1 contains the label 'A2, and cell A2 contains the number 5, then the function @@(A1) returns the value 5. If the label in cell A1 is changed to 'B10, and cell B10 contains the label "hi there", the function @@(A1) now returns the string value "hi there".

The argument of the @@ function must be a cell reference to the cell containing the indirect address. Similarly, the cell referenced by the argument of the @@ function must contain a string value that evaluates to a cell reference. This cell can contain a label, a string formula, or a reference to another cell, as long as the resulting string value is a cell reference.

The @@ function is primarily useful in situations where several formulas each have the same argument, and the argument must be changed from time to time during the course of the application. 1-2-3 lets you specify the arguments of each formula through a common indirect address. Figure 6.57 shows an example of this situation.

Fig. 6.57

Example of @@ function in a series of formulas.

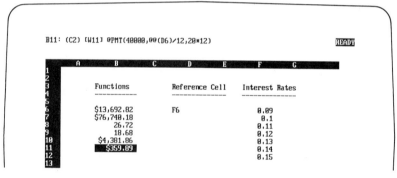

Cue:
Change interest rates for a variety of financial functions by indirect referencing with the @@ function.

In figure 6.57, column B contains a variety of financial functions, all of which use the @@ function to reference 1 of 7 interest rates in column F indirectly through cell D6. When you are ready to change the cell being referenced, you only have to change the label in cell D6 instead of editing all 6 formulas in column B. Figure 6.58 shows the results of the same formulas after the indirect address has been changed from 'F6 to 'F7.

Date and Time Functions

One of 1-2-3's most advanced features is its capacity to manipulate dates and times. This feature can be used for such things as mortgage analysis, aging of accounts receivable, and time management.

Reminder:
1-2-3's serial date numbers start at 1, for January 1, 1900.

All aspects of 1-2-3's date-handling capability are based on 1-2-3's power to represent any given date as a serial integer equal to the number of days from December 31, 1899, to the date in question. With this system, January 1,

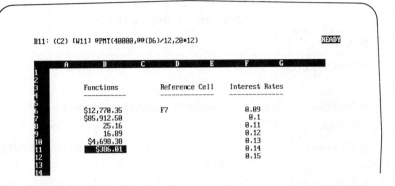

Fig. 6.58

Formulas using @@ after change of indirect reference.

1900, is represented by the number 1; January 2, 1900, is represented by the number 2; and so on. The maximum date that 1-2-3 can handle is December 31, 2099, represented by the serial number 73050.

1-2-3's time-handling capability is based on fractions of serial numbers. For instance, 8:00 a.m. is represented by the decimal fraction 0.333333 (or 1/3). Similarly, the decimal fraction for 10:00 p.m. is 0.916666. 1-2-3's serial numbering system allows you to devise an overall number representing both date and time, as shown in figure 6.59.

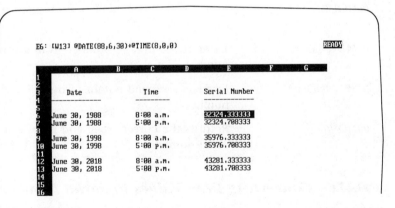

Fig. 6.59

Representing dates and times with serial numbers generated by the @DATE and @TIME functions.

The serial numbering system also lets you manipulate dates and times just like any other number in 1-2-3. For example, after setting the beginning date for a project and adding the number of days that the project should take to the beginning date, you can determine the completion date easily. Time values are just as easy to work with. For example, you can set up a complete schedule for the day by dividing it into hour increments.

The date and time functions available in 1-2-3 are summarized in table 6.10.

Table 6.10
Date and Time Functions

Function	Description
@DATE(y,m,d)	Converts a date value into a serial number
@DATEVALUE(date string)	Converts a date string into a serial number
@DAY(a)	Extracts the day number from a serial number
@MONTH(a)	Extracts the month number from a serial number
@YEAR(a)	Extracts the year number from a serial number
@TIME(h,m,s)	Converts a time value into a serial number
@TIMEVALUE(time string)	Converts a time string into a serial number
@HOUR(a)	Extracts the hour number from a serial number
@MINUTE(a)	Extracts the minute number from a serial number
@SECOND(a)	Extracts a second number from a serial number
@NOW	Returns the current date and time as a serial number

@DATE—Converting Date Values to Serial Numbers

Perhaps the most commonly used date function is @DATE. This function allows you to convert a date into an integer that 1-2-3 can interpret. The form of the @DATE function is

@DATE(year number,month number,day number)

Cue:
Use @DATE with the /Data Fill command to generate a range of dates.

The @DATE function can be used to produce a range of dates; one way to do this is to use the /Date Fill command. For example, to produce a range of the dates of all Mondays from August 3, 1987, to August 3, 1988, use the following steps:

1. Select /DF

2. Specify the range where you want the dates to appear, and press Enter

3. Enter @DATE(87,8,3) as the Start value, and press Enter

4. Enter 7 as the Step value, and press Enter

5. Enter @DATE(88,8,3) as the Stop value, and press Enter

6. Use **/R**ange Format **D**ate to display the range in whatever date format you choose, and expand the column widths as necessary

In figure 6.60, B5..E17 was selected as the range for the dates to appear, and then two additional steps were taken to improve appearances. First, columns were inserted between the columns containing the dates; then the inserted columns were reduced to a width of 5.

Fig. 6.60

Using the @DATE function.

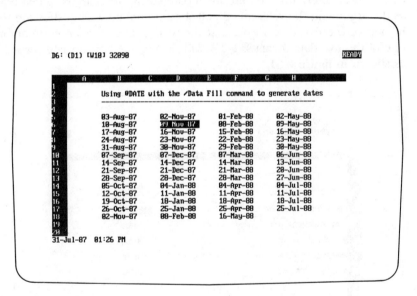

The numeric arguments of the @DATE function have certain restrictions. First, the year number must be between 0 (indicating the year 1900) and 199 (2099). Second, the month number must be between 1 and 12. Third, the day number must be one of the actual values for a given month (for example, 30 days for September and 31 days for December). Finally, 1-2-3 truncates all but the integer portion of the numeric arguments.

Once a date has been interpreted by 1-2-3 as an integer, you can use the **/R**ange Format **D**ate command to display the date in a more recognizable way, such as 01/01/88. (More information on 1-2-3's date and time formats may be found later in this chapter and also in Chapter 5.)

@DATEVALUE—Converting Date Strings to Serial Numbers

@DATEVALUE is a variant of @DATE producing a serial number from the month, day, and year information that you assign the function. But unlike the numeric arguments of @DATE, a string argument is assigned to @DATE-VALUE. The advantage of @DATEVALUE is that you don't have to remember the syntax of the @DATE function; you can enter the date string in any of the usual date formats. The general form of the function is

@DATEVALUE(date string)

The date string must be in any of the available date formats: D1, D2, D3, D4, or D5. As an alternative to entering a date string, you can use a cell reference as the argument; the referenced cell should contain a label showing the date in one of the five date formats. If the string or cell reference conforms to one of the five date formats, 1-2-3 will display the appropriate serial integer, as shown in figure 6.61.

Fig. 6.61

Converting dates in date format to serial numbers using the @DATEVALUE function.

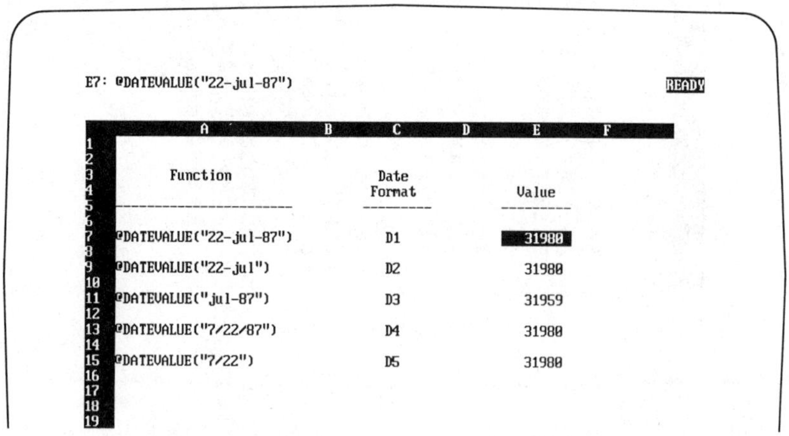

```
E7: @DATEVALUE("22-jul-87")                                          READY

                    A            B      C      D      E      F
1
2
3                Function              Date
4                                      Format       Value
5
6
7   @DATEVALUE("22-jul-87")            D1            31980
8
9   @DATEVALUE("22-jul")               D2            31980
10
11  @DATEVALUE("jul-87")               D3            31959
12
13  @DATEVALUE("7/22/87")              D4            31980
14
15  @DATEVALUE("7/22")                 D5            31980
16
17
18
19
```

Reminder:

Keep your system clock up-to-date and on-time to get accurate results from 1-2-3's date and time functions.

Notice that for the second and fifth date formats, 1-2-3 automatically supplies a serial integer that includes the year (1987), because July 22, 1987, was entered at the start of the day's session (when DOS prompted the user for a date) or as a response to the DOS DATE command. This is one reason why you should make sure that the date and time have been entered correctly with the DOS DATE command. If your system has an internal clock, you don't have to worry about entering the date and time.

Notice also that for the third function, 1-2-3 defaults to the first day in July as the day value.

If you decide to use @DATEVALUE with a date string entered in one of the Lotus International Date formats, the string must be in the same format as the one set in the /Worksheet Global Default Other International Date command. If the default format (MM/DD/YY) is in effect, you must enter the date string in month/date/year format (with slashes separating each component).

For example, entering the formula @DATEVALUE("7/22/87") results in the correct serial date value only if the /WGDOID setting is D4 (MM/DD/YY); otherwise the formula returns an ERR. If you separate the date components with hyphens or periods, for example, the function returns an ERR.

@DAY, @MONTH, and @YEAR—Converting Serial Numbers to Dates

The @DAY, @MONTH, and @YEAR functions allow you to extract parts of a date in integer form. The examples in figure 6.62 show the results of using these three functions.

Fig. 6.62

Comparing the @DAY, @MONTH, and @YEAR functions to the @DATE function

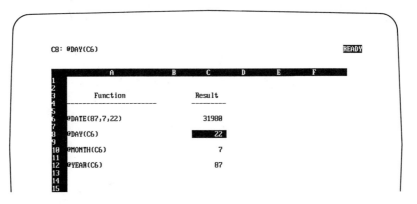

You can use the @DAY, @MONTH, and @YEAR functions for various time-related chores, such as aging accounts receivable and creating a schedule for amortizing a loan.

Displaying Dates

The five date functions already discussed are extremely useful for entering dates in the worksheet in a form that 1-2-3 can understand. The results of these functions, however, are integers that don't look like dates and are there-

Reminder:
Dates entered with date functions are stored as serial numbers.

fore hard to comprehend. For example, can you figure out the dates represented by the numbers 20124 and 32988?

The /**R**ange **F**ormat **D**ate command allows you to display dates in five different forms. As indicated earlier, dates are represented as integers that equal the number of days that have elapsed since December 31, 1899. The date format displays these integers in one of the five arrangements shown in figure 6.63.

Fig. 6.63

The five 1-2-3 date formats.

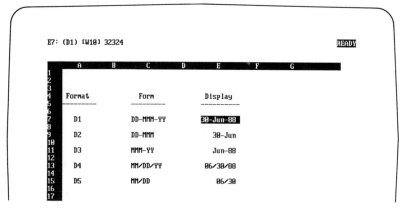

For all the examples shown in the figure, the integer 32324 is displayed in the worksheet prior to formatting, and still appears in the control panel when the formatted cell is highlighted.

Notice, too, that the first option (D1) creates a string 9 characters long—too long to be displayed in a column with the default width of 9. In general, you will need to expand any column containing dates formatted in the DD-MMM-YY format so that the column width is 10 or more characters. The [W10] in the control panel of figure 6.63 shows that the width of column E has been set at 10. Because the other date formats can be displayed in normal width columns, these formats (especially D4) can be used in place of the more detailed, but wider, DD-MMM-YY format.

@NOW—Finding Today's Date and Time

The @NOW function returns today's date and time as an integer. The number represents the number of days since December 31, 1899, and a fraction representing the time elapsed since 12:00 a.m. of the current day. This function is particularly useful for taking advantage of the timekeeping capability of an IBM PC, an IBM PS/2, and a PC-compatible.

If you have a clock that automatically supplies the date and time, or if you simply enter the date and time when you are prompted by DOS at the start of the day, the @NOW function will give you access to the date and time in the current worksheet. For example, if you enter the date 7-22-87 in response to the DOS date prompt, and 16:00 to the DOS time prompt (corresponding to 4:00 p.m.), the @NOW function will have the value

@NOW = 31980.66

You can use the @NOW function to stamp the date and time on your spreadsheets, as shown in figure 6.64. In the figure, @NOW is entered in both cells A1 and A2; cell A1 has been formatted with the /Range Format Date 1 command, and cell A2 has been formatted with the /Range Format Date Time 1 command. The [W12] in the control panel shows that the width of column A is set to 12 to accommodate the Time 1 format.

Cue:
Use @NOW to stamp the date and time on your spreadsheets.

Fig. 6.64

Using @NOW to stamp date and time on a spreadsheet.

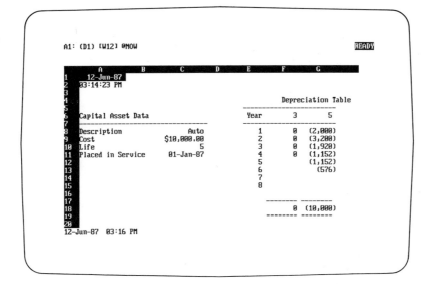

Date- and time-stamping is particularly useful when you need to keep track of multiple iterations of an application such as a budget. Each time you retrieve the file, @NOW returns the current date and time if you have kept your system clock up-to-date and on time.

Because the @NOW function is dependent on the PC DOS or MS-DOS system date and time for its value, you must always remember to enter at least the date, and preferably the date and time, in response to the operating system prompt before you enter 1-2-3. You can also use the DOS DATE and TIME commands to change the date and time.

Users of Release 1A of 1-2-3 may recognize @NOW as being similar to the @TODAY function. The only difference between the two functions is that @NOW includes the time as well as the date. Although @TODAY function is not available in Release 2, Release 1A spreadsheets using @TODAY still work because Release 2 automatically translates @TODAY to @NOW as it reads in the worksheet. Release 2.01 automatically translates @TODAY to @INT(@NOW).

@TIME—Converting Time Values to Serial Numbers

As mentioned earlier, 1-2-3 expresses time in fractions of serial numbers between 0 and 1. For example, .5 is equal to twelve hours (or 12:00 p.m.). In addition, 1-2-3 works on military time; 10:00 p.m. in normal time is 22:00 in military time. 1-2-3's timekeeping system may seem a little awkward at first, but you will soon grow used to it. Here are some general guidelines to help you:

Time increment		Numeric equivalent
1 hour	=	0.0416666667
1 minute	=	0.0006944444
1 second	=	0.0000115741

The @TIME function arrives at a serial number for a specified time of day. The general form of the function is

@TIME(hour number,minute number,second number)

Cue:
@TIME and the /Data Fill command can be used to generate a range of times.

The @TIME function can be used to produce a range of times just as the @DATE function can be used to generate a range of dates. One way to do this is to use the /Data Fill command. For example, to produce a range of times from 8:00 A.M. to 5:00 P.M. in 15 minute increments, use the following steps:

1. Select /DF

2. Specify the range where you want the times to appear, and press Enter

3. Enter @TIME(8,0,0) as the Start value, and press Enter

4. Enter @TIME(0,15,0) as the Step value, and press Enter

5. Enter @TIME(17,0,0) as the Stop value, and press Enter

6. Use /Range Format Date Time to display the range in whatever time format you choose, and expand the column widths as necessary

In figure 6.65, B5..E17 was selected as the range for the times to appear and the results were formatted with Time 2; then two additional steps were taken to improve appearances. First, columns were inserted between the columns containing the times; then the inserted columns were reduced to a width of 4.

Fig. 6.65

Using the @TIME function.

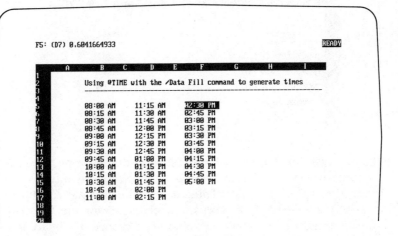

The numeric arguments have certain restrictions. First, the hour number must be between 0 and 23. Second, both the minute number and second number must be between 0 and 59. Finally, although 1-2-3 accepts numeric arguments that contain integers and decimals, only the integer portion is used.

Once a time has been interpreted by 1-2-3 as a fraction of a serial number, you can use the /Range Format Date Time command to display the time in a more recognizable way (for example, 10:42 p.m.). 1-2-3's time formats are discussed later in this chapter.

@TIMEVALUE—Converting Time Strings to Serial Values

Just like @DATEVALUE and @DATE, @TIMEVALUE is a variant of @TIME. Like @TIME, @TIMEVALUE produces a serial number from the hour, minute, and second information you give to the function. But unlike @TIME's numeric arguments, @TIMEVALUE uses string arguments. The general form of the function is

@TIMEVALUE(time string)

The time string must appear in one of the four time formats: T1, T2, T3, or T4. If the string conforms to one of the time formats, 1-2-3 will display the appropriate serial number fraction. (If you then format the cell, 1-2-3 will display the appropriate time of day.) Figure 6.66 shows the results of using the @TIMEVALUE function with the four different acceptable time strings.

Reminder:
The string argument of @TIMEVALUE must follow one of the four time formats available in 1-2-3.

Fig. 6.66

Using the @TIMEVALUE function.

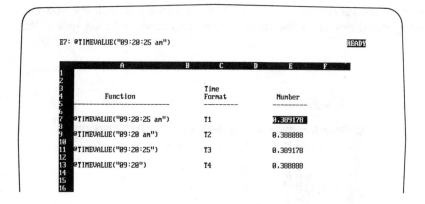

Fig. 6.66

Using the @TIMEVALUE function.

The first two time formats, T1 and T2, accept times from 12:00 a.m. to 11:59 a.m., and from 12:00 p.m. to 11:59 p.m. The second two time formats, called International Time formats by Lotus, accept military time from 00:00 (12 a.m.) to 23:59 (11:59 p.m.). The separator character for the International Time formats defaults to a colon (:), but you can change this by using the /Worksheet Global Default Other International Time command.

@SECOND, @MINUTE, and @HOUR—Converting Serial Numbers to Time Values

The @SECOND, @MINUTE, and @HOUR functions allow you to extract different units of time from a numeric time fraction. Figure 6.67 shows that these three functions are, in a sense, the reverse of the @TIME function, just as the @DAY, @MONTH, and @YEAR functions are the reverse of the @DATE function.

Fig. 6.67

Comparing the @SECOND, @MINUTE, and @HOUR functions to the @TIME function.

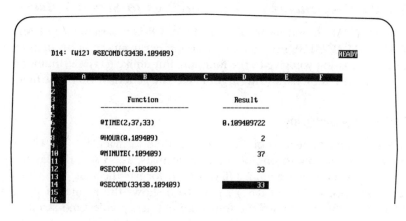

Notice that the argument includes both an integer and a decimal portion. Although the integer portion is important for date functions, it is disregarded for time functions, as shown with the second @SECOND function in the figure. You can use these functions for various time-related chores, one of which is developing a time schedule.

Displaying Times

You now have seen all of 1-2-3's time functions, but the resulting serial number fractions do not look familiar as expressions of time. The /**R**ange Format **D**ate **T**ime command allows you to display times in a more recognizable format. Lotus offers four different time formats, as shown in figure 6.68.

Fig. 6.68

The four ways to display time in 1-2-3.

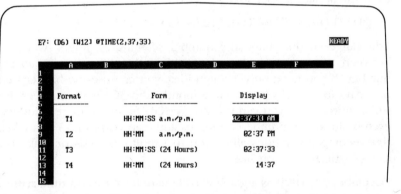

Before the cell is formatted, a fractional number is displayed in the worksheet as the result of using the @TIME function. In the first and third examples in figure 6.68, that number is 0.10940972; in the second and fourth examples, 12 hours later, the number is 0.60940972.

The first option (D6) creates a string of 11 characters that requires a column width of 12 in order to display the time in this format. For this reason, and because you may rarely use seconds, the D7 format is more useful for most people. Of course, you may find another of the four formats better suited to your needs.

General Comments on Date and Time Arithmetic

1-2-3's date and time arithmetic capabilities actually incorporate both a set of functions and a set of formats. Don't be confused by this mix. The functions, like @DATEVALUE, enter dates or times in the worksheet; the formats display these functions in an understandable form. Although the format can be used without the function, or the function without the format, the two tools are better used together.

In most cases date and time arithmetic will require simply subtracting one number from another. By subtracting, you can easily determine the number of days between dates, or hours between times. For example, subtracting @DATE(88,7,31) from @DATE(88,8,15) results in the value 15 (days). Similarly, subtracting @TIME(10,4,31) from @TIME(12,54,54) results in a value of 0.11832175 (2 hours, 50 minutes, and 23 seconds). To 1-2-3 these problems are as simple as subtracting the serial number for

@DATE(88,7,31)+@TIME(10,4,31) = 32355.4198

from the serial number for

@DATE(88,8,15)+@TIME(12,54,54) = 32370.5381

You can even determine the number of minutes, hours, weeks, and years between two serial numbers by dividing the difference by an appropriate number. If you need only a rough idea, you can use the banker's convention of 7 days in a week, 30 days in a month, and 360 days in a year. If you want to be more exact, you can use the @MOD function for remainders. You can even build in odd-numbered months and leap years. 1-2-3's date-keeping and timekeeping capabilities allow you to simplify analysis or make the analysis as sophisticated as you like.

December 31, 1899, is a good starting date for date and time arithmetic. The selection of an ending date must allow enough time for you to perform long-term analysis. The best choice is probably December 31, 2099, the latest date that the @DATE function can handle.

Cue:
Use date and time functions within logical functions for investment, project-planning, or product and service schedule applications.

As mentioned earlier, besides using date and time functions in arithmetic calculations, you can also use them in logical expressions, such as @IF(@DATE(88,15,05)>B2,C3,D4). In simple English this statement says: If the serial number equivalent to May 15, 1988, is greater than the value in cell B2, then assign the value in cell C3 to the current cell; otherwise, use the value in D4. This kind of test can be used to help keep track of investment portfolios or time performance.

String Functions

1-2-3 has a variety of functions that give the user significant power to manipulate strings. Strings are the opposite of values; they are labels or portions of labels. More specifically, strings are units of data consisting of connected characters (alphabetic, numeric, blank, and special) that are designated by quotation marks (" "). The functions specifically designated as string functions are not the only 1-2-3 functions that take advantage of the power and flexibility of strings. For example, data-management, logical, error-trapping, and special functions use strings as well as values. The string functions, however, are specifically designed to manipulate strings. Table 6.11 summarizes the string functions available in 1-2-3.

Table 6.11
String Functions

Function	Description
@FIND(search string, overall string,start number)	Locates start position of one string within another string
@MID(string,start number,n)	Extracts n characters from string, beginning with character start number
@LEFT(string,n)	Extracts leftmost n characters from string
@RIGHT(string,n)	Extracts rightmost n characters from string
@REPLACE(original string,start number, n,new string)	Substitutes n characters from the original string, with the new string at character start number
@LENGTH(string)	Displays number of characters in string
@EXACT(string1,string2)	Returns TRUE if string1 and string2 are exact matches; otherwise, FALSE
@LOWER(string)	Converts all characters in the string to lowercase
@UPPER(string)	Converts all characters in the string to uppercase
@PROPER(string)	Converts first character in each word in the string to uppercase, remaining characters to lowercase
@REPEAT(string,n)	Copies the string n times in a cell
@TRIM(string)	Extracts blank spaces from the string
@N(range)	Returns the value contained in the cell in the upper left corner of the range

Function	Description
@S(range)	Returns the string value of the cell in the upper left corner of the range
@STRING(a,n)	Converts a value to a string showing n decimal places
@VALUE(string)	Converts a string to a value
@CLEAN(string)	Removes nonprintable characters from the string
@CHAR(n)	Converts a code number into an ASCII/LICS character
@CODE(string)	Converts the first character in the string into an ASCII/LICS code

Reminder:
You can link strings to other strings using the concatenation operator (&). You cannot link strings to blank cells or to cells containing numeric values.

Strings can be linked to other strings by using the concatenation operator (&). The discussion of the individual string functions in this section shows several examples of the use of the concatenation operator, but you should remember this: you can't link strings to cells that contain numeric values or are blank. If you try, 1-2-3 returns an ERR.

Take particular care to avoid mixing data types in string functions. For instance, some functions produce strings, whereas others produce numeric results. Be careful not to combine functions from these two different groups unless you have taken all the precautions discussed throughout this section on string functions.

The numbering scheme for positioning characters in a label is also something to watch for when using string functions. These positions are numbered beginning with zero and continuing to a number corresponding to the last character in the label. The following example shows the position numbers (0 to 24) for a long label:

```
          1111111111122222
0123456789012345678901234
'two chickens in every pot
```

The prefix (') before the label does not have a number because the prefix is not considered part of the label. Nor are negative position numbers allowed. The importance of position numbers will become clearer in the next section.

@FIND—Locating One String within Another

One of the simplest string functions is @FIND, the best function for showing how position numbers are used in strings. The @FIND function locates the starting position of one string within another string. For instance, using the string that was just illustrated, suppose that you want to find at what position the string "every" occurs in this string. The general format of @FIND is

@FIND(search string,overall string,start number)

The search string is the string you want to locate. In this example the search string is "every". The overall string is the target string to be searched. In this example, "two chickens in every pot" is the overall string. Finally, the start number is the position number in the overall string where you want to start the search. If you wish to start at position 6 and you are using the overall string located in cell A2, the function you use is shown in figure 6.69.

Fig. 6.69

Using the @FIND function.

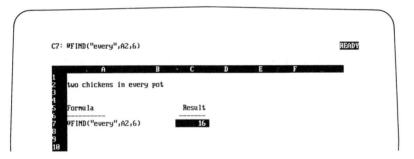

Your result is the number 16, the position of the first (and only) occurrence of "every" in the overall string. If the search string "every" was not found in the overall string, the ERR message would be displayed.

Notice that in our example, choosing the starting number of 6 has no bearing on the outcome of the function. You could just as easily choose 0 (or any other number less than or equal to 16) for the starting position of the search string. If "every" appeared more than once in the overall string, however, the start number could locate its occurrence elsewhere. Suppose that the following overall string appears in cell A2:

'two chickens in every pot, two cars in every garage

Now suppose that you decide to locate all the occurrences of "every" in the overall string. The function @FIND("every",A2,0) returns a value of 16, as before. Try changing the start number by adding 1 to the result of the original function (1 + 16 = 17). The appropriate function is now @FIND("every",A2,17). This new function returns the number 39, the starting location of the second occurrence of "every". Next, add 1 to the second result (1 + 39 = 40), and use @FIND("every",A2,40). The resulting ERR message tells you that you have found all the occurrences of the search string. Figure 6.70 shows the different results of using different position numbers.

Fig. 6.70

Using position numbers with the @FIND function.

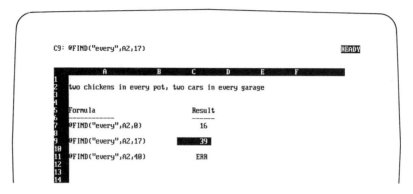

Keep in mind that @FIND (like string functions in general) is limited to 240 characters in a string. Another rule to remember is that any decimals in a start number will be ignored by 1-2-3.

Reminder:
@FIND performs only exact searches; upper- and lowercase is significant.

Still another rule to remember is that any search string must be entered exactly as you wish to find it because @FIND does not perform approximate searching. In the preceding example, if you had used a search string of "Every" instead of "every", you would get the ERR message instead of a number value.

@MID—Extracting One String from Another

Whereas @FIND helps you to locate one string within another, the @MID function lets you extract one string from another. This operation is called *substringing*. The general form of the function is

> @MID(string,start position,length)

The start position is a number representing the character position in the string where you wish to begin extracting characters. The length argument indicates the number of characters to extract. For example, to extract the first name from a label containing the full name "Page Davidson", use @MID("Page Davidson",0,4). This function extracts the string starting in position 0 (the first character) and continuing for a length of 4 characters—the string "Page".

Cue:
Use @MID with @FIND to extract first and last names from a list of full names.

Now suppose that you want to extract the first and last names from a column list of full names and to put those two names in a separate column. To accomplish this, use the @MID and @FIND functions together. Because you know that a blank space will always separate the first and last names, @FIND can locate the position of the blank in each full name. With this value, you can then set up the functions to extract the first and last names.

If cell A8 contains the full name "Ivan Andersen", place the function

@MID(A8,0,@FIND(" ",A8,0))

in cell B8. The value of this function will appear as "Ivan" because @FIND(" ",A8,0) will return a value of 4 for the length argument (see fig. 6.71).

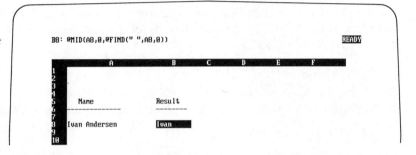

Fig. 6.71

Using the @MID function to extract a substring.

Next place the function

@MID(A8,@FIND(" ",A8,0)+1,99)

in cell C8. The @FIND function indicates that the start position is one character beyond the blank space. In addition, the length of the string to be extracted is 99 characters. Obviously, a length of 99 is overkill, but there is no penalty for this excess. The string that 1-2-3 extracts is "Andersen". Figure 6.72 shows the results.

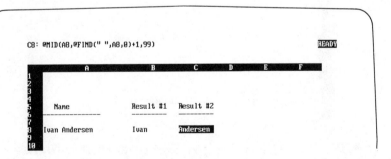

Fig. 6.72

Using @MID and @FIND to locate and extract first and last names.

Now that you have seen how the @MID and @FIND functions can separate first and last names, you may want to try using these functions in a case with a name containing a middle initial.

@LEFT and @RIGHT—Extracting Strings from Left and Right

@LEFT and @RIGHT are special variations of the @MID function and are used to extract one string of characters from another, beginning at the leftmost and rightmost positions in the underlying string. The general formats of the functions are

@LEFT(string,length)

@RIGHT(string,length)

Cue:
@RIGHT can be used to extract the ZIP code from an address.

The length argument is the number of character positions in a string to be extracted. For example, if you want to extract the ZIP code from the string "Cincinnati, Ohio 45243", use

@RIGHT("Cincinnati, Ohio 45243",5)

@LEFT works the same way as @RIGHT except that @LEFT extracts from the beginning of a string. For instance, extract the city in our example with

@LEFT("Cincinnati, Ohio 45243",10)

In most cases, however, use @FIND(",","Cincinnati, Ohio 45243",0) instead of 10 for the length in the function to extract the city from the address.

Figure 6.73 shows the results of using @LEFT and @RIGHT with varying length arguments.

Fig. 6.73

Changing the length argument for the @LEFT and @RIGHT functions.

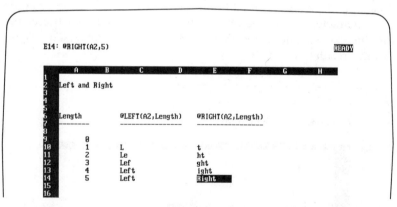

@REPLACE—Replacing a String within a String

The @REPLACE function removes a group of characters from a string and replaces the characters with another string using the same numbering scheme as @FIND. That is, @REPLACE numbers the character positions in a string, starting with zero and continuing to the end of the string (up to a maximum of 239). The general form of the command is

@REPLACE(original string,start number,length,replacement
string)

The start number argument indicates the position where 1-2-3 will begin removing characters in the original string. The length shows how many characters to remove, and the replacement string contains new characters to replace the removed ones. For example, suppose that the string "This is the original string" appears in cell A2. Figure 6.74 shows several examples of how to use @REPLACE to change words in the string.

Fig. 6.74

Using @REPLACE to alter a string.

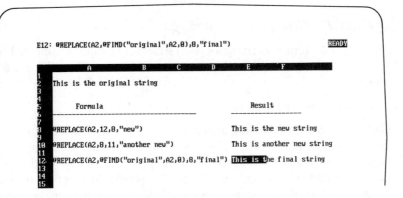

Notice in the third example in the figure that you can use the @FIND function to locate the string you want to replace instead of starting at 0 and counting up the 12 positions of the start number.

The @REPLACE function is a valuable tool for correcting a text entry without retyping the entire string.

@LENGTH—Computing the Length of a String

The @LENGTH function simply indicates the length of your strings. The general form of the function is

@LENGTH(string)

Figure 6.75 shows how @LENGTH can be used to find the length of a string. Notice that the function returns the value ERR as the length of numeric values or formulas, blank cells, and null strings.

Fig. 6.75

*Finding the length
of a string.*

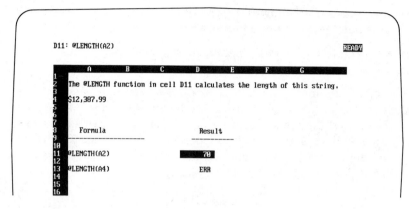

@EXACT—Comparing Strings

The @EXACT function compares two strings, returning a value of 1 for strings that are alike and 0 for strings that are unalike. The general form of the function is

@EXACT(string1,string2)

@EXACT's method of comparison is like the = operator in formulas except that the = operator checks for an approximate match, and the @EXACT function checks for an exact match. For example, if cell A2 holds the string "Marketing Function" and cell B2 holds the string "marketing function", the numeric value of A2=B2 is 1 because the two strings are an approximate match. Conversely, the numeric value of @EXACT(A2,B2) is 0 because the two functions are not an exact match.

Cue:
*Use the @S
function to ensure
that the argument
of @EXACT is a
string.*

The examples in figure 6.76 demonstrate the use of @EXACT. Notice in the third example that @EXACT cannot compare nonstring arguments. If you try to compare the entry in cell A6 with the blank cell C6, the value of @EXACT(A6,C6) is ERR. In fact, if either argument is a nonstring value of any type (including numbers), 1-2-3 will return the ERR message. (Note that the @S function, explained later in this chapter, can be used to ensure that the arguments of @EXACT have string values.)

@LOWER, @UPPER, and @PROPER— Converting the Case of Strings

1-2-3 offers three different functions for converting the case of a string value:

• @LOWER(string) converts all uppercase letters in a string to lowercase letters.

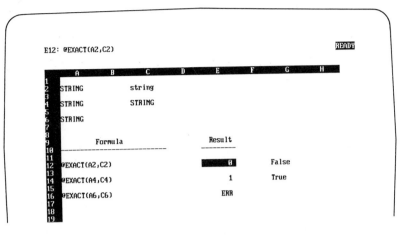

Fig. 6.76

Comparing strings with the @EXACT function.

- @UPPER(string) is the opposite of @LOWER; @UPPER raises all the letters in a string to uppercase letters.

- @PROPER(string) capitalizes the first letter in each word of a label. (Words are defined as groups of characters separated by blank spaces.) @PROPER goes on to convert the remaining letters in each word to lowercase.

Figure 6.77 gives an example of the use of each function.

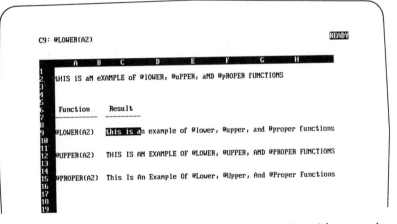

Fig. 6.77

Converting the case of alphanumeric strings.

As you might expect, none of these three functions works with nonstring values. For instance, if cell E9 contains a number or a null string (""), 1-2-3 will return ERR for each of these functions. (Note that using the @S function, explained later in this chapter, will ensure that the arguments of these functions have string values.)

@REPEAT—Repeating Strings within a Cell

@REPEAT repeats strings within a cell much as the backslash (\) repeats characters. But @REPEAT has some distinct advantages over the backslash. The general form of the function is

@REPEAT(string,number)

Reminder:
@REPEAT copies characters beyond the current column width.

The number argument indicates the number of times you wish to repeat a string in a cell. For example, if you want to repeat the string "COGS" three times, you can enter @REPEAT("COGS",3). The resulting string will be "COGSCOGSCOGS". This string follows 1-2-3's rule for long labels. That is, the string will display beyond the right boundary of the column, provided no entry is in the cell to the right. The technique for repeating labels with \ is different from that of @REPEAT because with \, 1-2-3 will fill the column to exactly whatever the column width may be.

You can set up a function to fill a cell almost exactly by using the @CELL and @LENGTH functions. If A3 is the cell you wish to fill by repeating the string "COGS", the first step is to enter @CELL("width",A3..A3) in an out-of-the-way cell, say, K4. The next step is to enter @LENGTH("COGS") in K5, another out-of-the-way cell. The final step is to enter

@REPEAT("COGS",K4/K5)

in cell A3. If the width of column A is 9 (the default column width), the label that appears in cell A3 is "COGSCOGS". Notice that since @REPEAT uses only the integer portion of the "number" argument, "COGS" is repeated only twice rather than 2.25 times.

The @REPEAT function in figure 6.78 shows you how to generate a dashed line that is one character less than the column width of the current cell. You can enter this formula in one cell and then /Copy it to any other appropriate cell in the spreadsheet.

Fig. 6.78

Using the @REPEAT function to generate dashed lines.

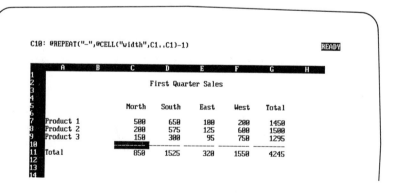

If you use this technique, you should remember two important points: (1) In the @CELL function, do not reference a cell that contains a formula, or a circular reference may result. (2) In Release 2.0 of 1-2-3, do not include a dashed line, or any other label, in a formula, or you will get an ERR; for example, do not enter the formula +C7+C8+C9+C10 in cell C11. Release 2.01 corrected this problem, and evaluates labels in formulas as 0.

@TRIM—Removing Blank Spaces from a String

The @TRIM(string) function can take out unwanted blank spaces from the beginning, end, or middle of a string. If more than one space occurs consecutively in the middle of a string, 1-2-3 removes all but one of the blank spaces. For example, the @TRIM function in figure 6.79 removes extra spaces from between the words of a sentence.

Fig. 6.79

Removing unwanted spaces with the @TRIM function.

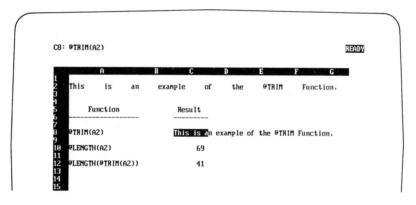

Notice that the value of @LENGTH(A2) is 69, but the value of @LENGTH(@TRIM(A2)) is 41. (For trimming other characters besides blank spaces, see the @CLEAN function described later in this chapter.)

@S and @N—Testing for Strings and Values

The @N and @S functions give you a way to test for the presence of strings or values. @N returns the value of a number or numeric formula found in a cell. If the cell is blank or contains a label, @N returns the value 0. @N will always have a numeric value.

The @S function returns the string value of a cell. If the cell contains a string or a formula that evaluates to a string, then @S returns this string. If the cell contains a number or is empty, @S returns the null string (""). @S will always have a string value.

The forms of the @N and the @S functions are

@N(range)

@S(range)

The argument must be a range or a single-cell reference. If you use a single-cell reference, 1-2-3 adjusts the argument to range format and returns the numeric or string value of the single cell. If the argument is a multicell range, @N and @S return the numeric or string value of the upper left corner of the range.

Figure 6.80 shows some results of using the @N and @S functions.

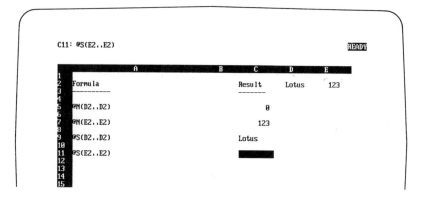

@STRING—Converting Values to Strings

The @STRING function lets you convert a number to a string so that the number can act with 1-2-3's string functions. For example, @STRING can override 1-2-3's automatic right-justification of numbers, and display a number justified to the left. The general form of the @STRING function is

@STRING(number to convert,decimal places)

1-2-3 uses the fixed-decimal format for the @STRING function. The decimal-places argument represents the number of places to be included in the string. For example, if the number-to-convert argument within cell A2 is 22.5, enter @STRING(J7,2) in cell C10. The resulting string 22.50 is displayed with left-justification, the default setting (see fig. 6.81).

Notice that in the first example in the figure, 1-2-3 rounds the number upward to 23, just as 1-2-3 rounds any number displayed in the fixed-decimal format.

The third example in the figure shows how to use the @STRING function to show a number as a percentage. The formula @STRING(A2,2)&"%" produces

Fig. 6.81

Converting a
number to a
string.

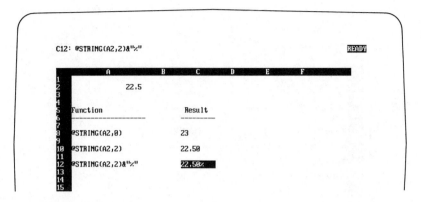

the string "22.50%". Note that to create a string from a number in any format other than fixed decimal, you must add the additional format characters yourself.

@VALUE—Converting Strings to Values

If you have been entering string data but need to use the data as numbers, use the @VALUE function. For example, suppose that you enter model numbers and their quantities in a database as labels. The information on model numbers works fine in the string format; but @VALUE will change the format of the quantity data to add different part quantities together. The general form of the function is

@VALUE(string)

Figure 6.82 shows several examples of converting labels to numeric values with the @VALUE function. Besides converting strings in the standard number format (the first example in the figure), @VALUE can also convert strings with decimal fractions as well as numbers displayed in scientific format. In the second example, the string "22 1/2" in cell C10 is converted by the function @VALUE(C10) to the number 22.5. Even if cell C10 contained the string "22 3/2", @VALUE would convert the string to the number 23.5. The final two examples in figure 6.82 show how @VALUE converts strings in percentage and scientific format.

A few rules should be remembered when you use @VALUE. Although 1-2-3 usually does not object to extra spaces left in a string, the program has trouble with some extra characters, such as trailing percent signs. Currency signs (such as $) that precede the string are acceptable, however. Try experimenting with different extra characters to see how @VALUE reacts. Another point to remember is that a numeric value as an argument for @VALUE will simply return the original number value.

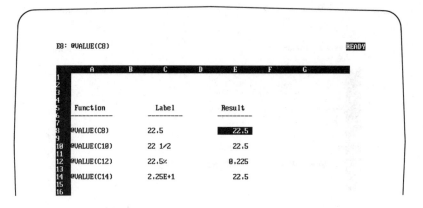

@CLEAN—Removing Nonprintable Characters from Strings

Cue:
@CLEAN removes nonprintable characters from data imported into your worksheet from other sources.

Sometimes when you import strings with /File Import (see Chapter 7), especially by way of a modem, the strings will contain nonprintable characters (ASCII codes below 32) interspersed throughout. The @CLEAN function removes the nonprintable characters from the strings (see fig. 6.83). The general format of the function is

@CLEAN(string)

Fig. 6.83

Using @CLEAN to remove nonprintable characters.

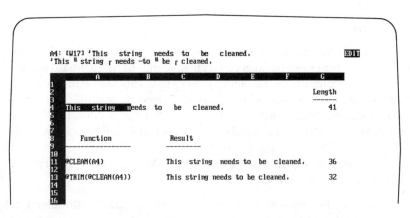

The argument of @CLEAN must be a string value or a cell reference to a cell containing a string value.

Functions Used with LICS

1-2-3 offers a few special functions for interfacing with the Lotus International Character Set (LICS), which Lotus calls "an extension of the ASCII printable character set." (Be aware that the ASCII code number for a given character may not correspond to its LICS code number.) Actually, the LICS can best be thought of as a new character set created by Lotus and superimposed on top of the ASCII character set.

The complete set of LICS characters is listed in the 1-2-3 reference manual and includes everything from the copyright sign to the lowercase *e* with the grave accent. Appendix C of this book shows you how to use the Alt-F1 (Compose) key to display the LICS characters.

@CHAR—Displaying ASCII/LICS Characters

The @CHAR function produces the ASCII/LICS equivalent of a number between 1 and 255 on-screen. The general form of the function is

@CHAR(number)

1-2-3 represents a ™ sign on-screen with a T. To display the trademark sign on screen, enter @CHAR(184) in a cell. What is more, a string formula can concatenate the trademark sign to a product name. For instance, enter the formula +"8080"&@CHAR(184) to produce the string "8080T". When you print the screen display, this string prints as 8080™. Figure 6.84 shows several other examples of the use of the @CHAR function.

Caution:
A character's ASCII code number may not be the same as the LICS code number.

Fig. 6.84

Displaying ASCII/ LICS characters with the @CHAR function.

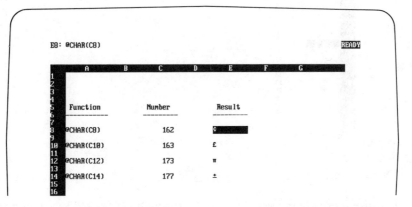

Keep in mind two simple rules when using @CHAR. First, if the numeric argument you are using is not between 1 and 255, 1-2-3 returns the ERR message. Second, if the argument you use is not an integer, 1-2-3 disregards the noninteger portion of the argument.

Cue:

Display ASCII/LICS characters with Alt-F1.

ASCII/LICS characters may also be displayed using the Alt-F1 (Compose) function key together with a compose sequence. See Appendix C for further information and for a list of LICS codes.

Nonprintable Characters in LICS

Be aware that not all the LICS characters are printable, nor will they always show up on the screen. More specifically, codes 1 through 31 are the problem area. But because these codes include all the characters necessary for making boxes and arrows in 1-2-3, you may want access to these characters.

You can get at these nonprintable characters with the Edit key. First, the /Data Fill command enters the numbers 1 through 31 in the range B1..B31. Then, after moving one column to the left, you enter @CHAR(B1) in cell A1 and copy that formula to the cells below. Finally, use the /Range Values command to convert the formulas in column A to the actual string values. Even though the cells in column A appear blank, you can see any one of the characters by moving the cursor to any cell in column A and pressing the Edit key. Figure 6.85 shows how the screen should appear.

Fig. 6.85

Using the F2 (Edit) key to view nonprintable characters.

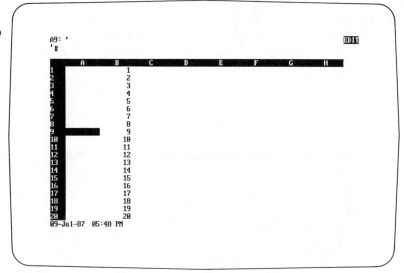

Because these characters @CHAR(1) through @CHAR(31) are nonprintable, only blanks will appear if you try to print them out.

@CODE—Computing the ASCII/LICS Code

The @CODE function performs as the opposite to @CHAR. Whereas @CHAR takes a number between 0 and 255 and returns an ASCII/LICS character, @CODE examines an ASCII/LICS character and returns a number between 0 and 255. The general form of the function is

@CODE(string)

Suppose that you want to find the ASCII/LICS code number for the letter *a*. You enter @CODE("a") in a cell, and 1-2-3 returns the number 97. If you had entered @CODE("aardvark"), 1-2-3 would still return 97, the code of the first character in the string. Figure 6.86 shows several other examples of the use of the @CODE function.

Reminder:
@CODE returns the ASCII/LICS code of the first character of the string used as the argument.

Fig. 6.86

Using @CODE to find ASCII/LICS numbers.

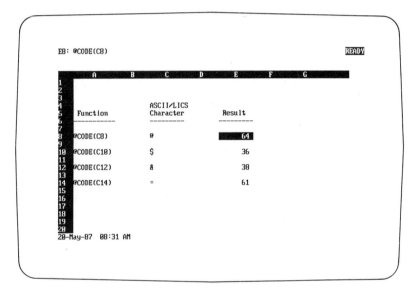

Remember that if you specify a number as the argument for @CODE (expressed as a number and not a string), 1-2-3 returns the ERR message.

Using HAL To Enter Functions into the Spreadsheet

Lotus HAL does not appreciably extend 1-2-3's function capabilities for all classes of functions, but does provide some interesting and useful capabilities for statistical functions and "what-if" analysis.

Using HAL with Statistical Functions

You can enter any 1-2-3 function into the spreadsheet by typing the function into HAL's Request Box and pressing the Insert key, but additional verbs are provided for making statistical requests. HAL's vocabulary contains the following synonyms for calculating statistics:

Function	HAL Synonym
@AVG	Average, Avg, Mean
@MAX	Maximize
@MIN	Minimize
@SUM	Add, Sum, Total
@STD	Standard deviation, Std
@VAR	Variance

HAL makes its computation for the current table and returns the result below the table, but you can specify a particular range for the computation and a cell destination for the result. Forgetting to specify a destination can sometimes be inconvenient or result in loss of data. For example, suppose that the current table is a column of numeric data in cells C1..C5. If you request \add, HAL sums the column, draws a dotted line in cell C6, and writes the total in cell C7, even if cell C7 already contains data.

In another example, if you request HAL to sum a current table that is a row of data from C1..F1, HAL will again draw a line under the last cell in the table; the line will appear in cell F2 and the result in cell F3. You probably would prefer the result to appear in cell G1, without a line. It's easy to get this result with HAL; you simply include the word *row* in your request.

You can also walk through a table row-by-row by adding the word *rows* to a statistical request. For example, if the range A3..G18 contains data, the following request will take the average of each row and write the results in the column H3..H18:

   \average rows 3 through 18

HAL will follow the same pattern for any of the statistical requests if you add the word *rows*.

The following examples show how you can make statistical requests for the range named SALES, and have HAL write the results in specific locations:

   \avg of sales in h25   \add sales in j25

   \max of sales in h27   \std of sales in j27

   \min of sales in h29   \variance of sales in j29

Using HAL for "What-If" Analysis

HAL extends 1-2-3's capabilities for "what-if" analysis by performing projections or forecasts automatically. If you instruct HAL to project, or increase, a column or row by a percentage or amount, HAL enters the correct formula and calculates the result. For example, if you want to see the impact of a ten-percent increase in sales on net income, you enter the request in HAL's Request Box, review the result, and then compare the result to the original values by using HAL's Undo key.

The following are valid HAL requests for projecting values in a column:

\project at 5%

\grow jan across by 10%

\proj col c at 5,000

In the first example, HAL multiplies the value in the current cell by five percent and places the result and formula in the cell directly to the right of the current cell. In the second example, HAL works across all labeled columns, beginning with the column labeled *Feb*; HAL increases the values in each column by ten percent over the preceding column. In the third example, the values in column C are added to 5,000 and placed in column D.

Similar requests can be made to have HAL make projections row-by-row.

You can see from these few examples that, if you use 1-2-3 for statistical analysis and model-building, HAL can significantly ease your workload and improve your work.

Chapter Summary

More than any of the previous chapters, this chapter should serve as a constant reference as you continue to work with 1-2-3. It is unlikely that one reading has produced complete comprehension, but one reading of this chapter and the book to this point will have given you a solid foundation for all the basics of building a spreadsheet. The versatility and power of functions will give you countless opportunities for expanding your use of 1-2-3.

You should now take a little time to learn the basics of managing 1-2-3 files, which is the topic of the next chapter. The next chapter also shows you how to transfer files between 1-2-3 and other programs, and between different versions of 1-2-3. If you have no present need for those operations, just learn the basic file operations and then go to Chapter 8. Chapter 8 presents a small spreadsheet model, as a review and as an opportunity to use your new skills in a step-by-step practice session.

7

Managing Files in 1-2-3

Storing, retrieving, and deleting files to and from disks are capabilities common to all spreadsheet programs. What makes 1-2-3 unique is its scale in performing these functions. Lotus lists the disk requirements for the program as either "two double-sided disk drives or one double-sided disk drive and a hard disk." Clearly, the program can function with less than these requirements (one double-sided disk drive is enough to squeak by), but this is not what Lotus had in mind. 1-2-3 was written for users who intend to mix and match many large files that will be moved in and out of storage quite frequently.

A complete listing of all file-operation commands can be found in the 1-2-3 Command Menu Map included at the back of this book, and a summary explanation of all file commands can be found in the 1-2-3 Command Reference located in the Quick Reference Section of this book.

This chapter will show you how to

- Save and name files

- Retrieve files

- Use passwords to protect files

- Retrieve portions of files

- Combine separate files

- Delete files

- List different types of files

- Import files, using the /File Import command

- Use the Translate Utility to transfer files and records between different releases of 1-2-3, and between 1-2-3 and other programs

A General Description of 1-2-3 Files

1-2-3 file names can be up to eight characters long with a three-character extension. The three basic rules for file names are

1. File names may include the characters A through Z, 0 through 9, and the underscore (_). Depending on your system, you may be able to use other special characters, but 1-2-3 will definitely not accept the characters <>, and *. Although 1-2-3 separates the file name from the three-letter extension, it does not accept the period (.) within the file name. For example, 1-2-3 will not accept the file name SALES1.1.TXT

2. File names may not contain blanks.

3. Lowercase letters are converted automatically to uppercase in file names.

Although you determine the eight-character name, 1-2-3 creates the extension automatically according to the type of file you are handling. The three possible file extensions are

.WK1 For worksheet files

.PRN For print files

.PIC For graph files

Experienced 1-2-3 users should note that Release 2 uses .WK1 as a file extension for worksheets rather than .WKS, used in previous releases. This difference allows 1-2-3 to distinguish between worksheets written by different releases and to prevent previous 1-2-3 releases from loading worksheets written by Release 2.

Release 2 easily reads older 1-2-3 worksheets with .WKS extensions and Symphony worksheets with .WR1 extensions, but writes them as new files with .WK1 extensions when the worksheet is saved. If you want to run .WK1 files with earlier versions of 1-2-3, you will need to use the Translate Utility, discussed later in this chapter.

In addition to creating files with the .WK1, .PRN, and .PIC extensions, 1-2-3 Release 2 lets you supply your own extension. To create a file name with your extension, enter the file name according to the rules listed above, enter a period, and then add an extension of one to three characters. Note that any file name with your own extension will not be displayed in the lists of .WK1, .PIC, or .PRN files. The /File **Retrieve** command, for example, will retrieve all .WK1 files but not files with your special extensions, unless you specify the extension. To retrieve your special file, type the file name and extension after the Name of file to retrieve: C:\ prompt.

To see a list of files with your own extension (along with all other files), use the /File **List Other** command. Although not fail-safe, creating file names with your own extensions can provide a level of security for those files for which you want to limit user access. Additional ways of limiting access to files are provided by Release 2's password system, described in the section on simple storage and retrieval.

Keep in mind that only one worksheet exists in a file, and that you can work on a worksheet only when it is in main memory.

Saving Files

The basic file function of storing files is easy to perform in 1-2-3. The /File **Save** command allows you to save an entire worksheet in a file on disk. The /File **Save** command makes an exact copy of the current worksheet, including all the formats, range names, and settings you have specified.

When you enter this command, 1-2-3 will try to help you by supplying a list of the current worksheet files on the disk. You can either point to one of the entries or enter a new file name. To enter a new file name, you must use the rules previously expressed. 1-2-3 will automatically supply a .WK1 extension, as shown in figure 7.1.

Reminder:
When you name a file, 1-2-3 automatically supplies the .WK1 extension.

Fig. 7.1
File name list during /File Save.

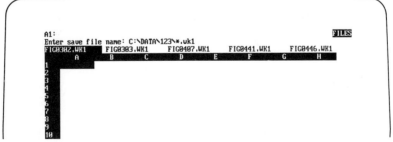

Naming and Saving Files

Remember to be expressive when thinking of a file name for the new file. True, you have only eight characters with which to name the file; but make those eight useful. In other words, choose a file name that relates something about the contents of the file. The following list provides some good examples of file names:

File name	Description
INVWS-06	Inventory worksheet for June
PRO_RRNT	Pro forma worksheet for the planned restaurant
EMPDPLST	Employee list for the Data Processing Department

If you work with many different worksheets that contain basically the same information, you'll need to make the names similar without, of course, using the same name. In the previous examples, the name INVWS-06 was given to an inventory worksheet for the month of June. Following this naming scheme, you would name the inventory worksheets for July and August INVWS-07 and INVWS-08, respectively. This naming technique will help you recall file names later.

After you've chosen the file name, type the name and press Enter. The file then is saved with the name given, and 1-2-3 assigns .WK1 as an extension.

Normally, the fact that 1-2-3 assigns the extension poses no problem because when 1-2-3 displays a list of files, only the files with the .WK1 extension are shown. At times, however, you may want to supply your own extension. For example, suppose that the file mentioned previously, PRO_RRNT, contains confidential information. When you type the file name, you can use an extension of .CFL to indicate that the file is confidential. In this case, the name is typed as PRO_RRNT.CFL.

Caution:
To save more than one version of the same worksheet, be sure to give each version a different file name.

Sometimes when you are creating a 1-2-3 model, you may want to save more than one version of the model on disk. If you want to keep more than one version of the same file, you'll need to save the file under different file names because each time you save a file under an existing name, the old file is replaced by the new one.

Suppose that you have been working on a cash management worksheet and have already saved it under the name CASHMGT. When you save the worksheet again, the name CASHMGT appears as the default name. 1-2-3 displays the last file name as the default, to save you typing time and trouble.

If you want to create a new file name at this point, you have two options. You could simply type the new name (such as CASHMGT2) and press Enter. The easier method, however, involves modifying the default name displayed by 1-2-3. Because changing the name to CASHMGT2 requires only that you add one character to the default name, you simply press the space bar once to change to EDIT mode; then you press the Backspace key, type *2*, and press Enter.

As you can tell from the mode indicator, 1-2-3 is in EDIT mode. At this stage, you can make any changes just as though you were editing a label in a worksheet cell. 1-2-3 assumes that if you are not going to use the current file name, you will type a completely new file name. By using the space bar, however, you can make minor changes to the path specification or the file name for the worksheet.

Cue:
When changing a file name, use the space bar to change to EDIT mode; then edit the current file name.

If you use a hard disk system, you may want to save your worksheets on floppy disks as well as on the hard disk. To do this, after you've saved the worksheet on the hard disk, issue /File Save again. When you see the file name you have just saved (as the file on the hard disk), press the Esc key until the prompt Enter save file name: is the only thing remaining. Then type the drive designation for the floppy disk and the new file name. Before pressing Enter, make sure that you have placed the correct floppy disk in the drive.

Checking Disk Space before Saving

As you use 1-2-3, you'll notice that before long you have several worksheet files that take up significant disk space. Hard disk users have less to worry about than floppy disk users in this respect. No matter what type of system you are using, however, you need to keep track of the amount of disk space used by your files. Nothing is worse than getting the message Disk full after working on an important worksheet and attempting to save it.

You can get around this problem by using 1-2-3's /System command. Whenever you type /s from READY mode, 1-2-3 "steps aside" and displays the DOS prompt. (Even though the DOS prompt is displayed, 1-2-3 and your worksheet are still in memory.) At the DOS prompt, you can enter the DOS CHKDSK command to see how much space is available on your disk. You can also use the FORMAT command to format a new disk.

Cue:
Use the /System command and the DOS CHKDSK command to check disk space before attempting to save a large worksheet.

Hard disk users also can use /System to exit to DOS so that they can check and format disks. If your hard disk is almost full, you may want to erase old files after you ensure that you have made a proper backup.

When you are finished with the DOS operations, type *exit* to return to the 1-2-3 worksheet. Now you can save the model on which you were working.

Warning:
After using the /System command, do not start a memory-resident program before attempting to return to 1-2-3; you will lose your work.

One point to remember: When you use /System to exit to DOS, *do not* start any program from DOS that will alter memory, such as a memory-resident program. If you do, you won't be able to return to the 1-2-3 worksheet, and you will lose any work that you had not saved.

Retrieving Files

To call a file back into memory from disk, use the /**File Retrieve** command. Again, 1-2-3 displays a list of all files currently on disk with the extensions .WK1 or .WKS.

Whenever you need to choose a file name, 1-2-3 helps you by displaying a list of the files on the current drive and directory. If the file name you want is in the list, you can select it by moving the cursor to that name and pressing Enter. Otherwise, you can type in the file name you want.

Cue:

To get a full-screen display of file names, press F3 while 1-2-3 is showing the list of file names.

While 1-2-3 is displaying the list of file names, you can show a full screen of file names by pressing the F3 (Name) key. For example, if you press the Name key when the screen shown in figure 7.1 is displayed, you'll get the full-screen display shown in figure 7.2. You will also see the date, time of creation, and file size of each file highlighted by the cell pointer.

Fig. 7.2

Full screen display of file names.

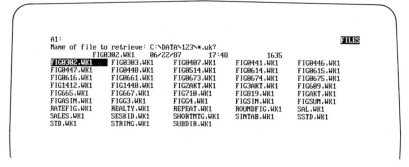

Using Wildcards for File Retrieval

When you are retrieving files, 1-2-3 allows the use of *wildcards*. These wildcards, the asterisk (∗) and the question mark (?), are helpful when you need to limit the number of files displayed on-screen or when you are unsure of the exact spelling of a file you want to retrieve.

The asterisk (∗) wildcard can be used in place of any combination of characters; the question mark (?) wildcard stands for any one character. The asterisk can be used only when it follows other characters or is used by itself. Following these rules, the name INVWS-∗.WK1 is acceptable, but ∗WS-06.WK1 is not. The question mark, on the other hand, can be used in any character position. Therefore, instead of the incorrect retrieval name ∗WS-06.WK1, you could enter ???WS-06.WK1.

Earlier in this chapter, we named an inventory worksheet INVWS-06 and then created several files that were named similarly and contained similar information. The additional files were named INVWS-07.WK1 and INVWS-08.WK1. If you want to use a wildcard character to retrieve these files, you can enter one of the following names in response to the prompt `Name of file to retrieve`:

INVWS-*.WK1
INVWS-??.WK1

Either of these names will retrieve the files you want. Similarly, to list all confidential files that have the extension .CFL, you can type *.CFL for the file name. All files with the .CFL extension will be listed.

Retrieving Files from Subdirectories

1-2-3 keeps track of subdirectory names as well as file names. These names are displayed in the current directory, with the subdirectories distinguished from files by the backslash (\ ) that appears after the subdirectory name (see fig. 7.3).

Fig. 7.3

Subdirectories in the current directory.

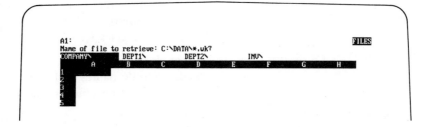

If you point to a subdirectory name and press Enter during a 1-2-3 file command, 1-2-3 switches to that subdirectory and displays a list of its files (see fig. 7.4). As you can see, the list includes any subdirectories of this subdirectory. You then can specify a file name in that subdirectory.

Fig. 7.4

Files in the selected subdirectory.

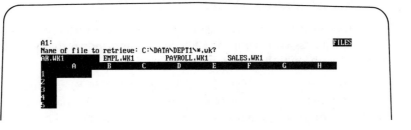

If you want to access a file on a different drive or in a directory that is not a subdirectory of the current directory, use the Esc key or the Backspace key. Pressing the Esc key once while the default path name shows on the control panel changes 1-2-3 to EDIT mode; you can then edit the file specification just as you would any label entry. Pressing the Esc key a second time erases the current drive and directory specification; you can then enter the specification for the drive and directory you want. (The /Worksheet Global Default Directory command is a small exception: for this command, the default path name appears on the control panel in EDIT mode; pressing the Esc key once erases the path name.)

Reminder:
Use the Backspace key to go to a higher level on the directory path; point to a name and press Enter to go forward on the path.

You can use the Backspace key to erase the path name, one directory at a time. To reverse the process, select a subdirectory name from the list of files and then press Enter.

Some valid file names, drive, and directory specifications are

B:\SAMPLE1.WK1	Worksheet file on drive B:
C:\123\SAMPLE1.WK1	Worksheet file in subdirectory 123 on drive C:
C:\123\DATA*.PIC	List of all .PIC files in subdirectory DATA of subdirectory 123 on drive C:. 1-2-3 displays the list and waits for you to select a specific file name.
A:*.*	List of all files on drive A:. 1-2-3 displays all file names and waits for you to select a specific file name.

If you want to find out more about DOS path names and subdirectories, you can consult *Using PC DOS* and *MS-DOS User's Guide*, 2nd Edition, both by Chris DeVoney; and *Managing Your Hard Disk*, by Don Berliner with Chris DeVoney; all published by Que Corporation. For more information on using 1-2-3 with subdirectories, see Appendix B.

Protecting Files with Passwords

You can protect your files by using 1-2-3's password protection system. You can create a password with the /File Save command so that your file can be retrieved with only the exact password.

To create a password, begin by selecting the /File Save command. At the Enter save file name: C:*.wk1 prompt, type the file name, leave a space, and then type *p*, as shown in figure 7.5. After you press Enter, you will see a password prompt; type your password and press Enter again. 1-2-3 then asks you to Verify password; type the password once more (see fig. 7.6). Any difference between the first and second passwords will result in nonacceptance.

Fig. 7.5

Indicating that a password will be entered.

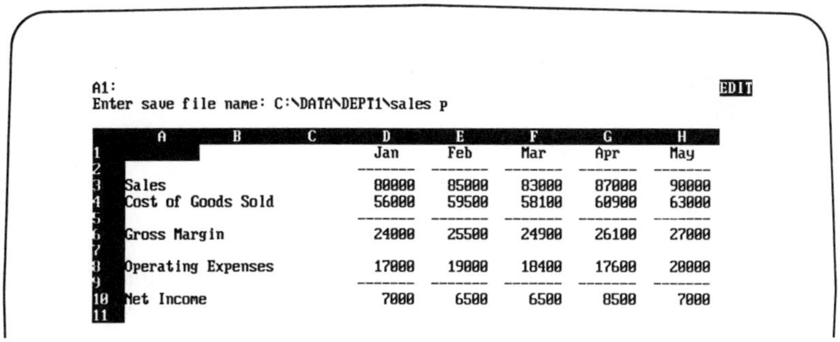

Fig. 7.6

Verifying the specified password.

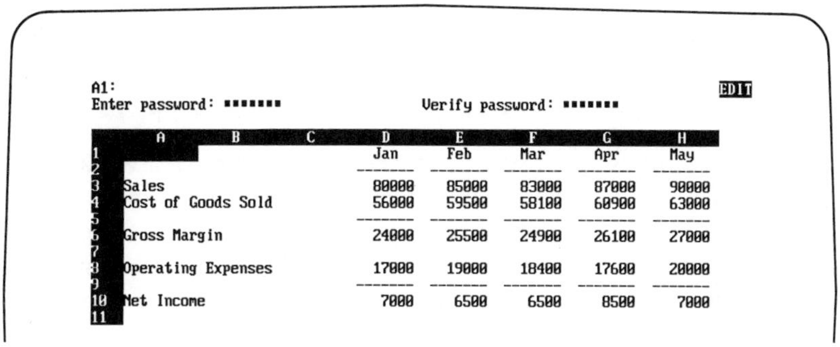

After you issue /**File Retrieve** and enter your password correctly, the worksheet will appear. But if you enter the password incorrectly, the words In-correct password will appear in the lower left corner of the screen, and the mode indicator will flash ERROR. Press Esc to return to a blank worksheet.

1-2-3 will accept any LICS character in a password, which can be as many as 15 characters long. You need to be careful, however, because 1-2-3 will accept the password only in the exact uppercase or lowercase letters you entered. For example, if you entered *pdfund* as your password, 1-2-3 would not retrieve the file if you typed *PDFUND* or *PDfund* or any other combination of uppercase and lowercase letters. Be sure not to forget your password.

Reminder:
To access a protected file, you must enter the password exactly.

You can delete a password by retrieving the file with the password you want to delete. Then, when you are ready to save the file, select the /**File Save** command. When the prompt appears, erase [PASSWORD PROTECTED] by pressing the Backspace or Esc key (see fig. 7.7). Proceed with the /File Save operation, and 1-2-3 will save the file without the password.

Fig. 7.7

*Removing
password
protection.*

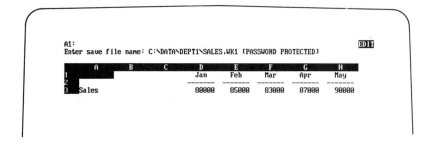

A1:
Enter save file name: C:\DATA\DEPT1\SALES.WK1 [PASSWORD PROTECTED]   EDIT

	A	B	C	D	E	F	G	H
				Jan	Feb	Mar	Apr	May
1								
2								
3	Sales			80000	85000	83000	87000	90000

To change a password, complete the first three steps for deleting the password name. After you have deleted [PASSWORD PROTECTED], press the space bar, type *p*, and press Enter. At this point, 1-2-3 will prompt you for a new password and ask you to verify it. Once you have completed these steps and saved the file, the new password will be stored.

Saving and Retrieving Partial Files

There will be times when you want to store only part of a worksheet (a range of cells, for instance) in a separate file on disk. For example, you can use the /File Xtract command to extract outlays from an expense report or revenues from an income statement. One of the best uses for a partial save is breaking up worksheet files that are too large to be stored on a single disk.

Conversely, you may have several worksheets with similar information. Suppose that you own a store in which each department is its own profit center. At the end of the month, you may want to combine each department's worksheet to get the overall picture of the store's profit and loss. The /File Combine command can be used to perform these operations.

Extracting Information

With the /File Xtract command, you can save part of the worksheet file—either the formulas existing in a range of cells or the current values of the formulas in the range, depending on the option you select. Both options create a worksheet file that can be reloaded into 1-2-3 with the /File Retrieve command. If you decide to save only the current values, however, the resulting worksheet file will contain numbers but no formulas. Selecting the Formulas option creates a file with all of the formulas intact.

The /**File Xtract** command requires also that you specify the portion of the worksheet you want to save. The range to be saved can be as small as a cell or as large as the entire worksheet. For example, consider the amortization table shown in figure 7.8. Suppose that you want to make a graphic comparison of one year's interest and principal payments for three different loans. Your Xtract range would be A28..G39.

Reminder:
/ File Xtract saves the formulas or the values from a specified range.

Fig. 7.8

Using /File Xtract on an amortization table.

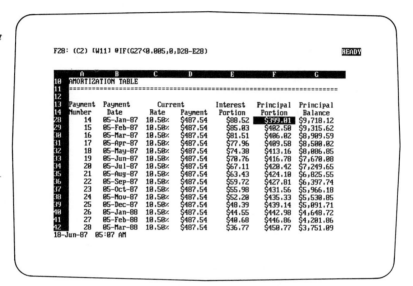

When you use the **Values** option with the /**File Xtract** command, you can "lock" the current values in a worksheet. To lock the values, issue the command and select the **Values** option. Next, specify the portion of the worksheet you need as the range to extract. You can select the entire worksheet as your range, if necessary. This will save the current values stored in the worksheet. You can think of this as taking a snapshot of the current worksheet.

The new, values-only file can be reloaded into the worksheet and printed or graphed, as previously mentioned. Figure 7.9 shows what the extracted portion of the worksheet looks like after it has been retrieved. If you compare the entry in the control panel with the same entry in figure 7.8, you can see that the calculated value has replaced the formula.

/**File Xtract Formulas** preserves any formulas that are in the extract range. This option can be particularly useful if your worksheet is too large to fit on one disk, because you can split the file across two disks and still preserve the formulas you need.

Cue:
Use / File Xtract Formulas to save a file that is too large to save on one disk.

Fig. 7.9

The extracted portion of the amortization table.

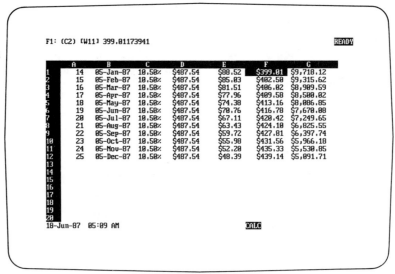

/File Xtract Formulas works like the /Copy command; formulas reference cells relative to their position. If you specify absolute addresses with Xtract, however, the formulas still use relative addressing. For example, if you extract the range E5..E10, the new file contains this range in A1..A6; any formulas in E5..E10 will appear in the extracted file with cell references relative to A1..A6, even if you specified absolute addresses. The absolute addressing specifications are extracted to the new file, however, and the cell references will be treated as absolute addresses in their new context.

Combining Files

Another function you will want to perform is that of making copies of certain ranges of cells from other worksheets and placing them into strategic spots in the current worksheet. For example, if you work for a large firm, you may want to combine several divisions' balance sheets and income statements in one consolidated worksheet.

Cue:
Use /File Combine to create a consolidated worksheet.

A simple technique for accomplishing this kind of consolidation is to start with and keep a copy of an "empty master." You will always have an empty master ready when it is time to perform a consolidation. When you start with an empty master, you can copy the first divisional worksheet onto the master, leaving the original copy of the divisional worksheet untouched.

Copying a range of cells can be helpful also when you want to combine quarterly data into a yearly statement. Again, the formats must be compatible, and you will benefit by keeping an empty master.

The command used to combine data in the preceding examples is /File Combine. This command gives you the following menu options:

Copy
: Pulls in an entire worksheet or a named range and causes the new contents to write over the corresponding cells in the existing worksheet. Cells in the worksheet that correspond to empty cells in the file or range being combined are not affected. (There is an important distinction here between empty cells and cells containing a blank in the combine file.)

Add
: Pulls in the values from an entire worksheet or a named range and adds these values to the corresponding cells in the current worksheet. The Add command affects only cells in the worksheet that are blank or contain numeric values. Cells containing formulas or labels are unchanged. Cells in the file being combined that contain labels or string formulas are not added.

Subtract
: Pulls in an entire worksheet or a named range and subtracts the values from the corresponding cells in the current worksheet. When an existing cell is empty, the incoming value is subtracted from zero. Like Add, Subtract affects only cells in the worksheet that are blank or contain numeric values. Cells containing formulas or labels in the current worksheet are unaffected, and cells from the worksheet being combined that contain labels or string formulas are not subtracted.

The specified worksheet or named range is combined into the current worksheet, with the current position of the cell pointer as the upper right corner of the combine range. For example, if the cell pointer is at cell A1, the specified worksheet or named range will be combined into the current worksheet, starting at cell A1. If the cell pointer is at cell AA100, the worksheet or range will be combined into the current worksheet, starting at cell AA100. Before you combine a range from another worksheet, be sure that your cell pointer is in the proper cell. Whatever is being copied, added, or subtracted will overwrite data that is currently in your worksheet.

When you use the /File Combine Copy command with worksheets or named ranges containing formulas, the cell references in those formulas are adjusted relative to the cell pointer location where the worksheet or range is combined, including absolute cell references. After the combining has been completed,

Reminder:
When you copy with /FCC, all cell references in formulas (even absolute references) are adjusted relative to their position in the new file.

the absolute cell references in cells that were combined into the current worksheet behave normally when you copy or move those cells.

Figures 7.10, 7.11, 7.12, and 7.13 show examples of the **Copy** and **Add** options. Figure 7.10 shows a worksheet that we created and stored on disk. Figure 7.11 shows a similar worksheet that is stored in 1-2-3's memory. Figure 7.12 shows the results of combining these two worksheets, using the **Copy** option with the cell pointer in A1. Notice that the copied range completely replaced the previous worksheet. Figure 7.13 shows the results of combining these two worksheets with the **Add** option, with the cell pointer in A1. The **Subtract** option is so much like the **Add** option that we did not include it here.

Fig. 7.10

Worksheet for /File Combine.

D3: 80000 READY

	A B C	D	E	F	G	H
1		Jan	Feb	Mar	Apr	May
2		--------	--------	--------	--------	--------
3	Sales	$80,000	$85,000	$83,000	$87,000	$90,000
4	Cost of Goods Sold	$56,000	$59,500	$58,100	$60,900	$63,000
5		--------	--------	--------	--------	--------
6	Gross Margin	$24,000	$25,500	$24,900	$26,100	$27,000
7						
8	Operating Expenses	$17,000	$19,000	$18,400	$17,600	$20,000
9		--------	--------	--------	--------	--------
10	Net Income	$7,000	$6,500	$6,500	$8,500	$7,000

Fig. 7.11

Another worksheet for /File Combine.

D3: 100000 READY

	A B C	D	E	F	G	H
1		Jan	Feb	Mar	Apr	May
2		--------	--------	--------	--------	--------
3	Sales	$100,000	$120,000	$130,000	$150,000	$160,000
4	Cost of Goods Sold	$78,000	$96,000	$112,000	$120,000	$123,000
5		--------	--------	--------	--------	--------
6	Gross Margin	$22,000	$24,000	$18,000	$30,000	$37,000
7						
8	Operating Expenses	$15,000	$16,000	$17,500	$18,000	$21,000
9		--------	--------	--------	--------	--------
10	Net Income	$7,000	$8,000	$500	$12,000	$16,000

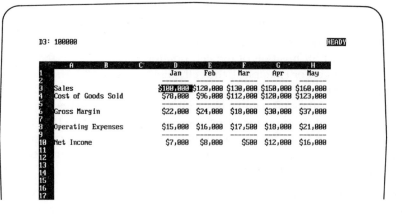

Fig. 7.12

Worksheet after /File Combine Copy.

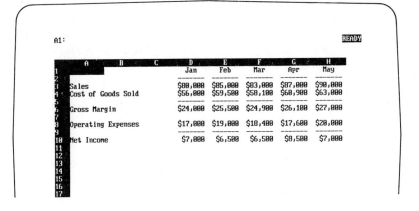

Fig. 7.13

Worksheet after /File Combine Add.

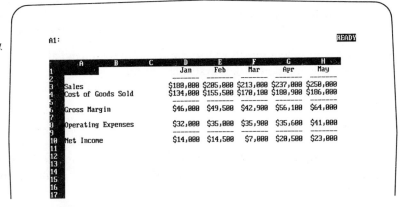

All three options (**Add**, **Subtract**, and **Copy**) are useful in combining worksheets. The **/File Combine Add** command, which can be used to consolidate one worksheet with another, is especially helpful. For example, /FCA could be used by a business with several divisions to consolidate the income statements for each division into a company-wide statement.

Deleting Files

When you save files to disk, you may sometimes find that the disk is full. To alert you, 1-2-3 flashes the message Disk full in the lower left corner of the screen. You can then either swap disks or delete one or more of the current files occupying space on the disk.

There are two ways to delete stored files in 1-2-3. The first way is to use the /File Erase command. When you issue /FE, a menu prompt will ask whether you want to erase a **Worksheet**, **Print**, **Graph**, or **Other** file. According to your choice (**W**, **P**, or **G**), 1-2-3 will show you only .WK1 files (created in Release 2) or .WKS files (if created in Release 1 or 1A), .PRN files, or .PIC files, respectively. If you choose **Other**, 1-2-3 will list all files. You can point to the file you want erased, or type its name and press Enter.

You can use the wildcard characters mentioned earlier to display all the files of a certain type that are to be deleted. These are the same wildcard characters used for DOS and other commands throughout 1-2-3, and they should look familiar. The following list shows some examples of using wildcard characters:

*   Matches the remaining characters of a file name. B* matches BOB, BARNEY, BOQUIST, etc.

?   Matches all characters in a single position in a file name. B?RD matches BARD, BIRD, and BYRD, but not BURT.

Warning:
Without a special utility program, you cannot recover information from a file that you have erased.

Be careful when you use the /File Erase command. Once a file has been deleted, that file cannot be recovered by conventional means. Always check and double-check that you really want to delete a file before you do so.

Another way to delete files is to use the /System command and the DOS DEL command. This method makes available the full power of DOS, but requires more time to suspend 1-2-3 execution, perform the DOS command, and return to 1-2-3.

SuperCalc users will recall that the command to format a single cell in SuperCalc is /FE. Because this same command in 1-2-3 begins the process of erasing a file, think twice about whether you should try to use the command to format a cell. There is a confirmation step to the /FE command in 1-2-3, but be careful.

Specifying a Drive

You use the /Worksheet Global Default Directory command to change the default drive and directory. Hard disk users can use the default directory setting to their advantage. For example, directories may be set up as shown in the diagram in figure 7.14. The default directory could then be set to C:\DATA. When a file is to be retrieved, the subdirectories \DATA\DEPT1, \DATA\DEPT2, and \DATA\COMPANY are displayed. After you've chosen the proper directory, the files stored in that directory are displayed again so that you can make a choice. Setting the default directory this way will save time if you use worksheets in different subdirectories.

There may be times, however, when you will want to override this setting temporarily. You may, for example, be doing a considerable amount of ex-

Fig. 7.14

Diagram of possible hard disk directories.

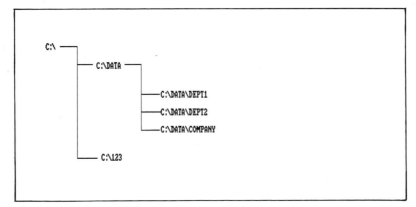

tracting, combining, and retrieving in one particular subdirectory on the hard disk. The /File Directory command lets you specify another drive for the duration of the current session.

Cue:
Use the /File Directory command to temporarily override the default directory.

If you're using a system that has two disk drives, you normally change the /Worksheet Global Default Directory setting to B:\ (Lotus sets the default to be A:\). This means that the root directory of drive B: is the active disk drive and directory for storing and retrieving files.

Listing Different Types of Files

1-2-3 can list all the names of a certain type of file on the active drive and directory with the /File List command. The choices for file types are

   Worksheet   Print   Graph   Other

Worksheet, **Print**, and **Graph** list the three types of 1-2-3 data files. The fourth choice, **Other**, lists all files of all types on the current drive and directory.

Which drive is the active drive depends on the /Worksheet Global Default Directory setting and whether that setting has been overridden by the /File Directory command. For a hard disk system, in which the default setting is C:\DATA\123\, a list of worksheet files might look like figure 7.15.

Transferring Files

A powerful feature of 1-2-3 is its capacity to interface with outside programs. To do this, you use the /File Import and /Print File commands or the Translate Utility. Although the kinds of files that can be transferred with these techniques are limited, this is only a minor setback because most files can be converted

Fig. 7.15

A list of 1-2-3 files with /File List.

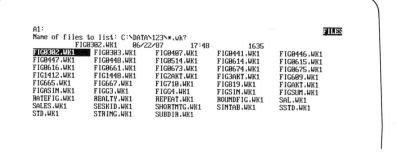

to the proper format one way or another. The following methods work well and, with a few small exceptions, are easy to use.

If you are an applications developer, Lotus provides you with an additional method of handling external files with 1-2-3's sequential file macro commands (see Chapter 15).

Transferring Files with /File Import

The /File Import command is used to copy standard ASCII files to specific locations in the current worksheet. .PRN (print) files are one example of standard ASCII text files. (.PRN files and their uses are covered in Chapter 9.) Other standard ASCII files include those produced by different word-processing and BASIC programs.

Figure 7.16 shows an example of an ASCII file. Notice that text is enclosed in quotation marks but that values are not. Notice also that each "field" is separated, or *delimited*, with commas.

Fig. 7.16

An example of a delimited ASCII file.

```
"Part Name","Part Number","Qty","Cost","Retail"
"Hammer","H0101",12,1.95,3.99
"Wrench","W0998",15,3.25,5.99
"Standard Screw Driver","S0099",30,1.07,1.99
"Phillips Screw Driver","S0101",25,1.27,2.09
"Hack Saw","00201",5,4.22,6.99
"Jig Saw","10020",5,22.94,29.99
```

To import the file in figure 7.16 into the current worksheet, you start by placing the cell pointer in the upper left corner of the range into which the data is to be imported and specifying /File Import. You then specify Text, and type the name of the file to import. Your worksheet should look like the one shown in figure 7.17. Notice that each line is imported as a long label and that the quotation marks and commas are imported as well.

Fig. 7.17

*ASCII file imported
into the worksheet.*

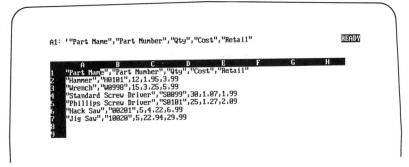

If you import the file as **Numbers**, it will look like the file shown in figure 7.18. Notice that no quotation marks or commas were imported and that each field is now contained in its own cell.

Fig. 7.18

*The ASCII file
imported as
Numbers.*

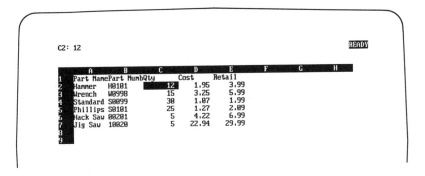

Generally, you should use the **Text** option for importing an ASCII file that was created with your word processor and that you want to use as documentation to create a report. Use the **Numbers** option when you import a delimited file. Remember that if you import a file with **Numbers**, any column headings that aren't enclosed in quotation marks will not be imported. Headings that are enclosed in quotation marks will be imported as labels.

Cue:
*Use the Text option
to import word-
processing files;
use the Numbers
option to import
ASCII delimited
files.*

ASCII files sometimes contain information in SDF format. If the information in figure 7.16 had been in SDF format, the file would look like the one shown in figure 7.19. ASCII files in SDF format should be imported as **Text**. The /**Data Parse** command can then be used to place each field in its own cell. (See Chapter 13 for an explanation of the /**Data Parse** command.)

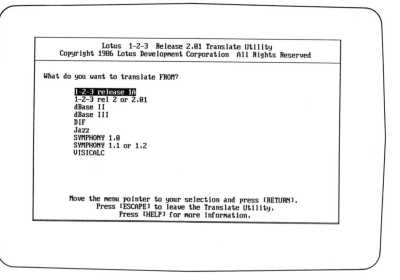

```
Part Name            Part Number  Qty    Cost   Retail
Hammer               H0101         12    1.95   3.99
Wrench               W0990         15    3.25   5.99
Standard Screw Driver S0101        30    1.07   1.99
Phillips Screw Driver S0101        25    1.27   2.09
Hack Saw             00201          5    4.22   6.99
Jig Saw              10020          5   22.94  29.99
```

In the early versions of 1-2-3, the /File Import command was used to import records from dBASE to 1-2-3. In Release 2, dBASE files can be transferred with the Translate Utility.

Transferring Files with the Translate Utility

The Translate Utility is used to import files from dBASE II, dBASE III, dBASE III Plus, and VisiCalc into 1-2-3, and to export 1-2-3 files in dBASE II, dBASE III, dBASE III Plus, and DIF formats (see fig. 7.20). This feature provides good communication with dBASE, including dBASE III Plus (which is not listed on the menu but can be accessed by selecting dBASE III). The Translate Utility also provides translation capabilities between all of Lotus's products, allowing free interchange of worksheets between 1-2-3 Release 2.01 and Symphony, Jazz, and earlier releases of 1-2-3.

Fig. 7.20

The Translate Utility screen.

```
              Lotus  1-2-3  Release 2.01 Translate Utility
        Copyright 1986 Lotus Development Corporation  All Rights Reserved

What do you want to translate FROM?

        1-2-3 release 1A
        1-2-3 rel 2 or 2.01
        dBase II
        dBase III
        DIF
        Jazz
        SYMPHONY 1.0
        SYMPHONY 1.1 or 1.2
        VISICALC




        Move the menu pointer to your selection and press [RETURN].
              Press [ESCAPE] to leave the Translate Utility.
                 Press [HELP] for more information.
```

If you are an advanced user, you may also want to export your 1-2-3 worksheet files in DIF format for use with other programs that can accept data in DIF format. Many presentation graphics packages, for example, accept data in DIF format. The Translate Utility allows you to take advantage of the more advanced statistical and plotting capabilities of these programs.

Basically, the Translate Utility involves the following steps:

1. Choose the format (program) from which to translate.

2. Choose the format (program) to translate to.

3. Choose the file from which to translate.

4. Type the name of the file to be created.

When you choose a file name, Translate gives you a list of files from which to choose, based on your choice of format. (As a format choice, for example, you may have chosen *.WK1 for 1-2-3 Release 2.0 or 2.01 or *.DBF for a dBASE file.) You can then choose one of the displayed file names or you can press Esc to edit the subdirectory or file name.

As you begin the translation process, an indicator appears on the screen, informing you of the progress of the translation.

Transferring Records between dBASE and 1-2-3

Aside from the obvious advantage of 1-2-3's spreadsheet capability, the primary reason to transfer dBASE records to or from 1-2-3 is that 1-2-3's data-sorting and querying capabilities are much faster and more easily implemented. If a database is large, only a portion of it can be imported because of 1-2-3's limitation on worksheet size. For small to medium-sized files that will be sorted and accessed frequently (such as address lists, telephone numbers, personnel files, etc.), there is a real advantage to using 1-2-3 over dBASE.

Lotus has put the Translate Utility to work in both directions. You can load a dBASE database into 1-2-3, process the database, and then write the database back into dBASE to use with dBASE procedures and reports. Why would you want to do this? As you may already know, although dBASE is particularly good at finding and processing one record at a time, 1-2-3 is best at making changes to whole sets of records, using full-screen editing techniques; block copy, move, insert, and delete commands; and formulas. An experienced dBASE application developer may find these dBASE translation capabilities the most exciting part of 1-2-3.

Cue:
To perform block operations on dBASE records, translate the dBASE file into 1-2-3, use 1-2-3's processing methods, and then translate back to dBASE.

Translating from dBASE to 1-2-3

To translate a dBASE file to 1-2-3, you enter the Translate Utility and specify that you are translating from dBASE II or dBASE III to 1-2-3 (choose dBASE III to translate from dBASE III Plus). Next you enter the name of the drive, the directory or directories, and the source file, and then the file name of the 1-2-3 worksheet to be created from the dBASE data file (see fig. 7.21). Then the Translate Utility quickly performs the translation.

Fig. 7.21

Translating from dBASE III.

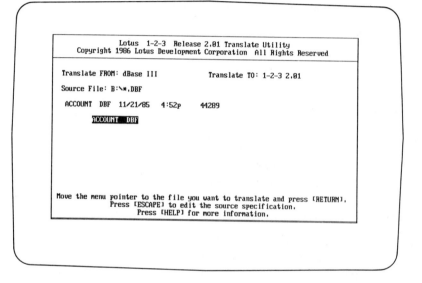

```
                 Lotus  1-2-3  Release 2.01 Translate Utility
        Copyright 1986 Lotus Development Corporation  All Rights Reserved

   Translate FROM: dBase III            Translate TO: 1-2-3 2.01

   Source File: B:\*.DBF

    ACCOUNT  DBF  11/21/85   4:52p      44289
          ACCOUNT   DBF




   Move the menu pointer to the file you want to translate and press [RETURN].
           Press [ESCAPE] to edit the source specification.
                  Press [HELP] for more information.
```

The translation is performed on dBASE records in the actual order they appear in the file, and only the first 8,191 records are translated. If you want the dBASE records from a file larger than 8,191 records or in some other order, you must sort or extract the records into another dBASE file before using the 1-2-3 Translate Utility.

The translation result is a 1-2-3 worksheet with one column for each field in the dBASE file. The first row of the worksheet holds the dBASE field names with column widths set to the widths of the dBASE fields. All the rows after the first row contain the data read from the dBASE file, one record per row, with the cells formatted according to the dBASE field specification. A dBASE character field changes to a 1-2-3 label, a dBASE numeric field translates to a number in fixed format, and a dBASE date field becomes a 1-2-3 date.

Translating from 1-2-3 to dBASE

You can translate an entire worksheet or just a named range in a worksheet to a dBASE file. To translate a worksheet or named range to a dBASE file, the worksheet must be in a specific format, corresponding closely to the way a dBASE file is translated to a 1-2-3 worksheet.

The field names must be located in the first row of the worksheet or named range. The remaining data, one record per row, should be placed in the second through last rows of the worksheet or named range. The values of any formulas in the worksheet or named range are translated to the dBASE file. The column widths in the worksheet establish the dBASE field widths, and the contents of the second row (the first row of data) establish the dBASE field types. Each cell in the second row, therefore, must hold a value or, if empty, be formatted. Watch out for second-row cells containing numbers that are not formatted. The number of decimal places displayed on-screen in 1-2-3 will determine the format of the dBASE field corresponding to this column.

Reminder:
Before you translate from 1-2-3 to dBASE, format the cells in the second row to establish the correct dBASE field type.

You can perform a translation from 1-2-3 to dBASE by selecting the Translate Utility and then specifying that you are translating from 1-2-3 to dBASE II or dBASE III (choose dBASE III to translate to dBASE III Plus). Next, enter the name of the drive, the directory or directories, and the file name of the 1-2-3 worksheet to be translated; and then enter the drive, directory or directories, and file name of the dBASE file to be created. The Translate Utility asks whether you want to translate the entire worksheet or just a named range, and then quickly performs the translation. Because the Translate Utility does not build or update dBASE index files, you must enter dBASE and rebuild any indexes after the translation is completed.

Lotus's Translate Utility offers a strong link between 1-2-3 worksheets and dBASE data files. A wish list for a perfect link would include direct links between the 1-2-3 worksheet and dBASE files by way of 1-2-3 commands. Ideally, these commands would allow you to create, index, and manipulate (directly from within the 1-2-3 worksheet) data in dBASE-formatted data files.

Using Lotus HAL To Simplify File Operations

As we have indicated throughout this book, Lotus HAL is a user-friendly interface for 1-2-3. By issuing simple English-style requests, you can perform 1-2-3 operations that would normally require a series of 1-2-3 commands. HAL is a memory-resident program that "pops up" over 1-2-3 when you press the backslash (\ ) key. This keystroke brings up HAL's request box, which appears in place of 1-2-3's control panel. Through this box, you communicate all your requests to HAL.

You can use HAL to perform the equivalent of 1-2-3's /File **R**etrieve, **S**ave, **L**ist, and **I**mport operations. In addition, HAL enhances 1-2-3's /File **C**ombine **A**dd command, which results in easier spreadsheet linking. In this section, we'll discuss HAL's four basic file functions, and then explain how you can use HAL to link spreadsheets.

Using HAL To Retrieve Files

HAL recognizes the following verbs for file retrieval operations: *retrieve*, *get*, and *load*. If you type any of these three words in HAL's request box, HAL will display a list of files in the third line of the control panel. You then have three options: typing a file name of up to eight characters and pressing Enter; selecting the file with the cursor-movement keys; or pressing F3 to display a full screen of file names. When the full screen of files is displayed, you use the cursor-movement keys to highlight the desired file; then press Enter. To retrieve a file, enter in HAL's request box either of the following requests:

    retrieve
    get incstmt

In response to the first request, which is similar to the /File **R**etrieve command, HAL displays in the third line of the control panel a list of spreadsheet files. The second request causes HAL to load the file INCSTMT into memory from the default disk and directory.

Using HAL To Save Files

With HAL, the operations of saving and retrieving files are similar. For saving files, HAL recognizes the verbs *file*, *keep*, *save*, and *store*. You then need to specify a file name by choosing an existing name (be careful—you may overwrite a needed file) or by entering a new file name. When you enter either of the following requests:

    file under incstmt
    save as budget88

into HAL's request box, the file will be saved successfully.

The first request causes HAL to save the file in memory to a file named INCSTMT.WK1 or INCSTMT.WKS, depending on which release of 1-2-3 you are using. Similarly, in the second request, HAL saves the current file under the name BUDGET88.WK1 or BUDGET88.WKS.

Using HAL To List Files

You can also use HAL to display your 1-2-3 file names. HAL displays your .WK1 (or .WKS), .PIC, or .PRN files when you begin a request with the verbs *directory*, *display*, and *list*.

The following HAL requests will list all the spreadsheet files in your current directory:

    dir
    display *.wk?

Similarly, you can use these requests to list all the graph files in the current directory:

    dir *.pic
    list pic

These requests list all the print (ASCII) files in the current directory:

    dir print
    display *.prn

Finally, HAL displays all files in the current directory when you issue the requests

    dir other
    list other
    display *.*

Using HAL To Import Files

Using HAL to import an ASCII file into a 1-2-3 spreadsheet requires a little more planning than a simple file-retrieve operation. First, although HAL's default is text, you can specify that the file be imported as numbers. Second, similar to standard 1-2-3 rules, the file can be up to 240 characters wide and 2,048 or 8,192 lines long, for Release 1A and 2, respectively. Third, because a copy of the print file will be imported into 1-2-3 at the current cell-pointer location, be sure to position the cell pointer at the desired spreadsheet location before executing the request. HAL recognizes the verb *import* at the beginning of a file-import request. The following HAL requests will import files as text:

    import products
    import list

The following HAL requests will import files as numbers:

    import data as numbers
    import sales as numbers

In addition, if you need to know all the ASCII file names in the current directory, the HAL request *import *.PRN* will create on-screen a list of all print files.

Using HAL To Combine Files

Another of HAL's enhancements to 1-2-3 is the capability of linking multiple spreadsheets. Linking spreadsheets helps you perform consolidations, uses less random access memory than one large spreadsheet, decreases the opportunity for spreadsheet errors, and enables you to quickly locate specific items in your applications.

HAL uses 1-2-3's \0 macro and /File Combine Add capabilities to link 1-2-3 spreadsheets. The cell to be linked in the current spreadsheet is the *target* cell, and the cell with the incoming value is the *source* cell. You can refer to the target and source cells by their cell addresses or range names, but you must follow this rule when using range names to link spreadsheets:

Source-cell range name + Source-file name < 13

In a request to link spreadsheets, HAL recognizes the verbs *attach*, *connect*, and *link*. The following are valid HAL link requests:

attach this cell to h20 in incstmt
connect b20 to b20..h20 in bal
link total to deprec in assets

After you create the link, you will want to make it permanent by saving the target spreadsheet. You can do this by using a HAL save request or /File Save. The next time you retrieve the spreadsheet it will automatically be updated by the source spreadsheet(s).

Keep in mind a few more rules as you use HAL's spreadsheet-linking feature. If you have a hard disk, the spreadsheets you want to link must be in the current directory, or HAL will flash an error message when you retrieve the spreadsheet with the target cells. Also, only one target cell or range can be linked to the same source cell at any one time. If you need to link multiple source cells or ranges to a single target cell or range, consider totaling target cells with @SUM. For example, you might have Division 1, 2, and 3's annual sales linked to rows five through seven in your spreadsheet and Total Sales in row nine.

In addition, if you are working with multiple linked spreadsheets, make sure that you've retrieved and saved all source spreadsheets before retrieving your target spreadsheet. Otherwise, the target spreadsheet may not have the most recent data. For example, consider the following example, in which a corporate financial statement is consolidated from divisional and plant results:

Corporate <=== Division <=== Plant

In a corporation-wide consolidation, you need to make sure that you've updated (retrieved and saved) the division-level spreadsheet. If you haven't, and you've made a change in the plant-level spreadsheet, the corporate consolidation will not reflect the most current financial data.

If you are working with a spreadsheet that is linked to other spreadsheets, you can make those links apparent by entering the following request:

show links

After you enter this request, HAL displays (three rows below the current table) a list of the link relationships. Because HAL puts the link information at that point, you must be careful if you have entered any data below the current table.

Finally, you can erase or remove a link by issuing a HAL *unlink* request and specifying a target-cell range or name. The following are valid HAL *unlink* requests:

unlink c10
unlink a20..g20
unlink total

HAL enables you to link 1-2-3 spreadsheets quickly and easily. Don't overlook this important feature of HAL as you plan and design your spreadsheets.

Using SQZ! To Compress Files and Assign Passwords

SQZ!, from Turner Hall Publishing, is a file-compression utility for 1-2-3 that can save you valuable disk space and speed up execution time when you are saving and retrieving 1-2-3 files.

SQZ! can be used on IBM PC, XT, AT, or compatible computers that have two floppy disk drives or one floppy and one hard disk drive. Because SQZ! is a memory-resident program that "pops up" over 1-2-3, your system must have a minimum of 256K.

The program has five options: four options that deal with file compaction and one that allows you to assign passwords to your files. When you want to activate SQZ!, you simply press the Alt key and the exclamation point (!). SQZ! responds by displaying the Status Window shown in figure 7.22.

Fig. 7.22

The SQZ! Status Window.

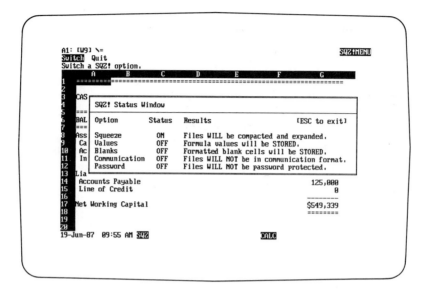

The SQZ! Status Window shows you the current status of each of the five options. You can then modify the settings by changing the status from ON to OFF or vice versa. The Results column shows what the status of each option means in relation to file operations.

The Squeeze option actually compresses the file. When this option is enabled and you save your worksheet file, SQZ! compacts the file as it is saved; when you retrieve the file, it expands to its original size. SQZ! saves the compressed file with the extension .WK! so that your .WK1 or .WKS files will not be altered or replaced.

The second option on the Status Window, Values, allows you to instruct SQZ! to save only the formulas on the worksheet. Normally, 1-2-3 saves both the formulas and the calculated values on the spreadsheet. The Values option can save you even more disk space by leaving out the values, but you must remember to press F9 to generate the values after you retrieve the file.

With the Blanks option, you can further compress a file by not saving blank cells. A formatted blank cell is a formatted cell that contains no data, labels, or formulas. Although you can save a significant amount of disk space with the Blank option, you should avoid using this option if your spreadsheet contains a data-entry area or macro that depends on blank, formatted cells.

The fourth option on the Status Window, Communication, formats a SQZ! file so that it can be transmitted over telephone or data lines. This option does not compress the file as much as the Squeeze option, but the file is compressed more than it would be if 1-2-3's /File Save command were used.

The Password option enables you to assign passwords to your spreadsheets. This option is particularly beneficial for users of 1-2-3 Release 1A; Release 2.0 and 2.01 users will need to remember that they can assign a password to a file by using either 1-2-3's or SQZ!'s password protection—but not both. One note of caution, however: If you use a password, make sure that you remember it. Otherwise, you won't be able to access your file.

SQZ! is a low-cost alternative to purchasing greater disk capacity. To show you how "compressed" a SQZ!-compressed file really is, we determined that Chapter 9, "Printing Reports," was originally a 42,517-byte file; now, after using SQZ!, the file uses a mere 11,730 bytes of RAM. That's a difference of 30,787 bytes. If you think that saving disk space or file-operation time is important, you'll find that SQZ! is an invaluable companion to 1-2-3.

Chapter Summary

1-2-3's file commands allow you to perform the basic operations of saving, retrieving, and deleting entire files. Although all other spreadsheet programs also perform these operations, 1-2-3 has even more to offer. You can store and retrieve parts of files, produce a list of all the files currently on a disk, and transfer files from other programs, such as Symphony and dBASE. All the file operations are effective and easy to use.

You have learned also about two powerful new 1-2-3 companion products: Lotus HAL and SQZ!. HAL enables you to communicate with 1-2-3 by using English requests instead of the 1-2-3 command menu. With SQZ!, you can compress your 1-2-3 worksheet files so that you save memory space and cut down on file save and retrieval time. Both of these products can help make your 1-2-3 file operations easier and more efficient.

Building a Model Spreadsheet: Hands-On Practice

This chapter will reinforce many of the concepts detailed in Chapters 1 through 7. As you work through this chapter, you will develop, store, retrieve, expand, and document the simple spreadsheet illustrated in figure 8.1.

Fig. 8.1

The CASHFLOW spreadsheet model.

```
          A         B              C           D           E           F
 1 CASHFLOW SCHEDULE
 2                               JAN         FEB         MAR         APR
 3        Collections on sales  $5,220.00   $6,280.00   $4,753.00   $6,721.
 4        New loans              1,000.00        0.00        0.00        0.
 5        Other inflows            375.50      730.00    2,358.00      439.
 6                              ----------  ----------  ----------  --------
 7 Total cash receipts           6,595.50    7,010.00    7,111.00    7,160.
 8
 9        Commissions paid         522.00      628.00      475.30      672.
10        Office expenses        4,860.20    5,374.00    5,677.00    4,982.
11        Loan/interest repayments    0.00        0.00    1,022.00        0.
12        Other outflows         1,400.60      987.00      127.00      658.
13                              ----------  ----------  ----------  --------
14 Total cash disbursements      6,782.80    6,989.00    7,301.30    6,312.
15
16 Cashflow excess (deficit)     (187.30)      21.00     (190.30)     847.
17
18 Beginning cash balance        1,100.80      913.50      934.50      744.
19 Ending cash balance            $913.50     $934.50     $744.20   $1,592.
20                              ==========  ==========  ==========  ========
21
22 Commission on cash collected    10.0%
```

Take a few moments to analyze the model. To keep typing to a minimum, we have included only a few general categories of cash receipts and cash disbursements in this model, which incorporates only six months of data. But in your own cashflow report, you can easily provide more detail by inserting additional rows and expanding the time period to a year.

The headings, cash receipts and cash disbursements titles, lines, and other subtitles are entered as labels. The numbers typed in the cash receipts (CR) and cash disbursements (CD) cells are assumed to be actual figures, already known to the user or calculated in another supporting schedule. If you were to expand and convert this spreadsheet to depict budgeted cashflows, the CR and CD figures could be generated by formulas. The formulas in this model produce the commissions paid, the CR and CD subtotals, the cash available, the beginning cash balances for all months but January, and the ending cash balances.

As you build this model, you will enter the three types of data, activate five of ten function keys, and use command sequences that start with 1-2-3's **Work-sheet**, **Range**, **Copy**, **Move**, and **File** options. (See the Command Menu map and the 1-2-3 Command Reference at the back of this book.)

Beginning To Build the Model

We will begin building the spreadsheet by establishing column-widths and formats for the CASHFLOW spreadsheet model. Then we will type the labels and the January values and enter the formulas for generating January subtotals.

Entering Labels

Before entering any data into the worksheet, first establish a 12-character global column width instead of the 9-character default width. After setting an individual width of 25 for column A, you will enter most of the labels (including the dashed lines) shown in figure 8.1. The labels will be automatically left-justified and displayed in the control panel with an apostrophe (') preceding the text. To right-justify a label as you enter it, precede the text with a single quotation mark ("). To center the cell contents, type a caret (^) before you type the label data. To enter the initial label contents in the CASHFLOW spreadsheet shown in figure 8.2, follow these steps (remember that boldface type indicates what keys should be pressed to execute the command):

1. Load the 1-2-3 program.

2. Access a blank worksheet with the screen in READY mode.

3. Select /**Worksheet** Global Column-Width **12**.

4. Position the cell pointer anywhere in column A.

5. Select /Worksheet Column Set-Width **25**.

6. Enter the following lines and text:

In cell:	*Enter:*
A1	CASHFLOW SCHEDULE
A3	Collections on sales
A4	New loans
A5	Other inflows
A7	Total cash receipts
A9	Commissions paid
A10	Office expenses
A11	Loan/interest repayments
A12	Other outflows
A14	Total cash disbursements
A16	Cashflow excess (deficit)
A18	Beginning cash balance
A19	Ending cash balance
B2	^JAN
B6	"----------
B13	"----------
B20	"==========

Note that each dashed line contains ten dashes.

Fig. 8.2

Initial label entry in column A.

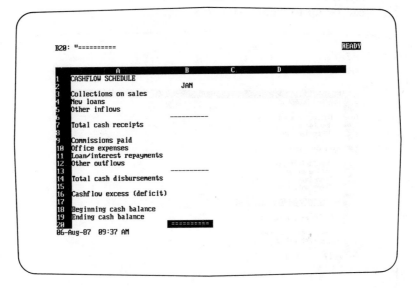

Now compare your spreadsheet to figure 8.2. If you made a mistake as you typed the cell contents, position the cell pointer on the cell containing the error and then retype the entry. (We will use EDIT mode, the alternative method for correction, later in this chapter.) If you typed an entry into a cell that should be blank, remove the unwanted entry by using /Range Erase and indicating which cell to erase.

To improve readability of the line-item descriptions, indent the individual CR and CD titles by inserting an extra column and moving all titles to the left (see fig. 8.3). To do so, follow these steps:

1. Position the cell pointer anywhere in column A.

2. Select /Worksheet Insert Column and press the Enter key.

3. Select /Worksheet Column Set-Width 3.

4. Select /Move. Enter **B1** as the FROM: range, followed by **A1** as the TO: range.

5. Select /Move. Enter **B7** as the FROM: range, followed by **A7** as the TO: range.

6. Select /Move. Enter **B14..B19** as the FROM: range, followed by **A14** as the TO: range.

7. Check to be sure that your screen matches figure 8.3.

8. Select /File Save. Enter **CASHFLOW** as the file name. (The file name can be up to eight characters long.)

Fig. 8.3

Label entry split between columns A and B.

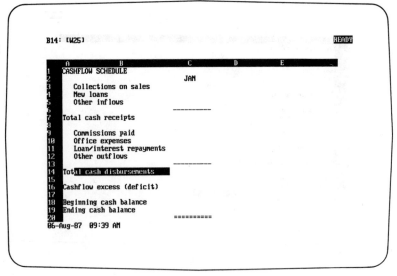

Periodically save your work! The Lotus program does not have an automatic save feature.

Because you have already saved your file, at this point you can do one of several things:

- /Quit 1-2-3

- Start to develop a new worksheet after having invoked the /Worksheet **Erase Yes** command sequence

- /File **Retrieve** a different file

- Continue working with the current CASHFLOW spreadsheet displayed on-screen

Let's continue to expand the current model.

Entering Numbers

Numbers will be right-justified automatically as you enter them in a spreadsheet. You need to determine the format of the numeric display for the worksheet as a whole or for any individual cells only if you want a format other than the default **General** format. (Refer to Chapter 5 for a complete presentation of the available options.)

For this model, we will establish comma (,) as the global format, **Currency** as the format for the first and last rows that display numbers, and **Percent** as the format for cell C22. Then we will add numeric data to the CASHFLOW spreadsheet. When this stage of the process is complete, your worksheet should look like the one in figure 8.4.

First, establish the spreadsheet formats by following these steps:

1. Select /Worksheet Global Format , (comma).

2. To complete the global format command, press the Enter key to accept the default 2 decimal places.

3. Select /**Range** Format **Currency 2**.

4. Specify **C3..H3** as the range to format the top numeric row.

5. Select /**Range** Format **Currency 2**.

6. Specify **C19..H19** as the range to format the bottom numeric row.

7. Select /**Range** Format **Percent 1**.

8. Specify **C22** as the cell to format.

Fig. 8.4

Number entry for
January.

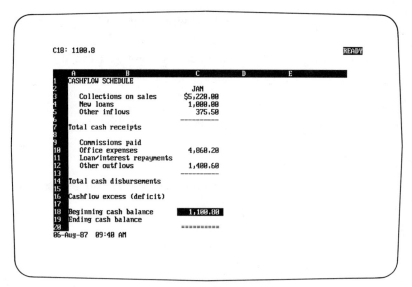

Fig. 8.4

Number entry for January.

Then enter the January values to the CASHFLOW spreadsheet by following these steps:

1. Enter the following numbers without commas or dollar signs.

In cell:	Enter:
C3	5220
C4	1000
C5	375.5
C10	4860.2
C12	1400.6
C18	1100.8

2. Select /File Save **CASHFLOW** Replace.

Your spreadsheet model now contains labels and numbers. To illustrate the power of an electronic spreadsheet compared to a hand-calculated one, you need to include one other type of input—formulas.

Entering Formulas and Deleting and Inserting Rows

1-2-3 calculates formulas automatically; you only need to specify which mathematical operations are to be performed and which cell locations will be involved in those operations. You create each part of a formula by either typing each cell address and mathematical operator involved, or by typing the math operators and pointing to the cells. You also can use 1-2-3's functions to automate common calculations. (Refer to Chapter 6 for a detailed discussion of functions.)

Take a moment to study figure 8.1 again. Suppose that, after having typed @SUM formulas for totaling the individual CR and CD with the initial spacing, you then decide to insert rows so that you can add new categories of receipts or disbursements. No problem! You can safely insert (and subsequently delete) rows or columns into (and from) formulas, provided that you do not disturb an end point of the formula range.

To insert two rows, so that your model looks like figure 8.5, follow these steps:

1. Position the cell pointer on cell C6.

2. Select /Worksheet Insert Row.

3. Press the ↓ once to highlight the range C6..C7; press the Enter key to complete the row insertions.

4. Enter the formula *@SUM(C3..C7)* in cell C9. Check the first nine rows on your screen to be sure that they match figure 8.5 and that cell C9 contains the correct sum.

Fig. 8.5

Inserted rows at the end of a formula range.

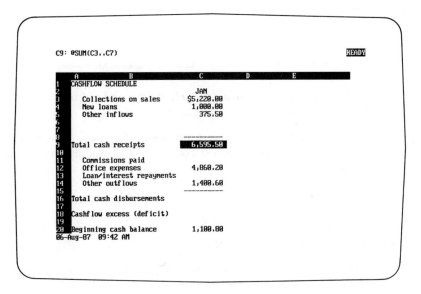

Now you will delete the inserted rows. Notice that the method you use to do so produces an ERR message (see fig. 8.6). Follow these steps:

1. Position the cell pointer on cell C6.

2. Select /**Worksheet** **Delete** **Row**.

3. Press the ↓ once to highlight the range C6..C7; press the Enter key to complete the row deletions.

4. Check the first seven rows on your screen to be sure that they match figure 8.6 and that cell C7 displays an ERR message.

Fig. 8.6

ERR result from deleting the end row of a formula range.

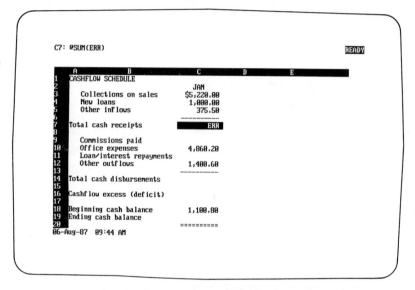

The ERR message occurs because you deleted the end point (C7) of the range used in the @SUM formula.

Repeat the entire process, but this time insert the extra rows in a different position (see fig. 8.7) and produce a correct @SUM calculation after deleting rows (see fig. 8.8).

To insert the rows

1. Position the cell pointer on cell C5.

2. Select /**Worksheet** **Insert** **Row**.

3. Press the ↓ once to highlight the range C5..C6; press the Enter key to complete the row insertions.

4. Enter the formula @**SUM(C3..C7)** in cell C9. Check the first nine rows on your screen to be sure that they match figure 8.7.

Fig. 8.7

Inserted rows avoiding the ends of a formula range.

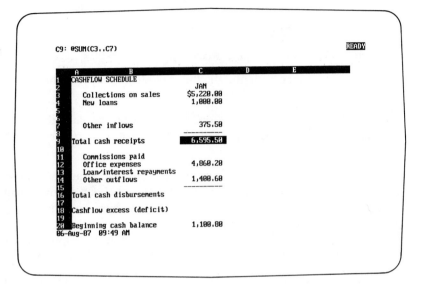

Fig. 8.8

Correct result deleting rows in a formula range.

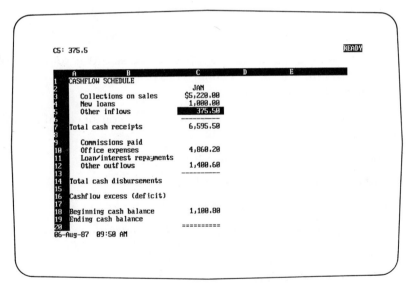

To delete the rows and produce a correct @SUM calculation

1. Position the cell pointer on cell C5.

2. Select /**W**orksheet **D**elete **R**ow.

3. Press the ↓ once to highlight the range C5..C6; press the Enter key to complete the row deletions.

4. Check the first seven rows on your screen to be sure that they match figure 8.8 and that cell C7 displays the correct result of @SUM.

You have not yet entered the numeric data for the January "Commissions paid." Let's assume that in this model the amount has been set by management as a percentage of each month's collections on sales, and that the current rate is 10%. That rate might change! You need to put data that may vary outside of the primary area of the worksheet, and reference the appropriate cell locations in any formula that includes the commission percentage figure.

In this illustration, put the percentage figure in cell C22 and reference cell C22 in the commissions-paid formula by following these steps:

1. Press the F5 (GoTo) key and respond **A22** to the request for an address.

2. Enter **Commission on cash collected** into cell A22.

3. Enter **.1** as the 10% commission figure in cell C22.

4. Enter **$C$22*C3** in cell C9. Check to be sure that your screen displays the calculated commissions-paid figure shown in cell C9 of figure 8.9.

To complete the January cashflow schedule, you need three additional formulas:

Total cash disbursements (in cell C14)

Cashflow excess (deficit) (in cell C16)

Ending cash balance (in cell C19)

To produce the results shown in figure 8.10, type the first two formulas:

1. Type **@SUM(C9..C12)** in cell C14.

2. Type **+C7-C14** in cell C16.

3. Check to be sure that your screen matches figure 8.10.

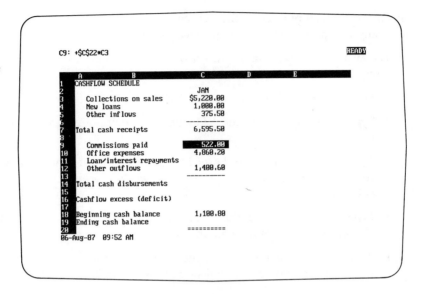

Fig. 8.9

Absolute and relative components of a formula.

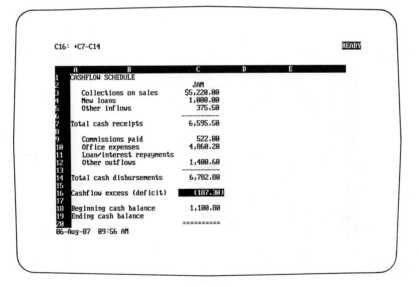

Fig. 8.10

Entering January formulas in cells C14 and C16.

Some people prefer using this "typing-only" method to enter relatively short formulas that contain only cells which are visible on the current screen. But as a general rule, a much safer way to enter formulas is the "type-and-point" method. In this method, you position the cell pointer where you want the formula to be entered; then type a plus sign, minus sign or open parenthesis, and move the cell pointer to the cell containing a value. Once you get used to typing and pointing, you may never enter a formula any other way!

To see what we mean, enter the third formula in cell C19 by typing and pointing:

1. Position the cell pointer on cell C19.

2. Type + and then press the ↑ key until the cell pointer rests on cell C16.

    Note: Do **NOT** press the Enter key while you create the formula; if you watch the control panel, you will see the formula being constructed.

3. Type + and then press the ↑ key until the cell pointer is on C18. The completed formula will appear in the control panel.

4. Press the Enter key to accept the +C16+C18 formula. Check to be sure that the ending cash balance figure is displayed in cell C19 on your screen (see fig. 8.11).

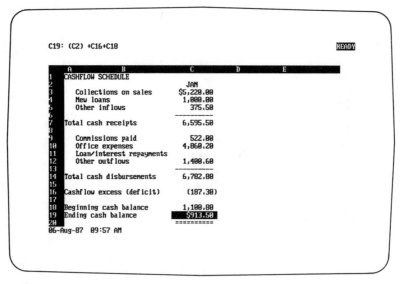

Fig. 8.11

Completing January formulas: cell C19.

You have completed the initial data entry for the CASHFLOW spreadsheet model. This section emphasized entering labels, numbers, and formulas for a single time period. The process involved using options from the **Worksheet**, **Range**, **Move**, and **File** submenus. In the following section, you will try other options from these submenus, work with the Copy command, and use additional function keys.

Expanding the Model

By setting up columns for 11 additional months of cashflow data, you can easily expand the spreadsheet model. To keep numeric entry to a minimum, you will add information for only February through June.

Refer once again to the total cashflow spreadsheet model shown in figure 8.1, and analyze the type of data entry needed to set up five additional months of information. The February through June headings (as well as the separating lines) must be entered as labels. You will enter all of the February through June CR and CD figures as numbers, with the exception of the commissions paid. To enter the beginning cash balance for February, you will specify the cell location of the ending cash balance for January. You will display all other figures by copying existing formulas or cell contents.

Typing Labels and the Remaining Numbers

Let's begin to expand the spreadsheet by entering the headings left-justified, using a single /Range command to center all the headings in the cells, and filling in the CR and CD numbers:

1. Enter the following headings in the appropriate cell locations:

In cell:	Enter:
D2	FEB
E2	MAR
F2	APR
G2	MAY
H2	JUN

2. Select /Range Label Center and enter **D2..H2** as the range of labels to center.

3. Enter the following numbers in the appropriate cell locations:

In cell:	Enter:
D3	6280
E3	4753
F3	6721
G3	5300
H3	4640
D4	0
E4	0
F4	0
G4	0
H4	800

D5	730
E5	2358
F5	439
G5	810
H5	478
D10	5374
E10	5677
F10	4982
G10	5222
H10	4891
C11	0
D11	0
E11	1022
F11	0
G11	0
H11	0
D12	987
E12	127
F12	658
G12	1500
H12	261

4. Check to be sure that your spreadsheet matches figure 8.12. Make any necessary corrections by retyping cell content.

Fig. 8.12

*Remaining
monthly headings
and numeric data.*

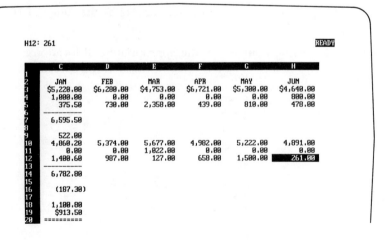

Now that you've finished the tedious job of entering data, you can use 1-2-3's Copy command to speed up the input of the remaining labels and formulas.

Copying Formulas and the Remaining Labels

At this point, you need separating lines at several additional places in rows 6, 13, and 20. Instead of entering each line as a separate label, you can copy the separating lines from cells C6, C13, and C20. The following steps show you the two methods for indicating the Copy FROM and the Copy TO ranges—typing cell addresses and moving the cell pointer.

1. Select /Copy and type **C6** as the range to copy FROM.

2. Complete the initial Copy command by typing **D6..H6** as the range to copy TO.

3. Position the cell pointer on C20 and select /Copy.

4. Press Enter to accept C20 as the range to copy FROM.

5. Press the → key once to position the cell pointer on D20. Then press the period (.) key to anchor cell D20 as the upper left corner of the range to copy TO. (D20..D20 appears after T0: in the control panel.)

6. Press the → key four times to highlight the range to copy TO. (D20..H20 appears after T0: in the control panel.)

7. Press the Enter key to accept D20..H20 as the TO: range.

8. Type or point to the ranges to copy from C13 to D13..H13. Or you might try copying from the range D6..H6 to the cell D13.

9. Check to be sure that your spreadsheet contains the separating lines in rows 6, 13, and 20 (see fig. 8.13).

In the next section, you will finish copying formulas in the spreadsheet. The FROM: and TO: ranges are provided, but step-by-step instructions to type or point the ranges in the Copy command are not included.

First, set a vertical title so that you will be able to keep the descriptions in columns A and B on the screen and still view the data for any month after March. Next, copy the formulas for January total CR (C7), Commissions paid (C9), total CD (C14), Cashflow excess (deficit) (C16), and Ending cash balance (C19) to the rest of their respective rows. Then set up and copy a formula to generate beginning cash balances based on the ending balance of the previous month.

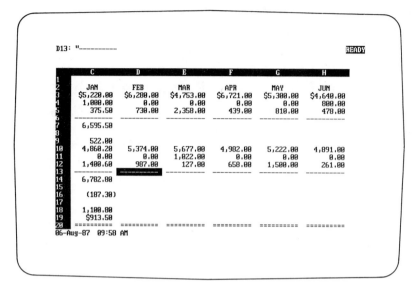

Fig. 8.13

Entering data by copying the separator lines.

Follow these steps:

1. Press the Home key and move the cell pointer to C1.

2. Select /Worksheet Title Vertical.

3. Enter +C19 in the FEB beginning cash balance cell (D18).

4. Execute six Copy commands, using the following ranges:

FROM:	TO:
C7	D7..H7
C9	D9..H9
C14	D14..H14
C16	D16..H16
D18	E18..H18
C19	D19..H19

5. Check to be sure that your screen displays the completed model, a portion of which is shown in figure 8.14.

6. Select /File Save **CASHFLOW** Replace.

Routine Maintenance of the Model

Now that your spreadsheet is complete, you will want to use it! You may need to update information by adding data or editing existing cell content.

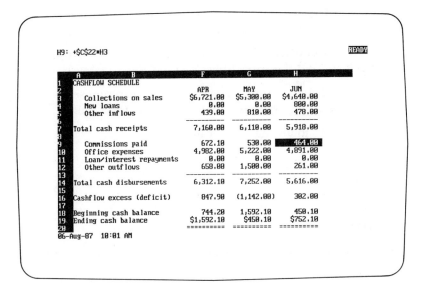

Fig. 8.14

Completing data entry by copying the formulas.

If you change numeric content that feeds into formulas, you may find that instant recalculation of every change slows down your editing session. As your spreadsheet increases in size, you may have difficulty remembering the cell coordinates for specific information. In this section, you will execute 1-2-3 commands with the aid of range names, invoke EDIT mode (the F2 key), and practice both manual and automatic recalculations.

Creating and Using Range Names

You have just completed a relatively small, simple worksheet with boundaries that extend beyond what can be seen on one screen. Most of the spreadsheets you develop on 1-2-3 will be even larger.

You can move the cell pointer quickly to any area in the worksheet by pressing the F5 (GoTo) key and responding with the appropriate cell location. Use the /Range Name command to define a cell or range of cells, and then specify the appropriate name when you use F5.

First, define several range names and then use these names with the F5 (GoTo) key and the F3 (Name) key to move the cell pointer quickly. Pressing the F3 key in POINT mode produces a menu of currently defined range names in alphabetical order. Complete the following steps:

1. Select /File Retrieve **CASHFLOW**, if the CASHFLOW spreadsheet is not the current worksheet.

2. Select /Worksheet Titles Clear so that you can move the cell pointer freely around the spreadsheet.

3. Select /Range Name Create; type **JUNE** in response to the request for a name; and type **H2** when prompted for a range.

4. Create the following range names:

Name:	Range:
COMM%	A22
CASHNET	A16
TITLE2	A24
TITLES	A1..B19

5. Press the F5 key. (Do not type a cell address response.)

6. Press the F3 key to access the list of range names.

7. Select any range name from the menu in the control panel.

8. Repeat the F5-F3 sequence and move to other defined ranges throughout the CASHFLOW spreadsheet.

9. Select /File Save **CASHFLOW R**eplace to store the range names as part of the CASHFLOW spreadsheet.

You can substitute a range name in any 1-2-3 operation that requires designation of a range. To copy TITLES to a blank area of the worksheet, follow these steps:

1. Select Copy and press the F3 key.

2. Select **TITLES** as the range to copy FROM.

3. Type **A24** as the range to copy TO. Make sure that the CASHFLOW titles have been copied to the range A24..B42.

Specifying a name by using the cursor-movement keys to move through the menu may be time-consuming if you have defined many range names. You can always type a range name, but you may not be sure that the spelling is correct or that the range name you indicate describes the location you need.

To simplify the process of specifying range names, you can create a table of range names within your worksheet. First, be sure that your worksheet contains enough blank cells to accept two columns of incoming data. Then follow these steps:

1. Select **/R**ange **N**ame **T**able.

2. Enter **C24** as the upper left corner of the table range.

3. Use the F5 (GoTo) key to move to cell C24. (Your screen should match the display in fig. 8.15.)

Fig. 8.15

Results of operations involving range names.

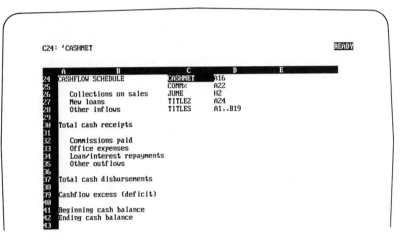

Using the F2 (Edit) Key

To alter data in the worksheet, simply retype the entire entry if the cell contents are relatively short or contain numerous errors. Otherwise, enter EDIT mode by pressing the F2 key. The following brief example illustrates the basic concepts of editing. You will change the heading from *JAN* to *January* and then restore it to its original spelling and position. To do so, follow these steps:

1. Enter **January** in cell C2.

2. Press the F2 key to bring the contents of cell C2 up into the control panel.

3. Press the Backspace key until only J remains.

4. Type **AN** and then press the Home key to bring the flashing cursor to the beginning of the entry you are editing.

5. Type ^

6. Press the Delete key to remove the apostrophe.

7. Press the Enter key to place the centered title in cell C2.

Recalculating the Model

If you change the contents of any cell while **Recalculation** is **Automatic** (the default), the worksheet will recalculate. For spreadsheets that are large and complex, recalculation may take a long time and you may want to change the **Recalculation** setting to **Manual**.

To show the effect of the different **Recalculation** settings, let's change the commission percentage in the CASHFLOW spreadsheet. First, we'll set up the screen display to keep monthly headings visible at all times and to show the June data as well as the January data. We will also hide the March, April, and May columns from display without removing the numbers from the calculations, as shown in figure 8.16.

Fig. 8.16

Rows 1 and 2 as a horizontal title on the screen.

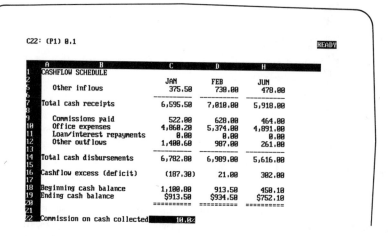

Follow these steps:

1. Press the Home key and position the cell pointer anywhere in row 3.

2. Select /Worksheet Titles Horizontal.

3. Select /Worksheet Column Hide.

4. Enter **E3..G3** as the range of columns to hide.

5. Position the cell pointer on C22, and then check your screen to be sure that it matches figure 8.16.

6. Change the contents of cell C22 to **.09** (instead of .1).

7. Check to be sure that your screen displays the recalculated figures for commissions paid (see row 9 of fig. 8.17).

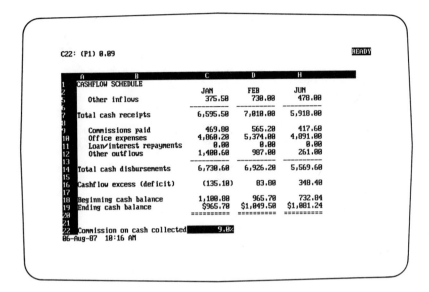

Fig. 8.17

Results of an automatic recalculation.

The 9% commissions-paid percentage is reflected in the ending cash balance for June ($1,081.24).

Before you restore the original 10%, use the following steps to set Recalculation to Manual. (If you change the contents of a cell while in Manual Recalculation, a CALC indicator will appear in the lower right corner of the screen to warn you that the necessary recalculation has not yet taken place.)

1. Select /Worksheet Global Recalculation Manual.

2. Enter **.1** in cell C22. (Note that the $1,081.24 in cell H19 still reflects a 9% commission rate, as illustrated in fig. 18.18.)

3. Press the F9 key to recalculate the worksheet and remove the CALC indicator. (Your screen should again match fig. 8.16.)

Even though the calculations are now correct for a 10% commissions-paid figure and the CALC indicator message has disappeared from the screen, recalculation is still set to Manual. (You cannot tell by looking at the screen whether the current recalculation mode is Manual or Automatic.)

Use the /Worksheet Status command to check the status of this global setting. Then restore Automatic recalculation, remove the frozen horizontal title, erase the extra set of titles and the table of range names, and display the hidden columns. To do so, use the following commands:

Fig. 8.18

The CALC *message that is displayed when recalculation is manual.*

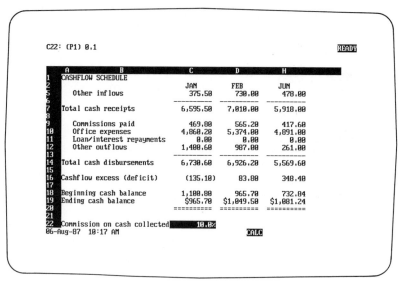

```
C22: (P1) 0.1                                                    READY

        A          B              C          D          H
    1  CASHFLOW SCHEDULE
    2                            JAN        FEB        JUN
    5         Other inflows     375.50     730.00     478.00
    6                         ---------  ---------  ---------
    7  Total cash receipts    6,595.50   7,010.00   5,918.00
    8
    9         Commissions paid   469.80     565.20     417.60
   10         Office expenses  4,860.20   5,374.00   4,891.00
   11         Loan/interest repayments  0.00     0.00       0.00
   12         Other outflows   1,400.60     987.00     261.00
   13                         ---------  ---------  ---------
   14  Total cash disbursements 6,730.60   6,926.20   5,569.60
   15
   16  Cashflow excess (deficit) (135.10)   83.80     348.40
   17
   18  Beginning cash balance  1,100.80     965.70     732.84
   19  Ending cash balance      $965.70   $1,049.50  $1,081.24
   20                         ==========  ========== ==========
   21
   22  Commission on cash collected    10.0%
   06-Aug-87  10:17 AM                           CALC
```

1. Select /**W**orksheet **S**tatus. Note that the Recalculation Method is Manual.

2. Press the Esc key to return to the spreadsheet.

3. Select /**W**orksheet **G**lobal **R**ecalculation **A**utomatic.

4. Select /**W**orksheet **T**itles **C**lear.

5. Select /**R**ange **E**rase **A24..D42**.

6. Select /**W**orksheet **C**olumn **D**isplay **E1..G1**.

7. Press the Home key and verify that the model matches the original figure 8.1.

8. Select /**F**ile **S**ave **CASHFLOW** Replace.

Protecting the Completed Model

A great deal of time and effort goes into developing, testing, and entering data into a model. Although you have saved your file on disk, and know that you should make an extra copy on another disk of important files, you may want to consider using some additional measures available in 1-2-3's **W**orksheet, **R**ange, and **F**ile options.

You can build protection into your worksheet, preventing entry into specified cells while permitting entry into others. You can extract all or part of the spreadsheet as values, so that the results of formulas (rather than the formulas themselves) will be stored. And you can extract the numeric fields from a completed model, leaving the labels and formulas to be stored as a blank model which can be used again. (Printing worksheet documentation is discussed in Chapter 9.)

Preventing Accidental Overwrite

The most recent version of your CASHFLOW file should match figure 8.1. Notice that the only cells you might want to change, to present a different year or variations of projected monthly cash movements, would be the CR and CD (except for the commissions paid). Once a model design has been developed and tested, be careful not to alter the labels and formulas.

Complete the following steps to selectively designate the ranges that you want to unprotect (C3..H5 and C10..H12), activate global protection for all remaining cells, check protection status, attempt to enter data in a protected cell, and restore the default protection settings:

1. Select **/Range** Unprotect **C3..H5**

2. Repeat the **/Range** Unprotect command and indicate the range **C10..H12**.

3. Select **/Worksheet** Global **Protection** Enable.

4. Select **/Worksheet** Status and note that global protection is On.

5. Press Esc to exit the status report.

6. Position the cell pointer on cell C7. Note that PR (protected cell) appears in the control panel.

7. Type **@SUM(C1..C5)** and press the Enter key. Note the mode change to ERROR and the message Protected cell in the lower left corner of the screen.

8. Press Esc to return to READY mode.

9. Select **/Worksheet** Global **Protection** Disable.

Preserving the Model on Disk

After you have created a spreadsheet and used it for a particular purpose, you may want to save the skeleton of the model for use with a different set of data.

One step you should take before saving the blank model is to save the data (with all current cell entries converted to values) of the current spreadsheet. To do this, use the following steps to extract all or part of your worksheet as values to a file with a different name (CASHDONE, in this example):

1. Select /File Retrieve **CASHFLOW** to display the CASHFLOW spreadsheet model that displays formula results (not the text of the formulas).

2. Select /File **X**tract **V**alues and enter **CASHDONE** in response to the prompt for a file name.

3. Enter **A1..H22** to indicate the range to be extracted. Wait for disk drive activity to cease.

If you retrieve CASHDONE, the screen will display the same values as CASHFLOW; but the cells that contain formulas in CASHFLOW will contain values in CASHDONE.

To create a blank model which you can reuse for other time periods, omitting all current numeric entry but retaining labels and formulas, follow these steps:

1. Select /File Retrieve **CASHFLOW** to view the CASHFLOW spreadsheet model that displays formula results (not text or values in place of formulas).

2. Make sure the cell pointer is located in cell A1; then select /File Combine Subtract Entire-File.

3. Enter **CASHFLOW** as the file to subtract.

4. Position the cell pointer on C7. Check your screen to make sure that it matches figure 8.19.

5. To save the file with the name MODEL, select /File **S**ave **MODEL**.

You can suppress the display of the zeros by using a /Worksheet Global Zero Yes command sequence. (Overwriting a formula cell by mistake is easy if you suppress the display of zeros. You may want to place global protection on a spreadsheet that is stored as a standard blank form.)

Chapter Summary

This chapter has given you hands-on experience with a spreadsheet—the powerful *1* of Lotus 1-2-3. You have entered and edited data, sometimes using Move and Copy commands. In addition, you have used five function keys and worked through examples of at least one option under every major submenu choice from the **W**orksheet, **R**ange, and **F**ile menus.

Fig. 8.19

Results of subtracting a file from itself.

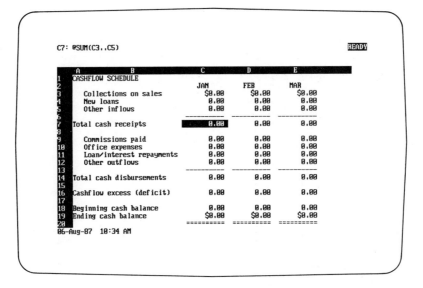

Continue to learn about 1-2-3 by using the program. Experiment with variations of menu choices that you have already practiced. For example, try your hand at using /Worksheet Window Unsync, which permits the two parts of a vertical or horizontal window to move independently of one another. Or try /File Combine Copy to bring a Named/Specified-Range from another file into a blank space in your current spreadsheet. Continue to experiment with other options. For example, you can try to /File List the files that you have stored.

Finally, don't forget to save your work frequently and often! In the following chapter, you will learn how to print your work.

Part II

Creating 1-2-3
Reports and Graphs

Includes

Printing Reports
Creating and Displaying Graphs
Printing Graphs
Creating Output: Hands-On Practice

Printing Reports

1-2-3 is a powerful tool for developing information presented in column-and-row format. You can enter and edit your spreadsheet and database files on-screen as well as store the input on disk. But to make good use of your data, you often need it in printed form: as a target production schedule, a summary report to your supervisor, or a detailed reorder list to central stores, for example.

By using 1-2-3's /Print command, you can access many sublevels of print options to meet your printing needs. You can elect to write directly from 1-2-3 to the printer by using the /Print Printer command sequence. Or use the alternate /Print File *filename* sequence to create a print (.PRN) file; later, you can produce a printout of the file from within 1-2-3 or from DOS, or you can incorporate the file into a word-processing file.

This chapter shows you how to

- Choose between /Print Printer and /Print File
- Print using default settings
- Print single or multiple pages
- Exclude segments within a designated print range
- Control paper movement
- Change the default settings
- Test the print format of large print ranges
- Print spreadsheet content cell-by-cell
- Prepare output for acceptance by other programs

321

Notice that printing graphs is not covered in this chapter, because you must use the PrintGraph program to print graphs; you cannot print them using the /Print command. Printing graphs is covered in Chapter 11.

Choosing Between /Print Printer and /Print File

You must start any /Print command sequence from 1-2-3's main menu. In figure 9.1, the Print option is highlighted on the control panel's second line; the third line explains the purpose of selecting the highlighted item.

Fig. 9.1

The menu for accessing a print operation.

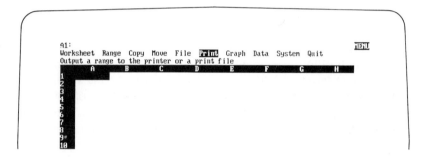

After initiating a /Print command from the main menu, you must select one of the two options shown in figure 9.2. To indicate that you want to use a printer on-line, choose Printer. Choose File to create a file on disk; later you can print the file from within 1-2-3 or incorporate it into a word-processing file.

Fig. 9.2

The initial print decision: print to the printer or to a disk file.

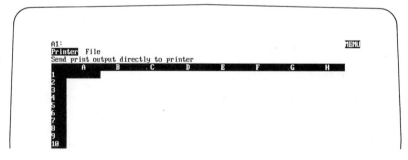

If you choose File, respond to the prompt for a print-file name by typing a name that is up to eight characters long. You don't need to add a file extension because 1-2-3 will automatically assign the .PRN (print file) extension. You can again incorporate the file into a 1-2-3 spreadsheet by using the /File

Import command, although the file will not be the same as your original worksheet file; imported .PRN files are all long labels. (**File Import** is discussed in Chapter 7.) You also can view a .PRN file by using the DOS TYPE command, a word-processor's print command, or a special printing routine.

After you select either **Printer** or **File**, the second line of the control panel will display the main **Print** menu (see fig. 9.3). This menu presents the following choices:

Menu Selection	*Description*
Range	Indicates what section of the worksheet is to be printed
Line	Adjusts the paper line-by-line in the printer
Page	Adjusts the paper page-by-page in the printer
Options	Makes available options to change default settings and enhance the appearance of the printout
Clear	Erases settings previously entered
Align	Signals the beginning of each page in the printer
Go	Starts printing
Quit	Exits the **Print** menu

Fig. 9.3

*Options on the main **Print** menu.*

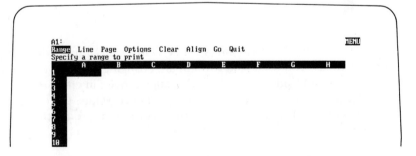

1-2-3 consistently positions the most frequently used (or least dangerous) command options to the left of a menu. In any /**Print** command sequence, you start with /**Print**, branch to either **Printer** or **File** *filename*, and proceed to a common main **Print** menu. Regardless of which branch you select, you must specify a **Range** to print, activate **Go**, and then select **Quit** to return to the worksheet. All other selections are optional.

Before you learn about specific selections from the **Print** main menu and submenu, you need a general understanding of 1-2-3's default print settings.

Understanding the Print Default Settings

To minimize the keystrokes necessary for a print operation, 1-2-3 makes certain assumptions about how you want your copy printed. The usual print operation produces 72 characters per line and 56 lines per page on 8 1/2-inch-by-11-inch continuous-feed paper, and uses the first parallel printer installed. You must know the current settings for your 1-2-3 program, however.

Current Printer Status

You should check the global default settings before you print. To do so, issue the /Worksheet Global Default command, which produces the menu shown in figure 9.4.

Fig. 9.4

The /Worksheet Global Default menu.

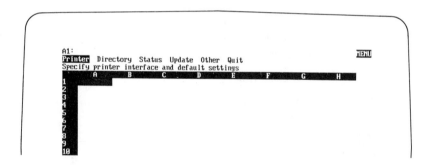

Three of the options in this menu (**Printer, Status,** and **Update**) directly pertain to print settings. You use **Printer** to initiate changing a setting for the current work session, and **Update** to make the change remain in effect every time you reload 1-2-3. To view the current settings, choose **Status**; the current printer settings will be displayed in a status report similar to that shown in figure 9.5.

Cue:

Use /WGD to check current default print settings.

The settings discussed in this chapter are in the upper left corner of the status screen: the first two settings contain hardware-specific information; the Margins and Page length sections show page layout; Wait...No is the setting for continuous-feed paper; no Setup string is in effect; and Name indicates which specific parallel printer is installed.

Fig. 9.5

A sample Global Default Status report.

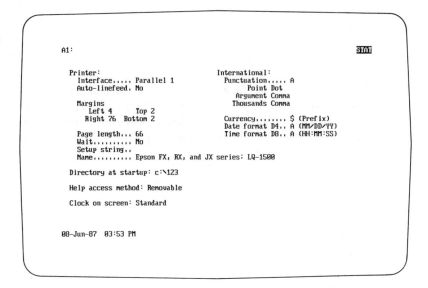

```
A1:                                                              STAT


        Printer:                         International:
            Interface..... Parallel 1        Punctuation..... A
            Auto-linefeed. No                      Point Dot
                                              Argument Comma
        Margins                           Thousands Comma
            Left 4      Top 2
            Right 76  Bottom 2            Currency........ $ (Prefix)
                                          Date format D4.. A (MM/DD/YY)
        Page length... 66                 Time format D8.. A (HH:MM:SS)
        Wait.......... No
        Setup string..
        Name.......... Epson FX, RX, and JX series; LQ-1500

        Directory at startup: c:\123

        Help access method: Removable

        Clock on screen: Standard


        08-Jun-87  03:53 PM
```

Global Default Hardware-Specific Options

If you want to change any of the print settings shown in the default status report, issue the /Worksheet Global Default Printer command. Notice that the first two options in the submenu shown in figure 9.6 are the same as the first two settings in the default status report: Interface and Auto-LF.

Fig. 9.6

The Global Default Printer submenu.

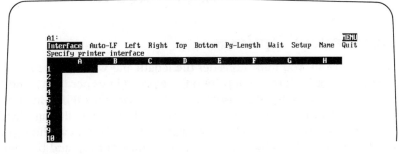

```
A1:                                                              MENU
Interface Auto-LF Left Right Top Bottom Pg-Length Wait Setup Name Quit
Specify printer interface
        A       B       C       D       E       F       G       H
1
2
3
4
5
6
7
8
9
10
```

Use the **Interface** option to specify one of eight possible connections between your computer and your printer:

1 First parallel port (the default)
2 First serial port
3 Second parallel port
4 Second serial port

5 DOS Device LPT1
6 DOS Device LPT2
7 DOS Device LPT3
8 DOS Device LPT4

Choices 5 through 8 are applicable only if your workstation is part of a local area network. If you select either serial port option (2 or 4), another submenu will appear. From this submenu, you must specify one of the following baud rates (data transmission speed—for example, a 1200 baud rate roughly equals 120 characters per second):

1 110 baud
2 150 baud
3 300 baud
4 600 baud
5 1200 baud
6 2400 baud
7 4800 baud
8 9600 baud
9 19200 baud

Check your printer manual for information about the type of interface and baud rate, if applicable.

Reminder:
*Set **A**uto-LF to **Yes*** *for double-spaced reports.*

The Auto-LF setting specifies the printer's end-of-line procedure; **Yes** signals the printer to automatically advance a line when it receives a carriage return; **No** means that the printer will *not* automatically advance a line when it receives a carriage return. With most printers, leave Auto-LF in its **No** default setting. If your reports are double-spaced, select **Yes**.

Page-Layout Options

For page layout, you must consider the length and width of the printer paper, the number of lines that will print on one page (lines per inch), and the *pitch* (characters per inch). Because 1-2-3 initially assumes 8 1/2-inch-by-11-inch paper and a printer output of 6 lines per inch, the default page length is 66 lines. Because of 1-2-3's default settings (2-line margins at the top and bottom), however, all 66 lines are not used if you want top and bottom margins on each page. Every line ordinarily contains 10 or 12 characters per inch, although you can vary the pitch by using setup strings, which are discussed later in this chapter.

Look again at figure 9.6. Five options determine default page-layout characteristics:

Option	Keystroke	Message
Left	**L**	Default left margin (0..240):4
Right	**R**	Default right margin (0..240):76
Top	**T**	Default top margin (0..32):2
Bottom	**B**	Default bottom margin (0..32):2
Pg-Length	**P**	Default lines per page (1..100):66

In each message, the numbers enclosed in parentheses indicate the minimum and maximum values you can select.

To calculate the width of your report, subtract the current left-margin setting (4) from the current right-margin setting (76). Your report will be printed with 72 characters per line.

To calculate how many lines of your worksheet will actually be printed, you need to subtract not only the lines for top and bottom margins, but also the lines that 1-2-3 automatically reserves for a header and a footer. If you are using all default settings, for example, the actual number of lines (or rows) from your worksheet that will be printed is 56. 1-2-3 assigns 2 lines each for the top and bottom margins, and reserves 3 lines each for a header and a footer. These 6 lines are reserved even if you do not enter a header or footer. Because the default page length is 66, you subtract 4 lines for top and bottom margins and 6 lines reserved for header and footer to get 56 lines printed. (To learn how to enter headers and footers on the printout, see the "Headers and Footers" section of this chapter.)

Reminder:
1-2-3 automatically reserves 3 lines each for a header and footer, even if you do not enter any.

Other Default Options: Wait, Setup, and Name

The final three options for default printer settings control the way paper is fed to the printer (**Wait**), the size and style of type (**Setup**), and the specific printer you use (**Name**).

If you are using continuous-feed paper, do not change the **Wait** option's default setting of **No**. If you are using single sheets of paper, select **Yes** to change the default setting; printing will then pause at the end of each page so that you can insert a new sheet of paper. After you insert the page, press Enter to continue printing.

Reminder:
*For printing on single sheets of paper, change the **W**ait option to **Yes** to have the printer pause after printing each sheet.*

The default setting for **Setup** is no setup string. No special printer-control codes, such as condensed print, 8 lines per inch instead of 6, or boldface type, are in effect. (For examples of setup strings, see the section "Changing the Print Options" in this chapter.)

The submenu that appears after you select **Name** depends on decisions made during installation. Suppose, for example, that you installed your 1-2-3 program

CASH FLOW PROJECTOR Copyright (C) 1987 Que Corporation

BALANCES IN WORKING CAPITAL ACCOUNTS

	Dec	Jan	Feb	Mar	Apr	May	Jun	Jul	Aug	Sep	Oct	Nov	Dec
Assets													
Cash	$17,355	$31,643	$34,333	$36,657	$35,614	$29,146	$20,000	$20,000	$20,000	$176,623	$186,131	$337,995	$582,796
Accounts Receivable	493,151	510,780	533,587	551,287	577,314	614,997	641,802	750,544	879,271	989,501	1,097,616	1,170,646	1,218,036
Inventory	163,833	169,209	176,671	180,246	206,788	228,828	269,990	296,527	324,230	345,629	352,687	358,926	358,926
Liabilities													
Accounts Payable	125,000	130,754	139,851	150,186	163,731	180,350	203,669	225,085	243,320	258,740	267,621	272,747	275,041
Line of Credit	0	0	0	0	0	0	1,834	8,327	2,035	0	0	0	0
Net Working Capital	$549,339	$580,878	$604,750	$627,003	$655,984	$692,620	$726,289	$833,659	$978,148	$1,153,013	$1,368,812	$1,594,820	$1,884,718

SALES

	Oct	Nov	Dec	Jan	Feb	Mar	Apr	May	Jun	Jul	Aug	Sep	Oct	Nov	Dec	Total
Profit Center 1	$27,832	$23,864	$26,125	$31,336	$37,954	$43,879	$51,471	$56,953	$53,145	$54,140	$53,614	$52,015	$48,902	$44,091	$42,536	$570,036
Profit Center 2	13,489	21,444	20,140	22,572	24,888	25,167	32,588	40,140	37,970	34,587	33,463	28,939	24,153	27,080	26,701	358,228
Profit Center 3	126,811	124,382	123,618	131,685	129,044	131,723	139,221	141,879	149,803	147,108	147,032	153,440	149,990	145,198	150,510	1,716,633
Profit Center 4	94,285	92,447	89,010	95,473	98,008	96,986	95,318	103,538	108,146	115,000	106,065	110,401	112,018	111,956	107,522	1,254,073
Profit Center 5										175,000	175,000	225,000	300,000	325,000	350,000	1,490,000
Total Sales	$262,417	$262,137	$258,893	$281,066	$289,894	$297,755	$318,598	$342,510	$349,064	$459,477	$515,174	$569,795	$635,063	$653,305	$677,269	$5,380,970

Percent of Collections																
Cash	10%															
30 Days	20%															
60 Days	50%															
90 Days	20%															

Cash Collections			$263,437	$267,077	$280,066	$292,571	$304,027	$322,258	$350,735	$386,447	$459,566	$526,948	$580,275	$629,878	$4,664,085

PURCHASES

Cost of Goods Sold

	%	Oct	Nov	Dec	Jan	Feb	Mar	Apr	May	Jun	Jul	Aug	Sep	Oct	Nov	Dec	Total
Profit Center 1	33%	$9,185	$7,875	$8,621	$10,341	$12,525	$14,480	$16,985	$18,794	$17,538	$17,866	$17,693	$17,165	$16,138	$14,550	$14,037	$188,112
Profit Center 2	29%	3,912	6,219	5,841	6,546	7,218	7,298	9,451	11,641	11,011	10,030	9,704	8,392	7,004	7,847	7,743	103,886
Profit Center 3	50%	63,406	62,191	61,809	65,843	64,522	65,862	69,611	70,940	74,902	73,554	73,516	76,720	74,995	72,599	75,255	858,317
Profit Center 4	67%	63,171	61,939	59,637	63,967	65,665	64,981	63,863	69,370	72,458	72,790	71,064	73,969	75,052	75,011	72,040	840,229
Profit Center 5	30%	0	0	0	0	0	0	0	0	0	34,500	52,500	67,500	90,000	97,500	105,000	447,000
Total Cost of Goods Sold		$139,673	$138,224	$135,908	$146,696	$149,930	$152,621	$159,910	$170,745	$175,908	$208,741	$224,476	$243,746	$263,189	$267,507	$274,075	$2,437,543

Inventory Purchasing Schedule																
0 Days in Advance	5%															
30 Days in Advance	50%															
60 Days in Advance	30%															
90 Days in Advance	15%															

Inventory Purchases	$138,873	$141,363	$148,015	$152,072	$157,391	$165,196	$177,452	$192,785	$217,071	$235,277	$252,180	$265,145	$270,247	$273,747	$274,075	$2,632,637

Payment Schedule																
Cash	30%															
30 Days	40%															
60 Days	30%															

Payment for Purchases	$142,612	$147,237	$152,451	$158,137	$166,531	$178,375	$195,471	$215,247	$234,886	$250,999	$262,786	$269,766	$272,795	$2,504,680

#		Oct	Nov	Dec	Jan	Feb	Mar	Apr	May	Jun	Jul	Aug	Sep	Oct	Nov	Dec	Total
74																	
75	**OPERATING EXPENSES**																
76																	
77	Profit Center 1	$20,458	$20,760	$20,963	$21,523	$22,329	$22,802	$23,108	$24,099	$24,422	$24,431	$25,060	$25,646	$25,515	$26,639	$26,881	$293,461
78	Profit Center 2	14,377	15,002	15,587	15,946	16,790	17,355	17,739	18,195	18,610	19,412	19,546	20,348	20,860	21,729	21,785	228,315
79	Profit Center 3	25,921	26,393	27,339	27,554	28,286	28,464	29,275	29,292	29,578	30,246	30,358	31,041	31,680	32,048	32,525	360,347
80	Profit Center 4	13,922	14,885	15,801	16,130	16,800	17,651	18,000	18,039	18,789	20,400	20,939	21,589	21,833	22,024	22,154	235,052
81	Profit Center 5					10,000	14,000	18,000	20,000	22,000	22,470	22,837	22,995	23,364	24,023	24,806	224,495
82																	
83	Corporate Overhead	14,944	15,262	15,801	16,332	16,474	16,933	17,616	18,575	18,640	19,278	19,544	20,225	21,142	21,565	22,378	228,702
84																	
85	Total Expenses	$89,622	$92,302	$95,491	$97,491	$110,679	$117,205	$123,777	$128,950	$132,954	$136,237	$138,284	$141,844	$145,394	$148,028	$150,529	$1,571,372
86																	
87	Payment Schedule — Cash	70%	70%	70%	70%	70%	70%	70%	70%	70%	70%	70%	70%	70%	70%	70%	
88	30 Days	20%	20%	20%	20%	20%	20%	20%	20%	20%	20%	20%	20%	20%	20%	20%	
89	60 Days	10%	10%	10%	10%	10%	10%	10%	10%	10%	10%	10%	10%	10%	10%	10%	
90																	
91	Total Payment for Expenses			$94,286	$96,572	$106,523	$113,928	$121,153	$126,741	$131,236	$134,852	$137,342	$140,571	$143,973	$146,883	$149,515	$1,549,288
92																	
93																	
94																	
95	**CASH FLOW SUMMARY**																
96																	
97	Collection of Receivables				$263,437	$267,077	$280,066	$292,571	$304,827	$322,258	$350,735	$386,447	$459,566	$526,948	$580,275	$629,878	$4,664,085
98	Other Cash Receipts				0	0	0	0	0	0	0	0	0	0	0	50,000	50,000
99																	
100	Cash Disbursements																
101	Payment for Purchases on Credit				147,237	152,451	158,137	166,531	178,375	195,471	215,247	234,886	250,999	262,786	269,766	272,795	2,504,680
102	Operating Expenses				96,572	106,523	113,928	121,153	126,741	131,236	134,852	137,342	140,571	143,973	146,883	149,515	1,549,288
103	Long-Term Debt Service				0	0	0	0	0	0	0	0	0	0	0	0	0
104	Interest Payment on Line of Credit																
105	Interest Rate			13.50%	13.50%	13.50%	13.50%	13.50%	13.50%	13.50%	13.50%	13.50%	13.50%	13.50%	13.50%	13.50%	
106	Payment				5,340	5,413	5,677	5,930	6,179	6,532	7,109	7,833	9,315	10,681	11,762	12,787	94,538
107	Income Tax Payments				0	0	0	0	0	0	21	94	23	0	0	0	137
108	Other				0	0	0	0	0	0	0	0	0	0	0	0	0
109																	
110	Total Cash Disbursements				249,149	264,387	277,742	293,614	311,295	333,238	357,228	380,154	400,908	417,440	428,411	435,077	4,148,643
111																	
112	Net Cash Generated This Period				$14,288	$2,690	$2,324	($1,043)	($6,468)	($10,980)	($6,493)	$6,293	$58,658	$109,508	$151,864	$244,801	$565,441
113																	
114																	
115																	
116	**ANALYSIS OF CASH REQUIREMENTS**																
117																	
118	Beginning Cash Balance				$17,355	$31,643	$34,333	$36,657	$35,614	$29,146	$20,000	$20,000	$20,000	$76,623	$186,131	$337,995	
119	Net Cash Generated This Period				14,288	2,690	2,324	(1,043)	(6,468)	(10,980)	(6,493)	6,293	58,658	109,508	151,864	244,801	
120																	
121	Cash Balance before Borrowings				31,643	34,333	36,657	35,614	29,146	18,166	13,507	26,293	78,658	186,131	337,995	582,796	
122	Minimum Acceptable Cash Balance				20,000	20,000	20,000	20,000	20,000	20,000	20,000	20,000	20,000	20,000	20,000	20,000	
123																	
124	Amount above/(below) Minimum Acceptable Balance				11,643	14,333	16,657	15,614	9,146	(1,834)	(6,493)	6,293	58,658	166,131	317,995	562,796	
125																	
126	Current Short-Term Borrowings				0	0	0	0	0	1,834	6,493	(6,293)	(2,035)	0	0	0	
127	Total Short-Term Borrowings				0	0	0	0	0	1,834	8,327	2,035	0	0	0	0	
128																	
129	Ending Cash Balance				$31,643	$34,333	$36,657	$35,614	$29,146	$20,000	$20,000	$20,000	$76,623	$186,131	$337,995	$582,796	
130																	

Fig 9.7

The Cash Flow Projector spreadsheet model.

to print on two different printers: the EPSON® printer you have at home and the Toshiba printer at work. And suppose that because each printer has only one parallel port, you set Interface to 1 (Parallel 1). In this case, selecting Name will produce a submenu with options 1 (the EPSON) and 2 (the Toshiba). If you are at home, choose 1; if you are at work, choose 2.

Reminder:
Use /WGD Update to make your new default settings "permanent."

Remember that if you use the /Worksheet Global Default Printer command to change print settings, the new settings remain in effect for the current work session. To have the settings remain the default whenever you start up 1-2-3, use the /Worksheet Global Default Update command after you have made the changes you want.

Basic Draft-Quality Printing

1-2-3's Print menu is designed for the simplest to most complex worksheet printing needs. You need only be concerned with the main Print menu if you want to quickly print a report that neither requires changing any default print settings (such as those for paper size) nor requires special enhancements (such as headers, footers, or different size and style of type). If you want to dress up your report or have special requirements for paper size, margins, or page length, then you'll need to use many of the commands available on menus that follow the main Print menu.

This section shows you how to print draft-quality reports quickly and easily by using a minimum of commands on the main Print menu. First, you'll learn how to print short reports of a page or less by using only two commands on the main Print menu. Then you'll learn how to print a report that spills onto more than one page, by using three commands from the main Print menu and one command from the Options menu. Later in the chapter, you'll learn how to use those commands that enhance reports, change type size and style, and automatically repeat border titles. You will also learn how to produce printouts of complete formulas rather than their resulting values.

Sample Cash-Flow Projector Spreadsheet

The large model in figure 9.7, which occupies the range A1..W130, is referenced throughout this chapter. This chapter focuses only on the printing options (and problems) associated with such a large spreadsheet. For a full explanation of the model, see Chapter 3 of Que's book *1-2-3 for Business*, 2nd Edition.

Quickly Printing One Screenful of Data (PrtSc)

Before you print any portion of a 1-2-3 spreadsheet, decide whether the output must be of "report" quality (suitable for official distribution or filing) or whether all you need is a "screen dump" (hard copy of the screen's contents).

Figure 9.8, for example, was produced by retrieving the Cash Flow Projector file and then pressing Shift-PrtSc.

Fig. 9.8

The result of using the DOS Shift-PrtSc key.

```
A1: [W9] \=                                                      READY

              A         B        C        D        E        F        G
 1   =========================================================================
 2
 3   CASH FLOW PROJECTOR                        Copyright (C) 1987 Que Corporation
 4
 5   =========================================================================
 6   BALANCES IN WORKING CAPITAL ACCOUNTS                          Dec
 7   ================================================================ =========
 8   Assets
 9     Cash                                                       $17,355
10     Accounts Receivable                                        493,151
11     Inventory                                                  163,833
12
13   Liabilities
14     Accounts Payable                                           125,000
15     Line of Credit                                                   0
16                                                                --------
17   Net Working Capital                                         $549,339
18                                                                ========
19
20
03-Aug-87   02:56 PM
```

The resultant screen dump captures everything on the screen, even such unwanted items as the contents of the highlighted cell A1 and the mode indicator. Such "quick and dirty" printouts may be adequate for interoffice memos and, because they capture the date-time display, for documenting model construction.

Cue:
"Screen dump" printing prints whatever is on the screen, including the date-time display.

Printing Draft-Quality Reports on One Page or Less

If you don't change any of the default print settings, and no other print settings have been entered during the current worksheet session, then printing a page or less involves only a few steps. These steps include:

1. Choosing to print to the printer or file

2. Highlighting on the worksheet the area you want printed

3. Choosing the command to begin printing

Two other steps may be necessary if another person uses your copy of 1-2-3 and has possibly changed either the default settings or has entered new settings in the **Print** menu during the current worksheet session. First, you can check the default settings by selecting /**Worksheet Global Default Status**. A quick review of the top left section of the **Status** screen will indicate whether the printer and page layout settings are the ones you need. Second, you can clear any special settings that may have been entered for **Print** commands by another user; select /**Print Printer Clear All** to erase any settings.

If you are certain that all default settings are correct and no other settings have been entered into the **Print** commands, you can easily print a report of a page or less by completing the following sequence of operations. First, check that your printer is on-line and that your paper is positioned where you want the data to print. Next choose /**Print Printer**. The main **Print** menu will then appear:

    Range   Line   Page   Options   Clear   Align   Go   Quit

Indicate what part of the worksheet you want to print by selecting **Range** and highlighting the area. Suppose that you want to print the *December* data for the *Balances in Working Capital* part of the Cash Flow Projector in figure 9.7. To print this small area, you specify the range A1..G17.

You can use the PgUp, PgDn, and End keys to designate ranges when you print. If you want to designate a range that includes the entire active area of the spreadsheet, anchor the left corner of the print range, press the End key, and then the Home key.

After you have highlighted the exact range you want to print, select **Go**. Selecting **Go** after entering the range A1..G17 for the Cash Flow Projector produces the printout shown in figure 9.9. If you accidentally press Enter after you have already used the **Go** option, the file will print a second time, which can be particularly disconcerting. If this happens, you can stop printing by pressing Ctrl-Break twice.

Fig. 9.9

The result of printing one page with default settings.

```
========================================================================
CASH FLOW PROJECTOR                  Copyright (C) 1987 Que Corporatio
========================================================================
BALANCES IN WORKING CAPITAL ACCOUNTS                              Dec
========================================================================
Assets
  Cash                                                        $17,355
  Accounts Receivable                                         493,151
  Inventory                                                   163,833

Liabilities
  Accounts Payable                                            125,000
  Line of Credit                                                    0
                                                             --------
Net Working Capital                                         $549,339
```

Printing Reports Longer than One Page

If the area of your worksheet has more rows and columns than can be printed on one page, you can use the basic steps discussed above for printing reports on a page or less. Setting the print range, however, so that a new page begins exactly where you want it to begin can sometimes be a bit tricky. Also, if you want to print a section of a large worksheet like the Cash Flow Projection in figure 9.7, you may need to use the /**Print Printer Options Border** command so that labels are repeated on each page.

To assure that information will be printed on the pages as you want them printed, remember that 1-2-3 treats numeric and text data differently when splitting data from one page to the next. Numbers will be printed complete because they can span only one cell. Text, on the other hand, such as long labels that lie across several cells, may be split in awkward places from one page to the next.

Suppose, for example, that you want to print six months of data from the *Balances in Working Capital Accounts* section on the Cash Flow Projector worksheet in figure 9.7. Suppose also that you want to print your report on 8 1/2-by-11-inch paper, the default paper size. To print the report on this size paper with the default margin settings and a pitch of 10 characters per inch, you need to print on two pages.

To print six columns of data from the *Balances in Working Capital Accounts* spreadsheet, you complete these steps. After first checking that your printer is on-line and that your paper is positioned where you want the printing to begin, choose the /**Print Printer** command. The main **Print** menu appears:

    Range   Line   Page   Options   Clear   Align   Go   Quit

Because you want the labels in A6 through A17 in figure 9.7 to print on both pages, you must use the **Options Borders** command. When you select **Options Borders**, 1-2-3 asks whether the labels you want repeated are located down a column or across a row. For our sample report, choose **Columns**. (To print a report on two or more pages and repeat labels that are displayed across a row, you select **Rows** after choosing **Options Borders**.)

After you choose **Columns**, the prompt Enter Border Columns: will appear. If your cell pointer is located in the column where the labels appear, press Enter; if not, move your cell pointer to the column and press Enter. To return to the main **Print** menu, select **Quit**. Once you have indicated which column or row of labels you want repeated on each page, you do not need to include those labels in your actual print range. 1-2-3 automatically places those labels in the first column or row on every page.

When you set the print range for reports that will print on more than one page, you highlight all columns or rows except those columns or rows that you entered using the **Options Borders** command. To print the January through June data for the *Balances in Working Capital Accounts* spreadsheet, you must highlight range H6..M18 (see fig. 9.7.). Notice that this range does not include A6..D18, which is the range that contains the labels.

Cue:

If you use Ctrl-Break to abort a print job, use /PP Align before you restart printing.

The last three steps involve moving the cursor to **Align** on the main **Print** menu, then selecting **Go**, and finally choosing **Quit** after printing is completed. Choosing **Align** assures that printing will begin at the top of all succeeding pages after the first. Make sure in particular that you reposition your printer paper and use the **Align** command whenever you have aborted a print job.

The resulting printed pages of the *Balances in Working Capital Accounts* spreadsheet are shown in figures 9.10A and 9.10B.

Fig. 9.10A

First page of a report printed on two pages.

```
BALANCES IN WORKING CAPITAL ACCOUNTS   Jan        Feb        Mar
====================================  =========  =========  =========
Assets
  Cash                                $31,643    $34,333    $36,657
  Accounts Receivable                 510,780    533,597    551,287
  Inventory                           169,209    176,671    189,246

Liabilities
  Accounts Payable                    130,754    139,851    150,186
  Line of Credit                            0          0          0
                                      --------   --------   --------
Net Working Capital                   $580,878   $604,750   $627,003
                                      ========   ========   ========
```

Fig. 9.10B

Second page of a report printed on two pages.

```
BALANCES IN WORKING CAPITAL ACCOUNTS   Apr        May        Jun
====================================  =========  =========  =========
Assets
  Cash                                $35,614    $29,146    $20,000
  Accounts Receivable                 577,314    614,997    641,802
  Inventory                           206,788    228,828    269,990

Liabilities
  Accounts Payable                    163,731    180,350    203,669
  Line of Credit                            0          0      1,834
                                      --------   --------   --------
Net Working Capital                   $655,984   $692,620   $726,289
                                      ========   ========   ========
```

Hiding Segments within the Designated Print Range

Because the /**Print** commands require the specification of a range to print, you can print only rectangular blocks from the spreadsheet. Nevertheless, you can suppress the display of cell contents within the range. You can eliminate one or more rows, hide one or more columns, or remove from view a segment that spans only part of a row or a column. The results of each of the following illustrations will print on one page, using default settings.

Excluding Rows

To exclude rows from printing, you must mark the rows for omission. Do this by typing a double vertical bar (‖) in the blank leftmost cell of the print range of each row you want to omit. Only one of these vertical bars appears on-screen and neither appears on the printout. A row marked in this way will not print, but the suppressed data remains in the spreadsheet and is used in any applicable calculations.

Suppose, for example, that you want to print the Cash Flow Summary line descriptions from the Cash Flow Projector model. When the /**Print Printer** command prompts you for a range to print, specify A94..D112. The printout of the contents of rows 94 through 112 is shown in figure 9.11A.

Fig. 9.11A

Printout of individual cash-disbursements rows.

```
=====================================
CASH FLOW SUMMARY
=====================================
Collection of Receivables
Other Cash Receipts

Cash Disbursements
 Payment for Purchases on Credit
 Operating Expenses
 Long-Term Debt Service
 Interest Payment on Line of Credit
  Interest Rate
  Payment
 Income Tax Payments
 Other

Total Cash Disbursements

Net Cash Generated This Period
```

Now suppose that you don't want the printout to show the cash-disbursements detail (rows 100 through 109). Do not use a worksheet command to delete the rows! Instead, omit the row from printing by typing a double vertical bar in the leftmost cell of each row to be omitted. Because the leftmost cell is not blank, however, you will need to make an adjustment. The simplest method is to insert a new column A and narrow it to a one-column width. Then type ‖ in cell A100 and copy that entry to cells A101..A109.

Cue:
If necessary, insert a new column A to provide blank cells for the double vertical bars.

When you execute the **Print** command, be sure to specify the expanded range A94..E112 (not A94..D112 or B94..E112). Figure 9.11B shows the resulting printout.

Fig. 9.11B

Individual cash-disbursements rows omitted.

```
=====================================
CASH FLOW SUMMARY
=====================================
Collection of Receivables
Other Cash Receipts

Total Cash Disbursements

Net Cash Generated This Period
```

To restore the spreadsheet after you have finished printing, delete the vertical bars from the leftmost cells of the marked rows and also delete column A.

Excluding Columns

As you learned from Chapter 4, you can use 1-2-3's /Worksheet Column Hide command to mark columns that you don't want to display on-screen. If these marked columns are included in a print range, they will not appear on the printout if the /Print Printer Options Other setting is As-Displayed.

Suppose, for example, that you are working with the Cash Flow Projector model and that you want to print only the descriptions and the January-through-March Sales/Cash Collections information contained in range A21..J40. Issue the /Worksheet Column Hide command and specify columns E1..G1 to suppress the October-through-December data. The resulting printout is shown in figure 9.12.

Fig. 9.12

The printout after hiding columns E, F, and G.

```
=====================================================================
SALES                                        Jan        Feb        Mar
=====================================================================
Profit Center 1                          $31,336    $37,954    $43,879
Profit Center 2                           22,572     24,888     25,167
Profit Center 3                          131,685    129,044    131,723
Profit Center 4                           95,473     98,008     96,986
Profit Center 5
                                        --------   --------   --------
Total Sales                             $281,066   $289,894   $297,755
                                        ========   ========   ========

                   Cash                      10%        10%        10%
Percent of         30 Days                   20%        20%        20%
Collections        60 Days                   50%        50%        50%
                   90 Days                   20%        20%        20%
                                        --------   --------   --------
Cash Collections                        $263,437   $267,077   $280,066
                                        ========   ========   ========
```

To restore the columns, select /Worksheet Column Display. When the hidden columns (marked with an asterisk) reappear on-screen, you can specify which column or columns to display.

Excluding Ranges

If you want to hide only a partial row, a partial column, or an area that partially spans one or more rows and columns, use the /Range Format Hidden command to mark the ranges.

Perhaps your spreadsheet includes documentation that you want to save on disk but omit from the printout. For example, you may want to omit the copyright message in the third row of the Cash Flow Projector model. To omit the message, issue the /Range Format Hidden command, and specify cell E3. (Although the message spans several cells, it is entered in E3.) Then print the range A1..G7 (see fig. 9.13).

Fig. 9.13

The printout after hiding range E3.

```
=========================================================================
CASH FLOW PROJECTOR
=========================================================================
BALANCES IN WORKING CAPITAL ACCOUNTS                         Dec
========================================================= =========
```

After you finish printing, select /**Range Format Reset** and then specify the range E3..E3 to restore the copyright message.

If you find yourself repeating print operations (hiding the same columns, suppressing and then restoring the same documentation messages, etc.), remember that you can save time and minimize frustration by developing and using print macros (see Chapter 14).

Cue:
Use print macros for repeated print operations.

Controlling Paper Movement

Unless you stipulate otherwise, the top of a page is initially marked by the print head's position when you turn on the printer and load 1-2-3. If you print a range containing fewer lines than the default page length, the paper will not advance to the top of the next page; the next print operation will begin wherever the preceding operation ended. If you print a range containing more lines than the default page length, 1-2-3 will automatically insert page breaks in the document between pages, but the paper will not advance to the top of the next page after the last page has printed.

If you don't want to accept 1-2-3's automatic paper-movement controls, you can change the controls from the keyboard. You can specify the "top" of a page in any paper position, advance the paper by line or by page, and insert page breaks exactly where you want them.

The Print Menu's Line, Page, and Align Options

If you are using continuous-feed paper, position the paper so that the print head is at the top of the page, and then turn on the printer. Do not advance the paper manually. Because 1-2-3 coordinates a line counter with the current page-length setting, any lines you advance manually are not counted, and page breaks will crop up in strange places.

If you want to advance the paper one line at a time (to separate several small printed ranges that fit on one page, for example), issue the /**Print Printer Line** command. This command sequence will cause the printer to skip a line.

If you want to advance to a new page after printing less than a full page, select the /**Print Printer Page** sequence. Whenever you issue this command, the printer will skip to a new page. (The following section shows how you can embed a page-break symbol in the print range to instruct 1-2-3 to advance automatically.)

In many cases, a faster way to advance the paper is to take the printer off-line, adjust the paper manually, put the printer on-line, and then issue the /**Print Printer Align** command. In fact, whether you adjust the paper off-line in this manner, or on-line with the paper-control commands, you should issue **Align**. **Align**, however, also resets the page counter, which you may not want to do if you are numbering pages in a header or footer (see the section on "Headers and Footers").

Whenever you begin a print job at the top of a page, it's good practice to select **Align** before selecting **G**o.

Reminder:
To print a footer on the last page of the printout, issue the /PP Page command at the end of the print session.

To print an existing footer option on the last page, use the **Page** command at the end of the printing session. If you select the **Quit** command from the /**Print** menu without issuing the **Page** command, this final footer will not print; although you can reissue the /**Print Printer** command, select **Page**, and the footer will still print.

Setting Page Breaks within the Spreadsheet

Look again at both figure 9.7, which shows the entire Cash Flow Projector model.

Suppose that you want to print three months of data (Oct.-Dec.) for the Sales and the Purchases Sections of the worksheet. To make sure that the Purchases section begins printing on a new page, you can insert a page break into the worksheet by using a command sequence or by typing a special symbol.

To enter a page break by using 1-2-3's commands, first move the cell pointer to column A and then to one row above the row at which you want the page break to occur. Then select the /**Worksheet Page** command, which automatically inserts a new blank row containing a page-break symbol (|::).

For example, to insert a page break just above the first separating line in the Cash Flow Projector model's Purchases section, position the cell pointer on A42 and then execute the command. Figure 9.14 shows the inserted row with the double-colon page-break symbol. To remove the inserted row and the page-break symbol after you finish printing, use the /**Worksheet Delete Row** command.

As an alternative, insert a blank row into your worksheet where you want a page break, and then type a page-break symbol (|::) into a blank cell in the

Fig. 9.14

Inserting a page-break symbol in the worksheet.

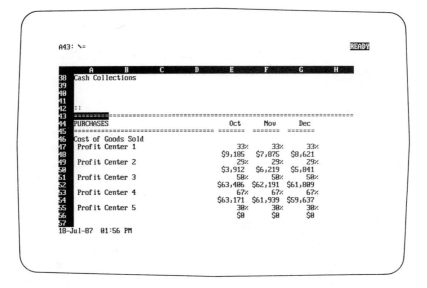

leftmost column of the print range in that row. The contents of cells in any row marked by the page-break symbol will not print.

Be careful when you alter a spreadsheet. You may alter formula results by inserting rows, or you may accidentally delete the wrong row after you finish printing. You may be able to avoid these problems by typing the page-break symbol into the leftmost column in the print range of a row that is already blank in your worksheet. First check to be sure the row is blank; use the End key and the arrow keys to scan across the row.

Caution:
Inserting a blank row for a page-break symbol may alter formulas or cause other problems.

Changing the Print Options

You can use the /**W**orksheet **G**lobal **D**efault **P**rinter command sequence to change the default print settings. The new default settings remain in effect for all print operations performed in the current work session. If you want the new settings to be in effect whenever you load 1-2-3, return to the **D**efault level of the command sequence and select the **U**pdate option (refer to fig. 9.4).

You can change print settings also by using the selections on the /**P**rint **P**rinter **O**ptions menu shown in figure 9.15. The **M**argins, **S**etup, and **P**g-Length options override the /**W**orksheet **G**lobal **D**efault **P**rinter settings for margins, setup strings, and page length. The **H**eader, **F**ooter, and **B**order margins are unique to this menu; they are provided to help you improve the readability of your reports.

Reminder:
*/**P**rint **P**rinter **O**ptions settings override corresponding /**W**orksheet **G**lobal **D**efault **P**rinter settings.*

Fig. 9.15

The /Print Printer (or File) Options submenu.

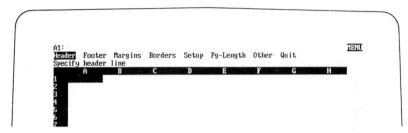

Whatever print settings you use for your worksheet are saved with the file when you execute **/File Save**. When you retrieve the file, the settings are still in effect.

Headers and Footers

As you know, 1-2-3 reserves three lines in a document for a header and an additional three lines for a footer. You can either retain the six lines (regardless of whether you use them) or eliminate all six lines by selecting **Other Unformatted** (illustrated later in this chapter) from the **/Print Printer Options** menu.

Technically, either the **Header** or **Footer** option lets you specify up to 240 characters of text within one line in each of three positions: left, right, and center. But from a practical standpoint, the overall header or footer line cannot exceed the number of characters printed per inch *multiplied by* the width of the paper in inches *minus* the right and left margins.

The header text, which is printed on the first line after any blank top margin lines, is followed by two blank header lines (for spacing). The footer text line is printed above the specified bottom-margin blank lines and below two blank footer lines (for spacing).

Although all features of the text can be entered manually, 1-2-3 provides special characters for controlling page numbers, the current date, and the positioning of text within a header or footer. These special characters are

Character	Function
#	Automatically prints page numbers, starting with 1
@	Automatically includes (in the form 29-Jun-87) the date that you entered when you loaded DOS
|	Automatically separates text: Absence of a | mark left-justifies all text. The first | mark centers text that follows. The second | mark right-justifies remaining text.

To illustrate, we will reprint the Cash Flow Projector range A1..G17 after adding a header that includes all the preceding special characters.

To add the header, select **/Print Printer**, specify **Range** A1..G17, and then select **Options Header**. At the prompt:

    Enter Header Line:

type:

    @|YOUR FIRM NAME|#

Then select **Quit** from the **/Print Printer Options** menu; signal the top of the page to the printer, if necessary, by selecting **Align**; and then select **Go**. If you compare the printed header line shown in figure 9.16 with figures 9.10A and 9.10B, you can see how the temporary changes improve the report's appearance.

Fig. 9.16

The result of specifying a header.

```
    03-Aug-87                     YOUR FIRM NAME                          1


    ===================================================================

    CASH FLOW PROJECTOR

    ===================================================================
    BALANCES IN WORKING CAPITAL ACCOUNTS                   Dec
    ===============================================     =========
    Assets
      Cash                                              $17,355
      Accounts Receivable                               493,151
      Inventory                                         163,833

    Liabilities
      Accounts Payable                                  125,000
      Line of Credit                                          0
                                                      ---------
    Net Working Capital                               $549,339
                                                      =========
```

Whenever the print range exceeds a single-page output, the header will be reproduced on each succeeding page and the page number will increase by one. If you have used the special page-number character (#) and want to print your report a second time before you leave the **Print** menu, you can reset the page counter and set the top of the form by simply selecting **Align** before you select **Go**.

Reminder:
*To print a report a second time, select **A**lign and then **G**o.*

If you have specified a header line, but the centered or right-justified text doesn't print, make sure that the right-margin setting is appropriate for the current pitch and paper width. To change the header, simply repeat the sequence to establish the text, press Esc to remove the display of the existing header from the control panel, and press Enter. (You can delete a header or footer without removing other specified options.)

Borders

A printed report of lines of figures can be difficult, if not impossible, to interpret if you don't know what those figures represent. You can make your report easy to understand by using a special 1-2-3 feature that lets you print specified columns and rows repeatedly on a multipage printout.

If you use the default **Print** settings to print the Cash Flow Projector model shown in figure 9.7, the report will contain all necessary information. But without descriptions of what each line of figures represents, some pages may be difficult to interpret.

Cue:

*Using **B**orders in printing is analogous to freezing titles on the worksheet.*

To improve the report, you need to add certain column or row headings—what 1-2-3 calls *borders*. Selecting **Borders Columns** produces a column that appears as a border to a set of rows; selecting **Borders Rows** produces a row that appears as a border to a set of columns. Setting borders in a printout is analogous to freezing titles in the spreadsheet: **Borders Columns** produces a border like a frozen vertical title display, and **Borders Rows** produces a column like a frozen horizontal title display.

To illustrate the process of creating borders, we will modify only a small portion of the report—the working-capital balances information in the range A1..S18 (refer to fig. 9.7). We'll omit the blank columns (E and F) as well as the initial December column (G), and we'll use the **Borders Columns** command to repeat the account names in columns A through D.

Select **/Print Printer**, specify **Range** H1..S18, and then select **Options Borders Columns**. When the message Enter Border Columns: appears in the control panel, specify A1..D1. As you can see from figures 9.17A through 9.17D, the account names are repeated to coincide with the January-through-December dollar amounts.

Fig. 9.17A

Page 1 of a printed column border.

```
==============================================================================
CASH FLOW PROJECTOR
==============================================================================
BALANCES IN WORKING CAPITAL ACCOUNTS     Jan        Feb       Mar
====================================  =========  =========  =========
Assets
 Cash                                   $31,643    $34,333    $36,657
 Accounts Receivable                    510,780    533,597    551,287
 Inventory                              169,209    176,671    189,246

Liabilities
 Accounts Payable                       130,754    139,851    150,186
 Line of Credit                               0          0          0
                                      ---------  ---------  ---------
Net Working Capital                    $580,878   $604,750   $627,003
                                      =========  =========  =========
```

Fig. 9.17B

Page 2 of the printed column border.

```
===============================================================

CASH FLOW PROJECTOR


BALANCES IN WORKING CAPITAL ACCOUNTS    Apr        May        Jun
===============================================================
Assets
  Cash                                $35,614    $29,146    $20,000
  Accounts Receivable                 577,314    614,997    641,802
  Inventory                           206,788    228,828    269,990

Liabilities
  Accounts Payable                    163,731    180,350    203,669
  Line of Credit                            0          0      1,834
                                     --------   --------   --------
Net Working Capital                  $655,984   $692,620   $726,289
                                     ========   ========   ========
```

Fig. 9.17C

Page 3 of the printed column border.

```
===============================================================

CASH FLOW PROJECTOR


BALANCES IN WORKING CAPITAL ACCOUNTS    Jul        Aug        Sep
===============================================================
Assets
  Cash                                $20,000    $20,000    $76,623
  Accounts Receivable                 750,544    879,271    989,501
  Inventory                           296,527    324,230    345,629

Liabilities
  Accounts Payable                    225,085    243,320    258,740
  Line of Credit                        8,327      2,035          0
                                     --------   --------   --------
Net Working Capital                  $833,659   $978,146 $1,153,013
                                     ========   ========   ========
```

Fig. 9.17D

Page 4 of the printed column border.

```
===============================================================

CASH FLOW PROJECTOR


BALANCES IN WORKING CAPITAL ACCOUNTS    Oct        Nov        Dec
===============================================================
Assets
  Cash                               $186,131   $337,995   $582,796
  Accounts Receivable              1,097,616  1,170,646  1,218,036
  Inventory                          352,687    358,926    358,926

Liabilities
  Accounts Payable                   267,621    272,747    275,041
  Line of Credit                           0          0          0
                                    --------   --------   --------
Net Working Capital              $1,368,812 $1,594,820 $1,884,718
                                    ========   ========   ========
```

If the designated border includes part of the print range, or the print range includes part of the border, you get the same information printed twice, which is probably not the result you want or expect.

If you want to print information with a horizontal border on every page, select the **B**orders **R**ows option. For example, you could use this option if you wanted to print out only the Liabilities information in rows 13 to 15.

Select the /**Print Printer Options Borders Columns** (or **Rows**) command sequence only when you want borders to be printed. If you select the sequence accidentally, the cell highlighted by the cell pointer will be entered as either the **Columns** or **Rows** you selected. Should this occur, remove the selection by using the /**Print Printer Clear Borders** command sequence.

Setup Strings

Setup strings are optional printer codes that you can use to change the size or style of type. To pass setup strings temporarily to the printer, use one of two methods. Either select the **Setup** option and specify the appropriate ASCII code, or embed the code in the spreadsheet. (Remember that you can establish a "permanent" or default setup string which will be used automatically whenever 1-2-3 is loaded. To do so, access the /**Worksheet Global Default** menu shown in fig. 9.4 and then select **Update**.)

We'll illustrate both temporary methods by printing portions of the Working Capital Accounts information in the Cash Flow Projector report. The examples assume that an EPSON printer is being used. (The *1-2-3 Reference Manual* contains a "Printer Control Codes" appendix.)

To use the first method, first send a setup string (the decimal code for ASCII must not exceed 39 characters) by executing a 1-2-3 command sequence. Assume that the print range is H1..S18 and that columns A1..D1 are established as a border at the left side of every printed page.

Access the /**Print Printer Options** menu, select **Setup**, type *015* to indicate condensed print on an EPSON printer, and then press Enter. At this point, if you were to **Quit** the **Options** menu and issue a **Go** command, the first printed page would contain only January-through-March amounts in condensed print.

Because you want the January-through-August amounts to fit on the page, you must establish margins that coincide with print pitch. Select **Margins Right** from the /**Print Printer Options** menu. Then specify *136* (8 1/2 inches multiplied by 16 characters per inch in condensed mode). The resulting printout is shown in figures 9.18A and 9.18B.

To remove the temporary setup string, select **Setup** from the /**Print Printer Options** menu, press Esc, and then press Enter. Exit the **Print Options** menu by selecting **Quit** or pressing Esc.

You use this method when you want all output from the current print operation to reflect the code condition. In the preceding illustration, for example, the contents in the entire print range, as well as the column borders, were printed in condensed mode.

```
==================================================================================

CASH FLOW PROJECTOR

==================================================================================
BALANCES IN WORKING CAPITAL ACCOUNTS   Jan       Feb       Mar       Apr       May       Jun       Jul       Aug
==================================================================================

Assets
  Cash                              $31,643   $34,333   $36,657   $35,614   $29,146   $20,000   $20,000   $20,000
  Accounts Receivable               510,780   533,597   551,287   577,314   614,997   641,802   750,544   879,271
  Inventory                         169,209   176,671   189,246   206,788   228,828   269,990   296,527   324,230

Liabilities
  Accounts Payable                  130,754   139,851   150,186   163,731   180,350   203,669   225,085   243,320
  Line of Credit                          0         0         0         0         0     1,834     8,327     2,035
                                   --------  --------  --------  --------  --------  --------  --------  --------
Net Working Capital               $580,878  $604,750  $627,003  $655,984  $692,620  $726,289  $833,659  $978,146
                                   ========  ========  ========  ========  ========  ========  ========  ========
```

```
===================================================================

CASH FLOW PROJECTOR

===================================================================
BALANCES IN WORKING CAPITAL ACCOUNTS   Sep       Oct       Nov       Dec
===================================================================

Assets
  Cash                              $76,623  $186,131  $337,995  $582,796
  Accounts Receivable               989,501 1,097,616 1,170,646 1,218,036
  Inventory                         345,629   352,687   358,926   358,926

Liabilities
  Accounts Payable                  258,740   267,621   272,747   275,041
  Line of Credit                          0         0         0         0
                                   --------  --------  --------  --------
Net Working Capital             $1,153,013 $1,368,812 $1,594,820 $1,984,718
                                   ========  ========  ========  ========
```

If you want only a portion within a print range to reflect a special printing characteristic, you can embed a setup string in the spreadsheet instead of issuing several separate print commands. In blank rows preceding and following the area that requires special treatment, type a double vertical bar (‖) and the appropriate ASCII code (or codes) separated by backslashes. (Insert a blank row, if necessary, making sure that it will not disturb any formulas in your worksheet.) The first vertical bar will not appear in the worksheet, and neither the bars nor the print codes will be printed. If you must embed a code in a row containing data, that data will not be printed.

If you want to print the first few rows of the Cash Flow Projector report in normal pitch, except for an enlarged title in row 3, you must first select **/Print Printer Clear All** to restore all print settings to default values. Then enter ‖\027\087\049 in the first cell of the first blank row (A2) to activate expanded print on an EPSON printer. Enter ‖\027\087\048 in the first cell of the next blank row (A4) to shut off expanded print. If you specify A1..F8 as the print range, the printed output will be similar to that shown in figure 9.19.

You can combine more than one print characteristic in a setup string if the combined setup code does not exceed the 39-character limit and your printer

Cue:

For special printing effects within a print range, embed setup strings in the spreadsheet.

Fig. 9.19

The results of embedding a setup string in the worksheet.

```
============================================================
CASH  FLOW  PROJECTOR
============================================================
BALANCES IN WORKING CAPITAL ACCOUNTS
============================================================
Assets
```

supports the combination. Check your printer manual for information about the compatibility of codes.

A setup string contains the print-enhancement codes found in the printer manual. Each code consists of a backslash and three digits. If the manual says, for example, to use ESC E to turn on emphasized mode, look up the decimal equivalent for ESC (27) and for uppercase E (69). Because each code must contain three digits and begin with a backslash, you use \027\069 as the setup string to turn on emphasized mode. (Note: do not include spaces in a setup string.)

Page Layout: Margins and Page Length

To change page layout temporarily, use the /**Print Printer Options** menu. If you want to change the margins, select the Margins option and then select **L**eft, **R**ight, **T**op, or **B**ottom from the submenu:

Menu Selection	Keystroke	Message
Left	**L**	Enter Left Margin (0..240):XX
Right	**R**	Enter Right Margin (0..240):XX
Top	**T**	Enter Top Margin (0..32):XX
Bottom	**B**	Enter Bottom Margin (0..32):XX

The XX at the end of each line denotes the current setting, which you can change. Before making any changes, review the "Understanding the Print Default Settings" section at the beginning of this chapter; and keep in mind general layout considerations such as the number of lines per page, the number of characters per inch, etc.

Reminder:
The right margin must be greater than the left margin.

Be sure that you set left and right margins that are consistent with the width of your paper and the established pitch (characters per inch). The right margin must be greater than the left margin. And make sure that settings for the top and bottom margins are consistent with the paper's length and the established number of lines per inch.

The specified page length must not be less than the top margin *plus* the header lines *plus* one line of data *plus* the footer lines *plus* the bottom margin, unless you use the /**Print Printer Options Other Unformatted** command to suppress all formatting. (Information about this command is included in the following section, "Printing a Listing of Cell Contents.") To maximize the output on every printed page of a large spreadsheet, you can combine the Unformatted option with setup strings that condense print and increase the number of lines per inch.

Printing a Listing of Cell Contents

You can spend hours developing and debugging a model spreadsheet and much additional time entering and verifying data. You should safeguard your work not only by making backup copies of your important files but also by printing the cell contents of important spreadsheets. Be aware, however, that this print job can eat up large chunks of time if you have a large worksheet.

You can print cell contents by selecting **Other** from the **/Print Printer Options** menu, and then selecting either **As**-Displayed or **Cell**-Formulas.

The two options are related. Choosing **Cell**-Formulas produces a listing that shows the width of the cell (if different from the default), the cell format, cell-protection status, and the contents of cells in the print range, with one cell per line. By subsequently selecting **As**-Displayed, you restore the default instructions to print the range as it appears on-screen.

Cue:
*Choose **Cell**-Formulas to print a listing of formulas in cells; the default, **A**s-displayed, prints the range as it appears on-screen.*

You can produce a cell-by-cell listing of only the first 7 columns and the first 18 rows of the Cash Flow Projector worksheet, for example, by selecting **/Print Printer**, specifying the range A1..G18, and then selecting **Options Other Cell**-Formulas. Return to the main **Print** menu by choosing **Quit** from the **Options** menu. Press **Align** and then **Go**. The resulting one-cell-per-line listing is shown in figure 9.20.

Notice that within the specified print range, the contents of each cell in the first row are listed before the next row is presented. Information enclosed by parentheses indicates a range format established independently of the global format in effect. For example, the (CØ) in cell G17 indicates that that cell was formatted (with a /**R**ange Format command) as Currency, with zero decimal places.

Information enclosed by square brackets indicates a column width set independently of the global column width in effect. For example, the [W11] in cell G17 indicates that column G was set specifically to be 11 characters wide. Cell content is printed after the column-width and format information. The formula in G17 results in the $549,339 shown in the printed spreadsheet in figure 9.8.

```
A1:  [W9]  \=
B1:  [W9]  \=
C1:  [W9]  \=
D1:  [W9]  \=
E1:  [W11] \=
F1:  [W11] \=
G1:  [W11] \=
A3:  [W9]  'CASH FLOW PROJECTOR
E3:  (H) [W11] 'Copyright (C) 1987 Que Corporation
A5:  [W9]  \=
B5:  [W9]  \=
C5:  [W9]  \=
D5:  [W9]  \=
E5:  [W11] \=
F5:  [W11] \=
G5:  [W11] \=
A6:  [W9]  'BALANCES IN WORKING CAPITAL ACCOUNTS
G6:  [W11] ^Dec
A7:  [W9]  \=
B7:  [W9]  \=
C7:  [W9]  \=
D7:  [W9]  \=
E7:  [W11] \=
F7:  [W11] \=
G7:  [W11] ' =========
A8:  [W9]  'Assets
A9:  [W9]  ' Cash
G9:  (C0) [W11] 17355
A10: [W9]  ' Accounts Receivable
G10: (,0) [W11] 493151
A11: [W9]  ' Inventory
G11: (,0) [W11] 163833
A13: [W9]  'Liabilities
A14: [W9]  ' Accounts Payable
G14: (,0) [W11] 125000
A15: [W9]  ' Line of Credit
G15: (,0) [W11] 0
G16: [W11] ' --------
A17: [W9]  'Net Working Capital
G17: (C0) [W11] +G9+G10+G11-G14-G15
G18: [W11] ' =========
```

If you need more extensive documentation and analysis, you may want to purchase an add-on auditing program. Chapter 4 contains descriptions of two such programs: *The Spreadsheet Auditor* and *The Cambridge Spreadsheet Analyst*. Lotus HAL also provides documentation and analysis features, as described in Chapter 4.

Clearing the Print Options

Selecting /**Print Printer Clear** lets you eliminate all or a portion of the **Print** options that you chose earlier. The **Clear** options are

    All   Range   Borders   Format

You can clear every **Print** option, including the print range, by selecting **All**, or you can be more specific by using the other choices:

Menu Selection	*Keystroke*	*Description*
Range	**R**	Removes the previous print-range specification

Borders	**B**	Cancels **C**olumns and **R**ows specified as borders
Format	**F**	Eliminates **M**argins, **P**g-Length, and **S**etup string settings

Remember that you can automate many routine print operations by setting up the print macros discussed in Chapter 14. **/Print Printer Clear All** is usually the first instruction in this type of macro.

Preparing Output for Acceptance by Other Programs

Many word-processing and other software packages accept ASCII text files. You can maximize your chances of successfully exporting 1-2-3 files to other programs if you select several **P**rint command sequences that eliminate unwanted specifications for page layout and page breaks.

Begin by selecting **/Print File**. Direct output to a .PRN file instead of to a printer by specifying a FILENAME. After specifying the **R**ange to print, choose **O**ptions **O**ther **U**nformatted. Selecting **U**nformatted removes all headers, footers, and page breaks from a print operation.

Cue:
In most cases, choose ***Unformatted*** *when printing to a file.*

Then **Q**uit the **O**ptions menu, create the .PRN file on disk by selecting **G**o, and **Q**uit the **/Print File** menu. Follow the instructions in your word-processing or other software package to import the specially prepared 1-2-3 disk files.

To restore the default printing of headers, footers, and page breaks, issue the **/Print Printer Options Other Formatted** command. You ordinarily choose **F**ormatted for printing to the printer and **U**nformatted when printing to a file.

Printing Reports with HAL

You can use the HAL verbs *print* and *write* to print reports quickly and easily. For example, instead of using the 1-2-3 **/Print Printer** command sequence, you can simply issue the command *print col a through col d* to print the active area in columns A through D. Or you can enter *write total* to print the range named TOTAL. To print the entire active area of the worksheet, you enter *print all* or *write all*. If you issue the commands without specifying a print area (e.g., *print*), HAL prints only the contents of the cell where the cell pointer is currently located.

To print a disk file using HAL, you use the requests *print to* or *write to*. For example, the HAL request *write total to income* prints the range named TOTAL to the file named INCOME.

In the preceding examples, HAL prints the specified areas using the current settings of the print options. You can use HAL also to change the settings. For example, you can specify the top, bottom, left, and right margins of your report by using the verb *set*. The following HAL requests illustrate how to set margins with HAL:

- \\set left margin to 5

- \\set right margin = 240

- \\set t margin = 2

- \\set bm to 10

You can use HAL to pass setup strings to the printer in one of two ways. You can enter the setup string directly into HAL's Request Box, or enter a HAL synonym for one or more of your printer's control codes. For example, the following HAL requests are valid for a Toshiba P351 printer:

- \\setup string is \\029\\091

- \\setup string is compress

In both examples, HAL instructs the printer to print in compressed pitch. For HAL to recognize the second request, you must add the synonym *compress* = *027\\091* to HAL's vocabulary prior to the request.

HAL uses the verbs *advance* and *adv* to advance continuous-feed paper in the printer. You can add a specific number of lines or pages to the request; for example, *advance 3 lines* or *adv 2 pages*. Although you can advance the paper easily with these requests, they do not remove the problem of keeping the paper properly aligned and the page-counter set properly. 1-2-3's /**Print Printer Align** command must still be used.

HAL is probably more useful in building worksheets than in printing reports, but HAL requests are generally easier to use than 1-2-3 commands. If you are accustomed to using HAL in the spreadsheet, you will find the printing requests a natural complement to the spreadsheet requests.

Using Sideways To Print Large Worksheets

Originally introduced in 1983, Sideways® was the first 1-2-3 add-on program. Sideways is a printing utility that allows you to print your spreadsheets on their sides by rotating them ninety degrees.

Spreadsheets quickly grow to sizes too large for your printer to accommodate. If you used the 1-2-3 /**Print** command to print the entire Cash Flow Projector report used in this chapter, for example, you would need to insert page breaks to produce a comprehensible printout. Even using compressed print does not solve the problem completely. Figure 9.7 showed an almost complete printout of the report using compressed print, but several rows in the PURCHASES account are incomplete. The missing entries were printed on a subsequent page (not shown in the figure), where they appeared to be stray numbers.

Figure 9.21 shows the first part of the same report printed with Sideways. The stray figures appear in their proper place in the report. Sideways reports have an added advantage: printed on continuous-feed paper, the reports fold out like pages in a book, making them easier to read and understand.

Sideways is easy to use because it employs slash commands and a menu structure similar to 1-2-3. The options that appear on the Sideways menu shown in figure 9.22 should look familiar to anyone who has printed reports from within 1-2-3.

The **O**ptions selection on the menu gives you access to commands for enhancing your printout with bold, underlined, and expanded type, as well as a choice of nine different character sizes. The report in figure 9.21 was printed using the 5×11 dot-matrix (Tiny) font.

Printing a report using Sideways may take a little longer than with the 1-2-3 /**Print** command, but the results are worth the wait. Sideways Version 3 will also operate as an add-in for Lotus Symphony and other popular spreadsheet and word-processing programs. Sideways is published by Funk Software.

Chapter Summary

This chapter showed you how to create printed reports from your 1-2-3 worksheets. You learned how to print quickly and easily using the default settings, and how to change the defaults. To customize your reports and make them more readable and understandable, you learned how to break the worksheet into pages; change the margins and page length; and provide headers, footers, and borders on the printout. You also discovered how to take full advantage of your printer's capabilities by passing setup strings to the printer.

Successfully printing large spreadsheets with a variety of options generally takes practice and some study of your printer manual. Use this chapter as a reference as you continue to experiment.

The next two chapters show you how to add visual effects to your reports. Chapter 10 shows you how to create graphs and view them on-screen; Chapter 11 shows how to print the graphs.

CASH FLOW PROJECTOR   Copyright (C) 1987 Que Corporation

BALANCES IN WORKING CAPITAL ACCOUNTS

Assets
- Cash
- Accounts Receivable
- Inventory

Liabilities
- Accounts Payable
- Line of Credit

Net Working Capital

	Oct	Nov	Dec
Cash			$17,355
Accounts Receivable			493,151
Inventory			163,833
Accounts Payable			125,000
Line of Credit			0
Net Working Capital			$549,339

SALES

	Oct	Nov	Dec	...	Nov	Dec	Total
Profit Center 1	$27,832	$23,864	$26,125		$44,091	$42,536	$570,036
Profit Center 2	13,489	21,444	20,140		27,060	26,701	358,228
Profit Center 3	125,811	124,382	123,618		145,198	150,510	1,716,633
Profit Center 4	94,285	92,447	89,010		107,522	107,522	1,254,073
Profit Center 5					325,000	350,000	1,490,000
Total Sales	$262,417	$262,137	$258,893		$653,305	$677,269	$5,388,970

Percent of Collections: Cash 10%, 30 Days 20%, 60 Days 50%, 90 Days 20%

| Cash Collections | $262,417 | $141,363 | $258,893 | | $580,275 | $629,878 | $1,664,085 |

PURCHASES

Cost of Goods Sold

	Oct	Nov	Dec	...	Nov	Dec	Total
Profit Center 1 (33%)	$9,185	$7,875	$8,621		$14,550	$14,037	$188,112
Profit Center 2 (29%)	$3,912	$6,219	$5,841		$7,847	$7,743	103,886
Profit Center 3 (50%)	$63,406	$62,191	$61,809		$72,599	$75,255	858,317
Profit Center 4 (67%)	$63,171	$61,939	$59,637		$75,011	$72,040	840,229
Profit Center 5 (30%)					$97,500	$105,000	447,000
Total Cost of Goods Sold	$139,673	$138,224	$135,908		$267,507	$274,075	$2,437,543

Inventory Purchasing Schedule: 0 Days in Advance 5%, 30 Days in Advance 50%, 60 Days in Advance 30%, 90 Days in Advance 15%

| Inventory Purchases | $138,873 | $141,363 | $148,015 | | $273,747 | $274,075 | $2,632,637 |

Payment Schedule: Cash 30%, 30 Days 40%, 60 Days 30%

| Payment For Purchases | $138,873 | $141,363 | $142,612 | | $269,766 | $272,795 | $2,504,680 |

OPERATING EXPENSES

	Oct	Nov	Dec	...	Nov	Dec	Total
Profit Center 1	$20,458	$20,760	$20,963		$21,565	$26,881	$229,461
Profit Center 2	14,377	15,002	15,587		21,565	26,881	228,315
Profit Center 3	25,921	27,329	27,230		32,048	32,525	360,347
Profit Center 4	13,922	14,885	15,801		24,023	24,806	236,052
Profit Center 5							224,495
Corporate Overhead	14,944	15,262	15,801		21,565	22,378	228,702
Total Expenses	$89,622	$92,302	$95,491		$148,028	$150,529	$1,571,372

Payment Schedule: Cash 70%, 30 Days 20%, 60 Days 10%

| Total Payment For Expenses | $94,266 | | | | $146,883 | $149,515 | $1,549,288 |

Fig. 9.21

The Cash Flow Projector report printed using Sideways.

Fig. 9.22

*The Sideways
command menu.*

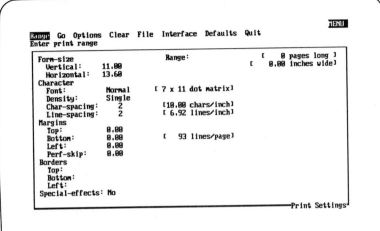

Fig. 9.22

*The Sideways
command menu.*

Range Go Options Clear File Interface Defaults Quit   MENU
Enter print range

```
 Form-size                     Range:              [     0 pages long ]
   Vertical:    11.00                              [   0.00 inches wide]
   Horizontal:  13.60
 Character
   Font:        Normal    [ 7 x 11 dot matrix]
   Density:     Single
   Char-spacing:    2     [10.00 chars/inch]
   Line-spacing:    2     [ 6.92 lines/inch]
 Margins
   Top:         0.00
   Bottom:      0.00      [   93 lines/page]
   Left:        0.00
   Perf-skip:   0.00
 Borders
   Top:
   Bottom:
   Left:
 Special-effects: No
                                                  Print Settings
```

10

Creating and Displaying Graphs

E ven if Lotus 1-2-3 provided only spreadsheet capabilities (the *1* in 1-2-3), the program would be extremely powerful. More information can be quickly assembled and tabulated electronically than could possibly be developed manually. But despite the importance of keeping detailed worksheets that show real or projected data, that data can be worthless if it can't be readily understood.

To help decision-makers who are pressed for time or unable to draw conclusions from countless rows of numeric data, and who may benefit from seeing key figures displayed graphically, Lotus offers graphics capabilities—the *2* in 1-2-3. The program offers five types of basic business graphs as well as limited options for enhancing the graphs' appearance. Although no match for the capabilities of many stand-alone graphics packages, 1-2-3's strength lies in its integration with the spreadsheet.

This chapter shows you how to do the following:

- Develop graphs using a minimum of commands
- Enhance the appearance of a graph
- Preserve the graph on disk
- Edit the current contents of a graph
- Reset some or all graph settings
- Select an appropriate graph type

- Develop all graph types

- Bypass selected 1-2-3 graph limitations

Draft- versus Final-Quality Graphs

Selecting /Graph from the initial 1-2-3 menu produces the main Graph menu:

Type X A B C D E F Reset View Save Options Name Quit

You can create graphs that display nothing more than unlabeled data points in bar (or stacked-bar), line (or XY), and pie forms. To do so, select a graph Type, specify a data range or ranges from choices **X A B C D E F**, and View the screen output. The result is a draft-quality graph that depicts relationships between numbers or trends across time.

To improve the appearance of your graphs and produce labeled final-quality output suitable for business presentations, you can select one or more Options. Select Save to store a graph for printing. And if you plan to recall specifications, use Name to store your graph specifications in the current spreadsheet.

Suppose that you want to make a quick on-screen comparison of specific data in your current worksheet—quarterly sales information in one range and the associated gross-profit figures in another range. By issuing the following command sequences, each on a separate line, you can produce the minimal graph shown in figure 10.1. (Note in the graph command sequences in this chapter that keys to be pressed to select menu options, and data to be entered, are shown in boldface type. Remember also that you do not press Enter when you make a menu selection, but you do press Enter after typing in data.)

> /Graph **Type Bar**
> **A N5..Q5** (Sales data range A)
> **B N8..Q8** (Gross Profit data range B)
> **View**

In this graph, the four sets of bars represent quarterly data. The bars are graphed in order from left to right, starting with the first quarter. Within each set, the left-hand bar represents Sales data and the right-hand bar, the corresponding Gross Profit figure. This minimal graph shows the upward movement of sales and gross profit throughout the first three quarters, followed by a downward trend in the fourth.

Suppose that you want to improve the appearance of this quarterly trend analysis before showing it to your colleagues. To produce the final-quality graph shown in figure 10.2, use the following command sequences:

/Graph Type **Bar**
      A N5..Q5   (Sales data range A)
      B N8..Q8   (Gross Profit data range B)
      X N3..Q3   (Quarterly headings below x-axis)
      Options Titles First **YOUR FIRM NAME**
              Titles Second **MIDWEST REGION**
              Titles X-Axis **1987 OPERATIONS**
              Titles Y-Axis **DOLLARS**
              Legend **A SALES**
              Legend **B GROSS PROFIT**
              Grid **Horizontal**
              Scale **Y** Scale Format Currency **0**

Fig. 10.1

A minimal, or draft-quality, sample graph.

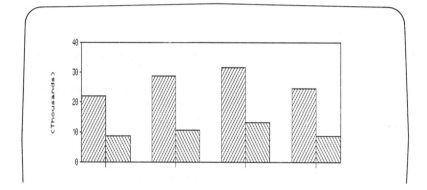

Fig. 10.2

A presentation-quality sample graph.

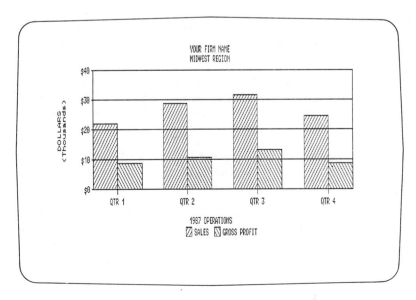

As you can see, even those who are unfamiliar with the data will be able to understand the contents of an enhanced graph.

In this chapter, you will learn how to apply all the options to one line graph. Then you'll learn how to construct all the other types of 1-2-3 graphs.

Basic Requirements for Creating a Graph

Before creating your first graph, you must determine whether your hardware supports viewing and printing graphs, whether your 1-2-3 software is correctly installed and loaded, and whether the spreadsheet on-screen contains data you want to graph. And you should understand which type of graph is best suited for presenting specific numeric data in picture form.

Hardware and Software Setup

We will use 1-2-3's graphics feature to create and view a graph, store its specifications for later use, and print it. Creating and storing a graph requires only that you have the Lotus system software installed on your equipment and that you correctly select options from the **Graph** menu.

Reminder:
To view a graph on-screen, you need a graphics monitor or a monitor with a graphics-display adapter.

To view a graph on-screen, you need a graphics monitor or a monitor with a graphics-display adapter. (Without such a monitor, you can construct and save a 1-2-3 graph, but you must print the graph to view it.) If you have two graphics monitors installed, one monitor will display the spreadsheet while the other displays the graph.

To print a graph, you need a graphics printer supported by 1-2-3 and a separate set of PrintGraph instructions. (These instructions are illustrated in Chapter 11.)

To create a graph, first load 1-2-3 and retrieve a worksheet file containing the data you want to graph. Suppose, for example, that you want to graph data from the 1987 CASH FLOW DATA spreadsheet, part of which is displayed in figures 10.3A and 10.3B.

To graph information from this spreadsheet's Working Capital Accounts section, you need to know which numeric data you can plot and which data (numeric or label) you may be able to use to enhance the graph.

Account names are displayed across columns A, B, and C. Monthly headings and amounts appear in columns D through O. The numeric entries in rows 7, 8, 9, 14, and 15, as well as the formula results in rows 11, 17, and 19, are suitable for graphing as data points.

Fig. 10.3A

The sample WORKING CAPITAL ACCOUNTS worksheet: January through June.

```
           A          B          C        D          E         F          G         H         I
 1 1987 CASH FLOW DATA
 2
 3 ================================================================================================
 4 WORKING CAPITAL ACCOUNTS      Jan        Feb        Mar        Apr       May       Jun
 5 ================================================================================================
 6 Current Assets:
 7   Cash                     $31,643    $34,333    $36,657    $35,614   $29,146   $20,000
 8   Accounts Receivable      510,780    533,597    551,287    577,314   614,997   641,802
 9   Inventory                169,209    176,671    189,246    206,788   228,828   269,990
10                            --------   --------   --------   --------  --------  --------
11     Total Current Assets   711,632    744,601    777,189    819,715   872,970   931,792
12
13 Current Liabilities:
14   Accounts Payable         130,754    139,851    150,186    163,731   180,350   203,669
15   Other Short-term Debt          0          0          0          0         0     1,834
16                            --------   --------   --------   --------  --------  --------
17     Total Current Liabilities 130,754  139,851   150,186    163,731   180,350   205,503
18
19 Net Working Capital       $580,878   $604,750   $627,003   $655,984  $692,620  $726,289
20                           ========   ========   ========   ========  ========  ========
```

Fig. 10.3B

The sample WORKING CAPITAL ACCOUNTS worksheet: July through December.

```
           A          B          C        J          K         L          M         N         O
 1 1987 CASH FLOW DATA
 2
 3 ================================================================================================
 4 WORKING CAPITAL ACCOUNTS      Jul        Aug        Sep        Oct       Nov       Dec
 5 ================================================================================================
 6 Current Assets:
 7   Cash                     $20,000    $20,000    $76,623   $186,131  $337,995  $582,796
 8   Accounts Receivable      750,544    879,271    989,501  1,097,616 1,170,646 1,218,036
 9   Inventory                296,527    324,230    345,629    352,687   358,926   358,926
10                            --------   --------   --------   --------  --------  --------
11     Total Current Assets 1,067,071  1,223,501  1,411,753  1,636,434 1,867,567 2,159,759
12
13 Current Liabilities:
14   Accounts Payable         225,085    243,320    258,740    267,621   272,747   275,041
15   Other Short-term Debt      8,327      2,035          0          0         0         0
16                            --------   --------   --------   --------  --------  --------
17     Total Current Liabilities 233,412  245,355   258,740    267,621   272,747   275,041
18
19 Net Working Capital       $833,659   $978,146 $1,153,013 $1,368,812 $1,594,820 $1,884,718
20                           ========   ========   ========   ========  ========  ========
```

To develop graphs to view on-screen, select **/Graph** from the main 1-2-3 menu to display the **Graph** menu. You will always use two options from the main **Graph** menu. You must indicate which **T**ype of graph you want. You must define at least one data series from the choices **X A B C D E F**. (You should use the **X** option as a data range only when you create an XY graph, which is explained later in this chapter.) To display the graph, assuming that you have a graphics-equipped monitor, you then select **V**iew.

Selecting a Graph Type

Selecting one of the five available graph types is easy. When you select **T**ype from the **Graph** menu, the following options are displayed:

Line   Bar   XY   Stacked-Bar   Pie

By selecting one of these options, you set that graph type and automatically restore the **Graph** menu to the control panel.

To understand which type will best display specific numeric data, you must know something about plotting points on a graph. Let's review the two basic terms (*x-axis* and *y-axis*) illustrated in figure 10.4.

Fig. 10.4

The graph's x and y axes.

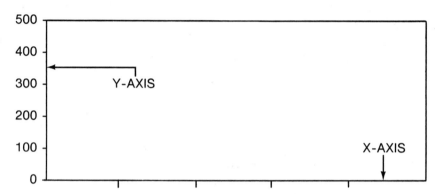

All graphs (except pie graphs) have two axes: the y-axis (the vertical left edge) and the x-axis (the horizontal bottom edge). 1-2-3 automatically provides tick marks for both axes. The program also scales the adjacent numbers on the y-axis, based on the minimum and maximum figures included in the plotted data range(s).

Every point plotted on a graph has a unique location (x,y): *x* represents the time period or the amount measured along the horizontal axis; *y* measures the corresponding amount along the vertical axis. The intersection of the y-axis and the x-axis is called the *origin*. Notice that the origin of the graph in figure 10.4 is zero (0). To minimize misinterpretation of graph results and to make graphs easier to compare, use a zero origin in your graphs. Later in this chapter, you will learn how to manually change the upper or lower limits of the scale initially set by 1-2-3.

Of the five 1-2-3 graph types, all but the pie graph display both x- and y-axes. Line, bar, and stacked-bar graphs display figures (centered on the tick marks) along the y-axis only. The XY graph displays figures on both axes. (A general statement about the use of each 1-2-3 graph type precedes the explanation of how to construct that type of graph.)

Specifying a Worksheet Data Range

1-2-3 does not permit you to type in data to be plotted on a graph. Do not confuse the process of plotting data points with that of typing descriptions, such as titles, which is illustrated later in this chapter.

Reminder:
You enter data
to be plotted
on a graph by
highlighting data
from the worksheet.

To create a graph, you must specify data from the currently displayed spreadsheet as a data series in range form. To enter a data series from the main **Graph** menu, choose one of the following options:

> X   A   B   C   D   E   F

Before you start building a graph, read the following general statements about the choice(s) required for each graph type:

Graph type	*Option(s)*
Line	Enter as many as six data series after you have accessed separately the **Graph** menu choices **A B C D E F**. You do not have to start with **A**. The data points in every data series are marked by a unique symbol (see table 10.1).
Bar	Enter as many as six data series after you have accessed separately the **Graph** menu choices **A B C D E F**. You do not have to start with **A**. Multiple data ranges appear on the graph from left to right in alphabetical order. Every data series displayed in black and white has unique shading. Every data series displayed in color is assigned one of three colors. (Shading and screen colors are summarized in table 10.1).
XY	To enter the data series being plotted as the independent variable, select **X** from the main **Graph** menu. Plot at least one dependent variable (you would usually select **A**). The unique symbols that mark the data points depend on which A-through-F data series is used with **X**. The symbols are the same as the **Line** symbols in table 10.1.
Stacked-Bar	Follow the Bar graph instructions. In a stacked-bar graph, multiple data ranges appear from bottom to top in alphabetical order.
Pie	Enter only one data series by selecting **A** from the main **Graph** menu. (To shade and "explode" pieces of the pie, also select **B**.)

As you build your own graphs, refer to the preceding comments (organized by graph type) and to the summary information (organized by data range) in table 10.1. This table (which can be found in the section "Using the Legend Option") shows each data range with the corresponding default assignments for line symbols, bar shading, and color.

Constructing the Default Line Graph

After you have selected the appropriate graph type for the data you will plot, producing a graph is easy. Using the Net Working Capital amounts in row 19 of figure 10.3A, you can create a line graph of the January-through-June amounts or the January-through December amounts. From 1-2-3's main menu, select /Graph to access the **Graph** menu.

Ordinarily, the next step would be to select **Type**. But because this is the initial graph created after you load 1-2-3, and **Line** is the default type, you don't have to make a selection.

To enter the first data range, choose **A** from the main **Graph** menu and then respond to the control-panel prompt by typing *D19..I19*.

By specifying the type of graph and the spreadsheet location of data to plot, you have completed the minimum requirements for creating a graph. If you press View, you'll see a graph similar to that shown in figure 10.5.

Fig. 10.5

A default line graph.

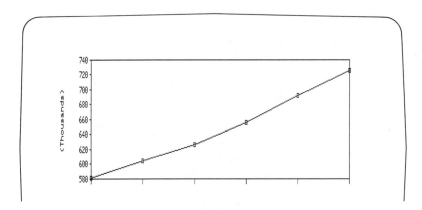

You know what this graph represents, but it won't mean much to anyone else. Although the six data points corresponding to the January-through-June figures have been plotted, none of the points has been labeled to indicate what it represents. And the two data points that rest on the graph's left and right vertical sides are difficult to see.

Because 1-2-3 sets a scale based on minimum and maximum values in the range, the program automatically displays the (Thousands) indicator along the y-axis. Notice, however, that the origin on this initial 1-2-3 line graph is not zero, which makes the upward trend seem larger than it really is.

Reminder:
1-2-3 automatically enters an indicator of units along the y-axis.

Before delving into the specific characteristics of each graph type, you should be aware of some of the available methods for improving the appearance of your graphs. These methods apply to all graph types, unless stated otherwise.

Enhancing the Appearance of a Basic Graph

As you know, you can create an on-screen graph by selecting from the main Graph menu a **Type**, the appropriate data series (**X A B C D E F**), and View. If you want to improve the appearance of your graph, select **Options** to access the following submenu:

Legend   Format   Titles   Grid   Scale   Color   B&W   Data-Labels   Quit

As you add enhancements to your graphs, check the results frequently. If you have only one monitor, select **Quit** to leave the **Graph Options** menu and return to the main **Graph** menu. Then select View to check the most recent version of the graph. Press any key to exit the graph display and restore the **Graph** menu to the screen.

To view the current graph from the worksheet's READY mode, press the F10 (Graph) key, which instantly redraws the graph with any updated information. Whenever you are not in MENU mode, you can use the F10 (Graph) key to "toggle" between the worksheet and the graph.

Reminder:
Use the F10 (Graph) key to toggle between displaying the worksheet and displaying the graph.

Adding Descriptive Labels and Numbers

To add descriptive information to a graph, you use the Legend, **Titles**, and **Data-Labels** options from the **Options** menu and the **X** option from the main Graph menu. Figure 10.6 shows where these additional items will appear on your graph.

As you can see, data labels appear within the graph. Descriptions entered with the **X** option appear immediately below the x-axis. You can enter as many as four titles: two at the top and one to describe each axis. Legends describing the shading, color, or symbols assigned to data ranges in line or bar graphs appear across the bottom of those graphs.

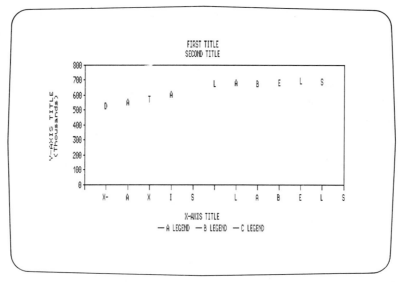

Fig. 10.6

Graph location of descriptive information.

Using the Titles Option

If you select /**Graph O**ptions **T**itles, the following options will be displayed in the control panel:

> First   Second   X-Axis   Y-Axis

Reminder:
The first title you enter with /Graph Options Titles will be printed twice the size of other titles.

You can enter one or two centered titles at the top of your graph. If you enter two titles, both will be the same size on-screen. But on the printed graph, the title you enter by selecting **F**irst will be twice the size of any other title specified. You can enter titles by typing a new description, by specifying a range name, or by referencing the cell location of a label or a number already in the worksheet.

Suppose that you want to enhance the basic line graph of the net working-capital amounts (refer to fig. 10.5). (Figures 10.3A and 10.3B contain the worksheet data for this graph.) You'll enter four titles, using cell references for two of the titles and typing new descriptions for the others.

Select **T**itles **F**irst and then, when 1-2-3 prompts you for a title, type *ABC Company.* Then press Enter. The **O**ptions menu (*not* the **T**itles submenu) will reappear.

Select **T**itles **S**econd and type \A*19* to make Net Working Capital (the contents of cell A19) the second top-centered title. Then, to reproduce 1987 CASH FLOW DATA beneath the x-axis, select **T**itles **X**-Axis and type \A*1*. To enter the fourth title, select **T**itles **Y**-Axis and then type *Actual Dollars.* Now check the graph by selecting **Quit** (to restore the main **Graph** menu) and then choosing **View**. Your graph should look like the enhanced graph in figure 10.7.

Fig. 10.7

Titles added to a line graph.

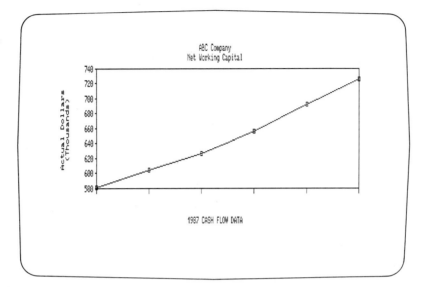

Although all titles appear on-screen in the same print style, when you print the graph you can select one font (such as italic) for the top title and another font for other titles and labels. (For a detailed discussion of this topic, see Chapter 11.)

Cue:
You can change fonts for printing each type of title.

To edit a title, use the command sequence that you used for creating the title. The existing text, cell reference, or range name will appear in the control panel, ready for editing. If you want to eliminate a title, press Esc and then press Enter.

The X-Axis and Y-Axis titles have no significance when you construct a pie graph.

Entering Labels within a Graph

After a data series has been graphed, you can enter values or labels to explain each point plotted on the graph. You do so by first selecting **Options Data-Labels** from the main **Graph** menu and then specifying the data series (**A B C D E F**) to which the data labels apply. Instead of typing the labels (as you typed the titles), you must specify each data-label range by pointing to an existing range in the worksheet, providing cell coordinates, and specifying a previously determined range name.

Continue to enhance your sample line graph by entering the January-through-June headings from row 4 of the worksheet (refer to fig. 10.3A). First, select /Graph Options Data-Labels. The following submenu choices will appear on-screen:

A   B   C   D   E   F   Quit

Below this menu, you'll see a line explaining that the highlighted **A** menu choice is used for specifying data labels for the A range. The only data range currently defined in the Working Capital line graph is the A range, which is defined as D19..I19.

To enter the six abbreviated monthly headings from row 4 in the worksheet, select **A** and then type *D4..I4* in response to the prompt for a label range. The following submenu will appear:

Center   Left   Above   Right   Below

From this menu, select only one option for each data-label range you are identifying. In other words, you cannot position one cell within a data-label range *above* its associated data point and another cell within that same data-label range *below* its associated data point.

To continue enhancing your graph, select **Above** and press **Quit**. Return to the main **Graph** menu by selecting **Quit** from the **Options** menu. To check the graph, select **View**. Your graph should resemble that in figure 10.8.

Fig. 10.8

Data-labels added within a line graph.

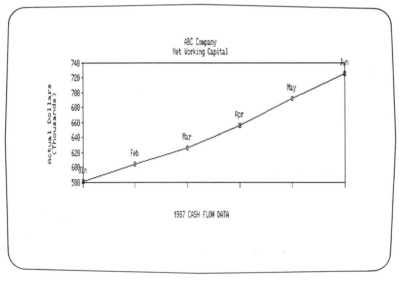

Placing labels within a graph often produces less than desirable results. Particularly on line graphs, the first and last labels tend to overlap the graph's edges. To solve this problem, you can expand any data ranges defined for a line graph by including blank cells at each end of the ranges defined.

If you graph more than one data series, attach the data labels to the data series with the largest figures. Then select **Above** to position the data labels above the data points plotted. To enter text or numbers as the plotted points, use the **Center** option with line graphs that display **Neither** lines nor symbols. (See the example in Chapter 12.)

To edit either the range or position of the data label, use the same command sequence you used to create the data label. Edit the current range, or specify a different position.

To eliminate a data label, use one of two methods. If you remember both the data series (**A B C D E F**) and the position (**Center, Left,** and so on) that you specified when you entered the data label, you can follow the original setup sequence, overriding the existing data-label range by substituting any single blank cell in the worksheet. (You cannot eliminate the existing range by pressing Esc, as you did to eliminate an unwanted title.)

To remove the January-through-June data labels from within the sample Working Capital graph, use the following sequence:

```
/Graph Options Data-Labels A        (data series)
    Enter D1        (to blank out the existing range)
    Select Above
```

Restore the main **Graph** menu by pressing **Quit** twice. Then press **View** to check the graph. The graph should again resemble that shown in figure 10.7.

The other method of removing data labels involves resetting the data series. Don't use this method if you want to remove only the labels. Because this method destroys not only associated options (such as data labels) but also the data, you would have to reenter the data series. (To learn more about resetting all or parts of graph settings, read this chapter's "Resetting the Current Graph" section.)

You cannot use the **Data-Labels** option for a pie graph.

Entering Labels Below the X-Axis

Instead of placing descriptive information within a graph, you may prefer to enter label information along the x-axis. The main **Graph** menu's **X** option has two distinct functions. Use it to position labels below the x-axis in line, bar, and stacked-bar graphs, or to enter a data series in an XY graph. (XY graphs are discussed later in this chapter.) You can use the **X** option also to identify slices of a pie chart.

Suppose, for example, that you want to enter the actual January-through-June Net Working Capital figures as labels below your sample graph's x-axis. Select **X** from the main **Graph** menu and type *D19..I19* when 1-2-3 prompts you for a range. Then select **View**. Your graph should look like that in figure 10.9.

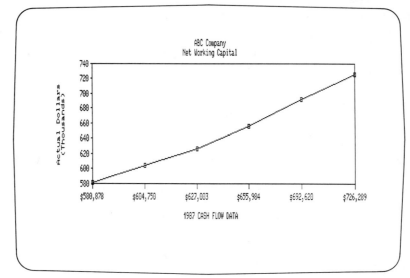

Notice that in this graph, the values used as descriptive labels below the x-axis display the same format shown in the worksheet.

You may remember that entries within the range you specify for descriptions can be either values or labels. To practice entering labels, you'll change the Net Working Capital descriptive amounts to January-through-June headings. To do so, select **X** from the main **Graph** menu, and then type *D4..I4* when 1-2-3 prompts you for a range. When you choose **View** to check the graph, your graph should resemble that shown in figure 10.10.

Caution:

If the x-axis labels or numbers are longer than 9 or 10 characters, parts of the descriptions may not be displayed.

If the x-axis labels or numbers are longer than 9 or 10 characters, parts of the extreme right or left descriptions may not be displayed. To edit the x-axis labels, select **X** from the main **Graph** menu and then override the current range by typing or pointing to a different range. To eliminate the x-axis labels, select **/Graph Reset X**.

You cannot use the **X** option to enter labels below the x-axis when you construct an XY or pie graph. (The x-axis can be used to place labels next to each pie slice in a pie graph, however.)

Fig. 10.10

Displaying labels below the x-axis.

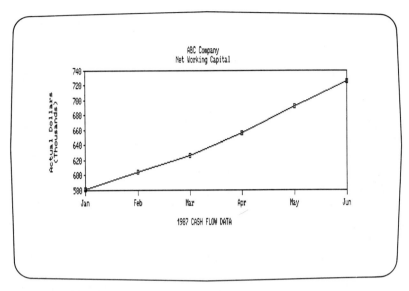

Using the Legend Option

Whenever a graph contains more than one set of data, you need to be able to distinguish between those sets. If you are using a color monitor and select Color from the main **Graph** menu, 1-2-3 differentiates data series with color. If the main **Graph** menu's default option **B&W** (black and white) is in effect, data series in line graphs will be marked with special symbols; data series in bar-type graphs will be marked with unique patterns of crosshatches. (See table 10.1 for a summary of the assignments specific to each data range.)

Table 10.1
Graph Symbols and Shading

Data Range	Line Graph Symbols	Bar Graph B&W Shading	On-Screen Color
A	□		Red
B	+		Blue
C	◊		White
D	△		Red
E	✕		Blue
F	▽		White

Caution:
Choose /Graph
Options B&W
before saving your
graph for printing,
to make sure that
data ranges are
shaded correctly.

If you intend to print the graph on a black-and-white printer, even if you have a color monitor, choose **B&W** before saving the graph. A graph saved under the **C**olor option will print on a black-and-white printer as all black.

You might pick a data series (**A B C D E F**) because you want certain symbols or shadings or, more often, to avoid using certain combinations of symbols or shadings. For example, if you entered only two data items in a line graph and used data ranges **D** and **F**, you would have difficulty distinguishing between the two three-sided assigned symbols—one pointing up and the other pointing down. On the other hand, pairing the A range (widely spaced crosshatches) with the D range (narrowly spaced crosshatches extending in the opposite direction) on a bar graph produces a distinctly different display. To provide explanatory text for data that is represented by symbols or shadings, use legends below the x-axis.

The most recent version of the sample Working Capital line graph displays the square symbol assigned to the data points entered as the A data series (refer to fig. 10.10). Suppose that you want to change the data to reflect two items, Total Current Assets (CA) and Total Current Liabilities (CL), rather than the single item reflecting Net Working Capital.

First, change the second title line to reflect the changed data. Select **/G**raph **O**ptions **T**itles **S**econd, press Esc to remove the current cell reference, and type *Components of Working Capital* as the new second title. You'll retain the A range, respecifying the data range as Current Assets, and add a second range, C, for the Current Liabilities. (Because you don't eliminate the A range, you don't use the **R**eset option.)

To enter the Total Current Assets figures for the first six months of the year, select **/G**raph **A** and then either type *D11..I11* or press Esc once and point to the range. If you remove the anchor from the data series range by pressing Esc, you must re-anchor it by pressing the period (.) key. When the main **G**raph menu reappears, select **C** and type *D17..I17* in response to the prompt for a range. Choose **O**ptions **L**egend **A** and, when 1-2-3 prompts you for a legend name, type *TOTAL CA*. Then select **L**egend **C** and type *TOTAL CL* at the prompt. Press **Q**uit to exit the **O**ptions menu. When you press **V**iew, 1-2-3 will display the modified graph (see fig. 10.11).

Reminder:
To edit a legend,
use the same
command
sequence you use
to create a legend.

If you want to edit a legend, use the same command sequence you used to create that legend. The existing text, cell reference, or range name will appear in the control panel, ready for you to edit. To eliminate a legend, press Esc and then press Enter.

Legends are appropriate only for graphs with two or more data series. You cannot use the **L**egend option for pie graphs, which can have only one data series.

Fig. 10.11

*Adding legends to
the line graph.*

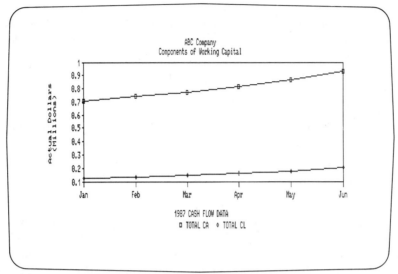

Altering the Default Graph Display

All the previously described enhancements involve adding label or number descriptions to the basic minimal graph. 1-2-3 supplies the additional default display items shown in figures 10.10 and 10.11.

For example, in both of these graphs the figures (scale) along the vertical y-axis were set automatically, taking into account the minimum and maximum values in the data ranges plotted. The amounts are displayed in General format. 1-2-3 also determines the parenthetical display of an indicator: (Thousands) in figure 10.10, (Millions) in figure 10.11. Within the graphs, 1-2-3 automatically centers the symbols on data points plotted; black lines are used to connect the symbols, leaving the background clear. All labels that were included in the x-axis range are displayed below the graphs.

You can change any of these additional default graph display items. To continue enhancing the appearance of a basic graph, you'll change the defaults in the simple line graph. (Additional illustrations are included in this chapter's explanations of how to develop all graph types.)

Specifying Connecting Lines or Symbols

A few choices on the **O**ptions menu do not apply to all graphs. For example, you've learned that **T**itles, **L**egend, and **D**ata-Labels are not applicable to pie graphs. The **F**ormat option, which is used to display connecting lines and symbols on a line-type graph, is appropriate for only two types of graphs: Line

*Reminder:
A few choices on
the **O**ptions menu
do not apply to all
graphs.*

and XY (a form of line graph). Do not confuse this **Format** option with the **Options Scale X-** (or **Y-**) **Axis Format** option. (Refer to the Command Menu Map if you are uncertain about the difference in the command sequences for these two **Format** options.)

Selecting **/Graph Options Format** produces this submenu:

Graph   A   B   C   D   E   F   Quit

You can control the lines and symbols for the entire line-type graph or for only a specific data range (or ranges). After you make a selection, this final submenu appears:

Lines   Symbols   Both   Neither

You'll use the graph shown in figure 10.10 to learn the mechanics of switching the default setting (**Both**) to **Lines** only. (You'll learn about specifying **Neither** or **Symbols** in this chapter's "Line Graphs" section.) Select **/Graph Options Format A Lines Quit**. Then choose **Quit** from the **Options** menu, and select **View** to check the graph. As you can see from figure 10.12, the square symbols centered on A range data points are no longer displayed.

Fig. 10.12

Suppressing the display of symbols in the line graph.

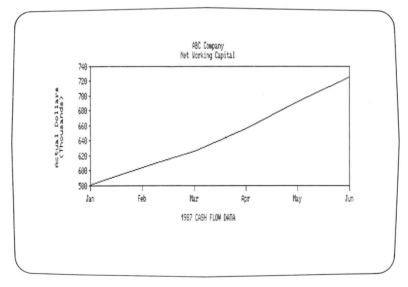

Experiment with different format displays by repeating the command sequences, first selecting the data range(s) that you want to change and then selecting a specific format. To restore the default format setting for the sample line graph, select **/Graph Options Format A B**oth. Returning to the main **Graph** menu and selecting **View** restores the graph shown in figure 10.10.

Note that you cannot use the Format option from the Graph Options menu for bar, stacked-bar, or pie graphs.

Setting a Background Grid

Ordinarily, you'll use the default (clear) background for your graphs. But there may be times when you'll want to impose a grid on a graph so that the data-point amounts are easier to read.

Selecting /**Graph O**ptions **Grid** produces this menu:

  Horizontal   Vertical   Both   Clear

The first option creates a series of horizontal lines across the graph, spaced according to the tick marks on the y-axis. The second option creates a series of vertical lines across the graph, spaced according to the tick marks on the x-axis. The third option causes both horizontal and vertical lines to appear, and the fourth clears all grid lines from the graph.

To add horizontal lines to the sample graph, select /**Graph O**ptions **Grid Horizontal**. Then select **Q**uit from the **O**ptions menu and press **View**. The graph should look like that shown in figure 10.13.

Reminder:
You cannot use the
Format option from
the Graph Options
menu for bar,
stacked-bar, or pie
graphs.

Fig. 10.13

Adding a horizontal grid to the line graph.

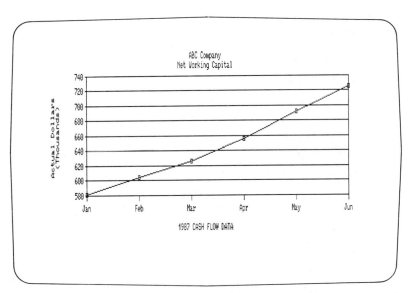

Experiment with different grids, repeating the command sequence and specifying other options. Whenever you want to eliminate a grid display, select /**Graph O**ptions **Grid Clear**.

Changing Axis Scale Settings

You can use the Scale option to alter three distinct default settings associated with the values displayed along a graph's x- and y-axes.

When a line, XY, bar, or stacked-bar graph is created, 1-2-3 automatically sets scale values displayed on the y-axis, taking into account the smallest and largest numbers in the data ranges plotted. (For XY graphs only, 1-2-3 also establishes x-axis scale values.)

You can change the upper and lower scale values. You cannot, however, determine the size of the increment between the maximum and minimum values (this increment is indicated by tick marks). For example, you cannot change the scale along the y-axis of the graph shown in figure 10.13 from the default increment of 20,000 to an increment of 25,000 on each tick mark (575, 600, 625, 650, 675, 700, 725, and 750). Furthermore, the increment displayed on the screen may not be the increment printed. As you will learn from Chapter 11, increments for scale values on printed graphs are the same as, or more closely spaced than, those displayed on-screen.

1-2-3 automatically sets the format of the scale values to General—the same default global numeric display that you see when you access a blank worksheet. Notice that dollar signs, commas, and decimal points are not displayed along the y-axis in figure 10.13. You can change the format to any of the styles available under the /Worksheet Global Format or /Range Format menus. Do not confuse the capability of altering the default format of the scale values with that of bringing in previously formatted worksheet numbers as data labels.

The third automatic scale-related display is the indicator that appears along the y-axis when a line, XY, bar, or stacked-bar graph is created. (On an XY graph, an indicator appears also along the x-axis.) This indicator appears as (Thousands) along the y-axis of the graph in figure 10.13.

Although you cannot change the indicator, you can suppress its display. To understand why you might want to suppress display of the indicator, imagine a worksheet that contains data with truncated trailing zeros (for example, a sales budget figure of 5,000,000 that has been entered in the worksheet as 5,000). Graphing the truncated figures will produce the y-axis indicator (Thousands), but you need (Millions). You can suppress display of the indicator and type an appropriate indicator as part of the y-axis title.

Select /Graph Options Scale to produce this menu:

   Y Scale   X Scale   Skip

To initiate changes in the upper or lower scale values, changes in the format of the scale values, or suppression of the scale indicator, select either of the first two options. (The Scale Skip command sequence is discussed in the following section.) Selecting either **Y** Scale or **X** Scale produces the following submenu:

Automatic   Manual   Lower   Upper   Format   Indicator   Quit

The **Automatic** and **Manual** options work as a set. To specify maximum (Upper) or minimum (**Lower**) axis values, select Manual; select Automatic to restore control to 1-2-3. When you select **Manual**, the entire submenu remains on the screen. Simply select Upper or Lower and respond to the prompt for a new figure.

If you elect to establish manual limits, remember that you must specify both upper and lower settings. Remember also that you can use negative figures for scale values in line, XY, and bar graphs, but not in stacked-bar or pie graphs.

Using the sample graph shown in figure 10.13, practice changing y-axis values by setting a minimum value of zero and a maximum value of 800,000. Select **/Graph Options Scale Y Scale Manual Lower** and then press Enter to accept the Ø displayed in the control panel. Immediately select **Upper**, and enter *800000* (without dollar signs or commas) as the upper limit. **Quit** the **Scale** submenu, **Quit** the **Options** menu, and press **View**. The graph should resemble that in figure 10.14.

Fig. 10.14

Changed y-axis upper and lower limits.

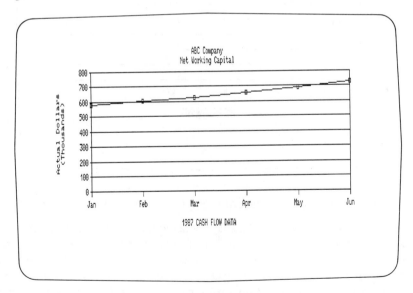

If you compare figures 10.13 and 10.14, you can see that setting the origin to zero (as should be done for most graphs) gives you a different perspective

on the magnitude of the increase in working capital. Notice also that 1-2-3 has changed the increment between tick marks from $20,000, in figure 10.13, to $100,000, in figure 10.14.

You can change scale format and suppress the scale indicator by using a few keystrokes. Suppose that you want to alter the y-axis title in the graph shown in figure 10.14 to indicate that the y-axis values are in thousands. Suppose also that you want to change the default **General** format to **Currency** format with zero decimal places and to suppress the automatic scale indicator.

Select **/Graph Options Titles Y-Axis** and type *(in thousands)* to add this information to the existing Actual Dollars title. Change the display format by selecting **Scale Y Scale Format Currency** and specifying zero decimal places. To suppress automatic display of the indicator, immediately select **Indicator** and then **No. Quit** the **Scale** submenu, **Quit** the **Options** menu, and **View** the graph (see fig. 10.15).

Fig. 10.15

Changed scale format and suppressed indicator.

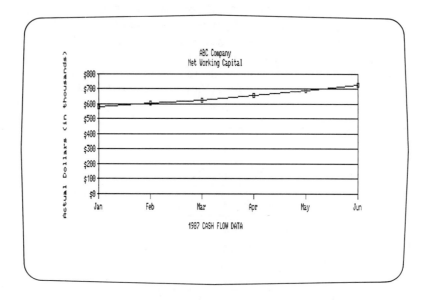

To see the changes, compare the graphs in figures 10.14 and 10.15.

Now restore the indicator display by selecting **/Graph Options Scale Y** (or **X**) **Scale Indicator Yes**. Change the format and manual limits by repeating the command sequences used to establish the first changes, this time selecting alternative formats or entering alternative minimum or maximum values. Restore the automatic scale limits by choosing **/Graph Options Scale Y** (or **X**) **Scale Automatic**.

Choose /**G**raph **O**ptions **S**cale **X** Scale only when the graph type is XY. Choose **Y** Scale for line, XY, bar, and stacked-bar graph types. The Format, Indicator, and **M**anual scale capabilities are not applicable to pie graphs.

Spacing Display of X-Axis Labels

You'll recall that selecting /**G**raph **O**ptions **S**cale produces the following options:

   Y Scale   X Scale   Skip

You've seen how to use the first two options. The **S**kip option determines the spacing of displayed labels—whether all labels or only every *n*th label you entered by selecting **X** from the main **G**raph menu will display below the x-axis. The default setting of 1 causes every label to display. If you set the skip factor to 3, every third label will be displayed.

If the labels are so long that they crowd together or overlap, use this option to improve the display. Technically, you can set a skip factor of 1 to 8,192, but you will seldom need to set the factor higher than 4.

Reminder:
Use /Graph Options Scale Skip when you cannot correctly display labels for the x-axis.

Suppose that the monthly headings below the x-axis in figure 10.15 were spelled out, which would tend to crowd the display. To set a skip factor other than the default, you would select /**G**raph **O**ptions **S**cale **S**kip and specify a factor of 2. Then return to the main **G**raph menu and press **V**iew. The changed spacing is shown in figure 10.16.

Fig. 10.16

Skipped labels on the x-axis.

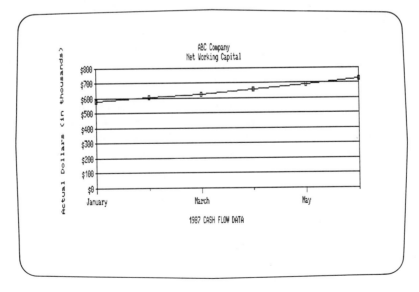

As you can see, only the January, March, and May x-axis labels are displayed. To retain the x-axis labels but restore the default setting of using every label in the range, repeat the command sequence, specifying a skip factor of 1.

Because using the main menu's **X** option to enter labels below the x-axis applies only to line, bar, and stacked-bar graphs, the **S**cale **S**kip command sequence does not apply to XY or pie graphs.

Viewing a Graph in Color

The /Graph **O**ptions **C**olor and **B**&W (black and white) options work as a set to control screen display of color. Setting colors to produce graph output on a color printer or plotter requires command input from the PrintGraph menu (see Chapter 11).

You can select the **B**&W option whether or not you have a color monitor installed. The initial setting when you load 1-2-3 is B&W. The connecting lines in XY or line graphs appear as white, amber, or green against a black background; bar or stacked-bar data ranges display a unique pattern of crosshatches. Refer to table 10.1 for a summary of the patterns of crosshatches assigned to each data range. (Pie graphs, which have unique capabilities for shading the portions of the single data range graphed, are illustrated in this chapter's "Pie Graph" section.)

To view graphs on-screen in color, you must use a color monitor. The connecting lines and symbols in XY or line graphs appear in the color assigned to the data range(s) in use; bar or stacked-bar segments reflect the color assigned to the data range(s) in use. Refer to table 10.1 for a summary of the colors assigned to each data range. (Pie graphs, which have unique capabilities for coloring the portions of the single data range graphed, are illustrated in this chapter's "Pie Graph" section.)

To illustrate 1-2-3's shading capabilities, you'll convert the line graph shown in figure 10.11 to a bar graph. (Note: Before you do this, you'll need to name the graph settings used to produce the graph in figure 10.11, if you haven't already done so.) Then, to produce the graph shown in figure 10.17, select **T**ype **B**ar.

Because the leftmost bar in each set represents Total Current Assets in the A data range, that bar is shaded for the A range. The rightmost bar in each set represents Total Current Liabilities, defined as the C data range, and is shaded accordingly. The legends at the bottom of the graph automatically reflect the appropriate black-and-white shading assignments.

If you have a color monitor, you can view this bar graph by selecting /Graph **O**ptions **C**olor. **Q**uit the **O**ptions menu and press **V**iew. As you can see from

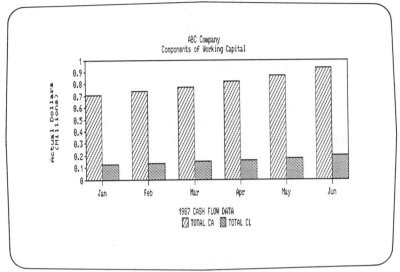

Fig. 10.17

Comparative bar graph in black and white.

the graph in figure 10.18, the shading in the bars is solid, which indicates that the Color option is in use.

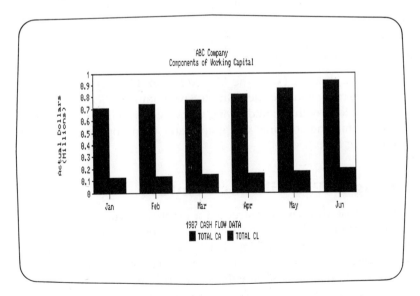

Fig. 10.18

Comparative bar graph in color.

In this graph, as in figure 10.17, the leftmost bar in each set represents Total Current Assets in the A data range. But on a color monitor, the entire bar would be filled in with the color red. The rightmost bar in each set, which represents Total Current Liabilities (defined as the C data range), would be filled in with white. The legends at the bottom of the graph would reflect the red and white color assignments.

A word of caution! If you can view (but not print) your graphs in color, restore the B&W setting by selecting /**Graph** **O**ptions **B&W** before you store your graphs.

The crosshatch shadings and colors assigned to data ranges **A B C D E F** do not apply to pie graphs which, unlike all other types, have only one possible data range (A). Coding input in the B data range determines the color or crosshatch shading assigned to each section of the pie (see this chapter's "Pie Graph" section).

Preserving the Graph on Disk

You have learned how to create a basic graph and how to use options to enhance display of that graph. All of the main **Graph** options (except **Reset**, **Save**, and **Name**) have been discussed in detail. In this section, we'll discuss the **Save** and **Name** options, which affect preserving the graph for future printing or recall to the screen. (The **Reset** option will be discussed just before we explain how to develop all graph types.)

Although using 1-2-3 to construct a graph from existing data in a spreadsheet is easy, having to rebuild the graph whenever you want to print or display it on-screen would be tedious.

Reminder:
Use /Graph Save
to save a graph file
for printing; use
/Graph Name to
view a graph later.
Always use /File
Save after using
/Graph Save or
/Graph Name to
store print and
display settings for
future use.

To create a disk file (with the file extension .PIC) that can be used only to print the graph, you use the /**Graph** **S**ave command. To save the graph specifications along with the underlying worksheet, you first use the /**Graph** **N**ame **C**reate command to name the graph, and then you save the worksheet by using /**File** **S**ave.

Saving a .PIC File for Printing

Suppose that you have constructed a graph that you want to store for subsequent printing through the PrintGraph program. (PrintGraph is discussed in Chapter 11.) After verifying that the graph type chosen is appropriate for your presentation needs, that the graph data ranges have been specified accurately, and that all desired enhancements have been added, choose /**Graph** **S**ave to create a .PIC file on disk. 1-2-3 prompts you for a file name and displays (in menu form across the top of the screen) a list of the .PIC files in the current directory.

You can either use the arrow keys to highlight an existing name or type a name that is as many as eight characters long. (1-2-3 will automatically add the extension.) If a .PIC file by the same name already exists in the current directory, you'll see a Cancel/**R**eplace menu similar to that which appears when you try to save a worksheet file under an existing name. To overwrite the contents of the existing .PIC file, select **R**eplace. To abort storage of the current graph as a .PIC file, select **C**ancel.

If you have set up subdirectories for disk storage, you can store the current graph as a .PIC file to other than the current subdirectory without first having to issue a **F**ile **D**irectory command to change directories. To store the graph, select /**G**raph **S**ave. Press Esc twice to remove all existing current-directory information. Then type the name of the new subdirectory in which you want to store this particular graph.

Remember two points: (1) /**G**raph **S**ave stores only an image of the current graph, locking in all data and enhancements, for the sole purpose of printing it with the PrintGraph program. When it is time to print, you cannot access this .PIC file to make changes such as adding a label or editing an underlying worksheet figure, although you can view the graph from the PrintGraph program. (2) You cannot recall the graph to screen in 1-2-3 unless you have named the graph if you created more than one graph and saved the worksheet. Naming graphs is described in the next section.

Creating Graph Specifications for Reuse

If you want to be able to view on-screen a graph that you created in an earlier graphing session (in which more than one graph was created), the graph must have been given a name when the graph was originally constructed (and the worksheet must have been saved, unless the same worksheet is still active). To name a graph, you issue the /**G**raph **N**ame command to access the following menu:

Use   Create   Delete   Reset

Only one graph at a time can be the *current* graph. If you want to save a graph that you have just completed (for subsequent recall to the screen) as well as build a new graph, you must first issue a /**G**raph **N**ame **C**reate command. The only way to store a graph for later screen display is to issue this command, which instructs 1-2-3 to remember the specifications used to define the current graph. If you don't name a graph and subsequently either reset the graph or change the specifications, you cannot restore the original without having to rebuild it.

When 1-2-3 prompts you for a graph name, provide a name that is up to 15 characters long. (You can use the same name for the .PIC file when you **S**ave the graph, and even for the worksheet file when you do a /**F**ile **S**ave; but remember that .PIC file names and .WK1 file names are limited to 8 characters each.)

You can use data from a single worksheet to create and name several different graphs. Just be sure to save the worksheet before you retrieve a different worksheet file or before you /**Q**uit 1-2-3. Graph specifications are stored with the worksheet file when you issue the /**F**ile **S**ave command.

To recall any named graphs from within the active spreadsheet, select /**G**raph **N**ame **U**se. When this command is issued, 1-2-3 displays a list of all the graph names stored in the current worksheet. You also can display the existing graph names by pressing the F3 (**N**ame) key. When the names are displayed, you can select the graph you want to redraw by either typing the appropriate name or pointing to the name on the list. By invoking **N**ame **U**se commands in rapid sequence, you create a "slide show" of 1-2-3 graphics.

To delete a single named graph, issue the /**G**raph **N**ame **D**elete command. Again, 1-2-3 will list all the graph names stored in the current worksheet. You can select the graph you want to delete by either typing the appropriate name or pointing to the name on the list.

If you want to delete all the graph names, issue the /**G**raph **N**ame **R**eset command. Be careful! This command does not have a Yes/No confirmation step. Using this command to delete the names of all graphs will also delete the parameters for all the graphs.

Keep in mind that /**G**raph **N**ame is like /**R**ange **N**ame: the name is available in a future worksheet session only if you have followed the **N**ame command with a /**F**ile **S**ave. /**G**raph **N**ame stores your graph settings in the current worksheet; /**F**ile **S**ave then stores the settings with the worksheet. Forgetting to use either /**G**raph **N**ame or /**F**ile **S**ave may result in extra work later.

Resetting the Current Graph

You may have noticed that, throughout this chapter, instructions for editing or removing options have been given at the end of each new topic. These instructions are important because 1-2-3 will continue to use an enhancement in the next version of the same graph, or in a new graph, unless you take specific actions to remove that enhancement. For example, you can build a series of six different bar graphs by specifying the graph **T**ype for only the first one. You'll recall that you did not have to respecify the titles you entered for the graph in figure 10.7 as you constructed the graphs in figures 10.8 through 10.10. Although you changed the second title to better explain the new data ranges in figure 10.11, that title was the only one of four that had to be changed.

If you want to make changes to only a few items in graph contents that involve enhancements, you can respecify or eliminate these items from the **Options** menu. However, if the next graph you'll construct is substantially different from the current one, you may want to use the /**Graph Reset** command. Selecting /**Graph Reset** produces this submenu:

Reminder:
Use /*Graph* **Reset** *when the next graph you want to construct is substantially different from the current one.*

Graph   X   A   B   C   D   E   F   Quit

Select **Graph** from this submenu only if you do not want to use any of the existing specifications in your new graph. This command, which ensures that no unwanted enhancements from a previous graph carry over into the current one, usually precedes any graph construction automated by macros. (Creating and using macros is discussed in Chapter 14.)

As an alternative to a total graph reset, you can specify removal of an individual data range. All data labels assigned to the reset data range will be eliminated also. By choosing **Reset X**, for example, you remove labels displayed below the x-axis, pie-slice labels, and x-axis information for an XY graph.

To illustrate the total graph-reset operation, as applied to the bar graph shown in figure 10.18, select /**Graph Reset Graph**. If you then select **View** from the main **Graph** menu, you'll hear a "beep" and see a blank screen. By removing the graph's data ranges, you have eliminated the essential ingredients for graph production.

The following sections of this chapter discuss how to construct each type of graph.

Developing Alternative Graph Types

You've learned that you can use 1-2-3 to build five types of graph: Line, Bar, XY, Stacked Bar, and Pie.

Because more than one type can accomplish the desired presentation, choosing the best graph form can sometimes be strictly a matter of personal preference. For example, selecting **Line**, **Bar**, or **Pie** would be appropriate if you plan to graph only a single data range. But, at other times, only one form will do the job. As you work through the remainder of this chapter, take a moment to learn or review the primary uses of each graph type.

Selecting an Appropriate Graph Type

You may want to review table 10.1 to refresh your memory about which data ranges are appropriate for each graph type. A brief summary of the use of each graph type follows:

Type:	*Purpose:*
Line	To show the trend of numeric data across time. Used, for example, to display monthly working-capital amounts during 1987.
Bar	To show the trend of numeric data across time, often comparing two or more data items. Used, for example, to display total current assets compared to total current liabilities for each month during 1987.
XY	To compare one numeric data series to another numeric data series, to determine if one set of values appears to depend on the other. Used, for example, to plot monthly Sales and Advertising Expenses to assess whether a direct relationship exists between the amount of sales and the dollars spent for advertising.
Stacked Bar	To graph two or more data series that total 100% of a specific numeric category. Used, for example, to graph three monthly data series—Cash, Accounts Receivable, and Inventory (displayed one above the other)—to depict the proportion each comprises of total current assets throughout the year. (Do not use this type of graph if your data contains negative numbers.)
Pie	To graph only one data series, the components of which total 100% of a specific numeric category. Used, for example, to graph the January Cash, Accounts Receivable, and Inventory amounts to depict the proportion each comprises of the January current assets. (Do not use this type of graph if your data contains negative numbers.)

Building All Graph Types

Although we've used line graphs to illustrate 1-2-3's general graph-enhancement options, most of the options can be used for all graph types. (As you may recall, we've pointed out which options don't apply to specific types of graphs.)

Now we'll focus on each graph type and discuss which enhancements are particularly useful when attached to a specific graph type. To do so, we'll use data in the "SALES (by Profit Center)" report shown in figures 10.19A and 10.19B. The Line, Bar, and Stacked Bar types are all appropriate for graphing this monthly sales-by-profit-center information.

Fig. 10.19A

Sample sales data by profit center (January through June).

```
                A        B        C         D         E         F         G         H
1  ==================================================================================
2  SALES                Jan      Feb       Mar       Apr       May       Jun
3  ==================================================================================
4  Profit Center 1   $31,336  $37,954   $43,879   $51,471   $56,953   $53,145
5  Profit Center 2    22,572   24,888    25,167    32,588    40,140    37,970
6  Profit Center 3   131,685  129,044   131,723   139,221   141,879   149,803
7  Profit Center 4    95,473   98,008    96,986    95,318   103,538   108,146
8                    ........  ........  ........  ........  ........  ........
9  Total Sales      $281,066 $289,894  $297,755  $318,598  $342,510  $349,064
10                   ======== ========  ========  ========  ========  ========
```

Fig. 10.19B

Sample sales data by profit center (July through December).

```
                A        B        I         J         K         L         M         N         O
1  ============================================================================================
2  SALES                Jul      Aug       Sep       Oct       Nov       Dec       Total
3  ============================================================================================
4  Profit Center 1   $54,140  $53,614   $52,015   $48,902   $44,091   $42,536   $570,036
5  Profit Center 2    34,587   33,463    28,939    24,153    27,060    26,701   $358,228
6  Profit Center 3   147,108  147,032   153,440   149,990   145,198   150,510 $1,716,633
7  Profit Center 4   108,642  106,065   110,401   112,018   111,956   107,522 $1,254,073
8                    ........  ........  ........  ........  ........  ........  ........
9  Total Sales      $344,477 $340,174  $344,795  $335,063  $328,305  $327,269 $3,898,970
10                   ======== ========  ========  ========  ========  ========  ========
```

Line Graphs

First, you'll use the worksheet data to create a line graph. Because you will be constructing a new graph, you'll want to reset the previous graph settings to ensure removal of any unwanted options that may have been carried over from the most recent graph operations. You must enter the four data series as ranges C4..N4, C5..N5, C6..N6, and C7..N7. Although you can choose any four of the menu's six **Range** options (**A B C D E F**), we recommend that you enter the data series in order (C4..N4 Profit Center 1 figures as the A range, C5..N5 Profit Center 2 figures as the B range, etc.) if you plan to specify also a corresponding legend. To produce a graph similar to that shown in figure 10.20, use the following command sequences:

/Graph Reset Graph
      Type   Line
      A C4..N4
      B C5..N5
      C C6..N6
      D C7..N7

Options Titles First **1987 SALES**
   Titles Second **SAMPLE COMPANY**
   Titles X-Axis **SALES BY PROFIT CENTER**
   Legend A \A4
   Legend B \A5
   Legend C \A6
   Legend D \A7
   Quit
View

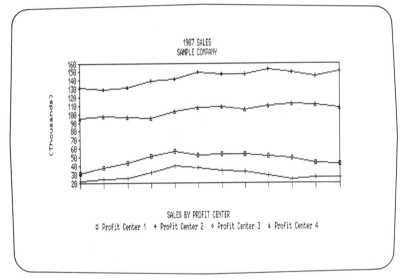

Fig. 10.20

An enhanced multiple-line graph.

Notice that the upper limit of the y-axis is set automatically at $160,000, which is slightly higher than the highest monthly sales figure ($153,440 September sales for Profit Center 3) in all the data ranges.

Reminder:
1-2-3 does not automatically set to zero the lower limit of a line graph's y-axis.

You'll recall that 1-2-3 does not automatically set to zero the lower limit of a line graph's y-axis. To make the graph easier to read, select **Options Scale Y Scale Manual Lower** and then specify a lower limit of zero (0). Because 1-2-3 requires that you set both limits if you switch to a manual setting, be sure to specify **Upper** *160000* immediately after you have set the lower limit.

Cue:
Always use legends for multiple-line graphs.

You'll notice that each of the four legends below the x-axis describes the symbol used for each line within the graph. Always use legends for multiple-line graphs. Without legends, you won't know which of the graph's lines represents a specific data series (unless you have memorized the symbols shown in table 10.1). If you prefer one symbol to another, pick the data range associated with that specific symbol when you select a data range or ranges from the main **Graph** menu. (You'll see how to do this for the set of graphs discussed in the following section.)

Stacked-Bar Graphs

You may want to experiment with different graph types when you plot multiple time-series data. If the data ranges combine in amount to produce a meaningful figure (for example, the combined January sales of each profit center equal total January sales), try using Stacked-bar as a graph type. The data ranges in a stacked-bar graph appear as bars; these bars are plotted in the order A B C D E F, with the A range closest to the x-axis. After having entered the command sequences to create figure 10.20, for example, you could create the stacked-bar graph shown in figure 10.21 by selecting **Type** Stacked-Bar from the main **Graph** menu and then selecting **View**.

Fig. 10.21

The initial stacked-bar graph.

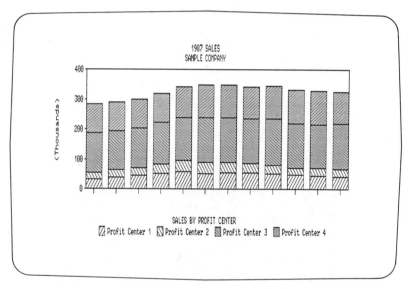

All the options that you set to produce the line graph in figure 10.20 are carried over to the new stacked-bar graph. The legends (which showed symbol assignments for the line graph) change automatically to display the crosshatches of a black-and-white bar graph. 1-2-3 also adjusts automatically the upper and lower limits of the y-axis. The new $400,000 upper limit in the current graph exceeds the highest total sales month ($349,064 in June). In a stacked-bar graph, the lower limit must always be zero.

Distinguishing between certain patterns of crosshatches can be difficult if those patterns appear together. For example, look at the patterns which represent Profit Centers 3 and 4 in the uppermost two bars for each month. To solve this problem, keep the profit center information in the order 1, 2, 3, and 4 but, instead of choosing data ranges A, B, C, and D, select data ranges A, C, E, and F. Then reset the B, C, and D ranges and create the new ranges C, E, and F. Finally, enter legends to show that C is Profit Center 2, E is Profit Center 3, and F is Profit Center 4. Assuming that the current graph is shown in figure 10.21, use the following command sequences to produce the graph shown in figure 10.22.

```
/Graph  Reset  B
               C
               D
               Quit
        C  C5..N5
        E  C6..N6
        F  C7..N7
        Options  Legend  C  \A5
                 Legend  E  \A6
                 Legend  F  \A7
                 Quit
        View
```

Fig. 10.22

The stacked-bar graph with revised patterns of crosshatches.

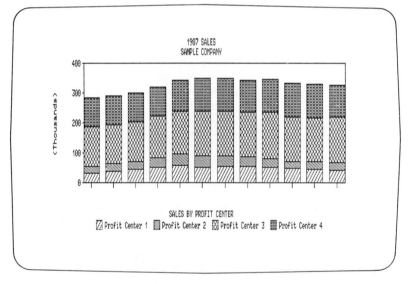

If you compare figures 10.21 and 10.22, you can see that changing the patterns of crosshatches by carefully selecting data ranges makes the information easier to read. If you intend to view the stacked-bar graph in color, be sure to assign different colors to consecutive bars; otherwise, you will not be able to differentiate between two distinct data items. (The colors in figure 10.22 would be displayed appropriately as: red [A range], white [C range], blue [E range], and white [F range].)

Bar and Comparative Bar Graphs

A bar graph is also appropriate for displaying the worksheet's sales-by-profit-center information (refer to figs. 10.19A and 10.19B). By plotting more than one data range, you can produce a comparative bar graph in which the bars are displayed in order of data series entered, with A in the leftmost position.

Assuming that the stacked-bar graph shown in figure 10.22 is the current graph, add monthly headings below the graph and then experiment with the bar graph type by entering the following command sequences:

> /Graph Type   Bar
>   X C2..N2
>   View

Your graph should be similar to that shown in figure 10.23.

Fig. 10.23

Four data ranges in a comparative bar graph.

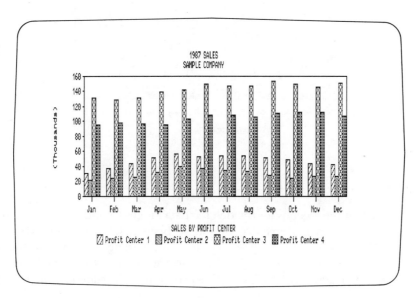

In this graph, each of the four bars clustered around a tick mark on the x-axis represents sales by profit center. In every set of bars, the leftmost bar represents data range A; the next, data range C; the next, E; and the rightmost bar represents data range F. Monthly headings are centered under the x-axis tick marks. And 1-2-3 has automatically revised (to $160,000) the upper scale of the y-axis.

Because the graph display seems crowded when you work with four data ranges, each of which contains 12 numbers, you may prefer to construct additional graphs, each of which compares fewer data series or contains only one data range. For example, to compare only the two top-ranked profit centers according to sales (data ranges E and F), use the following command sequences:

/Graph Reset A
                   C
                 Quit
       View

Compare your results to figure 10.24.

Fig. 10.24

Two data ranges in a comparative bar graph.

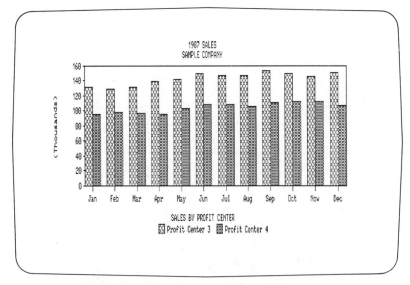

Notice that the legends for the deleted data ranges (A and C) are not displayed. Although you may think that they have been deleted with the data ranges, these legends are still assigned to the A and C ranges. If you use the A or C range for your next graph (without an intervening total graph reset), the associated legend will reappear. This problem is illustrated by the next graph.

Ordinarily, you will want to graph comparative information (that is, use more than one data series) when the numbers to be plotted are classified by region, division, product line, etc. By resetting one additional data range in the current example, however, you can produce a simple bar graph of only one profit center.

Suppose, for example, that you want to use data in the range O4..O7 to graph each profit center's contribution to total annual sales. To do so, you'll retain the bar graph type, X-labels, titles, and legends. But before you reestablish data range A as O4..O7, you'll reset all data ranges. Assuming that the graph in figure 10.24 is current, use the following command sequences to produce a graph similar to that shown in figure 10.25:

```
/Graph Reset E
             F
             Quit
       A O4..O7
       View
```

Fig. 10.25

A bar graph with an inappropriate legend.

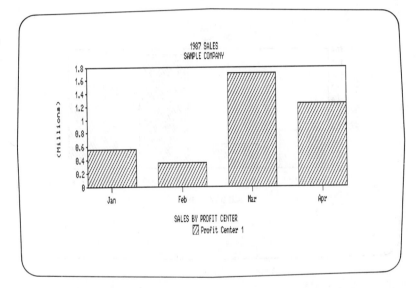

Because you have not changed the four legends used in figure 10.23, these legends are still established (as Profit Center 1, 2, 3, and 4), respectively, for data ranges A, C, E, and F. The legend (Profit Center 1) below the graph in figure 10.25 is inappropriate for two reasons: first, it no longer applies to the data being graphed; and second, a legend is needed only when more than one data series is being graphed. (To remove an unwanted legend, access the existing legend, press Esc, and then press Enter.) Furthermore, you need to revise the x-axis labels on this graph.

To correct the appearance of the graph shown in figure 10.25 and add a currency format to the scale numbers on the y-axis, use the following command sequences:

/Graph **X** A4..A7
    Options **Legend** **A**   Esc   Enter
                Scale **Y** **Scale** **Format** **Currency** **1**
                                Quit
            Quit
    View

The revised bar graph is shown in figure 10.26.

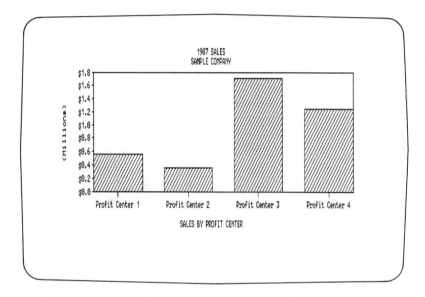

Reminder:
Use /Graph Options Data-Labels to display specific amounts as data-label descriptions within a graph or as x-labels below the graph.

When you graph summary information, especially when the figures are large, you may want to display specific amounts as data-label descriptions within the graph or as X-labels below the graph. For example, the graph in figure 10.26 would be easier to understand if each profit center's specific contribution to total annual sales were shown within the graph, above that center's bar. Recall that you can use /Graph Options Data-Labels to enter numbers as well as labels. In this case, raise the upper scale of the y-axis to make room for the data labels and then use the graphed range O4..O7 as a description. Then access the main **Graph** menu and apply the following command sequences to the previous settings to produce an improved graph (see fig. 10.27).

```
Options Scale Y Scale Manual
                    Upper 2000000
                    Quit
        Data-Labels A O4..O7 Above
                         Quit
            Quit
View
```

Fig. 10.27

*A bar graph with
numeric data
labels.*

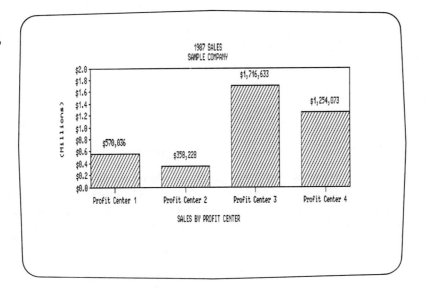

Fig. 10.27

*A bar graph with
numeric data
labels.*

Pie Graphs

Use a pie graph for plotting a single data series in a pie shape. The main **Graph** menu's **X** and **B** range options and the **Titles** and **Color** choices from the **Graph Options** menu are the only menu enhancements that apply to a pie graph.

You'll construct a pie graph by continuing to plot each profit center's contribution to total sales. If you select /**Graph Type Pie View**, carrying over the improved bar graph settings, the graph in figure 10.28 will be displayed.

1-2-3 automatically calculates and displays parenthetically the percentage of the whole represented by each pie wedge. (You cannot suppress these percentages.) Notice that the profit center labels, which you entered by using the main **Graph** menu's **X** option, have carried over from the previous bar graph.

Fig. 10.28

A basic pie graph.

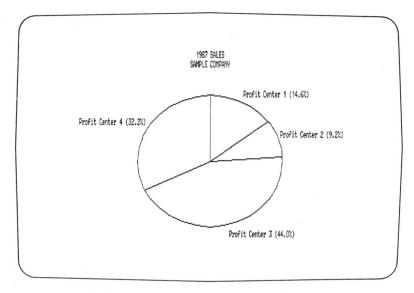

You can enhance this basic pie graph by adding shading or color. 1-2-3 provides eight different shading patterns for monochrome display, eight different colors for EGA color display, and four colors for CGA color display. Figure 10.29 shows the pie graph shading patterns associated with each code number.

Fig. 10.29

The crosshatch shading codes for pie graphs.

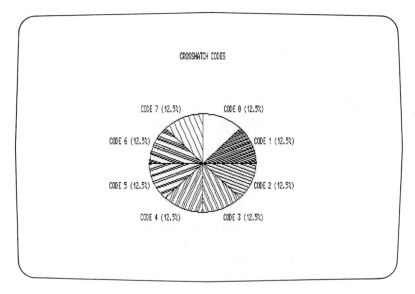

Use the **B** data range to specify the shadings or colors for each pie wedge. The B range can be any range of your worksheet that is the same size as the

A data range (in that worksheet) which you are plotting as a pie graph. To illustrate the process, enter codes 1, 2, 4, and 7 in cells P4, P5, P6, and P7 of the Sales by Profit Center worksheet (see fig. 10.30).

Reminder:
*Use the **B** data range to specify the shadings or colors for a pie wedge.*

Fig. 10.30

A worksheet containing initial shading codes.

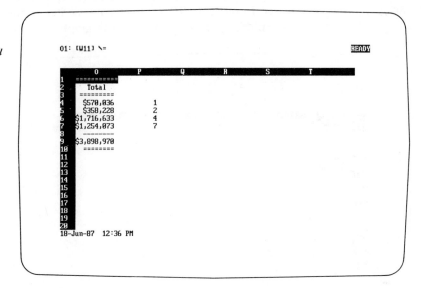

Assuming that all previous pie-graph settings are still in effect, select the **B** data range from the main **G**raph menu and specify P4..P7 as the B data range. Select **V**iew to see the enhanced pie graph (see fig 10.31).

Fig. 10.31

A shaded pie graph.

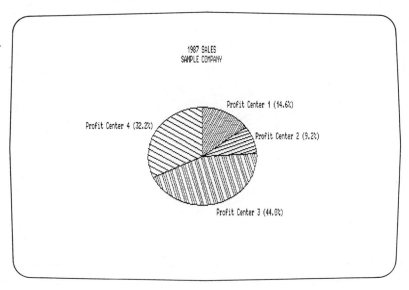

You can "explode" any or all of the wedges by adding 100 to the appropriate numeric shading code in the B range. To illustrate this feature, emphasize Profit Center 3's top performance by adding 100 to the code number in worksheet cell P6 (see fig. 10.32). Then press the F10 (Graph) key to view the graph. As you can see from figure 10.33, the Profit Center 3 portion of the pie is now offset (exploded) from the rest of the graph.

Fig. 10.32

A worksheet containing code to explode a pie wedge.

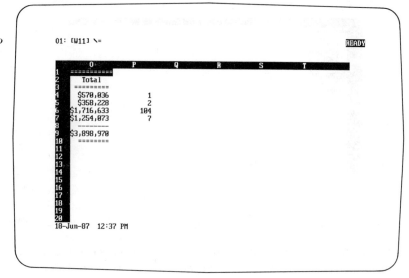

Fig. 10.33

A pie graph with an exploded wedge.

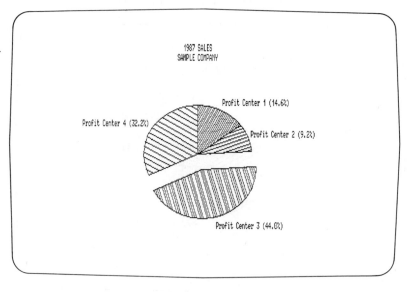

Marking each segment of the pie with an appropriate label is essential. In this case, you must label each profit center.

XY Graphs

The XY graph, often called a *scatter plot*, is a unique variation of a line graph. In this type of 1-2-3 graph, two or more different data items from the same data range can share the same X value. Instead of showing time-series data, XY graphs illustrate the relationships between different attributes of data items—age and income, for example, or educational achievements and salary. You must think of one data item as the independent variable and consider the other item to be dependent on the first. Use the main **Graph** menu's **X** data range to enter the independent variable, and one of the **A B C D E F** options to enter the other item. If the relationship between the two items is strong, the symbols which represent each item tend to cluster in a straight-line pattern.

Suppose that you want to create a graph which shows a correlation between the amount a profit center spends on advertising and the sales generated by that profit center. Imagine that, somewhere in the spreadsheet, information is being tabulated to record each profit center's share of advertising dollars spent. To create an XY graph for Profit Center 1, use the sample % of Advertising Budget data for Profit Center 1 (see fig. 10.34) and the monthly Sales data for Profit Center 1 from the worksheet in figures 10.19A and 10.19B.

Fig. 10.34

A sales spreadsheet containing advertising data.

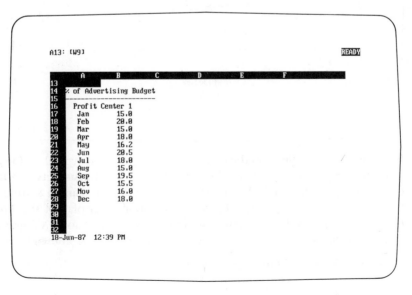

Using the amount of advertising dollars expended as the independent variable, with sales the dependent item, you'll construct an XY graph that includes titles and labels. To do so, access the main **Graph** menu and then issue the following command sequences:

> **Reset Graph**
> **Type XY**
> **A C4..N4**
> **X B17.B28**
> **Options Titles First SALES vs SHARE OF ADVERTISING**
>   **Titles Second PROFIT CENTER 1**
>   **Titles X-Axis % of Advertising Budget**
>   **Quit**
> **View**

The initial XY graph should look like the one shown in figure 10.35.

Fig. 10.35

An initial XY graph with connecting lines.

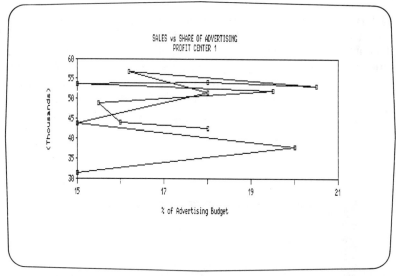

Because this graph displays the default lines and symbols typical of line graphs, using the graph to determine whether a relationship exists between the two data series plotted would be difficult, at best. But by using a setting that is frequently applied to XY graphs, you can suppress display of the lines and make the graph easier to read. Assuming that the previous XY graph with connecting lines is the current graph, issue the following command sequences:

Cue:

To create a scatter plot, use an XY graph without lines connecting the data points.

> **Options Format Graph Symbols**
>   **Quit**
>   **Quit**
> **View**

The revised graph should resemble that shown in figure 10.36.

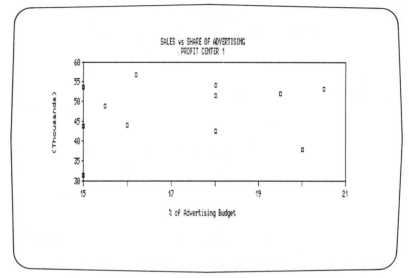

Fig. 10.36

An XY graph that displays symbols only.

This XY graph, without lines connecting the data points, is called a scatter plot. If the symbols in a scatter plot seem to cluster along a single, imaginary straight line fitted among the data points, a strong relationship exists.

At first glance, the widely scattered data points in figure 10.36 seem to indicate no strong dependency of sales dollars on advertising dollars spent. Before you draw conclusions, however, manually set the lower scale limits of both axes to zero. To avoid distortion in the graph due to scale differences, use the following command sequences:

Options Scale Y Scale **Manual**
                        Upper 60000
                        Lower 0
                        Quit
           Scale X Scale **Manual**
                        Upper .22
                        Lower 0
                        Quit
                Quit
    View

Then compare the results to figure 10.37.

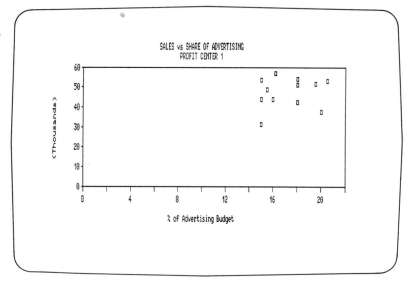

Fig. 10.37

An XY graph with the origin set at zero.

Aren't you glad you didn't jump to conclusions? As you can see, the revised graph seems to show a significant correlation between the sales generated and the advertising dollars expended for Profit Center 1 during 1987. (If you want to calculate data for a regression line to plot through the scattered symbols, use the **Data Regression** command discussed in Chapter 13.)

Bypassing Selected 1-2-3 Limitations

Now that you have learned when to use and how to construct the five 1-2-3 graph types and how to use options to enhance them, you should be able to create most of your graphs by accepting the program's graphics defaults and selecting other menu options.

A few common problem areas exist, however. For example, you may find that the worksheet data you want to graph is not in a continuous range. Or you may not like the size of a single-range bar graph, or the way 1-2-3 positions data points on a line graph's axes. Perhaps you'd like the moveable title capability found in many stand-alone graphics software programs, which is not an option on 1-2-3 menus. With a little experimentation, you may be able to overcome these apparent limitations.

Graphing Noncontinuous Ranges

Although 1-2-3 requires that a graph's data ranges be continuous, you can get around this limitation by creating continuous ranges in a blank area of the spreadsheet. Suppose that the Sales by Profit Center spreadsheet included not only monthly data but also quarterly summary information (see figs. 10.38A and 10.38B).

Cue:
To graph noncontinuous ranges, use blank areas of the worksheet.

Fig. 10.38A

The Sales spreadsheet with quarterly summary data (January to June).

	A	B	C	D	E	F	G	H	I	J
1	===									
2	SALES		Jan	Feb	Mar	Qtr1	Apr	May	Jun	Qtr2
3	==================	=========	=========	=========	===========	=========	=========	=========	===========	
4	Profit Center 1		$31,336	$37,954	$43,879	$113,169	$51,471	$56,953	$53,145	$161,569
5	Profit Center 2		22,572	24,888	25,167	72,627	32,588	40,140	37,970	110,698
6	Profit Center 3		131,685	129,044	131,723	392,452	139,221	141,879	149,803	430,903
7	Profit Center 4		95,473	98,008	96,986	290,467	95,318	103,538	108,146	307,002
8			--------	--------	--------	----------	--------	--------	--------	-----------
9	Total Sales		$281,066	$289,894	$297,755	$868,715	$318,598	$342,510	$349,064	$1,010,172
10			========	========	========	==========	========	========	========	===========

Fig. 10.38B

The Sales spreadsheet with quarterly summary data (July to December).

	A	B	K	L	M	N	O	P	Q	R
1	===									
2	SALES		Jul	Aug	Sep	Qtr3	Oct	Nov	Dec	Qtr4
3	==================	=========	=========	=========	===========	=========	=========	=========	===========	
4	Profit Center 1		$54,140	$53,614	$52,015	$159,769	$48,902	$44,091	$42,536	$135,529
5	Profit Center 2		34,587	33,463	28,939	$96,989	24,153	27,060	26,701	$77,914
6	Profit Center 3		147,108	147,032	153,440	$447,580	149,990	145,198	150,510	$445,698
7	Profit Center 4		108,642	106,065	110,401	$325,108	112,018	111,956	107,522	$331,496
8			--------	--------	--------	----------	--------	--------	--------	-----------
9	Total Sales		$344,477	$340,174	$344,795	$1,029,446	$335,063	$328,305	$327,269	$990,637
10			========	========	========	==========	========	========	========	===========

If you wanted to graph only the monthly sales information for Profit Center 1, you might be tempted to hide columns F, J, N, and R and then specify the range C4..R4. Try it! Because the cell entries in hidden columns are graphed, the result will be a line, bar, or pie graph with 16 data points plotted, not the 12 data points you need.

You can create continuous ranges by pointing to data in noncontinuous ranges. To illustrate this procedure, enter the cell contents in the range A12..F16 by typing *+A4* in cell A13 and then copying from cell A13 to A14..A16, repeating the process as shown in figure 10.39.

To verify that your screen display reflects the quarterly summary figures created in continuous ranges, compare your screen and figure 10.40.

If you want to create a comparative bar graph of the quarterly sales information, use the following command sequences:

```
/Graph Reset Graph
        Type  Bar
        A  C13..F13
        B  C14..F14
        C  C15..F15
        D  C16..F16
        X  C12..F12
```

Options Titles First **1987 SALES**
Titles Second **SAMPLE COMPANY**
Titles X-Axis **SALES BY PROFIT CENTER**
Legend A \A13
Legend B \A14
Legend C \A15
Legend D \A16
Quit

View

The new graph will be similar to that shown in figure 10.41.

Fig. 10.39

Cell contents (in text format) for continuous ranges.

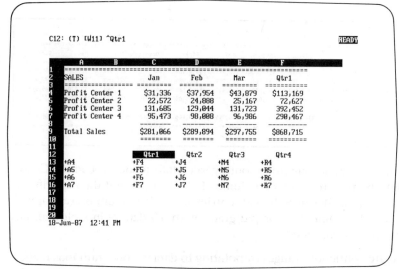

Fig. 10.40

A cell display after creating continuous ranges.

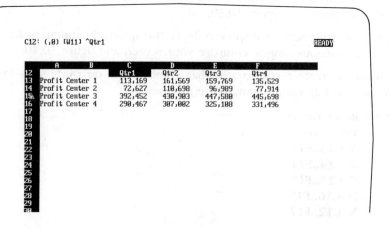

Fig. 10.41

A bar graph that uses newly created continuous ranges.

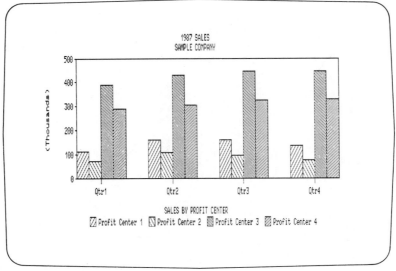

Using Blank Cells To Alter Spacing

You can use blank cells or ranges to improve the default appearance of many 1-2-3 graphs. Notice that, in figure 10.41, the leftmost and rightmost bars rest against the left and right sides of the graph. If this were a line graph, the first and last data points in each range would be plotted on the graph's right and left sides, respectively. Either graph would be easier to read if each data range were preceded and followed by a blank cell.

To illustrate the concept, you'll use the quarterly summary data from figure 10.39. First, move the range C12..F16 one column to the right (to D12..G16). Expand each data range to include six cells (a blank, four quarterly figures, and another blank). Then apply the following command sequences to the current graph:

```
/Graph  A  C13..H13
        B  C14..H14
        C  C15..H15
        D  C16..H16
        X  C12..H12
        View
```

The graph displayed on your screen should look like the slightly revised comparative bar graph shown in figure 10.42.

You can change the display also by using totally blank ranges. For example, if you were to use data from figure 10.40 to graph quarterly data only for

Fig. 10.42

*Using blank cells
to alter bar-graph
display.*

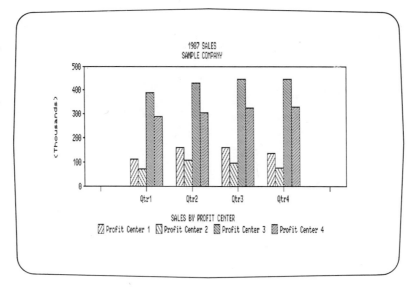

Profit Center 1 (adjusting the options accordingly), the resulting graph would resemble that shown in figure 10.43.

Fig. 10.43

*A bar graph
created by
referencing
noncontinuous
data.*

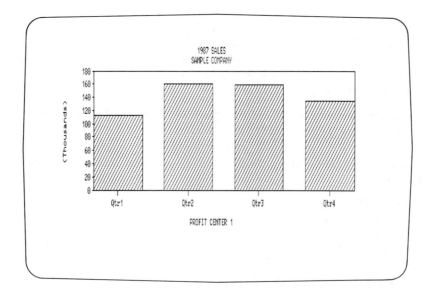

Cue:

*To narrow the bars
of a bar graph, add
blank data ranges.*

To improve the appearance of this graph, you can narrow the bars by adding additional blank data ranges. If you simply add one range of blank cells as the B range (a single blank cell, such as C17 in the current example, will do), the results will be less than satisfactory (see fig. 10.44).

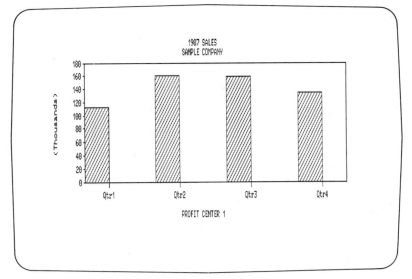

Fig. 10.44

A graph displaying the wrong way to change bar width.

Although the bars in figure 10.44 are narrower than the original bars, each new bar is situated slightly to the left of the corresponding x-axis tick mark. The location of the bars suggests that data which ought to be graphed is missing. To keep the data range centered on the tick marks, add an equal number of blank ranges on both sides of each data range. For example, graph the data range C13..F13 as the B range, enter a blank A range (any blank cell such as C17), and then enter a blank C range (any blank cell such as C17). Figure 10.45 reflects the addition of an even number of blank ranges.

Now compare the default display (which is shown in fig. 10.42) to the revised display in figure 10.45. Both are "correct." Deciding which to use is a matter of individual preference. However, you should avoid creating bar graphs such as that shown in figure 10.44, in which the bars do not appear centered on the tick marks. Inadvertently creating a blank range is easy if the cell pointer is currently positioned on a blank cell and, after accessing one of the **A B C D E F** choices from the main Graph menu, you press Enter instead of Esc to leave the submenu without specifying a range.

Using Blank Cells To Create Moveable Titles

Although some software packages offer a moveable title option for positioning descriptive information anywhere within a graph, 1-2-3 does not. As you've learned, you can use 1-2-3's options to create only four titles: two centered above the graph, one to the left of the y-axis, and one below the x-axis.

Fig. 10.45

*A graph displaying
bars positioned
correctly over tick
marks.*

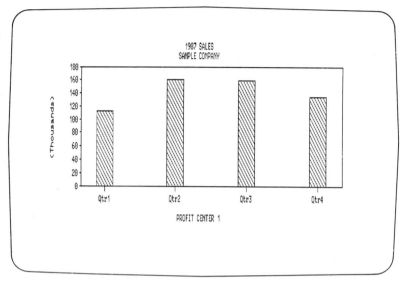

Cue:
*For more freedom
in placing titles, use
blank spaces with
the Data-Labels
option.*

You can use 1-2-3's Data-Labels option to place text selectively within the graph, however. For example, suppose that the reduced fourth-quarter sales for Profit Center 1 (refer to fig. 10.44) were due to the bad publicity of a product recall, and that you want to include this explanatory text in the graph, close to the fourth-quarter data. To do so, first type the description *PRODUCT RECALL* in a blank area of the worksheet (cell F18, for example). (Be sure that this area of the worksheet has three blank cells to the left above the first, second, and third quarter data, which doesn't need extra explanation.) Then, to produce the moveable title shown in figure 10.46, enter the Data-Labels command sequences that set the B range to include the blank cells (C18..F18) positioned above the bars.

Using HAL To Produce Graphs

One of HAL's most attractive benefits is the ease with which you can produce graphs. Even weathered old 1-2-3 diehards can tire of the multitude of settings you must go through in order to produce different types of graphs. In graphing, as in other application areas, HAL acts as a natural-language processor, allowing you to type English requests and produce the types of graphs you want without going through a myriad of 1-2-3 commands.

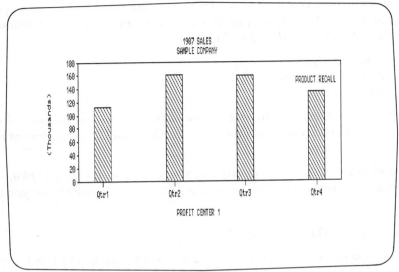

Fig. 10.46

*Setting a moveable
title within the
graph.*

Creating Graphs

HAL creates graphs from columns of data in the current table. (In HAL, a *table* is any continuous rectangular block of data; the *current table* is the table at which the cell pointer is located. You communicate the graph request for bar, line, and pie graphs by using the verbs *draw*, *graph*, *plot*, and *view*. For XY graphs, you use the words *against* or *versus* in requests. In XY graphs, the first data range is used as the y-axis, and the second data range is used as the x-axis. The following HAL requests can be used to create graphs:

    draw this
    plot qtr1 to qtr4 as line
    view a10..g10 as pie
    graph 1987 against 1986

The first request creates a bar graph from columns of data in the current table. The second request creates a line graph from columns labeled Qtr1, Qtr2, Qtr3, and Qtr4. The third request creates a pie graph from the data in the range A10..G10. The last request creates an XY graph from the data in columns labeled 1987 and 1986.

Editing Graph Settings

After you have created a basic graph from a HAL request, you can specify data ranges and modify the x-axis label. HAL recognizes the verbs *make* and *set* in a data-range request. You can also delete, or reset, data ranges by using the verb *reset*. You must also refer to the data range by its letter (A through F, and X) or by number (1st through 6th). For example, the following are valid HAL requests for editing graphs:

    make A range col c
    make X-range be row 3
    reset A range

In the first request, column C becomes the A range; in the second request, the data in row 3 becomes the labels for the x-axis. The last request removes the graph's A range.

After entering the editing request, you can issue the *graph*, *plot*, or *view* request or press the F10 (Graph) key to have HAL redraw the graph.

Enhancing a Graph

You also can use HAL requests to add titles to the x- and y-axis and to the graph itself. You can add titles to graphs by using the verbs *label* and *title*. Some valid *title* requests are

    label graph Net Income
    title 2nd line 1982-1987
    label x-axis Year

Titles can be up to 39 characters long. Remember to issue an appropriate HAL request or press F10 to redraw the graph.

Naming Graphs

For naming graphs, HAL recognizes the phrases *call graph*, *name graph*, and *rename graph*. The following are valid *naming* requests:

    call graph sales87
    name graph incstmt
    rename graph assets

You then need to save the graph with the spreadsheet file by using 1-2-3's /File Save command or by issuing a HAL file-save request. After you have saved the graph, you can view it again by entering *call up graph*, *get graph*, *load graph*, or *retrieve graph*. The following requests recall the named graph:

    call up graph sales87
    get graph incstmt
    load graph assets

Creating .PIC Files

Before you can print graphs with 1-2-3's PrintGraph program, you must save them to disk as .PIC files. HAL can do that for you, if you enter the requests *keep graph*, *save graph*, or *store graph*. You also need to specify an eight-character file name when you enter the request. The following HAL requests save the previously named graphs as .PIC files:

> keep graph incstmt
> save graph assets

You also can use the request *file graph* to display all .PIC files in your current directory.

This section has described the basics of graphing with HAL. As you can see, creating 1-2-3 graphs can be a trouble-free, almost effortless process when you let HAL communicate your commands to 1-2-3.

Using Freelance Plus

Lotus's Freelance Plus is a graphics program that you use to create presentation-quality graphs from 1-2-3 .PIC files. With Freelance Plus, you can enhance your 1-2-3 graphs by shading, moving, or deleting existing graphic elements, adding symbols from the program's library of 500 graphic objects, or drawing freehand.

Unlike other 1-2-3 companion products, Freelance Plus is a stand-alone program; it does not operate in your computer's memory along with 1-2-3. Freelance Plus is an extremely powerful and versatile program with many applications, and can be used to create graphs independent of 1-2-3. The discussion in this section will cover only using Freelance Plus to enhance 1-2-3 graphs.

After installing Freelance Plus for your computer system, you use the program's multiple-level command menus to retrieve a 1-2-3 .PIC file (see fig. 10.47).

The file appears in the Freelance Plus work area, which occupies the majority of your computer's screen. The program's commands appear across the top of the screen, as in 1-2-3, and an information panel appears on the right side of the screen.

You Select an existing graph to Edit, and then you position the cross-hairs where you want to make changes. You control the cross-hairs with the cursor-movement keys, a mouse, or a digitizer tablet. You can move and change headings, change fill colors, extract bars and wedges, explode areas, change

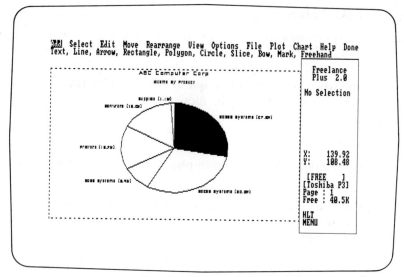

line widths, or make a variety of other changes. You also can change symbols, by drawing your own or copying ready-made ones from the Symbol library.

For example, consider the pie graph in figure 10.48, which was generated using 1-2-3 and the PrintGraph program.

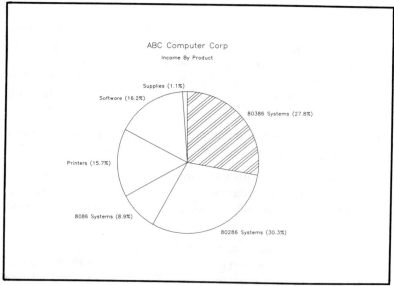

Figure 10.49 shows the same graph enhanced by Freelance Plus.

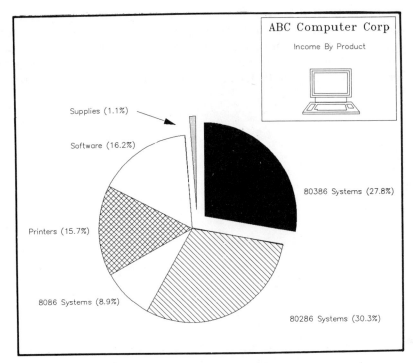

Fig. 10.49

*The 1-2-3 graph
enhanced by
Freelance Plus.*

In the Freelance Plus graph, one of the pie's wedges has been moved, other wedges shaded, and an arrow added to draw attention to each segment of the graph and to add a dramatic effect to the entire subject.

Freelance Plus is easy to learn and use, but has a few minor drawbacks. Some menus contain commands that begin with the same first letter, which can cause inconvenience. In addition, Freelance Plus does not display colors and fonts accurately on a monochrome screen. Although the program will print these attributes correctly, you'll need an IBM Enhanced Color Display and an EGA board with 128K for an equivalent screen display. More important, a Freelance Plus graph generated from a 1-2-3 .PIC file cannot be updated automatically if you make changes in your spreadsheet. You have to Save the graph again in 1-2-3, import the new .PIC file into Freelance Plus, and then start your enhancements from the beginning.

Despite these limitations, if you need boardroom-quality graphs, or want to draw organizational charts, design office layouts, or just add your company's logo to your graphs, Freelance Plus is definitely worth considering.

Chapter Summary

You have learned a great deal about 1-2-3 graphs from this chapter: how to create and enhance all five graph types, how to store graphs for printing as well as for subsequent recall to the screen, and how to use your imagination to produce alternative graph displays. The next chapter explains how to print graphs. (See Chapter 12 for additional practice in using 1-2-3 graphs.)

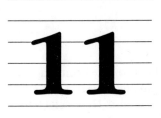

11

Printing Graphs

Chapter 10 showed you how to use 1-2-3 to create and display graphs. Because the main 1-2-3 program cannot print graphics, you must use the PrintGraph program to print the graphs you saved in graph (.PIC) files. You can use the PrintGraph program for quick and easy printouts of graphs; you can also choose from a variety of optional print settings for enhancing the appearance of printed graphs. This chapter shows you how to

- Access the PrintGraph program

- Use the status screen

- Print a graph by using PrintGraph default settings

- Change graph size, font, and color settings

- Select or alter hardware-related settings

- Control paper movement from the keyboard

- Establish temporary PrintGraph settings

Accessing the PrintGraph Program

To access PrintGraph directly from DOS, type *pgraph* at the DOS prompt. (The PrintGraph program should reside in the current directory for a hard disk system; for a floppy disk system, the disk containing the PrintGraph program should be in the active drive.) If you use a driver set other than the default 1-2-3 set, you must also type the name of that driver set (*pgraph hp*, for example) to reach the main **PrintGraph** menu.

However, you are more likely to use PrintGraph immediately after you have created a graph. If you originally accessed 1-2-3 by typing *lotus*, select **/Quit Yes** to return to the Access menu. Then select **PrintGraph** instead of exiting to the DOS prompt. If you are using 1-2-3 on a floppy disk system, you will be prompted to remove the 1-2-3 System disk and insert the PrintGraph disk, unless you use a member of the IBM PS/2 family. For the PS/2, the PrintGraph program resides on the System disk.

Warning:
Save your worksheet before you use the 1-2-3 /System command.

Alternatively, if you have sufficient RAM, you can use PrintGraph after you have issued the **/System** command. Then, instead of having to reload 1-2-3 after you leave PrintGraph, you can return directly to 1-2-3 by typing *exit* at the system prompt. *But be careful.* Before you use this technique, save your worksheet. And, because you must have at least 256K of remaining RAM to run PrintGraph and 1-2-3 simultaneously without overwriting your worksheet, use the **/W**orksheet **S**tatus report to check remaining internal memory (RAM) before you attempt to use **/S**ystem.

Producing Basic Printed Graphs

Reminder:
*Printing a graph can be as easy as selecting the image to be printed and then choosing **Go**.*

Printing a graph can be a simple procedure if you accept PrintGraph's default print settings. If the correct hardware configuration has been specified, you can produce a half-size, block-font, black-and-white graph on 8 1/2-inch-by-11-inch continuous-feed paper simply by marking a graph for printing and then printing it.

When you select **PrintGraph** from the 1-2-3 Access menu or type *pgraph* at the DOS prompt, the following menu appears:

    Image-Select   Settings   Go   Align   Page   Exit

You choose **Image-Select** to mark a graph for printing, and **Go** to print the graph.

Suppose, for example, that you want to print the line graph saved in the WCLINE.PIC file. Make sure that the current printer and interface specifications accurately reflect your hardware, that you're using continuous-feed paper, and that the printer is on-line and positioned at the top of a page. Then you can print the default graph shown in figure 11.1 by issuing the following command sequences:

    Image-Select **WCLINE**
    Go

This graph is centered upright (zero degrees rotation) on the paper and fills about half of an 8 1/2-inch-by-11-inch page. The titles are printed in the default BLOCK1 font (character style).

Fig. 11.1

Sample graph printed at default settings.

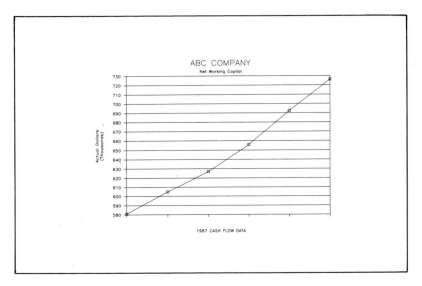

If you want to enhance this default graph, you can do so by using any or all of PrintGraph's many special features. These special capabilities (which are not available in the main 1-2-3 program) include the production of high-resolution output on special printers and plotters; enlargement, reduction, and rotation of graph printouts; and the use of several additional colors and font types.

To illustrate what happens if you use PrintGraph's size and font options with the same hardware settings that you used for the graph in figure 11.1, issue the following command sequences:

> **Image-Select WCLINE**
> **Settings Image Size Full**
> > > **Quit**
> > > **Font 1 ITALIC1**
> > > **Font 2 ROMAN1**
> > > **Quit**
> > **Quit**
> **Align**
> **Go**

The resulting graph is printed automatically on its side (90 degrees rotation) and almost fills an 8 1/2-inch-by-11-inch page (see fig. 11.2). The top center title is printed in the italic font; the other titles, in the roman font. (These font options, as well as other nondefault settings, are described in detail later in this chapter.)

Fig. 11.2

Sample graph printed with font and size changes.

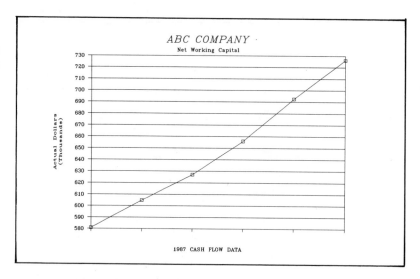

Comparing On-Screen to Printed Graphs

Reminder:
The printed graph will not be exactly the same as the screen display you see with /Graph View.

A printed graph looks different from its on-screen display. For example, if you compare figure 11.3 (which captures the on-screen display of a stacked-bar graph) with figure 11.4 (which shows the same graph printed), two differences are immediately apparent.

Fig. 11.3

Screen display of a sample stacked-bar graph.

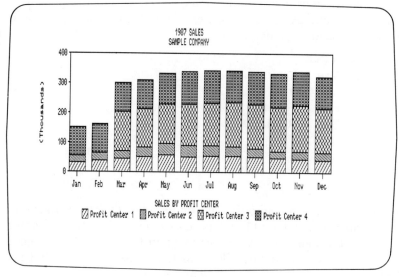

Fig. 11.4

*The printed sample
stacked-bar graph.*

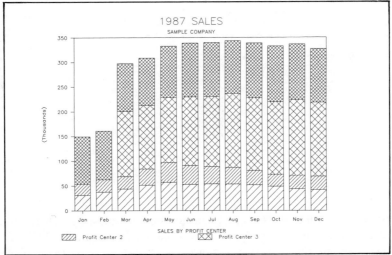

You can see at a glance that the two top-center titles in the on-screen version appear to be the same size (or pitch) but that, in the printed graph, the first title has been changed automatically to a larger pitch. Notice also the difference in the y-axis—the tick marks in the on-screen version are scaled in increments of $100,000; the printed graph provides additional detail in increments of $50,000. These revisions, which generally improve graph appearance, cannot be altered.

Notice a third difference between the two graphs—the legends. Although the four legends in figure 11.3 are centered neatly below the graph, the legends in figure 11.4 are spread out so that the first and last legends are not printed. You can solve this problem by reducing the amount of text in each legend.

Cue:
To ensure that all the legends appear in the printout, keep the amount of legend text at a minimum.

Using the PrintGraph Menu and Status Report

PrintGraph is entirely menu-driven. The menu screens provide not only instructions for printing graph (.PIC) files but also information about current print conditions. If you are using a hard disk, the screen displayed when you enter the PrintGraph program will be similar to that shown in figure 11.5.

The first three text lines, which display a copyright message and two levels of current menu options, always remain on-screen. In the PrintGraph status-report area below the double solid line, option selections are continually updated. (The status report, which also remains on-screen, disappears temporarily when you select a printer, graphs to print, and a font style.)

```
Copyright 1986 Lotus Development Corp. All Rights Reserved. Release 2.01  MENU

Select graphs for printing
Image-Select  Settings  Go  Align  Page  Exit

   GRAPH      IMAGE OPTIONS                    HARDWARE SETUP
   IMAGES     Size            Range Colors       Graphs Directory:
   SELECTED   Top       .395    X Black            C:\123\DATA
              Left      .750    A Black          Fonts Directory:
              Width    6.500    B Black            C:\123
              Height   4.691    C Black          Interface:
              Rotate    .000    D Black            Parallel 1
                                E Black          Printer Type:
              Font              F Black            Toshiba P1350
              1  BLOCK1                          Paper Size
              2  BLOCK1                            Width      8.500
                                                  Length    11.000

                                               ACTION OPTIONS
                                                 Pause: No   Eject: No
```

Before you select the Go command to begin printing a graph, get in the habit of checking the status report. As you can see from figure 11.5, the settings displayed in the status report are organized in four areas: GRAPH IMAGES SELECTED, IMAGE OPTIONS, HARDWARE SETUP, and ACTION OPTIONS. Each of these areas is directly related to either the Image-Select or Settings option on the PrintGraph menu.

For example, a list of graphs that can be selected for printing appears under GRAPH IMAGES SELECTED, on the left side of the status report. (In fig. 11.5, no graphs have been selected for printing.) To make changes in the other three status-report areas, you first select Settings from the main PrintGraph menu. When you select Settings, the following menu appears:

   Image   Hardware   Action   Save   Reset   Quit

If you choose Image, you can change the size, font, and color of the graph; the updated revisions are displayed in the status report's IMAGE OPTIONS area. (The settings shown in fig. 11.5 will produce a black-and-white, half-size graph in which all titles, labels, and legends are printed in block style.)

To alter the paper size, printer, or disk-drive specifications displayed in the HARDWARE SETUP area, you select Hardware. (The instructions in fig. 11.5 tell PrintGraph to look for .PIC files in the C:\123\Data subdirectory, to look for font program files in the C:\123 directory on drive C, to print on standard-size paper, and to use a Toshiba printer.)

If you have finished printing a graph and want to move (eject) to a new page, pausing while you change the specifications for the next graph, select Action from the Settings menu. Then update the ACTION OPTIONS section of the status report by changing both the Pause and Eject options from No to Yes.

Before you learn how to change each setting, you should explore the details of using the PrintGraph program.

Establishing the Physical Print Environment

The physical print environment includes: the disk drives containing files applicable to the graph-printing operation; the printer type and name; paper size; and printer actions to control print delay and paper movement. Updates to these print environment settings are displayed in the status report's rightmost column.

In figure 11.5, current physical-environment settings are displayed under HARDWARE SETUP and ACTION OPTIONS. For example, the HARDWARE SETUP information shows that the files to be graphed are located in the subdirectory C:\123\DATA and that the printer will not pause (Pause: No) between printing two or more selected graph images.

Before you select any graphs for printing, and before you select options that will affect the printed image, you should understand each Hardware and Action option.

When you select **P**rintGraph **S**ettings **H**ardware, you'll see the following menu:

Graphs-Directory Fonts-Directory Interface Printer Size-Paper Quit

The **G**raphs-Directory and **F**onts-Directory options pertain to disk-drive specifications; **I**nterface and **P**rinter determine the current printer name and type; and Size-Paper permits you to specify paper length and width in inches.

Changing the Graphs Directory

In figure 11.5, the current Graphs Directory is C:\123\DATA, which is the correct setting for a hard disk system with .PIC files on a directory named *DATA* that is a subdirectory of a directory named *123*. If you aren't sure whether you want to load a few .PIC files from a floppy disk onto your hard disk, you can insert the floppy disk in your system's A: drive and temporarily instruct PrintGraph to look for the graph files on drive A:.

Reminder:
The graphs you want to print must be located on the current Graphs Directory.

First, select **S**ettings **H**ardware **G**raphs-Directory from the main **P**rintGraph menu. Type *a:* at the prompt:

Enter directory containing picture files

(Before typing the new information, you don't have to erase the previous setting by pressing Esc or the Backspace key.) The revision will be updated immediately in the upper right corner of the status report (see fig. 11.6).

To restore C:\123\DATA as the current Graphs Directory, type *c:\123\data* after repeating the command sequence.

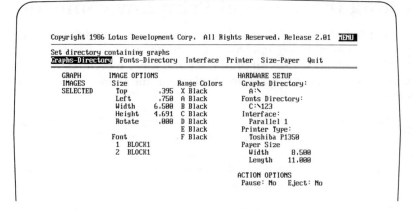

```
Copyright 1986 Lotus Development Corp. All Rights Reserved. Release 2.01  MENU

Set directory containing graphs
Graphs-Directory  Fonts-Directory  Interface  Printer  Size-Paper  Quit

    GRAPH     IMAGE OPTIONS                    HARDWARE SETUP
    IMAGES    Size             Range Colors    Graphs Directory:
    SELECTED  Top        .395  X Black           A:\
              Left       .750  A Black         Fonts Directory:
              Width     6.500  B Black           C:\123
              Height    4.691  C Black         Interface:
              Rotate     .000  D Black           Parallel 1
                              E Black         Printer Type:
              Font            F Black           Toshiba P1350
              1  BLOCK1                       Paper Size
              2  BLOCK1                         Width     8.500
                                               Length   11.000

                                             ACTION OPTIONS
                                               Pause: No   Eject: No
```

On a dual floppy system, you ordinarily establish drive B: as the drive location of your graph files.

Changing the Fonts Directory

Whenever you print a graph, you use PrintGraph's font files, which contain program instructions for font styles; these files are located on the same disk that holds the PrintGraph program. (Available font styles are discussed in this chapter's "Selecting Fonts" section.) As you can see from figure 11.5, the location of the Fonts Directory is C:\123. This is the correct setting for a hard disk system that has PrintGraph installed in a directory named *123*.

Lotus delivers the PrintGraph program with the default drive for the Fonts Directory as A:\. To change to C:\123, you issue the following command:

Settings Hardware Fonts-Directory **C:\123**

Setting the Type and Name of the Current Printer

To specify the printer or plotter that you'll use to print the selected graph images, you must coordinate two Settings Hardware submenu options: **Interface** and **Printer**. The former sets the type of connection to a graphics printer; the latter establishes a specific type of printer.

You can direct the graph output to one of two parallel printers, one of two serial printers, or one of four DOS devices (usually set up as part of a local area network). If you need to determine whether a printer is parallel or serial, consult your printer manual.

Selecting **Settings Hardware Interface** produces eight menu choices, labeled 1 through 8, which represent the physical connections between your computer and your printer:

1	Parallel 1	5	DOS Device LPT1
2	Serial 1	6	DOS Device LPT2
3	Parallel 2	7	DOS Device LPT3
4	Serial 2	8	DOS Device LPT4

In figure 11.7, option 3 (Parallel 2) is highlighted on the **Settings Hardware Interface** submenu. (The default setting is Parallel 1.)

Fig. 11.7

The Settings Hardware Interface submenu.

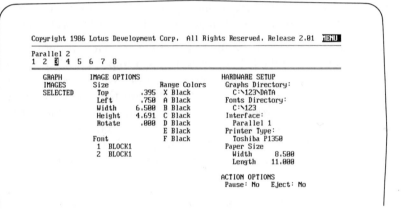

If you specify a serial interface, you must also select a baud rate. Baud rates determine the speed at which data is transferred. (See Chapter 9 for the available baud rates.) Because each printer has specific requirements, consult your printer manual for the appropriate rate. Many serial printers accept more than one baud rate. A general guideline is to choose the fastest rate your printer will accept without corrupting the data. A baud rate of 1200 is normally a safe choice.

After you have specified the appropriate interface number for the current graph-printing operation, PrintGraph again displays the Hardware submenu so that you can name the printer attached to the designated interface.

To select a printer, you must have installed one or more printers when you set up 1-2-3. If you installed three printers (an Epson MX100, an IBM Graphics, and a Toshiba) to run with 1-2-3, a list of these printers will be displayed when you select **Printer** from the **Settings Hardware** menu (see fig. 11.8).

Fig. 11.8

The Settings Hardware Printer display.

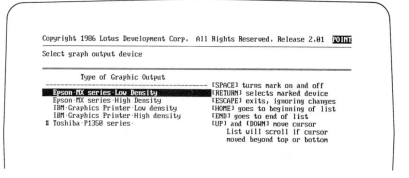

```
Copyright 1986 Lotus Development Corp. All Rights Reserved. Release 2.01  POINT

Select graph output device

        Type of Graphic Output
------------------------------------------------  [SPACE] turns mark on and off
  Epson·MX series·Low Density                      [RETURN] selects marked device
  Epson·MX series·High Density                     [ESCAPE] exits, ignoring changes
  IBM·Graphics Printer·Low density                 [HOME] goes to beginning of list
  IBM·Graphics Printer·High density                [END] goes to end of list
# Toshiba·P1350 series·                            [UP] and [DOWN] move cursor
                                                        List will scroll if cursor
                                                        moved beyond top or bottom
```

Cue:
Use a low-density option for faster, draft-quality printing.

Notice that the list includes not three, but five options. You can print at either high or low density (dark or light print). If you use a high-density option, the printed graph will be of high quality but printing will take more time.

Instructions for moving the highlighted bar to mark an option are displayed on the right half of the Printer screen. For example, [SPACE] tells you to press the space bar to mark or unmark a selection with a # sign. The highlighted line, # Epson MX series Low Density, tells you that the current printer is an Epson MX and that you have chosen to print at low density. If you want to select another printer, press the space bar to remove the # mark from the Epson MX and then reposition the highlighted bar. Then follow the [RETURN] instructions—mark and select the new device by pressing Enter.

Changing the Paper Size

The default paper size is 8 1/2-by-11 inches, but you can print your graph on paper of another size by selecting the Settings Hardware submenu's Size-Paper option. (The option is named Size-Paper to avoid confusion. If it were named **Paper**, it might be confused with the **Printer** option on the same submenu; if the option were named **Size**, it might be confused with an **Image** option used to change the size of a graph.)

When you select Size-Paper, the following options are displayed:

    Length   Width   Quit

Reminder:
*The **S**ize-paper option tells PrintGraph to print on different paper size, but does not change the size of the graph.*

After selecting **Length** or **Width**, specify the appropriate number of inches. To adjust the paper size to the 14-inch-wide paper used in wide-carriage printers, for example, select Settings Hardware Size-Paper Width and then type *14*. Remember that this command changes the size of the paper, not that of the graph. (Changing the size of a graph is discussed in this chapter's "Adjusting Size and Orientation" section.) Be sure to select a paper size that can accommodate the specified graph size.

Making the Printer Pause between Graphs

If you have selected more than one .PIC file for a single print operation, you can make the printer pause between printing the specified graphs. If you are using a manual sheet-feed printer, for example, you can pause to change the paper. Or you may want to stop printing temporarily so that you change the hardware settings, directing the output to a different printer. (You cannot change the font, color, and size options during the pause.)

If you want the printing operation to pause, select Settings Action Pause Yes before you select Go from the main PrintGraph menu. After each graph has been printed, the printer will pause and the computer will beep. To resume printing, press the space bar.

To restore the default setting so that all currently specified graphs will print nonstop, choose Settings Action Pause No.

Ejecting the Paper To Start a New Page

The other Action option applies to "batching" several graphs in one print operation. When you select Settings Action Eject Yes, continuous-feed paper advances to the top of a new page before the next graph is printed. Use the alternate default setting, Eject No, to print two (or more) half-size (or smaller) graphs on a single page.

Do not confuse the Settings Action Eject Yes command sequence with the main PrintGraph menu's Page command. (The Page option is described in this chapter's "Completing the Print Cycle" section.) Both commands advance the paper to the top of a new page. Settings Action Eject Yes is appropriate when you use a single Go command to print more than one selected graph; the paper advances automatically after each graph has been printed. You select PrintGraph Page, on the other hand, whenever you want to advance the paper one page at a time before or after a printing session.

Reminder:
The Eject option is not the same as Page. Eject advances the paper automatically between the printing of selected graphs; Page allows you to advance the paper manually from the keyboard.

Controlling the Appearance of the Printed Graph

Review the initial PrintGraph status report shown in figure 11.5. You've learned about the physical print environment needed to produce a graph: the printer type and name, the disk-drive location of required files, and the paper size and movement. Now that you're familiar with the mechanics of producing a graph, you'll learn about options that affect the printed graph's appearance. These options are displayed in the middle of the status screen, under IMAGE OPTIONS.

If you select **Settings Image**, you'll see the following submenu:

Size   Font   Range-Colors   Quit

Use these options to change the size of a graph, to specify one or two print styles on a single graph, and to select colors. (As you know, you use the 1-2-3 /**Graph** commands to enter graph enhancements such as titles, legends, and labels.)

Adjusting Size and Orientation

The **Image** menu's **Size** option lets you adjust the size of graphs and decide where, and at what angle, they will be printed on a page. You determine the size of the graph by specifying the desired **Width** and **Height**, and set the graph's position on the page by specifying the **Top** and **Left** margins. You can also **Rotate** the graph a specified number of degrees on the page.

When you select **Settings Image Size**, you'll see the menu shown in figure 11.9.

Fig. 11.9

*The Settings Image
Size submenu.*

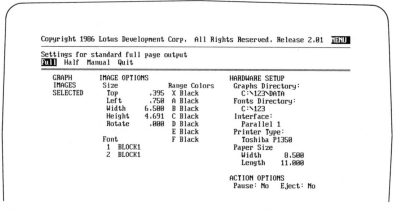

```
Copyright 1986 Lotus Development Corp. All Rights Reserved. Release 2.01  MENU

Settings for standard full page output
Full  Half  Manual  Quit

GRAPH       IMAGE OPTIONS                      HARDWARE SETUP
IMAGES      Size                               Graphs Directory:
SELECTED    Top        .395    Range Colors        C:\123\DATA
            Left       .750    X Black          Fonts Directory:
            Width     6.500    A Black             C:\123
            Height    4.691    B Black          Interface:
            Rotate     .000    C Black             Parallel 1
                               D Black          Printer Type:
            Font               E Black             Toshiba P1350
            1  BLOCK1          F Black          Paper Size
            2  BLOCK1                              Width      8.500
                                                  Length    11.000

                                               ACTION OPTIONS
                                               Pause: No   Eject: No
```

The default **Half** option automatically produces a graph that fills half of a standard-size 8 1/2-inch-by-11-inch page (refer to fig. 11.1). Figure 11.9 shows the default assignments:

Top	.395 (inches)
Left	.750 (inches)
Width	6.500 (inches)
Height	4.691 (inches)
Rotate	.000 (degrees)

Because these settings are the default, you don't have to use the **Size** option to print a graph of these dimensions centered upright on a standard-size page.

Width refers to the horizontal graph dimension produced on a page. The width of the half-size graph shown in figure 11.1 is the x-axis. In a zero-rotation graph, the ratio of x-axis size (Width) to y-axis size is 1.386 to 1.

The Full option automatically determines a combination of the width, height, top, left, and rotation settings to produce a graph that fills an 8 1/2-inch-by-11-inch page (refer to fig. 11.2). The top of this horizontal graph (90 degrees rotation) lies along the left edge of the paper. The automatic assignments for a full-size graph are

Top	.250 (inches)
Left	.500 (inches)
Width	6.852 (inches)
Height	9.445 (inches)
Rotate	90.000 (degrees)

The y-axis of the full-size graph shown in figure 11.2 is printed across the width of the paper. The y-axis has been changed automatically to 6.852 inches. In a graph rotated 90 degrees, the ratio of x-axis size (Height) to y-axis size is 1.378 to 1.

If you want to change any or all of the size settings, select Manual from the Settings Image Size submenu. Then select one or more of the following options:

Top   Left   Width   Height   Rotation   Quit

To position a printed graph at a location other than the automatic distances from the edges of the paper, change the margin settings. If you want to center a half-size graph at the top of 11-inch-by-14-inch paper, for example, specify a different left margin by selecting Settings Image Size Manual Left and typing *3.5* as the revised number of inches. When you press Enter, the updated left-margin specification will be displayed in the status report.

Determine the appropriate number of inches by working from the default values. You know that a half-size graph is centered automatically on an 8 1/2-inch page and that changing to paper 14 inches wide will add 5 1/2 inches to the width. Add half of the increase (2.75 inches) to the default left margin (.75 inches) to calculate the total number of inches (3.5) for the new dimension.

When you change the Width and Height settings, be sure to maintain the basic x- to y-axis ratio of approximately 1.38 to 1. For example, suppose that you want to produce an upright (zero rotation) graph that is only three inches high. You know that the x-axis dimension should exceed the y-axis dimension and that, at zero rotation, the x-axis is the width. Multiply the desired height

Cue:
The x- to y-axis ratio should remain at 1.38 to 1 for every combination of Width and Height setting.

of 3 inches by 1.38 to calculate the proportionate width (4.14 inches) of the graph.

Be sure that the combined dimensions (margin, width, and height) do not exceed the size of the paper. If a graph exceeds the physical bounds of the paper, 1-2-3 will print as much of the graph as possible and then truncate the rest.

Although you can set rotation anywhere between zero and 360 degrees, you will use three settings (zero, 90, or 270) for most graphs. To print an upright graph, use zero; to position the graph's center titles along the left edge of the paper, use 90; use 270 to position the graph's center titles along the right edge of the paper.

Selecting Fonts

You can use different character types, or *fonts*, in a printed graph. For example, you can print a graph's top center title in one character type (Font 1) and then select a different font (Font 2) for the remaining titles, data-labels, x-labels, and legends. If you want to use only one print style, your Font 1 choice will be used for all descriptions.

When you select Settings Image Font 1, you'll see the options shown in figure 11.10.

Fig. 11.10

The Settings Image Font 1 options.

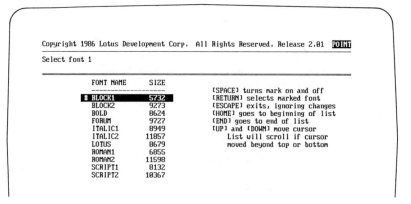

BLOCK1 is the default font. The number after the font name indicates the darkness (density) of the printed characters. Notice that four of the fonts permit alternative print-density specifications. If you choose BLOCK2, for example, the printed characters will be darker than those produced by choosing BLOCK1. Figure 11.11 shows a sample of each font style.

Fig. 11.11

Samples of fonts available in PrintGraph.

This is BLOCK1 type

This is BLOCK2 type

This is BOLD type

This is FORUM type

This is ITALIC1 type

This is ITALIC2 type

This is LOTUS type

This is ROMAN1 type

This is ROMAN2 type

This is SCRIPT1 type

This is SCRIPT2 type

Two of these fonts (italic and script) may be difficult to read, especially on half-size graphs produced on a dot-matrix printer. Before you print a final-quality draft in darker density, print the graph at the lower density so that you can determine whether the font and size settings are correct.

Cue:
Print the graph at the faster, low-density setting to check font appearance before you print the final version at the high-density setting.

Choosing Colors

If you have a color printing device, you can use the PrintGraph program to assign colors to all parts of a graph. Select **Settings Image Range-Colors** to produce the following submenu:

   X   A   B   C   D   E   F   Quit

For all graph types except Pie, use the **X** option to assign a single color to the edges of the graph, any background grid, and all displayed options other than legends and data-labels. Use **A**, **B**, **C**, **D**, **E** and **F** to assign a different color to every data range used. The color set for an individual data range is used also for any data-label or legend assigned to that data range.

Reminder:
*Use the **A** through **F** settings to assign a different color to each data range.*

You use a different method to determine the print colors for a pie graph. Because you create a pie graph by using only data in the A range, and because each wedge of the pie is assigned a B-range shading code, you must use the appropriate shading codes to determine which colors will print. First, associate each code with the following Image Range-Colors menu options:

Range-Colors Option	B-range Shading Code
X	Shading code ending in 1 (101 or 1)
A	Shading code ending in 2
B	Shading code ending in 3
C	Shading code ending in 4
D	Shading code ending in 5
E	Shading code ending in 6
F	Shading code ending in 7

When you select an option from the **Settings Image Range-Colors** submenu, a menu of colors will be displayed. The number of colors displayed depends on the capabilities of the current printer (named in the hardware setup area of the PrintGraph status report). If your printer does not support color printing, only the **B**lack option will appear. To choose a color for each range, highlight that color and press Enter. In figure 11.12, the assigned colors are listed in the IMAGE OPTIONS section of the PrintGraph status report.

Fig. 11.12

Sample status report after Range-colors have been selected.

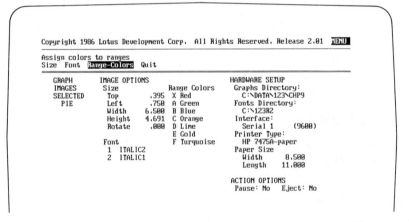

If you know that you will print a specific graph in color, select /**Graph O**ptions **C**olor before you store that graph as a .PIC file. If you store the graph in black and white and then print it in color, the crosshatch markings and the colors assigned to the ranges both will print.

Reminder:

If you intend to print a graph in color, select the 1-2-3 command /Graph Options Color before saving the graph specifications.

Saving and Resetting PrintGraph Settings

After you have established current Hardware, Action, and Image settings and completed the current printing operation, you will select one of two options from the Settings menu: Save or Reset. Both of these options apply to the entire group of current settings.

If you choose Save, the current options will be stored in a file named PGRAPH.CNF, which will be read whenever PrintGraph is loaded. Select Reset to restore all Hardware, Action, and Image settings to PrintGraph's default settings or to the options saved during the current session, whichever occurred most recently. Image-Selected graphs are not reset.

Completing the Print Cycle

After you have accepted the default options or selected other Hardware, Action, and Image options, you access the main PrintGraph menu to complete the printing operation. From this menu, you select the graph(s) to be printed, adjust the paper alignment, and select Go.

Previewing a Graph

To preview a graph, select Image-Select from the main PrintGraph menu. The menus and the status report area disappear temporarily from the screen; in their place, you see a list of the .PIC files in the current Graphs Directory (see fig. 11.13).

Fig. 11.13

List of .PIC files displayed after choosing Image-Select.

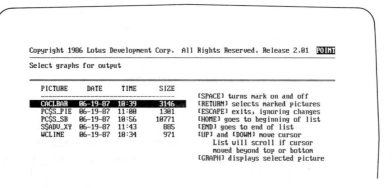

Instructions for selecting graphs are displayed on the right side of the screen. The last item (GRAPH) on the list of instructions indicates that pressing the F10 (Graph) key causes the highlighted graph to appear on the screen. To verify that the graph shown is the one you want to print, use the Graph key to preview every graph listed. Size and font options are not displayed in this preview, and you can't see rotation or half-size results. But the preview does give a good idea of what the printed graph will look like—in some instances, a better idea than /Graph View. For example, legend titles that are too wide to print will appear complete when viewed on-screen with /GV, but not with the F10 preview.

Selecting a Graph

Selecting graphs that you want to print from the list of .PIC files is easy—to mark the files for printing, simply follow the directions on the right side of the screen. Use the cursor-movement keys to position the highlighted bar on the graph that you want to select. Then press the space bar to mark the file with a # symbol. The space bar acts as a toggle key; use the same action to remove any unwanted marks. If necessary, continue to mark additional graphs. (In fig. 11.14, two graphs have been marked for printing.) After you press Enter to accept the currently marked graphs for printing, the updated status report will again be displayed.

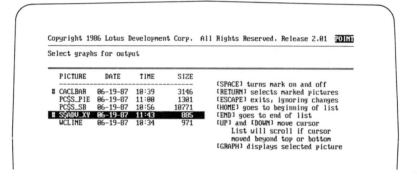

Fig. 11.14

.PIC files marked for printing.

Controlling Paper Movement from the Main Menu

The main PrintGraph menu's Align option sets the program's built-in, top-of-page marker. When you choose Align, PrintGraph assumes that the paper in the printer is aligned correctly at the top of the page. Using the page-length information you provided when you installed the graphics device, PrintGraph then inserts a form feed at the end of every page. Regularly selecting Align before selecting Go is a good practice.

The **P**age option advances the paper one page at a time. At the end of a printing session, this useful option advances continuous-feed paper to help you remove the printed output.

While you are using the PrintGraph program, control the movement of paper from the keyboard, not from the printer. Although many printers have controls that allow you to scroll the paper one line at a time, PrintGraph does not recognize these controls. For example, if you scroll the paper three lines but do not realign it, PrintGraph will be three spaces off when you issue the next form-feed command.

Go (and Wait!)

To print a graph, you must select **G**o from the main **PrintGraph** menu. After you select **G**o, you will see in the screen's menu area messages indicating that picture and font files are loading. Then the graphs will be printed. Printing a graph takes much longer than printing a similar-sized worksheet range, especially if you are printing in high-density mode.

If you want to interrupt the process of printing a graph or series of graphs, use the Ctrl-Break key combination. Then press Esc to access the PrintGraph menu options.

Cue:
To stop PrintGraph while printing is in progress, press Ctrl-Break.

Exiting the PrintGraph Program

To leave the PrintGraph program, choose **Exit** from the main **PrintGraph** menu. The next screen to appear depends on the method you used to access PrintGraph. If you entered PrintGraph from the 1-2-3 Access System, the Access menu reappears. Select **Exit** to restore the DOS prompt, or select another Access menu option. If you entered PrintGraph by typing *pgraph* from the DOS prompt, the DOS prompt is restored.   ·

If you want to enter 1-2-3 after you have exited PrintGraph and restored the DOS prompt, remember how you originally accessed the DOS prompt (before you typed *pgraph*). If you were using 1-2-3 and selected /**S**ystem to reach the DOS prompt, type *exit* and press Enter to return to the 1-2-3 worksheet. If you were not using 1-2-3 before the PrintGraph session, type *123* or *lotus* and then select **123** from the Access menu.

Chapter Summary

The mechanics of printing a graph are simple. The PrintGraph utility program provides a menu-driven approach to mark graphs for printing, to select image options unavailable when creating graphs, and to specify settings involving the physical print environment. Producing the printed graph in a reasonable amount of time is not so simple. You must initially create and store the graphs within the 1-2-3 program, correctly install hardware that supports the desired options, and patiently await the results.

With the conclusion of this chapter, you have learned all the fundamentals of 1-2-3. The hands-on practice session in Chapter 12 provides an opportunity to reinforce what you have learned about printing reports and creating and printing graphs. Part III, which begins with Chapter 13, will introduce you to advanced 1-2-3 topics: database management, creating keyboard macros, and using the Lotus Command Language. Many users do not approach the advanced topics until they have used 1-2-3 for a while. If that is your preference, keep this book handy as a reference as you continue to use 1-2-3, and then return to Part III when you are ready.

12

Creating Output: Hands-On Practice

You can use 1-2-3's integrated graphing capabilities to create graphs based on information in 1-2-3 spreadsheets and databases, and then store the graph specifications as part of the .WK1 files. You can also use 1-2-3's printing capabilities to print your worksheet and database files. To print graphs, you use the PrintGraph utility program.

This chapter's hands-on practice sessions reinforce concepts that you have already learned. If you want to review a concept in greater detail as you work through the practice sessions in this chapter, refer to the appropriate chapter:

- Printing (Chapter 9)
- Creating graphs (Chapter 10)
- Printing graphs (Chapter 11)

The practice sessions provide step-by-step instructions for:

- On-line printing of all or part of a .WK1 file
- Creating and storing several graphs
- Printing graphs using default or enhanced settings

433

Entering the Practice-Session Spreadsheet

This chapter gives you an opportunity to practice both printing reports and creating and printing graphs; the reports and graphs are based on the complex financial worksheet shown in figure 12.1. As you can see, this worksheet is extensive, containing income and ratio-analysis data for a company with five divisions. So that you can enter every number manually, this section shows you how to quickly create a "dummy" worksheet by entering only a few values and formulas and then using the /Copy command to fill the worksheet with data.

Before you begin to create the worksheet, however, take a minute to examine its structure.

Rows 1 through 39 of the model display income-related text and numbers, including monthly figures and annual totals for Sales, Cost of Goods Sold, Operating Expenses, and Net Income.

Rows 44 through 50 display the percentage relationship of Gross Profit (Sales less Cost of Goods Sold) to Sales.

Rows 52 through 58 display the percentage relationship of Net Income to Sales.

(For spacing purposes, illustrated in the graph section, columns B and O have been left blank.)

If you intend to use this chapter only for practice creating and printing graphs, you can skip to those sections and enter only the data that is specifically used in creating the graphs. Also, if you choose, you can practice printing reports with a worksheet that contains only the labels shown in figure 12.1, perhaps along with values in column P and in row 58. To get a better idea of how to print reports, however, follow the instructions in this section to enter the data into the worksheet.

This section will not give instructions in complete detail for entering the data into the worksheet. If you have not done the spreadsheet practice session (Chapter 8), we suggest you do so before you begin this session.

The spreadsheet in figure 12.1 is designed to allow you extensive use of the /Copy command to enter the data. A good way to proceed is as follows:

1. Enter the labels (leaving columns B and O blank) and adjust column widths as necessary. Notice that you can use the /Copy command for dashed lines and for the repeated labels Northeast, Southeast, Central, Northwest, and Southwest.

		Jan	Feb	Mar	Apr	May	Jun	Jul	Aug	Sep	Oct	Nov	Dec	TOTAL
1	======================	===	===	===	===	===	===	===	===	===	===	===	===	=====
2	REGIONAL INCOME REPORT													
3	======================	===	===	===	===	===	===	===	===	===	===	===	===	=====
4	Sales													
5	Northeast	$31,336	$34,370	$37,404	$40,438	$43,472	$46,506	$49,540	$52,574	$55,608	$58,642	$61,676	$64,710	$576,276
6	Southeast	30,572	33,606	36,640	39,674	42,708	45,742	48,776	51,810	54,844	57,878	60,912	63,946	$567,108
7	Central	131,685	134,719	137,753	140,787	143,821	146,855	149,889	152,923	155,957	158,991	162,025	165,059	$1,780,464
8	Northwest	94,473	97,507	100,541	103,575	106,609	109,643	112,677	115,711	118,745	121,779	124,813	127,847	$1,333,920
9	Southwest	126,739	129,773	132,807	135,841	138,875	141,909	144,943	147,977	151,011	154,045	157,079	160,113	$1,721,112
10														
11	Total Sales	414,805	429,975	445,145	460,315	475,485	490,655	505,825	520,995	536,165	551,335	566,505	581,675	5,978,880
12														
13	Cost of Goods Sold													
14	Northeast	10,341	11,274	12,207	13,140	14,073	15,006	15,939	16,872	17,805	18,738	19,671	20,604	185,670
15	Southeast	6,546	7,479	8,412	9,345	10,278	11,211	12,144	13,077	14,010	14,943	15,876	16,809	140,130
16	Central	65,843	66,776	67,709	68,642	69,575	70,508	71,441	72,374	73,307	74,240	75,173	76,106	851,694
17	Northwest	63,967	64,900	65,833	66,766	67,699	68,632	69,565	70,498	71,431	72,364	73,297	74,230	829,182
18	Southwest	72,314	73,247	74,180	75,113	76,046	76,979	77,912	78,845	79,778	80,711	81,644	82,577	929,346
19														
20	Total Cost of Goods Sold	219,011	223,676	228,341	233,006	237,671	242,336	247,001	251,666	256,331	260,996	265,661	270,326	2,936,022
21														
22	Operating Expenses													
23	Northeast	21,529	23,470	25,411	27,352	29,293	31,234	33,175	35,116	37,057	38,998	40,939	42,880	386,454
24	Southeast	15,946	17,887	19,828	21,769	23,710	25,651	27,592	29,533	31,474	33,415	35,356	37,297	319,458
25	Central	27,554	29,495	31,436	33,377	35,318	37,259	39,200	41,141	43,082	45,023	46,964	48,905	458,754
26	Northwest	16,130	18,071	20,012	21,953	23,894	25,835	27,776	29,717	31,658	33,599	35,540	37,481	321,666
27	Southwest	32,361	34,302	36,243	38,184	40,125	42,066	44,007	45,948	47,889	49,830	51,771	53,712	516,438
28														
29	Total Operating Expenses	113,520	123,225	132,930	142,635	152,340	162,045	171,750	181,455	191,160	200,865	210,570	220,275	2,002,770
30														
31	Net Income													
32	Northeast	(534)	(374)	(214)	(54)	106	266	426	586	746	906	1,066	1,226	4,152
33	Southeast	8,080	8,240	8,400	8,560	8,720	8,880	9,040	9,200	9,360	9,520	9,680	9,840	107,520
34	Central	38,288	38,448	38,608	38,768	38,928	39,088	39,248	39,408	39,568	39,728	39,888	40,048	470,016
35	Northwest	14,376	14,536	14,696	14,856	15,016	15,176	15,336	15,496	15,656	15,816	15,976	16,136	183,072
36	Southwest	22,064	22,224	22,384	22,544	22,704	22,864	23,024	23,184	23,344	23,504	23,664	23,824	275,328
37														
38	Total Net Income	82,274	83,074	83,874	84,674	85,474	86,274	87,074	87,874	88,674	89,474	90,274	91,074	1,040,088
39														
40														
41	======================	===	===	===	===	===	===	===	===	===	===	===	===	=====
42	REGIONAL RATIO ANALYSIS													
43	======================	===	===	===	===	===	===	===	===	===	===	===	===	=====
44	Gross Profit on Sales													
45	Northeast	67.0%	67.2%	67.4%	67.5%	67.6%	67.7%	67.8%	67.9%	68.0%	68.0%	68.1%	68.2%	67.8%
46	Southeast	78.6%	77.7%	77.0%	76.4%	75.9%	75.5%	75.1%	74.8%	74.5%	74.2%	73.9%	73.7%	75.3%
47	Central	50.0%	50.4%	50.8%	51.2%	51.6%	52.0%	52.3%	52.7%	53.0%	53.3%	53.6%	53.9%	52.2%
48	Northwest	32.3%	33.4%	34.5%	35.5%	36.5%	37.4%	38.3%	39.1%	39.8%	40.6%	41.3%	41.9%	37.8%
49	Southwest	42.9%	43.6%	44.1%	44.7%	45.2%	45.8%	46.2%	46.7%	47.2%	47.6%	48.0%	48.4%	46.0%
50	Total	47.2%	48.0%	48.7%	49.4%	50.0%	50.6%	51.2%	51.7%	52.2%	52.7%	53.1%	53.5%	50.9%
51														
52	Return on Sales													
53	Northeast	-1.7%	-1.1%	-0.6%	-0.1%	0.2%	0.6%	0.9%	1.1%	1.3%	1.5%	1.7%	1.9%	0.7%
54	Southeast	26.4%	24.5%	22.9%	21.6%	20.4%	19.4%	18.5%	17.8%	17.1%	16.4%	15.9%	15.4%	19.0%
55	Central	29.1%	28.5%	28.0%	27.5%	27.1%	26.6%	26.2%	25.8%	25.4%	25.0%	24.6%	24.3%	26.4%
56	Northwest	15.2%	14.9%	14.6%	14.3%	14.1%	13.8%	13.6%	13.4%	13.2%	13.0%	12.8%	12.6%	13.7%
57	Southwest	17.4%	17.1%	16.9%	16.6%	16.3%	16.1%	15.9%	15.7%	15.5%	15.3%	15.1%	14.9%	16.0%
58	Total	19.8%	19.3%	18.8%	18.4%	18.0%	17.6%	17.2%	16.9%	16.5%	16.2%	15.9%	15.7%	17.4%

Fig. 12.1
Contents of the Regional Income and Ratio Analysis file.

2. Enter the values (except the totals) for Sales (C5..C9), Cost of Goods Sold (C14..C18), and Operating Expenses (C23..C27) into column C only.

3. Enter the formula **+C5+3034** into cell D5; then /Copy D5 to D6..D9 and to E5..N9.

4. Enter the formula **+C14+933** into cell D14; then /Copy D14 to D15..D18 and to E14..N18.

5. Enter the formula **+C23+1941** into cell D23; then /Copy D23 to D24..D27 and to D23..N27.

All the fictitious values have now been entered. The next steps involve entering and copying formulas.

1. Enter the formula **+C5-C14-C23** into cell C32; then /Copy cell C32 to C33..C36 and to D32..N36.

2. Enter the function **@SUM(C5..C10)** into cell C11; then /Copy cell C11 to D11..N11, C20..N20, C29..N29, and C38..N38.

To enter the formulas for computing the totals in column P, follow these steps:

1. Enter the function **@SUM(C5..N5)** into cell P5; then /Copy cell P5 to P6..P9, P14..P18, P23..P27, and P32..P36.

2. Enter the function **@SUM(P5..P10)** into cell P11; then /Copy cell P11 to cells P20, P29, and P38.

For the REGIONAL RATIO ANALYSIS:

1. Enter the formula **(C5-C14)/C5** into cell C45; then /Copy cell C45 to C46..C49, D45..N49, and P45..P49.

2. Enter the formula **(C11-C20)/C11** into cell C50; then /Copy cell C50 to D50..N50 and to P50.

3. Enter the formula **+C32/C5** into cell C53; then /Copy cell C53 to C54..C57, D53..N57, and P53..P57.

4. Enter the formula **+C38/C11** into cell C58; then /Copy cell C58 to D58..N58 and to P58.

Your data entry is now complete. To make your spreadsheet look like figure 12.1, use the /**Range** Format command, selecting Currency **0** (C5..P5), comma (,) **0** C6..P38), and **Percent 0** (C45..P58), as appropriate.

Printing a .WK1 (Worksheet) File

You use 1-2-3's **Print** commands to print spreadsheet and database files, which are stored as .WK1 files. In this section of the chapter, you will practice sending output directly to the printer. First, using the default print settings, you will print a portion of the regional income-related data. Then, using several print options, you will print the entire file. Before you begin, make sure that:

▶ Your printer is installed correctly and on-line

▶ You have cleared all previous print settings from the on-screen model—use **/Print Printer Clear All**; then select **Quit** to return to the worksheet

Printing a Partial Report

To print data from a spreadsheet or database file, you simply specify a **Range** and then activate the main Print menu's **Go** command.

This first example shows you how to print only the Sales totals for each region of the sample company (rows 1 through 11 of figure 12.1), omitting the monthly detail. The printed output is displayed in figure 12.2.

Fig. 12.2

One-page printout produced by specifying only the print range.

```
===============================================
REGIONAL INCOME REPORT              TOTAL
===========================         ======
Sales
    Northeast                    $576,276
    Southeast                     567,108
    Central                     1,780,464
    Northwest                   1,333,920
    Southwest                   1,721,112
                                 --------
    Total Sales                 5,978,880
```

To print this portion of the spreadsheet, and then eject the paper to the top of a new page, follow these steps:

1. Press **/** to activate the main 1-2-3 menu.

2. Select **/Print Printer Range**.

3. At the prompt for a print range, enter **P1..P11**

4. When the main Print menu appears, select **Options Borders Columns**.

5. Enter the range **A1..B1** to indicate that you want the labels in column A and the space in column B printed to the left of the data in range P1..P11.

6. Choose **Quit** to return to the main Print menu.

7. Check your printer, making sure that it is on-line and that the print head is aligned at the top of a page.

8. Select **Align**.

9. Select **Go**.

10. Check the printed output, which should match figure 12.2.

11. Select **Page** to advance the paper in the printer.

12. Select **Quit** to restore the screen to READY mode.

Printing a Full Report with Enhancements

In this section, you will print the entire Regional Income and Ratio Analysis file using several of the enhancements from the Options menu. You'll use options to add a header, adjust the margins, add a border, and print in condensed mode. The printed output will look like figure 12.3.

To print the entire file on only two pages, adding page numbers and descriptive information that repeats on each page, follow these steps:

1. Select **/Print Printer Clear All** to remove any previous print settings.

2. Select **Options Header** to specify a one-line message across the top of each page.

3. At the prompt for a header line, type |**SAMPLE COMPANY**|#

   Note: The vertical bars (|) position text within a header. On the printout, SAMPLE COMPANY will be centered, and the page numbers will be printed in the upper right corner of the 8 1/2-inch-by-11-inch page.

4. Select **Borders Columns**.

5. Enter the range **A1..B1** to repeat (on each printed page) the column A account names and regions as well as the spacing column (B).

6. Select **Setup**.

7. At the prompt, type the appropriate printer code for condensed print. (For example, you'd type **\015** for an EPSON printer; check your printer manual for the correct code for your printer.)

8. Select **Margins Right**.

SAMPLE COMPANY

REGIONAL INCOME REPORT

	Jan	Feb	Mar	Apr	May	Jun	Jul	Aug	Sep	Oct	Nov	Dec	TOTAL
Sales													
Northeast	$31,336	$34,370	$37,404	$40,438	$43,472	$46,506	$49,540	$52,574	$55,608	$58,642	$61,676	$64,710	$576,276
Southeast	30,572	33,606	36,640	39,674	42,708	45,742	48,776	51,810	54,844	57,878	60,912	63,946	$567,108
Central	131,685	134,719	137,753	140,787	143,821	146,855	149,889	152,923	155,957	158,991	162,025	165,059	$1,780,464
Northwest	94,473	97,507	100,541	103,575	106,609	109,643	112,677	115,711	118,745	121,779	124,813	127,847	$1,333,920
Southwest	126,739	129,773	132,807	135,841	138,875	141,909	144,943	147,977	151,011	154,045	157,079	160,113	$1,721,112
Total Sales	414,805	429,975	445,145	460,315	475,485	490,655	505,825	520,995	536,165	551,335	566,505	581,675	5,978,880
Cost of Goods Sold													
Northeast	10,341	11,274	12,207	13,140	14,073	15,006	15,939	16,872	17,805	18,738	19,671	20,604	185,670
Southeast	6,546	7,479	8,412	9,345	10,278	11,211	12,144	13,077	14,010	14,943	15,876	16,809	140,130
Central	65,843	66,776	67,709	68,642	69,575	70,508	71,441	72,374	73,307	74,240	75,173	76,106	851,594
Northwest	63,967	64,900	65,833	66,766	67,699	68,632	69,565	70,498	71,431	72,364	73,297	74,230	829,182
Southwest	72,314	73,247	74,180	75,113	76,046	76,979	77,912	78,845	79,778	80,711	81,644	82,577	929,346
Total Cost of Goods Sold	219,011	223,676	228,341	233,006	237,671	242,336	247,001	251,666	256,331	260,996	265,661	270,226	2,935,922
Operating Expenses													
Northeast	21,529	23,470	25,411	27,352	29,293	31,234	33,175	35,116	37,057	38,998	40,939	42,880	386,454
Southeast	15,946	17,887	19,828	21,769	23,710	25,651	27,592	29,533	31,474	33,415	35,356	37,297	319,458
Central	27,554	29,495	31,436	33,377	35,318	37,259	39,200	41,141	43,082	45,023	46,964	48,905	458,754
Northwest	16,130	18,071	20,012	21,953	23,894	25,835	27,776	29,717	31,658	33,599	35,540	37,481	321,666
Southwest	32,361	34,302	36,243	38,184	40,125	42,066	44,007	45,948	47,889	49,830	51,771	53,712	516,438
Total Operating Expenses	113,520	123,225	132,930	142,635	152,340	162,045	171,750	181,455	191,160	200,865	210,570	220,275	2,002,770
Net Income													
Northeast	(534)	(374)	(214)	(54)	106	266	426	586	746	906	1,066	1,226	4,152
Southeast	8,080	8,240	8,400	8,560	8,720	8,880	9,040	9,200	9,360	9,520	9,680	9,840	107,520
Central	38,288	38,448	38,608	38,768	38,928	39,088	39,248	39,408	39,568	39,728	39,888	40,048	470,016
Northwest	14,376	14,536	14,696	14,856	15,016	15,176	15,336	15,496	15,656	15,816	15,976	16,136	183,072
Southwest	22,064	22,224	22,384	22,544	22,704	22,864	23,024	23,184	23,344	23,504	23,664	23,824	275,328
Total Net Income	82,274	83,074	83,874	84,674	85,474	86,274	87,074	87,874	88,674	89,474	90,274	91,074	1,040,088

REGIONAL RATIO ANALYSIS

	Jan	Feb	Mar	Apr	May	Jun	Jul	Aug	Sep	Oct	Nov	Dec	TOTAL
Gross Profit on Sales													
Northeast	67.0%	67.2%	67.4%	67.5%	67.6%	67.7%	67.8%	67.9%	68.0%	68.0%	68.1%	68.2%	67.8%
Southeast	78.6%	77.7%	77.0%	76.4%	75.9%	75.5%	75.1%	74.8%	74.5%	74.2%	73.9%	73.7%	75.3%
Central	50.0%	50.4%	50.8%	51.2%	51.6%	52.0%	52.3%	52.7%	53.0%	53.3%	53.6%	53.9%	52.2%
Northwest	32.3%	33.4%	34.5%	35.5%	36.5%	37.4%	38.3%	39.1%	39.8%	40.6%	41.3%	41.9%	37.8%
Southwest	42.9%	43.6%	44.1%	44.7%	45.2%	45.8%	46.2%	46.7%	47.2%	47.6%	48.0%	48.4%	46.0%
Total	47.2%	48.0%	48.7%	49.4%	50.0%	50.6%	51.2%	51.7%	52.2%	52.7%	53.1%	53.5%	50.9%
Return on Sales													
Northeast	-1.7%	-1.1%	-0.6%	-0.1%	0.2%	0.6%	0.9%	1.1%	1.3%	1.5%	1.7%	1.9%	0.7%
Southeast	26.4%	24.5%	22.9%	21.6%	20.4%	19.4%	18.5%	17.8%	17.1%	16.4%	15.9%	15.4%	19.0%
Central	29.1%	28.5%	28.0%	27.5%	27.1%	26.6%	26.2%	25.8%	25.4%	25.0%	24.6%	24.3%	26.4%
Northwest	15.2%	14.9%	14.6%	14.3%	14.1%	13.8%	13.6%	13.4%	13.2%	13.0%	12.8%	12.6%	13.7%
Southwest	17.4%	17.1%	16.9%	16.6%	16.3%	16.1%	15.9%	15.7%	15.5%	15.3%	15.1%	14.9%	16.0%
Total	19.8%	19.3%	18.8%	18.4%	18.0%	17.6%	17.2%	16.9%	16.5%	16.2%	15.9%	15.7%	17.4%

Fig. 12-3

Two-page printout reflecting Print options.

9. Type **132** to accommodate the 16-characters-per-inch printed across the 8 1/2-inch-wide paper.

10. Select **Margins Top** and enter **0** (zero).

11. Select **Margins Bottom** and enter **0**. (Steps 9 and 10 ensure that all of the spreadsheet's rows will fit on one page.)

12. Select **Margins Left** and enter 0. **Quit** the Print Options menu.

13. Select **Range** from the main Print menu.

14. Enter **C1..P58** to print the entire file. (Note that you exclude the A and B border columns from the print range.)

15. Check the printer, making sure that it is on-line and that the print head is aligned at the top of the page.

16. Select **Align** to signal 1-2-3 that the print head is at the top of the page, and to reset the page counter.

17. Select **Go**.

18. Check the printed output to make sure that it matches figure 12.3.

19. Select **Page** to advance the paper in the printer.

20. Select **Quit** to restore the screen to READY mode.

You have practiced printing one page with the default settings, and using several print options to print a two-page spreadsheet. You probably will want to experiment, using different settings to see how they affect your printed .WK1 files. When you find a combination of settings that you want to use repeatedly, you may want to capture the necessary keystrokes in macros (see Chapter 14). Then use the macros to automate printing.

Creating Graphs

In this section, you will construct several graphs and use almost every available option to "dress up" their appearance. If you want to be a "sidewalk supervisor," you can see how each graph is developing by periodically selecting View from the main Graph menu. (Do this after you have specified the graph type and the data ranges, but before you have completed all of the steps.) You will store all of the graphs for printing as well as for subsequent recall to the screen.

Before you begin, make sure that your screen displays:

▶ The Regional Income and Ratio Analysis spreadsheet

▶ The READY mode indicator

If you have not yet entered data into the worksheet, use a blank worksheet and enter at least the contents of the cells (or ranges of cells) used in the graphs. Refer to figure 12.1 for the labels and numbers needed to complete each graph.

Creating a Simple Bar Graph

You'll begin by creating a graph that displays the monthly Sales and Net Income figures of the model's Southwest Region (see fig. 12.4). Using only a few options, you will add to the graph:

• Titles that describe the graph's contents

• Legends to differentiate the two data series

• X-axis labels to specify the time series (monthly data)

Fig. 12.4

On-screen view of a basic bar graph.

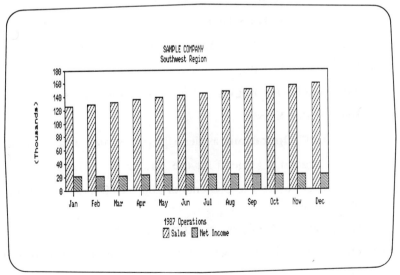

To construct this graph, use the following steps (remember that you do not press Enter after selecting a menu option, but you do press Enter after typing information). The first series of steps involves choosing the /Graph command and selecting the type of graph you want to display.

1. Press / to activate the main 1-2-3 menu.

2. Select **Graph** to access the main Graph menu.

3. Select **Reset Graph** to ensure that no previous graph settings remain.

4. Select **Type** from the main Graph menu.

5. Specify **Bar**. (The main Graph menu will again be displayed.)

In the second series of steps, you indicate the ranges of values for bars on your graph.

1. Select **A** as the first data range.

2. Enter **C9..N9** (monthly Sales for the Southwest Region).

3. Select **C** as the second data range.

4. Enter **C36..N36** (monthly Net Income for the Southwest Region). (Because you want a specific crosshatch shading pattern for the second range, you use C, not B, as this range.)

The third stage involves entering titles at the top and bottom of the graph, indicating labels (legends) to identify the cross-hatching patterns on the graph, and finally indicating the labels for each x-axis point.

1. Select **Options Titles First**.

2. Type **SAMPLE COMPANY** as the the graph's top-center title.

3. Select **Titles Second**.

4. Type **Southwest Region** as the second top-center title.

5. Select **Titles X-Axis**.

6. Type **1987 Operations** as descriptive text below the x-axis.

7. Select **Legend A** (legend for the A range).

8. Enter **\A4** to use the contents of cell A4 (Sales) as text for the first legend.

9. Select **Legend C** (legend for the C range).

10. Enter **\A31** (Net Income) as text to describe the second data range.

11. **Quit** the Options submenu.

12. Select **X** from the main Graph menu.

13. Enter **C2..N2** as the range to input monthly headings below the x-axis.

You are now ready to view your graph, name it, save the specifications for printing the graph, and save the worksheet file.

1. Select **View** and check the displayed graph. (It should match figure 12.4.)

2. Press any key to restore the main Graph menu.

3. Select **Name Create.**

4. Type **87S_WEST** as the name under which you will store your graph specifications in the spreadsheet.

5. Select **Save.**

6. Type **87S_WEST** (the graph file name) to create a .PIC file on disk. (You will use this .PIC file to print the graph.)

7. Select **Quit** to return to the worksheet.

8. Issue a **/File Save** command to save the spreadsheet (if you have finished working on the graph in the current file).

Creating Enhanced Graphs

You will practice using other 1-2-3 enhancements as you create two additional graphs:

- A stacked-bar graph of the components of annual sales-dollars by region (total Cost of Goods Sold, total Operating Expenses, and total Net Income)

- A line graph of the monthly percentage return on Sales

Figure 12.5 shows the screen display of the initial stacked-bar graph with its data labels and legends.

In this section, you will have the chance to again practice the commands used to create the bar graph in the preceding section. In addition, you can practice the commands for changing the format of numbers, changing the scale of the y-axis, and solving problems with legends.

To create the initial stacked-bar graph, use the following series of steps. Begin by clearing current graph settings and then selecting the type of graph:

1. Issue a **/Graph Reset** command.

2. Select **Graph** to remove all previous graph settings.

3. Select **Type Stacked-Bar.**

Fig. 12.5

The initial on-screen view of a stacked-bar graph.

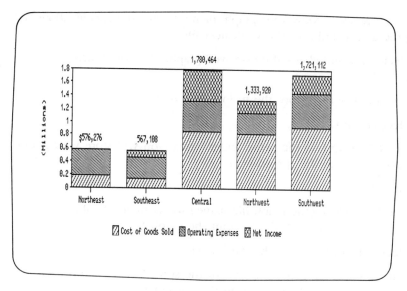

Next, enter the data range for your graph:

1. Select **A** for the first data range.

2. Enter **P14..P18** as the regional Cost of Goods Sold data.

3. Select **C** for a second data range. (Ignore the part of the prompt that indicates `third data range`.)

4. Enter **P23..P27** as the regional Operating Expense data.

5. Select **E** for a third data range.

6. Enter **P32..P36** as the regional Net Income data.

7. Select **X**.

The next stage includes identifying the range for x-axis labels, identifying labels to be used as legends for cross-hatching indicators, and specifying data labels that will appear above each stacked bar.

1. Specify the range **A14..A18** (the regional names) for the labels below the x-axis.

2. Select **Options Legend A**.

3. Enter **\A13** to use this cell's contents as the legend description.

4. Select **Legend C**.

5. Enter **\A22** as the legend description for the second data range.

6. Select **Legend E.**

7. Enter **\A31** as the legend description for the third data range.

8. Select **Data-Labels E** to initiate setting labels above the top bar (your third data range) in the stacked-bar graph.

9. Enter the range **P5..P9** to use the actual regional sales figures as data labels.

10. Select **Above** to complete setting the Data-Labels.

11. Select **Quit** to exit the Data-labels submenu.

You can now view the stacked-bar graph you have just created:

1. Select **Quit** from the Graph Options menu.

2. Select **View** from the main Graph menu.

3. Check to be sure that your graph matches figure 12.5.

4. Press any key to restore the main Graph menu.

On this graph, only the Northeast region's data label is displayed in currency format (the other regional figures lack the dollar sign). In addition, the Central region's data label rests on the top edge of the graph. You can improve the display by raising the upper scale of the y-axis, standardizing the format of the data, and adding titles. And you can reduce the size of the legend titles before you save the graph to print; if you don't, part of the legend display will not print.

To improve the appearance of the stacked-bar graph, so that it looks like the graph in figure 12.6, use the following series of steps. Begin by displaying values in **Currency** format:

1. **Quit** the main Graph menu.

2. Select **/Range Format Currency.**

3. Type **0** (zero) as the number of decimal places.

4. Enter the range **P6..P9** to complete the format change of the total regional sales figures.

Next, add titles and legends to your graph by completing these steps:

1. Select **/Graph Options Titles First.**

2. Type **SAMPLE COMPANY** as the graph's top center title.

3. Select **Titles Second.**

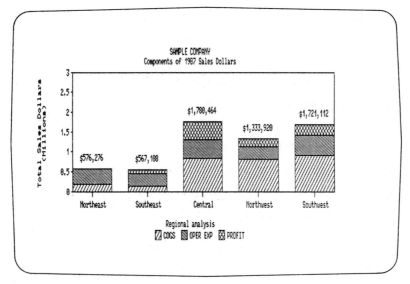

Fig. 12.6

On-screen view of the stacked-bar graph with improved format and scale.

4. Type **Components of 1987 Sales Dollars** as the second top center title.

5. Select Titles **X-Axis**.

6. Type **Regional Analysis** as descriptive text below the x-axis.

7. Select Titles **Y-Axis**.

8. Type **Total Sales Dollars** as descriptive text along the y-axis.

9. Select Legend **A**

10. Press Esc to erase the current setting; then type **COGS** as the text for the first legend.

11. Select Legend **C**

12. Press Esc, and then type **OPER EXP** as the text for the second data range.

13. Select Legend **E**

14. Press Esc, and then type **PROFIT** as the text for the third data range.

You can change the scale of your graph by completing the following steps:

1. Select Scale **Y Scale Manual Upper**.

2. Enter **3000000** (3 million, without commas) as the new upper limit.

3. **Quit** the Scale submenu.

Finally, display your graph, name it, and save the graph in the .PIC format for printing. Also, don't forget to save the worksheet file.

1. **Quit** the Options submenu.

2. Select **View** and check your screen to make sure that it matches figure 12.6.

3. Press any key to restore the main Graph menu.

4. Select **Name Create.**

5. Enter **SALES$** as the graph name to store graph specifications to the spreadsheet.

6. Select **Save.**

7. At the prompt, respond with the graph file name **SALES$** to create a .PIC file on disk. (This file will be used only for printing the graph.)

8. Select **Quit** to return to the worksheet.

9. Issue a **/File Save** to save the graph settings with the file.

Now you will construct a line graph, of a single data range, which shows monthly percentage return on Sales (see fig. 12.7). (The graph shows unmistakably that the future of the SAMPLE COMPANY is not too bright.) As you begin to create this graph, you will use a total graph reset to remove previous graph settings. (On this new line graph, the first title line is the only item that duplicates an option on the stacked-bar graph.)

Fig. 12.7

On-screen view of a basic line graph.

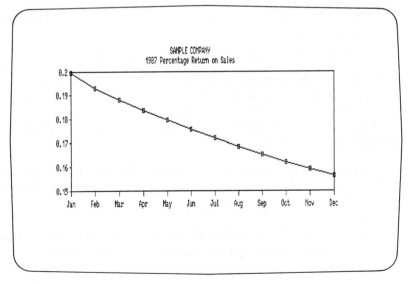

To produce this basic line graph, complete the following series of steps. First clear all current settings, and enter data for the single range in your line graph:

1. Select **Reset** from the main Graph menu.

2. Select **Graph** to remove all previous graph settings.

3. Select **A** as the only data range.

4. At the prompt, respond **C58..N58** to enter the monthly total percentage return on Sales. (In this example, you do not have to specify a graph type after resetting the graph; Line is the default graph type.)

Next, enter the titles you want to appear at the top of your graph, and indicate the range of dates on your worksheet to be used as x-axis labels.

1. Select **Options Titles First**.

2. Type **SAMPLE COMPANY** as the graph's top center title.

3. Select **Titles Second**.

4. Type **1987 Percentage Return on Sales** as the second top center title.

5. **Quit** the Options submenu.

6. Select **X** from the main Graph menu.

7. Enter **C2..N2** as the range to input monthly headings below the x-axis.

8. Select **View** so that you can check whether your screen matches figure 12.7.

9. Press any key to restore the main Graph menu.

You can make this default line graph look like the graph in figure 12.8. You will do so by setting the origin (the intersection of the x- and y-axes) to zero; by expanding the data range to include blank cells at both ends (to move the Jan. and Dec. data points off the edges of the graph); and by using data labels to display specific percentages.

To alter the graph's appearance, proceed as follows. Use the first series of steps to enter a space before the first data point and after the last data point.

1. Select **A** from the main Graph menu.

2. Enter **B58..O58** to replace the current C58..N58. (This expanded range adds a blank cell to each end of the data range.)

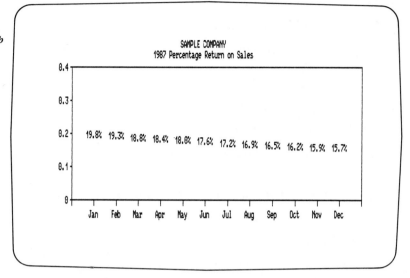

Fig. 12.8

On-screen view of the line graph with data labels and altered scale.

3. Select **X** from the main Graph menu.

4. Enter **B2..O2** to move the monthly headings over so that they line up with the monthly entries.

To change your line graph's format from a connected line to a series of percentages, follow these steps:

1. Select **Options Format Graph** to access a submenu of display options for line and XY graphs only.

2. Select **Neither** to remove connecting lines and symbols.

3. Select **Quit** to exit the Format submenu.

4. Select **Data-Labels** from the Graph Options menu.

5. Select **A** to set up labels for the graph's only data range.

6. Enter the range **B58..O58** to use the percentage values in row 58 as labels. (Note that the data-label range must include also a blank cell at either end so that it matches the length of the associated data range.)

7. Choose **Center** to position the data-labels on the plotted data points.

8. **Quit** the Data-label submenu.

Change the scale of your y-axis by completing the following steps:

1. Select **Scale Y** Scale **Manual Upper.**

2. Reenter the upper limit of **.32.** (Because selecting **Manual** causes both the upper and lower scale limits to display as Ø, you need to respecify only the upper limit.)

3. **Quit** the Scale submenu.

4. **Quit** the Options submenu.

Finally, display and name your graph, save it for printing, and save the entire worksheet.

1. Select **View** and check your screen, which should match figure 12.8.

2. Press any key to restore the main Graph menu.

3. Select **Name Create.**

4. Enter the graph name **SALESROR** to store these graph specifications in the spreadsheet.

5. Select **Save.**

6. At the prompt, respond with **SALESROR** to create a .PIC file on disk. (This file will be used only for printing the graph.)

7. **Quit** the main Graph menu.

8. Select **/File Save.**

9. Enter the file name **REGION87** to store the Regional Income and Ratio Analysis data as well as the specifications of the three named graphs (87S_WEST, SALES$, and SALESROR).

10. End the 1-2-3 session by selecting **Quit Yes** from the main command menu.

The final section of this chapter shows you how to print two of the graphs you've created.

Printing .PIC (Graph) Files

To print graphs, you must access a utility program called PrintGraph. Only graphs that have been stored as .PIC files can be printed. You will access the PrintGraph program from the disk operating system (DOS) prompt or from the 1-2-3 Access menu. Then you will print, one at a time, two graphs: one at default settings and another that alters image-related options. These graphs are displayed on-screen as figures 12.4 and 12.6, respectively.

Before you begin this practice session, make sure that:

▶ The PrintGraph hardware setup (Printer, Fonts-Directory, Graphs-Directory, and Paper size) is appropriate for your equipment. (Hardware setup is explained in Chapter 11.)

Using Default PrintGraph Settings

Only a few keystrokes are needed to produce a default half-size graph displaying block style print. You'll print the default comparative bar graph showing Southwest Region data (see fig. 12.9).

Fig. 12.9

A bar graph printed using default settings.

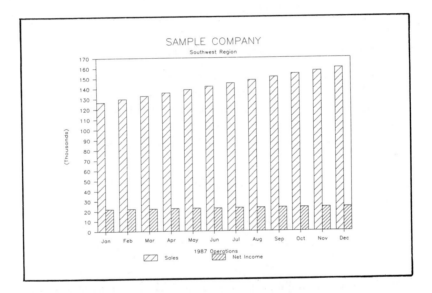

To print this graph, use the following command sequences:

1. Type **pgraph** at the DOS prompt (C⟩ or A⟩, with the PrintGraph program in the current directory or on the disk currently in the A drive)

   or

   Type **lotus** at the DOS prompt (C⟩ or A⟩, with 1-2-3 on the current directory or with the 1-2-3 System disk in drive A); then select **PrintGraph** from the Access System menu.

2. Choose **Image-Select** from the main PrintGraph menu.

3. Position the highlighted bar on 87S_WEST and press Enter. (This step automatically marks [with a # symbol] the highlighted .PIC file name for printing and restores the main PrintGraph menu to the screen.)

4. Check the printer, making sure that it is on-line and that the print head is at the top edge of the paper.

5. Select **Align** to ensure that 1-2-3 recognizes the current top-of-page.

6. Select **Go**, and wait for the half-size graph to print.

7. Check the output, which should match figure 12.9.

8. Select **Page** from the main PrintGraph menu to advance the paper to the top of the next page.

Changing PrintGraph Settings

You use the main PrintGraph menu's Settings option to alter print options. Most of the Settings options deal with establishing a specific print environment (location of files, type of printer, etc.) and are not illustrated here. In this final practice session, you will use two options (**Font** and **Size**) to change the default graph's image and produce a full-size graph with two font styles (see fig. 12.10).

To produce this full-size stacked-bar graph, use the following command sequences:

1. Choose **Image-Select** from the main PrintGraph menu.

2. Position the highlighted bar on 87S_WEST and press the space bar to unmark the 87S_WEST graph.

3. Position the highlighted bar on SALES$ and press Enter. (The highlighted .PIC file name will be marked [#] automatically for printing and the main PrintGraph menu will be restored to the screen.)

4. Select **Settings Image Size Full**.

5. Select **Quit** to exit the Size submenu.

6. Select **Font 1** to access a list of 1-2-3 font styles.

7. Press the space bar to unmark the default BLOCK1 font style.

8. Position the highlighted bar on FORUM and press Enter to specify a print style for the top center title.

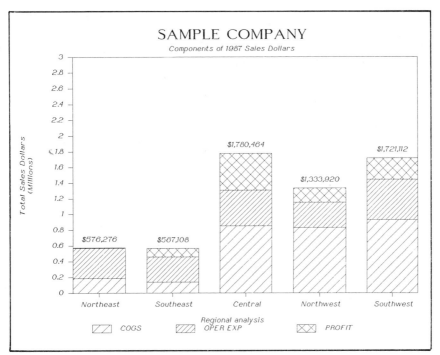

Fig. 12.10

A stacked-bar graph, printed with size and font changes.

9. Select **Font 2** and press the space bar to unmark the default BLOCK1 font style.

10. Position the highlighted bar on LOTUS and press Enter to specify the print style for the remaining descriptive text.

11. **Q**uit the Image submenu.

12. **Q**uit the Settings menu.

13. Select **G**o from the main PrintGraph menu and wait while the graph is printed.

14. Check the printed full-size graph to be sure that it matches figure 12.10.

15. Select **P**age twice from the main PrintGraph menu to eject the graph from the printer.

16. Select **E**xit to return to the DOS prompt.

Chapter Summary

This chapter has given you a chance to practice printing spreadsheet and database (.WK1) files and graph (.PIC) files. Review the detailed print and graph information in Chapters 9, 10, and 11, and check this book's troubleshooting section for additional printing information. And remember— One .PIC is worth a thousand WK1s!

Part III

Customizing 1-2-3: Databases, Macros, and the Command Language

Includes

Data Management

Using Macros To Customize Your Spreadsheet

Introduction to the Command Language

13

Data Management

In addition to the electronic spreadsheet and business graphics, 1-2-3 has a third element: data management. Because the entire 1-2-3 database resides in the spreadsheet within main memory (RAM), 1-2-3's database feature is fast, easy to access, and easy to use.

The speed results from a reduction in the time required to transfer data to and from disks. By doing all the work inside the spreadsheet, 1-2-3 saves the time required for input and output to disk.

The 1-2-3 database is easily accessed because Lotus Development Corporation has made the entire database visible within the spreadsheet. You can view the contents of the whole database by using worksheet windows and cursor-movement keys to scroll through the database.

The ease of use is a result of integrating data management with the program's spreadsheet and graphics functions. The commands for adding, modifying, and deleting items in a database are the same ones you have already seen for manipulating cells or groups of cells within a worksheet. And creating graphs from ranges in a database is as easy as creating them in a spreadsheet.

This chapter shows you how to

- Create a 1-2-3 database
- Enter, modify, and maintain data records
- Carry out **Sort** and **Query** operations
- Load data from ASCII files and other programs
- Apply data with other /**Data** commands
- Use database statistical functions

What Is a Database?

A *database* is a collection of data organized so that you can list, sort, or search its contents. The list of data might contain any kind of information, from addresses to tax-deductible expenditures.

In 1-2-3, the word *database* means a range of cells that spans at least one column and more than one row. This definition, however, does not distinguish between a database and any other range of cells. Because a database is actually a list, its manner of organization sets it apart from ordinary cells. Just as a list must be organized to be useful, a database must be organized to permit access to the information it contains.

Remember nonetheless that in 1-2-3 a database is similar to any other group of cells. This knowledge will help you as you learn about the different /**Data** commands that are covered in this chapter. There are many instances in which you can use these database commands in what you might consider "non-database" applications.

The smallest unit in a database is a *field*, or single data item. For example, if you were to develop an information base of present or potential corporate contributors for a not-for-profit organization, you might include the following fields of information:

Company Name
Company Address
Contact Person
Phone Number
Last Contact Date
Contact Representative
Last Contribution Date

A database *record* is a collection of associated fields. For example, the accumulation of all contributor data about one company forms one record.

In 1-2-3, a *record* is a row of cells within a database, and a *field* is a single cell.

A database must be set up so that you can access the information it contains. Retrieval of information usually involves key fields. A database *key field* is any field on which you base a list, sort, or search operation. For example, you could use *Zipcode* as a key field to sort the data in the contributor database and assign contact representatives to specific geographic areas. And you could prepare a follow-up contact list by searching the database for the key field *Last Contact Date* in which the date is less than one year ago.

What Can You Do with a 1-2-3 Database?

Reminder:
The 1-2-3 database resides in the spreadsheet's row-and-column format.

The 1-2-3 database resides in the spreadsheet's row-and-column format. Figure 13.1 shows the general organization of a 1-2-3 database.

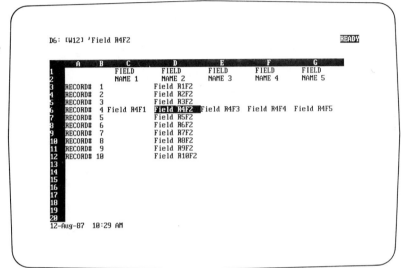

Fig. 13.1

General organization of the 1-2-3 database.

Labels (*field names*) describing the data items appear as column headings. Information about each specific data item (field) is entered in a cell in the appropriate column. In figure 13.1, the highlighted cell (D6) represents data for the second field name in the database's fourth record.

In the Marketing Research database shown in figure 13.2, the highlighted row (row 5) contains all fields of information concerning the first record.

Reminder:
You must load the entire 1-2-3 database into memory before you can perform any data-management operations.

The major disadvantage of Lotus's approach is the limitation it imposes on the size of the database. With some popular database programs, you can get by with loading only portions of your database at once; with 1-2-3, the entire database must be in memory before you can perform any data-management operations.

Theoretically, the maximum number of records you can have in a 1-2-3 database corresponds to the maximum number of rows in the spreadsheet (8,192 rows minus 1 row for the field names). Realistically, however, the number of records in a specific database is limited by the amount of available memory: internal memory (RAM), disk storage, and the room needed within the database to hold data extracted by **Query** commands.

Fig. 13.2

The highlighted record.

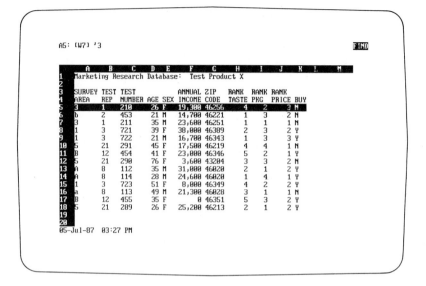

```
A5: [W7] '3                                                    FIND

        A    B    C    D   E    F      G    H    I    J    K  L    M
1  Marketing Research Database:   Test Product X
2
3  SURVEY TEST TEST             ANNUAL ZIP   RANK RANK RANK
4  AREA   REP  NUMBER AGE SEX INCOME CODE  TASTE PKG  PRICE BUY
5  3      1    210    26  F   19,300 46256   4    2     3 N
6  b      2    453    21  M   14,700 46221   1    3     2 N
7  3      1    211    35  M   23,600 46251   1    1     1 N
8  1      3    721    39  F   38,000 46309   2    3     2 Y
9  1      3    722    21  M   16,700 46343   1    3     3 Y
10 5      21   291    45  F   17,500 46219   4    4     1 N
11 B      12   454    41  F   23,000 46346   5    2     1 Y
12 5      21   290    76  F    3,600 43204   3    3     2 N
13 A      8    112    35  M   31,000 46020   2    1     2 Y
14 A      8    114    28  M   24,600 46020   1    4     1 Y
15 1      3    723    51  F    8,000 46349   4    2     2 Y
16 A      8    113    49  M   21,300 46028   3    1     1 N
17 B      12   455    35  F        0 46351   5    3     2 Y
18 5      21   289    26  F   25,200 46213   2    1     2 Y
19
20
05-Jul-87  03:27 PM
```

If your computer has 640K of internal memory, you can store in a single database only about 1,000 400-byte (character) records or 8,000 50-byte records. (To provide a frame of reference, each record in the Marketing Research database shown in fig. 13.2 contains 67 characters.) Disk operating system commands and the 1-2-3 program instructions occupy the remaining memory. For large databases, you need to extend the internal memory capacity beyond 640K.

Reminder:

If you use floppy disks to store database files, you are limited to a total of 360,000 characters. If you use a hard disk, you are limited to 4 million characters.

If you use floppy disks for external storage of database files, you are limited to files that total approximately 360,000 characters (1.2 million characters on a high-density disk). On a hard disk, a database of 8,000 500-byte records occupies four million characters, or four megabytes.

When you estimate the maximum database size you can use on your computer equipment, be sure to include enough blank rows to accommodate the maximum output you expect from extract operations.

If you can deal with 1-2-3's memory constraints and the somewhat time-consuming method of using menu options to manipulate data, you'll have a powerful data-management tool.

As you may know, you access the submenu of **/Data** commands from the main 1-2-3 menu. Because all the options (**Worksheet, Range, Copy, Move, File,**

Print, and **G**raph) that precede **D**ata on the main menu work as well on databases as they do on spreadsheets, the power of 1-2-3 is at your fingertips.

If you prefer to use a stand-alone program such as dBASE for your database, use 1-2-3's file-translation capabilities (see Chapter 7) to take advantage of 1-2-3's data and graph commands.

Cue:
You can translate files between 1-2-3 and dBASE for your database applications.

When you select **D**ata from the 1-2-3 main menu, the following options are displayed in the control panel's second menu line:

  Fill **T**able **S**ort **Q**uery **D**istribution **M**atrix **R**egression **P**arse

The **S**ort and **Q**uery (search) options are true data-management operations. Both are described in detail early in this chapter. The other options (**F**ill, **T**able, **D**istribution, **M**atrix, **R**egression, and **P**arse) are considered, more appropriately, data-creation operations. They too are described in this chapter.

Creating a Database

You can create a database as a new database file or as part of an existing spreadsheet. If you decide to build a database as part of an existing worksheet, choose a worksheet area that will not be needed for anything else. This area should be large enough to accommodate the number of records you plan to enter during the current session and in the future. If you add the database to the side of the spreadsheet, be careful about inserting or deleting spreadsheet rows that might also affect the database. If you add a database below an existing spreadsheet, be careful not to disturb predetermined column widths in the spreadsheet portion when you adjust column widths to the widths of database fields.

Caution:
Locate your database where it won't be affected by inserting or deleting columns or rows and by changing column widths in other applications.

After you have decided which area of the worksheet to use, you create a database by specifying field names across a row and entering data in cells as you would for any other 1-2-3 application. The mechanics of entering database contents are simple; the most critical step in creating a useful database is choosing your fields accurately.

Determining Required Output

1-2-3's data-retrieval techniques rely on locating data by field names. Before you begin typing the kinds of data items you think you may need, write down the output you expect from the database. You'll also need to consider any source documents already in use that can provide input to the file. For example, you might use the following information from a sample database:

Company Name
Company Address
Contact Person
Phone Number
Last Contact Date
Contact Representative
Last Contribution Date

When you are ready to set up these items in your database, you must specify for each information item a field name, the column width, and the type of entry.

You might make a common error in setting up your database if you choose a field name (and enter data) without thinking about the output that you want from that key field. For example, suppose that you establish GIFTDATE as a field name to describe the last date a contribution was made. Then you enter record dates as labels, in the general form XX/XX/XX. Although you can search for a GIFTDATE that matches a specific date, you won't be able to perform a math-based search for all GIFTDATEs within a specified period of time or before a certain date. To get maximum flexibility from 1-2-3's **Data** commands, enter dates in your databases in the following form (see Chapter 6 for more information):

@DATE(year number,month number,day number)

Reminder:
The format of your data (date, labels, numbers) will affect how the data can be sorted and searched.

You then need to choose the level of detail needed for each item of information, select the appropriate column width, and determine whether you will enter data as a number or as a label. For example, if you want to be able to sort by area code all records containing telephone numbers, you should enter telephone numbers as two separate fields: area code (XXX) and the base number XXX-XXXX. Because you will not want to perform math functions on telephone numbers, enter them as labels.

To save memory and increase data-entry speed and accuracy, code as much information as possible. For example, if you need to query only about workloads, plan to use the first, middle, and last initials of each contact representative in the database instead of printing a list of their full names.

If you enter database content from a standard source document, such as a marketing research survey form, you can increase the speed of data entry by setting up the field names in the same order as the corresponding data items on the form.

Be sure to plan your database carefully before you establish field names, set column widths and range formats, and enter data.

Entering Data

After you have planned your database, you can build it. To help you understand how the process works, we will create a Marketing Research database as a new database on a blank worksheet (in READY mode). After we select the appropriate area of the worksheet for the database, we enter the field names across a single row (see fig. 13.3).

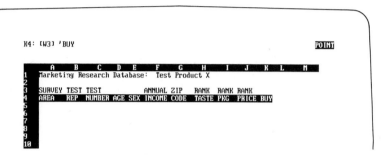

Fig. 13.3

Creating field names in a database.

The highlighted bar rests on row 4, the field name row. The field names must be labels, even if they are the numeric labels '1, '2, etc. Although you can use more than one row for the field names, 1-2-3 processes only the values that appear in the bottom row. For example, the first field name in the Marketing Research database (rows 3 and 4 of column A) is SURVEY AREA. Only the AREA (the portion in row 4) will be referenced as a key field in sort or query operations.

Keep in mind that all field names should be unique; any repetition of names confuses 1-2-3 when you search or sort the database. The field names in figure 13.3 are acceptable because, although the words in row 3 are repeated (two TESTs and three RANKs), each key-field name in row 4 is unique.

Reminder:
Keep all field names unique; any repetition of field names will confuse 1-2-3.

To control the manner in which cells are displayed on the screen, use 1-2-3's Format and Column Set-Width options. In figure 13.2, notice that the range format in column F is , (comma) with zero decimal places, and that column widths on the worksheet vary from 4 to 7 characters.

Note also that whenever a right-justified column of numeric data is adjacent to a left-justified column of label information (AGE..SEX or INCOME..CODE, for example), the data looks crowded. You can insert blank columns to change the spacing between fields, but if you plan to search values in the database, do not leave any blank rows.

Cue:
Insert blank columns between fields to prevent crowding data.

After you have altered the column widths, entered title and field names, and added spacing columns, you can add records to the database. To enter the first record, move the cursor to the row directly below the field-name row and then enter the data across the row in the normal manner.

In the sample Marketing Research database, the contents of the AREA, REP, NUMBER, SEX, CODE, and BUY fields are entered as labels; the contents of the AGE, INCOME, TASTE, PKG, and PRICE fields are entered as numbers. Figure 13.4 shows the initial data and the column spacing for this database.

Fig. 13.4

The newly created Marketing Research database.

A1: [W7] 'Marketing Research Database: Test Product X   READY

	A	B	C	D	E	F	G	H	I	J	K	L	M	N
1	Marketing Research Database: Test Product X													
2														
3	SURVEY	TEST	TEST				ANNUAL		ZIP	RANK	RANK	RANK		
4	AREA	REP	NUMBER	AGE		SEX	INCOME		CODE	TASTE	PKG	PRICE		BUY
5	3	1	210	26		F	19,300		46256	4	2	3		N
6	b	2	453	21		M	14,700		46221	1	3	2		N
7	3	1	211	35		M	23,600		46251	1	1	1		N
8	1	3	721	39		F	38,000		46389	2	3	2		Y
9	1	3	722	21		M	16,700		46343	1	3	3		Y
10	5	21	291	45		F	17,500		46219	4	4	1		N
11	B	12	454	41		F	23,000		46346	5	2	1		Y
12	5	21	290	76		F	3,600		43204	3	3	2		N
13	A	8	112	35		M	31,000		46020	2	1	2		Y
14	A	8	114	28		M	24,600		46020	1	4	1		Y
15	1	3	723	51		F	8,000		46349	4	2	2		Y
16	a	8	113	49		M	21,300		46028	3	1	1		N
17	B	12	455	35		F	0		46351	5	3	2		Y
18	5	21	289	26		F	25,200		46213	2	1	2		Y
19														
20														

05-Jul-87 03:29 PM

This sample Marketing Research database will be used periodically throughout the chapter to illustrate the results of using **D**ata commands. In this book, the fields are limited to a single screen display. In "real life" applications, however, you would track many more data items. You can maintain 256 fields (the number of columns available) in a 1-2-3 database.

In the AREA field, letters code the shopping-center test locations, and numbers indicate the locations of college-campus product testing. The entries in the TASTE and PKG fields reflect options 1 through 5 (1 = most favorable); the entries in the PRICE field reflect options 1 through 3 (1 = too high).

Modifying a Database

After you have collected the data for your database and decided which field types, widths, and formats to use, creating a database is easy. Thanks to 1-2-3, maintaining the accuracy of the database content is easy also.

To add and delete records in a database, use the same commands for inserting and deleting rows that you use for any other application in 1-2-3. Because records correspond to rows, you begin inserting a record with the /**W**orksheet

Insert **R**ow command. You then fill in the various fields in the rows with the appropriate data. Figure 13.5 shows an example of inserting a record in the middle of a database. Instead of inserting a record in the middle of a database, however, you probably will use 1-2-3's sorting capabilities, illustrated in the next section, to rearrange the physical order of database records.

Fig. 13.5

Inserting a record row in the database.

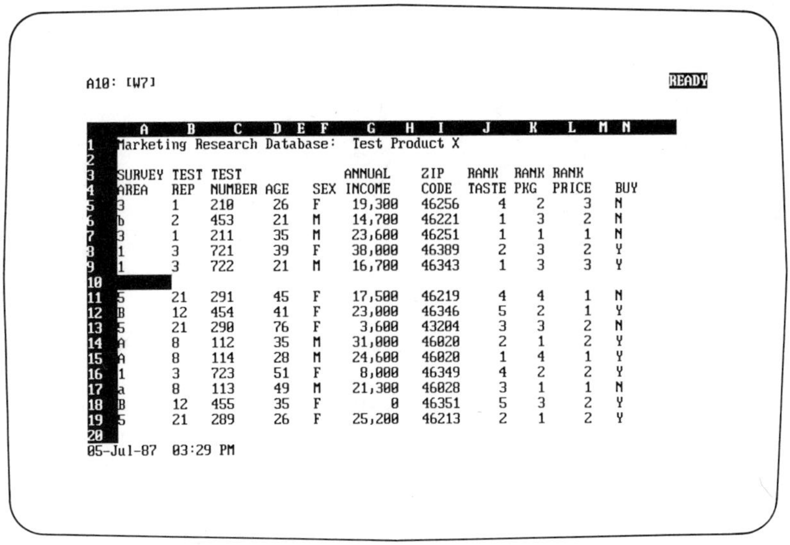

A10: [W7]   READY

	A	B	C	D	E	F	G	H	I	J	K	L
1	Marketing Research Database: Test Product X											
2												
3	SURVEY	TEST	TEST			ANNUAL	ZIP	RANK	RANK	RANK		
4	AREA	REP	NUMBER	AGE	SEX	INCOME	CODE	TASTE	PKG	PRICE	BUY	
5	B	1	210	26	F	19,300	46256	4	2	3	N	
6	b	2	453	21	M	14,700	46221	1	3	2	N	
7	B	1	211	35	M	23,600	46251	1	1	1	N	
8	1	3	721	39	F	38,000	46389	2	3	2	Y	
9	1	3	722	21	M	16,700	46343	1	3	3	Y	
10												
11	5	21	291	45	F	17,500	46219	4	4	1	N	
12	B	12	454	41	F	23,000	46346	5	2	1	Y	
13	5	21	290	76	F	3,600	43204	3	3	2	N	
14	A	8	112	35	M	31,000	46020	2	1	2	Y	
15	A	8	114	28	M	24,600	46020	1	4	1	Y	
16	1	3	723	51	F	8,000	46349	4	2	2	Y	
17	a	8	113	49	M	21,300	46028	3	1	1	N	
18	B	12	455	35	F	0	46351	5	3	2	Y	
19	5	21	289	26	F	25,200	46213	2	1	2	Y	
20												

05-Jul-87 03:29 PM

To delete records, move your cell pointer to the row or rows that you want to delete and use the /**W**orksheet **D**elete **R**ow command. Because you will not have an opportunity to verify the range before you issue the command, be extremely careful when you specify the records to be deleted. If you want to remove only inactive records, consider first using the **E**xtract command to store the extracted inactive records in a separate file before you delete the records. (This chapter will teach you how.)

Cue:
*Archive inactive records with the **E**xtract command before you delete them from the main database.*

The process of modifying fields in a database is the same as that for modifying the contents of cells in any other application. As you learned in Chapter 3, you change the cell contents either by retyping the cell entry or by using the F2 (Edit) key and editing the entry.

To add a new field to a database, position the cell pointer anywhere in the column that will be to the right of the newly inserted column. Issue the /**W**orksheet **I**nsert **C**olumn command, and then fill the field with values for each record. For example, to insert a DATE field between the NUMBER and AGE fields in the Marketing Research database, position the cell pointer on any cell in the AGE column, issue the **I**nsert **C**olumn command, and then type the new field name in D3 and D4 (see fig. 13.6).

Reminder:
*Add new fields to your database with /**W**orksheet **I**nsert **C**olumn; delete fields with /**W**orksheet **D**elete **C**olumn.*

Fig. 13.6

Inserting a column for a new field.

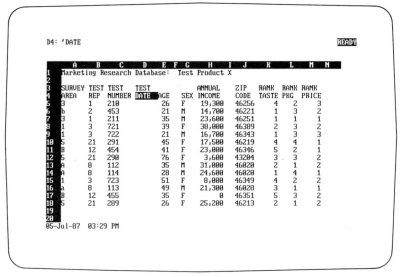

```
D4: 'DATE                                                                READY

        A    B    C    D E F G    H    I  J    K    L    M  N
  1 Marketing Research Database:  Test Product X
  2
  3 SURVEY TEST TEST TEST          ANNUAL  ZIP  RANK RANK RANK
  4 AREA   REP  NUMBER DATE  AGE  SEX INCOME  CODE TASTE PKG PRICE
  5 3      1    210          26   F   19,300  46256  4   2    3
  6 b      2    453          21   M   14,700  46221  1   3    2
  7 3      1    211          35   M   23,600  46251  1   1    1
  8 1      3    721          39   F   38,000  46389  2   3    2
  9 1      3    722          21   M   16,700  46343  1   3    3
 10 5      21   291          45   F   17,500  46219  4   4    1
 11 B      12   454          41   F   23,000  46346  5   2    1
 12 5      21   290          76   F    3,600  43204  3   3    2
 13 A      8    112          35   M   31,000  46020  2   1    2
 14 A      8    114          28   M   24,600  46020  1   4    1
 15 1      3    723          51   F    8,000  46349  4   2    2
 16 a      8    113          49   M   21,300  46020  3   1    1
 17 B      12   455          35   F       0   46351  5   3    2
 18 5      21   289          26   F   25,200  46213  2   1    2
 19
 20
05-Jul-87  03:29 PM
```

Because maintaining data is expensive, you may not feel justified keeping certain seldom-used data fields in the database. To delete such a field, position the cell pointer anywhere in the column you want to remove and then use the /**W**orksheet **D**elete **C**olumn command.

All other commands, such as those for moving cells, formatting cells, displaying the contents of worksheets, etc., are the same for both database and other spreadsheet applications.

Sorting Database Records

1-2-3's data management capability lets you change the order of records by sorting them according to the contents of the fields. Selecting /**D**ata **S**ort produces the following command menu:

    Data-Range   Primary-Key   Secondary-Key   Reset   Go   Quit

Reminder:
Do not include the field-name row when you are designating a Data-Range for sorting your database.

To sort the database, start by designating a **D**ata-Range. This range must be long enough to include all of the records to be sorted and wide enough to include all of the fields in each record. Remember not to include the field-name row in this range. (If you are unfamiliar with how to designate ranges or how to name them, see Chapter 4.)

The **D**ata-Range does not necessarily have to include the entire database. If part of the database already has the organization you want, or if you don't want to sort all the records, you can sort only a portion of the database.

(Remember: When you sort, do not include the field names in your Data-Range.)

After choosing the Data-Range, you must specify the keys for the sort. *Keys* are the fields to which you attach the highest precedence when the database is sorted. The field with the highest precedence is the Primary-Key, and the field with the next highest precedence is the Secondary-Key. You must set a Primary-Key, but the Secondary-Key is optional.

After you have specified the range to sort, the key field(s) on which to base the reordering of the records, and whether the sort order, based on the key, is ascending or descending, select Go to execute the command. As a useful step for restoring the file to its original order, /File Save the database to disk before you issue a Sort command.

Caution:
Use /File Save before sorting your database, in case you need to restore the original order.

The One-Key Sort

One of the simplest examples of a database sorted according to a primary key (often called a single-key database) is the white pages of the telephone book. All the records in the white pages are sorted in ascending alphabetical order using the last name as the primary key. This ascending alphabetical-order sort can be used to reorder the records in the Addresses database shown in figure 13.7.

Fig. 13.7

The unsorted Addresses database.

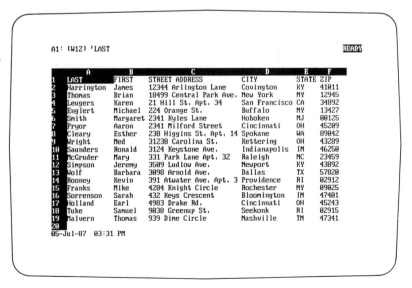

Use 1-2-3's Sort capability to reorder records alphabetically on the LAST name field. Select /Data Sort Data-Range. At the prompt for a range to sort, respond with *A2..F19*. After you specify the range, the /**D**ata **S**ort menu returns to the screen. This is one of 1-2-3's "sticky" menus. (The /**P**rint **P**rinter menu is another.) Sticky menus remain displayed and active until you enter **Q**uit. This sticky menu is helpful because you don't have to enter /**D**ata **S**ort at the beginning of each command.

After choosing the **D**ata-Range, select **P**rimary-Key and then enter or point to the address of any entry (including blank or field-name cells) in the column containing the primary-key field. For example, enter *A1* as the **P**rimary-Key in the Addresses database. 1-2-3 then asks you to enter a sort order (**A** or **D**). *A* stands for Ascending and *D* for Descending. For this example, choose **A**scending order and press Enter. Finally, you enter **G**o from the menu to execute the sort. Figure 13.8 shows the Addresses database sorted in ascending order by last name.

Fig. 13.8

The Addresses database sorted by LAST name.

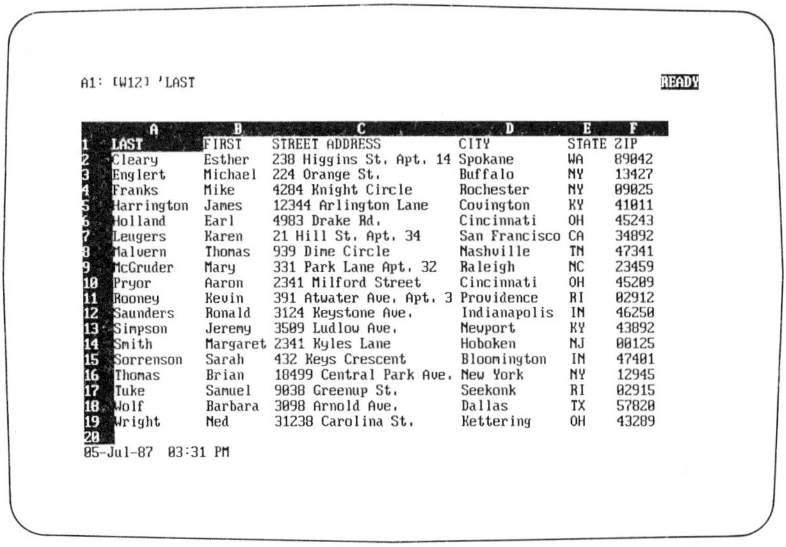

You can add a record to an alphabetized name-and-address database without having to insert a row manually to place the new record in the proper position. Simply add the new record to the bottom of the current database, expand the **D**ata-Range, and then sort the database again by last name.

Cue:

Add a new record to a sorted database by entering the record at the bottom of your database and then re-sorting the database.

The Two-Key Sort

A double-key database has both a primary and secondary key. In the telephone book's Yellow Pages, records are sorted first according to business type (the primary key) and then by business name (the secondary key). As an example of a double-key sort (first by one key and then by another key within the first sort order), we will reorder the Addresses database first by state and then by city within state.

Designate the range *A2..F19* as the **Data-Range**. Select **Primary-Key** from the **Sort** menu and enter *E1* as the field location of the initial sort. (Remember that you can specify any cell in column E.) Enter *A* for ascending order for the sort by STATE. Select **Secondary-Key**, enter *D1*, and choose *A* for ascending sort order by CITY. Figure 13.9 shows the results of issuing the **Go** command after you have specified the two-key sort.

Fig. 13.9

The Addresses database sorted by CITY within STATE.

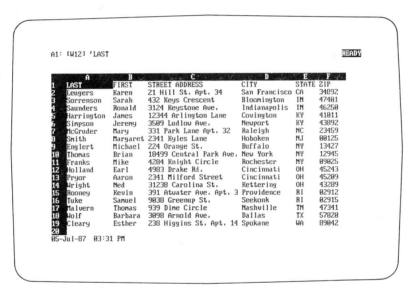

```
A1: [W12] 'LAST                                                          READY

        A          B        C                        D              E     F
1  LAST        FIRST    STREET ADDRESS            CITY           STATE ZIP
2  Leugers     Karen    21 Hill St. Apt. 34      San Francisco  CA    34092
3  Sorrenson   Sarah    432 Keys Crescent        Bloomington    IN    47401
4  Saunders    Ronald   3124 Keystone Ave.       Indianapolis   IN    46250
5  Harrington  James    12344 Arlington Lane     Covington      KY    41011
6  Simpson     Jeremy   3589 Ludlow Ave.         Newport        KY    43892
7  McGruder    Mary     331 Park Lane Apt. 32    Raleigh        NC    23459
8  Smith       Margaret 2341 Kyles Lane          Hoboken        NJ    00125
9  Englert     Michael  224 Orange St.           Buffalo        NY    13427
10 Thomas      Brian    18499 Central Park Ave.  New York       NY    12945
11 Franks      Mike     4284 Knight Circle       Rochester      NY    09025
12 Holland     Earl     4983 Drake Rd.           Cincinnati     OH    45243
13 Pryor       Aaron    2341 Milford Street      Cincinnati     OH    45289
14 Wright      Ned      31238 Carolina St.       Kettering      OH    43289
15 Rooney      Kevin    391 Atwater Ave. Apt. 3  Providence     RI    02912
16 Tuke        Samuel   9038 Greenup St.         Seekonk        RI    02915
17 Malvern     Thomas   939 Dine Circle          Nashville      TN    47341
18 Wolf        Barbara  3098 Arnold Ave.         Dallas         TX    57020
19 Cleary      Esther   238 Higgins St. Apt. 14  Spokane        WA    89042
20
05-Jul-87  03:31 PM
```

As you can see, records are now grouped first by state in alphabetical order (California, Indiana, Kentucky, etc.) and then by city within state (Bloomington, Indiana, before Indianapolis, Indiana). When you determine whether to use a primary or secondary key, be sure to request a reasonable sort. For example, do not try to sort first on city and then on state within city. Also, whenever possible, you may want to have the key fields as the leftmost fields in your database. By having the key fields as the first one or two fields in the database, you won't have to hunt for the results of the sort. As in our example, however, you'll find that this visual advantage isn't always feasible.

Sorts on More Than Two Keys

Although 1-2-3 seems to limit you to sorting on only two keys, you can bypass this apparent limitation by using the program's *string* capabilities. For example, suppose that you want to reorder the four fields of student information in the College database shown in figure 13.10.

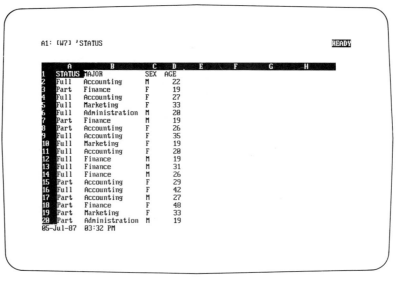

You can reorder the records to focus first on MAJOR field of study, then on SEX within each field of study, and then on AGE within each group of male or female students. Although subdividing each age group into the STATUS of full- or part-time student is not particularly significant in this small sample database, you can add additional sorts within sorts when appropriate.

To generate accurate sorts by using 1-2-3 string capabilities, you must follow certain rules. You must create a new field and enter a string formula. All fields joined in the string operation must either be labels or be converted to labels. If the contents of the stringed fields are not all the same size, you must make appropriate adjustments to the string formula. You must copy the string formula to all records involved in the sort and convert the resultant formulas to values. After you complete the string setup, you will sort on the new field.

To illustrate the concept of using string capabilities to sort on more than two keys, we will reorder the records in the College database. We will sort first on MAJOR, then on SEX within major, followed by AGE within sex, and then STATUS within age.

As the first step in the sort process, we will create a new field and enter a string formula (see fig. 13.11).

To create the new field name, enter *SORT-KEY* in cell E1. Then enter the formula *+B2&" "&C2&" "&@STRING(D2,0)&" "&A2* in cell E2. Notice that

Fig. 13.11

Entering a string formula for a multiple-key sort.

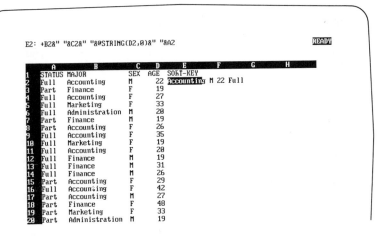

the formula appears in the upper left corner of the control panel and that the results of the formula display the label fields concatenated (strung together) in the highlighted cell.

The following listing breaks down the formula in cell E2 so that you can better understand it:

Formula piece	Description
+B2	Indicates the initial sort on MAJOR
&	String concatenation symbol
" "	Places a space after the contents of B2
&C2&" "	Indicates the secondary sort on SEX
&@STRING	Begins to add a third sort dimension on AGE; @STRING converts a numeric field to a label field; all stringed fields must be labels or the formula will return an ERR message
(D2,0)&" "	Required completion of the @STRING function to enclose the numeric field D2 in parentheses, followed by a comma and specification of decimal places (in this case, zero decimal places)
&A2	Adds a fourth sort dimension on STATUS

As the next step in setting up a sort that uses string capabilities, you need to copy the new formula to all the other fields in column E that fall within the specified data range. Figure 13.12 shows the results of copying the formula in E2 to the range E3..E20. (The cell pointer has been moved to E4 to show that the cell contents produced in the copy are currently in formula form.)

Fig. 13.12

The results of copying the string formula.

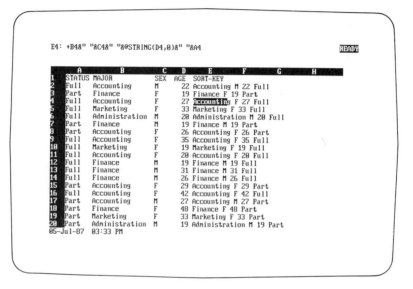

```
E4: +B4&" "&C4&" "&@STRING(D4,0)&" "&A4                    READY

     A        B            C   D     E         F       G       H
 1 STATUS  MAJOR          SEX AGE  SORT-KEY
 2 Full    Accounting      M   22  Accounting M 22 Full
 3 Part    Finance         F   19  Finance F 19 Part
 4 Full    Accounting      F   27  Accounting F 27 Full
 5 Full    Marketing       F   33  Marketing F 33 Full
 6 Full    Administration  M   20  Administration M 20 Full
 7 Part    Finance         M   19  Finance M 19 Part
 8 Part    Accounting      F   26  Accounting F 26 Part
 9 Full    Accounting      F   35  Accounting F 35 Full
10 Full    Marketing       F   19  Marketing F 19 Full
11 Full    Accounting      F   20  Accounting F 20 Full
12 Full    Finance         M   19  Finance M 19 Full
13 Full    Finance         M   31  Finance M 31 Full
14 Full    Finance         M   26  Finance M 26 Full
15 Part    Accounting      F   29  Accounting F 29 Part
16 Full    Accounting      F   42  Accounting F 42 Full
17 Part    Accounting      M   27  Accounting M 27 Part
18 Part    Finance         F   48  Finance F 48 Part
19 Part    Marketing       F   33  Marketing F 33 Part
20 Part    Administration  M   19  Administration M 19 Part
05-Jul-87  03:33 PM
```

For the string sort to work properly, the new formulas in column E must be converted to values. Use /**R**ange **V**alue and specify E2..E20 as both the range to copy FROM and the range to copy TO. This step converts all the formulas to values. As you can see from figure 13.13, the column E display does not change. But if you compare figures 13.12 and 13.13, you will notice that the control panel in the former displays cell E4's formula content whereas the control panel in the latter displays the contents of cell E4 as nonformula data. Setup of the stringed sort is now complete.

To begin the sort operation, select /**D**ata **S**ort **D**ata-Range and specify A2..E20 as the range to sort. Select **P**rimary-Key, enter any cell in column E (E1, for example) and then choose **A**scending order. Then select **G**o to execute this sort on more than two keys. Your screen should look like the one shown in figure 13.14.

Notice that major fields of study are grouped alphabetically, that study fields are subdivided into female and male categories, and that each of these subgroups is further sorted by age. For example, the six female accounting majors rank in age from 20 to 42 years. Splitting a duplicate age (Finance M

Fig. 13.13

Changing the new string formulas to values.

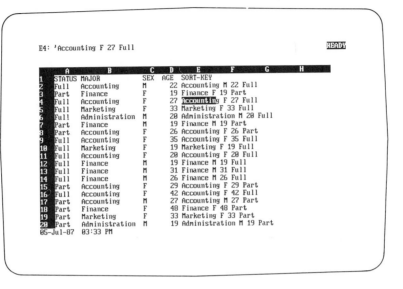

Fig. 13.14

The results of executing a multiple-key sort.

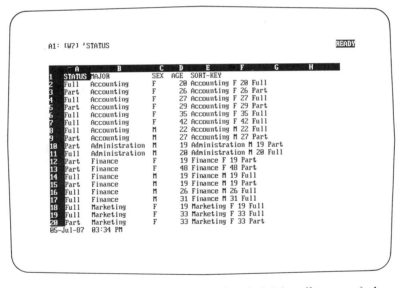

19 or Marketing F 33, for example) into a fourth subdivision (by status) does not produce meaningful data.

You can bypass 1-2-3's limited menu selections by stringing together any three (or more) meaningful sort keys. For example, try a different string sort on the College database shown in figure 13.11. This time, use full or part-time STATUS as the Primary-Key, followed by SEX within STATUS, and then by

MAJOR within SEX. The control panel in figure 13.15 displays the string formula required to set up this sort.

Fig. 13.15

Entering an alternative sort-string formula.

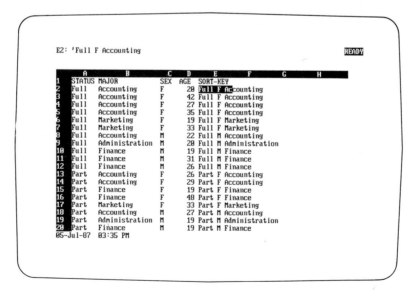

```
E2: +A2&" "&C2&" "&B2                                    READY

     A        B          C    D    E         F        G        H
1  STATUS  MAJOR        SEX  AGE  SORT-KEY
2  Full    Accounting    M    22  Full M Accounting
3  Part    Finance       F    19
4  Full    Accounting    F    27
5  Full    Marketing     F    33
6  Full    Administration M   20
7  Part    Finance       M    19
8  Part    Accounting    F    26
9  Full    Accounting    F    35
10 Full    Marketing     F    19
11 Full    Accounting    F    20
12 Full    Finance       M    19
13 Full    Finance       M    31
14 Full    Finance       M    26
15 Part    Accounting    F    29
16 Full    Accounting    F    42
17 Part    Accounting    M    27
18 Part    Finance       F    40
19 Part    Marketing     F    33
20 Part    Administration M   19
05-Jul-87  03:34 PM
```

If you copy the formula down column E, change the formulas to values, and execute the sort, the results of this alternative sort on more than two keys should look like figure 13.16.

Fig. 13.16

The results of the alternative string sort.

```
E2: 'Full F Accounting                                   READY

     A        B          C    D    E         F        G        H
1  STATUS  MAJOR        SEX  AGE  SORT-KEY
2  Full    Accounting    F    20  Full F Accounting
3  Full    Accounting    F    42  Full F Accounting
4  Full    Accounting    F    27  Full F Accounting
5  Full    Accounting    F    35  Full F Accounting
6  Full    Marketing     F    19  Full F Marketing
7  Full    Marketing     F    33  Full F Marketing
8  Full    Accounting    M    22  Full M Accounting
9  Full    Administration M   20  Full M Administration
10 Full    Finance       M    19  Full M Finance
11 Full    Finance       M    31  Full M Finance
12 Full    Finance       M    26  Full M Finance
13 Part    Accounting    F    26  Part F Accounting
14 Part    Accounting    F    29  Part F Accounting
15 Part    Finance       F    19  Part F Finance
16 Part    Finance       F    40  Part F Finance
17 Part    Marketing     F    33  Part F Marketing
18 Part    Accounting    M    27  Part M Accounting
19 Part    Administration M   19  Part M Administration
20 Part    Finance       M    19  Part M Finance
05-Jul-87  03:35 PM
```

Determining the Collating Sequence

The order in which the records appear after the sort depends on the ASCII numbers of the contents of the primary and secondary keys. For this reason, you should not include blank rows past the end of the database when you designate the **Data-Range**. Because blanks have precedence over all the characters in a sort, these blank rows will appear at the top of your sorted database.

By using the Install program, you can determine the order of precedence that 1-2-3 uses for sorting text strings. The three choices are

1. Numbers First (the default sort order if you do not specify another sort order during installation)

2. Numbers Last

3. ASCII

The ASCII and Numbers First options both sort in the following order:

Blank spaces

Special characters (!, #, $, etc.)

Numeric Characters (1, 2, 3, 4, etc.)

Alpha Characters (A, b, etc.)

Special Compose Characters (International Characters)

When you've specified numbers as labels, a problem can occur because 1-2-3 sorts from left to right, one character at a time. For example, if you were to sort the Marketing Research database in ascending order according to the representative who administered the test (REP, in column B), the results of the sort would resemble those in figure 13.17.

Although you would expect the records to be sorted in ascending order on the REP field, notice that the 12 in rows 7 and 8 appears before the 2 in row 9, and that 21 appears before 3. This problem occurs because 1-2-3 sorts the numbers one character at a time when sorting labels.

To bypass the problem, enter a zero (0) before each single-character REP field. Figure 13.18 shows the corrected sort of the edited single-character REP fields.

Restoring the Presort Order

If you sort the original contents of the database on any field, such as the REP field shown in figure 13.17, you cannot restore the records to their original order. If you add a "counter" column to the database before any sort, however,

Caution:
*Do not include blank rows past the end of the database when you designate the **Data-Range** for a sort.*

Reminder:
You can use the Install program to change the order of precedence that 1-2-3 uses for sorting.

Cue:
Add a "counter" field to your database in case you want to restore records to their original order.

Fig. 13.17

An erroneous ascending sort.

```
B4: [W5] 'REP                                                          READY

        A    B    C   D E F     G      H    I    J     K    L M N
1  Marketing Research Database:   Test Product X
2
3  SURVEY TEST TEST                ANNUAL  ZIP  RANK RANK RANK
4  AREA   REP  NUMBER AGE  SEX  INCOME  CODE TASTE PKG PRICE  BUY
5  3      1    211    35   M    23,600  46251  1    1    1    N
6  3      1    210    26   F    19,300  46256  4    2    3    N
7  B      12   455    35   F         0  46351  5    3    2    Y
8  B      12   454    41   F    23,000  46346  5    2    1    Y
9  b      2    453    21   M    14,700  46221  1    3    2    N
10 5      21   290    76   F     3,600  43204  3    3    2    N
11 5      21   291    45   F    17,500  46219  4    4    1    N
12 5      21   289    26   F    25,200  46213  2    1    2    Y
13 1      3    723    51   F     8,000  46349  4    2    2    Y
14 1      3    721    39   F    38,000  46309  2    3    2    Y
15 1      3    722    21   M    16,700  46343  1    3    3    Y
16 a      8    113    49   M    21,300  46028  3    1    1    N
17 A      8    114    28   M    24,600  46020  1    4    1    Y
18 A      8    112    35   M    31,000  46020  2    1    2    Y
19
20
05-Jul-87  03:37 PM
```

Fig. 13.18

The corrected ascending sort.

```
B4: [W5] 'REP                                                          READY

        A    B    C   D E F     G      H    I    J     K    L M N
1  Marketing Research Database:   Test Product X
2
3  SURVEY TEST TEST                ANNUAL  ZIP  RANK RANK RANK
4  AREA   REP  NUMBER AGE  SEX  INCOME  CODE TASTE PKG PRICE  BUY
5  3      01   210    26   F    19,300  46256  4    2    3    N
6  3      01   211    35   M    23,600  46251  1    1    1    N
7  b      02   453    21   M    14,700  46221  1    3    2    N
8  1      03   723    51   F     8,000  46349  4    2    2    Y
9  1      03   721    39   F    38,000  46389  2    3    2    Y
10 1      03   722    21   M    16,700  46343  1    3    3    Y
11 a      08   113    49   M    21,300  46028  3    1    1    N
12 A      08   114    28   M    24,600  46020  1    4    1    Y
13 A      08   112    35   M    31,000  46020  2    1    2    Y
14 B      12   454    41   F    23,000  46346  5    2    1    Y
15 B      12   455    35   F         0  46351  5    3    2    Y
16 5      21   290    76   F     3,600  43204  3    3    2    N
17 5      21   291    45   F    17,500  46219  4    4    1    N
18 5      21   289    26   F    25,200  46213  2    1    2    Y
19
20
05-Jul-87  03:37 PM
```

you will be able to reorder the records on any field and then restore the original order by resorting on the counter field.

Figure 13.19 shows the counter field NUM, which has been added in column A. After you have sorted the database on a particular column, you can sort again on the NUM field to restore the records to their original order.

Fig. 13.19

Inserting a counter field in an original database.

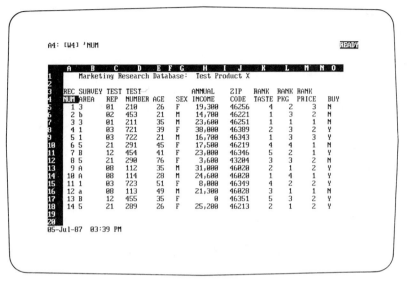

```
A4: [W4] 'NUM                                                              READY

      A   B    C    D    E F G    H       I    J    K     L    M  N  O
1         Marketing Research Database:   Test Product X
2
3     REC SURVEY TEST TEST            ANNUAL   ZIP  RANK  RANK RANK
4     NUM AREA   REP  NUMBER AGE  SEX INCOME   CODE TASTE PKG  PRICE  BUY
5      1  3     01   210    26   F   19,300   46256  4    2    3     N
6      2  b     02   453    21   M   14,700   46221  1    3    2     N
7      3  3     01   211    35   M   23,600   46251  1    1    1     N
8      4  1     03   721    39   F   38,000   46389  2    3    2     Y
9      5  1     03   722    21   M   16,700   46343  1    3    3     Y
10     6  5     21   291    45   F   17,500   46219  4    4    1     N
11     7  B     12   454    41   F   23,000   46346  5    2    1     Y
12     8  5     21   290    76   F    3,600   43204  3    3    2     N
13     9  A     00   112    35   M   31,000   46020  2    1    2     Y
14    10  A     00   114    28   M   24,600   46020  1    4    1     Y
15    11  1     03   723    51   F    8,000   46349  4    2    2     Y
16    12  a     00   113    49   M   21,300   46020  3    1    1     N
17    13  B     12   455    35   F        0   46351  5    3    2     Y
18    14  5     21   289    26   F   25,200   46213  2    1    2     Y
19
20
05-Jul-87  03:39 PM
```

Searching for Records

You have learned how to use the main **D**ata menu's **S**ort option to reorganize information from the database by sorting records according to key fields. In this section of the chapter, you will learn how to use **Q**uery, the menu's other data-retrieval command, to search for records and then edit, extract, or delete the records you find.

We will use the Tools Inventory database shown in figure 13.20 to illustrate the basic concepts of 1-2-3's search (also called *query*) operations.

Looking for records that meet certain conditions is the simplest form of searching a 1-2-3 database. To determine when to reorder items, for example, you can use a search operation to find any records with an on-hand quantity of less than four units.

Once you have located the information you want, you can extract the found records from the database to another section of the worksheet separate from the database. For example, you can extract all records with a purchase order (P.O.) date, and print the newly extracted area as a record of pending purchases.

With 1-2-3's search operations, you also have the option of looking for only the first occurrence of a specified field value in order to develop a unique list of field entries. For example, search the ISSUE field to extract a list of the different units of measure. Finally, you can *delete* all inventory records

Fig. 13.20

The initial Tools Inventory database.

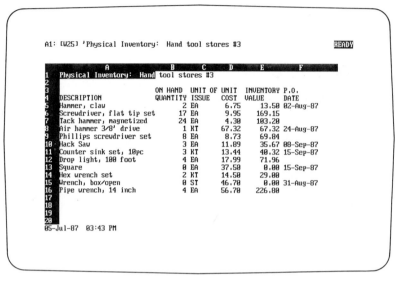

```
A1: [W25] 'Physical Inventory: Hand tool stores #3                    READY

        A              B      C     D      E         F
1   Physical Inventory: Hand tool stores #3
2
3                      ON HAND  UNIT OF UNIT  INVENTORY P.O.
4   DESCRIPTION        QUANTITY ISSUE   COST  VALUE    DATE
5   Hammer, claw            2  EA       6.75     13.50 02-Aug-87
6   Screwdriver, flat tip set  17  EA   9.95    169.15
7   Tack hammer, magnetized   24  EA    4.30    103.20
8   Air hammer 3/8' drive    1  KT     67.32     67.32 24-Aug-87
9   Phillips screwdriver set  8  EA     8.73     69.84
10  Hack Saw                 3  EA     11.89     35.67 08-Sep-87
11  Counter sink set, 10pc   3  KT     13.44     40.32 15-Sep-87
12  Drop light, 100 foot     4  EA     17.99     71.96
13  Square                   0  EA     37.50      0.00 15-Sep-87
14  Hex wrench set           2  KT     14.50     29.00
15  Wrench, box/open         0  ST     46.70      0.00 31-Aug-87
16  Pipe wrench, 14 inch     4  EA     56.70    226.80
17
18
19
20
05-Jul-87  03:43 PM
```

for which quantity on-hand equals zero (if you don't want to reorder these items).

Minimum Search Requirements

To initiate any search operation, you need to select the operation from the /**Data** Query menu:

Input Criterion Output Find Extract Unique Delete Reset Quit

You can use the first three options to specify ranges applicable to the search operations. **Input** and **Criterion**, which give the locations of the search area and the search conditions, respectively, must be specified in all **Query** operations. An output range must be established only when you select a **Query** command that copies records or parts of records to an area outside the database.

The last two options signal the end of the current search operation. **Reset** removes all previous search-related ranges so that you can specify a different search location and conditions. **Quit** restores the main **Data** menu.

The four options in the middle of the **Query** menu perform the following search functions:

Option	Keystroke	Description
Find	**F**	Moves down through a database, and positions the cursor on records that match given criteria. You can enter or change data in the records as you move the cursor through them.
Extract	**E**	Creates copies, in a specified area of the worksheet, of all or some of the fields in certain records that match given criteria.
Unique	**U**	Similar to **Extract**, but recognizes that some of the field contents in the database may be duplicates of other cell entries in the same fields. Eliminates duplicates as entries are copied to output range.
Delete	**D**	Deletes from a database all the records that match given criteria and shifts the remaining records to fill in the gaps that remain.

To perform a **Query** operation, you must specify both an input range and a criterion range and select one of the four search options. (Before issuing a Unique or Extract command, you must also specify an output range.)

Determining the Input Range

The input range for the /Data **Query** command is the range of records you want to search. The specified area does not have to include the entire database. In the Tools Inventory database shown in figure 13.20, specifying an input range of A4..F16 defines the area of search as the entire database. Entering A1..F9 as the input range for the sorted College database in figure 13.14 limits the search area to the records for the accounting majors.

Whether you search all or only a part of a database, you *must* include the field-name row in the input range. (Remember that you must *not* include the field names in a sort operation.) If field names occupy space on more than one row, specify only the bottom row to start the input range. In the Tools Inventory database, for example, even though rows 3 and 4 both contain portions of the field names, you would start the input range with row 4 (by entering A4..F16 instead of A3..F16).

Reminder:
You must include the field name in the input range whether you search all or only a part of a database.

Select /**D**ata **Q**uery **I**nput, and specify the range by typing or pointing to a range or by using an assigned range name. You do not have to specify the range again unless the search area changes.

Determining the Criterion Range

In previous 1-2-3 applications, you learned to communicate cell locations to 1-2-3. Similarly, when you want 1-2-3 to search for records that meet certain criteria, you must be able to talk to 1-2-3 in terms the program will understand.

Suppose that you want to identify all records in the Addresses database that contain OH in the STATE field. When the database is on-screen and 1-2-3 is in READY mode, type *STATE* in cell H2 and *OH* in cell H3 (see fig. 13.21). Type *Criterion Range* in cell H1 only if you want the documentation it provides; cell H1 is not directly involved in the search command.

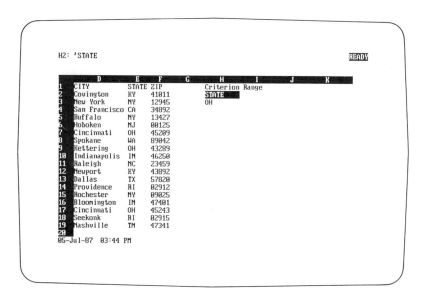

Select /**D**ata **Q**uery, and specify A1..F19 as the input range. The **Q**uery submenu will be displayed in the control panel as soon as you enter the input range. Select **C**riterion, and then type, point to, or name the range H2..H3 as the location of your search condition. The **Q**uery menu will again return to the screen.

You can use numbers, labels, or formulas as criteria. A criterion range can be up to 32 columns wide and two or more rows long. The first row must contain the field names of the search criteria, such as STATE in row 2 of figure 13.21. The rows below the unique field names contain the actual criteria, such as OH in row 3. The field names of the input range and the criterion range must match.

By entering the input and criterion ranges, you have completed the minimum requirements for executing a **F**ind or **D**elete command. Be sure to enter the specific field names above the conditions in the worksheet (in READY mode) before you use the /**D**ata **Q**uery **C**riterion command sequence.

Caution:
The criterion range must include the field name(s) in the first row, and criteria in the second row.

Issuing the Find Command

When you select **F**ind from the **Q**uery menu, a highlighted bar will rest on the first record (in the input range) that meets the conditions specified in the criterion range. In the current example, the highlighted bar rests on the first record that includes OH in the STATE field (see fig. 13.22).

Fig. 13.22

The first record highlighted in a Find operation.

```
A7: [W12] 'Pryor                                                      FIND

      A          B        C                       D            E      F
1   LAST       FIRST    STREET ADDRESS          CITY         STATE  ZIP
2   Harrington James    12344 Arlington Lane    Covington    KY     41011
3   Thomas     Brian    18499 Central Park Ave. New York     NY     12945
4   Leugers    Karen    21 Hill St. Apt. 34     San Francisco CA    34092
5   Englert    Michael  224 Orange St.          Buffalo      NY     13427
6   Smith      Margaret 2341 Kyles Lane         Hoboken      NJ     00125
7   Pryor      Aaron    2341 Milford Street     Cincinnati   OH     45209
8   Cleary     Esther   238 Higgins St. Apt. 14 Spokane      WA     89042
9   Wright     Ned      31238 Carolina St.      Kettering    OH     43289
10  Saunders   Ronald   3124 Keystone Ave.      Indianapolis IN     46250
11  McGruder   Mary     331 Park Lane Apt. 32   Raleigh      NC     23459
12  Simpson    Jeremy   3509 Ludlow Ave.        Newport      KY     43092
13  Wolf       Barbara  3098 Arnold Ave.        Dallas       TX     57820
14  Rooney     Kevin    391 Atwater Ave. Apt. 3 Providence   RI     02912
15  Franks     Mike     4204 Knight Circle      Rochester    NY     09025
16  Sorrenson  Sarah    432 Keys Crescent       Bloomington  IN     47401
17  Holland    Earl     4903 Drake Rd.          Cincinnati   OH     45243
18  Tuke       Samuel   9030 Greenup St.        Seekonk      RI     02915
19  Malvern    Thomas   939 Dine Circle         Nashville    TN     47341
20
05-Jul-87  03:45 PM
```

By using the ↓ cursor key, you can position the highlighted bar on the next record that conforms to the criterion. You can continue pressing the ↓ key until the last record that meets the search conditions has been highlighted (see fig. 13.23). Notice that the mode indicator changes from READY to FIND during the search.

The ↓ and ↑ cursor keys let you position the cursor to the next and previous records that conform to the search criteria set in the criterion range. The Home and End keys can be used to position the cursor on the first and last records in the database, even if those records do not fit the search criteria. In FIND mode, you can use the → and ← cursor keys to move the single-

Reminder:
The up and down cursor keys let you highlight the previous and next records that conform to the search criteria.

Fig. 13.23

The last record highlighted in a Find operation.

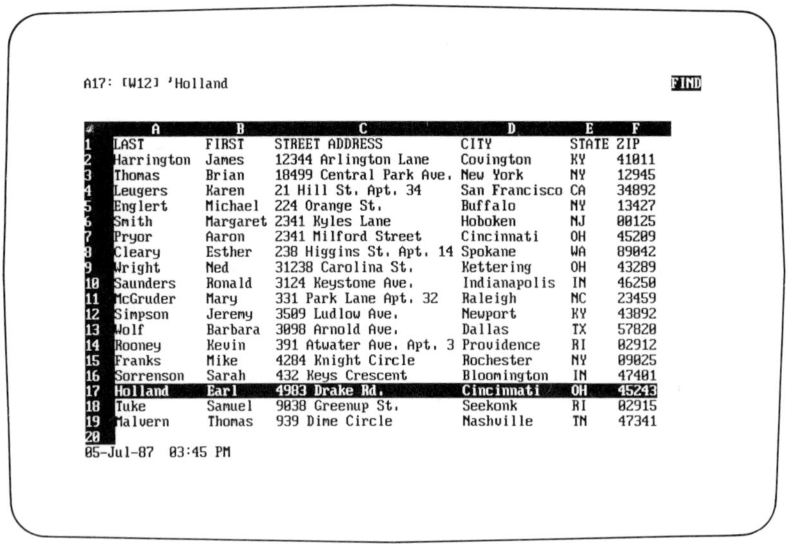

```
A17: [W12] 'Holland                                                    FIND

  #      A          B            C                  D           E      F
  1  LAST       FIRST     STREET ADDRESS         CITY         STATE  ZIP
  2  Harrington James     12344 Arlington Lane   Covington    KY     41011
  3  Thomas     Brian     18499 Central Park Ave.New York     NY     12945
  4  Leugers    Karen     21 Hill St. Apt. 34    San Francisco CA    34892
  5  Englert    Michael   224 Orange St.         Buffalo      NY     13427
  6  Smith      Margaret  2341 Kyles Lane        Hoboken      NJ     00125
  7  Pryor      Aaron     2341 Milford Street    Cincinnati   OH     45209
  8  Cleary     Esther    230 Higgins St. Apt. 14 Spokane     WA     89042
  9  Wright     Ned       31238 Carolina St.     Kettering    OH     43289
 10  Saunders   Ronald    3124 Keystone Ave.     Indianapolis IN     46250
 11  McGruder   Mary      331 Park Lane Apt. 32  Raleigh      NC     23459
 12  Simpson    Jeremy    3509 Ludlow Ave.       Newport      KY     43092
 13  Wolf       Barbara   3098 Arnold Ave.       Dallas       TX     57820
 14  Rooney     Kevin     391 Atwater Ave. Apt. 3 Providence  RI     02912
 15  Franks     Mike      4204 Knight Circle     Rochester    NY     09025
 16  Sorrenson  Sarah     432 Keys Crescent      Bloomington  IN     47401
 17  Holland    Earl      4903 Drake Rd.         Cincinnati   OH     45243
 18  Tuke       Samuel    9038 Greenup St.       Seekonk      RI     02915
 19  Malvern    Thomas    939 Dime Circle        Nashville    TN     47341
 20
05-Jul-87  03:45 PM
```

character flashing cursor to different fields in the current highlighted record. Then enter new values or use the Edit key to update the current values in the field. One caution: If you change the record so that it no longer satisfies the Find criteria and then move away from that record, you cannot use the ↓ or ↑ key to return to the record during the Find operation.

To end the Find operation and return to the Data Query menu, press Enter or Esc. To return directly to READY mode, press Ctrl-Break.

Listing All Specified Records

Cue:
Copy extracted records to a new file by using /File Xtract.

The Find command has limited use, especially in a large database, because the command must scroll through the entire file if you want to view each record that meets the specified criterion. As an alternative to the Find command, you can use the Extract command to copy to a blank area of the worksheet only those records that meet the conditions. (Before you issue the command, you must define the blank area of the worksheet as an output range.) You can view a list of all the extracted records, print the range of the newly extracted records, or even use the /File Xtract command to copy only the extracted record range to a new file on disk.

Defining the Output Range

Choose a blank area in the worksheet as the output range to receive records copied in an extract operation. Designate the range to the right of, or below, the database. In figure 13.24, for example, both the criterion range and the output range have been placed below the records in the Addresses database.

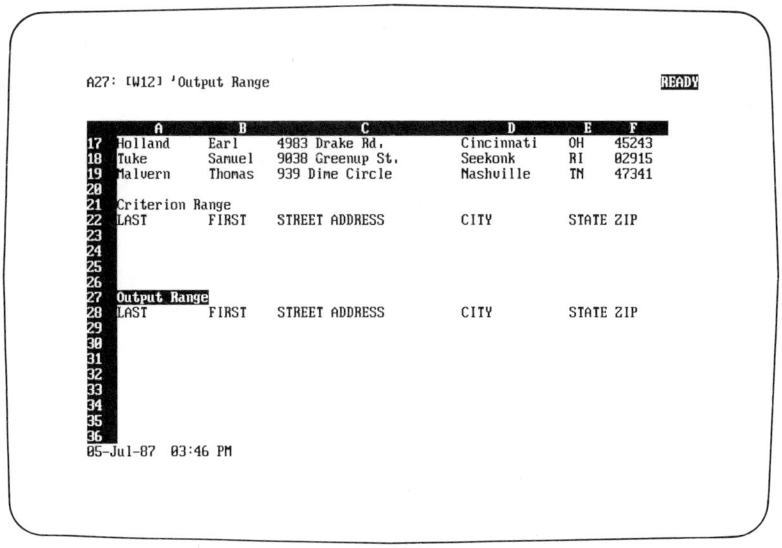

Fig. 13.24

*The criterion range
and output range
below the
database.*

```
A27: [W12] 'Output Range                                          READY

        A          B           C                 D          E      F
17  Holland      Earl      4983 Drake Rd.     Cincinnati   OH    45243
18  Tuke         Samuel    9038 Greenup St.   Seekonk      RI    02915
19  Malvern      Thomas    939 Dime Circle    Nashville    TN    47341
20
21  Criterion Range
22  LAST         FIRST     STREET ADDRESS     CITY         STATE ZIP
23
24
25
26
27  Output Range
28  LAST         FIRST     STREET ADDRESS     CITY         STATE ZIP
29
30
31
32
33
34
35
36
05-Jul-87  03:46 PM
```

In the first row of the output range, copy the names of only those fields whose contents you want to extract. You do not have to copy these names in the same order as they appear in the database. (In fig. 13.24, the Output Range entry in cell A27 is for documentation purposes only, and all field names in row 28 have been reproduced in the existing order of the database.)

The field names in both the criterion and output ranges must match the corresponding field names in the input range. To avoid mismatch errors, use the /Copy command to copy the database field names in the criterion and output ranges.

Select /**D**ata **Q**uery **O**utput; then type, point to, or name the range location of the output area. You can create an open-ended extract area by entering only the field-name row as the range, or you can set the exact size of the extract area.

To limit the size of the extract area, enter the upper-left to lower-right cell coordinates of the entire output range. The first row in the specified range must contain the field names; the remaining rows must accommodate the maximum number of records you expect to receive from the extract operation. Use this method when you want to retain additional data that is located below the extract area. For example, as you can see in figure 13.24, naming

Reminder:
*Field names in the
criterion and output
ranges must match
the corresponding
field names in the
input range.*

Caution:
*If you do not allow
sufficient room in
the output range for
extracted records,
the extract
operation will abort.*

A28..F36 as the output range limits incoming records to eight (one row for field names and one row for each record). If you do not allow sufficient room in the fixed-length output area, the extract operation will abort and the message too many records will be displayed on-screen.

To create an open-ended extract area that does not limit the number of incoming records, specify as the output range only the row containing the output field names. For example, by naming A28..F28 as the output range in figure 13.24, you define the area to receive records from an extract operation without limiting the number of records.

Caution:
The extract
operation will
overwrite all
existing data in the
output range.

An extract operation first removes all existing data from the output range. If you use only the field-name row to specify the output area, all data below that row will be destroyed to make room for the unknown number of incoming extracted records.

Executing the Extract Command

To execute an **Extract** command, you must type the search conditions in the worksheet, type the output field names in the worksheet, and set the input, criterion, and output ranges from the **Data Query** menu.

To accelerate what seems to be a time-consuming setup process, establish standard input, criterion, and output areas and then store the range names for these locations. Keeping in mind the limit of 32 criterion fields, you might establish a single criterion range (such as the range A22..F23 in fig. 13.24) that encompasses all the key fields on which you might search. By establishing such a range, you will save the time needed to respecify a criterion range for each extract on different field names; but if the criterion range contains many unused field names, you will lose some speed of execution.

To illustrate the extract process applied to the Addresses database, create a list of all records with OH in the STATE field. Assuming that rows 22 and 28 contain the field names, enter *OH* in cell E23. Select /**Data Query** and specify the input (A1..F19), criterion (A22..F23), and output ranges (A28..F28). Then choose **Extract** from the **Query** menu. The output range in figure 13.25 contains three extracted records, each of which meets the condition of STATE = OH.

You do not have to extract entire records or maintain the order of field names within the extracted records. For example, you can combine the first- and last-name fields in a new field (NAME) and then extract only the NAME and CITY information from records that have OH in the STATE field. To do this, type *NAME* in cell G1 and then type the string formula +*B2&" "&A2* in cell G2 (see fig. 13.26).

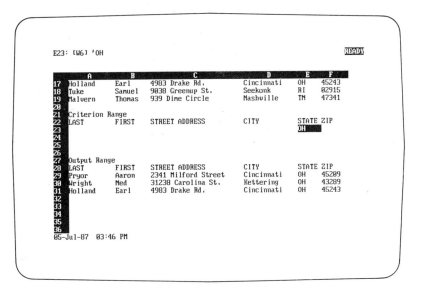

Fig. 13.25

A full-record extract on an "exact match" label condition.

```
E23: [W6] 'OH                                                    READY

         A          B           C                 D            E      F
17   Holland     Earl      4983 Drake Rd.      Cincinnati     OH    45243
18   Tuke        Samuel    9038 Greenup St.    Seekonk        RI    02915
19   Malvern     Thomas    939 Dime Circle     Nashville      TN    47341
20
21   Criterion Range
22   LAST        FIRST     STREET ADDRESS      CITY           STATE ZIP
23                                                            OH
24
25
26
27   Output Range
28   LAST        FIRST     STREET ADDRESS      CITY           STATE ZIP
29   Pryor       Aaron     2341 Milford Street Cincinnati     OH    45209
30   Wright      Ned       31238 Carolina St.  Kettering      OH    43289
31   Holland     Earl      4983 Drake Rd.      Cincinnati     OH    45243
32
33
34
35
36
05-Jul-87  03:46 PM
```

Fig. 13.26

Creating the NAME field in the Addresses database.

```
G2: +B28" "&A2                                                  READY

         C                  D             E      F     G        H
1    STREET ADDRESS       CITY          STATE  ZIP    NAME
2    12344 Arlington Lane Covington     KY     41011  James Harrington
3    18499 Central Park Ave. New York   NY     12945
4    21 Hill St. Apt. 34  San Francisco CA     34092
5    224 Orange St.       Buffalo       NY     13427
6    2341 Kyles Lane      Hoboken       NJ     00125
7    2341 Milford Street  Cincinnati    OH     45209
8    230 Higgins St. Apt. 14 Spokane    WA     89042
9    31238 Carolina St.   Kettering     OH     43289
10   3124 Keystone Ave.   Indianapolis  IN     46250
11   331 Park Lane Apt. 32 Raleigh      NC     23459
12   3509 Ludlow Ave.     Newport       KY     43892
13   3098 Arnold Ave.     Dallas        TX     57020
14   391 Atwater Ave. Apt. 3 Providence RI     02912
15   4204 Knight Circle   Rochester     NY     89025
16   432 Keys Crescent    Bloomington   IN     47401
17   4983 Drake Rd.       Cincinnati    OH     45243
18   9038 Greenup St.     Seekonk       RI     02915
19   939 Dime Circle      Nashville     TN     47341
20
05-Jul-87  03:47 PM
```

After you have copied the contents of cell G2 to the range G3..G19, use the **R**ange **V**alue command to convert the formulas in G2..G19 to values.

Next, **R**ange **E**rase the field names in row 28. Type the new field *NAME* in cell A28, skip column B (for spacing purposes), and enter the second output field *CITY* in cell C28. Then respecify the output range as A28..C28. Expand both the input and criterion ranges to include the new column G. This operation extracts the name and city information for all records of individuals living in Ohio (see fig. 13.27).

Fig. 13.27

A partial-record extract on a single label condition.

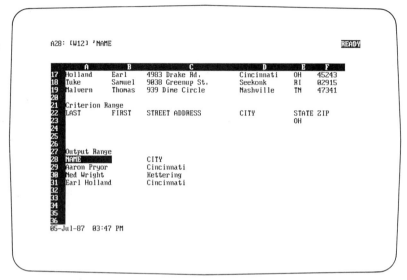

More Complicated Criterion Ranges

In addition to an "exact match" search on a single label field, 1-2-3 permits a wide variety of record searches: on exact matches to numeric fields; on partial matches of field contents; on fields that meet formula conditions; on fields that meet all of several conditions; and on fields that meet either one condition or another.

Let's look first at variations of queries on single fields.

Wildcards in Criterion Ranges

Reminder:
You can use wildcards for matching labels in database operations.

You can use 1-2-3's wildcards for matching labels in database operations. The characters ?, *, and ~ have special meaning when used in the criterion range. The ? character instructs 1-2-3 to accept any character in that specific position, and can be used only to locate fields of the same length. The * character, which tells 1-2-3 to accept any and all characters that follow, can be used on field contents of unequal length. By placing a tilde (~) symbol at the beginning of a label, you tell 1-2-3 to accept all values *except* those that follow. Table 13.1 illustrates how you can use wildcards in search operations.

Table 13.1
Using Wildcards in Search Operations

Enter	To find
N?	NC, NJ, NY, etc.
BO?L?	BOWLE but not BOWL
BO?L*	BOWLE, BOWL, BOLLESON, BOELING, etc.
SAN*	SANTA BARBARA, SAN FRANCISCO
SAN *	SAN FRANCISCO only
~N*	Strings in specified fields that *do not* begin with the letter *N*

Use the ? and * wildcard characters when you are unsure of the spelling used in field contents. Be sure that the results of any extract operation which uses a wildcard are what you need. And be extremely careful when you use wildcards in a **Delete** command. If you are not careful, you may remove more records than you intend.

Formulas in Criterion Ranges

To set up formulas that query numeric fields in the database, you can use the following relational operators:

>	Greater than
>=	Greater than or equal to
<	Less than
<=	Less than or equal to
=	Equal to
<>	Not equal to

Create a formula that references the first field entry in the numeric column you want to search. 1-2-3 will test the formula on each cell down the column until the program reaches the end of the specified input range.

You can place the formula anywhere below the criterion range's field-name row (unlike text criteria, which must appear directly below the associated field name). For example, you can use a formula based on information already in the Marketing Research database in figure 13.4 to extract the records of test participants who are at least 45 years old. First, type the formula +*D5*>=*45* in cell D22 (see fig. 13.28).

Notice that the formula is displayed in the control panel and that a zero (0) is displayed in cell D22. The formula checked whether the contents of cell

Fig. 13.28

Extracting records with a relative formula condition.

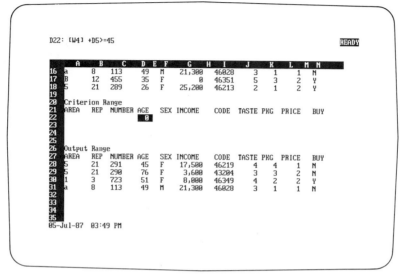

D5 (AGE = 26) were greater than or equal to 45 and returned the zero (0) to indicate a false condition. (To better understand the search condition, you could use the **Range Format Text** command to change the display from 0 to the formula. But the AGE column in this example is so narrow that the full formula cannot be displayed.)

After you have specified the input, criterion, and output ranges correctly, executing an extract operation produces four records for which AGE equals or exceeds 45 years. A criterion of +D5>45 would extract only three records; the formula +D5=45 would extract only one record.

To reference cells outside the database, use formulas that include absolute cell addressing. (For addressing information, refer to Chapter 4.) For example, suppose that immediately after you issue the preceding command (to extract records based on AGE), you want to extract the records of those Marketing Research database respondents whose income exceeds the average income of all respondents. To do this, you must first return to READY mode. Then determine the average income by entering *@AVG(G5..G18)* in a blank cell (G24) away from all database ranges (see fig. 13.29).

Next, type the formula *+G5>$G$24* as the criterion under INCOME in cell G22. The +G5 tells 1-2-3 to test (starting in cell G5) income contents against the average income in cell G24 and to continue down column G to the end of the input range (row 18), testing each subsequent income cell against the average income in cell G6.

Fig. 13.29

Extracting records with a mixed formula condition.

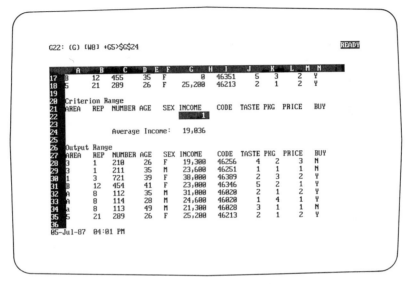

With the program still in READY mode, press the F7 (Query) key to repeat the most recent query operation (Extract, in this example) and eliminate the need to select **/Data Query Extract**. Use the shortcut method only when you do not want to change the locations of the input, criterion, and output ranges. As you can see from figure 13.29, the extracted records indicate that eight of the Marketing Research database participants have incomes greater than the average income of all respondents.

AND Conditions

Now that you have seen how to base a **Find** or **Extract** operation on only one criterion, you will learn how to use multiple criteria for your queries. You can set up multiple criteria as AND conditions (in which *all* the criteria must be met) or as OR conditions (in which any *one* criterion must be met). For example, searching a music department's library for sheet music requiring drums AND trumpets is likely to produce fewer selections than searching for music appropriate for drums OR trumpets.

Reminder:
You can set up multiple criteria for your queries with AND conditions or OR conditions.

Indicate two or more criteria, ALL of which must be met, by specifying the conditions on the criterion row immediately below the field names. The multiple criteria in row 24 of the College database requests those records for which MAJOR equals Accounting and SEX equals Male (see fig. 13.30). If you then issue an **Extract** command, 1-2-3 will extract two records that meet both conditions.

When you maintain a criterion range that includes many fields, you can quickly extract records based on an alternative condition. For example, access READY

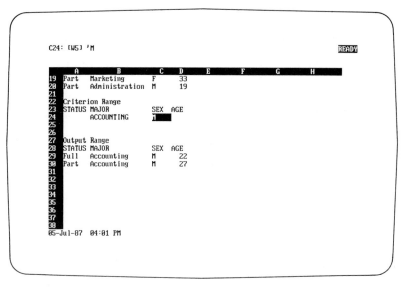

Fig. 13.30

An initial two-field logical AND search.

mode, change *M* to *F* in cell C24 (under SEX), and press the F7 (Query) key. 1-2-3 will immediately copy the records of female accounting majors to the extract range (see fig. 13.31).

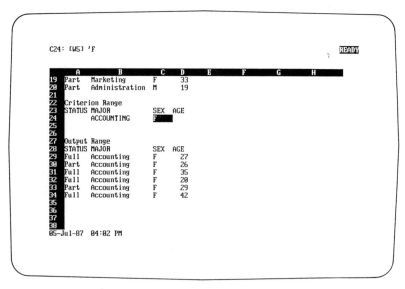

Fig. 13.31

A revised two-field logical AND search.

You can continue to add conditions that must be met. Enter the additional criteria only in the row immediately below the field-name row. For example, the extracted records in figure 13.32 are limited to female accounting majors under 30 years old.

Fig. 13.32

A three-field logical AND search.

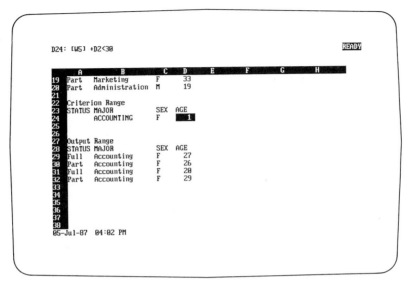

OR Conditions

Criteria placed on the *same* row have the effect of a logical AND; they tell 1-2-3 to find or extract on this field condition AND this field condition AND this field condition, etc. Criteria placed on *different* rows have the effect of a logical OR; that is, find or extract on this field condition OR that field condition, and so on. You can set up a logical OR search on one or more fields.

Searching a single field for more than one condition is the simplest use of an OR condition. To illustrate the concept, we will extract from the Tools Inventory database (refer to fig. 13.20) those records whose unit of issue is either KT (kit) or ST (set).

Under the ISSUE criterion field, type one condition immediately below the other (see fig. 13.33). Be sure to expand the criterion range to include the additional row. As you can see from the output range in figure 13.33, four records in the Tools database have either KT or ST for a unit of issue.

Caution:
Make sure your criterion range includes all rows containing the multiple criteria.

You can also specify a logical OR condition on two or more different field conditions. For example, suppose that you want to search the Marketing Research database for records in which age is greater than 50 OR in which income exceeds $25,000. Figure 13.34 shows the setup of the criterion in rows 22 and 23.

Type *+D5>50* in cell D22. In the next row, enter *+G5>25000* in cell G23. (Remember that you can type formulas under any field name; you could have

Fig. 13.33

A logical OR search within a single field.

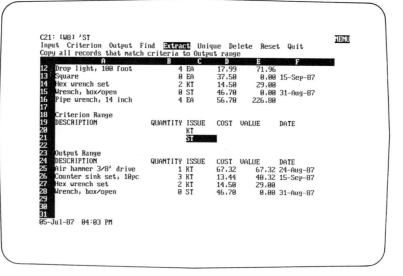

```
C21: [W8] 'ST                                                    MENU
Input  Criterion  Output  Find  Extract  Unique  Delete  Reset  Quit
Copy all records that match criteria to Output range
          A              B   C    D      E        F
12 Drop light, 100 foot       4 EA   17.99   71.96
13 Square                     0 EA   37.50    0.00 15-Sep-87
14 Hex wrench set             2 KT   14.50   29.00
15 Wrench, box/open           0 ST   46.70    0.00 31-Aug-87
16 Pipe wrench, 14 inch       4 EA   56.70  226.80
17
18 Criterion Range
19 DESCRIPTION          QUANTITY ISSUE  COST VALUE    DATE
20                               KT
21                               ST
22
23 Output Range
24 DESCRIPTION          QUANTITY ISSUE  COST VALUE    DATE
25 Air hammer 3/8' drive       1 KT   67.32   67.32 24-Aug-87
26 Counter sink set, 10pc      3 KT   13.44   40.32 15-Sep-87
27 Hex wrench set              2 KT   14.50   29.00
28 Wrench, box/open            0 ST   46.70    0.00 31-Aug-87
29
30
31
05-Jul-87  04:03 PM
```

Fig. 13.34

A logical OR search on two fields.

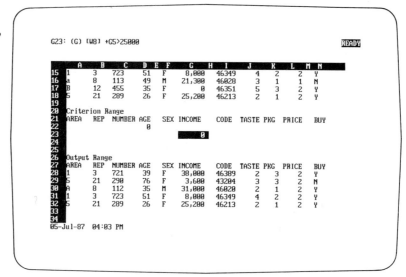

```
G23: (G) [W8] +G5>25000                                         READY
     A   B    C   D E F   G      H    I     J K   L M N
15 1    3  723  51  F   8,000  46349   4   2    2 Y
16 a    8  113  49  M  21,300  46028   3   1    1 N
17 B   12  455  35  F      0   46351   5   3    2 Y
18 5   21  289  26  F  25,200  46213   2   1    2 Y
19
20 Criterion Range
21 AREA REP NUMBER AGE  SEX INCOME  CODE TASTE PKG PRICE  BUY
22                   0
23                           0
24
25
26 Output Range
27 AREA REP NUMBER AGE  SEX INCOME  CODE TASTE PKG PRICE  BUY
28 1    3  721  39  F  38,000  46389   2   3    2 Y
29 5   21  290  76  F   3,600  43204   3   3    2 N
30 A    8  112  35  M  31,000  46020   2   1    2 Y
31 1    3  723  51  F   8,000  46349   4   2    2 Y
32 5   21  289  26  F  25,200  46213   2   1    2 Y
33
34
05-Jul-87  04:03 PM
```

entered the two formulas in cells A22 and A23, for example.) Adjust the criterion range to include the OR condition established by expanding the criterion range down a row. When you issue the **Extract** command, five records are copied to the output range. Although rows 29 and 31 in figure 13.34 do not reflect INCOME contents exceeding $25,000, they do contain AGE contents over 50. Only one condition OR the other had to be met before the copy was made.

To add additional OR criteria, drop to a new row, enter each new condition, and expand the criterion range. If you reduce the number of rows involved in an OR logical search, be sure to contract the criterion range.

Although no technical reason prevents you from mixing AND and OR logical searches, the results of such a mixed query operation may not be of much use. Follow the format of placing each AND condition in the row immediately below the criterion field name row, and each OR condition in a separate row below. For example, if you want to search the Marketing Research database for records in which BUY equals Y (Yes) and INCOME is either less than $10,000 or greater than $30,000, erase the AGE search condition in cell D22 and then enter the AND/OR conditions in the following cells:

	G	H	I	J	K	L	M	N
22	+G5<10000							Y
23	+G5>30000							Y

By specifying these conditions, you tell 1-2-3 to search for records in which INCOME is less than $10,000 and the BUY response is "Yes" (row 22) OR for records in which INCOME is greater than $30,000 and the BUY response is "Yes" (row 23). The criterion range (A21..N23) remains unchanged. Repeating the Y in cell N23 is critical (even though you have entered Y in cell N22) because if 1-2-3 finds a blank cell within a criterion range, the program selects all records for the field name above that blank cell.

We recommend that you test the logic of your search conditions on a small sample database in which you can verify search results easily by scrolling through all records and noting which of them should be extracted. For example, if the Marketing Research database contained hundreds of responses, you could test the preceding AND/OR search conditions on the small group of 14 records shown in figure 13.4. (Issuing an **Extract** command should copy to the output area only the records in rows 8, 13, 15, and 17.)

String Searches

If you want to search on the partial contents of a field, you can use functions in a formula. For example, suppose that you can remember only the street name "Keystone" for a record you want to extract from the Addresses database. If you can safely assume that all street addresses start with a number and have a space before the street name (XXX Streetname), you can use the formula shown in the control panel of figure 13.35 as the search criterion in cell C23.

Cue:
Use string functions to search on the partial contents of a field.

The double quotation marks (" ") in the formula instruct 1-2-3 to start the search after a blank space is encountered (between the street number and street name). The 1,8 portion of the formula instructs the program to search

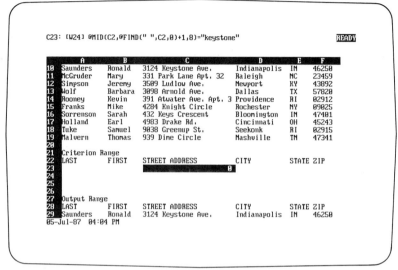

Fig. 13.35

Using a function condition to search a string.

on the first through the eighth character positions matching "Keystone," thereby eliminating any need to know whether "Street," "Ave.," "Avenue," etc., is part of the field. Issuing the Extract command produces one record in the output range (row 29). You also could use compound criteria and search on both CITY and part of the STREET ADDRESS field. (See Chapter 6 for an in-depth description of functions.)

Special Operators

To combine search conditions within a single field, use the special operators *#AND#* and *#OR#*. Use the special operator *#NOT#* to negate a search condition.

Use #AND# or #OR# to search on two or more conditions within the same field. For example, suppose that you want to extract from the Tools Inventory database all records with an August, 1987, purchase-order date (DATE). Establish the criterion by requesting an extract of all dates later than July 31, 1987, AND earlier than September 1, 1987. In figure 13.36, the formula condition has been entered in cell A20. (Keep in mind that you do not have to type a formula under the associated field name—DATE, in this example.) The extracted records are displayed in rows 25 through 27.

You use the #AND#, #OR#, and #NOT# operators to enter (in one field) conditions that could be entered some other way (usually in at least two fields). For example, you could enter +C5="KT"#OR#C5="ST" in a single cell in row 20 (any cell in the criterion range A19..F20) as an alternative criterion

Fig. 13.36

Extracting records with the special operator #AND#.

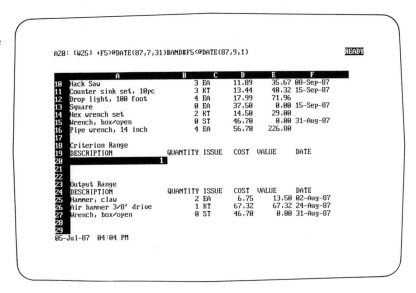

```
A20: [W25] +F5>@DATE(87,7,31)#AND#F5<@DATE(87,9,1)              READY

              A                B    C       D      E         F
10  Hack Saw                   3 EA     11.89    35.67 08-Sep-87
11  Counter sink set, 10pc     3 KT     13.44    40.32 15-Sep-87
12  Drop light, 100 foot       4 EA     17.99    71.96
13  Square                     0 EA     37.50     0.00 15-Sep-87
14  Hex wrench set             2 KT     14.50    29.00
15  Wrench, box/open           0 ST     46.70     0.00 31-Aug-87
16  Pipe wrench, 14 inch       4 EA     56.70   226.80
17
18  Criterion Range
19  DESCRIPTION          QUANTITY ISSUE  COST  VALUE     DATE
20                                1
21
22
23  Output Range
24  DESCRIPTION          QUANTITY ISSUE  COST  VALUE     DATE
25  Hammer, claw               2 EA      6.75    13.50 02-Aug-87
26  Air hammer 3/8' drive      1 KT     67.32    67.32 24-Aug-87
27  Wrench, box/open           0 ST     46.70     0.00 31-Aug-87
28
29
05-Jul-87  04:04 PM
```

entry for producing figure 13.33 (unit of issue as KT or ST in the Tools Inventory database).

Use #NOT# at the beginning of a condition to negate that condition. For example, if the Tools Inventory database had only three units of issue—KT, ST, and EA (each)—you could produce the results shown in figure 13.33 by specifying the criterion *#NOT#"EA"* in cell C20 of the criterion range A19..F20.

Other Types of Searches

Reminder:
Use the /Data
Unique command
to copy only the
first occurrence of
a record in the
output range.

In addition to the **Query** and **Find** commands, you can use the **Data** menu's **Unique** and **Delete** commands for searches. By issuing the **Unique** command, you can produce (in the output range) a copy of only the first occurrence of a record that meets a specified criterion. And you can update the contents of your 1-2-3 database by deleting all records that meet a specified criterion. After entering the conditions, you need to specify only the input and criterion ranges before you issue the **Delete** command.

Searching for Unique Records

Ordinarily, the **Unique** command is used to copy into the output area only a small portion of each record that meets the criterion. For example, if you want a list of measurements used in the Tools Inventory database, set up an output range that includes only the unit of ISSUE (see fig. 13.37). To search all records, leave blank the row below the field-name row in the criterion range A19..F20. Then, with the input range defined as A4..F16 and the output range set at A24, select **Unique** to produce (in rows 25 through 27) a list of the three units of measure.

Fig. 13.37

The results of issuing a Unique command.

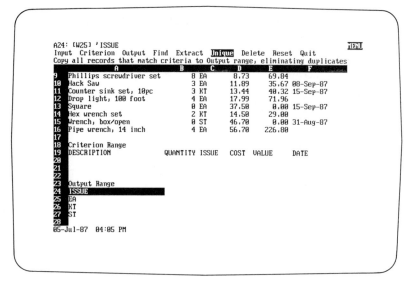

As another example, you can produce (from the College database) a list of the majors selected by current students. To do so, you specify in the output area only the field name MAJOR, leave blank the row under field names in the criterion range, and execute the Unique command.

Deleting Specified Records

As you know, you can use the /**Worksheet Delete Row** command sequence to remove records from a spreadsheet. If you want a fast alternative to this "one-by-one" approach, use the **Delete** command to remove unwanted records from your database files. Before you select **Delete** from the **Query** menu, simply specify the range of records to be searched (input range) and the conditions for the deletion (criterion).

For example, suppose that you want to remove from the Addresses database all records with a STATE field beginning with the letter *N*. To do so, specify an input range of A1..F19, a criterion range of A22..F23, and use the criterion N* in cell E23 (see fig. 13.38). Then issue the **Delete** command to remove all records for states that begin with *N*. As you can see from the figure, the remaining records pack together in rows 2 through 14, and the input range automatically adjusts to A1..F14.

Be extremely careful when you issue the **Delete** command. To give you the opportunity to verify that you indeed want to select the **Delete** command,

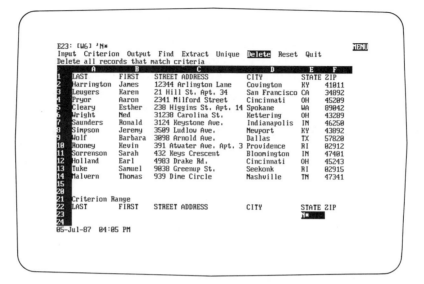

Fig. 13.38

The results of issuing a Delete command.

1-2-3 displays the following menu on which the leftmost, least dangerous command is highlighted:

Cancel   Delete

Choose **Cancel** to abort the delete command. Select **Delete** to verify that you want to execute the delete operation.

You can guard against deleting the wrong records by doing one (or both) of two things. Before you issue a **Query Delete** command, you can

1. /File Save the database, using a name such as TEMP, to create a copy of the original. Then, if the logic of the delete conditions proves faulty, you will be able to retrieve this copy.

2. Perform an **Extract** on the delete conditions, view the records to verify that they are to be removed, and then perform the **Delete** operation.

Loading Data from Other Programs

Lotus provides several means of importing data from other applications. The Translate utility (see Chapter 7) has options for converting data directly to 1-2-3 spreadsheets from VisiCalc, DIF, dBASE II, and dBASE III files. You then can access the data by using the /File Retrieve or /File Combine commands from the current spreadsheet.

Use the /File Import command to read into a current spreadsheet the data stored on disk as a text file. Depending on the format, these files may be read directly to a range of cells or a column of cells. Specially formatted "numeric" data can be read directly to a range of spreadsheet cells. ASCII text can be stored as long labels in a single column with one line of the report per cell. You must then disassemble these labels into the appropriate data values or fields by using @functions or the /Data Parse command.

Finally, you can use certain commands from the Command Language (see Chapter 15) to read and write an ASCII sequential file directly from within 1-2-3 Command Language programs.

The /Data Parse Command

Reminder:
Use /Data Parse to split long labels imported from text files into separate text, number, or date fields.

The /Data Parse command is a flexible and easy method of extracting numeric, string, and date data from long labels and placing it in separate columns. For example, suppose that you typed inventory data in a report composed with the WordStar word-processing program and you want to load the print-image file in 1-2-3. After you load the file by using the /File Import command, you must reformat the data by using the /Data Parse command.

Executing the Parse Command

The /File Import command loads the inventory data into the range A1..A16 (see fig. 13.39). Visually, the data is formatted in a typical spreadsheet range such as A1..G16, but the display is misleading. The current cell-pointer location is A5; the entire contents of the row exist only in that cell as a long label.

To break down the long label to columns, move the cursor to the first cell to be parsed and select /Data Parse. The following menu then appears:

Format-Line   Input-Column   Output-Range   Reset   Go   Quit

Use Format-Line to Create or Edit a newly inserted line in the data to be parsed. The Format command line specifies the pattern or patterns for splitting the long labels into numbers, labels, and dates.

Use Input-Column for specifying the range of cells to be parsed. The output range denotes the upper left corner cell of a block of cells that will hold the parsed data.

Reset clears the previously set Input-Column and Output-Range. Go performs the parse, based on the specified Input-Column, Format-Lines, and Output-Range.

Fig. 13.39

Results of a File Import command.

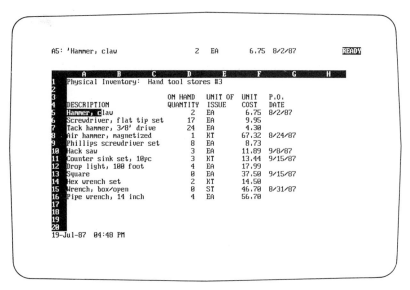

```
A5: 'Hammer, claw            2   EA       6.75  8/2/87              READY

     A      B        C        D        E        F        G        H
1  Physical Inventory:  Hand tool stores #3
2
3                              ON HAND   UNIT OF   UNIT    P.O.
4  DESCRIPTION                 QUANTITY  ISSUE     COST    DATE
5  Hammer, claw                    2     EA        6.75   8/2/87
6  Screwdriver, flat tip set      17     EA        9.95
7  Tack hammer, 3/8' drive        24     EA        4.30
8  Air hammer, magnetized          1     KT       67.32   8/24/87
9  Phillips screwdriver set        8     EA        8.73
10 Hack saw                        3     EA       11.89   9/8/87
11 Counter sink set, 10pc          3     KT       13.44   9/15/87
12 Drop light, 100 foot            4     EA       17.99
13 Square                          0     EA       37.50   9/15/87
14 Hex wrench set                  2     KT       14.50
15 Wrench, box/open                0     ST       46.70   8/31/87
16 Pipe wrench, 14 inch            4     EA       56.70
17
18
19
20
19-Jul-87  04:48 PM
```

To parse the data in figure 13.39, follow these steps:

1. Move the cursor to A3, which is the first cell that has the data you want to break into columns. (You do not have to parse the title in cell A1.)

2. Parse the column headings in cells A3..A4, using one format line; and then parse the data in A5..A16, using another format line.

Different format lines are necessary because the data is a mixture of label, numeric, and date data, and because all the headings are labels. Select Format-Line Create. A suggested format line is inserted in the data at A3, in a step that moves the remaining worksheet content down one line.

After creating a format line, you can edit it by selecting Format-Line again and choosing Edit. Use the format line to mark the column positions and the type of data in those positions. Parse uses the format line to break down the data and move it to its respective columns in the output range.

Combinations of certain letters and special characters comprise format lines. The letters denote the beginning position and the type of data; special symbols define the length of a field and the spacing.

Symbol	Purpose
D	Marks the beginning of a **D**ate field.
L	Marks the beginning of a **L**abel field.

S	Marks the beginning of a **S**kip position.
T	Marks the beginning of a **T**ime field.
V	Marks the beginning of a **V**alue field.
>	Defines the continuation of a field. Use one > for each position in the field (excluding the first position).
*	Defines blank spaces (in the data below the format line) that may be part of the block of data in the following cell.

Add as many format lines as you need in your data. In the inventory example, you need to enter another format line at cell A6 and specify the format criteria for the data records that follow. Suggested format lines are shown in figure 13.40. To restore the **P**arse menu, press Enter after you finish editing.

Fig. 13.40

Editing a format line in a Parse operation.

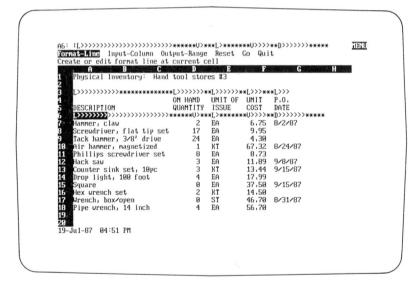

After setting up two format lines in the Physical Inventory example (see fig. 13.40), select **I**nput-Range from the **P**arse menu. Point to or type the range A3..A18, which includes format lines, column headings, and data. Continue by selecting **O**utput-Range from the **P**arse menu and by specifying A20 as the upper left corner of a blank range to accept the parsed data. Complete the operation by selecting the **G**o option (see fig. 13.41).

The data displayed in individual cells may not be exactly what you want. You can make a few changes in the format and column width, and you can also add or delete information to make the newly parsed data more usable. These

Fig. 13.41

Unsatisfactory results from a Parse operation.

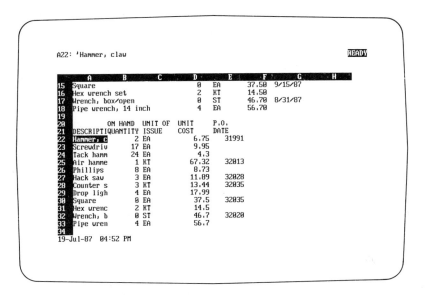

enhancements are not part of the **Parse** command, but they usually are necessary after importing and parsing data.

To produce the final inventory database shown in figure 13.42, follow these steps:

Fig. 13.42

Improving the appearance of parsed data.

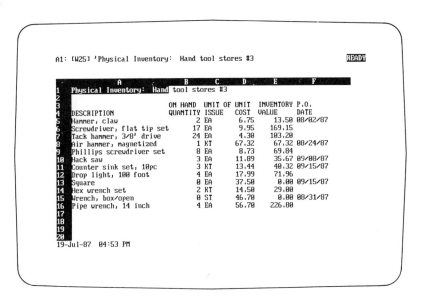

1. Delete rows A3..A19 to remove the unparsed data and to move the parsed data up under the title.

2. Expand column A to make it 25 characters wide, and contract column C to make it 8 characters wide.

3. Reformat the P.O. DATE range in column E to the Date 4 format.

4. Insert at column E a column for the inventory value.

5. Widen the new column E to 10 characters (the P.O. DATE should be column F).

6. Add the INVENTORY and VALUE headings in cells E3 and E4, respectively.

7. Enter in cell E5 the formula that will compute the inventory value (+B5*D5).

8. Copy the formula in cell E5 to cells E6..E16.

9. /Range Format D5..E16 to the comma (2 decimal places) display.

Cautions about Using /Data Parse

Caution:
Make sure the column widths are wide enough to accept the complete value or label you want in the field.

If you are parsing a value that continues past the end of the field, the data is parsed until a blank is encountered or until the value runs into the next field in the format line. This means that if you parse labels, you need to make sure that the field widths in the format line are wide enough so that you can avoid losing data because of blanks. If you parse values, the field widths are less critical.

Experiment on small amounts of data until you are comfortable using the /Data Parse command. After you understand how this important command works, you will find many more applications for it. Every time you develop a new application, you should consider whether existing data created on another software program can be imported and then changed to 1-2-3 format by using the /Data Parse command.

Database Statistical Functions

1-2-3's database statistical functions are similar to the spreadsheet statistical functions but have been modified to manipulate database fields. These functions are another unique feature of 1-2-3.

Like the standard statistical functions, the database statistical functions perform in one simple statement calculations that would otherwise require several statements. This efficiency and ease of application make these excellent tools. They include the following functions:

@DCOUNT	Gives the number of items in a list
@DSUM	Sums the values of all the items in a list
@DMIN	Gives the minimum of all the items in a list
@DMAX	Gives the maximum of all the items in a list
@DSTD	Gives the standard deviation of all the items in a list
@DVAR	Gives the variance of all the items in a list
@DAVG	Gives the arithmetic mean of all the items in a list

The general form of these functions is

@DFUN(input range, offset, criterion range)

The input and criterion ranges are the same as those used by the /Data Query command. The input range specifies the database or part of a database to be scanned, and the criterion range specifies which records are to be selected. The offset indicates which field to select from the database records; the offset value must be either zero or a positive integer. A value of zero indicates the first column, a one indicates the second column, and so on.

Now we present an example that uses the database statistical functions. The example involves computing the mean, variance, and standard deviation of the average interest rates offered by money market funds for a given week. If you are unfamiliar with the concepts of mean, variance, and standard deviation, you can read more about them in Chapter 6. At this point, we assume that you know what these terms mean, and we simply show you how to use them for database applications.

Figure 13.43 shows the Money Market Returns database and the results of the various database functions. Notice that the functions to find the maximum and minimum rates of return are also included.

The functions and their ranges are

Count	@DCOUNT(A3..B20,1,D13..D14)
Mean	@DAVG(A3..B20,1,D13..D14)
Variance	@DVAR(A3..B20,1,D13..D14)
Std. Dev.	@DSTD(A3..B20,1,D13..D14)

Fig. 13.43

*Statistical
functions used
with Money Market
database.*

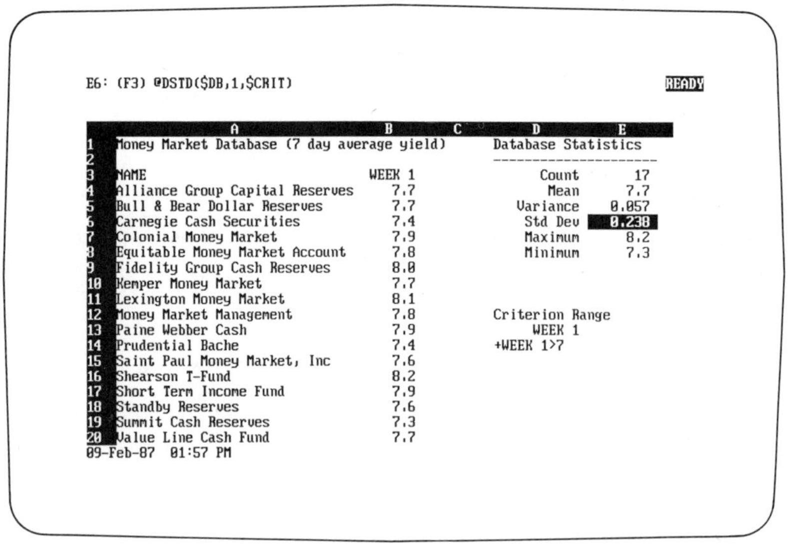

	A	B	C	D	E
1	Money Market Database (7 day average yield)			Database Statistics	
2					
3	NAME	WEEK 1		Count	17
4	Alliance Group Capital Reserves	7.7		Mean	7.7
5	Bull & Bear Dollar Reserves	7.7		Variance	0.057
6	Carnegie Cash Securities	7.4		Std Dev	0.238
7	Colonial Money Market	7.9		Maximum	8.2
8	Equitable Money Market Account	7.8		Minimum	7.3
9	Fidelity Group Cash Reserves	8.0			
10	Kemper Money Market	7.7			
11	Lexington Money Market	8.1			
12	Money Market Management	7.8		Criterion Range	
13	Paine Webber Cash	7.9		WEEK 1	
14	Prudential Bache	7.4		+WEEK 1>7	
15	Saint Paul Money Market, Inc	7.6			
16	Shearson T-Fund	8.2			
17	Short Term Income Fund	7.9			
18	Standby Reserves	7.6			
19	Summit Cash Reserves	7.3			
20	Value Line Cash Fund	7.7			

E6: (F3) @DSTD($DB,1,$CRIT)   READY

09-Feb-87 01:57 PM

Maximum	@DMAX(A3..B20,1,D13..D14)
Minimum	@DMIN(A3..B20,1,D13..D14)

Figure 13.43 shows that the week's mean return for 17 different money market funds works out to an annual percentage rate of 7.7 (cell E4) with a variance of .057 (cell E5). This result means that about 68 percent of the money market funds return between 7.46 and 7.94 percent annually.

One Std. Dev. below mean 7.7 .238 7.46

One Std. Dev. above mean 7.7 .238 7.94

The result of the @DMIN function (cell E8) shows that Summit Cash Reserves returns the lowest rate at 7.3 percent. This value is almost two standard deviations below the mean. That figure—two standard deviations below the mean—is computed as follows:

Two Std. Devs. below mean 7.7 - (2 × .238) = 7.22

Because approximately 95 percent of the population falls within plus or minus two standard deviations of the mean, Summit Cash Reserves is close to being in the lowest 2.5 percent of the population of money market funds for that week; 5 percent is divided by 2 because the population is assumed to be normal. (See Chapter 6 for a further discussion of how to interpret the statistical functions.)

Conversely, the Shearson T-Fund returns 8.2 percent, the highest rate. The @DMAX function has determined the highest rate (cell B16) to be just over two standard deviations above the mean, the highest 2.5 percent of the population.

By setting up the proper criteria, you can analyze any portion of the database you want. How do the statistics change if funds returning less than 7.5 percent are excluded from the statistics? Figure 13.44 gives the answer.

Fig. 13.44

Money Fund analysis with funds earning less than 7.5 percent excluded.

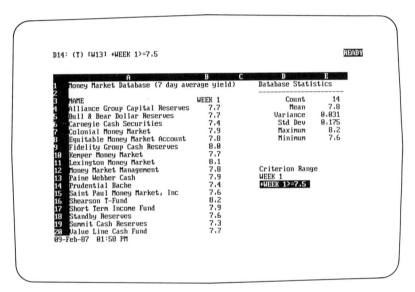

Obviously, the database statistical functions can tell you a great deal about the database as a whole and about how to interpret the values contained in it. If you add several more weeks' data to the database, as shown in figure 13.45, the database statistical functions can also be used to analyze all or part of the larger database.

You can use all the methods you have seen so far to interpret the statistics in figure 13.45. The input, offset, and criterion ranges used for the data from the third week of our example are as follows:

Input range	A3..G20
Offset	3 (for the fourth column)
Criterion range	I13..I14

From this information, you can determine how the formulas have been set up for each week. The criterion range displayed in figure 13.45 (I13..I14) shows the criteria used to select the values for the third week.

Fig. 13.45

*Additional Money
Fund data.*

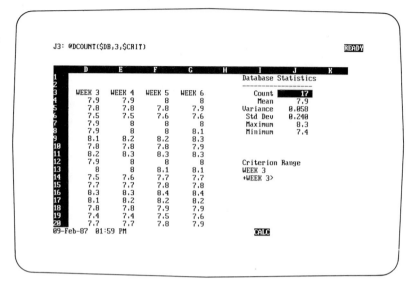

```
J3: @DCOUNT($DB,3,$CRIT)                                              READY

      D         E         F         G       H     I        J        K
1                                                     Database Statistics
2                                                     --------------------
3   WEEK 3    WEEK 4    WEEK 5    WEEK 6              Count        17
4    7.9       7.9       8         8                   Mean       7.9
5    7.8       7.8       7.8       7.9             Variance     0.058
6    7.5       7.5       7.6       7.6             Std Dev      0.240
7    7.9       8         8         8               Maximum       8.3
8    7.9       8         8         8.1             Minimum       7.4
9    8.1       8.2       8.2       8.3
10   7.8       7.8       7.8       7.9
11   8.2       8.3       8.3       8.3
12   7.9       8         8         8               Criterion Range
13   8         8         8.1       8.1             WEEK 3
14   7.5       7.6       7.7       7.7             +WEEK 3>
15   7.7       7.7       7.8       7.8
16   8.3       8.3       8.4       8.4
17   8.1       8.2       8.2       8.2
18   7.8       7.8       7.9       7.9
19   7.4       7.4       7.5       7.6
20   7.7       7.7       7.8       7.9
09-Feb-87  01:59 PM                                          CALC
```

Table Building

Reminder:
*Table building
automates the
"what if" process.*

Table building is an extended version of the "what if" process. In fact, you could duplicate the functions performed by the table-building feature by performing repeated "what if" analyses. Doing so would take a prohibitive amount of time, however. Table building automates the "what if" process so that you can make a thorough analysis with a minimal amount of effort. The /Data Table command is the host command for the table-building function, which makes 1-2-3 a superior program for performing "what if" analyses.

Table building automates the "what if" process through iteration: 1-2-3 takes sets of values and substitutes them one at a time for existing values in the worksheet. You provide the values for substitution and tell 1-2-3 where to substitute them. The program automatically records the results.

This procedure may sound mysterious, but it is actually simple; 1-2-3 does most of the work internally. All you have to know is how to set up the appropriate ranges; 1-2-3 takes care of the rest.

Although the /Data Table command may take some time to learn, you will find it to be one of the most powerful commands in 1-2-3. In fact, the strength of this command rivals similar commands in more sophisticated mainframe decision-support systems. When you consider the command's strength with its ease of implementation, you'll find that the /Data Table command is an excellent feature of 1-2-3.

The purpose of the /**D**ata **T**able command is to structure the "what if" analysis. The command lets you build a table of input values that the program substitutes one at a time into your model. 1-2-3 then records the results in the table next to the input values.

We can demonstrate a simple example by building a table of interest rates and showing their effect on the monthly payments of a 30-year mortgage, as shown in figure 13.46.

Fig. 13.46

Worksheet for monthly payment analysis.

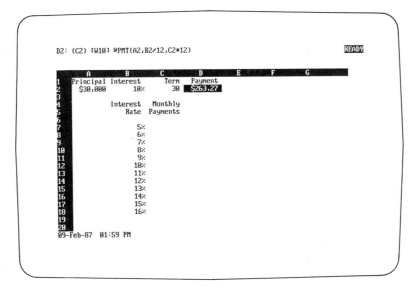

By using the /**D**ata **T**able **1** command, you can have 1-2-3 substitute in appropriate input cells the interest rates you have entered in a column. After calculating the results, 1-2-3 lists the monthly payments in the column next to the interest rates.

Before entering the /**D**ata **T**able **1** command, you enter the interest-rate values in a column. (To enter those values, we used the /**D**ata **F**ill command, which is covered in the next section.) Cells B7..B18 hold the interest rates. For the next step, you need to enter either the appropriate formula for calculating the results or the cell address from which to draw those results. This entry goes next to the column of interest rates and one row above the first entry.

We entered +D2 in cell C6, as shown in figure 13.47, but we could have entered in C6 the formula for computing the value. The formula in cell D2 is @PMT(A2,B2/12,C2*12). +D2 appears because the /**R**ange Format Text command was issued for cell C6, causing the formula rather than the value to be displayed.

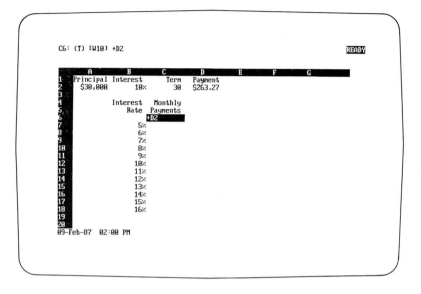

After we issue the /Data Table 1 command, 1-2-3 prompts us to indicate a *table range*, a range of cells that includes the column of interest rates and the column where the results are to appear. In this example, we enter B6..C18. Notice that this range specification includes the formula row (see fig. 13.48). Then the program prompts us to enter an *input cell*. This is the cell to which all the values in the column of interest rates correspond. The entry here is *B2*.

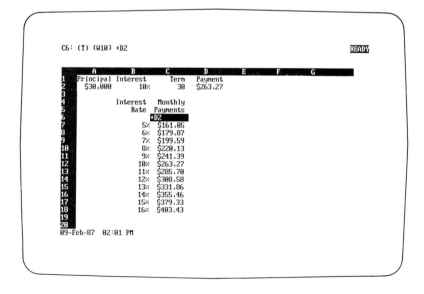

While 1-2-3 calculates the results, the WAIT mode indicator flashes in the upper right corner of the screen. When the calculation is finished, the sign changes to READY. Now the table contains all the payment values.

If you would like to try some other input values, you can change the values and then press the F8 (Table) key to recalculate the table automatically. When the table is recalculated, 1-2-3 uses the command parameters you specified in the previous /Data Table command.

A more complicated example, shown in figure 13.49, uses the /Data Table 2 command, which requires two input variables instead of one. Using more variables increases the breadth of the sensitivity analyses we can perform. This example is designed to show the effects of changes in order quantity and order point on total cost. We are after that combination of order point and order quantity that minimizes "Cumulative Costs to Date" at the end of a 12-month period.

Fig. 13.49

Inventory analysis with /Data Table command.

	A	B	C	D	E	F	G	H	I	J	K	L	M
1	Month	Jan	Feb	Mar	Apr	May	Jun	Jul	Aug	Sep	Oct	Nov	Dec
2	....												
3	Beginning Inventory	43	15	39	28	10	38	18	45	21	11	39	20
4	Past Demand for Month	28	16	11	18	12	20	13	24	10	12	19	22
5	Ending Inventory	15	-1	28	10	-2	18	5	21	11	-1	20	-2
6	Quantity Ordered	0	40	0	0	40	0	40	0	0	40	0	40
7	Setup Costs ($10 per order)	$0.00	$10.00	$0.00	$0.00	$10.00	$0.00	$10.00	$0.00	$0.00	$10.00	$0.00	$10.00
8	Inventory Costs ($.2/unit)	$3.00	$0.00	$5.60	$2.00	$0.00	$3.60	$1.00	$4.20	$2.20	$0.00	$4.00	$0.00
9	Shortage Costs ($1/unit)	$0.00	$1.00	$0.00	$0.00	$2.00	$0.00	$0.00	$0.00	$0.00	$1.00	$0.00	$2.00
10	Total Costs for Month	$3.00	$11.00	$5.60	$2.00	$12.00	$3.60	$11.00	$4.20	$2.20	$11.00	$4.00	$12.00
11	Cum Cost From Last Month	$0.00	$3.00	$14.00	$19.60	$21.60	$33.60	$37.20	$48.20	$52.40	$54.60	$65.60	$69.60
12	Cumulative Costs to Date	$3.00	$14.00	$19.60	$21.60	$33.60	$37.20	$48.20	$52.40	$54.60	$65.60	$69.60	$81.60
13													
14													
15	Order Quantity Input Cell	40											
16	Order Point Input Cell	8											

	DATA TABLE 1 -->	Order Quant	Cumulative Cost		DATA TABLE 2 -->		Order Quantity					
		.....	.....			38	39	40	41	42	43	Average
21			+N13		+N13	38	39	40	41	42	43	Average
22		25	$104.00		1	$91.20	$103.80	$96.40	$96.00	$93.20	$91.60	$95.37
23		26	$109.60		2	$91.20	$103.80	$96.40	$93.80	$93.20	$91.60	$95.00
24		27	$106.40		3	$91.20	$86.40	$96.40	$93.80	$93.20	$91.60	$92.10
25		28	$98.00		4	$91.20	$86.40	$96.40	$93.80	$93.20	$91.60	$92.10
26		29	$99.60		5	$90.40	$86.40	$81.60	$93.80	$84.80	$91.60	$88.10
27		30	$102.40		6	$90.40	$86.40	$81.60	$93.80	$94.80	$91.60	$89.77
28		31	$95.20		7	$90.40	$86.40	$81.60	$81.60	$94.80	$91.60	$87.73
29		32	$91.60		8	$93.20	$89.40	$81.60	$81.60	$94.80	$87.00	$87.93
30		33	$94.60	o	9	$93.20	$93.60	$81.60	$81.60	$85.20	$87.00	$87.03
31		34	$95.60	r	10	$93.20	$93.60	$87.20	$81.60	$85.20	$97.00	$89.63
32		35	$86.60	d	11	$93.20	$93.60	$94.00	$88.60	$85.20	$90.00	$90.77
33		36	$88.80	e	12	$88.80	$93.60	$94.00	$88.60	$93.60	$90.00	$91.43
34		37	$84.60	r	13	$88.80	$93.60	$94.00	$88.60	$93.60	$92.60	$92.87
35		38	$93.20		14	$96.40	$93.60	$94.00	$96.80	$93.60	$98.60	$95.50
36		39	$93.60	P	15	$110.40	$100.20	$100.80	$103.80	$100.80	$106.00	$103.67
37		40	$81.60	o	16	$110.40	$108.60	$100.80	$103.80	$100.80	$106.00	$105.07
38		41	$81.60	i	17	$110.40	$108.60	$100.80	$103.80	$109.20	$106.00	$106.47
39		42	$85.20	n	18	$110.40	$116.40	$108.80	$103.80	$109.20	$106.00	$109.10
40		43	$87.00	t	19	$110.40	$116.40	$108.80	$103.80	$109.20	$106.00	$109.10
41		44	$90.00		20	$110.40	$116.40	$114.40	$112.00	$109.20	$114.60	$112.83
42		45	$88.40		21	$110.40	$116.40	$122.40	$112.00	$109.20	$114.60	$114.17
43		46	$86.80		22	$110.40	$116.40	$122.40	$112.00	$117.60	$114.60	$115.57
44		47	$86.40		23	$110.40	$116.40	$122.40	$112.00	$117.60	$114.60	$115.57
45		48	$88.40		24	$110.40	$116.40	$122.40	$128.40	$117.60	$123.20	$119.73
46		49	$90.40		25	$110.40	$116.40	$122.40	$128.40	$117.60	$123.20	$119.73
47		50	$98.00		26	$118.00	$116.40	$122.40	$128.40	$117.60	$123.20	$121.00

The lower left portion of figure 13.49 shows the result of using the /Data Table 1 command to calculate the effect of different order quantities on cost. The /Data Table 2 command creates a much more extensive table, as shown in the lower right portion of the figure. This table shows the effect on cost of order point and order quantity. The result is a more complete analysis. This is the advantage of the /Data Table 2 command.

To use the /Data Table 2 command, you enter the values for Variable 2 (order quantity, in this example) in the row just above the first entry of Variable 1 (order point). In our example, these values begin in cell F21. Notice also that you enter +N13, the address of the formula for Cost to Date, in the row directly above the first entry of Variable 1, cell E21 in our example. Again, the Text format is used so that the cell displays +N13.

When you issue the /Data Table 2 command, 1-2-3 calls for a table range and input cells for Variables 1 and 2. You enter the following information for these parameters:

Table Range E21..K47

Input Cell Variable 1 B16

Input Cell Variable 2 B15

After you enter this information, 1-2-3 begins building the table of results. Although you may have to wait for the /Data Table 2 command to work, the results will be well worth your time. The table in figure 13.49 took about two minutes to calculate on an IBM PC. To duplicate manually what 1-2-3 does would take much longer. If you plan to use the /Data Table command often, you may want to invest in an 8087 or 80287 coprocessor for your computer.

Note that we find no one correct answer concerning the effect of changes in order quantity and order point on total cost. Our limited analysis, however, shows that on average an order point of about 9 and an order quantity of about 41 are best.

The advantage of the /Data Table command is that it allows you to perform extensive sensitivity analyses and display the results in a tabular format. You can perform analyses that you might not otherwise perform, given the time required. The power you gain from combining this command with macros and special database statistical functions can be great.

Filling Ranges with Numbers

The command for filling ranges is /Data Fill. /Data Fill is useful when combined with the other database commands mentioned earlier in this chapter, especially /Data Table and /Data Sort.

Reminder:
Use the /Data Fill command to automate the process of entering a series of numbers or dates that increment at the same value.

/Data Fill fills a range of cells with series of numbers that increase or decrease by a specified increment or decrement. For an example of the use of /Data Fill, look at the year numbers used as titles in the sales forecast shown in figure 13.50.

Fig. 13.50

Entering year numbers with /Data Fill.

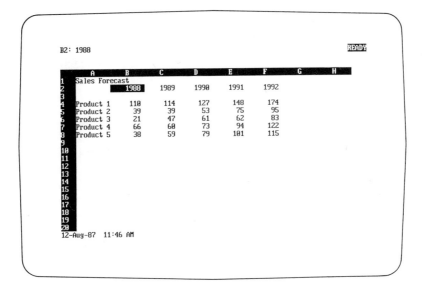

When you issue the /Data Fill command, 1-2-3 first prompts you for the starting number of the series. The program then asks for the step (or incremental) value to be added to the previous value. Finally, 1-2-3 prompts you for the ending value.

To enter a sequence of year numbers for a five-year forecast beginning in 1988, you need to start by specifying the range of cells to be filled. For this example, we chose B2..F2 and then entered the beginning value, 1988. The incremental or step value in this example is one. The ending value is 1992 for a five-year forecast.

One disadvantage of the /Data Fill command for year numbers is that you can't center or left-justify the numbers after you have created them. As numbers, they will always be right-justified. If you like your year numbers centered or left-justified, you should type them in as labels instead.

Cue:
Combine /Data Fill with /Data Table to build a list of interest rates.

The /Data Fill command can also work with the /Data Table command to build a list of interest rates, as shown in figure 13.46. In that figure, the column of interest rate values was entered with the /Data Fill command. We specified B7..B18 for the range of cells to be filled, .05 for the starting value, and .01 for the step value. For the ending value, we let 1-2-3 default to 8,192, which is far beyond the ending value we actually needed. The /Data Fill command, however, fills only the specified range and doesn't fill cells beyond the end of the range.

Cue:
Use /Data Fill to create a "counter" field in your database in case you need to restore the database to its original order after sorting.

The /Data Fill command is useful with /Data Sort. Suppose that you're going to /Data Sort a database, and you want to be able to restore the records to their original order if you make a mistake in sorting them. All you need to do is add a field to the database and use /Data Fill to fill the field with consecutive numbers. Then you can sort your database. If you find that the results of the sort are unacceptable, you simply sort the database on the new field in order to return the database to its original order. Figure 13.51 shows an example before the /Data Sort operation; figure 13.52 shows the result.

Reminder:
You can use formulas and functions in beginning, step, and end values in /Data Fill.

In our examples, we have used regular numbers for the beginning, incremental, and ending values, but we can also use formulas and functions. If we want to fill a range of cells with incrementing dates, after the range has been set, we can use the @DATE function to set the start value, for example @DATE(87,6,1). We can use also a cell formula, such as +E4, for the incremental value. In this case, E4 may contain the increment 7 so that there can be increments of one week at a time. We can enter the stop value

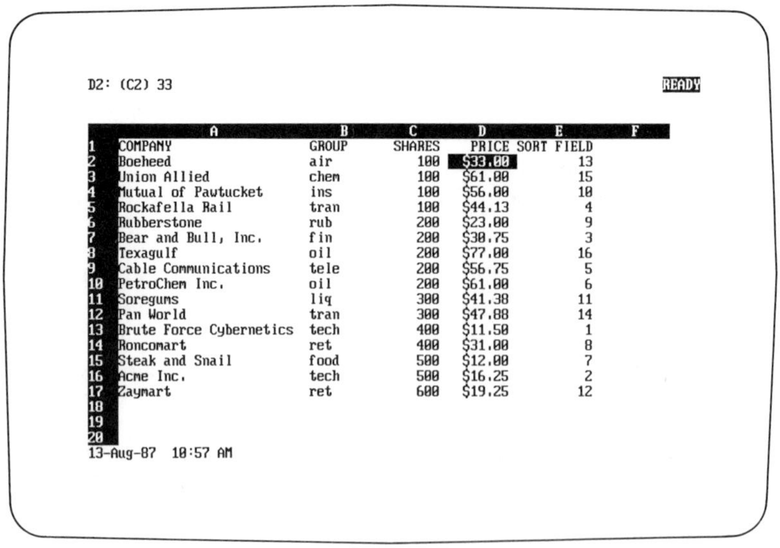

Fig. 13.51

Stocks database sorted by number of shares.

```
D2: (C2) 33                                                    READY

          A                    B       C       D        E       F
 1  COMPANY                  GROUP   SHARES    PRICE SORT FIELD
 2  Boeheed                  air       100   $33.00         13
 3  Union Allied             chem      100   $61.00         15
 4  Mutual of Pawtucket      ins       100   $56.00         10
 5  Rockafella Rail          tran      100   $44.13          4
 6  Rubberstone              rub       200   $23.00          9
 7  Bear and Bull, Inc.      fin       200   $30.75          3
 8  Texagulf                 oil       200   $77.00         16
 9  Cable Communications     tele      200   $56.75          5
10  PetroChem Inc.           oil       200   $61.00          6
11  Soreguns                 liq       300   $41.38         11
12  Pan World                tran      300   $47.88         14
13  Brute Force Cybernetics  tech      400   $11.50          1
14  Ronconart                ret       400   $31.00          8
15  Steak and Snail          food      500   $12.00          7
16  Acme Inc.                tech      500   $16.25          2
17  Zaymart                  ret       600   $19.25         12
18
19
20
13-Aug-87  10:57 AM
```

Fig. 13.52

*Stocks database
returned to
original order.*

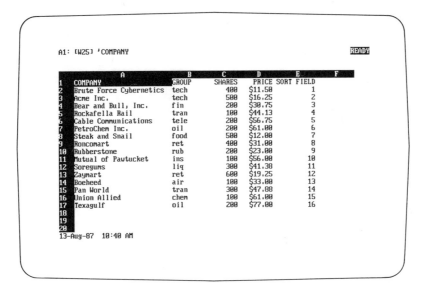

```
A1: [W25] 'COMPANY                                              READY

        A                    B        C        D       E         F
1  COMPANY               GROUP    SHARES    PRICE SORT FIELD
2  Brute Force Cybernetics tech      400   $11.50         1
3  Acme Inc.             tech       500   $16.25         2
4  Bear and Bull, Inc.   fin        200   $30.75         3
5  Rockafella Rail       tran       100   $44.13         4
6  Cable Communications  tele       200   $56.75         5
7  PetroChem Inc.        oil        200   $61.00         6
8  Steak and Snail       food       500   $12.00         7
9  Roncomart             ret        400   $31.00         8
10 Rubberstone           rub        200   $23.00         9
11 Mutual of Pawtucket   ins        100   $56.00        10
12 Soreguns              liq        300   $41.38        11
13 Zaymart               ret        600   $19.25        12
14 Boeheed               air        100   $33.00        13
15 Pan World             tran       300   $47.88        14
16 Union Allied          chem       100   $61.00        15
17 Texagulf              oil        200   $77.00        16
18
19
20
13-Aug-87  10:40 AM
```

@DATE(87,10,1), for example; or, if the stop date is in a cell, we can give that cell address as the stop value. 1-2-3 allows many different combinations of commands.

Frequency Distributions

The command for creating frequency distributions in 1-2-3 is the /**Data Dis**tribution command. A *frequency distribution* describes the relationship between a set of classes and the frequency of occurrence of members of each class. A list of consumers with their product preferences illustrates use of the /**Data Distribution** command to produce a frequency distribution (see fig. 13.53).

To use the /**Data Distribution** command, you first specify a values range, which corresponds to the range of Taste Preference numbers in this example. After specifying B3..B18 for the values range, you set up the range of intervals at D3..D7, in what 1-2-3 calls the *Bin* range. If you have evenly spaced intervals, the /**Data Fill** command can be used to enter the values for the Bin range. If the intervals were not evenly spaced, you could not use the /**Data Fill** command to fill the range.

When you specify these ranges and enter the /**Data Distribution** command, 1-2-3 creates the Results column (E3..E8) to the right of the Bin range (D3..D7). The Results column, which shows the frequency distribution, is always in the column segment to the right of the Bin range and extends one row farther down.

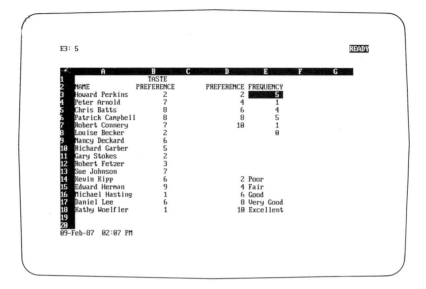

Fig. 13.53

*Using /Data
Distribution to
analyze Taste
Preference data.*

The values in the Results column represent the frequency of distribution of the numbers in the Values range for each interval. The first interval in the Bin range is for values greater than zero and less than or equal to two; the second, for values greater than two and less than or equal to four, etc. The last value in the Results column, in cell E8 just below the corresponding column segment, shows the frequency of leftover numbers (that is, the frequency of numbers that don't fit into an interval classification).

The /Data Distribution command can help you create understandable results from a series of numbers. The results are easily graphed, as shown in figure 13.54.

A manufacturer looking at this graph would probably start looking for another product or start trying to improve the taste of the current product.

The /Data Regression Command

The /Data Regression command gives you a free multiple-regression analysis package within 1-2-3. Most people will probably never use this advanced feature. But if you need to use it, 1-2-3 saves you the cost and inconvenience of buying a stand-alone statistical package for performing a regression analysis.

Use /Data Regression when you want to determine the relationship between one set of values (the dependent variable) and one or more other sets of values (the independent variables). Regression analysis has a number of uses in a business setting, including relating sales to price, promotions, and other

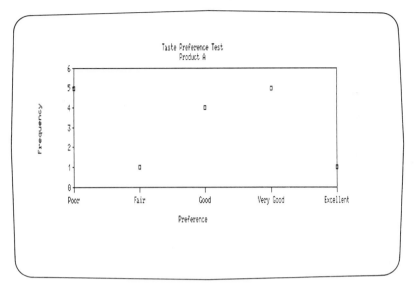

Fig. 13.54

*Graph of results
from the /Data
Distribution
command.*

market factors; relating stock prices to earnings and interest rates; and relating
production costs to production levels.

Think of linear regression as a way of determining the "best" line through a
series of data points. Multiple regression does this for several variables simultaneously, determining the "best" line relating the dependent variable to
the set of independent variables. As an example, we will use a data sample
showing Annual Earnings versus Age. Figure 13.55 shows the data; figure 13.56
shows the data plotted as an XY graph.

The /**D**ata **R**egression command can simultaneously determine how to draw
a line through these data points and how well the line fits the data. When
you invoke the command, the following menu appears:

   X-Range   Y-Range   Output-Range   Intercept   Reset   Go   Quit

Use the **X**-Range option to select one or more independent variables for the
regression. The /**D**ata **R**egression command can use as many as 16 independent variables. The variables in the regression are columns of values, which
means that any data in rows must be converted to columns with /**R**ange
Transpose before the /**D**ata **R**egression command is issued. In this example,
the X-Range is A7..A20.

The **Y**-Range option specifies the dependent variable. The **Y**-Range must be
a single column; we therefore select C7..C20.

The **Output-Range** option specifies the upper left corner of the results range.
This should be an unused section of the worksheet, because the output is
written over any existing cell contents.

Fig. 13.55

Annual Earnings versus Age data.

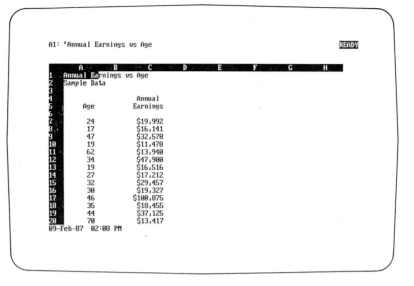

Fig. 13.56

XY graph of Annual Earnings versus Age.

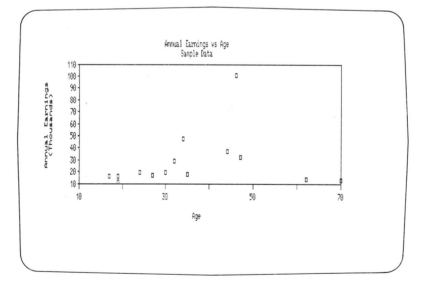

The Intercept option lets you specify whether you want the regression to calculate a constant value. Calculating the constant is the default, but it may be necessary in some applications to exclude a constant.

Figure 13.57 shows the results of using the /Data Regression command in the Annual Earnings versus Age example. The results include the value of the constant and the coefficient of the single independent variable that we specified with the **X**-Range option. The results also include a number of regression statistics that describe how well the regression line fits the data. In this case, the R-Squared value and the standard errors of the constant and the regression coefficient all indicate that the regression line does not explain much of the variation in the dependent variable.

Fig. 13.57

Results of /Data Regression on Annual Earnings versus Age.

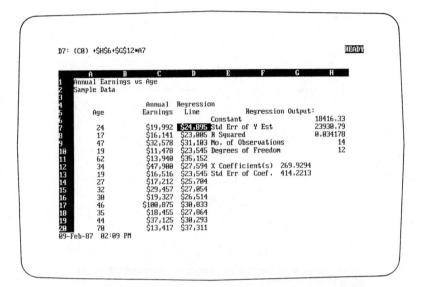

The new data in column D is the computed regression line. These values consist of the constant plus the coefficient of the independent variable times its value in each row of the data. This line can be plotted against the original data, as shown in figure 13.58.

Looking at the Annual Earnings versus Age plot, you notice that income appears to rise with age until about age 50; then income begins to decline. You can use the /Data Regression command to fit a line that describes such a relationship between Annual Earnings and Age. In figure 13.59, we have added a column of data in column B containing the square of the age in column A. To include this new column in the regression, specify the range A7..B20 for the **X**-Range and recalculate the regression. Note that the regression statistics are much improved over the regression of Annual Earnings versus Age. This means that the new line fits the data more closely than the old one. (However, the regression statistics indicate that the regression only "explains" about one-third of the variation of the dependent variable.)

You must add the new regression coefficient to the equation that generates the regression line, and sort the data by age, to generate the new plot in figure 13.60. (You have to sort the data by age to plot the curved line on the XY

Fig. 13.58

Plot of Annual Earnings versus Age data, with regression line.

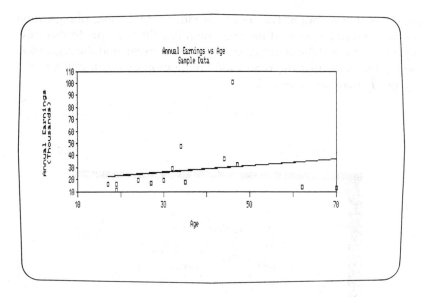

Fig. 13.59

Annual Earnings versus Age and the square of Age.

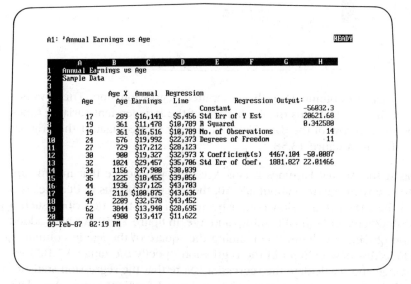

graph.) Note that the regression line is now a parabola that rises until age 45, then declines. The regression line generated by a multiple regression may or may not be a straight line, depending on the independent variables that are used.

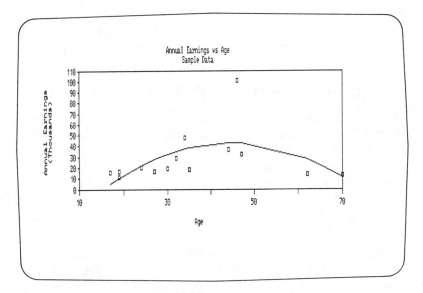

Fig. 13.60

Plot of Annual Earnings versus Age, with revised regression line.

The /Data Matrix Command

The /Data Matrix command is a specialized mathematical command that lets you solve systems of simultaneous linear equations and manipulate the resulting solutions. This command is powerful but has limited application in a business setting. If you are using 1-2-3 for certain types of economic analysis or for scientific or engineering calculations, you may find this command valuable.

The /Data Matrix command has a menu with two options: Invert and Multiply. The Invert option lets you invert a nonsingular square matrix of up to 90 rows and columns. Just select the Invert option and highlight the range you want to invert. Then select an output range to hold the inverted solution matrix. You can place the output range anywhere in the worksheet, including on top of the matrix you are inverting.

The time required to invert a matrix is proportional to the cube of the number of rows and columns. A 10-by-10 matrix takes about 6 seconds, and a 90-by-90 matrix takes almost one hour on an IBM PC with no numeric coprocessor. If you are going to use 1-2-3 to invert matrices, you may want to invest in an 8087 or 80287 coprocessor for your computer.

The Multiply option allows you to multiply two rectangular matrices together in accordance with the rules of matrix algebra. The number of columns in the first matrix must equal the number of rows in the second matrix. The result matrix has the same number of rows as the first matrix, and the same number of columns as the second.

When you select /Data Matrix Multiply, 1-2-3 prompts you for three ranges: the first matrix, the second matrix, and the output range. Multiply is fast compared to Invert, but may still take some time if you multiply large matrices.

Practice Set: Selected Data Commands

Use the following examples to reinforce the mechanics involved in issuing the first four commands on the /Data menu and calculating a total based on a criterion being met. All of the exercises access existing data or create new data in a Deductible Expenses database that has 14 records (rows 3 through 16) and the field headings DATE, ITEM, AMOUNT, and CATEGORY, located in row 2 and columns A, C, D, and E, respectively. The entries for May, June, and July have been entered initially in order of occurrence, as shown here.

Column:	A	B	C	D	E
Row 1			Deductible Expenses Database		
Row 2	DATE		ITEM	AMOUNT	CATEGORY
Row 3	17-May-87		Wall Street Journal	$ 96.00	Subscription
Row 4	25-May-87		Airfare to Phoenix	$650.00	Travel
Row 5	28-May-87		Secretarial Help	$150.00	Employment
Row 6	02-Jun-87		Airfare to NY	$560.00	Travel
Row 7	09-Jun-87		Business Luncheon	$40.00	Entertainment
Row 8	09-Jun-87		InfoWorld	$32.00	Subscription
Row 9	09-Jun-87		DOS 3.1	$67.00	Software
Row 10	14-Jun-87		1-2-3	$495.00	Software
Row 11	22-Jun-87		Computerworld	$45.00	Subscription
Row 12	24-Jun-87		PC Magazine	$26.00	Subscription
Row 13	27-Jun-87		Airfare to Denver	$525.00	Travel
Row 14	27-Jun-87		Tax Prep book	$14.95	Tax Prep
Row 15	03-Jul-87		PC World	$22.00	Subscription
Row 16	07-Jul-87		Secretarial Help	$150.00	Employment

Practice: The Sort Command

Use the following steps to sort the records in the Deductible Expenses database alphabetically, based on the description in the ITEM field.

1. Select /Data Sort Data-Range.

2. Respond *A3..E16* to the prompt for the data sort range.

3. Select Primary-Key and enter any cell in column C.

4. Specify Ascending order, and press Enter.

5. Select **G**o to execute the sort.

6. Be sure that your screen displays the records sorted in alphabetical order by ITEM (see fig. 13.61).

Fig. 13.61

Practice: Sorting on one key.

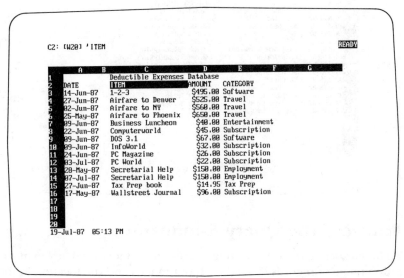

You can easily sort on two different keys by changing the primary key and adding a secondary key. To illustrate, reorder the records in the Deductible Expenses database first by CATEGORY and then by AMOUNT within category. You do not have to respecify the unchanged data-range. Complete these steps:

1. Select **/D**ata **S**ort.

2. Select **P**rimary-Key, and enter any cell in column E.

3. Specify **A**scending order, and press Enter.

4. Select **S**econdary-Key, and enter any cell in column D.

5. Specify **D**escending order, and press Enter.

6. Select **G**o to execute the sort.

7. Be sure that your screen displays the records sorted in alphabetical order by CATEGORY and by descending AMOUNT within category (see fig. 13.62).

Fig. 13.62

Practice: Sorting on two keys.

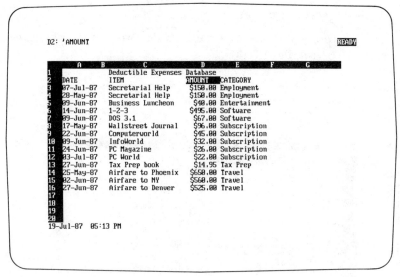

Practice: The Query Command

To find or delete records meeting conditions, remember that you must specify only a range of records to search (**Input range**) and the location in the worksheet of the search criterion (**Criterion range**). To extract all the specified records or only the first occurrence of each record, you must also provide a display area (**Output-range**).

Create a criterion range and an output range below the records in the Deductible Expenses database by entering the cell contents of rows 18, 19, 23, and 24 (see fig. 13.63). You can copy the field headings from A2..E2 to both the criterion range A19..E19 and the output range A24..E24.

To illustrate the extraction of all records that exactly match a single criterion, produce a list of subscription purchases by following these steps:

1. Enter *Subscription* in cell E20 as the specific criterion under the field name CATEGORY.

2. Select **/Data Query**.

3. Select **Input** and enter *A2..E16*, including all records and the field headings.

4. Select **Criterion** and enter the entire range *A19..E20*, instead of only the limited current criterion range E19..E20.

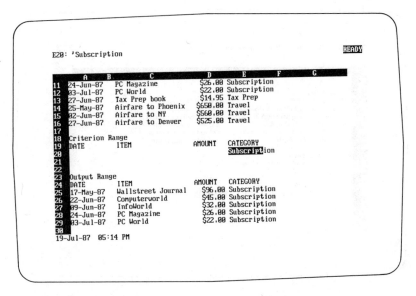

Fig. 13.63

Practice: Finding an "exact match."

```
E20: 'Subscription                                              READY

      A     B          C              D       E          F       G
11 24-Jun-87   PC Magazine          $26.00  Subscription
12 03-Jul-87   PC World             $22.00  Subscription
13 27-Jun-87   Tax Prep book        $14.95  Tax Prep
14 25-May-87   Airfare to Phoenix  $650.00  Travel
15 02-Jun-87   Airfare to NY       $560.00  Travel
16 27-Jun-87   Airfare to Denver   $525.00  Travel
17
18 Criterion Range
19 DATE          ITEM               AMOUNT  CATEGORY
20                                          Subscription
21
22
23 Output Range
24 DATE          ITEM               AMOUNT  CATEGORY
25 17-May-87   Wallstreet Journal   $96.00  Subscription
26 22-Jun-87   Computerworld        $45.00  Subscription
27 09-Jun-87   InfoWorld            $32.00  Subscription
28 24-Jun-87   PC Magazine          $26.00  Subscription
29 03-Jul-87   PC World             $22.00  Subscription
30
19-Jul-87  05:14 PM
```

5. Select **Output** and specify only the field-heading output range *A24..E24* to extract an unlimited number of records.

6. Select **Extract** to transfer to the output area the copy of records that have Subscription as the entry in the category field.

7. **Quit** the Query menu, and be sure that your screen displays five extracted records, as shown in rows 25 through 29 (refer to fig. 13.63).

You have two choices for determining the total dollars spent on subscriptions to-date: set up an @SUM function to total the numeric output (D25..D29) from the previous **Query Extract** command, or eliminate having to extract the data first by entering the formula *@DSUM((A2..E16),3,(A19..E20))*, as shown in cell D36 (see fig. 13.64).

The previous practice **Query Extract** command copied entire records to the output area, as determined by the field headings in the output range. Practice extracting only portions of records meeting a formula criterion by following these steps:

1. **Range Erase** cell E20 to remove the previous criterion.

2. Enter the formula *+D3>100* in cell D20.

3. Erase the field headings in A24..E24, and enter *ITEM* in cell A24 and *AMOUNT* in cell D24.

4. Press the F7 (Query) key to repeat the last query operation.

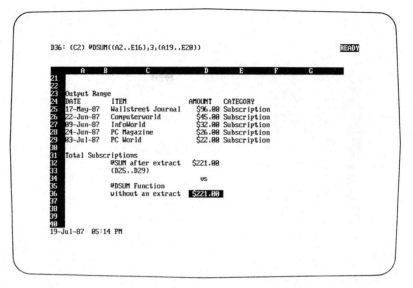

Fig. 13.64

Practice: Using the @DSUM function.

5. Be sure that your screen displays only the ITEM and AMOUNT information for six records that meet the condition of having an amount in excess of $100 (see fig. 13.65).

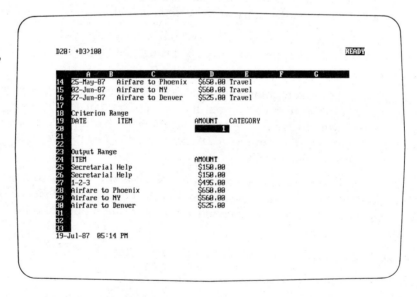

Fig. 13.65

Practice: Using a formula as search criterion.

Suppose that you want to extract full records for which the amount is either greater than $600 or less than $50. You could expand the current criterion range to include an extra row 21 and then enter an "OR" condition below the first condition.

In row 19, enter AMOUNT; in row 20 enter +D3>600, and in row 21 enter +D3<50. If you use this format, however, you must expand the criterion range from A19..E20 to A19..E21.

As an alternative, enter both conditions in a single cell separated by the relational operator #OR#:

1. Copy the field header row A19..E19 to the output range A24..E24 to restore the full record extract.

2. **Range Erase** the previous criterion in cell D20.

3. Enter the formula *+D3>600#OR#D3<50* in cell A20. (Remember that formula criterion does not need to be positioned under the field-name heading. The numeric content is used in the search operation. Also, remember that the criterion range should include only A19..E20.)

4. Press the F7 (Query) key to repeat the last query operation.

5. Be sure that your screen displays seven records that meet the condition of having an amount greater than $600 or less than $50, as shown in rows 25 through 31 (see fig. 13.66).

Fig. 13.66

Practice: Using the #OR# relational operator.

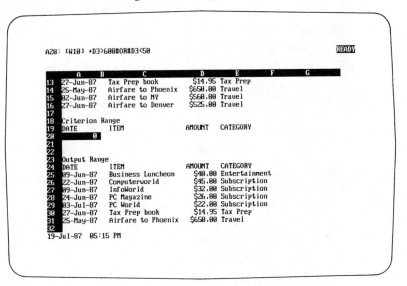

Use the **Query Unique** command to produce a listing of only the first record (or part of a record) within the input range that meets the specified criterion.

For example, you can use the **Unique** command to produce a list of category types in the Deductible Expenses database by following these steps:

1. Erase the contents in the criterion row 20 and the output rows 24 through 31 to remove unwanted criterion and output field names as well as the previous extract results.

2. Enter *CATEGORY* in cell A24 as the only field name desired in the output range; leave blank all criterion cells in row 20 to search all records.

3. Select /**Data Query Unique**. (The Input range and Criterion range remain unchanged.)

4. Quit the Query menu and be sure that your screen displays six category types, as shown in rows 25 through 30 (see fig. 13.67).

Fig. 13.67

Practice: Listing unique records.

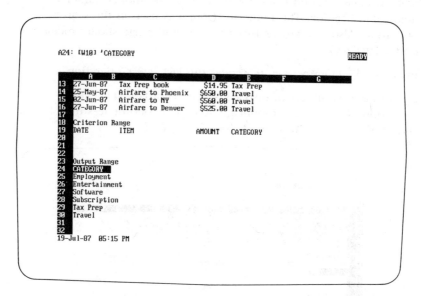

Deleting records by using a **Query** command can be dangerous if you do not specify correctly the criterion for the deletion. As a precaution, you first might extract records meeting the conditions entered and view the extracted records to verify the accuracy of the criterion before you continue the deletion. First extract and then delete all May records from the Deductible Expenses database by following these steps:

1. Copy the field headings in A19..E19 to the output area A24..E24 to restore extract of full records.

2. Enter the formula *+A3<@DATE(87,6,1)* in cell A20 as the criterion to search for records with a date before June 1, 1987 (all the May records, in this database).

3. Select **/Data Query Extract**, and be sure that three records with May dates appear in rows 25 through 27 (see fig. 13.68).

Fig. 13.68

Practice: Extracting records to verify a delete.

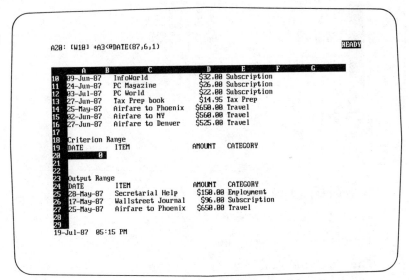

4. Select **Delete** from the Query submenu, and select **Delete** again to execute the command. (The alternative is canceling the **Delete** command.)

5. **Quit** the Query menu, and be sure that the Deductible Expenses database has only 11 June and July records (see fig. 13.69). The Input range is adjusted automatically to A2..E13, but the criterion or output ranges do not move.

Practice: The Fill Command

Use the **/Data Fill** command to generate a series of numbers that change by a specified amount. For example, prepare to set up a table of 1-2-3 software prices, assuming 5 to 25 percent discounts on a $495 stated retail price. First **Range Format** G4..G8 to **Percent 0**, and then format H4..H8 to **Currency 2**. Use the **Fill** command to enter the percentages shown in column G (see fig. 13.70):

Fig. 13.69

Practice: Executing a Query Delete command.

```
A20: [W10] +A3<@DATE(87,6,1)                                    READY

      A    B         C              D        E         F        G
1                Deductible Expenses Database
2   DATE         ITEM            AMOUNT   CATEGORY
3   07-Jul-87    Secretarial Help  $150.00 Employment
4   09-Jun-87    Business Luncheon  $40.00 Entertainment
5   14-Jun-87    1-2-3            $495.00 Software
6   09-Jun-87    DOS 3.1          $67.00 Software
7   22-Jun-87    Computerworld    $45.00 Subscription
8   09-Jun-87    InfoWorld        $32.00 Subscription
9   24-Jun-87    PC Magazine      $26.00 Subscription
10  03-Jul-87    PC World         $22.00 Subscription
11  27-Jun-87    Tax Prep book    $14.95 Tax Prep
12  02-Jun-87    Airfare to NY    $560.00 Travel
13  27-Jun-87    Airfare to Denver $525.00 Travel
14
15
16
17
18  Criterion Range
19  DATE         ITEM            AMOUNT   CATEGORY
20        0
    19-Jul-87   05:16 PM
```

1. Select /Data Fill, and enter *G4..G8* as the fill range.

2. Enter *.95* as the start value.

3. Enter *-.05* as the step value.

4. Enter *0* as the stop value (or enter any number less than the .75 desired ending value).

Fig. 13.70

Practice: Filling a range with values.

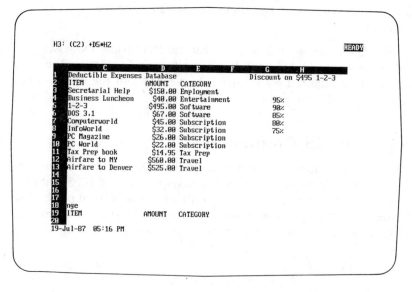

```
H3: (C2) +D5*H2                                               READY

      C              D        E         F       G        H
1   Deductible Expenses Database            Discount on $495 1-2-3
2   ITEM            AMOUNT   CATEGORY
3   Secretarial Help  $150.00 Employment
4   Business Luncheon  $40.00 Entertainment        95%
5   1-2-3           $495.00 Software               90%
6   DOS 3.1          $67.00 Software               85%
7   Computerworld    $45.00 Subscription           88%
8   InfoWorld        $32.00 Subscription           75%
9   PC Magazine      $26.00 Subscription
10  PC World         $22.00 Subscription
11  Tax Prep book    $14.95 Tax Prep
12  Airfare to NY    $560.00 Travel
13  Airfare to Denver $525.00 Travel
14
15
16
17
18  nge
19  ITEM            AMOUNT   CATEGORY
20
    19-Jul-87  05:16 PM
```

Practice: The Table Command

Create a table of values based on changes in one variable by using a **Table 1** command. For example, generate the prices to be paid for 1-2-3 software, assuming payment at 75 to 95 percent of the stated $495 retail price:

1. Enter the formula *+D5*H2* in cell H3, which is the cell immediately above and to the right of the first percentage variable (see fig. 13.70).

2. Select /Data Table **1**.

3. Enter *G3..H8* when prompted for the table range.

4. Enter the blank cell *H2* when prompted for the input cell. (Remember that the input cell must be included in the formula.)

5. Wait until the table values are entered automatically in the range H4..H8 (see fig. 13.71).

Fig. 13.71

Practice: Creating a table with one variable.

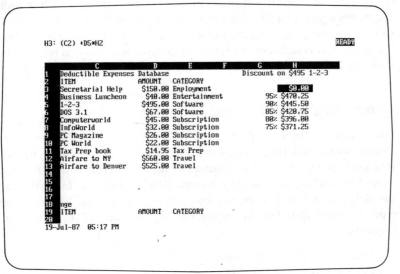

Managing Data with Lotus HAL

As you have seen in other chapters, Lotus HAL can be used to streamline many tedious 1-2-3 tasks. One of HAL's biggest advantages is its enhancement of 1-2-3 database functions. HAL simplifies sorting and data table management operations and makes using 1-2-3's database querying commands—/Data

Query Extract, Unique, and Delete—an easy job. This section explains how you can use HAL to write simple requests to create, sort, and query 1-2-3 data tables.

Sorting a Database

When you want to use HAL to sort a database, you can use requests beginning with the verbs *arrange, group, organize,* or *sort.* After you enter the request, HAL sorts the current table in ascending order, using the leftmost field as the primary key field on which to sort. You do have the option of specifying sort ranges and of selecting a secondary key field. The following list shows some valid HAL requests:

>   sort a3..g20
>   group by population -
>   org by col a then by col b

The first request sorts the range A3..G20 in ascending order; the second request sorts the Population fields in descending order (which is indicated by the minus sign); and the third request, which includes two criteria, tells HAL to sort the current table by column A and then by column B. (Remember that if the sort results are not what you'd expected, you can restore the spreadsheet to its previous state by pressing Undo.)

Querying a Database

When you use HAL to perform 1-2-3's /Data Query Extract, Unique, and Delete commands, HAL creates the criterion and output ranges for you. Before HAL creates the criterion and output ranges, however, HAL erases the spreadsheet from below the database to row 8192. Although HAL will warn you of the deletion before it happens, you need to be careful when executing this type of command. The following list shows some HAL *extract* and *delete* requests:

>   extract records whose balance > 100
>   match unique asset in a200
>   delete col g = paid

The first request extracts records in which the value of the Balance field is greater than 100. The second request uses the *unique* qualifier to specify that only records with unique Asset entries be copied to cell A200. The third request tells HAL to delete all records in which the value *paid* appears in column G.

Creating Database Reports

HAL's *report* requests really shine. In addition to HAL's sort and query capabilities, HAL has access to all of 1-2-3's statistical functions. HAL recognizes the phrase *report on* as the beginning of a report request. The following gives you an example of a valid HAL *report* request:

   report on person and sales

The request groups records by the Person fields, places a dashed line below the last value in each Sales field, sums each individual's sales amounts below the dashed line, and places the report three rows below the database.

Using HAL with Data Tables

HAL also can generate new data tables or calculate previously created data tables. For this function, HAL recognizes *create a table*, *crosstabulate*, *tabulate*, and *make a table*, among other requests. The following example shows a valid HAL data table request:

   create a table of product totaling $(000)

In response to the request, HAL creates a data table containing a list of products from the Product fields and totals from the $(000) fields.

You also can have HAL fill in, or calculate, data tables you have previously created. (Note: If you name the range you want to fill before entering the request, you can save the typing required in entering lengthy cell ranges.) The following are valid requests for calculating data tables:

   crosstab exp_data
   \xtab checks summing amounts

The first request calculates the data table previously created in the range EXP_DATA; the second calculates the data table previously created in the range named Checks and totals the Amounts field.

This section has provided a brief overview of HAL's data management functions. HAL makes these powerful 1-2-3 commands easy to learn and efficient to use. Because of the complexity of 1-2-3's data management features and their comparable HAL procedures, a full chapter could be devoted to explaining them. (For more information on HAL's data management operations, see *Using Lotus HAL*, by Que Corporation.)

Chapter Summary

The data-management chapter addresses all eight options on the /Data menu. The first two options, **Sort** and **Query**, which are described extensively in the first half of the chapter, are true data-management commands that require the database organization by field name. The other six choices—**Fill**, **Table**, **Distribution**, **Matrix**, **Regression**, and **Parse**—create data and can be used in database or spreadsheet applications.

Data management is one of the advanced capabilities of 1-2-3. If you have mastered data management, you are a true "power user," and you probably are already using 1-2-3 macros. If not, be sure to continue your learning—Chapter 14 presents the creation and use of keyboard macros, and Chapter 15 introduces you to the powerful Lotus Command Language.

14

Using Macros To Customize Your Spreadsheet

In addition to all of the capabilities available from the commands in 1-2-3's main menu, two other features make 1-2-3 the most powerful and popular integrated spreadsheet, graphics, and database program available today. Using 1-2-3's macros and Command Language, you can automate and customize 1-2-3 for your particular applications. First, you can reduce multiple keystrokes to a two-keystroke operation with 1-2-3 macros: Press two keys, and 1-2-3 does the rest, whether you're formatting a range, creating a graph, or printing a spreadsheet. Second, you can control and customize worksheet applications with 1-2-3's powerful Command Language.

You can best think of macros as the building blocks for Command Language programs. When you begin to add commands from the Command Language to simple keystroke macros, you can control and automate many of the actions required to build, modify, and update 1-2-3 models. At its most sophisticated level, 1-2-3's Command Language can be used as a full-fledged programming language for developing custom business applications.

This chapter introduces the concept of macros; explains how to create, use, and debug macros; and provides numerous examples which you can copy for your own applications. In the next chapter, you will be introduced to the Command Language, learn the functions and applications of its commands, and learn how to create Command Language programs.

What Is a Macro?

Before releasing 1-2-3 to the general public in 1983, Lotus decided to describe macros as *typing alternatives*. This name was later de-emphasized in favor of the term *macros*. In its most basic form, a macro is simply a collection of keystrokes. These keystrokes can be commands or simple text and numeric entries. Macros provide an alternative to typing data and commands from the keyboard—hence the name "typing alternative."

By creating a simple macro, for example, you can automate the sequence of seven keystrokes necessary for formatting a cell in Currency format—you can execute the seven keystrokes by pressing two keys.

The Elements of Macros

A macro is nothing more than a specially named *text cell*. All macros are created by entering the keystrokes (or representatives of those strokes) to be stored into a worksheet cell. For example, suppose that you want to create the very simple typing alternative macro which will format the current cell to appear in the currency format with no decimal places. The macro would look like this:

    '/rfcØ~~

You enter this macro into the worksheet in exactly the same way that you would any other label: by typing a label prefix, followed by the characters in the label. The label prefix informs 1-2-3 that what follows should be treated as a label. If this prefix were not used, 1-2-3 would automatically interpret the next character, /, as a command to be executed immediately instead of stored in the cell. Any of the three 1-2-3 label prefixes (', ", or ^) would work equally well. (We chose ' because we're used to seeing labels aligned at the left edge of the cells.)

All macros that begin with a nontext character (/, \, +, -, or any number) must be started with a label prefix. Otherwise 1-2-3 will interpret the characters that follow as numbers or commands.

The next four characters represent the command used to create the desired format. After all, /rfc is simply shorthand for /**R**ange **F**ormat **C**urrency. The Ø ("zero") informs 1-2-3 that we want no digits to be displayed to the right of the decimal. If you were entering this command from the keyboard, you would type the *0* in response to a prompt. In the macro, the Ø is simply assumed by 1-2-3.

At the end of the macro are two characters called *tildes*. When used in a macro, the tilde (~) represents the Enter key. In this case, the two tildes signal that the Enter key should be pressed twice. Think about this for a moment. If you were entering this command from the keyboard, you would have to press Enter twice: after supplying the 0 for the number of decimals, and again to signal that the format applied to the current cell. If you have your 1-2-3 program handy, try this procedure to see what we mean.

1-2-3 also uses symbols other than the ~ to stand for keystrokes. For example, look at the following macro:

```
'/rfc0~.{END}{RIGHT}~
```

This macro is similar to the one we just looked at, except that the command here causes the cursor to move. This command can be used to format an entire row instead of just one cell.

Once again, notice the ' at the beginning of the macro and the ~ symbol at the end. Notice also the phrase {END}{RIGHT} in the macro. The {END} in this phrase stands for the End key on the keyboard. The {RIGHT} represents the right-arrow key. This phrase has the same effect in the macro as these two keys would have if they were typed in sequence from the keyboard. The cursor would move to the next boundary between blank and nonblank cells in the row.

Symbols like these are used to represent all of the special keys on the IBM PC and PS/2 keyboards. In every case, the name of the function key (that is, RIGHT for the right arrow, or CALC for function key F9) is enclosed in braces. For example, {UP} represents the up-arrow key, the symbol {END} stands for the End key, and {GRAPH} represents the F10 graph key. Release 2 also uses braces to enclose the Command Language. The Command Language is discussed in the next chapter. If you enclose in braces a phrase that is not a key name or a command keyword, 1-2-3 will return the error message

```
Unrecognized key Range name{...}(A1)
```

where {...} represents the invalid key name and (A1) says the error occurred in cell A1.

Table 14.1 shows the complete list of special key representations.

Function Key Grammar

To specify more than one use of a special key, you can include repetition factors inside the braces of a special-key phrase. For example, you can use the following statements:

Reminder:
You can include a repetition factor within cursor-movement keywords.

| {PGUP 3} | Press the PgUp key three times in a row. |
| {RIGHT JUMP} | Press the right-arrow key the number of times indicated by the value in the cell called JUMP |

Table 14.1
Special Key Representations in Macros

Function Keys	Action
{EDIT}	Edits contents of current cell (same as F2)
{NAME}	Displays list of range names in the current worksheet (same as F3)
{ABS}	Converts relative reference to absolute (same as F4)
{GOTO}	Jumps cursor to cell coordinates (same as F5)
{WINDOW}	Moves the cursor to the other side of a split screen (same as F6)
{QUERY}	Repeats most recent query operation (same as F7)
{TABLE}	Repeats most recent table operation (same as F8)
{CALC}	Recalculates worksheet (same as F9)
{GRAPH}	Redraws current graph (same as F10)

Cursor-Movement Keys

{UP}	Moves cursor up one row
{DOWN}	Moves cursor down one row
{LEFT}	Moves cursor left one column
{RIGHT}	Moves cursor right one column
{BIGLEFT}	Moves cursor left one screen
{BIGRIGHT}	Moves cursor right one screen
{PGUP}	Moves cursor up 20 rows
{PGDN}	Moves cursor down 20 rows
{HOME}	Moves cursor to cell A1
{END}	Used with {UP}, {DOWN}, {LEFT}, or {RIGHT} to move cursor to next boundary between blank and nonblank cells in the indicated direction. Used with {HOME} to move cursor to lower right corner of the defined worksheet.

Function Keys	*Action*

Editing Keys

{DELETE} or {DEL}	Used with {EDIT} to delete a single character from a cell definition
{INSERT}	Toggles the editor between insert and overtype modes
{ESCAPE} or {ESC}	Esc key
{BACKSPACE} or {BS}	Backspace key

Special Keys

~	Enter key
{~}	Causes tilde to appear as ~
{{} and {}}	Causes braces to appear as { and }

Creating, Using, and Debugging Macros

The best macros are simple macros. Most users are better off using macros to automate simple, repetitive tasks. If you want to create a sophisticated program with 1-2-3, do what you would normally do before writing a program in any other language: plan it carefully and be prepared to spend time documenting and debugging your macros.

When you start to use macros in your worksheets, keep several considerations in mind. Developing a macro involves careful planning. You begin by defining which actions you want that macro to perform; then you determine the sequence of keystrokes necessary to accomplish those actions.

After planning your macro, you face the problem of where to put it; you'll want your macros out of the way, but easily accessible from your main work area. You'll want to document your macro when you enter it so that you'll still understand what it does if, after three months, you decide to change it. After entering a macro, you need to name it so that you can execute it. And, if you're like us, your macro probably won't work right the first time and will need "debugging." The following sections of this chapter deal with these considerations.

Planning Your Macro

Reminder:
Step through the series of actions you want a macro to perform before you start creating it.

As discussed previously, a macro can be thought of as a substitute for keyboard commands. Because a macro is a substitute for keystrokes, the best way to plan a macro is to step through the series of instructions you intend to include in the macro from the keyboard, one keystroke at a time. Do this before you start creating the macro. Take notes about each step as you go, and then translate the keystrokes that you've written down into a macro that conforms to the syntax rules.

The keystroke approach usually works well for simple macros. Stepping through an operation at the keyboard is an easy way to build simple macros.

For more complex macros, the best approach is to break a large macro into smaller macros that execute in series. Each small macro performs one simple operation; the series of simple operations together perform the desired application.

This approach starts with an application's results. What is the application supposed to do or to produce? What form must the results take? If you start with the desired results and work backward, you lower the risk of producing the wrong results with your application.

Next, consider input. What data is needed? What data is available, and in what form? How much work is involved in going from the data to the results?

Finally, look at the process. How do you analyze available data and, using 1-2-3, produce the desired results? How can necessary calculations be divided into a series of tasks, each of which a simple macro can perform?

This "divide and conquer" method of breaking a complex task into simpler pieces is the key to successful development of complex worksheets, whether or not they include macros. Although this method entails initial work, as you analyze and plan your macros, less work is required by the time your application functions properly.

Where To Put the Macro

Caution:
Locate your macros in a worksheet area outside your main model.

In most cases, you will want to place your macros outside the area that will be occupied by your main model. This will help to keep you from accidentally overwriting or erasing part of a macro as you create your model.

Depending on how much space you want to leave on your worksheet for applications, you can reserve either the topmost rows of the worksheet or a few columns to the right of the area where you build most applications.

We frequently put macros in column AA in our models. We selected this column for several reasons. First, because our models rarely require more than 26 columns, we don't have to worry about overwriting the macros area with the model. Second, column AA is close enough to the origin that the macros area can easily be reached with the Tab key.

There is no rule that says you must place your macros in the same place in every model. In models that you'll use more than once, you'll want to place the macros wherever it is most convenient. In small models, you may want to put your macros in column I, which lies just off the home screen when all of the columns have a width of 9.

We typically apply the range name MACROS to the area of our sheet that contains the macros. This allows us to get at the macros quickly with the GOTO command and the range name MACROS.

Experienced 1-2-3 users should note that, because Lotus has reworked the way that 1-2-3 uses memory, placing your macros outside the basic rectangle which contains your model no longer consumes large amounts of memory. However, placing macros outside the normal rectangle will cause the End-Home key sequence to place the cursor at the right corner of the overall spreadsheet, including the macro area, instead of at the lower right corner of the model. This makes the End-Home key sequence less useful.

Documenting Your Macros

Professional programmers usually write programs that are *self-documented*, or *internally documented*. This means that the program contains comments which help to explain each step in it. In BASIC, these comments are in REM (for REMark) statements. For example, in the following program, the REM statements explain the action taken by the other statements.

```
10 REM This program adds two numbers
20 REM Enter first number
30 INPUT A
40 REM Enter second number
50 INPUT B
60 REM Add numbers together
70 CAB
80 REM Display Result
90 Print C
```

It is also possible to document your 1-2-3 macros. The best way to do this is to place the comments next to the macro steps in the column to the right of the macro. For example, in the simple macro in figure 14.1, the macro name is in column AA, the macro itself is in column AB, and the comments are in column AC.

Fig. 14.1

A suggested macro layout.

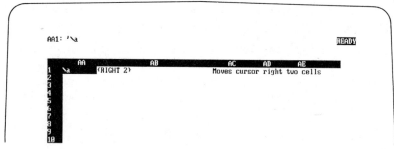

Cue:

Documenting your macros makes debugging and modifying them easier.

Including comments in your macros will make them far easier to use. Comments are especially useful when you have created complex macros that are important to the overall design of the worksheet. Suppose that you have created a complex macro but have not looked at it for a month. Then you decide that you want to modify the macro. Without built-in comments, you might have a difficult time remembering what each step of the macro does.

Naming Macros

A macro that has been entered in the worksheet as a label (or a series of labels) must be given a name. Ranges containing macros are assigned names just like every other range. The only difference is that the name you assign to a macro which you will invoke directly from the keyboard must meet certain special conditions: it must be only one character, it must be an alphabetic character (or 0), and it must be preceded by a backslash (\ ).

You can assign any legal range name to a macro that will be either used only as a subroutine or called with a BRANCH statement from another macro. Table 14.2 shows several macro names that can be invoked from the keyboard, and others that can be invoked only by other macros.

For example, suppose that you had just built the macro shown in figure 14.2.

Now you need to name this macro so that you can invoke it from the keyboard. Although you could give the macro any one-letter name, it is always a good idea to choose a name that in some way describes the macro. Obviously, it is difficult to create descriptive one-letter names. In this case, for example,

Table 14.2
Invoking Macro Names

Invoked from Keyboard	Invoked Only from Macros
\a	\ABC
\b	ABC
\0	\?
	\1

Fig. 14.2

Naming a macro.

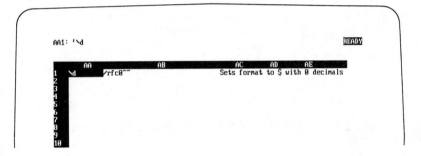

you could choose the name \d (for dollar) or \f (for format). Probably the best name for this macro would be \$, but because the symbol $ is not a letter, \$ is not a legal macro name.

Suppose that we decided to name the macro \d. To assign the name, we would issue the command /Range Name Create. Next, we would type the name we had selected—\d—and press the Enter key. Finally, 1-2-3 would prompt us for the range to name. If the cursor were currently on cell AB1, we could simply press Enter to assign the name to the cell. Otherwise, we would move the cursor to the desired cell or type the cell coordinates from the keyboard.

Some macros require more than one row in the spreadsheet. For example, look at the simple two-row macro in figure 14.3.

To name this macro, we need to assign a name to only the first cell in the range that contains the macro. In this case, we would assign the name \c to cell AB1. There is no reason, however, why a name cannot be assigned to the entire range AB1..AB2.

1-2-3's /Range Name command is remarkably flexible. For example, one cell can be part of several different named ranges.

Fig. 14.3

A simple two-row macro.

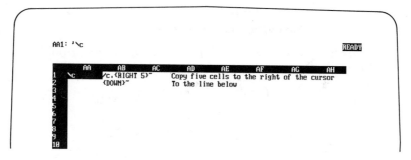

There is another variation on the /Range Name Labels command that can be very useful when you want to name a macro. The **Right** option of this command (found in the /Range Name Labels menu) allows you to name a range, using the contents of the cell immediately to its left. For example, suppose that you had created the macro in figure 14.4.

Fig. 14.4

Naming a macro with /Range Name Labels.

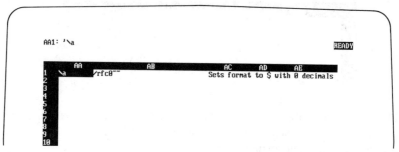

With your cell pointer on cell AA1, you can name your macro by using the /Range Name Labels Right command, which would assign the name \a to the range AB1.

The /Range Name Labels command can be used in a variety of ways. If you are documenting your macros properly, you will already have the names in the sheet; therefore, using the Labels option is a simple and convenient way to name the macros.

If you import macros from an external library file, you can use the Labels command to create quickly names for the imported macros. In fact, one of the macros in this chapter automatically imports a worksheet file and names all of the macros in the file.

Executing Macros

All macros except those named \0 (which are executed automatically when their file is retrieved) are executed, or invoked, by pressing the Alt key and at the same time pressing the letter name of the macro. For example, if the macro we wanted to use were named \a, we would invoke it by pressing Alt-a. The \ symbol in the name is a representation of the Alt key.

As soon as the command is issued, the macro starts to run. If there are no bugs or special instructions built into the macro, it will continue to run until it is finished. You will be amazed at its speed. The commands are issued faster than you can see them.

Many macro keystrokes or commands can be stored in a single cell. Some that are especially long or include special commands must be split into two or more cells, like the example shown in figure 14.3. This is no problem. When 1-2-3 starts executing a macro, the program continues in the first cell until all the keystrokes stored there are used. 1-2-3 then moves down one cell to continue execution. If the cell below is blank, the program stops. If that cell contains more macro commands, however, 1-2-3 will continue reading down the column until it reaches the first blank cell.

Automatic Macros

As mentioned earlier, 1-2-3 offers an exciting macro feature called *automatic macro execution*. This technique allows the user to create a special macro that will execute automatically when the sheet is loaded. This macro is created just like any other macro. The only difference is in its name. The macro that you want to execute automatically must have the name \0 ("backslash zero").

Reminder:
Macros named \0 are executed automatically when their file is retrieved.

An even more powerful feature of 1-2-3 is its ability to load a model automatically into the 1-2-3 worksheet. When 1-2-3 loads, it automatically searches the current disk drive for a special worksheet file named AUTO123.WK1. If this file is on the disk, 1-2-3 will automatically load it into the worksheet. If the file contains a macro named \0, the macro will automatically execute.

You can use these features of 1-2-3 to create completely self-contained programs in the 1-2-3 worksheet. Pressing the Alt key is not required to start the macro in this case. When combined with menus and the other useful macro commands, the automatic execution feature makes macros a remarkably user-friendly tool.

Note one thing about the automatic macro: it cannot be executed by the Alt-0 key combination. If you need to be able to execute the macro from the keyboard, however, there is no reason why the macro you've named \0 could

Cue:
*To invoke a \0
macro manually,
name the macro
with \ and a letter
in addition to
naming it \0.*

not also have another name, such as \a. One macro then becomes, in effect, two: one that executes automatically, and one that can be executed from the keyboard.

There can be only one automatic macro in each worksheet. This macro can be as large as you want, however, and can include as many steps as you wish. It can also include subroutine calls that access other macros in the sheet.

Common Errors

Like all computer programs, macros are literal creatures. They have no ability to discern an error in the code. For example, you will recognize immediately that {GOTI} is a misspelling of {GOTO}. But a macro cannot do this. It will try to interpret the misspelled word and, being unable to, will deliver an error message.

Caution:
*Misplaced spaces
and tildes (~) will
cause problems
when running your
macro.*

This means that you must be extremely careful when you build your macros so that they have no errors. Even misplaced spaces and tildes can cause difficulty for 1-2-3. No matter how careful you are, however, some errors are going to slip through.

The biggest problem most beginners have with macros is forgetting to represent all of the required Enter keystrokes in the macros. This can lead to some dismaying results. For example, the missing ~ after the {RIGHT 5} in the macro in figure 14.5 will cause the {DOWN} command to be included in the definition of the FROM range of the /Copy command, instead of defining the TO range. The result of running this macro is shown in figure 14.6. As you can see, the /Copy command in the macro stopped in the middle of its execution because of the missing keystroke (tilde).

Caution:
*Cell references in
macros do not
change when
changes are made
in the worksheet.*

Another big problem with 1-2-3 macros is that the cell references included in macros are always absolute. They do not change when, for example, cells are moved about or deleted from the sheet. For example, this simple macro erases the contents of cell A6:

        '/re~A6~

Fig. 14.5

*A macro with a
missing ~.*

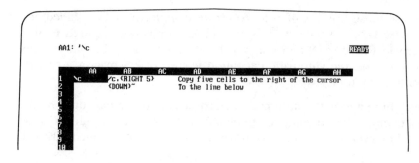

```
AA1: '\c                                                                READY

         AA      AB        AC       AD        AE      AF      AG      AH
      1  \c      /c.{RIGHT 5}        Copy five cells to the right of the cursor
      2          {DOWN}~             To the line below
      3
      4
      5
      6
      7
      8
      9
     10
```

Fig. 14.6

The result of running the macro with the missing ~.

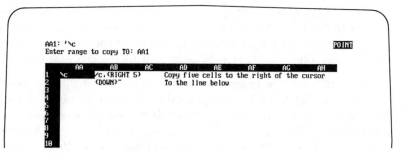

But suppose that we move the contents of the macro so that it now lies one cell to the right. This would be done by pressing the /Move command, pressing Enter, pressing the right-arrow key, and pressing Enter once more. Because we still want to blank the same contents from the sheet, we might expect our macro to say

    '/re~B6~

If you try this example, however, you will see that the macro has *not* changed.

If you think about it for a second, this makes perfect sense. A macro is nothing but a label. You wouldn't expect other labels to change when the sheet is changed. For example, if you created the label

    'A15A15A15A15

you wouldn't expect it to change to

    'C15C15C15C15

if you inserted two columns in the sheet to the left of column A. Macros are no different.

The absolute nature of cell references within macros is a strong argument in favor of using range names. Because a range name remains associated with the same range even if the range is moved, range names within macros (and other formulas) will follow the cells to which they apply, eliminating the kind of problem we saw above.

Cue:
Use range names rather than cell references to avoid reference problems in macros.

Debugging a Macro

Almost no program works perfectly the first time. In nearly every case, there are errors that will cause the program to malfunction. Programmers call these problems *bugs* and the process of eliminating them *debugging the program.*

Like programs written in other programming languages, 1-2-3 macros usually need to be debugged before they can be used. 1-2-3 has an extremely useful

Reminder:
1-2-3's STEP mode (Alt-F2) allows you to run a macro one step at a time.

tool that helps make debugging much simpler: the Step function. When 1-2-3 is in STEP mode, all macros are executed one step at a time. 1-2-3 literally pauses between each keystroke stored in the macro. This means that the user can follow along step by step with the macro as it executes.

Let's step through the buggy macro we developed in the previous section. The macro in figure 14.5 was supposed to copy the contents of five cells to the next line. If we attempted to run this macro, we would see the screen in figure 14.6. There is no indication in figure 14.6 that the line below has been included in the FROM range. All you know is that the macro ends with the program waiting for you to specify the TO range.

Once an error is discovered, you must first get out of the macro and into READY mode by pressing Esc one or more times. When the mode indicator says READY, you can start debugging the macro.

If we assume that we don't know what the problem is with the macro, our next step is to enter STEP mode and rerun the macro. To invoke the single-step mode, press Alt-F2. When you do this, the mode indicator will change to the message STEP. This message will change to SST as soon as you execute the Alt-C macro. In execution after the command, the macro will move forward only one step at a time. After each step, the macro will pause and wait for you to type any keystroke before going on. Although any key can be used, we prefer using the space bar to step through a macro.

As you step through the macro, which was executed with the cursor in cell AA5, you will see each command appear in the control panel. In our example, just before the error occurs, the control panel would look like that in figure 14.7.

Fig. 14.7

The macro does not perform as was intended.

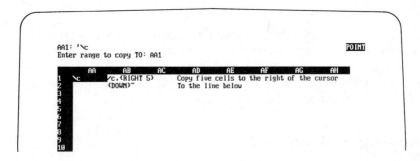

Thanks to single-step mode, when the error occurs, it is easy to pinpoint the location in the macro. Once the error is identified, you can exit STEP mode by pressing Alt-F2 again. Then abort the macro by pressing Esc one or more times.

Editing the Macro

You are now ready to repair the error. Fixing an error in a macro is as simple as editing the cell that contains the erroneous code. You don't need to rewrite the cell. You need only to change the element in error.

In our example, we would first move the cursor to cell AB1, then press F2 to enter EDIT mode. Because the error is a missing ~, fixing the macro is easy. Just type ~ and press Enter to exit from EDIT mode.

Although editing complex macros can be tougher than editing a simple one like this one, the concept is exactly the same. Just use 1-2-3's cell editor (F2) to correct the cell that contains the error.

Creating Simple Macros

Now that you have been introduced to the elements of macros and to some of the considerations in using macros, it's time for you to create some simple but useful macros of your own. The following examples provide simple typing alternative macros. In the next chapter, you'll learn how to use the macro command language to go beyond the simple typing alternative. The macros discussed here are useful in various situations and can significantly enhance your productivity as a 1-2-3 user.

Examples of Macros

The 1-2-3 novice may want to avoid macros until he or she is fairly comfortable with 1-2-3 in general. But you do not need to know everything about 1-2-3 before you begin to use macros. This section contains a number of macros that you can use right away.

If you have experience with BASIC or another programming language, the macros will be easier to learn and use. But even the advanced programmer will find some obstacles with 1-2-3's macros. First, macros can be difficult to debug. However, the single-step feature that allows the macro to be executed one step at a time helps to alleviate this problem.

A Macro To Format a Range

One of the macros that we have already created makes an excellent open-ended macro. The "typing alternative" macro to format the cell as currency,

```
'/rfc0~~
```

can be converted to an open-ended macro by removing the second tilde from the end of the macro,

`'/rfcØ~`

This macro works precisely like its closed brother, except that here the macro does not complete the formatting command. Instead, it ends, leaving the command open and waiting for a range to be provided. You would enter the range from the keyboard and then press Enter.

This feature can be very useful. For example, in many worksheets, you want some cells formatted as dollars and others as integers. In one case, you may have only one cell to format. In another, you want to format a whole row. This macro can be used in either situation. For example, if you want to format only one cell, you can place the cursor on the cell to be formatted and execute the macro. When the macro is finished, you can press Enter to complete the command. This applies the format to the current cell. On the other hand, if you want to format an entire row, you can use the arrow keys to POINT to the range to be formatted after the macro is completed.

Open-ended macros frequently specify every part of the command except the range to which the command applies. The range is provided from the keyboard.

In effect, the open-ended macro allows you to apply a format or a command to any range of the sheet. Many of the /**R**ange commands can be simplified by condensing them into open-ended macros.

A Macro To Erase a Range

For an example of how to simplify a /**R**ange command with an open-ended macro, consider the following:

`'/re`

This macro starts the /**R**ange **E**rase command but stops prior to assigning the range for the command. The range is supplied from the keyboard. This macro becomes a quick way to erase any portion of the worksheet.

A Simple Pointing Macro

Cue:
*Use pointing
macros to create
formulas.*

One of the most useful types of macros is a pointing macro. For example,

`'+{RIGHT 3}+{DOWN 2}`

inserts in the current cell a formula that is equal to the cell three cells to the right plus two cells below. If we start in cell C17, the formula would be

`+F17+C19`

Notice that this macro includes nothing but mathematical symbols and cursor-key representations.

Entering Text with Macros

Although normally you enter the Macro utility from 1-2-3's READY mode, you can invoke a macro also from MENU mode or while you are entering a label or formula into the sheet. These alternatives allow you to create macros that enter commonly used phrases into the worksheet. For example, suppose that the word "expense" will occur a number of times in a given sheet. The word will sometimes occur by itself or in combination with other words, as in "sales" expense and "office expense."

You can create a macro that enters the word "expense" in the current cell. The macro would look like this:

Cue:
Create a macro to enter words used frequently in your spreadsheets.

   ' expense

Notice that an extra space appears at the beginning of the macro. This space separates the word "expense" from any other word in the cell when the macro is invoked. You will notice also that this is an open-ended macro. Other words can be appended in the cell after "expense."

Suppose that you are defining cell A55 as containing the label "expense—miscellaneous". First, invoke the macro to enter the label "expense" into the cell. Next, simply complete the phrase from the keyboard. The completed cell will look like this:

   ' expense—miscellaneous

Press Enter to close out the cell. To enter the label "Telephone expense (Local)", type *Telephone*, execute the macro, and follow the macro with "(Local)" before pressing Enter.

This kind of macro can save time when you set up a large worksheet. You should create a number of "common word" macros to use when you want to enter labels throughout the sheet.

A Macro To Create Headers

The simple macro in figure 14.8 can be used to create a row of column headers in the worksheet. Each cell contains the abbreviation of the name of a month.

Essentially, this macro scrolls across a row, inserting the name of one month in each cell before moving on. Notice the use of {RIGHT} to stand for the right-arrow key ($\rightarrow$).

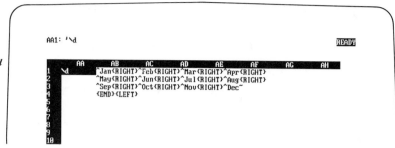

Fig. 14.8

A macro for entering abbreviated months as centered column heads.

A Macro To Date the Worksheet

Thanks to 1-2-3's built-in date functions, you can date your worksheets with the @NOW function. The obvious way to date a sheet is to enter the @NOW function in an appropriate cell. But there is a problem with dating a worksheet this way. When the sheet is reloaded into memory after being saved, the program will automatically recalculate, changing the date before you view it and defeating the purpose of dating the sheet in the first place.

There is a macro solution to this problem. The simple macro in figure 14.9 automatically dates the sheet and ensures that the current date remains in the sheet.

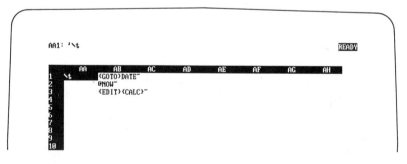

Fig. 14.9

A macro that enters the system date in a cell with the range name DATE.

This macro assumes that the range name DATE has been assigned to a single cell somewhere in the sheet. The macro goes to the range with the name DATE and inserts the value of @NOW there. The cell DATE can be formatted in any way you choose for the best display of the date.

The third line is our old friend, the formula-to-value conversion macro. This line converts the contents of the DATE cell from the @NOW function to the actual numeric value of the @NOW function. This conversion keeps the date from being updated automatically the next time the sheet is loaded.

The one problem with this macro is that it doesn't automatically return you to the point from which you started. Instead, the macro leaves the cursor on the DATE cell. This can be remedied, however, with the use of /rncHERE in a help macro.

A Macro To Name Macros

Although using the /**R**ange **N**ame **L**abel command is a convenient way to name macros, we can speed up the process by creating a macro that automatically names another. This macro condenses the /**R**ange **N**ame command into a single keystroke:

    '/rnlr~

Before you execute this macro, you must move the cursor to the cell that contains the *name* of the macro you want to name. For example, in the worksheet in figure 14.10, you would move the cursor to cell A1 before issuing the command. After the macro is complete, the name \w would be assigned to cell B1.

Fig. 14.10

Using the naming macro.

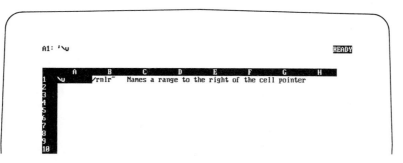

Creating a standard macro area in your worksheet will make the naming macro even simpler to use. For example, suppose that you decide to store your macros always in column AB. This means that the name for the macros will lie in column AA. You could then modify our range-naming macro to look like figure 14.11.

Fig. 14.11

A modified macro-naming macro.

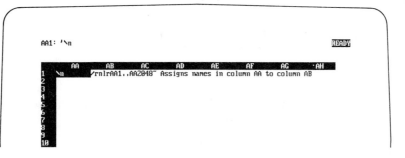

This macro names every cell in column AB with the cell references found in column AA. If you use this macro, however, make sure that there is no "garbage" in column AA, but only true macro names. Otherwise, the wrong names will be assigned to the macros in column AB.

Printing with a Macro

Cue:

Save time by automating worksheet printing with a macro.

Macros can be used to automate complex tasks that are repeated frequently. Printing a large worksheet is such a task. There are several steps involved in readying the worksheet for printing: specifying the print range; aligning the paper in the printer; and specifying such options as borders, headers, footers, and margins. Although the design of a printing macro will vary from application to application, the sample model in figure 14.12 demonstrates many of the ways a macro can help with this task.

Fig. 14.12

A basic print macro.

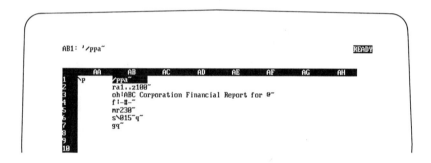

This macro looks complex, but it is really very simple. The first line invokes the 1-2-3 **/Print Printer Align** command, which informs 1-2-3 about the location of the top of form. The second line supplies the range for the print job. This range can be predetermined and entered in the macro or can be specified at execution time with a {?} command (for example, r{?}~).

The next lines assign values to the 1-2-3 print options. Line three inserts a centered title (including the current date) in the report. Line four adds a footer that supplies the page number. The next command sets the right margin to 230, and the following line instructs the printer (in this case an Epson FX-100™) to print in a compressed mode. The q~ command makes the macro step up one level in the print menu so that the g~ (GO) command in the next line can be issued. The final q~ returns 1-2-3 to READY mode after the report is printed.

Note that this macro cannot be used for every model, but you can create a macro like it to print your frequently used reports.

Creating a Macro Library

Once you have become comfortable with macros and have developed a few that you find yourself using repeatedly, you will want to develop what we call a *macro library*. A macro library is a worksheet that contains several macros. It typically also includes the name labels associated with each macro and any internal documentation you have written.

If you decide to create a macro library, you will need the simple macro shown in figure 14.14. This macro loads into memory a set of macros that you have on disk and names each macro in the set. For example, suppose that you have a macro library which contains the following macros:

```
\a    /rfc0~~
\b    /re.
```

and that this library is stored on disk in a worksheet file called LIBRARY.WK1. Now suppose that you are creating a new model and want to include the library in the model. The macro in figure 14.13 will do the trick.

Fig. 14.13

A macro for loading a macro library.

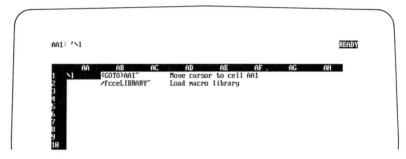

This macro performs two operations. First, it moves the cursor to cell AA1; then it loads the file LIBRARY.WK1. The macros will be loaded into cells AA1 and AA3.

We can now combine this macro with the one in figure 14.11 to create the macro shown in figure 14.14.

Fig. 14.14

A macro for loading and naming a macro library.

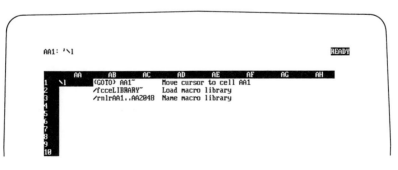

This macro will load and name the macro library. (Although columns AA and AB are used here, you can use any range you want to store your macros.)

Going Beyond Typing-Alternative Macros

As this chapter explains, the simplest macros are typing-alternative macros. After you master creating and using these macros, you can move beyond these simple keystroke macros to more sophisticated ones containing commands from the Lotus Command Language. The Command Language tremendously expands the power of simple keystroke macros by allowing you to link macros, call macros as subroutines, design menus and prompts, and perform a wide variety of other tasks.

Chapter 15 provides a detailed explanation of the Command Language, but to help you begin to understand how the Command Language enhances 1-2-3 macros, consider the sample macro that follows.

Suppose, for example, that you have created in column A a column of row headers that is similar to figure 14.15, and that you later decide to indent each label one character. Indenting a single label is not difficult. You simply edit the cell by pressing the F2 key, moving the cursor to the far left of the cell by pressing the Home key, positioning the cursor one character to the right by pressing →, and then typing a space. Finally, you press Enter to end the edit. Repeating this process 20 times, however, can be tedious.

Fig. 14.15

A column of row headers.

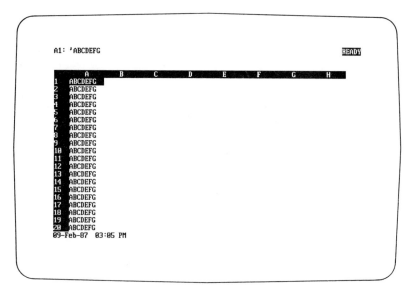

To automate this process, you can create a macro that contains the sequence of keystrokes for indenting and also uses one of the commands from 1-2-3's Command Language (see fig. 14.16). The first two lines of the macro are simply keystroke selections, but the third line includes the command BRANCH. This command causes the macro to loop, and the sequence of keystrokes will repeat nonstop. When you run the macro, it will automatically indent the entire column of heads (see fig. 14.17).

Fig. 14.16

A macro for inserting a space in a column of row headers.

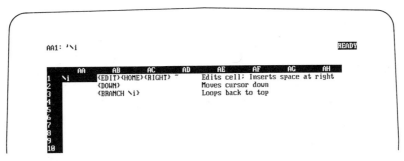

Fig. 14.17

Row headers after running the macro.

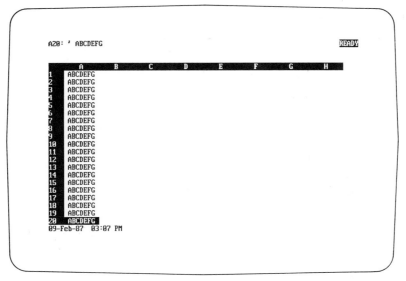

More specifically, here's what each element in the macro does: After you press Alt-i, the macro begins by invoking EDIT mode and then moving the cursor to the first space in the cell. Line two of the macro moves the cursor down one row.

The statement in line three tells the macro to continue processing at the cell named \i. If you remember that this macro is named \i, you'll realize that line three is telling the macro to start over again. This kind of device is called a *loop* in programming jargon. This loop will cause the program to continue running until you stop it manually.

Once all the labels are indented, you stop the macro. The simplest way to do this is to press Ctrl-Break. The Ctrl-Break keys can always be used to stop a macro.

This macro points out another valuable use for macros: *editing* the worksheet. At times, we have created complex macros that added and deleted rows or columns throughout the worksheet. Editing macros are most useful when the editing task must be performed repeatedly. In this case, try to create a macro that will perform the job automatically.

Creating and Using HAL Macros

Hal macros are similar to macros you build directly in 1-2-3 because both are a series of labels entered in cells down a column. HAL macros, however, are much easier to create and debug because they use plain English phrases as command lines rather than using special representations for command sequences, function keys, cursor keys, etc. Consider, for example, the difference between the standard 1-2-3 macro and HAL macro for formatting a range as currency shown in figure 14.18.

Fig. 14.18

A standard 1-2-3 macro and a HAL macro for formatting a range.

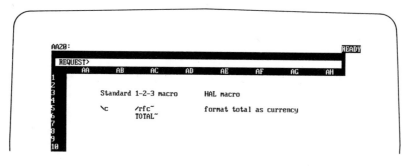

The 1-2-3 macro on the left uses the conventions necessary for all standard 1-2-3 macros: single keystroke representations for command sequences (/rfc), special symbol to represent ENTER (~), and special macro name (\c). The HAL macro, on the other hand, is the English language command for performing the range format operation. Another difference between HAL macros and standard 1-2-3 macros is that HAL macros do not need to be named to execute them.

To run a HAL macro, you can simply indicate the cell address. Rather than having to name the macro with the backslash and a letter as you do with standard 1-2-3 macros, HAL macros are invoked by typing one of HAL's accepted words for running a macro (run, do, execute) and the cell address of the macro.

To run the HAL macro in figure 14.18, you first access the HAL prompt line by pressing the backslash (\ ) and then type

> run ae5

Figure 14.19 shows the HAL prompt line with this command.

Fig. 14.19

*Running a HAL
macro from the
prompt line.*

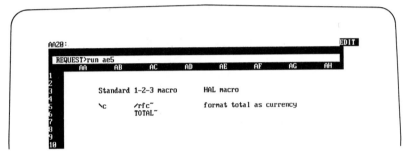

Even though you don't need to use a special macro name like \c for HAL macros, these macros can use regular 1-2-3 range names. Range names are, in fact, easier to remember. If you named cell AE5 in figure 14.19 with the range name FORMAT, you could invoke the HAL macro by entering *run format* in the HAL prompt line. It's especially easier to use a single range name with a HAL macro that goes beyond one cell than trying to remember the whole range for the macro.

HAL macros are easier to create and debug than standard 1-2-3 macros. Suppose that you want to create a HAL macro that will date the worksheet at the end of a session, will format the cell containing the date, calc the worksheet, and save the worksheet file. Creating a HAL macro to perform these operations involves first finding an area in the worksheet that won't interfere with your spreadsheet or database applications. Next, you type each operation as a separate English language command.

*Cue:
HAL macros are
easier to create
and debug than
standard 1-2-3
macros.*

As shown in figure 14.20, you enter each line in successive rows down a single column. Note that the first line tells HAL to enter today's date in A1. The second line directs HAL to format the cell in date format. To make sure the date is displayed, the third line widens the column width. The worksheet is finally calculated and saved through the HAL commands in the fourth and fifth lines.

To name your HAL macro, access the HAL prompt line and type the command

> name ab2..ab6 date

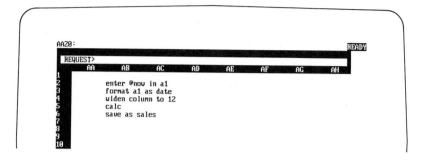

As soon as the macro is named, you run it by accessing the HAL prompt line
and entering *run date*. The result of the macro is shown in figure 14.21.

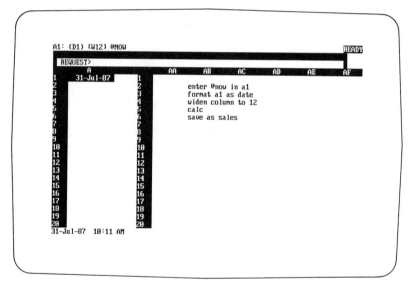

Debugging a HAL macro is much easier than debugging 1-2-3 macros. If HAL
cannot interpret one of your command lines, the macro stops, and the cursor
automatically moves to the cell containing the error. As shown in figure 14.22,
HAL displays a message as soon as it comes upon an error or a command
that it can't interpret.

When you press RETURN, you can then easily edit the cell by using the F2
edit key or typing over the existing text.

Overall, HAL macros provide numerous benefits beyond the capabilities of
standard 1-2-3 macros, although there can be a noticeable difference in how
quickly HAL macros are executed versus standard 1-2-3 macros. As illustrated

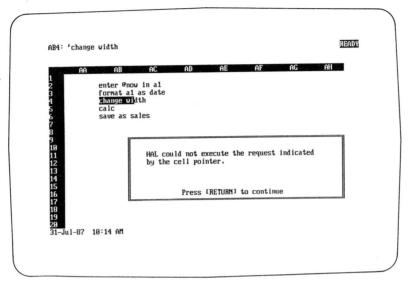

Fig. 14.22

The HAL message for macro errors or commands that HAL can't interpret.

```
AB4: 'change width                                              READY

      AA      AB      AC      AD      AE      AF      AG      AH
1
2             enter @now in a1
3             format a1 as date
4             change width
5             calc
6             save as sales
7
8
9
10                ┌──────────────────────────────────────────┐
11                │ HAL could not execute the request indicated│
12                │ by the cell pointer.                       │
13                │                                            │
14                │                                            │
15                │          Press [RETURN] to continue        │
16                └──────────────────────────────────────────┘
17
18
19
20
31-Jul-87  10:14 AM
```

above, HAL macros are easier to create and debug because they use the same vocabulary that can be used for any HAL command. HAL macros can take advantage of functions that are available in HAL but not in 1-2-3. You can, for example, create "what if" macro applications that use HAL's Undo feature, not available in 1-2-3. If you're currently using HAL but haven't investigated its macro capabilities, try taking advantage of this capability.

Chapter Summary

By establishing the habit of creating macros for your most frequent 1-2-3 tasks, you'll save time and increase efficiency. Think of the operations you perform most often, jot down the series of keystrokes needed to complete each operation, and begin your own macro library. As you become experienced in creating and using keystroke macros, begin experimenting with the Command Language. Turn to Chapter 15 and learn about 1-2-3's Command Language.

15

Introduction to the Command Language

In addition to 1-2-3's keyboard macro capabilities, the program contains a powerful set of commands offering many features of a full-featured programming language. This set of commands, which includes the original Release 1A /x commands plus 41 other commands, is called 1-2-3's Command Language. With the Command Language, you can customize and automate 1-2-3 for your worksheet applications.

In the preceding chapter, you learned how to automate keystrokes to save precious time by streamlining work functions. This chapter explains the various Command Language commands you can use to perform a variety of programming tasks. This chapter is not designed to teach programming theory and concepts, but rather to introduce you to the capabilities of programming with the Command Language.

If you have a burning desire to try your hand at programming, or you want to become your company's 1-2-3 expert (creating models to amaze every department), or if you are interested in developing template models to distribute on the open market, you should begin by reading this chapter.

Why Use the Command Language?

Programs created with the Command Language give you added control and flexibility in the use of your 1-2-3 worksheets. With the Command Language, you control such tasks as accepting input from the keyboard during a program, performing conditional tests, repeatedly performing a sequence of commands, and creating user-defined command menus.

You can use the Command Language as a full-featured programming language to develop custom worksheets for specific business applications. For example, by developing Command Language programs that teach users exactly how to enter and change data on a worksheet, you can ensure that data is entered correctly. With this type of program, novice users of an application will not have to be familiar with all 1-2-3 commands and operations.

There's nothing mysterious about using the Command Language. After learning the concepts and the parts of the Command Language discussed in this chapter, you'll be ready to develop programs that

- Create menu-driven spreadsheet/database models
- Accept and control input from a user
- Manipulate data within and between files
- Execute tasks a predetermined number of times
- Control program flow
- Set up and print multiple reports
- Make intelligent decisions based on user input
- Execute multiple programs based on decisions made within programs

As you become more experienced with the Command Language, you'll be able to take advantage of its full power to

- Disengage or redefine the function keys
- Develop a complete business system—from order entry to inventory control to accounting
- Operate 1-2-3 as a disk-based database system—limiting the size and speed of the file operation only to those of the hard disk

If you want to take 1-2-3 to its practical limits, the Command Language is the proper vehicle and your creativity can be the necessary fuel.

What Is the Command Language?

The 1-2-3 Command Language is a set of over 40 invisible commands. These commands are called *invisible* because, unlike the command instructions that are invoked through the 1-2-3 menu and function keys, the Command Language's commands cannot be invoked from the keyboard. These commands can be used only within Command Language programs.

The program in figure 15.1 illustrates how you can use the Command Language. With commands such as MENUBRANCH and BRANCH, you can create custom menus to assist and prompt the user. The program in figure 15.1 begins by creating a range name wherever the user has positioned the cell pointer prior to invoking the program. The second line continues by displaying a custom help screen. The third line uses the MENUBRANCH command to display a menu with three options: to select the next help screen, to select the previous help screen, or to return to the original cell-pointer position in the worksheet. The BRANCH command in the last line of the first two options causes the program to redisplay the menu after the user has selected either the next or the previous help screen.

Fig. 15.1

Command Language program using MENUBRANCH and BRANCH.

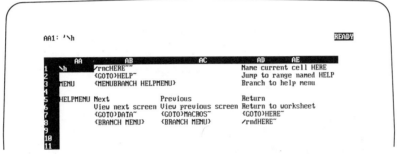

As you read this chapter, you will learn about the commands for accepting input (see table 15.1); for program control (see table 15.2); for decision-making operations (see table 15.3); for data manipulation (see table 15.4); for program enhancement (see table 15.6); and for file manipulation (see table 15.7).

1-2-3's /x Commands

In addition to the Command Language's more than 40 commands, 1-2-3 includes a set of eight /x commands. These commands were included in the original 1-2-3 Release 1A to provide a "limited" programming capability that went beyond simple keystroke macros. All eight /x commands have Command Language counterparts. The eight /x commands and their Command Language counterparts include:

/x Command	Description	Command Language Alternative
/xi	If-then-else command	IF
/xq	Command for quitting execution	QUIT

/x Command	Description	Command Language Alternative
/xg	Command for instructing the program to continue	BRANCH
/xc	Command for accessing a subroutine	{name}
/xr	Command for processing on the next line following the /xc in the calling program	RETURN
/xm	Command for creating menus	MENUBRANCH
/xn	Input command accepting only numeric entries	GETNUMBER*
/xl	Input command accepting only labels	GETLABEL*

* See the discussion that follows of the differences between /xn and GETNUMBER and between /xl and GETLABEL.

Six of these commands work exactly like their Command Language counterparts. For example, /xq performs exactly like the Command Language's QUIT. When inserted into a program, both commands will produce the same result. Other commands that function like their Command Language counterparts include /xi, /xg, /xc, /xr, and /xm.

The remaining /x commands (/xn and /xl) work a little differently than their comparable Command Language commands. These commands are used to prompt the user for text and numeric data and then place the data in the current cell. Before their Command Language counterparts (GETLABEL and GETNUMBER) will be able to do the same tasks, some tricky programming is required. /xn, unlike GETNUMBER, will not allow users to enter characters (except range names and cell addresses), nor will /xn let the user simply press Enter in response to the prompt.

Except in the special instances in which /xn and /xl perform differently from their Command Language counterparts, the /x commands should not be used in new programs developed in Release 2. /x commands are beneficial, however, because they enable you to run and easily modify in Release 2 programs originally developed in Release 1A.

The Elements of Command Language Programs

The commands discussed in this chapter are used most often with the keyboard macros discussed in Chapter 14. In the examples that follow, you will see how to use macros with the Command Language commands to produce complete, efficient programs that take 1-2-3's macro capability far beyond simply automating keystrokes.

Command Language programs contain the Command Language commands and all the elements that can be included in macros. Programs can include

1. Keystrokes used for selecting 1-2-3 commands (for example, /rfc0).

2. Range names and cell addresses.

3. Keywords for moving the cell pointer (see Chapter 14 for a list of keywords).

4. Keywords for function keys (see Chapter 14).

5. Keywords for editing (see Chapter 14).

6. Key representation for Enter: ~

7. Command Language commands.

Command Language Syntax

Like the keywords used in macros (discussed in Chapter 14), all commands in the Command Language are enclosed in braces. Just as you must represent the right-arrow key in a macro as {RIGHT}, you must enclose a command such as QUIT in braces, such as

{QUIT}

Many commands, however, require additional arguments within the boundaries of the braces. The arguments that follow commands have a grammar similar to the grammar used in 1-2-3 @functions. The general format of commands that require arguments is

{COMMAND argument1,argument2,. . . ,argumentN}

An argument can consist of numbers, strings, cell addresses, range names, formulas, and functions.

The commands and arguments are separated by a space and, for most commands, arguments are separated by commas (with no spaces). As you study the syntax for the specific commands described in this chapter, keep in mind the importance of following the conventions for spacing and punctuation. For example, when you use the BRANCH command to transfer program control to a specific location in the program, you must follow the word *BRANCH* with the cell address or range name indicating where the program should branch.

Creating, Using, and Debugging
Command Language Programs

With Command Language programs, as with macros, you must keep several considerations in mind to ensure that your programs are efficient and error-free. You begin by defining which actions you want the program to perform and determining the sequence of actions. Then you develop the program, test it, and, if necessary, debug it.

If you have created keyboard macros, you have a head start toward creating Command Language programs. These programs share many of the conventions used in the keyboard macros presented in Chapter 14. If you haven't experimented with 1-2-3 macros, we recommend that you begin with simple keystroke macros before you try to develop Command Language programs. We recommend also that you review Chapter 14's detailed discussions of creating, using, and debugging macros because many of the concepts are related to Command Language programs. For readers who have created macros and read Chapter 14, the following paragraphs contain a brief overview.

Like keyboard macros, Command Language programs should be carefully planned and positioned on the worksheet. As recommended in Chapter 14, reserve for the programs either the topmost rows of your worksheet or a few columns to the right of the area in which you enter most applications.

You enter Command Language programs just as you enter macros—as text cells. You must start with a label prefix any line that begins with a nontext character (such as /, \, (, +, -) so that 1-2-3 will not interpret the characters that follow as numbers or commands.

After you have decided where to locate your program and have begun to enter program lines, keep several considerations in mind.

First, remember to document your Command Language programs as you would document macros—to the right of each program line. Because Command Language programs are usually more complex than macros, documenting each line is essential. A documented program is easier to debug and change than an undocumented one.

Second, remember that Command Language programs must be named in the same way that macros are named. Names must begin with the backslash (\) and be followed by a single letter; for example, \a is an acceptable name for a Command Language program. If you want the program to be invoked automatically as soon as you open the worksheet file, use a two-character name that begins with a backslash (\), followed by 0 (zero). (For additional information about names, see Chapter 14's "Automatic Macros" section.) Enter the program name in the cell directly to the left of the program's first line. Use 1-2-3's /**R**ange **N**ame command to name your Command Language program. (The "Macro To Name Macros" described in Chapter 14 provides an easy way to name your programs.)

All programs except those named with \0 are invoked by pressing and holding the Alt key while pressing the appropriate letter key. If you want to start an automatic program from the keyboard, give it a another name in addition to \0.

After you have developed and started to run your program, you may need to debug it. Like macros, Command Language programs are subject to such problems as missing tildes (~), misspelled keywords, or the use of cell addresses that remain absolute in the program but have changed in a worksheet application. You can solve the cell-address problem by using range names in place of cell addresses wherever possible.

To debug Command Language programs, you use 1-2-3's STEP mode as you would for simple keyboard macros. Before you execute the program, press Alt-F2 to invoke STEP mode. Then execute your Command Language program. Press any key or the space bar to activate each operation in the program. When you discover the error, press Alt-F2 to turn off STEP mode, press Esc, and edit your program.

The Command Language

Using the power of the program's Command Language, you can make 1-2-3 applications easier to use; you can enhance the features of 1-2-3's regular commands; and you can customize 1-2-3 for special worksheet applications. In the following sections, the Command Language commands are grouped into six categories: accepting input, decision-making operations, data manipulation, program enhancement, and file manipulation.

Commands for Accepting Input

The {?}, GET, GETLABEL, GETNUMBER, and LOOK commands provide for all possible types of input into a 1-2-3 file (see table 15.1). These commands can be used also to provide the operator with a more user-friendly interface than that of 1-2-3's standard commands and operations. For example, you can use these commands to create prompts that help the user enter data more easily and quickly. These commands also make it easy to perform simple edit checks on the input before storing it in the spreadsheet.

Table 15.1
Commands for Accepting Input

Command	Description
{?}	Accepts any type of input
{GET}	Accepts a single character into <location>
{GETLABEL}	Accepts a label into <location>
{GETNUMBER}	Accepts a number into <location>
{LOOK}	Places first character from type-ahead buffer into <location>

The {?} Command

The {?} command causes the program to pause while you enter any type of information. During the pause, no prompt will be displayed in the control panel; you can move the cell pointer, thus directing the location of the input. The program will continue executing after you press the Enter key. The format for the {?} command is

   {?}   Accepts any type of input

For example, the following one-line program combines macro commands and a Command Language command to create a file-retrieve program:

   /fr{Name}{?}~

This program displays all files in the current drive, and then pauses to accept input from the user. In this instance, you can either type the name of a viewed file or simply move the cell pointer to a file name and press Enter.

The GET Command

The GET command places a single keystroke into a target cell. The keystroke can then be analyzed or tested in a number of ways, and the results of these tests can be used to determine the flow of the program. The format for the GET command is

{GET location}   Accepts single keystroke into range defined by
                        <location>

In the example shown in figure 15.2, the GET statement traps individual keystrokes in a cell named CAPTURE. Line two evaluates CAPTURE. If the keystroke in CAPTURE is the letter Q, the file is saved automatically. If CAPTURE contains any other keystroke, /fs~r is ignored. In either case, control is passed to line three of the program, which places the cell pointer in cell F25.

Fig. 15.2

*Using the GET
command to trap
keystrokes.*

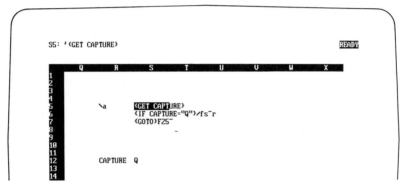

A more involved use of GET is shown in figure 15.3. Suppose that you are writing an inventory program and want to prompt the user to make a one-keystroke choice to enter data on premium- or regular-quality widgets. Figure 15.3 shows the program you might use in such an application.

Fig. 15.3

*Using the GET
command to allow
one-character
input.*

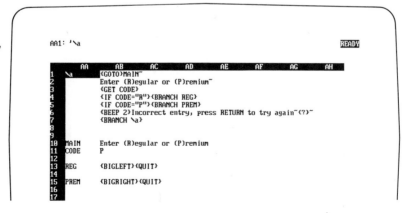

In this example, the GET command is used to pause the program while the user enters a single letter from the keyboard and to store that entry in a cell named CODE. Notice that the program enters the user-prompt in the cell named MAIN. If you want a prompt to appear in the control panel rather than in the spreadsheet, you must use the GETLABEL or GETNUMBER commands.

The GETLABEL Command

The GETLABEL command accepts any type of entry from the keyboard. The prompt (which must be a string enclosed in quotation marks) is then displayed in the control panel. With this command, the entry will be placed in the target cell as a label when the user presses the Enter key. The format for the GETLABEL command is

{GETLABEL prompt,location}   Accepts label into <location>

In the example in figure 15.4, the GETLABEL statement displays a prompt and accepts a label date into cell R19. Line two places in cell R20 a formula that converts the label date to a numerical date and then formats the cell to appear as a date.

Fig. 15.4

Using the GETLABEL command to allow input of a label date.

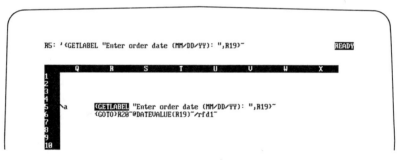

Figure 15.5 shows how to use GETLABEL with the IF, BRANCH, and BEEP commands (discussed later in this chapter) to prompt the user for a part description.

Fig. 15.5

Using the GETLABEL command with other commands for more complex string input.

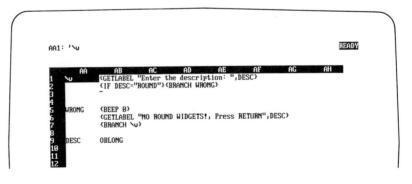

You can add a second GETLABEL command to this program so that if you make an incorrect entry, an error message will display and the program will pause until you press any key. Remember, however, that whatever you enter in response to the prompt will be stored in DESC.

GETLABEL versus /xl

Both forms of this command are identical except for one /xl command feature. If you write the /xl command as

/xlprompt~~

the label entered in response to the prompt will be placed at the cell pointer's current location. You cannot do this with the GETLABEL command because 1-2-3 will give you an error message if there is no location argument. Using the /xl command is much more convenient than using the GETLABEL command, for example, in a subroutine in which the location of the destination cell changes with each subroutine call. By using /xl in such a situation, you don't have to specify the location at which the label will be placed.

The GETNUMBER Command

The GETNUMBER command accepts only numerical entries. The prompt (which must be a string enclosed in quotation marks) is displayed in the control panel, and the entry is placed in the cell when you press Enter. The format for the GETNUMBER command is

{GETNUMBER prompt,location}~   Accepts the number into <location>

In the example in figure 15.6, the GETNUMBER statement displays a prompt and accepts a numerical entry into cell S10. Line two then copies that numerical entry into the next available row in column A (the @COUNT function finds the next open row in column A).

Fig. 15.6

Using the GETNUMBER command for numerical input.

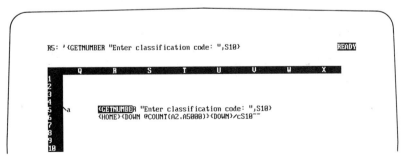

Figure 15.7 shows how GETNUMBER can be used in an inventory program. Here GETNUMBER prompts the user for a part number. If the user does not enter a number between 0 and 9999, the program displays the message INVALID PART NUMBER! press Return and the user is prompted to enter another number.

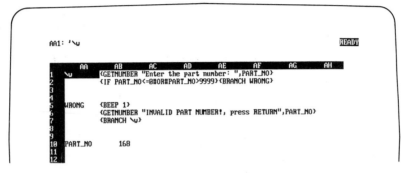

Fig. 15.7

GETNUMBER used in an inventory application.

GETNUMBER versus /xn

The GETNUMBER and /xn commands work differently. With GETNUMBER, a blank entry or a text entry has a numeric value of 0. With /xn, however, if the entry is a blank or a text entry, an error message occurs, and the user is again prompted for a number. This difference can be very useful in some applications. If, for example, you accidentally press *Q* (a letter) instead of the *1* key, the /xn command will return an error message. The /xn command can be used also in the form

   /xnprompt~

to read a numeric value into the current cell instead of into a specified location. (See the discussion at the end of the GETLABEL section.)

The LOOK Command

The LOOK command checks 1-2-3's type-ahead buffer. If any keys have been pressed since the program execution began, the first keystroke will be placed in the target cell location. The LOOK command frequently is used to interrupt processing until you press a key. The general form of the command is

   {LOOK location}   Places first character from type-ahead buffer into
                                      <location>

When the LOOK command is executed, the keyboard type-ahead buffer is checked, and the first character is copied into the indicated location. This means that you can type a character at any time and the program will find it when the LOOK command is executed. The contents of location can then be tested with an IF statement. Because the character is not removed from the type-ahead buffer, you must make provisions to use it or dispose of it before the program needs keyboard input or ends.

In the program in figure 15.8, the LOOK statement examines 1-2-3's type-ahead buffer and places the first keystroke in the cell named CAPTURE. If no keys have been pressed, the LOOK statement blanks the cell, leaving only a label prefix. Although program execution is not halted by this statement, lines two and three of the sample program force the program to pause. Line three forms a looping structure until a key is pressed, satisfying the IF condition in line two. This is the most common use of the LOOK statement. (For more information, see the IF and BRANCH commands.)

Fig. 15.8

Use of the LOOK command.

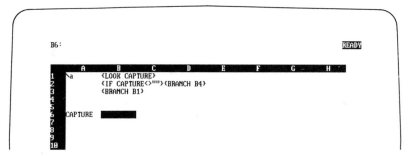

As a simple test of the LOOK command, try the example in figure 15.9. This program causes the speaker to beep until you press any key. Each time the LOOK command is encountered, 1-2-3 checks the keyboard buffer and copies into location INTERRUPT the first character found. Then an IF statement checks the contents of INTERRUPT and branches accordingly. The GETLABEL command at the end serves to dispose of the keystroke that interrupted the loop.

Fig. 15.9

Using the LOOK command to stop a beeping program.

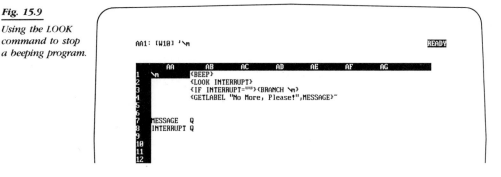

The LOOK command is more helpful when you have built a lengthy program to process, such as a stock-portfolio database, and you want to be able to stop processing at certain points in the program. You can enter a LOOK command, followed by an IF statement similar to that in figure 15.9, at several places in the program. Then, if you press a key, the program stops the next time a LOOK is executed. If you do not touch the keyboard, the program continues processing. In this example, the LOOK command is preferable to the GET command, which always stops the program to wait for an entry.

Commands for Program Control

The commands shown in table 15.2 (BRANCH, MENUBRANCH, MENUCALL, RETURN, QUIT, ONERROR, BREAKOFF, BREAKON, WAIT, DISPATCH, DE-FINE, and RESTART) allow varying degrees of control in 1-2-3 programs. These commands, used alone or in combination with decision-making commands, afford the programmer extremely specific control of program flow.

Table 15.2
Commands for Program Control

Command	Description
{BRANCH}	Program continues at <location>
{MENUBRANCH}	Prompts user with menu found at <location>
{MENUCALL}	Like MENUBRANCH except that control returns to the statement after the MENUCALL
{RETURN}	Returns from a program subroutine
{QUIT}	Ends program execution
{ONERROR}	Traps errors, passing control to <branch>
{BREAKON}	Enables {BREAK} key
{BREAKOFF}	Disables {BREAK} key
{WAIT}	Waits until specified time
{DISPATCH}	Branches indirectly via <location>
{DEFINE}	Specifies cells for subroutine arguments
{RESTART}	Cancels a subroutine

The BRANCH Command

The BRANCH command causes program control to pass unconditionally to the cell address indicated in the BRANCH statement. The program begins reading commands and statements at the cell location indicated in <location>. Program control does not return to the line from which it was passed unless directed to do so by another BRANCH statement. The general format of the BRANCH command is

> {BRANCH location}   Continue program execution in cell
>   specified by <location>

In the example in figure 15.10, line one places the cell pointer in cell R34 and then enters an @COUNT function. Line two passes program control to cell F13, regardless of any commands that may follow the BRANCH command (in either the same cell location or the cell below). Program commands are read beginning in cell F13.

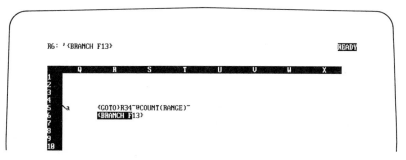

Fig. 15.10

Using the BRANCH command to pass program control to cell F13.

BRANCH is an unconditional command unless it is preceded by an IF conditional statement, as in the example that follows (the IF statement must be in the same cell to act as a conditional testing statement). For more information, see the IF command.

> {IF C22="alpha"}{BRANCH G24}
> {GOTO}S101~

Suppose, for example, that three separate companies are under your corporate umbrella, and that you have written a program for adding and modifying records in a corporate personnel database. Depending on how the user of the program responds to the Enter Company (R, A, or C): prompt, you want the program to branch to a different place in the program and prompt the user further for data specific to that company. Figure 15.11 shows a portion of the program.

The BRANCH statements in the \m program cause the flow of program execution to shift to the different company routines. In this example, the

Fig. 15.11

Using BRANCH in a database application.

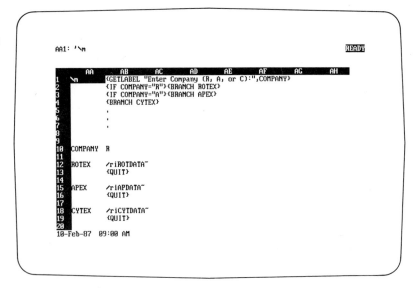

```
AA1: '\m                                                          READY

          AA        AB        AC        AD        AE        AF        AG        AH
1    \m       {GETLABEL "Enter Company (R, A, or C):",COMPANY}
2             {IF COMPANY="R"}{BRANCH ROTEX}
3             {IF COMPANY="A"}{BRANCH APEX}
4             {BRANCH CYTEX}
5                       .
6                       .
7                       .
8
9
10   COMPANY   R
11
12   ROTEX     /riROTDATA~
13             {QUIT}
14
15   APEX      /riAPDATA~
16             {QUIT}
17
18   CYTEX     /riCYTDATA~
19             {QUIT}
20
10-Feb-87   09:00 AM
```

BRANCH statements are coupled with IF statements to shift execution conditionally, depending on the user's response. After the program executes a company routine, the QUIT statement at the end of the routine causes program execution to stop.

You may prefer that execution return to the \m program or to another program after completing the company routine. This can be done in one of two ways: (1) you can replace the {QUIT} statements at the end of subroutines with {BRANCH \m} statements to return to \m; or (2) you can replace the BRANCH statements in \m with subroutine calls (discussed later in this chapter); then, in the subroutine you can include a BRANCH to the point where execution should continue.

You need to remember two important points about BRANCH statements. First, they cause a permanent shift in the flow of statement execution (unless you use another BRANCH statement). Second, BRANCH statements are most often used in combination with IF statements.

The MENUBRANCH Command

The MENUBRANCH command defines and displays in the control panel a menu-selection structure from which as many as eight individual programs may be initiated. You select the desired menu item as you would make a selection from a 1-2-3 command menu. The form of the MENUBRANCH command is

{MENUBRANCH location}   Executes menu structure at <location>

The menu invoked by the MENUBRANCH command consists of one to eight consecutive columns in the worksheet. Each column corresponds to one item in the menu. The upper left corner of the range named in a MENUBRANCH statement must refer to the first menu item; otherwise, you will receive the error message Invalid use of Menu macro command.

Each menu item consists of three or more rows in the same column. The first row is the menu option name. Try to keep the option name items short so that they will all fit on the top line of the control panel. If the length of the option name exceeds 80 characters, 1-2-3 will display the error message Invalid use of Menu macro command.

Be careful to choose option names that begin with different letters. If two or more options begin with the same letter and you try to use the first-letter technique to access an option, 1-2-3 will select the first option it finds with the letter you specified.

The second row in the menu range contains descriptions of the menu items. The description is displayed in the bottom row of the control panel when the cell pointer highlights the name of the corresponding menu option. Each description may contain up to 80 characters of text. The description row must be present, even if it is blank.

The third row begins the actual program command sequence. Once the individual programs have been executed, program control must be directed by statements at the end of each individual program.

No empty columns can exist between menu items; the column immediately to the right of the last menu item must be empty. You can supplement the 1-2-3 menu structure by creating a full-screen menu (for enhancement purposes only).

In figure 15.12, the MENUBRANCH statement produces a menu structure that begins in cell AB4. The individual programs begin in row 6 in each cell. Each of these programs must contain a statement to continue once the main task has been completed. For example, suppose that you are using the corporate personnel database and that you have entered the program shown in figure 15.12.

When the MENUBRANCH statement is executed, 1-2-3 displays in the control panel the menu beginning at the cell ROTEX_MENU. (Note: The /**R**ange **N**ame **L**abel **R**ight command was used to assign the name ROTEX_MENU to the cell in which the label Production resides. Production is the first menu item.)

You can select the desired menu item either by moving the cell pointer with the arrow keys or by pressing the first letter of the menu item. The bottom line of the control panel contains a description of the menu item currently

Fig. 15.12

Program using the MENUBRANCH command.

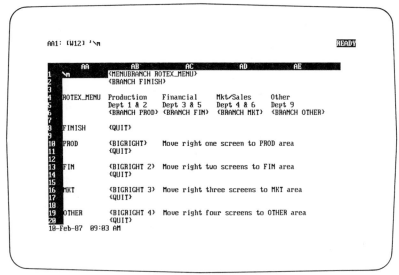

highlighted by the user. For instance, when you move the cell pointer to Financial, the capsule description Dept 3 & 5 appears.

Now suppose that you want to select the second menu item (Financial). You select it the same way you do any 1-2-3 menu item, by pressing Enter after you've positioned the cell pointer on your choice, or by entering the first letter of the menu item. The menus that you create with the MENU-BRANCH command are just like the 1-2-3 command menus.

After you've selected Financial from the menu, the next statement to be executed is {BRANCH FIN}. If, instead of selecting a menu item, you press the Esc key, 1-2-3 stops displaying the menu items and executes the next program command after the MENUBRANCH command, {BRANCH FINISH}.

Modeling Tip: If you have a multilevel menu structure, you can make the Esc key function as it does in the 1-2-3 command menus (backing up to the previous menu). After the current MENUBRANCH command, place a BRANCH to the previous level's MENUBRANCH. When you press the Esc key, this BRANCH will back you up to the previous menu.

The MENUCALL Command

The MENUCALL command is identical to the MENUBRANCH command except that 1-2-3 executes the menu program as a subroutine. Once the individual menu programs have been executed, program control returns to the cell immediately below the cell containing the MENUCALL statement. The format of the MENUCALL command is

{MENUCALL location}   Like MENUBRANCH except MENUCALL
                        acts as a subroutine

Suppose that you replace the MENUBRANCH command in figure 15.12 with a MENUCALL. The results are shown in figure 15.13.

Fig. 15.13

Use of the MENUCALL command in place of MENUBRANCH.

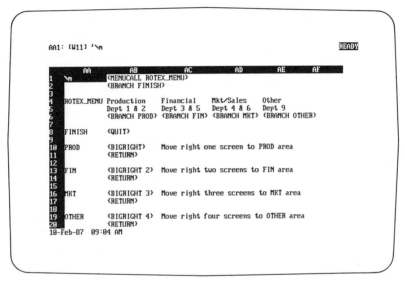

When you use a MENUCALL, 1-2-3 returns to the statement immediately following the MENUCALL whenever it reads a blank cell or a {RETURN}. For example, suppose that you select the Financial menu option, which causes 1-2-3 to branch to FIN. The first statement in FIN moves the cell pointer over two screens. When 1-2-3 encounters the RETURN statement, though, the flow of execution shifts back to the statement following the MENUCALL, the {BRANCH FINISH} statement.

Keep in mind that pressing Esc has the same effect with MENUCALL as it does with MENUBRANCH. Execution shifts to the statement following the MENUCALL statement. You can use only the technique described in the MENUBRANCH command modeling tip (using the Esc key) if this is also what you want to do when the MENUCALL command finishes executing.

The advantage of MENUCALL is that you can call the same menu from several different places in a program and continue execution from the calling point after the MENUCALL is finished. This is the advantage you get from using subroutines in general.

Subroutines {name}

The MENUCALL statement should give you some feel for calling sub-routines. However, quite a bit more can be involved in calling standard (nonmenu) subroutines.

A subroutine is an independent program that can be run from within the main program. Calling a subroutine is as easy as enclosing the name of a routine in braces ({SUB}). When 1-2-3 encounters a name in braces, the program passes control to the named routine. Then, when the routine is finished (when 1-2-3 encounters a blank cell or a {RETURN}), program control passes back to the command in the cell below the cell that called the subroutine.

Why use subroutines? You can duplicate a simple subroutine by using two BRANCH commands. But by using a subroutine, you can execute the subroutine from any number of locations within the main program.

The RETURN Command

The RETURN command indicates the end of subroutine execution and returns program control to the cell immediately below the cell that called the sub-routine. When 1-2-3 reads the RETURN, it returns to the main program (or other subroutine) at the location after the subroutine call. Do not confuse RETURN with QUIT, which ends the program completely. RETURN can be used with the IF statement to return conditionally from a subroutine. The form of this command is

{RETURN}   Returns control from a subroutine

In figure 15.14, line one places the cell pointer in AA101 and then calls the subroutine {SUB}. After {SUB} is executed, the RETURN command passes control to the next command after the subroutine call, placing the cell pointer in the HOME position and then copying the range of cells entered by the subroutine into the range identified by the HOME position as its upper left corner.

1-2-3 also ends a subroutine and returns to the calling routine when the program encounters, while executing the subroutine, a cell that either is blank or contains a numeric value. Although this method of returning from a sub-routine works, the RETURN command is preferred because it documents the fact that a particular set of macro keywords and command language instructions is intended to be a subroutine.

Fig. 15.14

Using the RETURN command.

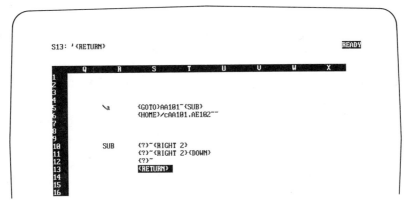

The QUIT Command

The QUIT command forces the program to terminate unconditionally. Even without a QUIT command, the program will terminate if it encounters (within the program sequence) a cell that is empty or contains an entry other than a string. However, it is good practice to always put a QUIT statement at the end of your programs to indicate that you intend execution to stop. (Conversely, do not put a QUIT command at the end of a program that you intend to call as a subroutine.) The form of the QUIT command is

{QUIT}   Halts program execution

In the following example, the QUIT command forces the program sequence to terminate unconditionally:

{HOME}/fs~r {QUIT}

This is not the case when QUIT is preceded by an IF conditional testing statement (see fig. 15.15).

Fig. 15.15

Using the QUIT command with an IF statement.

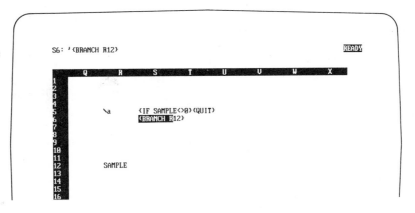

The ONERROR Command

The processing of Command Language programs is normally interrupted if a system error (such as Disk drive not ready) occurs during execution. By sidestepping system errors that would normally cause program termination, the ONERROR command allows programs to proceed. The general format of the command is

{ONERROR branch,[message]}   Traps errors, program control passes
                                          to <branch>

The ONERROR command passes program control to the cell indicated by the first argument; any errors can be recorded in the message cell (the second argument).

As a general rule, you should always make sure that your ONERROR statement is executed by the program before an error takes place. Therefore, you may want to include an ONERROR statement near the start of your programs. Because you can have only one ONERROR statement in effect at a time, you should take special precautions to write your programs so that the right message appears for each error condition.

In figure 15.16, the ONERROR statement acts as a safeguard against leaving drive A empty or not closing the drive door. If an error occurs, program control will pass to S10 and the error message in V10 will be displayed. Because S10 is the file-save sequence, this program will not continue until drive A contains a disk and the drive door has been closed.

The best place to put an ONERROR statement is directly above where you think an error may occur. For example, suppose that your program is about to copy a portion of the current spreadsheet to a disk file, using the /File Xtract command. A system error will occur if the drive is not ready or the disk is full. Therefore, you should include a strategically placed ONERROR command (see fig. 15.17).

In this example, the ONERROR statement will cause the program to branch to a cell called BAD_DRV if an error occurs. A copy of the error message that 1-2-3 issues is entered in a cell called BAD_DRV_MSG. (This argument is optional.) Then, the first statement in the BAD_DRV routine positions the cell pointer to an out-of-the-way cell (cleverly called OUT_OF_WAY_CELL). Next, the message Disk drive is not ready is entered in the spreadsheet, followed by Prepare drive and press Return to continue. The program pauses for the user to press Return (Enter). Finally, the program branches back to \p to try again.

Ctrl-Break presents a special problem for the ONERROR statement. Because Ctrl-Break actually causes an error condition, the ONERROR statement is auto-

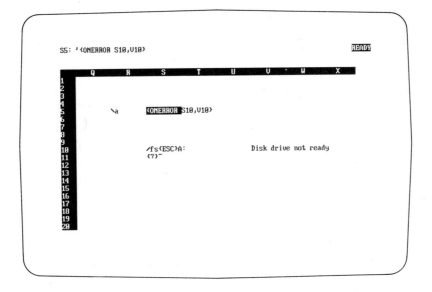

Fig. 15.16

Using the ONERROR command to prompt users to close the drive door.

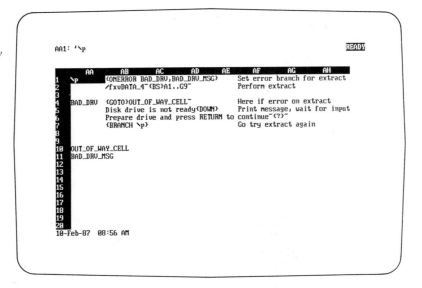

Fig. 15.17

Using an ONERROR statement to retry disk access.

matically invoked. Therefore, a good technique when you plan to use the ONERROR statement is to disable Ctrl-Break after you have debugged your program. (See the following discussion of the BREAKOFF command.) By disabling Ctrl-Break, you can prevent the confusion that might arise with an untimely error message.

The BREAKOFF Command

The easiest way to stop a program is to issue a Ctrl-Break command. However, 1-2-3 can eliminate the effect of a Ctrl-Break while a program is executing. By including a BREAKOFF command in your program, you can prevent the user from stopping the program before its completion. Note: Before you use a BREAKOFF statement, you must be certain that the program has been fully debugged.

The BREAKOFF command disables the Ctrl-Break command during program execution. The form of the BREAKOFF command is

{BREAKOFF}   Disables Ctrl-Break sequence

Note: When a menu structure is displayed in the control panel, you can halt program execution by pressing Esc, regardless of the presence of a BREAKOFF command.

BREAKOFF is used primarily to prevent the user from interrupting a process and destroying the integrity of data in the spreadsheet. You will not need to use BREAKOFF unless you are developing extremely sophisticated programs; but, in such applications, BREAKOFF can be an important safeguard against user-caused problems.

The BREAKON Command

To restore the effect of Ctrl-Break, use the BREAKON command. The form of this command is

{BREAKON}   Enables Ctrl-Break sequence

You will probably want a simple one-line program that issues a BREAKON, just in case something happens to your original program during execution. You may also want to make sure that the last statement in your program before QUIT is BREAKON.

Because any Ctrl-Break commands in the keyboard buffer will be executed as soon as the BREAKON command is executed, be sure that the BREAKON is at a place where the program can safely stop. Figure 15.18 demonstrates how you can use the BREAKOFF and BREAKON commands.

The WAIT Command

The WAIT command causes the program to pause until an appointed time. The general form of the WAIT command is

{WAIT argument}   Waits until time or time elapsed
                         specified by <argument>

Fig. 15.18

Use of the BREAKON and BREAKOFF commands.

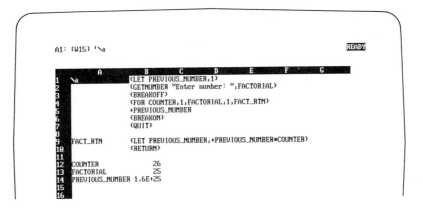

Fig. 15.19

Using the WAIT command to display messages.

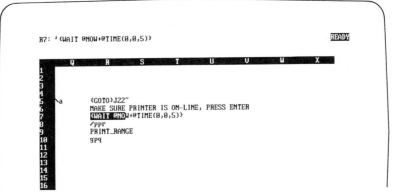

The WAIT statement in figure 15.19 allows the message to be displayed for 5 seconds.

The serial-time-number must contain a date plus a time. If you want the program to wait until 6:00 PM today to continue, you can use the expression {WAIT @INT(@NOW)+@TIME(18,00,00)}. To make the program pause for 50 seconds, use the expression {WAIT @NOW+@TIME(00,00,50)}.

The DISPATCH Command

The DISPATCH command is similar to the BRANCH command. The DISPATCH command, however, branches indirectly to a location specified by the value contained in the location pointed to by the argument. The form of the command is

{DISPATCH location}   Branches indirectly via <location>

The location given as the DISPATCH argument should contain a cell address or range name that is the destination of the DISPATCH. If the cell referred to by location does not contain a valid cell reference or range name, an error occurs and program execution either stops with an error message or transfers to the location in the current ONERROR command.

The location must be a cell reference or range name that points to a single cell reference. If the location is either a multicell range or a range that contains a single cell, the DISPATCH acts like a BRANCH statement and transfers execution directly to location.

In figure 15.20, the DISPATCH statement selects the subroutine to be executed, based on the input in the cell number generated by the GETLABEL statement. The string formula in the DISPATCH command concatenates the word SUB and the menu selection number entered by the user. Because the name of every subroutine begins with the word SUB, the DISPATCH command passes program control to the subroutine specified by the user.

Fig. 15.20

Example of the DISPATCH command.

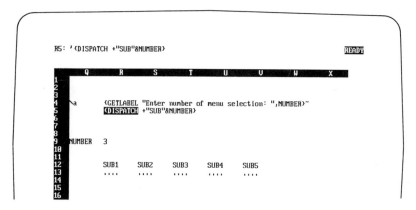

The DEFINE Command

An important subroutine feature of 1-2-3 is the capability of passing arguments, using the keyword version of the subroutine call only. A subroutine called with arguments must begin with a DEFINE statement that associates each argument with a specific cell location. The form of the subroutine call with arguments is

{DEFINE loc1:Type1, . . . }   Specifies cells for subroutine arguments

where loc1, loc2, etc. are names or cell references for the cells in which to place the arguments passed from the main program. One or more arguments, separated by commas, can be used. Type is either STRING or VALUE. Type is optional; if not present, the default is STRING.

If an argument is of type STRING, the text of the corresponding argument in the subroutine call is placed in the indicated cell as a string value (label).

If an argument is of type VALUE, the corresponding argument in the subroutine call is treated as a formula, and its numeric or string value is placed in the argument cell. An error will occur if the corresponding argument in the subroutine call is not a valid number, string, or formula. You do not, however, have to put a string in quotation marks or have a leading + sign in a formula that uses cell references.

Suppose that you have an application where you must repeatedly convert strings to numbers and display the numbers in Currency format. Rather than enter the same code at several different places in the program, you decide to write a subroutine. Figure 15.21 shows how the subroutine might appear.

Fig. 15.21

Example of a subroutine call with parameters.

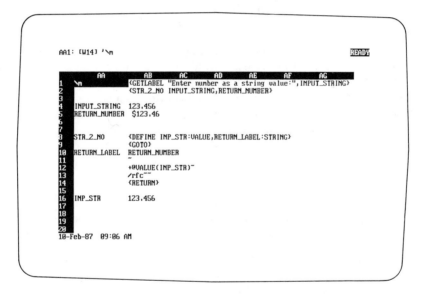

Note that the /**R**ange **N**ame **L**abel **R**ight command has been used to define all the range names in this example.

The first statement in the MAIN part of the program is a GETLABEL statement that reads a string value into the cell named INPUT_STRING. The second statement in the MAIN routine calls a subroutine named STR_2_NO and passes the arguments INPUT_STRING (the name of the cell containing the input string) and RETURN_NUMBER (the name of the cell where the formatted number is to be stored).

The STR_2_NO subroutine begins with a DEFINE statement, which defines where and how the arguments passed to the subroutine from the MAIN part of the program are to be stored. Any subroutine that receives arguments passed from its calling macro must begin with a DEFINE statement.

The DEFINE statement in STR_2_NO specifies two cells, INP_STR and RETURN_LABEL, that will hold the two arguments passed from the caller. Note that if the number of arguments in the subroutine call does not agree with the number of arguments in the DEFINE statement, an error will occur.

The DEFINE statement specifies that the first argument in the subroutine call is to be evaluated and its value placed in INP_STR. Since the first argument is the cell reference INPUT_STRING, the value in cell INPUT_STRING—the string "123.456"—is placed in INP_STR.

The DEFINE statement specifies that the text of the second argument in the subroutine call is to be placed into cell RETURN_LABEL as a string. Because the text of the second argument is RETURN_NUMBER, the string RETURN_NUMBER is placed in cell RETURN_LABEL.

The cell containing the second argument is located in the body of the subroutine. This technique is used to allow the subroutine to return a value to a location designated by the caller. In our example, the location RETURN_NUMBER is passed to the subroutine as a string value. The subroutine uses the passed value as the argument of a {GOTO} statement that places the cell pointer on the output cell. This technique is one of two primary ways to return information to the calling routine. The other way to return information is to place it in a specified cell that is used every time the subroutine is called.

After the subroutine places the cell pointer on the output cell, it continues by converting the string in INP_STR to a number and placing the resulting numeric value in the output cell.

Passing arguments to and from subroutines is important if you want to get the most out of 1-2-3's subroutine capabilities. Subroutines with arguments simplify program coding and make the resulting macros easier to trace. Subroutine arguments are almost essential when you are developing a subroutine to perform a common function that you will use again and again. They are also one of the trickiest parts of the 1-2-3 Command Language commands.

The RESTART Command

Just as you can call subroutines from the main program, you can also call one subroutine from another. In fact, as 1-2-3 moves from one subroutine to the next, the program saves the addresses of where it has been. This technique is called *stacking*, or saving addresses on a stack. By saving the addresses on a stack, 1-2-3 can trace its way back through the subroutine calls to the main program.

If you decide that you don't want 1-2-3 to return by the path it came, you can use the RESTART command to eliminate the stack. In other words, the RESTART command allows a subroutine to be canceled at any time during execution. You will not need to use this command until you are an expert at writing Command Language programs. Once you reach this point, though, this command is very helpful. The RESTART command is normally used with an IF statement under a conditional testing evaluation. The format for this command is

{RESTART}   Cancels a subroutine

Figure 15.22 illustrates how RESTART can be used to prevent a user from omitting data in a database. This example combines the GETLABEL, GET-NUMBER, and BRANCH commands to produce a simple database application for entering product information. GETLABEL and GETNUMBER are used to prompt the user for product data; if the product item number and price are omitted, RESTART prevents the user from continuing to enter new data; in the last line, BRANCH loops to repeat the process for entering a new record.

Fig. 15.22

Using RESTART in a database application.

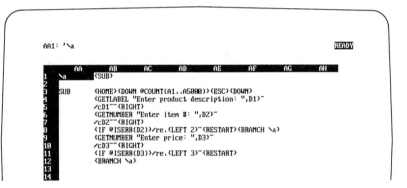

Let's look at the program, line-by-line. The first line simply begins the sub-routine (named SUB) in cell AB3. The subroutine begins by determining exactly where to move the cell pointer in the product database. Notice that @COUNT is used in AB3 to count the number of records in the database. After the cell pointer moves to an empty cell, line AB4 prompts the user for a product description and enters this data in cell D1. The Copy command in AB5 copies the product description to the appropriate cell in the database.

The commands in AB6 through AB11 prompt the user for the product item number and price, copy the data to the appropriate locations in the database, and check that the item number and price have actually been entered. If the data has not been entered, the RESTART command clears the stack, allowing the subroutine to be canceled. AB8 checks to make sure that item numbers are entered. If a user forgets to include a number, the program prompts the user to reenter product information. Cell AB9 checks price data. If price information is omitted, RESTART again clears the stack, allowing the subroutine to be canceled.

Decision-making Commands

The Command Language's decision-making commands, shown in table 15.3, give you the capabilities of true programming languages such as BASIC. With the three commands (IF, FOR, FORBREAK) presented in the following sections, you can test for numeric and string values. The IF command provides the kind of conditional logic available in many high-level languages. FOR and FORBREAK offer a conditional looping capability, allowing you to control how many times a group of commands is activated.

Table 15.3
Decision-making Commands

Command	Description
{IF}	Conditionally executes statements after IF
{FOR}	For Loop Command. Loop count is placed in <counter>
{FORBREAK}	Terminates a {FOR} loop

The IF Command

The IF statement uses IF-THEN-ELSE logic to evaluate the existence of certain numeric and string values. Commonly used to control program flow and enable the program to perform based on criteria provided by the user, the Command Language's IF command is the functional equivalent of the IF command in BASIC. The form of the IF command is

{IF condition}{true}	Executes true or false statements based on
{false}	result of condition

If the logical expression is true, then the remaining commands on the same line are executed. (These commands would ordinarily include a {BRANCH} command to skip the {false} statements.) If the expression is false, execution skips the commands (after the IF command) on the current line and continues on the next line.

As the following examples illustrate, IF statements can check for a variety of conditions including the position of the cell pointer, a specific numeric value, or a specific string value. In figure 15.23, for example, the IF statement checks to see whether the current location of the cell pointer is on row 200. If it is, program control is passed to cell R8, where a QUIT command is executed. If the cell pointer is not on row 200, the cell pointer will move down a row, accept input, then branch back to cell R5, where the IF statement will again check to see whether the cell pointer is located on row 200.

Fig. 15.23

Using IF to check the cell pointer.

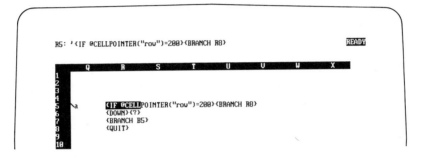

Figure 15.24 illustrates how IF can be used to evaluate a cell's value. The IF statement evaluates the value in cell R18. If cell R18 contains a negative value, the program converts that value to 0, and program execution is halted. If the value in cell R18 is 0 or greater, line two replaces the value in cell R18 with the value representing the equation (R18*.55).

Fig. 15.24

Using IF to evaluate a cell value.

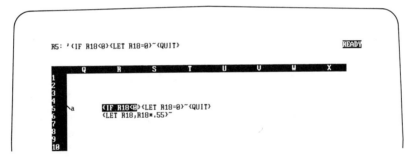

The IF command can also evaluate a string value entered by the user. You can, for example, develop IF statements that complete certain operations depending on whether the user enters *Y* (Yes) or *N* (No).

Suppose, for example, that you want to test the value in a single-cell range called NEW_RECORD. If the value in NEW_RECORD is Y (for Yes), you want to add a new record to a database. Otherwise, you want to modify an existing record in the database. Your program will include the following statements:

```
{IF NEW_RECORD="Y"}{BRANCH NEW_ROUTINE}
{BRANCH MOD_ROUTINE}
```

The first line is contained in a single cell. The part of the cell following the IF portion is called the THEN clause. The THEN clause is executed only if the result ot the logical test is true. In this case, the THEN clause contains the keyword BRANCH, followed by the range name NEW_ROUTINE. (BRANCH is often used with IF.) The program will branch to NEW_ROUTINE if the value of NEW RECORD is equal to Y (or y; the test is not case-sensitive).

The second line contains the ELSE clause, which is executed only if the result of the logical statement in the IF statement is false (because the THEN clause contains a branch to NEW_ROUTINE). If the program statements in the THEN clause do not transfer control, the line below the IF statement (the ELSE clause) will be executed after the statement(s) in the THEN clause. In this example, the ELSE clause also contains a BRANCH statement, but the range to branch to is called MOD_ROUTINE.

The IF statement adds significant strength to 1-2-3's Command Language. However, the one disadvantage of the IF statement is that if you want to execute more than one command after the logical test, the THEN clause must contain a branching statement or a subroutine call. What's more, if the code in the THEN clause does not branch or execute a QUIT command, the program will continue its execution right through the ELSE clause.

The FOR Command

The FOR command is used to control the looping process in a program by calling a subroutine to be executed a certain number of times. FOR enables you to define the exact number of times the subroutine will be executed. The form of the FOR command is

{FOR counter,start,stop,step,routine}   Activates a loop a specific
                                        number of times

The FOR statement contains five arguments. The first argument is a cell that acts as the counter mechanism for the loop structure. The second argument is the starting number for the counter mechanism; the third, the completion number for the counter mechanism. The fourth argument is the incremental value for the counter mechanism; and the fifth, the name of the subroutine. Arguments 2, 3, and 4 can be values, cell addresses, or formulas. Arguments 1 and 5, however, must be range names or cell addresses. Because multiple loops are permitted, you need to be careful of the logical flow of multiple looping structures.

Notice how FOR is used in the simple example in figure 15.25. FOR in the first line of the program controls how many times the program loops to format a column of values. The FOR statement begins by using the range named COUNT, located at B5, as a counter to keep track of how many times the program should loop. The second argument, 1, is the start-number for the counter; the next argument, 5, is the stop-number. The program keeps track of the looping process by comparing the counter against the stop-number, and stops executing if the counter value is larger than the stop-number.

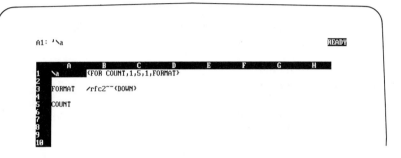

Fig. 15.25

Using FOR to control the number of loops in a formatting program.

The FOR statement's next argument, 1, is the step-number; this is the value by which the counter is to be incremented after each loop. The last argument, FORMAT, is the name of the routine to be executed.

If you want to end the processing of a FOR command based on something other than the number of iterations, such as a conditional test, you can use the FORBREAK command. When you use this command, 1-2-3 interrupts the processing of the FOR command and continues execution with the command following the FOR.

Data Manipulation Commands

The LET, PUT, CONTENTS, and BLANK commands allow precise placement of data within worksheet files. These commands, which are listed in table 15.4, function similarly to such menu commands as Copy, Move, and Erase but provide capabilities that go beyond simple copy, move, and erase operations.

Table 15.4
Data Manipulation Commands

Command	Description
{LET}	Places value of expression in <location>
{PUT}	Puts value into col, row within range
{CONTENTS}	Stores contents of <source> to <destination>
{BLANK}	Erases the cell or range

The LET Command

The LET command places a value or string in a target cell location without the cell pointer actually being at the location. LET is extremely useful, for example, for placing criteria in a database criterion range. The form of the LET command is

{LET location,expression}   Places value of expression in
                      <location>

In the program in figure 15.26, the LET statement in line one is executed only if the condition in the IF statement is true. Regardless of the outcome of line one, the LET statement in line two will be executed. Line one will place a label in a cell, whereas line two will place a value representing the formula (in the program) in a cell.

Fig. 15.26

Using the LET command with an IF statement.

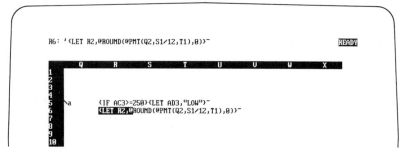

Figure 15.27 shows how to use LET in an application that takes a master file and saves it under a new name, that of a client code number. The program begins with a GETLABEL statement that prompts the user for a client code number and places the number in cell B3. The LET statement then duplicates the client code number in the cell named CODE, which lies within the program in R6.

Fig. 15.27

Using the LET command in a program for saving files.

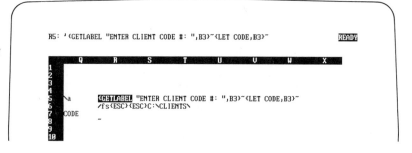

You can use a string value with the LET command. In fact, you can even use a string formula. For example, if the cell named FIRST contains the string "Robert" and LAST holds the string "Hamer", the statement

{LET NAME,first&" "&last}

will store "Robert Hamer" in NAME.

Like the DEFINE command, the LET command allows you to specify :STRING and :VALUE suffixes after the argument. The STRING suffix stores the text of the argument in the location, whereas the VALUE suffix evaluates the argument as a string or numeric formula and places the result in the location. When a suffix is not specified, LET stores the argument's numeric or string value if it is a valid formula; otherwise, the text of the argument is stored. For example

{LET name,first&" "&last:VALUE}

will store "Robert Hamer" in NAME, whereas

{LET name,first&" "&last:STRING}

will store the string *first&" "&last* in NAME.

The LET command can be duplicated by moving the cell pointer to the desired location with {GOTO} and entering the desired value into the cell. However, the LET command has the major advantage that it does not disturb the current location of the cell pointer. The /Data Fill command can also be used to enter numbers, but not to enter string values. Overall, the LET command is a convenient and useful means for setting the value of a cell from within a program.

The PUT Command

The PUT command places a value in a target cell location determined by the intersection of a row and a column in a defined range. The form of the PUT command is

{PUT range,col,row,value}   Places value into cell within range

The PUT statement contains four arguments. The first argument defines the range into which the value will be placed. The second argument defines the column offset within the range; the third, the row offset within the range. The fourth indicates the value to be placed in the cell location. Argument 1 may be a range name or cell address. Arguments 2, 3, and 4 may be values, cell references, or formulas.

For example, the following PUT statement

{PUT TABLE,S1,S2,ARG4}

will place the contents of the cell named ARG4 in the range named TABLE at the intersection defined by the values in cells S1 and S2.

Figure 15.28 shows the results of different variations of this command. Keep in mind that the row and column offset numbers follow the same conventions followed by functions (the first column is number 0, the second is number 1, etc.).

Fig. 15.28

Using the PUT command to enter numbers and labels.

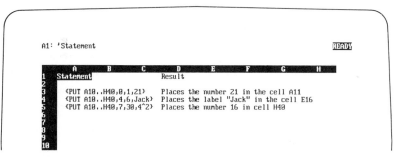

The CONTENTS Command

The CONTENTS command stores the contents of the source cell in the destination cell, optionally assigning an individual cell width and/or cell format. If width or format are not specified, the CONTENTS command uses the column width and format of the source location to format the string. The form of the CONTENTS command is

{CONTENTS destination,source,[width],[format]}   Stores contents of
                                                  <source> to
                                                  <destination>

For example, the following CONTENTS statement

{CONTENTS THERE,HERE,11,121}

will place the contents of the cell named HERE in the cell named THERE, give the individual cell a width of 11, and format the entry as a full international date (121).

Suppose, for example, that you want to copy the number 123.456, which resides in cell A21, to cell B25, and change the number to a string while you copy. The statement for this step is

{CONTENTS B25,A21}

The contents of cell B25 will be displayed as the string '123.456 with a left-aligned label-prefix character.

Next, suppose that you want to change the width of the string when you copy it. Rather than have the string display as "123.456", you want it to display as "123.4". You will get the desired result if you change the statement to

{CONTENTS B25,A21,6,1}

This second statement uses a width of 6 to display the string. The least significant digits of the number are truncated to create the string. If the number cannot be displayed in the specified width using the specified format, a string of asterisks "*****" is placed in the cell instead. (This works just like 1-2-3's normal spreadsheet formatting commands.)

Finally, suppose that you want to change the display format of the string while you copy it and change its width. The following string will change the display format to **Currency 0**.

{CONTENTS B25,A21,5,32}

The number used for the format number in this statement was taken from the list of CONTENTS command format numbers that appears in table 15.5. The result of the statement is the number $123.

In the following examples of the CONTENTS command with 123.456 as the number in cell A21, the width of column A is 9, and the display format for cell A21 is **Fixed 2**.

{CONTENTS B25,A21}	Displays the number 123.46 in cell B25.
{CONTENTS B25,A21,4}	Displays the number, using a width of 4 and the **Fixed 2** format. The result is "****".
{CONTENTS B25,A21,5,0}	Displays the number 123 in cell B25, using the **Fixed 0** format.

The CONTENTS command is rather specialized but very useful in situations that require converting numeric values to formatted strings. CONTENTS can convert long numeric formulas to strings, using the **T**ext format. This application is particularly useful for debugging purposes.

The BLANK Command

The BLANK command will erase a range of cells in the spreadsheet. Although this command works similarly to the /**R**ange **E**rase command, there are a few advantages to using BLANK over /**R**ange **E**rase in your Command Language programs. BLANK is faster than /**R**ange **E**rase because /**R**ange **E**rase requires a sequence of operations (selecting **R**ange; then selecting **E**rase) initiated

Table 15.5
Numeric Format Codes for CONTENTS Command

Code	Destination String's Numeric Display Command
0	Fixed, 0 decimal places
1-15	Fixed, 1 to 15 decimal places
15-31	Scientific, 0 to 15 decimal places
32-47	Currency, 0 to 15 decimal places
48-63	Percent, 0 to 15 decimal places
64-79	Comma, 0 to 15 decimal places
112	+/- Bar Graph
113	General
114	D1 (DD-MMM-YY)
115	D2 (DD-MM)
116	D3 (MMM-YY)
121	D4 (Full International)
122	D5 (Partial International)
119	D6 (HH:MM:SS AM/PM time format)
120	D7 (HH:MM AM/PM time format)
123	D8 (Full International time format)
124	D9 (Partial International time format)
117	Text format
118	Hidden format
127	Current window's default display format

through the 1-2-3 menu. BLANK, on the other hand, works outside of the menu structure. The form of the BLANK command is

{BLANK location}   Erases range defined by <location>

In the example in figure 15.29, the BLANK statement erases RANGE1. Line two executes the BLANK RANGE2 statement only if the conditional IF statement tests true.

Fig. 15.29

Using the BLANK command to erase a range.

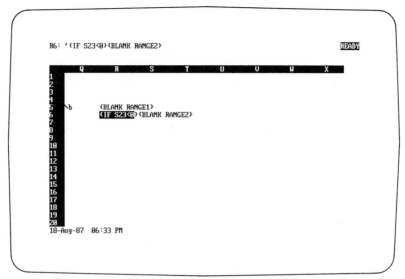

Program Enhancement Commands

The commands shown in table 15.6 (BEEP, PANELOFF, PANELON, WINDOWSOFF, WINDOWSON, INDICATE, RECALC, and RECALCCOL) can "dress up" your program or recalculate a portion of your worksheet. With skillful placement, these commands can add the polish that a solid program structure needs to become a smooth, easy-to-use application. This catch-all group of maintenance-oriented commands includes commands to sound your computer's speaker, control the screen display, and selectively recalculate portions of the spreadsheet. Two commands in this group (WINDOWSOFF and PANELOFF) can increase significantly the execution speed of large Command Language programs.

The BEEP Command

The BEEP command activates the computer's speaker system to produce one of four tones. Each argument (1-4) produces a different tone. The BEEP command is commonly used to alert the user to a specific condition in the program or to draw the user's attention. The form of the BEEP command is

    {BEEP [number]}   Sounds one of the computer's four beeps
      or
    {BEEP}

The following BEEP statement

    {IF A35>50}{BEEP 2}

Table 15.6
Program Enhancements Commands

Command	Description
{BEEP}	Sounds one of the computer's four beeps
{PANELOFF}	Suppresses display of control panel
{PANELON}	Displays control panel
{WINDOWSOFF}	Suppresses redisplay of current window
{WINDOWSON}	Enables redisplay of current window
{INDICATE}	Resets control panel indicator to <string>
{RECALC}	Recalculates a specified portion of the worksheet row-by-row
{RECALCCOL}	Recalculates a specified portion of the worksheet column-by-column

will produce a sound if the condition presented in the IF statement is true. If not, program control will pass to the next cell below the IF statement.

The PANELOFF Command

The PANELOFF command freezes the control panel, prohibiting the annoying display of program commands in the control panel during program execution. This command can be used effectively to display messages in the control panel, regardless of the cell pointer's current location. Be aware, however, that the PANELOFF command will prevent the display of prompts from GETLABEL and GETNUMBER statements. The form of the PANELOFF command is

{PANELOFF}   Suppresses display of control panel

In the following example,

{PANELOFF}
/cC27..E39~AB21~

the PANELOFF command suppresses display in the control panel of the copy command in the second line.

The PANELON Command

The PANELON command unfreezes the control panel. This command is commonly used immediately before a GETLABEL or GETNUMBER command. The form of the PANELON command is

{PANELON}   Displays control panel

In figure 15.30, the PANELON command reactivates the control panel so that the prompt for the GETLABEL statement is displayed.

Fig. 15.30

Using PANELON with GETLABEL.

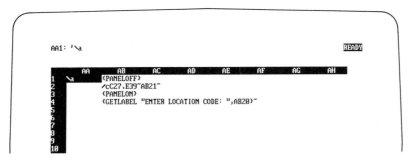

The WINDOWSOFF Command

By using the WINDOWSOFF command, you can freeze the lower part of the screen and have just the control panel show the changes that occur as a result of the commands activated in your program. The WINDOWSOFF command freezes the current screen display, regardless of whether the program is executing. WINDOWSOFF is particularly useful when you are creating applications that will be used by novice 1-2-3 users. WINDOWSOFF enables you to display only those screen changes that the user must see, freezing other changes that might confuse the novice. The form of the WINDOWSOFF command is

{WINDOWSOFF}   Suppresses screen display

In the example,

{WINDOWSOFF}
/cS24~Z12~ {CALC}

the WINDOWSOFF command prevents the automatic screen-rebuilding associated with the /Copy command or the Calc key.

Using the WINDOWSOFF and PANELOFF commands can have a significant effect on program execution time. In one complex application, use of the WINDOWSOFF and PANELOFF commands to completely freeze the screen reduced execution time by 50 percent, from 5 to 2 1/2 minutes. Speed improvement will depend, of course, on the particular application.

You can use WINDOWSOFF with PANELOFF to create a graph "slide show" for business meetings. These commands allow you to display a sequence of graphs uninterrupted by intervening worksheet screens.

The program in figure 15.31 demonstrates how to use the WINDOWS-OFF and PANELOFF commands to eliminate screen shifting and to reduce execution time for such a presentation. The PANELOFF and WINDOWSOFF commands in AB1 suppress redrawing of the window and panel. The following lines, AB2-AB5, display four different graphs. In line AB6, the PANELON and WINDOWSON commands restore redrawing of the window and panel (see the following sections). The program ends in line AB7 by returning the worksheet display with the cell pointer located at the HOME position.

Fig. 15.31

*Using
WINDOWSOFF and
PANELOFF for a
graphics slide
show.*

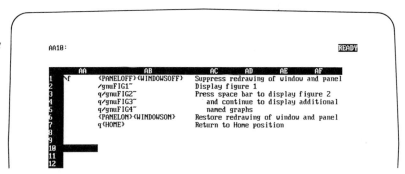

Be aware that if something goes wrong with your program while the WINDOWSOFF command is in effect, you can get into trouble. Unless you have a simple one-line program already preset for issuing the WINDOWSON command (see the following section), you may have to reboot 1-2-3 and start your application all over again to recover the use of the screen. Therefore, it is wise to develop and test your programs without the WINDOWSOFF and WINDOWSON commands; add these commands to the debugged and tested program.

The WINDOWSON Command

The WINDOWSON command unfreezes the screen, allowing display of executing program operations. This command is commonly used to allow display of the Lotus menu structures. The form of the WINDOWSON command is

{WINDOWSON}   Displays screen

In figure 15.31, the WINDOWSON command in AB6 activates display of the worksheet screen after all graphs have been shown.

The INDICATE Command

The INDICATE command alters the mode indicator in the upper right corner of the 1-2-3 screen. This command is commonly used to provide custom indicators. The INDICATE command will accept a string argument of up to five characters. If the string is longer, 1-2-3 uses only the first five characters. When you use the INDICATE command, you have to enter a string. You cannot use a cell address or range name. The form of the INDICATE command is

{INDICATE string}   Resets mode indicator to <string>

Suppose, for example, that you want to display the message START in the upper right corner of the screen. You can use the following INDICATE command

{INDICATE START}

Unless you clear your indicator, using the command

{INDICATE}

will display the START message until you exit 1-2-3.

To blank out the indicator completely, you can use the command

{INDICATE ""}

Controlling Recalculation

Two macro commands, RECALC and RECALCCOL, allow you to recalculate a portion of the worksheet. This feature can be useful in large spreadsheets where recalculation time is long and where you need to recalculate certain values in the worksheet before you proceed to the next processing step in your macro. The commands for partial recalculation have the form

{RECALC location,condition,iteration-number}

and

{RECALCCOL location,condition,iteration-number}

in which location is a range or range name that specifies the cells whose formulas are to be recalculated. The condition and iteration-number arguments are optional.

If the condition argument is included, the range is recalculated repeatedly until condition has a logical value of TRUE (1). Remember that condition must be either a logical expression or a reference to a cell within the recalculation range that contains a logical expression. If condition is a reference to a cell outside the recalculation range, then the value of condition, either TRUE (1) or FALSE (0), will not change, and condition will not control the partial recalculation.

If the iteration-number argument is included, the condition argument must also be specified (the value 1 makes condition always TRUE). The iteration-number specifies the number of times that formulas in the location range are to be recalculated.

The RECALC and RECALCCOL commands differ in the order in which cells in the specified range are recalculated. The RECALC command performs the calculations by row—all the cells in the first row of the range, then all the cells in the second row, etc. The RECALCCOL command performs the calculations by column—all the cells in the first column of the range, followed by all the cells in the second column, etc. In both commands, only cells within the specified range are recalculated.

Use RECALC to recalculate the range when the formulas in the range refer only to other formulas in rows above or to the left of themselves in the same row in that range. Use RECALCCOL to recalculate the range when formulas in the range refer only to other formulas in columns to the left or to cells above themselves in the same column.

Just a word of caution here: You may have to use CALC if formulas in the range refer to other formulas located below and to their right, or if formulas refer both to cells in rows above and to the right and to cells in columns below and to the left.

You need to include in the range only those cells you want to recalculate. The formulas in the recalculation range can refer to values in cells outside the range; however, those values are not updated by the RECALC or RECALCCOL.

When either the RECALC or RECALCCOL command is executed, the partial recalculation occurs immediately. However, the results do not appear on screen until the screen is redrawn. Program execution may continue for some time before a command that updates the screen is executed. In the interim, the recalculated numbers, although not visible on screen, are available for use in calculations and conditional tests.

If the program ends and you want to be sure that the recalculated numbers are on screen, use the PgUp and PgDn keys to move the window away from and back to the recalculated range. The act of looking away and back again will update the screen and display the current values in the recalculated range.

You may need to use CALC, RECALC, or RECALCCOL after commands such as LET, GETNUMBER, and ?, or after 1-2-3 commands such as /Range Input within a program. You do not need to recalculate after invoking 1-2-3 commands such as /Copy and /Move; 1-2-3 automatically recalculates the affected ranges after such commands, even during program execution.

Caution: Recalculating a portion of the worksheet can cause some formulas (those outside a recalculated range that reference formulas within the range) to fail to reflect current data. If this should occur in your application, be sure to perform a general recalculation at some point before the end of your program.

File Manipulation Commands

Eight commands give 1-2-3 the capability of opening, reading, writing, and closing a sequential data file containing ASCII text data. This capability allows 1-2-3 applications to read and write files used by other business applications. Although the /File Import and /Print File commands provide a limited capability to manipulate foreign files, the file-manipulation commands shown in table 15.7 provide a capability equal to the sequential file commands in BASIC or other programming languages.

Table 15.7
File Manipulation Commands

Command	Description
{OPEN}	Opens file for reading, writing, or both
{CLOSE}	Closes a file opened with {OPEN}
{READ}	Copies specified characters from the {OPEN} file to <location>
{READLN}	Copies next line from file to <location>
{WRITE}	Copies a string to the open file
{WRITELN}	Copies a string plus a carriage-return line-feed sequence to the open file
{SETPOS}	Sets a new position for the file pointer
{GETPOS}	Records file pointer position in <location>
{FILESIZE}	Records size of open file in <location>

Warning: The file manipulation commands are programming commands. To read from and write to foreign files successfully, you must understand exactly how these commands work and how the sequential files you are manipulating are organized. If you write to a file containing another application, be sure to back up the file before trying to write to it from within 1-2-3.

If you keep this warning in mind, this group of commands can open up the world of outside files to your 1-2-3 applications. Should you need to process external data files, these commands make it possible to do the job, using 1-2-3.

The OPEN Command

The OPEN command opens a disk file, providing access so that you can write to or read from that file. The access-mode argument is a single character string that specifies whether you want to read only ("R"), write only ("W"), or both read from and write to the file ("M").

Note that 1-2-3 will allow only one file to be open at a time. If you want to work with more than one file in your application, you will have to open each file before using it, and then close it again before opening and using the next file. Note also that the "M" (modify) argument cannot create a new file.

The form of the OPEN command is

{OPEN filename,access mode}   Opens file for reading, writing, or both

The filename argument is a string, an expression with a string value, or a single-cell reference to a cell that contains a string or a string expression. The string must be a valid DOS file name or path name. A file in the current directory can be specified by its name and extension. A file in another directory may require a drive identification, a subdirectory path, or a complete DOS path in addition to the file name and extension.

The access-mode argument is a single character string that specifies whether you want to read only ("R"), write only ("W"), or both read from and write to the file ("M").

"R" (Read)	Read access opens an existing file and allows access with the READ and READLN commands. You cannot write to a file opened with Read access.
"W" (Write)	Write access opens a new file with the specified name and allows access with the WRITE and WRITELN commands. Any existing file with the specified name will be erased and replaced by the new file.
"M" (Modify)	Modify access opens an existing file with the specified name and allows both read (READ AND READLN) and write (WRITE and WRITELN) commands.

The OPEN command succeeds if it is able to open the file with the access you requested. If the OPEN command succeeds, program execution continues with the cell below the OPEN. Any commands after the OPEN in the current cell are ignored.

The OPEN command will fail with an ERROR if the disk drive is not ready. You should use an ONERROR command to handle this contingency.

If the access mode is READ or MODIFY but the file does not exist on the indicated directory, the OPEN command fails, and program execution continues with the commands after the OPEN command in the current cell. You can place one or more commands after the OPEN command in the same cell in order to deal with the failure. The most common practice is to place a BRANCH or a subroutine call after the OPEN to transfer to a macro that deals with the failure.

Here are some examples (with explanations) of the OPEN command

{OPEN "PASTDUE","R"}{BRANCH FIXIT}
Open the existing file named PASTDUE in the current directory for reading. If the file cannot be opened, branch to the routine FIXIT.

{OPEN "C:\DATA\CLIENTS.DAT",w}
Open the new file named CLIENTS.DAT in drive C, subdirectory DATA, for writing.

{OPEN file,m}{BRANCH RETRY}
Open the file whose name is in cell FILE for Modify access. If the file cannot be opened, branch to the routine RETRY.

Figure 15.32 shows an example of using all of the file commands except the READ and WRITE commands (which are similar to the READLN and WRITELN commands). The program named \o uses the OPEN command to open a user-specified file. This program illustrates how to deal with `disk drive not ready` and `file not found` errors. After prompting you for the file name, an ONERROR command sets the error jump to the routine that handles such problems as the drive not being ready. Next, the OPEN command is used with the BRANCH that follows it. This BRANCH handles such problems as a `file not found` error.

The CLOSE Command

The CLOSE command closes a currently open file. If no file is open, the CLOSE command has no effect. CLOSE does not take an argument. The CLOSE command is particularly important for files that you are writing or modifying. You can lose the last data written to a file that you don't close. The form of the CLOSE command is

{CLOSE}   Closes a file opened with {OPEN}

Fig. 15.32

A program that uses the file commands.

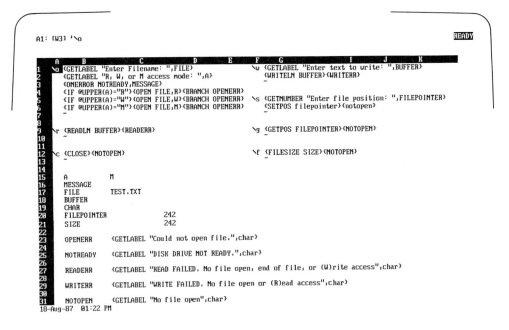

Although, under most circumstances, 1-2-3 automatically takes care of a file that you do not close, you should make it a practice to use CLOSE when you are finished using any file opened with OPEN. Better safe than sorry. Use of the CLOSE command is illustrated in the program labeled \c in figure 15.32.

The READ Command

The READ command reads a specified number of characters from the currently open file, beginning at the present file pointer location. The characters read from the file are placed in the spreadsheet at the cell <location> indicated. The form of the READ command is

{READ bytecount,location}   Copies specified number of characters
                              from file to <location>

in which bytecount is the number of bytes to read, starting at the current position of the file pointer, and location is the cell to read into. READ places the specified number of characters from the file into the location cell as a label. Bytecount can be any number between 1 and 240, the maximum number of characters in a 1-2-3 label. If bytecount is greater than the number of characters remaining in the file, 1-2-3 reads the remaining characters into location. After the READ command finishes, the file pointer is positioned at the character following the last character read.

For example, the statement

    {READ NUM,INFO}

transfers information from the open file into the cell location named INFO. The amount of information transferred is determined by the contents of the cell named NUM, which can contain either a value or a formula.

The READ command is useful primarily when you want to read a specific number of characters into the buffer. A data file that contains fixed-length records, for example, is read conveniently by the READ command with bytecount equal to the record length.

READ generally should not be used with ASCII text files from a word processor or text editor. Such files generally have variable length lines terminated with a carriage-return, line-feed sequence and are read better with the READLN command. Although figure 15.32 does not contain an example of the READ command, READ is used much like the READLN in the figure's \r program.

The READLN Command

The READLN command reads one line of information from the currently open file, beginning at the file pointer's current position. The characters read are placed in the cell <location> in the current spreadsheet. The READLN command form is

    {READLN location}   Copies next line from file to <location>

For example, the statement

    {READLN HERE}

will copy a line from an open file into the cell named HERE. The line will be determined by the SETPOS command. (SETPOS is discussed later in the chapter.)

Use READLN to read a line of text from a file whose lines are delimited by a carriage-return, line-feed combination. You would, for example, use READLN to read the next line from an ASCII text file. ASCII text files are created with 1-2-3's **/Print File** command. Also referred to as print files, these files are assigned the .PRN file extension by 1-2-3. READLN is best suited to reading files that are print images. The program labeled \r in figure 15.32 illustrates the use of READLN.

Using READ and READLN

If you attempt to read past the end of the file, if no file is open, or if the file was opened with Write access, the READ or READLN command is ignored and program execution continues in the same cell. Otherwise, after the READ or READLN command is completed, program execution continues on the next line. This allows you to place a BRANCH or subroutine call after the READ or READLN to handle the problem of an unexecuted READ or READLN statement.

The WRITE Command

The WRITE command writes a string of text to the currently open file. The WRITE command has the form

{WRITE string}

The argument string can be a literal string, a range name or cell reference to a single cell that contains a string, or a string expression. Because WRITE does not place a carriage-return, line-feed sequence at the end of the string, multiple WRITEs can be made to concatenate text on a single line. WRITE is well suited to creating or updating a file that contains fixed-length database records. Although there is no example of the WRITE command in figure 15.32, the WRITE command is used in much the same way as is the WRITELN command in the \w program.

If the file pointer is not at the end of the file, 1-2-3 overwrites the existing characters in the file. If the file pointer is at the end of the file, 1-2-3 extends the file by the number of characters written. And if the file pointer is past the end of the file (see discussion of the SETPOS command, later in this section), before writing the characters, 1-2-3 extends the file by the amount indicated.

The WRITELN Command

The WRITELN command is identical to the WRITE command except that it places a carriage-return, line-feed sequence after the last character written from the string. The WRITELN command form is

{WRITELN string}

WRITELN is useful when the file being written or updated uses the carriage-return line feed to mark the end of its lines or records. (The WRITE command is also useful.) In many applications, several WRITEs are used to write a line to the file; then a WRITELN is used to mark the end of the line. The WRITELN command is illustrated in the \w program in figure 15.32.

The SETPOS Command

The SETPOS command sets the position of the file pointer to a specified value. The form of the command is

{SETPOS file-position}

File-position is a number, or an expression resulting in a number, that specifies the character at which you want to position the pointer. The first character in the file is at position 0, the second at position 1, and so on.

As an example, suppose that you have a database file with 100 records which are each 20 bytes long. To access the first record, you can use the commands

{SETPOS 0}
{READ 20,buffer}

To read the 15th record, you can use the commands

{SETPOS (15-1)*20}
{READ 20,buffer}

Nothing prevents you from setting the file pointer past the end of the file. If the file pointer is set at or past the end and a READ or READLN command is executed, the command does nothing, and program execution continues with the next command on the same line (error branch). If the file pointer is set at or past the end and a WRITE or WRITELN command is executed, 1-2-3 will first extend the file to the length specified by the file pointer, then, starting at the file pointer, will write the characters.

Warning: If you inadvertently set the file pointer to a large number with SETPOS and write to the file, 1-2-3 will attempt to expand the file and write the text at the end. If the file will not fit on the disk, the WRITE command does nothing, and program execution continues with the next command on the same line (error branch). If the file will fit on the disk, 1-2-3 extends the file and writes the text at the end.

If a file is not currently open, SETPOS does nothing, and execution continues with the next command on the same line as the SETPOS command. Otherwise, when the SETPOS command is completed, execution continues on the next line of the program. This allows you to place a BRANCH command or a subroutine call after the SETPOS command to handle the problem of an unexecuted statement. SETPOS is illustrated in the \s program in figure 15.32.

The GETPOS Command

The GETPOS command allows you to record the file pointer's current position. The form of this command is

{GETPOS location}

The current position of the file pointer is placed in the cell indicated by location, where location is either a cell reference or a range name. If location points to a multicell range, the value of the file pointer is placed in the upper left corner of the range.

The GETPOS command is useful if you record in the file the location of something you want to find again. You can use GETPOS to mark your current place in the file before you use SETPOS to move the file pointer to another position. You can use GETPOS to record the locations of important items in a quick-reference index. GETPOS is illustrated in the \g program in figure 15.32.

The FILESIZE Command

Another file-related command, FILESIZE, returns the length of the file in bytes. The form of the command is

{FILESIZE location}

The FILESIZE command determines the current length of the file and places this value in the cell referred to by location. Location can be a cell reference or range name. If location refers to a multicell range, the file size is placed in the cell in the upper left corner of the range. FILESIZE is illustrated in the \f program in figure 15.32.

A Command Language Application

Although 1-2-3's **Print** menu provides most of the capabilities needed for a variety of worksheet printing tasks, you cannot use the **Print** menu to print multiple copies of a single report automatically. To print multiple copies of the same report, you must repeatedly select the commands for aligning paper and beginning the print operation. With 1-2-3's Command Language, you can create a program for printing multiple copies of the same report automatically. And you can enhance the program by adding help screens and prompts that will help users solve problems that may occur during the print operation.

Figure 15.33 illustrates a Command Language program for printing multiple copies of a report. Notice that this program includes 11 of the commands discussed in the previous sections of this chapter. These commands include

Commands for Accepting Input: GET, GETNUMBER, and LOOK

Commands for Program Control: BRANCH, MENUCALL, QUIT, and BREAKOFF

Decision-making Commands: IF and FOR

Program Enhancement Commands: BEEP and PANELOFF

Fig. 15.33

A Command Language program that prints multiple copies.

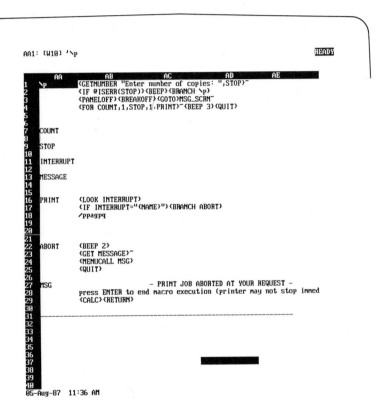

```
AA1: [W10] '\p                                                          READY

        AA          AB              AC          AD          AE
1  \p        {GETNUMBER "Enter number of copies: ",STOP}~
2            {IF @ISERR(STOP)}{BEEP}{BRANCH \p}
3            {PANELOFF}{BREAKOFF}{GOTO}MSG_SCRN~
4            {FOR COUNT,1,STOP,1,PRINT}~{BEEP 3}{QUIT}
5
6
7  COUNT
8
9  STOP
10
11 INTERRUPT
12
13 MESSAGE
14
15
16 PRINT      {LOOK INTERRUPT}
17            {IF INTERRUPT="{NAME}"}{BRANCH ABORT}
18            /ppagpq
19
20
21
22 ABORT      {BEEP 2}
23            {GET MESSAGE}~
24            {MENUCALL MSG}
25            {QUIT}
26
27 MSG                        - PRINT JOB ABORTED AT YOUR REQUEST -
28            press ENTER to end macro execution (printer may not stop immed
29            {CALC}{RETURN}
30
31 ------------------------------------------------------------------
32
33
34
35
36
37
38
39
40
05-Aug-87  11:36 AM
```

In the first line, the GETNUMBER command lets the user enter the number of copies to be printed. For example, if you want three copies you would enter that number in response to the prompt Enter number of copies:. Then the GETNUMBER command stores the number in cell AB9, which has the range name STOP. Notice the companion error-checking routine for GETNUMBER in the program's second line (AB2).

In line 3, PANELOFF prevents movement on the control panel (so that the user won't be distracted); {BREAKOFF} disables Ctrl-Break; and a message screen (with the range name MSG_SCRN) is incorporated into the worksheet.

This message screen informs the user that the print job is in progress and explains what to do if something goes wrong (see fig. 15.34). Notice that cell AI8 in figure 15.34 uses a string formula to tell the user how many copies are to be printed.

Fig. 15.34

The message displayed by the print program.

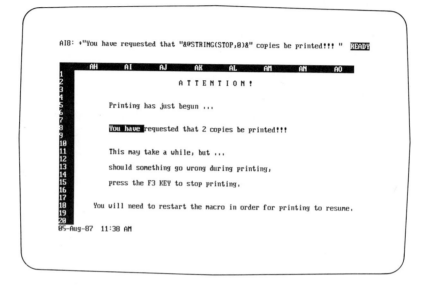

As you can see from figure 15.33, two additional range names (INTERRUPT and MESSAGE) appear in lines 11 and 13, respectively. The PRINT subroutine contains a LOOK statement followed by an IF statement, both of which use the range INTERRUPT. Two other subroutines, ABORT and MSG, are used also. (The range to be printed must be predefined.)

When you run the program, the following actions take place. First, the prompt Enter number of copies: is displayed in the control panel (see fig. 15.35). After you enter a number, the message screen shown in figure 15.36 appears. The string formula in cell AI8 is updated with the value entered in STOP, confirming the number of copies to be printed. You are told to wait a while and to press F3 if you want to interrupt the print operation. At this point, printing begins.

Now let's see how the procedure for canceling printing works. Suppose that you requested the wrong number of copies to be printed. As soon as you press F3, the computer beeps, the menu message PRINT JOB ABORTED AT YOUR REQUEST appears in the control panel, and you are instructed to Press ENTER to end program execution (see fig. 15.37). You are advised also that the printer may not stop immediately. This delay will occur if your printer has

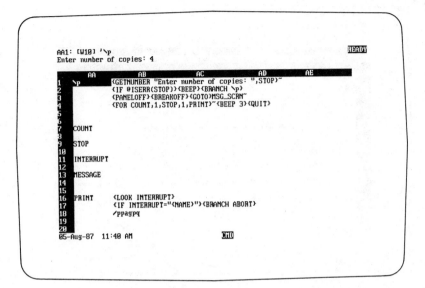

Fig. 15.35

The prompt for number of copies to be printed.

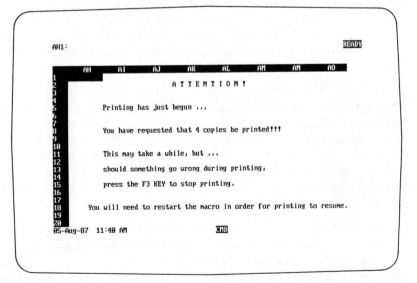

Fig. 15.36

Message screen indicating number of copies.

a print buffer; the text to be printed will have already been transferred from the computer to the buffer.

How did all this happen? The essential elements in this method of stopping the program are the LOOK and IF statements in the subroutine PRINT.

LOOK checks the type-ahead buffer to see whether anything was typed during program execution. If something was typed, the first character is copied into

Fig. 15.37

Message showing that the print job has been aborted.

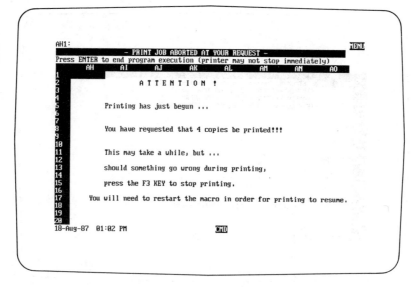

```
AH1:                                                                    MENU
              - PRINT JOB ABORTED AT YOUR REQUEST -
Press ENTER to end program execution (printer may not stop immediately)
         AH      AI      AJ      AK      AL      AM      AN      AO
1
2                    A T T E N T I O N !
3
4
5        Printing has just begun ...
6
7
8        You have requested that 4 copies be printed!!!
9
10
11       This may take a while, but ...
12
13       should something go wrong during printing,
14
15       press the F3 KEY to stop printing.
16
17       You will need to restart the macro in order for printing to resume.
18
19
20
18-Aug-87  01:02 PM                       CMD
```

the range named INTERRUPT. If a function key was pressed, the name representation for that function key is stored in INTERRUPT. In this program, each time LOOK is executed, 1-2-3 checks INTERRUPT to see whether anything is stored there. For instance, if you had pressed F3, the character {NAME} would be stored in INTERRUPT.

INTERRUPT is then evaluated by the IF statement, which indicates that if INTERRUPT contains the string {NAME}, the program should branch to the subroutine ABORT; otherwise, the program should print the worksheet. Note that you must press F3 to stop printing. Pressing any other key will cause a false condition in the IF statement, and the print routine will be executed. Because both LOOK and IF are part of PRINT, these two commands are executed whenever the FOR statement executes the loop; INTERRUPT is checked on every pass.

When program control next moves to ABORT, no additional reports are printed. ABORT causes the computer to beep and issues the GET command to clear the keyboard buffer (LOOK doesn't do this). ABORT then displays the menu message stored in MSG. Because {MENUCALL MSG} is used, the {RETURN} in the MSG subroutine sends the program back to ABORT when you press Enter. The {QUIT} is then executed, ending the program and re-enabling Ctrl-Break.

Figure 15.38 shows what happens if you press F3 during program execution. Because you pressed F3, the range name INTERRUPT contains the string {NAME}. Notice that the range name MESSAGE also contains {NAME} (GET put the string there). Because {NAME} has already done its job with LOOK and is now useless, MESSAGE is nothing more than the "wastebasket" where GET sends all unwanted characters.

Fig. 15.38

The print program after the F3 key has been pressed.

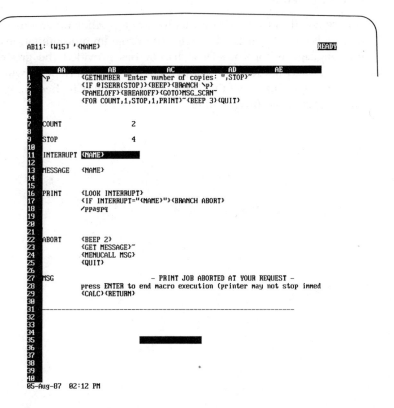

This is a sophisticated program for a special application that uses many strong Release 2 capabilities, including string formulas and keyword commands. You will probably want to use this program if you occasionally print multiple copies of long reports (or even if you print multiple copies of short reports).

Chapter Summary

As you work with the 1-2-3 Command Language, you soon will discover that your powerful spreadsheet program has an extremely powerful programming language.

Although 1-2-3's Command Language makes many things possible, be aware of some practical limitations. For example, because 1-2-3 is RAM-based, you must limit the size of your files. In addition, 1-2-3 may not always execute programming commands with lightning speed. There is almost always a tradeoff of capabilities; the most difficult applications may take a good deal of time to execute.

If you are an adventurer who wants to develop efficient, automated, customized models, and if you can live with the programming limitations, the Command Language is for you. This chapter has provided the groundwork for developing such models. As you become more experienced with the Command Language, turn to other Que titles for help in becoming an expert Command Language programmer.

Part IV

Quick Reference Guide
to 1-2-3

Includes

Troubleshooting Section
Troubleshooting Index
1-2-3 Command Reference

Troubleshooting
Section

This section addresses many of the problems you can encounter while using 1-2-3, and offers a variety of creative solutions. First-time users of 1-2-3 will find that this section can help them untie knots that seem hopelessly snarled but are really only minor inconveniences when understood correctly.

Experienced users will undoubtedly derive even greater benefit from the problems and solutions presented here. As your use of the program becomes increasingly complex and sophisticated, so do the problems and errors that you encounter. Although first-time users face problems that momentarily seem insurmountable, the most perplexing problems in using 1-2-3 are those faced by power users who push the program to its limits.

We suggest you use this section in two different ways:

1. Read the entire section after you have read the rest of the book and have begun to use 1-2-3; or use the same method segment-by-segment. Most people learn 1-2-3 in segments—learning how to build a simple spreadsheet before they learn to incorporate complex formulas and functions; later learning how to print reports, and then to create graphs; much later, perhaps, learning how to create and use macros or to use the program's database management capabilities. You can use this section the same way: after you learn the basics of one area of the program, read through the applicable portion of the troubleshooting section. Reading this section before you encounter problems will help you avoid those problems.

2. Refer to this section as you encounter problems. The section is arranged to provide easy reference. The running heads at the upper right corner of the right-hand page contain the name of the general area of problems covered on that page (e.g., **SPREADSHEET PROBLEMS**). As each problem is introduced, a more specific designation (e.g., **DATA ENTRY PROBLEM #1**) appears in the left margin, followed by a brief description of the problem. A quick scan of the heads and the margins will take you

621

to the area that describes your problem. Using this section as a reference will be even easier, of course, if you have already read the section, as recommended in the first method. As an additional aid, a separate Troubleshooting Cross-Reference Index is provided at the end of this section.

The topics in this troubleshooting section are arranged as they appear in the book, in the following order:

1. *Installation*: this section in particular should be read *before* you install 1-2-3. Some potentially disastrous installation problems cannot be remedied—they can only be avoided. Some installation problems, however, can be remedied after they occur. This section covers both initial installation problems and later problems, such as those encountered when you later decide to create and use your own driver sets or install different printers.

2. *Spreadsheet*: covers problems in the basic spreadsheet environment—the environment in which you will probably encounter your first problems and surprises.

3. *Commands*: covers the use of 1-2-3 commands in the spreadsheet.

4. *Functions*: solves a variety of basic and highly complex problems associated with functions.

5. *File operations*: particularly addresses problems encountered while transferring and combining data from different files, using different directories, and saving and retrieving files.

6. *Printing*: a troublesome area for most people, who struggle to "get their reports to look exactly like they're supposed to look." This section answers many printing problems and provides many creative and useful tips.

7. *Graphing*: the wide variety of graphing options make this area as difficult as printing. This section helps you through the maze.

8. *Data Management*: possibly the most troublesome section of all. Many of the highly sophisticated database management systems (DBMS) on the market are much more powerful than this capacity of 1-2-3. Nevertheless, 1-2-3's capabilities are considerable, complex, and unfamiliar to many users, who enter this area reluctantly. Once you do start to use 1-2-3's database capabilities, you quickly and frequently encounter problems. Overcoming these problems, with the help of this section, can open doors to a much more extensive and rewarding use of 1-2-3.

9. *Macros*: macros and the Lotus Command Language (LCL) are among 1-2-3's most powerful features. This is an area that many users have fun with, because they can learn a little at a time, building their skills slowly. As the skills build, so do the problems. This section helps you with many of those problems.

The Troubleshooting reference section cannot be, and is not meant to be, a comprehensive listing of all 1-2-3 problems. This section sometimes echoes and reinforces the explanations given elsewhere in the book. More often, this section extends your knowledge and your skills beyond the explanations given elsewhere. The ultimate solver of problems must be the individual user, but this section can help, by solving specific problems and by showing a pattern of creative thinking for solving problems as they occur.

Other books extend the assistance given here. We especially recommend *1-2-3, Tips, Tricks, and Traps*, 2nd Edition; *1-2-3 for Business*, 2nd Edition; *1-2-3 Macro Library*, 2nd Edition; and *1-2-3 Command Language*; all published by Que.

Troubleshooting Installation

Problems with Drivers

DRIVER PROBLEM #1:

You can't print, and you can't display graphs on a color monitor.

EXPLANATION: The program requires a file, called a *driver set*, that describes the equipment used in your system. This file must have the extension .SET. When you execute 1-2-3, the program looks for a file (called 123.SET) containing the driver set. The System disk contains an initial driver set called 123.SET. This driver set uses a Universal Text Display driver that works with almost any display but has no support for printers and can't display graphs.

SOLUTION: Run the Install program and follow the prompts to describe your computer system. If you don't give the driver set a special name, Install names it 123.SET.

NOTE: If you use different displays on your computer system, you may need several driver sets. You can use Install to set up different driver sets and give them individual names. To tell the program to use a driver set other than 123.SET, specify the name of the driver .SET file when you execute the program.

For example, if you run Install and name a driver set COLOR.SET, you must specify this name whenever you run a 1-2-3 program. Instead of typing *123* (or *lotus* or *pgraph*) at the DOS prompt, type *123 color* (or *lotus color* or *pgraph color*).

If you always use the same display with your system, let Install name your driver set 123.SET. Then you can forget about it when you execute 1-2-3.

DRIVER PROBLEM #2:

The system hangs at the copyright screen, forcing you to reboot.

EXPLANATION: The default Universal Text Display driver works with almost any display. However, if you have a color monitor and try to start the program with a driver set for a monochrome monitor, or vice versa, you hang the system.

SOLUTION: First, if the driver set is not called 123.SET, make sure that you specified the proper driver set when you executed 1-2-3. Suppose, for example, that 123.SET is set for monochrome and that you have the color-monitor driver in a file called COLOR.SET. Be sure to specify COLOR when you use a color monitor. If you are using 123.SET, rerun Install and check the driver set.

If the driver set seems to be correct, test to see if the original driver set on the System (or Backup) disk runs correctly. If you execute the program from the hard disk, put the System or Backup disk in drive A and, at the C:> prompt, type:

    123 A:123

If the original driver set runs correctly, you can be certain that you specified an incorrect driver set and must rerun Install. If the computer still hangs, the problem must involve the switch setting for the math coprocessor.

ALTERNATE EXPLANATION: Two sets of switches located within an IBM Personal Computer tell the computer what kind of monitor you have, how much memory and how many floppy disk drives you have, and so on. The XT contains one set of switches. Although the AT has no switch settings, its SETUP program serves the same purpose.

One of the switch settings on the PC or XT tells the computer whether you have a math coprocessor chip installed. This special chip can perform math functions many times faster than the regular microprocessor in your computer. In most cases, a computer with a math coprocessor executes faster than a computer without one. The amount of time saved in a worksheet recalculation depends on the kinds of calculations in the worksheet. In a PC or XT, the math coprocessor is an 8087 chip; in an AT, it is an 80287 chip.

Until recently, virtually no programs were capable of using the math coprocessor. Beginning with Release 2, 1-2-3 uses the math coprocessor if one is installed. If you do not have a math coprocessor but the switch settings indicate that you do, the system hangs as soon as you try to run the program.

You may have owned a PC for years and not been aware that this switch setting was not set properly, because your computer operates properly as long as you do not run programs that try to use the math coprocessor. Some editions of the *IBM Guide to Operations* show the switch settings reversed.

ALTERNATE SOLUTION: If you do not have a math coprocessor, set the switch indicated in your guide to the ON position, even if the guide states otherwise.

If you have an AT, run its SETUP program, making sure that you have not indicated that you have a math coprocessor if none is installed. If you have a Personal System/2, this error cannot occur because there are no switch settings or SETUP programs to run.

DRIVER PROBLEM #3:

When you use a 1-2-3 template that uses the extended graphics characters, the screen looks weird.

EXPLANATION: Many companies used the extended graphics characters to make their screens look fancy or customized. These graphics characters were an undocumented feature in Release 1A of 1-2-3. Many of these characters were used to create the Release 1A start-up screen shown. (See fig. T.1 for an example of a screen using these characters.)

Fig. T.1

Extended characters in Release 1A.

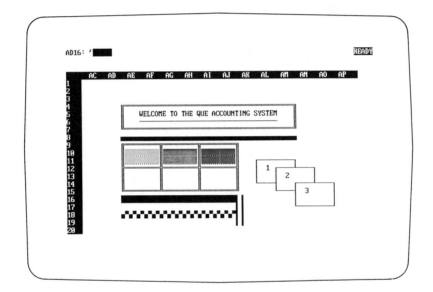

In Release 2, however, all the graphics characters have been redefined as the Lotus International Character Set (LICS). If you use the Release 1A template with Release 2, the start-up screen will look like that shown in figure T.2.

SOLUTION: If you've converted your Release 1A templates that use extended graphics characters, you can use them with Release 2 by selecting a special text-display driver: the Universal Text Display —ASCII— No LICS. To select this driver, run Install and choose Advanced Options, Modify Current Driver Set, Text Display. Then select the driver, as shown in figure T.3. This special driver can be used with any monitor and does not interfere with displaying graphs.

DRIVER PROBLEM #4:

You have access to several printers and plotters that you use occasionally for printing worksheets and graphs, but keeping track of all the driver sets for these different configurations is difficult.

Fig. T.2

Extended characters converted to LICS in Release 2.

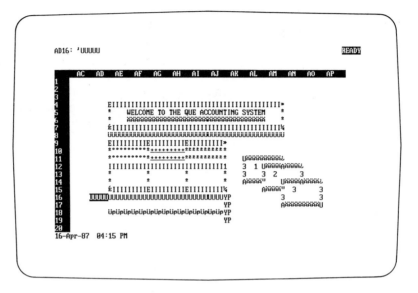

Fig. T.3

The ASCII text display driver.

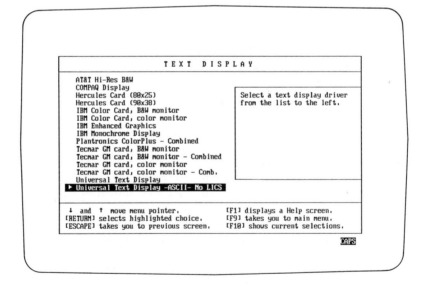

EXPLANATION: 1-2-3 lets you use only the printers and plotters in your driver set. If you put all your output devices in different driver sets, you must remember which driver set to use whenever you execute the program.

SOLUTION: Do not set up different driver sets for each printer or plotter. Put them all in one set.

You must use more than one driver set only when you change either the physical display or the way 1-2-3 displays information, which is an option with some display systems. (With a Hercules card, for example, you can display text as either 25×80 or 38×90.)

If you switch equipment and use different printers and plotters, you can install them all in one driver set. Whenever you specify a text printer, Install asks whether you have another printer. If you sometimes attach another printer to your system, answer *Yes* and then select the other printer. You can complete this step for as many as four different printers that you might attach to your computer. Repeat the step for any printers or plotters that you might attach to your computer for printing graphs.

You are not limited to four graphics printers. Because the program does not expect more than one printer or plotter to be used at a time, you can install more than one, even when only one is attached. Then, while you're working in 1-2-3, use the /Worksheet Global Default Printer Name command to select the printer currently attached to your computer. If the printer you select as the default printer is to remain the default, you must select Update from the /Worksheet Global Default menu. This command saves the defaults to disk; then, whenever you start 1-2-3, the same defaults are in effect.

If you attach printers to different ports on your computer, you must use the /Worksheet Global Default Printer Interface command to tell 1-2-3 which printer interface to use. Parallel printers usually are Parallel 1. If you have more than one parallel-printer port, you must specify the one to which the printer is connected. If you use a serial printer, you must specify which serial port (interface) you're using (usually Serial 1). If you use a local area network and printed output is redirected to another computer, you may have to specify DOS Device LPT1: to LPT4:.

In PrintGraph, use Settings Hardware Printer to specify the printer or plotter. 1-2-3 then lists all the graph printers and plotters that you included in your driver set (see fig. T.4). Use Settings Hardware Interface to specify the correct LPT or COM port. After you make the changes, use Settings Save to make the new settings the default.

Problems with Hard Disk Installation

WARNING:

Problems with copy protection on a hard disk can cost you the use of the System disk. This can happen in the following instances: if your hard disk fails completely; if you restore the entire hard disk; or, possibly, if you use a utility program to reorganize your hard disk.

Fig. T.4

A list of all graph output devices in the driver set.

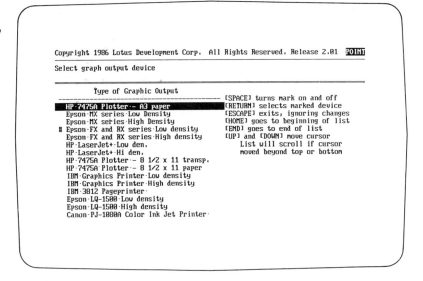

```
Copyright 1986 Lotus Development Corp. All Rights Reserved. Release 2.01  POINT

Select graph output device
_____

        Type of Graphic Output
----------------------------------------------- [SPACE] turns mark on and off
  HP-7475A Plotter -- A3 paper                   [RETURN] selects marked device
  Epson-MX series-Low Density                    [ESCAPE] exits, ignoring changes
  Epson-MX series-High Density                   [HOME] goes to beginning of list
# Epson-FX and RX series-Low density             [END] goes to end of list
  Epson-FX and RX series-High density            [UP] and [DOWN] move cursor
  HP-LaserJet+-Low den.                                List will scroll if cursor
  HP-LaserJet+-Hi den.                                 moved beyond top or bottom
  HP-7475A Plotter -- 8 1/2 x 11 transp.
  HP-7475A Plotter -- 8 1/2 x 11 paper
  IBM-Graphics Printer-Low density
  IBM-Graphics Printer-High density
  IBM-3812 Pageprinter-
  Epson-LQ-1500-Low density
  Epson-LQ-1500-High density
  Canon-PJ-1080A Color Ink Jet Printer-
```

You must troubleshoot this problem before it happens. If you run COPYHARD or use Install to move the copy protection to a hard disk, you must be careful not to lose the protection information permanently.

HARD DISK PROBLEM #1:

You used the DOS BACKUP and RESTORE commands to restore your hard disk, and now you can't execute 1-2-3.

EXPLANATION: The copy protection files written to the hard disk by COPYHARD or Install are known as hidden, read-only files. Because they are DOS files, these hidden files are backed up if you back up the entire hard disk. If you restore the hard disk from a floppy disk and, in the process, restore the hidden files, the copy protection information appears to be invalid to 1-2-3. You must use your Backup System disk and contact either your dealer or Lotus for a replacement disk.

SOLUTION: If you have backed up your entire disk, you must use the /P parameter when you use the DOS RESTORE command. (This parameter indicates that you want DOS to prompt you before it restores any files that have been changed or that are marked read-only.) Then you can answer *no* to the Restore any read-only files? prompt.

ALTERNATE SOLUTION: A safer solution is to use Install's Advanced Options to remove the copy protection from the hard disk before you start a full disk backup. After you again install the program on a hard disk, back up only your data directories.

NOTES: 1. If your hard disk fails, you may not be able to recover the copy protection. Before a hard disk fails completely, you usually receive warnings that something is wrong. If you start receiving data errors, seek errors, or other disk errors, immediately remove the copy protection. Use the System disk to start 1-2-3 until you have either replaced your hard disk or made sure that it is not failing.

2. Hard disks are most vulnerable to failure when they are new. Do not use COPYHARD or Install to install the copy protection on a hard disk unless you have used the disk for at least two weeks with no disk-related errors.

3. Because you cannot restore the copy protection information from a backup floppy disk to a hard disk, you cannot restore this information to another hard disk. If you must move the 1-2-3 program to a different hard disk, you must remove the copy protection information from the first disk and reinstall it on the other disk.

4. Many of the hard-disk utilities available on the market can optimize disk performance, recover lost files, and rearrange files and directories. Some of these utilities may also destroy the 1-2-3 copy protection information.

Before you use one of these hard-disk utilities, ask your vendor whether the utility has been tested on 1-2-3 Release 2 or later. If you have any doubt, remove the copy protection information before you use the utility to reorganize your hard disk.

Troubleshooting the 1-2-3 Spreadsheet

Problems with Data Entry

DATA ENTRY PROBLEM #1:

After you type a label that starts with a number, the program beeps and puts you in EDIT mode.

EXPLANATION: When you begin typing information in a cell, 1-2-3 changes the READY mode indicator in the screen's upper right corner to either LABEL or VALUE. If the first character you type is a number or a symbol used in a formula, the program assumes that you are typing a value. If you then type any character that is invalid for a value entry, 1-2-3 beeps, moves the cursor to the first character it rejected, and switches to EDIT mode.

SOLUTION: To type a label such as **353 Sacramento Street**, you must first type a label prefix, such as an apostrophe ('), so that 1-2-3 knows you are working with a label. If you forget to enter the prefix, and 1-2-3 beeps, press Home and insert the apostrophe.

If the label is a valid numeric entry, instead of an error you'll get a numeric calculation that you don't want. For example, if you type *(317)-842-7162* as a telephone number, 1-2-3 evaluates the entry as a formula and displays -7687. Edit the field to change it from a number to a label.

DATA ENTRY PROBLEM #2:

When you finish writing a complex formula, 1-2-3 switches to EDIT mode. If you can't find the error immediately, you have to press Esc. You lose the entire formula and have to start again.

EXPLANATION: When you type an invalid formula, the program refuses to accept the entry and switches to EDIT mode. You must provide a valid entry before you can continue.

SOLUTION: Make the formula a valid entry by converting it to a label: press the Home key, type an apostrophe, and press Enter. Then you can work on the problem until you find and correct the error. Or you can work on another part of the worksheet and return to the formula later.

You may have used a range name in the formula without having created the name. If you forgot to create a range name, convert the formula to a label, create the range name, and then edit the formula to remove the label prefix.

NOTE: Here is a method for debugging complex formulas. For example, suppose that you enter this formula in a cell:

@IF(@ISERR(A1/A2),@IF(A2=0),0,@ERR),A1/A2)

When you press Enter, 1-2-3 beeps and switches to EDIT mode. If the error isn't obvious, you are stuck. You cannot exit EDIT mode unless you either fix the error or press Esc, erasing the contents of the cell. But because the program accepts anything as a label, you can insert a label prefix at the beginning of the entry and then press Enter. Then copy the formula to another cell and work on it until you find the error.

In this case, begin by eliminating the compound @IF from the formula. To do so, copy the formula to a blank cell (a work area) and then erase the middle @IF statement, replacing it with a zero:

@IF(@ISERR(A1/A2),0,A1/A2)

Because this formula works, the problem must be in the @IF statement that you erased. Again, copy the original formula to the work area. Now delete everything except the middle @IF:

@IF(A2=0),0,@ERR

You can see that you should erase the right parenthesis that follows A2=0. Make the change and test it:

@IF(A2=0,0,@ERR)

When this segment works, erase the work cell and correct the original formula:

@IF(@ISERR(A1/A2),@IF(A2=0,0,@ERR),A1/A2)

You may write formulas that are longer and more complex than this example. To debug them, simply convert them to labels and test them, one part at a time.

Problems with Circular References

CIRCULAR REFERENCE PROBLEM #1:
The CIRC indicator suddenly appears after you enter a formula.

EXPLANATION: Whenever the worksheet is recalculated and a CIRC indicator appears at the lower right corner of the screen, 1-2-3 is warning you about a *circular reference*. Circular references are formulas that refer to themselves, either directly or indirectly. Because they usually are errors, you should correct circular references as soon as they occur.

An example of the most common direct circular reference is shown in figure T.5. In this example, the @SUM function includes itself in the range to be summed. Whenever the worksheet recalculates, this sum increases.

Fig. T.5

A direct circular reference.

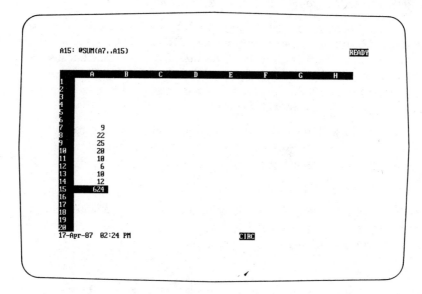

SOLUTION: Change the @SUM formula to include the cells through A14, but excluding A15; the CIRC indicator will disappear.

CIRCULAR REFERENCE PROBLEM #2:

The CIRC indicator appears after you enter a formula, but the formula does not refer to itself.

EXPLANATION: 1-2-3 is warning you about an indirect circular reference, which is tricky to find and to fix. No formula refers to itself, but two or more formulas refer to each other. For example, each formula in figure T.6 seems reasonable, but A1 refers to A3, A2 refers to A1, and A3 refers to A2. You have no way of evaluating these formulas. The numbers increase whenever the worksheet recalculates.

SOLUTION: If you can't find an obvious reason for the CIRC indicator, use /Worksheet Status to find the cell location of the circular reference (see fig.

Fig. T.6

An indirect circular reference.

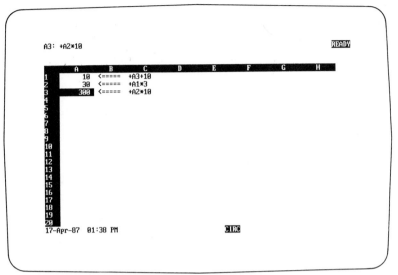

T.7). If, after looking at the formula in the cell, you still cannot find the problem, write down the formula and check the contents of every cell referenced. You eventually will track down the problem.

Fig. T.7

/Worksheet Status shows a circular reference.

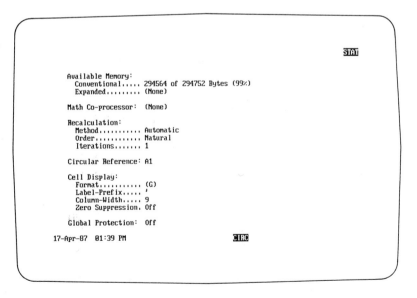

ALTERNATE EXPLANATION: @CELL("width") can cause an annoying circular reference if you use the cell address that contains this function to determine the width of the column that contains the formula. For example, if cell C9 contains the formula:

@CELL("width",C9..C9)

it is considered a circular reference.

ALTERNATE SOLUTION: Because all the cells in the column must be the same width, change the formula to refer to another cell in the same column:

@CELL("width",C8..C8)

CIRCULAR REFERENCE PROBLEM #3:

You have a formula that is supposed to be a circular reference and you don't know how many times to recalculate to get the correct answer.

EXPLANATION: Even deliberate circular references can be a problem. Figure T.8 shows a profit calculation in which total profit depends on the amount of the executive bonus, but the bonus is based on profits—a legitimate circular reference. Every time 1-2-3 recalculates, the profit figure comes closer to the right answer. The problem lies in knowing how many recalculations you need. The general answer is that you must recalculate until the change in the results is insignificant.

Fig. T.8

A deliberate circular reference.

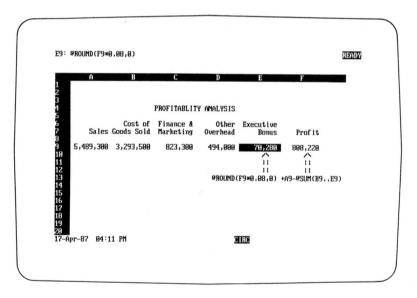

SOLUTION: You can recalculate manually if this is a one-time calculation and the worksheet is small. Use @ROUND to set the required precision. In figure T.8, the bonus is rounded to whole dollars. Then press F9 (Calc) to calculate the worksheet until the profit number does not change. In the example shown in figure T.8, you must calculate the worksheet four times before the profit figure stops changing.

ALTERNATE SOLUTION: If the circular reference is part of a large worksheet, recalculation may take an inordinate amount of time. Use the macro in figure T.9 to recalculate only part of the worksheet until you get the correct answer.

Fig. T.9

A macro with a {RECALC} that resolves a circular reference.

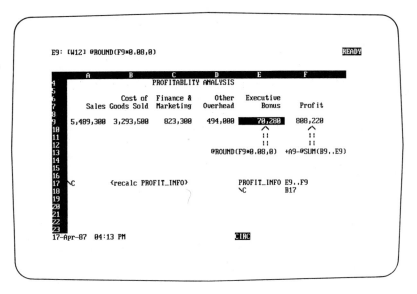

If the numbers change often and you want to recalculate automatically, use the macro in figure T.10 to recalculate the profit information until PROFIT is equal to OLD PROFIT in cell F5. Figure T.10 shows the result of executing the macro. In most cases, cell F5 would be hidden. This macro works because {RECALC} proceeds row-by-row and F5 is above PROFIT. If OLD PROFIT were below PROFIT, this macro would not work because the two numbers would always be the same and the macro would stop at the first {RECALC}.

CIRCULAR REFERENCE PROBLEM #4:

An ERR is created in one of the cells in an intentional circular reference, which causes all the cells in the circular reference also to return ERR. You remove the source of the ERR, but the remaining cells continue to show an ERR.

EXPLANATION: Cells that depend on a cell which returns an ERR will also return an ERR. If two or more cells with ERR refer to each other, the result is always ERR. Once the cells in the circular reference have been contami-

Fig. T.10

A macro that automatically solves a circular reference.

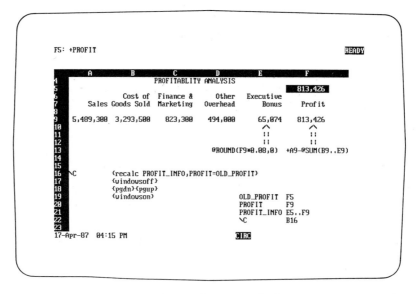

nated, you may not be able to eliminate all the ERRs no matter how many times you recalculate after you correct the original error.

SOLUTION: First break the circular reference; then correct the error and recalculate. The fastest way to break the circular reference is to copy the cells that evaluate to ERR to a work area and then erase the original cells in ERR. Then calculate the worksheet, which should cause the ERR indicators to disappear. Finally, copy the formulas back to the original cells and erase the work area.

Avoiding ERR

ERR PROBLEM #1:

A formula that had been working correctly suddenly changes to ERR.

EXPLANATION: A valid formula can be destroyed by certain subsequent entries. When the program can't evaluate part of a formula, it changes that part of the formula to ERR, and the result is ERR.

Moves, deletions, and certain entries can destroy a formula or make it invalid. If you move a cell or a range to a cell referenced in a formula, the program replaces the reference with ERR (see fig. T.11).

SOLUTION: If you want to move a *value* into a cell after you refer to that cell in a formula, you cannot use the /Move command. Instead, you must /Copy the cell and then erase the original cell.

Fig. T.11

Moving turns a formula to ERR.

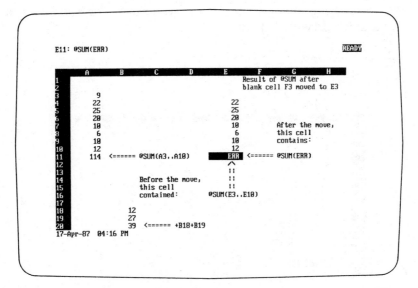

If you want to move a *formula* to a cell after you have referred to the cell in a formula, you again cannot use the /Move command. Instead, you must use the /Copy command, following these four steps:

1. Edit the formula to convert it to a label

2. Copy the label to the cell

3. Edit the label to convert it back to a formula

4. Erase the original cell

You have to convert the formula to a label to prevent relative cell references from changing when you copy the formula.

If you want the cell references to change when you copy the formula to its new location, just copy the cell as a formula.

ERR PROBLEM #2:

Formulas change to ERR after you delete a row or a column somewhere else in the worksheet.

EXPLANATION: Although you seldom deliberately delete a row or column containing information used in formulas, deleting such information accidentally is not unusual. The /Worksheet Delete Row or Column command deletes the entire row or column without giving you a chance to inspect the entire row or column; you can see only the usual screenful. Information contained in the row or column may be somewhere off-screen. Figure T.12 shows the effect of deleting row 18. As in the move example of figure T.11, the referenced cell changes to ERR.

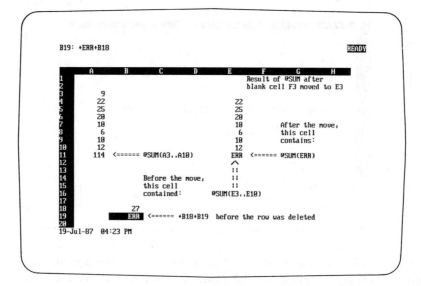

SOLUTION: Avoid this problem by checking the worksheet carefully before you delete rows or columns. To check a row, move the cell pointer to the row and then press End left-arrow and End right-arrow. If the cell pointer moves from column A to column IV, the row must be empty. Use End up-arrow and End down-arrow to see whether a column is empty from row 1 to row 8192.

Even this method is not foolproof. A formula can legitimately refer to a blank cell in a row or column that is completely blank. Perhaps the cell will contain data that has not yet been entered. If you delete this blank row or column, the formula that refers to the cell in that row or column changes to ERR.

The most foolproof way to avoid this error is to

1. Save the worksheet.

2. In a blank cell, put an @SUM formula that sums the entire active area (from A1 to {End}{Home}).

3. Delete the row or column and, if recalculation is set to manual, Calc the worksheet.

If your @SUM formula changes to ERR, you know that somewhere a cell changed to ERR when you deleted the row or column. Search the worksheet until you find the ERR. If the formula is in error, correct it. If the deleted row or column is needed, then retrieve the worksheet you saved before the deletion.

ERR PROBLEM #3:

String formulas change to ERR after you erase a cell or a range.

EXPLANATION: With numeric formulas, it usually does not matter whether a cell contains a number or a string or whether it is blank. Blank cells and cells containing strings are treated as zeros in numeric calculations. (In Release 2.0, however, these cells are not always treated as zeros. One of the reasons Lotus upgraded Release 2 to Release 2.01 is that in Release 2, numeric formulas result in ERR when any referenced cell contains a string formula.)

But, even in Release 2.01, string formulas are not as forgiving as numeric formulas. A string formula results in ERR if any referenced cell is blank or contains numeric values. If you erase a cell used in a string formula, the string formula changes to ERR. This may be an acceptable change if you plan to enter new data in the cell. Figure T.13 shows some examples of numeric and string formulas.

Fig. T.13

Blank cells and numbers cause ERR in string functions.

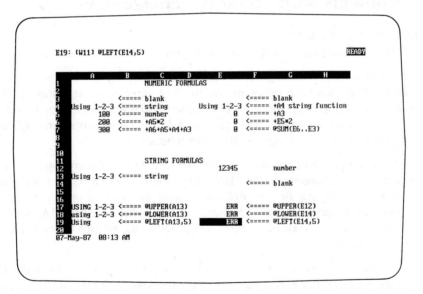

SOLUTION: If you are sure that you will complete the blank cells before you print the worksheet, nothing needs to be done. In fact, you can leave the ERR to remind you that data is missing.

If the data is optional, you must trap the possible error in the formula. You can test for a null string in the cell before referencing the cell in the formula.

A blank cell is treated as though it contains a null string (""). For example, the formula

    +A1&B1

concatenates the strings in A1 and B1 if both contain strings. If A1 always contains a string and B1 can be blank, change the formula to

    +A1&@IF(B1="","",B1)

If A1 is either blank or a number, the result is ERR, and the program warns you that something is wrong. If B1 is blank, no error occurs and the formula equates to the contents of A1.

Here's another formula that behaves in a similar manner:

    +A1&@S(B1..B1)

The @S function avoids errors, filtering out anything that is not a string. This formula works if B1 contains a label, number, or is blank.

Problems with Memory Management

MEMORY PROBLEM #1:
While working on a large worksheet, you run out of memory.

EXPLANATION: Running out of memory is one of the most common problems in 1-2-3. Because the program was the first spreadsheet to allow the full use of 640K of memory, most users assumed that they would never run out of memory. They kept building bigger worksheets, eventually ran out of memory, and then had to redesign their entire worksheets.

Part of the problem was solved when Release 2 provided an improved method of memory management for blank cells. Some worksheets that were too big for Release 1A can fit into Release 2, with its better memory management. However, because Release 2 is much bigger than Release 1A, leaving less memory for the worksheet, some worksheets that fit into Release 1A are too big for Release 2.

SOLUTION: There are several ways to avoid running out of memory. But because none of them is foolproof, use /Worksheet Status to check available memory while you build large worksheets.

Proper worksheet design is the best way to avoid memory problems. Don't try to put an entire accounting system into one worksheet. And don't try to use one worksheet for all your product-line forecasts, even if the worksheets for all the products lines are identical. Instead, build separate worksheets based on a single template. Not only do properly designed worksheets save memory; they also speed recalculation. (The larger the worksheet, the longer you must wait whenever you recalculate.)

Sophisticated analysis models can require a dozen or more separate worksheets. Each of these worksheets can either print a detailed report or (for a smaller, consolidated report) extract data to be combined into a summary report.

ALTERNATE SOLUTION: Another way to avoid memory problems is to make sure that your computer has the maximum amount of memory. If you want to build large worksheets, you need at least 640K, the maximum amount of memory that normal programs can use. Memory has become so inexpensive that most of the new computers on the market, including the IBM Personal System/2, include at least 640K of standard memory. If your computer comes with 256K, you can add 384K for as little as $100 to $150.

Because 1-2-3 users wanted to build increasingly larger worksheets, Lotus (working with Intel and Microsoft) developed the LIM expanded memory specification (EMS). This hardware and software specification lets a program use memory that exceeds the 640K limit. To use expanded memory, a program must know about EMS. Although you cannot use EMS with older programs, you can use as many as four megabytes of expanded memory with 1-2-3 Release 2 and later. Because a normal memory board doesn't work with more than 640K, however, you must buy a special memory expansion board designed to be an EMS board.

Expanded memory works in both the PC (and compatibles) and the AT (and compatibles). AST Research, Inc., has devised an extended EMS called EEMS. Both EMS and EEMS boards provide the same expansion capabilities for 1-2-3 worksheets.

Using expanded memory does not solve all memory problems. Although certain parts of worksheets—labels, formulas, decimal numbers, and integers larger than 32,767—use expanded memory, everything else must be in regular memory (up to 640K). And you must have four bytes in regular memory for every cell stored in expanded memory. You can have a maximum of approximately 100,000 individual cell entries before you run out of conventional memory, which means that you can run out of memory and still have megabytes of expanded memory that you have not used (and cannot use).

ALTERNATE SOLUTION: Because formulas take up more space than numbers, you can use formulas to build a worksheet and then, using the /Range Value command, convert the formulas to numbers. Use this method with any numbers that will not change when you update the worksheet. (Be sure to save the original template with the unconverted formulas, in case you later discover that you need the formulas.)

Because the results of the /Data Table command are numbers, not formulas, you can save memory by converting large tables of formulas to data tables. Then repeat the /Data Table command to recalculate the tables if the values in the input cells change. Do not use this technique in a large worksheet if you frequently need to recalculate the data table—it could take several minutes or even hours.

ALTERNATE SOLUTION: The shape of the active area also can affect the total amount of memory used by the worksheet. The active area is defined as a rectangle starting in cell A1 and ending in the last row and last column that (1) contains either data or a range format or (2) is unprotected. For example, a worksheet with a value in G3 and a format in A12 has an active area from A1 to G12. A worksheet with cell AF4 unprotected and a label in B300 has an active area from A1 to AF300.

The shape of the active area, critical in release 1A, is less important in Release 2. Although Lotus says that the Release 2 memory-management scheme uses no memory for empty cells, this statement does not appear to be true. For example, putting the number *1* in cells A1, A2, B1, and B2 uses 32 bytes of memory. Putting the number *1* in cells A1, A8192, IV1, and IV8192 uses 65,506 bytes of memory. (In fact, simply formatting or unprotecting those four cells uses 65,506 bytes—even though you enter no data at all in the worksheet.)

If memory is a problem, keep the shape of the occupied cells in your worksheet as small as possible. To move the cursor to the lower right corner of the active area of any worksheet, press End-Home. You may be surprised to discover that a stray entry is costing you quite a bit of memory.

ALTERNATE SOLUTION: If you frequently move, insert, and delete rows and columns when you build large worksheets, you may run out of memory. When you move data or delete rows and columns, not all the memory is recovered. You usually can recover the memory by saving the worksheet and retrieving it again.

Troubleshooting 1-2-3 Commands

Problems with Range Names

RANGE NAMES PROBLEM #1:

A range name that was valid suddenly results in an ERR.

EXPLANATION: Moving and deleting cells and ranges can change formulas to ERR (see the PROBLEMs on "Avoiding ERR"). These operations also cause the loss of range names. Both ranges and range names are identified by the upper left corner cell and the lower right corner cell. If you move a cell or a range of cells to one of these corner cells, the range name is lost. Suppose, for example, that you are working with the range name table shown in figure T.14. After a few move and delete operations, your range name table changes (see fig. T.15). As you can see, you have lost only those range names in which the cells in the upper left or lower right corners were affected.

Fig. T.14

A range name table.

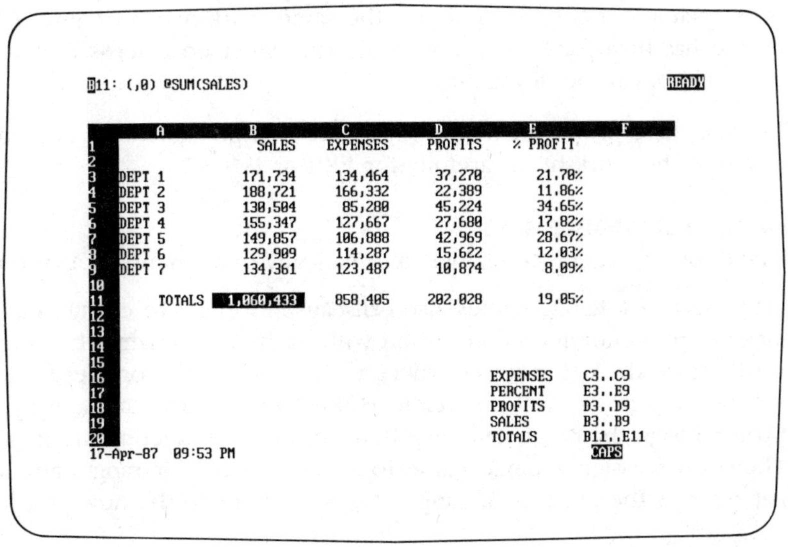

```
B11: (,0) @SUM(SALES)                                              READY

         A          B          C          D          E          F
1                 SALES     EXPENSES    PROFITS    % PROFIT
2
3   DEPT 1        171,734    134,464     37,270     21.70%
4   DEPT 2        188,721    166,332     22,389     11.86%
5   DEPT 3        130,504     85,280     45,224     34.65%
6   DEPT 4        155,347    127,667     27,680     17.82%
7   DEPT 5        149,857    106,888     42,969     28.67%
8   DEPT 6        129,909    114,287     15,622     12.03%
9   DEPT 7        134,361    123,487     10,874      8.09%
10
11    TOTALS    1,060,433    858,405    202,028     19.05%
12
13
14
15
16                                      EXPENSES    C3..C9
17                                      PERCENT     E3..E9
18                                      PROFITS     D3..D9
19                                      SALES       B3..B9
20                                      TOTALS      B11..E11
17-Apr-87  09:53 PM                                          CAPS
```

Fig. T.15

A range name table after moving and deleting.

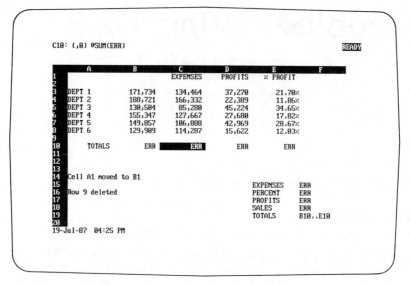

SOLUTION: Although both ranges and range names are lost in the same manner, using range names provides an easy way to audit these errors. Keep a current range name table in all your worksheets. After you make any changes, re-create the range name table and look for ERR.

CAUTION: If you lose a range name, and then save and later retrieve the file, something strange happens—the lost range names no longer are lost. Any cell that was erased or had data moved into, however, is changed to cell IV8192. As an example, figure T.16 shows the same worksheet as figure T.15 after the file has been saved and retrieved. The effect on macros that use these range names can be disastrous.

To avoid these problems, frequently create a range name table and check the table and the worksheet carefully for ERR or IV8192.

RANGE NAMES PROBLEM #2:

A valid formula seems to change automatically to an incorrect cell reference.

EXPLANATION: Range names also can cause formulas to change incorrectly. For example, a common convention with macros is to name the current cell HERE, move the cell pointer wherever it's needed to complete the macro, and then return the cell pointer to HERE. This process can cause problems if you reassign the range name HERE instead of first deleting the range name. When you reassign a range name to a different cell or range, any formulas that refer to the old cell or range change to refer to the new cell or range.

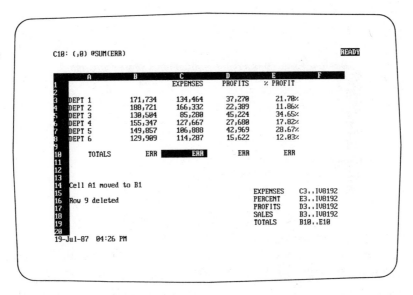

Fig. T.16

A range name table after the file is saved and retrieved.

In figure T.17, cell A10 is named HERE, and the formula in A12 refers to A10. Figure T.18 shows the same worksheet after the name HERE has been reassigned to refer to C10. Notice that the formula in A12 now refers to C10.

SOLUTION: To avoid this problem, always use /**R**ange **N**ame **D**elete before you use /**R**ange **N**ame **C**reate to reassign a range name.

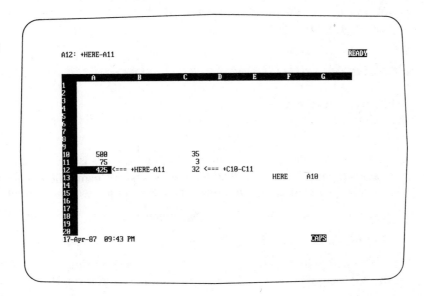

Fig. T.17

A formula using the range name HERE.

Fig. T.18

*The formula after
HERE is reassigned.*

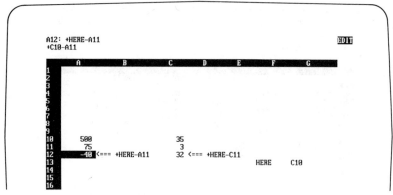

RANGE NAMES PROBLEM #3:

A range name looks correct in the range name table, but the macros and formulas that refer to the named range do not work properly.

EXPLANATION: This problem occurs when you use a range name that is also a cell address. If you set up a complex report and give the individual pages the range names P1, P2, and P3, the printed report will contain only the cells P1, P2, and P3. If you give a macro the range name GO2 and then {BRANCH GO2}, the macro will branch to cell GO2 and, probably, stop at a blank cell.

SOLUTION: Never name a range with a combination of one or two letters and a number. Don't even use a range name such as TO4; a range name that is not a valid cell address in the current version of 1-2-3 may be a valid cell address in a future release.

Problems with Relative and Absolute Addressing

ADDRESSING PROBLEM #1:

After you copy a formula to other cells, the copied formulas are incorrect—the addresses are wrong.

EXPLANATION: One of 1-2-3's handiest built-in features is the automatic formula adjustment for relative cell addressing when a formula is copied. Relative addressing is so natural and automatic that you no longer think about it.

For example, consider the following formula in cell A4:

+A1+A2-A3

When the cell pointer is positioned in A4, the program displays this formula on the top line of the control panel. You think of the formula as

Add the contents of A1 and A2 and subtract the contents of A3.

If you copy the formula from A4 to B4, it becomes

+B1+B2-B3

This result, which is exactly what you would expect after you have gained some experience in using 1-2-3, depends on what is called relative addressing. Each formula is stored with addresses relative to the cell that contains the formula. Internally, 1-2-3 interprets the formula in A4 as:

Add the contents of the cell three rows up and the cell two rows up and subtract the contents of the cell one row up.

This is the same formula originally in A4 and copied into B4.

You frequently do not want the cell references to change when you copy a formula. If you copy the cell references as relative addresses, you get the wrong formula. In figure T.19, for example, the formula for percent of total was written in C2 and copied to C3..C13. The relative addressing adjustment changes the formula in C3 from +B2/B14 to +B3/B15.

Fig. T.19

Relative and absolute addressing.

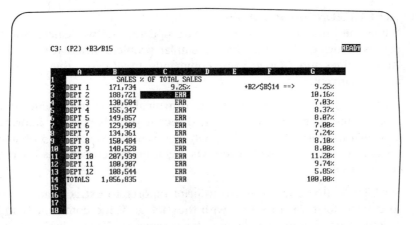

SOLUTION: Specify an address as absolute when you write the formula, not when you copy it. To make an address absolute, precede the column and the row by a dollar sign ($). If you use the pointing method to specify a range or a cell address, make the address absolute by pressing F4—the ABS or Absolute key— when you point to the cell. If you type a cell address manually, make the address absolute by pressing F4 after you type the address.

The formula in C2 should be +B2/$B$14. When you copy this formula, the relative address (B2) changes, but the absolute address ($B$14) does not change. The correct formulas are shown in column G.

Problems with Recalculation

RECALCULATION PROBLEM #1:

As your worksheets become larger, recalculation becomes annoyingly slow.

EXPLANATION: Whenever you add or change a cell, 1-2-3 recalculates the entire worksheet. At first, this recalculation is almost instantaneous, and you can ignore the delay. As you add formulas and include more complex formulas and string functions, the delay increases noticeably and becomes annoying. Your work can slow down dramatically if you add data to many cells in a large worksheet.

SOLUTION: The first solution is to change recalculation to manual by using the /Worksheet Global Recalculation Manual command. You experience no delay the next time you make an entry, because no recalculation occurs. To warn you that the information in some of the cells may be incorrect, the CALC indicator appears at the bottom of the screen.

Press the F9 (Calc) key when you want the program to recalculate the worksheet. The CALC indicator disappears until you make another entry.

RECALCULATION PROBLEM #2:

When you print reports after you have updated the worksheet, some of the data is incorrect. You may have a similar problem when you use the /File Xtract Values and /Range Value commands. In all cases, the resulting values are not current.

EXPLANATION: When recalculation is manual, the current values of any formula in the worksheet may be incorrect if you change the information in cells that the formula uses. Generally, you cannot expect 1-2-3 commands to recalculate the worksheet (even when getting the correct answer requires a recalculation).

SOLUTION: If you use a macro to print reports, to extract data as values, or to convert formulas to values with the /Range Value command, add {CALC} to the macro before it executes the commands. If you don't use a macro, press F9 to recalculate manually.

RECALCULATION PROBLEM #3:

When you use the /File Combine Add (or Subtract) command to transfer information from another worksheet, the transferred data is not current.

EXPLANATION: This problem is related to the preceding one. If you save a file that recalculates manually and later combine all or part of that file into another worksheet, the current values of the formulas may be incorrect (even if the current worksheet is set for automatic recalculation).

The /File Combine Add (and Subtract) commands use the current values of the formulas in the source file. Unless these formulas are recalculated, the values combined with the /FCA or /FCS commands may be incorrect. On the other hand, the /File Combine Copy command brings formulas, not current values, into the worksheet. Therefore, you do not have to be concerned about whether the source file has been recalculated.

SOLUTION: In this case (unlike the preceding problem, in which you can calculate the worksheet immediately before executing the command), you must calculate the source worksheet before saving it. If you use a macro to save your worksheet, add {CALC} to the macro before it saves the file. If you don't use a macro, recalculate manually by pressing the F9 (Calc) key before you save the file.

RECALCULATION PROBLEM #4:

You want to see only a few values on a large worksheet that takes a long time to recalculate, but you are spending an inordinate amount of time recalculating.

EXPLANATION: On large, complex models that can take several minutes to recalculate, you almost always use manual recalculation. If you build or change the model or enter data in one section, however, you often want to see the current values in only that area. Continually pressing the F9 (Calc) key causes you to lose time while you wait for the program to recalculate the entire worksheet.

SOLUTION: You can recalculate only part of a worksheet in one of several ways.

To recalculate a single cell, simply edit the cell. Press F2 (Edit) and then press Enter.

To recalculate a range of cells, copy the range to itself. Figure T.20 shows a range that is part of a large worksheet. To recalculate the cells in only the range BC65..BH75, copy the range BC65..BH75 to BC65. All the cells in the range recalculate when 1-2-3 copies them to themselves.

To recalculate part of a worksheet inside a macro, use the macro commands {RECALC} and {RECALCCOL}.

RECALCULATION PROBLEM #5:

Because your worksheet is large, you keep recalculation on manual and use the partial-recalculation methods described in the preceding solution. But the partial recalculation sometimes produces incorrect results.

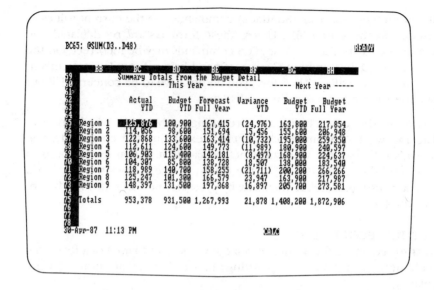

EXPLANATION: When you recalculate the entire worksheet, 1-2-3 uses natural-order calculation as the default. In other words, unless you change the recalculation order to Rowwise or Columnwise, 1-2-3 always calculates a cell after calculating the results of all the cells to which that cell refers. This step avoids problems that occurred in older spreadsheet programs, which could calculate only across rows or down columns. With natural-order calculation, formulas can be anywhere in the worksheet; with other calculation methods, formulas are correct after one recalculation *only* when they refer to cells above or to the left of the cell being recalculated. Formulas that refer to a cell address below and to the right of the cell being recalculated are known as *forward references*.

The worksheet shown in figure T.21 contains forward references. When you press F9 (Calc), the program calculates the correct answer. Figures T.22A, T.22B, and T.22C show the results of different methods of partial recalculation. Certain combinations produce correct results, but others are incorrect.

Figure T.22A shows the same formulas as figure T.21 before any calculation. Figure T.22B shows the results after a Copy or {RECALCCOL} recalculates the formulas by column. The formula in A2 is incorrect because it was calculated while cell B1 still contained a value of 1. Later, Column B was calculated and cell B1 became 101, but it was too late to change the value in A2. The other formulas are correct.

Figure T.22C shows the results after a {RECALC} recalculates the formulas by row. The formula in B3 is incorrect because it was calculated while cell A4

Fig. T.21

A worksheet with forward references.

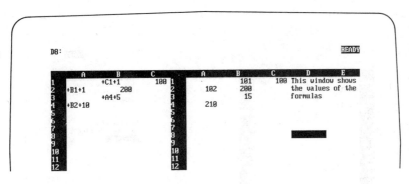

Fig. T.22A

A worksheet with forward references before recalculation.

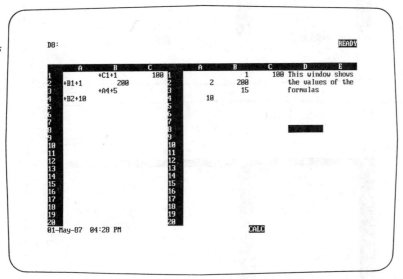

still contained a value of 10. Later, row 4 was calculated and cell A4 became 210, but it was too late to change the value in B3. The other formulas are correct.

SOLUTION: No complete solution to the problem exists. The only way to get complete natural-order recalculation is to recalculate the entire worksheet. If you know the structure of the data and the formulas, however, you can make sure that you get the correct answer from partial recalculation.

First, be sure to recalculate all the cells that are referenced by the formulas in the area you want to recalculate. Suppose, for example, that you want to recalculate part of a large worksheet (see fig. T.23). If you change the discount rate in BA60 and then recalculate the range BD65..BD75, you'll get an in-

Fig. T.22B

*Forward references
after recalculation
by column.*

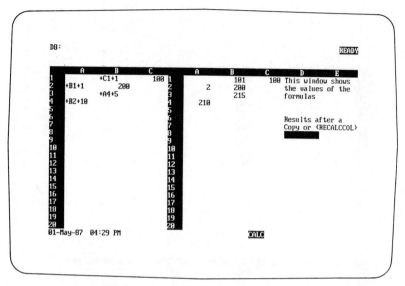

Fig. T.22C

*Forward references
after recalculation
by row.*

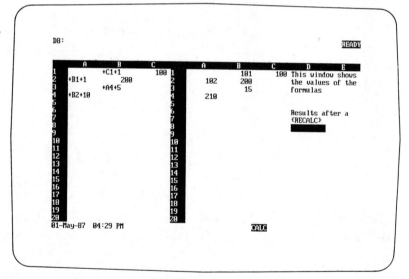

correct answer because the average discounts are not recalculated. To get
the correct answer, recalculate the range BC65..BD75. (Note that you do not
have to include cell BA60 in the recalculation because that cell contains a
number and is not affected by a recalculation.)

Try to avoid forward references in the area in which you want partial recalculation. If no forward references are present, the partial recalculations can
work.

Fig. T.23

A range that is part of a large worksheet.

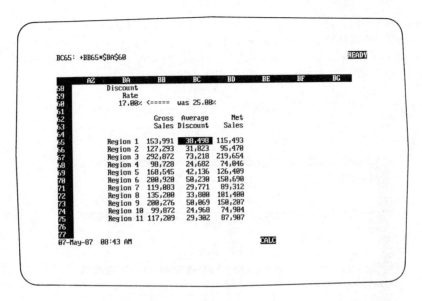

If you cannot avoid forward references, you can still get the correct answer if you pay attention to how partial recalculation proceeds. When you copy a range or use {RECALCCOL}, the program recalculates each cell, starting at the upper left corner of the range and continuing down each column. When it reaches the bottom of each column, 1-2-3 starts recalculating at the top of the next column in the range.

If you use {RECALC}, the program recalculates each cell, starting at the upper left corner of the range and continuing across each row. When it reaches the rightmost cell of each row, 1-2-3 starts recalculating at the leftmost cell in the next row.

The following rules apply to partial recalculation:

1. If you use Copy or {RECALCCOL} for a partial recalculation, the results may be incorrect for a formula which refers to another formula that is either in a column to its right or below it in the same column.

2. If you use {RECALC} for a partial recalculation, the results may be incorrect for a formula which refers to another formula that is either in a row below it or to its right in the same row.

3. Formulas that refer to cells containing values are correct using any recalculation method.

If you must use partial recalculation on a range with forward references, the only solution involves more than one recalculation. You must {RECALC} or

{RECALCCOL} once for every *nested forward reference* in the range. A nested forward reference is a formula that refers forward to a formula that refers forward (and so on) to a cell. Figure T.24 shows a series of forward references. Each {RECALC} resolves one additional forward reference.

Fig. T.24

A series of forward references.

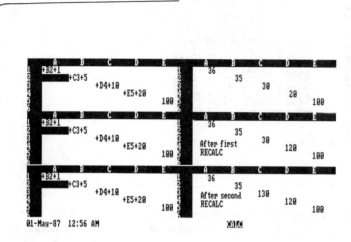

After you have determined how many nested forward references you need to recalculate, add that number of {RECALC} or {RECALCCOL} statements to your macro.

Miscellaneous Problems

SPLIT SCREEN PROBLEM #1:

When you split the screen into two windows to look at two parts of the worksheet simultaneously, the second window moves with the first one, and you can't control the second window.

EXPLANATION: You split the 1-2-3 screen for one of two basic reasons: to keep part of a large table in sight at all times, or to look at two completely different parts of a worksheet at the same time. The first of these reasons is the more common of the two. Figure T.25 shows an example of this kind of split screen. The totals are always displayed in the bottom window. When you scroll the top window, the bottom window scrolls with it, ensuring that the columns in both windows always match (see fig. T.26). This *synchronized scrolling* is the default (the Sync option) when you split the screen (horizontally or vertically) into two windows. In a vertical split, the same rows are displayed in the left and right windows.

E7: 150222 READY

	A	B	C	D	E	F	G
1		BUDGET SUMMARIES					
2							
3							
4							
5		January	February	March	April	May	June
6		-------	-------	-------	-------	-------	-------
7	Region 1	129,767	136,256	143,069	150,222	157,733	165,620
8	Region 2	125,297	131,562	138,140	145,047	152,300	159,915
9	Region 3	114,807	120,547	126,575	132,903	139,548	146,526
10	Region 4	121,220	127,281	133,645	140,327	147,343	154,710
11	Region 5	135,937	142,734	149,871	157,364	165,233	173,494
12	Region 6	113,055	118,708	124,643	130,875	137,419	144,290
13	Region 7	130,880	137,424	144,295	151,510	159,085	167,039
14	Region 8	100,345	105,362	110,630	116,162	121,970	128,068
15	Region 9	106,299	111,614	117,194	123,054	129,207	135,667
16	Region 10	125,816	132,106	138,712	145,647	152,930	160,576
17	Region 11	135,100	141,855	148,948	156,395	164,215	172,426
18	Region 12	105,713	110,999	116,549	122,377	128,495	134,920
	A	B	C	D	E	F	G
49	TOTALS	4,989,312	5,238,778	5,500,717	5,775,753	6,064,540	6,367,768

01-May-87 01:22 AM CAPS

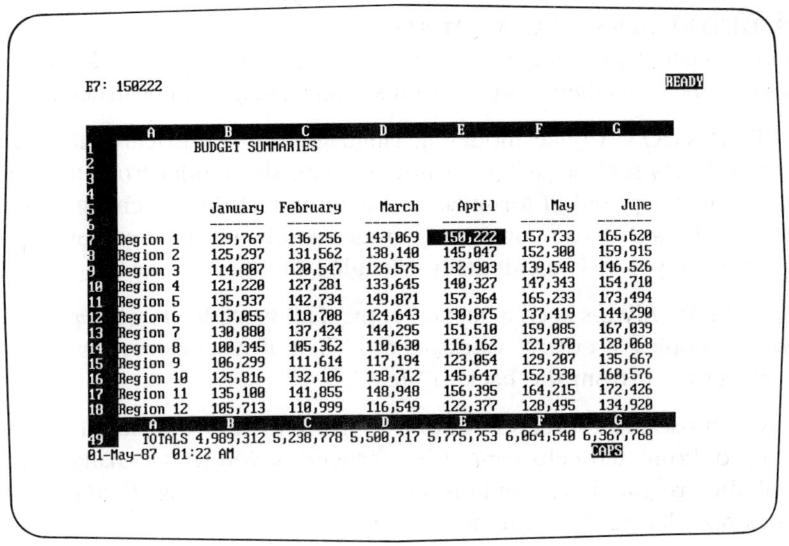

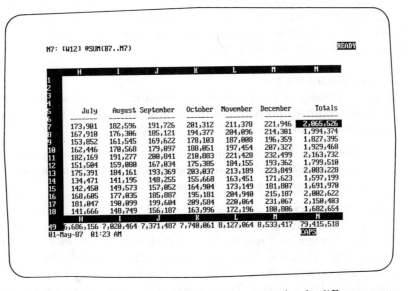

Fig. T.25

The display split into two windows.

N7: [W12] @SUM(B7..M7) READY

	H	I	J	K	L	M	N
1							
2							
3							
4							
5	July	August	September	October	November	December	Totals
6	-------	-------	-------	-------	-------	-------	--------
7	173,901	182,596	191,726	201,312	211,378	221,946	2,065,526
8	167,910	176,306	185,121	194,377	204,096	214,301	1,994,374
9	153,852	161,545	169,622	178,103	187,008	196,359	1,827,395
10	162,446	170,568	179,097	188,051	197,454	207,327	1,929,468
11	182,169	191,277	200,841	210,883	221,428	232,499	2,163,732
12	151,504	159,080	167,034	175,385	184,155	193,362	1,799,510
13	175,391	184,161	193,369	203,037	213,189	223,849	2,083,228
14	134,471	141,195	148,255	155,668	163,451	171,623	1,597,199
15	142,450	149,573	157,052	164,904	173,149	181,807	1,691,970
16	168,605	177,035	185,887	195,181	204,940	215,187	2,002,622
17	181,047	190,099	199,604	209,584	220,064	231,067	2,150,403
18	141,666	148,749	156,187	163,996	172,196	180,806	1,682,654
	H	I	J	K	L	M	N
49	6,686,156	7,020,464	7,371,487	7,740,061	8,127,064	8,533,417	79,415,518

01-May-87 01:23 AM CAPS

Fig. T.26

The windows scroll in sync.

However, when you split the screen to look at two completely different parts of a worksheet (data and macros, for example), you do not want to use synchronized scrolling. You want to be able to move the cursor around the data area in one window while the other window remains fixed on a specific macro.

SOLUTION: To eliminate the default synchronized scrolling, you must specify /Worksheet Window Unsync after you split the screen into two windows.

DATA DESTRUCTION PROBLEM #1:

Occasionally, by making a mistake with /Copy, /Move, or /Delete, you destroy part of the worksheet and then must painstakingly reconstruct it.

EXPLANATION: Unlike modeling languages and statistical-analysis packages, spreadsheets such as 1-2-3 do not separate the model from the data. (The *model* is composed of formulas and macros that do not change. The *data* is the numbers that you continually enter and change.) When you use 1-2-3 to enter data, you risk accidentally changing the model as well.

SOLUTION: Always keep a backup copy of all worksheets. (Keep two or three backup copies of critical worksheets.) Then, if you destroy a worksheet, you can recover it from the backup file.

You can use the Protection option to prevent the worksheet from being destroyed. Protected cells cannot be changed. If you try to change a protected cell, the program beeps and displays the warning message Protected cell but does not change the contents of the cell.

Use the /Range Unprotect command to unprotect the cells you want to change. After you have completed the worksheet and are ready to use it, turn on the protection feature by issuing the /Worksheet Global Protection Enable command before you enter data.

TEMPLATE PROBLEM #1:

At the beginning of every month, you must carefully erase all the data from the past month to prepare for the new month. If you leave old data, the information for the new month will be incorrect.

EXPLANATION: This problem is related to the preceding one. Because 1-2-3 does not distinguish between the model and the data, the program can't present a blank model for the next month's data.

SOLUTION: Although 1-2-3 can't distinguish between the model and the data, you can. Build a model, or *template*: a worksheet that contains all necessary formulas, formats, and macros but no data. Save this worksheet and make a backup copy. Then use this model every month to start the new month. After you've added data to the file, always be sure to save it under a different name from that of the template. For example, you might name a budget template BUDGET. Retrieve BUDGET every month, saving it as BUD0887 in August, 1987; BUD0987 in September, 1987; and so on.

Troubleshooting Functions

FUNCTIONS PROBLEM #1:

You get apparent rounding errors, even when you have not rounded off.

EXPLANATION: When you use formats such as Fixed, Comma (,), and Currency with a fixed number of decimal places, 1-2-3 keeps the number to 15 decimal places but rounds off the display. Examples of the resulting *apparent* rounding errors are shown in figure T.27.

Fig. T.27

A worksheet with rounding errors.

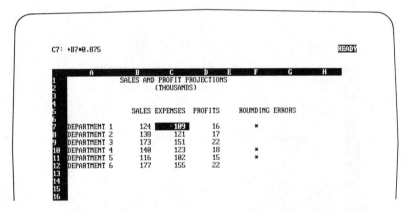

SOLUTION: To avoid such rounding errors, use the @ROUND function to round off numbers to the same precision shown in the display (see fig. T.28).

FUNCTIONS PROBLEM #2:

Two numbers that should be equal sometimes test as unequal.

EXPLANATION: This can be a sneaky problem. Figure T.29 shows what should be two identical columns of numbers. Column A was created by using /Data Fill; column B, by using a formula. The @IF formula in column C indicates that some of the numbers are not equal. This problem can occur with fractions because computers process numbers in binary, and then convert the numbers to decimal to display them. The problem does not occur with integers.

SOLUTION: Use @ROUND when you compare two fractions.

Fig. T.28

Rounding errors eliminated by @ROUND.

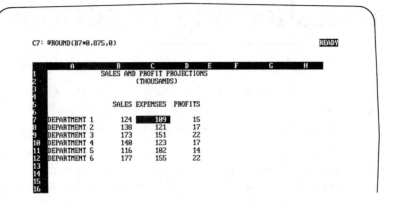

Fig. T.29

Numbers that should be equal may not test equal.

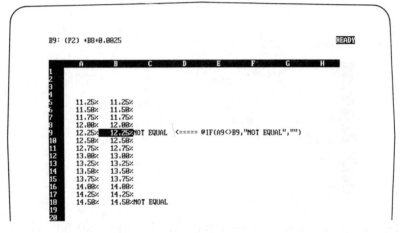

FUNCTIONS PROBLEM #3:

You get ERR when you try to combine numbers and strings.

EXPLANATION: Although Release 2 of 1-2-3 has a full complement of string functions, you cannot mix strings and numbers in the same function. Figure T.30 shows the effect of trying to build an address by using words from strings and a number for the ZIP code.

SOLUTION: Use the @STRING function to convert a number to its equivalent string (see fig. T.31). Then you can use the converted number in a string function.

Fig. T.30

An error when numbers mix with strings.

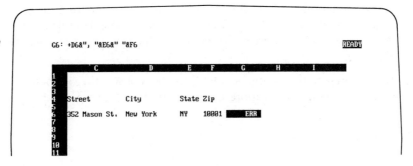

Fig. T.31

A function that converts a number to a string.

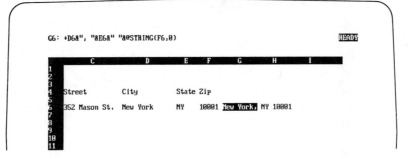

FUNCTIONS PROBLEM #4:

You want to use string functions on a field, but you are not sure whether a number or a string will be entered in the field.

EXPLANATION: All functions work on either strings or numbers, but not on both. If you don't know what a cell contains, and you guess incorrectly, you risk getting ERR or an incorrect result.

SOLUTION: You can test a cell to see whether it contains a number or a string and then, depending on the contents of the cell, use the appropriate functions. Suppose, for example, that you want to concatenate the contents of A1 and B1. The formula is

   +A1&B1

The ampersand (&), which is a string concatenation operator, causes an error if either A1 or B1 is blank or contains a number. Let's assume that you are sure that A1 contains a string but that you don't know whether B1 contains a string, a number, or is blank. To concatenate B1 to A1 only if B1 contains a string, use the following formula:

   +A1&@S(B1)

The @S function (a filter) does nothing if the cell contains a string, but returns a null string if the cell does not contain a string. The formula therefore results in either A1 (if B1 does not contain a string) or in A1&B1 (if B1 contains a string).

To concatenate the contents of B1 regardless of whether it contains a number or a string, you need a more complex formula (see fig. T.32).

Fig. T.32

A formula that handles numbers, strings, or blank cells.

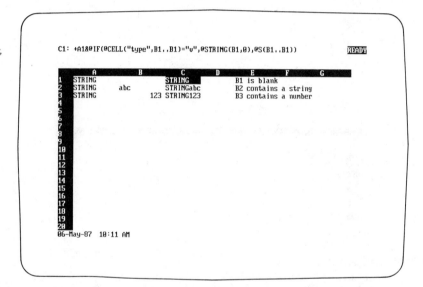

In this formula, if the type is "v" (for value), the contents of the cell are converted to a string. If the cell is blank, the @S function filters it out and the cell is ignored. If the cell contains a string, the @S function does nothing and the two strings are concatenated.

Troubleshooting File Operations

FILE PROBLEM #1:

Your hard disk contains so many files that finding the files you want is difficult; whenever you perform a file operation, long delays occur.

EXPLANATION: A single hard disk can hold hundreds—even thousands—of files. If that many files were placed in one subdirectory, however, keeping track of them would be impossible. And DOS slows down significantly if you have more than approximately 112 or 224 files (depending on which version of DOS you use) in one subdirectory.

If you try to put all the files in the root directory, DOS reaches an absolute limit and won't let you save additional files.

SOLUTION: Set up separate subdirectories for different applications and users.

The default directory should contain the subdirectory of files that you use most often. To specify the name of this subdirectory, use the /Worksheet Global Default Directory command.

To reach files in other subdirectories, use the /File Directory command. This command changes the directory until you either use /File Directory again or return to the default directory by quitting and reentering 1-2-3.

FILE PROBLEM #2:

You want to retrieve a file that is not in the default directory, but you don't remember which directory contains the file.

EXPLANATION: You can see only the files in the current directory. The file you want is in another subdirectory, but 1-2-3 does not list all of the disk's subdirectories.

SOLUTION: Select /File List, and choose Worksheet, Print, Graph, or Other, depending on the type of file you're looking for. 1-2-3 displays a list of all files of that type and all subdirectories on the current directory. To search forward through a chain of directories, move the cursor to the directory you want and press Enter. To search backwards through the chain of directories, use the Backspace key. When you locate your file, use the /File Directory and File Retrieve commands to retrieve the file.

ALTERNATE SOLUTION: Use the /System command to suspend 1-2-3 temporarily and return to DOS. This method makes the DOS TREE command available to you; you can use the TREE, CD, and DIR commands to find the subdirectory and file that you want.

After you have located the file, return to 1-2-3 by typing *exit* at the DOS prompt. Then you can use the **/File Directory** and **/File Retrieve** commands to read the file.

FILE PROBLEM #3:

While building a large worksheet, you fear making a mistake that will destroy part of the worksheet and cost you hours of work.

EXPLANATION: Sooner or later, everyone destroys part or all of an important worksheet. The greater your proficiency in 1-2-3, the larger and more complex the worksheets you can build—and the more disastrous the errors you can make.

SOLUTION: There may be no solution once you destroy the worksheet; you may not be able to restore it. The only solution may be to avoid the problem by preparing for it.

You can best prepare for this problem by saving your worksheet frequently when you make many changes or write macros. Be sure to save the worksheet under a different name. (If you were to use the same file name, you might save the file two or three times after making a disastrous error before discovering that you had made an error.)

If you are developing a worksheet, for example, save it under a name that includes a sequence number (such as BUDGET1, BUDGET2, BUDGET3, and so on). When you reach BUDGET10 and have done some testing, you can consider erasing BUDGET1. At least once during each development session, save the worksheet to a floppy disk. This backup copy is an additional safeguard.

If you enter data in a worksheet daily, save the worksheet under a name that includes the date (BUD0809 or BUD0810, for example).

Remember that time spent storing data is minimal compared to the time you might have to spend reentering lost data and rebuilding lost macro-driven worksheets.

FILE PROBLEM #4:

Some of the formulas brought in by **/File Combine Copy** are meaningless.

EXPLANATION: Using **/File Combine Copy** is similar to using **/Copy** within a worksheet. The same rules about relative addressing apply in both instances. If you combine (pull in) part of another worksheet that contains formulas which refer to cells in the combined area, the formulas stay the same in relation to the cells they refer to. If you combine formulas that refer to cells outside the combined area, however, these formulas become references to cells somewhere else in the current worksheet. These formulas may become meaningless, leading to incorrect results.

For example, figure T.33 shows the result of combining the data in J10..K15. Because the formula in K10 refers to cell G10, which is a blank cell in this worksheet, the result in K10 is zero. In the original worksheet, the corresponding cell contained a price and the formula gave a correct result.

Fig. T.33

Formulas may be meaningless after File Combine.

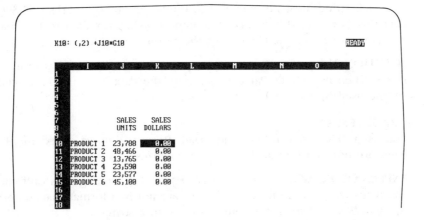

SOLUTION: You can use /File Combine Add to combine into the current worksheet the values from another worksheet. The formulas in the other worksheet are converted to numbers. If you don't want any of the formulas from the other worksheet, simply use /File Combine Add for the entire range. If you want some of the formulas from the other worksheet, first use /File Combine Copy to get the formulas. Then, to get the numbers, use /File Combine Add on a different range.

OTHER: /File Combine Add has pitfalls of its own. As 1-2-3 executes the /File Combine Add command, the program checks each cell in the current worksheet. If a cell is blank or contains a number, the corresponding value from the file being combined is added to that cell. If the cell in the current worksheet contains a formula, 1-2-3 skips that cell, regardless of what the corresponding cell in the file being combined may contain. And /File Combine Add combines in only numeric values—not strings.

FILE PROBLEM #5:

You used /File Combine Add and got old values.

EXPLANATION: Before combining them, /File Combine Add converts to values any formulas in the range to be combined. If the file is set for manual recalculation and was saved without a recalculation, some of the formulas may not reflect current values.

SOLUTION: If you intend to use a worksheet later for /File Combine Add (or Subtract), always calculate the worksheet before saving it.

FILE PROBLEM #6:

After you use /File Import Numbers to read in an ASCII file, some of the information is lost and some of it looks scrambled.

EXPLANATION: /File Import Numbers works only when the data in the ASCII file is in a precise format. Each field must be separated by commas or spaces, and each string must be enclosed in double quotation marks. 1-2-3 ignores data that is not in this format, but imports whatever data that it finds and recognizes as numbers. Ordinarily, the result is a useless mess.

SOLUTION: Using /File Import Text, read in the ASCII data as a series of long labels. Then use /Data Parse to separate the data into individual cells that can be used by 1-2-3.

FILE PROBLEM #7:

You used /File Import Text and /Data Parse to import a text file, but the dates are not in a format that 1-2-3 recognizes.

EXPLANATION: When you use /Data Parse, 1-2-3 recognizes only numbers and dates with certain formats. If dates are not in a format that the program recognizes as a date, 1-2-3 converts them to a string.

SOLUTION: In many cases, no solution is necessary. You can leave the dates as labels unless you plan to use date arithmetic on them. If you need to convert the labels to dates, however, you can do so by using string functions and @DATEVALUE.

Figure T.34 shows a directory listing that was redirected to a text file, imported into 1-2-3, and parsed. The dates in column L are labels because, with the hyphens (-) between the date fields, 1-2-3 did not recognize them as dates.

The string function in the control panel converts the string to a valid 1-2-3 date format. Next, @DATEVALUE converts to a date the string that looks like a date. Then you use the /Range Format Date command to format the cell so that it looks like a date.

FILE PROBLEM #8:

To save a backup copy, you use /File Directory to change the directory to A:\ and then use /File Save to save the file. Later, you notice that the file was not saved on drive A.

EXPLANATION: You have used procedures that work in Release 1A of 1-2-3 but not in Release 2. When you save a file in Release 2, 1-2-3 remembers the entire path that was last used to save the file or, if you haven't saved the file,

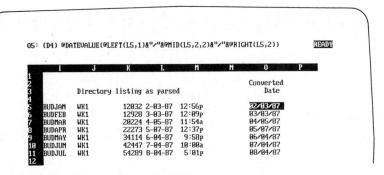

Fig. T.34

*String functions
and @DATEVALUE
to convert a date.*

to retrieve it. The program does not consider the current directory. By changing the directory and executing a /File Save, you saved the file in the original directory.

Suppose, for example, that your file BUD0810 was read from the default directory: C:\DATA\123.

You change the directory to A:\, and then use /File Save. 1-2-3 ignores the fact that the current directory is A:\ and displays the default path:

```
Enter save file name: C:\DATA\123\BUD0810
```

If you were using Release 1A, no path would display and you could now press Enter to save the file in A:\. But in Release 2, the file is saved again in C:\DATA\123.

SOLUTION: Clear the entire old path explicitly by pressing Esc three times and retyping the file name. Because you gain nothing by changing the current directory, leave it alone and include drive A in the file name. In this example, after you use /File Save you'll see the prompt:

```
Enter save file name: C:\DATA\123\BUD0810
```

Pressing Esc once displays:

```
Enter save file name: C:\DATA\123\*.WK1
```

Pressing Esc again displays:

```
Enter save file name: C:\DATA\123\
```

When you press Esc a third time, you see:

```
Enter save file name:
```

At this prompt, type *A:\BUD0810* and then press Enter. The file will be saved on drive A.

Caution: The next time you save this file, it will be saved on drive A unless you reverse the process and type the old path in drive C.

Troubleshooting Printing

PRINTING PROBLEM #1:

You have a multiple-page report that spans different sections of the worksheet. Specifying all the different print ranges is a laborious task.

EXPLANATION: The program remembers only the last print range specified. If a report has multiple print ranges, you must specify each one whenever you print the report.

SOLUTION: Create a macro. If you are not familiar with macros, read Chapters 14 and 15 to learn how to write a simple macro for printing a report, and generally how to write macros and use the Lotus Command Language.

Give each page or print range a descriptive name (PAGE1, PAGE2, and so on) and then instruct your macro to print each page (see fig. T.35). Although you may make a few errors the first time you write the macro, the finished macro will always print an error-free report.

Fig. T.35

A simple print macro.

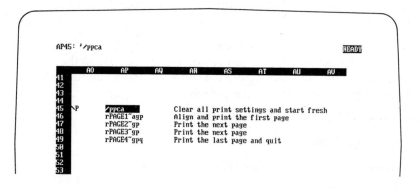

PRINTING PROBLEM #2:

Your print macro usually works as you want it to, but after you change the print options (to print a different report), the standard reports print incorrectly.

EXPLANATION: 1-2-3 remembers the print settings from the last report you printed. If you print a special report on wider paper, or with different margins, headers, footers, and setup strings, for example, these settings affect the next report that you print with the macro.

SOLUTION: At the beginning of your print macro, use the /**Print Printer Clear All** command to reset all printer options to their defaults and to clear everything else (see fig. T.35). Then have the macro specify the printer options you want. In this way, you can include in one worksheet several print macros that won't interfere with one another.

PRINTING PROBLEM #3:

After you have made changes to the worksheet, your reports sometimes print data that is not current.

EXPLANATION: In manual recalculation mode, 1-2-3 prints the worksheet as of the last recalculation.

SOLUTION: If you specify the printing options manually, press F9 (Calc) before you start the /**Print** command. If you use a macro to print, begin the macro with {CALC}.

PRINTING PROBLEM #4:

Although you calculated correctly the number of lines per page when you set up your print ranges, the report runs off the end of the page and then skips a page.

EXPLANATION: You must tell the program the exact length (in print lines) of a page. The default for six lines per inch on 11-inch paper is 66 lines. But because 1-2-3 automatically reserves three lines at the top and three lines at the bottom of each page, the maximum print range on a page is only 60 lines. (These extra lines provide one line for a header or a footer—even if none is specified—and two lines between the print range and the header or footer.) If you specify top and bottom margins, you must subtract them from 60 (not 66) to determine the maximum number of lines in a one-page print range.

SOLUTION: If you are not trying to pack the maximum number of lines into each page, you can adjust your print ranges to fit the number of available lines.

If you don't use headers, footers, or borders, you can recover the use of the six lines by using the /**Print Options Other Unformatted** command. This print setting eliminates automatic page breaks, headers, footers, and borders.

To skip to the next page, you can specify page breaks manually with the /**Print Printer Page** command. You can also specify page breaks manually by inserting page-break codes into the worksheet with the /**Worksheet Page** command. Neither of these **Page** commands is affected when you print with the **Unformatted** option.

PRINTING PROBLEM #5:

When you set up your print ranges, you considered margins and the six lines mentioned in the preceding problem. But the program occasionally skips a page between pages.

EXPLANATION: You can use one of two methods to skip to the next page when you print reports: you can specify a long report and let 1-2-3 skip automatically to a new page whenever it prints a full page or encounters a page-break code, or you can specify individual print ranges for each page and use the **P**age command to tell the program to skip to the next page. Under certain conditions, the two methods conflict and *both* send a page break to the printer, which results in a blank page.

With top and bottom margins of zero, you can have a one-page print range of as many as 60 lines. If 1-2-3 encounters a print range of exactly 60 lines, the program automatically tells the printer to skip to the next page. If your macro also sends a page break, you get a blank page.

SOLUTION: Either restrict your print ranges to 59 lines (minus the number of lines for top and bottom borders) or do not issue a **P**age command after a 60-line page.

PRINTING PROBLEM #6:

You do not want to print certain information that's in the middle of a print range.

EXPLANATION: You've documented assumptions, shown intermediate results that clarify a calculation, and added comments to make your worksheets easier to understand. You may not want to include this information in your final printed reports.

SOLUTION: This problem has several solutions. Pick those that best meet your needs.

Two solutions skip only rows:

- You can specify multiple print ranges that skip any rows you do not want printed. (This method is practical only if you use a macro to print and if you do not add comments after completing the worksheet.)

- You can use a special label prefix, the vertical bar (|), to tell 1-2-3 not to print a row. (This symbol is located on the backslash key.) Whenever 1-2-3 sees this label prefix in the leftmost cell of a row in a print range, the program skips that row. Except for printing, this label prefix and the left-aligned label prefix (') act in the same way. The contents of the cell are displayed normally.

To skip one or more columns in the middle of a print range:

- Use the /Worksheet Column **H**ide command to hide the column before you print it. Then, after you have printed the range, "unhide" the column by using the /Worksheet Column **D**isplay command.

PRINTING PROBLEM #7:

You want to print a report twice, but the second copy, instead of starting at page 1, begins with the next page number of the first copy.

EXPLANATION: With 1-2-3, you can build a report from many separate sections of a worksheet. If you use page numbers in headers or footers, every page starts with the next page number because the program assumes that you are producing one report.

SOLUTION: Issue the **A**lign command after a **P**age command to instruct 1-2-3 to start again at page 1. Because **A**lign also tells the program that you have adjusted the paper to the top of the page, always issue the **P**age command before the **A**lign command to prevent your pages from being misaligned.

PRINTING PROBLEM #8:

You don't want to bother specifying individual print ranges for a long report.

EXPLANATION: If your report is more than five pages long, setting up the range names and writing the macro to print the report can be a tedious process. And if the report will grow longer as time passes (if it contains year-to-date details, for example), you want to avoid having to continue adding range names and changing the macro.

SOLUTION: Let 1-2-3 automatically break up your report. 1-2-3 forces a page break after every full page and automatically inserts any headers or footers that you specify. If you specify borders, 1-2-3 prints them on every page; you simply specify one print range.

1-2-3 also splits vertically a report that is too wide to print on a single page. The program prints as much material as possible on one page and then prints the "right side" of the report on separate pages. You can leave these pages separate or tape them together to make a wide report.

PRINTING PROBLEM #9:

You let 1-2-3 handle page breaks automatically, but the program separates information that you want kept on one page.

EXPLANATION: When you specify a long report and let the program separate it automatically into pages, every page has the same number of print lines.

However, the report may contain information that you do not want separated: paragraphs of explanation, or multiple-line descriptions of accounts, for example.

SOLUTION: Leave the report as one print range, and insert page-break characters manually wherever you want a page to end. To insert a page-break character, move the cell pointer to the cell in the leftmost column of the row at which you want to start a new page. Then use the /Worksheet Page command to instruct 1-2-3 to insert a row above the cell pointer and put a page-break character (|::) in the cell.

PRINTING PROBLEM #10:

When you used the /Worksheet Page command to specify a page break, the command inserted a row through a macro or a database in the same row as the print range.

EXPLANATION: 1-2-3 inserts a page break by inserting a row across the entire worksheet. The blank row is inserted through anything that spans that row.

SOLUTION: Instead of using /Worksheet Page to insert a page break, you can indicate where you want the new page by typing the page-break character as a label.

In the leftmost column of the row where you want the new page, type the page-break character—a vertical-bar label prefix followed by two colons (|::). 1-2-3 treats this label as a page-break character, except that no blank row is inserted in the worksheet. *Remember that you must type the page-break character in a blank line in your print range because the row with the page-break character does not print.*

PRINTING PROBLEM #11:

You used the Setup string to tell the printer to print compressed print. But the report wraps to a new line after 72 characters, even though additional space remains on the line.

EXPLANATION: Because 1-2-3 cannot interpret a setup string, it does not recognize either the size of the characters you print or the width of the paper you use. The print settings indicate to the program the amount of material that can fit on a line and on a page.

SOLUTION: Whenever you change the print pitch, change the right margin. With a default left margin of 4 and a default right margin of 76, the 72-character print line matches the standard 72 data characters that 1-2-3 displays on the screen.

If you change the line spacing to something other than six lines per inch, you also must change the Pg-Length to match the new setting.

Troubleshooting Graphing

GRAPHING PROBLEM #1:

Because your worksheet uses many different graphs, selecting the graph ranges and other specifications is a slow, tedious process.

EXPLANATION: 1-2-3 has one current active graph. To use many different graphs in one worksheet, you must spend time specifying each one separately.

SOLUTION: Although the program has only one current active graph, you can save a library of graphs within the worksheet. After you have specified a graph completely, use the /**Graph Name Create** command to save the specification under a name you choose.

Repeat the process for each graph, giving each a different name. Then, to recall any graph, issue the /**Graph Name Use** command and either type the name of the appropriate graph or point to its name in the list of graph names.

When you save the worksheet, the graph names and settings are saved also. Be sure you save the worksheet; if you forget to save, the names and settings will be lost.

GRAPHING PROBLEM #2:

You don't like the patterns used by some of the graph ranges.

EXPLANATION: 1-2-3 has a fixed set of patterns for each graph range (A through F). If a graph displays the A and B ranges next to one another, looking at the two patterns may strain your eyes (see fig. T.36).

SOLUTION: If you have fewer than six ranges to graph, simply skip those ranges whose patterns you don't want to use. You do not have to specify the ranges in order. Figure T.37 shows the preceding graph with ranges A and C specified (and with no B range).

GRAPHING PROBLEM #3:

You want to separate the bars in your graphs but the program automatically puts them side by side.

EXPLANATION: In a bar graph with multiple ranges, each graph range touches the one next to it even if there is ample room to separate them.

Fig. T.36

The A and B ranges can be hard on your eyes.

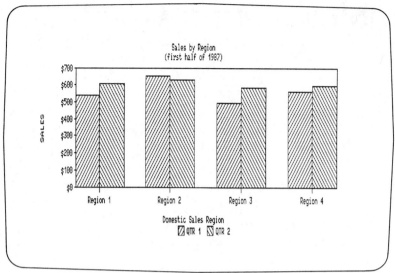

Fig. T.37

Using just the A and C ranges.

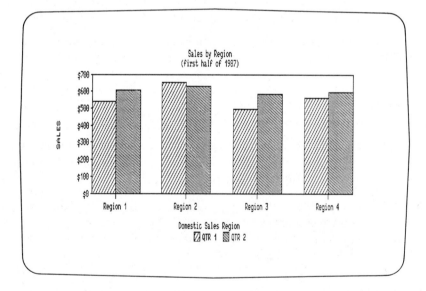

SOLUTION: You can specify a range of blank cells (or zeros) as a dummy graph range. 1-2-3 displays this dummy range as a bar with zero height, which is the same as a space between the bars. The bar graph in figure T.38 shows that the A and C ranges, which contain data, are separated by B and D ranges of blank cells. To widen the space between the Regions, you also must include blank cells in the X-axis.

Fig. T.38

A blank B and D range adds spacing to the graph.

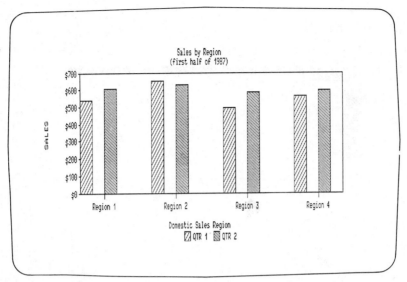

GRAPHING PROBLEM #4:

You are graphing data (in thousands) in which numbers higher than 1,000 represent millions. 1-2-3 automatically scales the data and adds the deceiving notation (Thousands) to the Y-axis.

EXPLANATION: This problem can be extremely confusing. 1-2-3 assumes that all the numbers you graph represent units. If the largest numbers are greater than 1,000, 1-2-3 automatically scales the numbers into thousands and adds the notation (Thousands) to the Y-axis. You cannot stop this automatic scaling.

If you graph information that is already in thousands (or millions, or more) in the worksheet (such as you might find on a financial statement), the (Thousands) indicator on the graph will be incorrect.

Figure T.39A shows a table of sales data for the first three quarters. The numbers are in thousands of dollars. Note that one of the numbers in the table (in cell D5) is larger than 1000. Figure T.39B shows the graph of this data with the incorrect Y-axis labels.

SOLUTION: Although you cannot stop the automatic scaling, you can turn off the indicator. To do so, use the /Graph Options Scale Y-Scale Indicator command and, when 1-2-3 asks for a yes or no answer, press *N*. Then use either /Graph Options Titles Second (or Y-Axis) to insert the correct scaling indicator (see fig. T.40).

Fig. T.39A

Data with numbers in thousands.

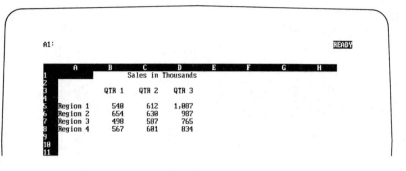

Fig. T.39B

An incorrect scaling notation.

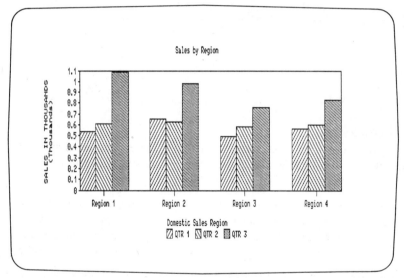

GRAPHING PROBLEM #5:

Your graph's X-axis ranges overlap.

EXPLANATION: You can fit only a limited number of X-axis labels or numbers on a graph before they start to overlap (see fig. T.41).

SOLUTION: Use the /Graph Options Scale Skip command to skip a specific number of X-axis entries between the entries displayed on the graph. Figure T.42 shows the preceding graph after you have specified Skip *2*.

GRAPHING PROBLEM #6:

After waiting 30 minutes while a graph prints, you discover an error and must print the graph again.

EXPLANATION: This is a common problem. The graph display does not show exactly what the printed graph will look like. For example, the display doesn't

Fig. T.40

A graph with the scaling indicator turned off.

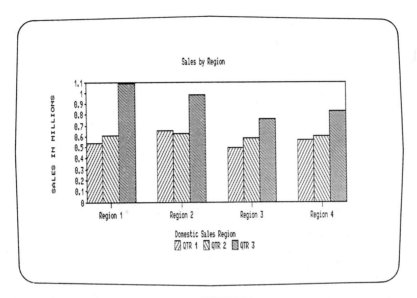

Fig. T.41

Overlapping X-axis labels.

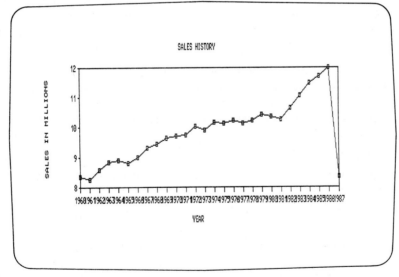

show the different type fonts you can specify for the text portion of your graph. And you can easily overlook missing legends or incorrect data on the display.

SOLUTION: Speed up the process of printing a graph by specifying the lowest possible density for your printer. Select **Settings Hardware Printer** from the PrintGraph menu to look at a list of all the printers and densities you included in your driver set (see fig. T.43). Most printers have at least two densities;

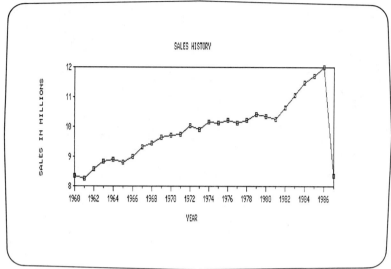

some have three or four. Depending on the density, the difference in print time for one full-page graph can be a few minutes or an hour or more. Although the lowest density may not be acceptable for printing material that you show to someone else, you can use it for a quick test print.

Or you can get a quick test print by specifying an unusually small size. To do so, choose Settings Image Size Manual from the PrintGraph menu and then specify a small **Width** and **Height** for the test print. To produce a graph that covers one-sixteenth of a page, for example, specify a **Width** of 2.345 inches and a **Height** of 3.5 inches. These numbers are half the sizes that you would specify for a half-page graph.

When you are confident that the graph is correct, print it full-size in the print density you want.

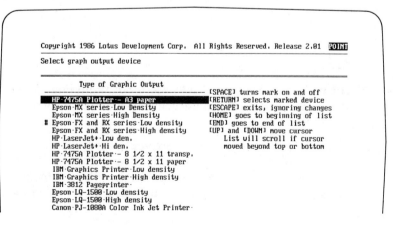

Troubleshooting Data Management

DATA MANAGEMENT PROBLEM #1:

You set up a Criterion range, but all the records are selected.

EXPLANATION: When you choose /Data Query Find, Extract, Unique, or Delete, 1-2-3 uses the Criterion range as a filter to select records from the database. If the Criterion range is not exact, these Query commands do not work correctly.

SOLUTION: Reissue the /Data Query Criterion command. When 1-2-3 highlights the old range, check it carefully, looking for the following errors:

1. *Does the first row of the Criterion range contain field names?* If not, the Criterion Range does nothing.

2. *Do the field names match exactly the field names in the database?* If any field names in the Criterion range do not match the names in the database, the label and number matches in those fields are ignored. Don't take chances with incorrect field names when you build your Criterion range. Copy the field names from the database to ensure that the names are identical.

3. *Does the Criterion range contain any blank rows?* This is the most common error in Criterion ranges that select all records. Each row is a separate selection test; if a record in the database passes any one test, that record is selected. Because a blank row has no tests, *all* records are selected.

4. *Do any compound tests use #NOT# or <> (not equal)?* These compound tests, which can be extremely tricky, can produce results that are just the opposite of the results you are trying to produce. Here is an example of an erroneous compound test:

    +B5<>100#OR#B5<>200

The purpose of this test is to select all records except those in which the value in column B is either 100 or 200. This written statement makes sense, but the effect of the test (the formula) is to select all records in which the value in column B is anything *but* 100 or 200. The test selects all records because if the value is 100, it passes the test because it is not 200; if the value is 200, it passes the test because it is not 100. The correct way to write the test is

+B5<>100#AND#B5<>200

DATA MANAGEMENT PROBLEM #2:

You set up a Criterion range, but none of the records is selected.

EXPLANATION: Each field in a row in a Criterion range can be a separate test. To be selected, a record must pass all the tests in the same row. If you write the selection tests incorrectly, it may be impossible for a record to pass all of them. This problem is most common when you use the #AND#, #OR#, and #NOT# operators in your selection tests.

SOLUTION: Carefully check the selection tests in your Criterion range for tests such as:

+B5>100#AND#B5<0

This test tells 1-2-3 to select records only when the value in column B is both greater than 100 and less than zero. Because this result is impossible, no records are selected.

Also, make sure that the test's format matches the data in the field you are testing. If you use label matches or string functions on numeric data, or if you use number matches on strings, nothing is selected.

DATA MANAGEMENT PROBLEM #3:

You set up a Criterion range, but either *only* the first record is selected or all the records *after* the first one are selected.

EXPLANATION: The addresses used in formula matches are treated as relative addresses, based on the first record in the database. Therefore, any cell addresses in formula matches use the first record in the database. If your Criterion range includes the following test:

+B5>100

row 4 contains the field names for this database, and row 5 is the first record in the database. When the Criterion range is used to select records, 1-2-3 first tests the first record. If the value in B5 is greater than 100, the record is selected; if not, the record is not selected.

Then 1-2-3 adjusts the formula and moves down one row to the next record. At the second record, the test is

+B6>100

The cell addresses change for each record in the database, as though you had copied the formula down one row before making the test. The program handles this step automatically.

Suppose that you want to compare a field in the database (B5) to a field outside the database (AG67). The test might be

+B5>AG67

1-2-3 handles the test on the first record in the manner shown in the preceding example, selecting the record if the test is true. But when the program moves to the second record, the test is changed to

+B6>AG68

AG68 may either be blank or contain data that does not pertain to the values in column B in your database.

SOLUTION: If you make the cell references that address cells outside the database absolute, they won't adjust as 1-2-3 moves down the data records. For example, if you change the test in the preceding example to

+B5>$AG$67

1-2-3 will compare all the values in column B to the contents of AG67.

DATA MANAGEMENT PROBLEM #4:

A /Data Query Find command works correctly, but /Data Query Extract (or Unique) does not.

EXPLANATION: You can use the same settings for Find, Extract, or Unique. Because Find ignores the Output range, you can test whether the problem lies in the Criterion range or in the Output range. If Find works but Extract or Unique does not, something is wrong with the Output range.

SOLUTION: The field names in the Output range must match the field names in the database. If the names do not match, 1-2-3 selects the correct records but does not copy any fields to the Output range. To ensure that the field names match, copy them from the database.

DATA MANAGEMENT PROBLEM #5:

As your database grows, the output from Extract commands grows also. You keep filling the Output range and getting an error message.

EXPLANATION: When you define an Output range, you can define the number of rows that you want 1-2-3 to use. If the output of the Extract (or Unique)

commands contains more records than you have specified, the **Query** stops and you see an error message:

```
Too many records for Output range.
```

You must enlarge the size of the **Output** range and then rerun the **Extract**.

SOLUTION: Specify as the **Output** range only the row containing the field names. 1-2-3 treats this specification as allowing the use of as many rows as necessary for **Extract** or **Unique**.

If you use this solution, however, be sure not to put anything below the **Output** range. If you do, you will lose valuable data because the next time you issue an **Extract** or **Unique** command, 1-2-3 will erase everything below the field names before copying the selected records. (The program will even erase data which is far below the area needed for copying in the selected records.)

Troubleshooting Macros

MACRO PROBLEM #1:

You write a macro. But when you press the Alt key and the letter of the name of the macro, nothing happens.

EXPLANATION: You must use a precise name format for macros that you execute from the keyboard (by using the Alt key). The range name must be exactly two characters: the first is always a backslash; the second, a letter (from A to Z) or 0 (for macros that are executed automatically). If you name your macro anything else and try to execute it by pressing the Alt key, 1-2-3 cannot recognize it as a macro.

SOLUTION: Use /**R**ange **N**ame **C**reate to check the macro's range name. 1-2-3 lists, in alphabetical order, all the range names in the worksheet. Range names that start with a backslash are at the end of the list. If you don't see the range name listed, you haven't named your macro. Even experienced programmers make this seemingly trivial mistake, which is the most common reason a macro won't work.

If the range name is in the list, make sure that you have included the backslash. For example, although the letter *A* is a valid range name, it is not a valid name for a macro that is used with the Alt key.

Another common error is to use a slash (/) instead of a backslash (\) when you name a macro. If the range name is on the list, check carefully to make sure that it starts with a backslash.

If the macro name is listed and looks valid, highlight it and press Enter. 1-2-3 highlights the range with that name. The range should contain only one cell—the first cell of the macro. The contents of the macro must be a label or a string-valued function. If the cell is blank or contains a numeric value, the macro will not work.

MACRO PROBLEM #2:

After you write a few macros, you move some data. The macros now refer to the wrong addresses.

EXPLANATION: Macros are not like formulas; the addresses in macros do not change automatically when you move data that is used by the macro. In fact, a macro is nothing more than a label. 1-2-3 does not adjust the contents of labels when you move data because the program does not know that labels contain addresses.

SOLUTION: *NEVER* use cell addresses in macros. Always give range names to all of the cells and ranges you use in macros and use these range names in the macros. Then, if you move these ranges or insert and delete rows and columns, the range names will adjust automatically and the macro will continue to refer to the correct cells and ranges.

MACRO PROBLEM #3:

Your macro seems to work correctly, but after you execute the macro the display is wrong.

EXPLANATION: 1-2-3 does not update the display or recalculate the worksheet during certain macro commands. Figure T.44 shows a macro (\A) that has just been executed. Although the contents of cell A1 should be 100, the cell is blank. And although the worksheet is set for automatic recalculation, the CALC indicator is on.

Fig. T.44

The macro does not update the display.

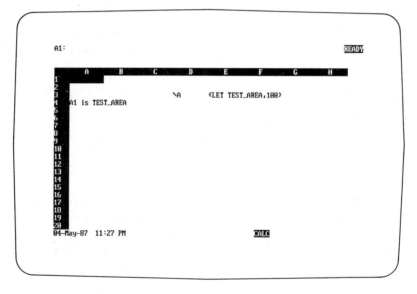

SOLUTION: To display the update, add a tilde (~) to the end of the macro. If you add a tilde to the macro shown in figure T.44, 1-2-3 displays 100 as the contents of A1, and the CALC indicator vanishes (see fig. T.45). Other macro commands such as {RECALC} and {RECALCCOL} require other commands that force 1-2-3 to update the display. The PgDn-PgUp key combination (in a macro, use {PgDn} and {PgUp}) is the easiest way to accomplish this (refer to fig. T.10).

Fig. T.45

*A ~ at the end
updates the display.*

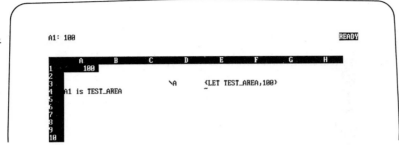

MACRO PROBLEM #4:

Although the logic of your macro appears correct, the macro never works properly. Critical values do not seem to be current, even when recalculation is on automatic.

EXPLANATION: On a large worksheet, macros would execute slowly if 1-2-3 recalculated the entire worksheet after every macro command. 1-2-3 seldom recalculates the worksheet while a macro executes. If critical values change during execution, the macro uses the old values—not the current ones.

SOLUTION: Determine which cells and ranges must be recalculated to make the macro work correctly, and then add {RECALC} or {RECALCCOL} statements to the macro where necessary. A complete worksheet recalculation with {CALC} works also, but usually is extremely slow.

The macro shown in figure T.46 tests incorrectly for a valid entry. In this macro, {GETNUMBER} finds the old value because the test in IP_TEST (cell C12) is not updated after {GETNUMBER}. To correct the problem, add a {RECALC} to the macro (see fig. T.47). In this case, a tilde works if the worksheet is set for automatic recalculation. A {RECALC} or {RECALCCOL} is required in manual recalculation mode.

In figure T.47, the macro branches to PROCESS if the test in C12 is 1 (true) and branches to ERROR_ROUTINE if the test is not 1 (false). These routines will perform whatever processing you need in your worksheet.

MACRO PROBLEM #5:

You need to change a macro that you wrote earlier, but you can't remember how it works.

EXPLANATION: This common problem surprises users when they first start to work with macros. After having painstakingly written, tested, and debugged a macro, you use it successfully in your worksheet. Because you wrote the

Fig. T.46

A macro that requires recalculation to work correctly.

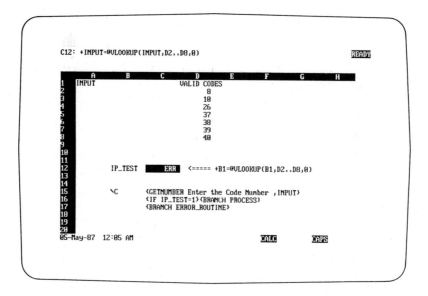

Fig. T.47

A macro with {RECALC}.

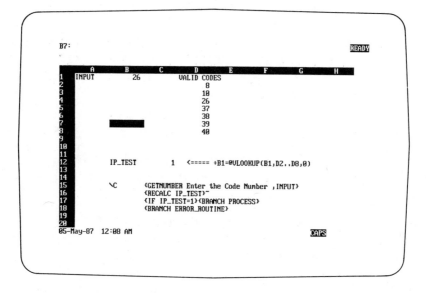

macro, you know exactly what it does and how it operates. When you have to change it, you are amazed that you can't remember how it works.

Even people who write 1-2-3 macros for a living have this problem. They think that they can quickly write a macro and remember how it works. They write the macro quickly but have difficulty figuring it out a few months later.

SOLUTION: Structure and document your macros carefully and consistently. Keep each macro short, and design it to perform only one operation. Instead of trying to cram the entire macro onto one line, keep each line of macro code short. Put all the range names to the left of the cell with that name, and put comments to the right of each macro statement. Write your comments in plain language, and explain *why* the macro does what it does.

To make your macros easy to read, use uppercase and lowercase letters consistently. Always use lowercase letters for commands and uppercase letters for range names and functions. Macro key words can be either uppercase or lowercase, but be consistent in all your macros. (For example, all key words in this book are uppercase.)

As you can see from the following example:

\h   /rncHERE~~{GOTO}HELP~{?}{ESC}{GOTO}HERE~/rndHERE~

a poorly constructed, undocumented macro is confusing. This macro is a subroutine that provides the operator with a page of help text (at the range name HELP). When the operator reads the information and presses Enter, the macro returns the cursor to range name HERE (its position before the macro executed). The use of this macro is explained more fully in Chapter 15.

Figure T.48 shows the same macro code after its structure has been improved and documented.

Fig. T.48

A well-constructed macro.

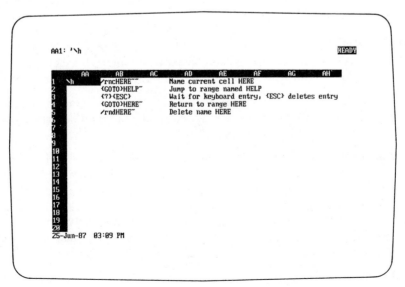

MACRO PROBLEM #6:

Although your macro seems correct, it starts to beep in the middle of some commands and puts some commands as a label in a cell.

EXPLANATION: The macro may look correct, but 1-2-3 is not interpreting the macro in the way you anticipated. Either something is missing or the macro contains extraneous keystrokes.

SOLUTION: This problem commonly occurs if you forget to include tildes (to indicate *Enter*) in a macro. You can use one of two methods to find errors:

1. Press Alt-F2 to put macro execution in single-step mode. When you execute the macro, 1-2-3 executes only one keystroke and then waits for you to press any key (which key doesn't matter). When you press a key, you signal the program to execute the next macro keystroke. As you watch the macro execute in slow motion, you usually can see exactly where the error lies. (With some macros, this single-step approach can be painfully slow.)

2. Play "computer" and execute the macro manually. First, print the macro; then replay it from the keyboard, doing exactly as the macro indicates, keystroke by keystroke. Unless this is a recalculation problem that happens only during macro execution, you will find the error if you follow the script faithfully. If the macro works when you execute it manually, change recalculation to manual and try again.

MACRO PROBLEM #7:

You have written a series of handy macros for your worksheet but you can't remember all their names. You may even run out of letters for macro names.

EXPLANATION: You can name only 27 macros (A to Z plus 0) for execution from the keyboard per worksheet. Even remembering 20 or more macros in several worksheets boggles the mind.

SOLUTION: Use menus to execute macros. Menus are easier to learn than many of the macro key words. You can have a large macro-driven worksheet with hundreds of macros, only one of which (\M) is executed from the keyboard. This one macro is used to bring up the main menu. A series of hierarchical menus can contain any number of macros, each of which can have any valid range name. (Only macros executed from the keyboard require special names that start with a backslash.)

If you use more than five macros, even if they are for your own use only, put them in a menu so that you won't have to remember their names.

MACRO PROBLEM #8:

You wrote a macro containing an error. It destroyed your worksheet.

EXPLANATION: A macro can do anything that you can do from the keyboard. A macro can erase all or part of the worksheet, quit 1-2-3, and erase a file on the disk. If you don't prepare for possible catastrophic errors, you can lose hours—even days—of work.

SOLUTION: Always save your worksheet before you test a macro. Then, if the macro destroys something, you still have the data on disk. If part of the macro saves the file, make sure that you first save it with a different name. Saving the file is futile if the macro erases most of the worksheet and then saves the destroyed file with the name of the original file.

In fact, using a macro to save a file automatically is so dangerous that you should save your files manually until you are completely familiar with macro programming and the Lotus Command Language. Some people believe that it is too dangerous to ever do file saves from a macro.

Troubleshooting Index

1-2-3 Command Reference

Worksheet Commands /W

The /Worksheet commands control the display formats, screen organization, protection, and start-up settings for the *entire* worksheet. If you want to change these settings for only a *portion* of the worksheet, look at the options available in the /Range command menu. To change settings that affect the entire worksheet, however, use the /Worksheet commands shown in the following illustration.

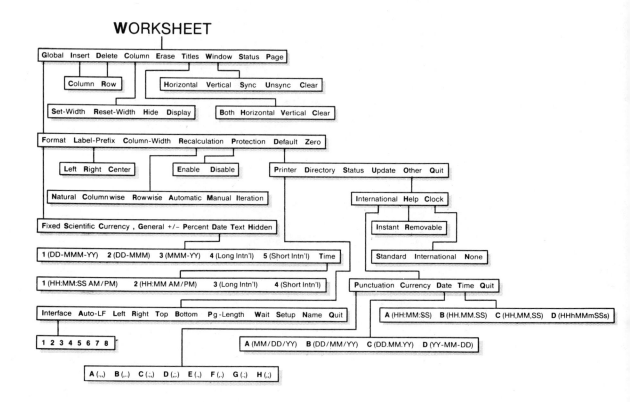

Worksheet Global Format

/WGF

Purpose

Selects how most numeric values and formula results should appear.

/WGF formats the *entire* worksheet, but previously entered values and formulas do not change.

Reminders

• Decide on a format for numeric data before you use /WGF.

• If you want to format only a portion of the worksheet, use instead /**R**ange Format.

• Use the **D**ate format option of the /WGF command when most values on your spreadsheet are dates; otherwise, use /**R**ange Format **D**ate.

Procedures

1. Type /wgf

2. Use → and ← to select a Format menu choice. The second menu line displays examples of how the format appears.

3. Select one of the following formats:

Menu Item	Keystroke	Description
Fixed	**F**	Fixes the number of decimal places displayed. For 3 decimals, 1.2345 appears as 1.235.
Scientific	**S**	Displays in scientific notation large or small numbers. For example, for a 2-decimal format, 950000 appears as 9.50E+05.
Currency	**C**	Displays the default currency symbol (e.g., $ or £) and commas. Often used for the first row and the bottom line of financial statements. For example, for a 2-decimal format, 24500.254 appears as $24,500.25.
		Marks thousands and multiples of thousands. For 2 decimals, 24500.254 appears as 24,500.25.

General	**G**	Suppresses zeros after the decimal point; uses scientific notation for large or small numbers; and serves as the default decimal display.
+/-	**+**	Creates horizontal bar graphs or time duration graphs on computers that do not have graphics. A positive number displays as + symbols; a minus number, as - symbols. For example, 6.23 appears as ++++++.
Percent	**P**	Displays a decimal number as a whole percentage number with a percent sign (%). For 2 decimal places, .346 appears as 34.60%.
Date	**D**	Displays the date in customary formats. One selection under **Date** formats the **Time** display.

Date
1. DD–MMM–YY   12–Jan–51
2. DD–MMM   12–Jan
3. MMM–YY   Jan–51
4. MM/DD/YY   01/12/51
5. MM/DD   01/12

Time
1. HH:MM:SS AM/PM   1:04:34 PM
2. HH:MM AM/PM   1:04 PM
3. HH:MM:SS   13:04:34
4. HH:MM   13:04

Text	**T**	Evaluates formulas as numbers but displays formulas as text. Numbers in cells appear in General format.
Hidden	**H**	Hides cell contents from display and printing but evaluates contents. Use this command to hide confidential notes or variables.

4. After you select Fixed, **S**cientific, **C**urrency, comma (,), or **P**ercent, enter the number of decimal places. 1-2-3 normally truncates trailing zeros, but these appear for the number of decimal places you set.

5. Press Enter.

Important Cues

- Use /**R**ange Format to format only a portion of the worksheet.

- Use **T**ext format to display formulas used in Data Tables and to document formulas and their locations.

- If you enter a number too large for the formatted cell, it fills with asterisks. To remove them, move the pointer to the cell, select /**W**orksheet Column Set-Width, and press → until the column is wide enough to display the entire number.

- /WGF commands round only the display of numbers. Stored numbers are retained to 15-decimal precision; the stored numbers, not the displayed numbers, are used in calculations.

- To display non-USA formats with commands, use /**W**orksheet Global **D**efault **O**ther. Type /wgd and select one of the following formats:

Menu Item	*Keystrokes*	*Changes*
Other Int'l Punctuation	**OIP**	Numeric punctuation
Other Int'l Currency	**OIC**	Currency symbol
Other Int'l Date	**OID**	International date formats
Other Int'l Time	**OIT**	International time formats

Cautions

- ▶ /WGF rounds displayed numbers to the specified decimal setting, but calculations are performed to 15-decimal precision. To keep apparently wrong values from being displayed, use @ROUND to round formula results so that calculated results match displayed values.

- ▶ Other users may enter percentage values incorrectly if you use **Percent** format. Include, therefore, a screen prompt to remind users to place a percent sign (%) after percentages. 1-2-3 automatically divides the entry by 100.

*For more information, see **Range Format**, **Worksheet Global Default**, and Chapter 5.*

Worksheet Global Label-Prefix /WGL

Purpose

Selects how you want text labels aligned throughout the worksheet.

Labels narrower than cell width can be aligned to the left, right, or center. Labels longer than cell width are left-aligned. Previously entered labels do not change.

Reminders

• Decide how to align the labels before you begin building the worksheet. Use /Worksheet Global Label-Prefix to select left (the default setting), right, or center alignment.

• If you use /WGL after you begin to build the worksheet, existing labels are not affected. Any alignment previously set with /Range Label is not altered by /WGL.

• To change the alignment of labels in a single cell or a range of cells, use /Range Label.

Procedures

1. Type /wgl

2. Select one of the following:

Menu Item	*Keystroke*	*Description*
Left	**L**	Aligns label with cell's left edge
Right	**R**	Aligns label with cell's right edge
Center	**C**	Centers label in a cell

3. Type the labels as you want them to appear on the worksheet.

Important Cues

■ Align labels in a cell by entering one of the following prefixes *before* you type the label:

Label Prefix	*Function*
' (apostrophe)	Aligns label to the left (default)
" (quotation mark)	Aligns label to the right
^ (caret)	Centers label in the cell
\	Repeats character to fill the cell

Note: The backslash (\ ) label prefix cannot be selected with /WGL.

- The label prefix appears as the first character in the control panel when the cell pointer is positioned on a cell that contains a label. Use /Worksheet Status to show the global label prefix.

- You must enter a label prefix in front of labels that begin with a number or formula symbol. For example, you must supply a prefix for an address or part number, as shown in the following list:

Correct	*Incorrect*
'2207 Cheyenne Dr.	2207 Cheyenne Dr.
"34-567FB	34-567FB

- Use EDIT mode to turn a number into a label. To do this, position the cell pointer on the number you want to change and press the F2 (Edit) key. Then press the Home key to move the cursor to the beginning of the number, type the label prefix, and press Enter.

- Because every line of macro code must be entered as a string, a label prefix must precede text used as macro code. For example, if your macro line begins with the command sequence /ppooc, you must precede the entry with a label prefix, such as '/ppooc; otherwise, the keystrokes in the macro will select the command instead of typing macro code.

- Preserve a formula with an unidentified error by adding a label prefix before the formula. For example, if you enter the formula:

  +B5*@PMT(B16B12/12,B14*12)

  1-2-3 signals an error and enters EDIT mode. (The problem is a missing comma after B16.) If you can't find the error, press the Home key to move to the beginning of the formula. Type an apostrophe and press Enter. The formula will then be accepted as a text label. You can return to it later to look for the error and make the correction. Delete the apostrophe and press Enter after you make the correction.

- Document formulas by temporarily adding a label prefix and then copying the label to another part of the worksheet. To do this, move the cell pointer to the formula and press the F2 (Edit) key. Next, press the Home key to move the cell pointer to the front of the formula, type an apostrophe, and press Enter. The formula is changed to text, and you can copy the text-formula to a documentation area of your spreadsheet. Use the Edit, Home, and Del keys to remove the apostrophe on the original formula so that it can operate normally.

- To turn a numeric label into a number, use EDIT mode and delete the label prefix.

| *Caution* | Numbers or formulas preceded by a label prefix have a zero value when evaluated by a numeric formula. In a database query, you must use text searches to search for numbers with a label prefix. |

For more information, see Chapters 4 and 14.

Worksheet Global Column-Width /WGC

| *Purpose* | Sets column width for the entire worksheet. |

| *Reminder* | Before you use /WGC, decide the column widths you need for the worksheet, and position the cell pointer so that an average column width is displayed. |

| *Procedures* | 1. Type /wgc |

2. Enter a number for the column width used most frequently, or press → or ← to increase or decrease column width, respectively.

3. Press Enter.

| *Important Cues* | ■ Use /Worksheet Column Set-Width to set individual columns so that numbers and labels display correctly. When the column width is too narrow for the value entered, asterisks are displayed in the cell (see fig. W.1). |

■ Any global column width can be set to a new width with /Worksheet Column Set-Width. Column widths previously set with /Worksheet Column Set-Width will keep their original setting.

■ The default column width for all columns is 9 characters. Column width settings can range from 1 to 240 characters.

■ You can see the current setting for the global column width by selecting /Worksheet Status.

Fig. W.1

Asterisks displayed in a column that is too narrow.

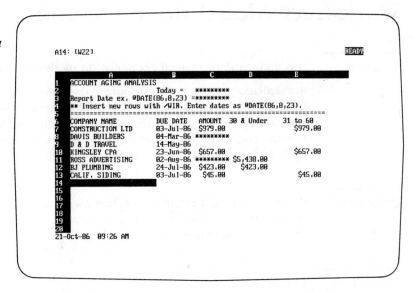

Caution

If you use a split worksheet and change the column width in one or both windows, settings used in the bottom or right windows are lost when the windows are cleared. 1-2-3 keeps the column widths used in the top window of a horizontal split or the left window of a vertical split.

For more information, see Chapter 4.

Worksheet Global Recalculation   /WGR

Purpose   Sets automatic or manual recalculation modes for the entire worksheet.

Recalculation can be set to **Automatic** or **Manual**. Manual recalculation should be used to increase data-entry speed on large spreadsheets or databases. You can have 1-2-3 calculate formulas in a particular order by selecting either the **Columnwise** or **Rowwise** options. /WGR can also be used to calculate a formula multiple times to ensure correct results.

Reminder   If you change recalculation to **Columnwise** or **Rowwise**, enter formulas in a specific order so that they will be calculated correctly. 1-2-3's default settings are **Natural** and **Automatic** recalculation.

Procedures   1. Type /wgr

2. Select one of the following:

Menu Item	Keystroke	Description
Natural	**N**	Calculates formulas in the order the results are needed (the normal worksheet setting for the order of recalculation)
Columnwise	**C**	Starts at the top of column A and recalculates downward; then moves to column B
Rowwise	**R**	Starts at the beginning of row 1 and recalculates to the end; then continues through the following rows
Automatic	**A**	Recalculates whenever cell contents change (the normal worksheet setting for when recalculation occurs)
Manual	**M**	Recalculates only when you press the F9 (Calc) key or when {CALC} is encountered in a macro. The CALC indicator appears at the bottom of the screen when recalculation is advised.
Iteration	**I**	Recalculates the worksheet a specified number of times

3. If you select **Iteration**, enter a number from 1 to 50. The default setting is 1. **Iteration** works with **Columnwise** and **Rowwise** recalculations or with **Natural** recalculation when the worksheet contains a circular reference.

4. If you select **Columnwise** or **Rowwise** recalculation, you may need to repeat Step 1 and select **Iteration** in Step 2. In Step 3, enter the number of recalculations necessary for correct results. **Columnwise** and **Rowwise** recalculations often require multiple calculations for all worksheet results to be correct.

Important
Cues

■ Display the current recalculation setting by selecting **/Worksheet Status**. Figure W.2 shows **Manual** recalculation selected for **Rowwise** calculation with 1 **Iteration**.

Fig. W.2

Recalculation settings for the worksheet.

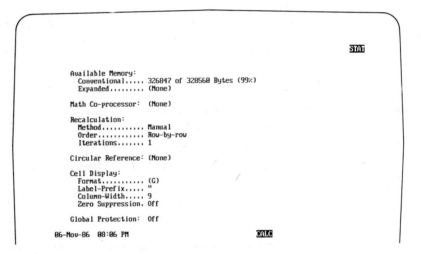

```
                                                                    STAT
         Available Memory:
           Conventional..... 326847 of 328560 Bytes (99%)
           Expanded......... (None)

         Math Co-processor: (None)

         Recalculation:
           Method.......... Manual
           Order........... Row-by-row
           Iterations...... 1

         Circular Reference: (None)

         Cell Display:
           Format.......... (G)
           Label-Prefix.... "
           Column-Width.... 9
           Zero Suppression. Off

         Global Protection: Off

      06-Nov-86  08:06 PM                        CALC
```

■ **Columnwise** or **Rowwise** recalculation often requires multiple recalculations. Set the number of automatic recalculations by selecting **/WGR** and choosing **Iteration**.

Caution

When you use **Manual** recalculation, the screen display is not valid when the CALC indicator appears at the bottom of the screen. This indicator means that changes have been made on the worksheet, and you need to press the F9 (Calc) key so that 1-2-3 will recalculate the worksheet to reflect the changes.

For more information, see Chapter 4.

Worksheet Global Protection   /WGP

Purpose | Protects the entire worksheet from being changed.

Reminder | Save time by making sure that your worksheet is complete before you enable worksheet protection. After the worksheet is protected, you will have to disable protection or unprotect a range before you can modify the worksheet.

Procedures | 1. Type /wgp

2. Select one of the following options:

Menu Item	Keystroke	Description
Enable	**E**	Protects the worksheet. Only cells specified with /**R**ange Unprotect can be changed.
Disable	**D**	Unprotects the worksheet. Any cell can be changed.

Important Cues

■ Before or after you protect the entire worksheet, you can use /**R**ange Unprotect to specify cells that can be modified.

■ While /**W**orksheet Global Protection is enabled, use /**R**ange Unprotect to indicate the cells that can be changed.

■ Protected cells display a PR on the status line. Unprotected cells display a U on the status line.

■ /**W**orksheet Global **P**rotection works with the /**R**ange Unprotect and /**R**ange Input commands to restrict the cell pointer to unprotected cells. This keeps inexperienced users from entering data in cells that already store information.

■ Use /**W**orksheet Global Protection **D**isable on a data table before you execute /**D**ata Table. Otherwise, the data table can be disabled.

Cautions

▶ Macros that change cell content can change only unprotected cells. When programming macros, include in the macro code the commands necessary to enable or disable protection.

▶ /**W**orksheet Erase is one of the few commands that can be used while /**W**orksheet Global **P**rotection is enabled.

*For more information, see Chapter 4 and **Worksheet Erase**.*

Worksheet Global Default   /WGD

Purpose

Specifies display formats and start-up settings for hardware.

With this command, you can control how 1-2-3 works with the printer; which disk and directory are accessed automatically; which international displays are used; and which type of clock is displayed. The settings can be saved so that each time you start 1-2-3, the specifications go into effect. For temporary changes, see the /**File** or /**Print** menu options.

Reminder

Before you set the interface to serial printers, find out the baud rate of your printer. The printer should be set to standard MS-DOS serial printer settings of 8 bits, no parity, and 1 stop bit (2 stop bits at 110 baud). These printer settings can be set with microswitches (DIP switches in your printer) and are normally preconfigured at the factory.

Procedures

1. Type /wgd

2. Select the setting you want to change:

Menu Item	*Keystroke*	*Description*
Printer	**P**	Specifies printer settings and connections. Choose from the following options:

    Interface – Select parallel or serial port.
    Auto-LF – If printer is printing double spaces, choose **Yes**.
    Left – Margin (default 4, 0-240)
    Right – Margin (default 76, 0-240)
    Top – Margin (default 2, 0-32)
    Bottom – Margin (default 2, 0-32)
    Pg-Length – (default 66, 1-100)
    Wait – Pause for page insert.
    Setup – Initial printer-control code
    Name – Select from multiple printers.
    Quit – Return to the Printer menu.

Directory	**D**	Specifies directory for read or write operations. Press Esc to clear. Type new directory and press Enter.
Status	**S**	Displays settings for /**Worksheet Global Default**.

Update	U	Saves to disk the current global defaults for use during the next startup.
Other	O	**International** lets you specify display settings for **Punctuation**, **Currency**, **Date**, and **Time**.
		Help lets you choose whether the Help file is immediately accessible from disk (**Instant**) or whether the Help disk can be removed (**Removable**).
		Clock lets you choose between **Standard** and **International** date and time formats or to have **None** displayed on the screen.
Quit	Q	Returns you to the worksheet.

Important Cues

Changes made with /Worksheet Global Default are good only while 1-2-3 is running. To save the settings so that they load automatically at start-up, select /Worksheet Global Default Update. On a disk-based system, make certain that the 1-2-3 System disk is in the current drive. Use the DIR command to verify that the 123.CNF file has been updated.

Caution

When you use /Worksheet Global Other Help Instant, if you remove the Help file disk before you press F1, you receive the message `Cannot find the 123.HLP help file` and the system may lock up.

For more information, see Chapter 5.

Worksheet Global Zero   /WGZ

Purpose   Suppresses zeros in displays and printed reports so that only nonzero numbers appear.

When /Worksheet Global Zero is in effect, zeros from formulas and typed entries are hidden.

Reminder   Protect hidden zeros in the worksheet by using the /Worksheet Global Protection and /Range Unprotect commands. This prevents users new to 1-2-3 from typing over or erasing necessary hidden zero values or formulas.

Procedures   1. Type /wgz

2. Choose **Yes** or **No**.

Important Cues
- The worksheet's default setting is No so that zeros are displayed in normal operation.

- Suppressed zeros in formulas and typed entries still are evaluated as zeros by other formulas.

Caution   If zeros are suppressed, you can easily erase or write over portions of the worksheet that appear blank but contain suppressed zeros. To prevent accidental erasures and type-overs, use /Worksheet Global Protection Enable and /Range Unprotect.

*For more information, see **Worksheet Global Protection**, **Range Protect/ Unprotect**, and Chapter 4.*

Worksheet Insert Column/Row   /WI

Purpose

Inserts one or more blank columns or rows in the worksheet.

Use this command to add space for formulas, data, or text.

Reminders

Before you use /WI:

- Place the cell pointer in the column you want to move to the right when one or more columns are inserted;

or

- Place the cell pointer in the row you want to move down when one or more rows are inserted.

Procedures

1. Type /wi

2. Select one of the following:

Menu Item	***Keystroke***	***Description***
Column	**C**	Inserts column(s) at cell pointer. Moves current column right.
Row	**R**	Inserts row(s) at cell pointer. Moves current row down.

3. Insert more than one column by moving the cell pointer right to highlight one cell for each additional column. Insert more than one row by moving the cell pointer down to highlight one cell for each additional row. Figure W.3 shows the cell pointer highlighting rows B9 to B11 so that three blank rows will be inserted after row 8.

Fig. W.3

Specifying the number of rows to be inserted.

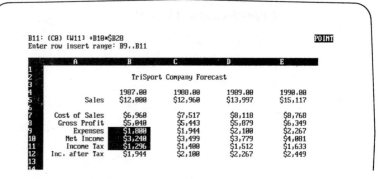

4. Check to make sure that the number of highlighted cells equals the number of columns or rows you want inserted.

5. Press Enter. Figure W.4 shows the worksheet after the rows have been inserted.

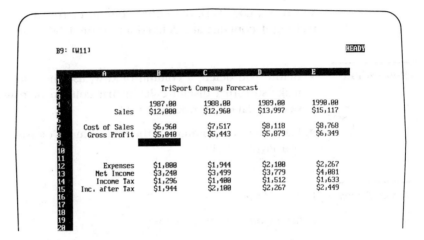

Important Cues

■ Addresses and ranges adjust automatically to the new addresses created when columns or rows are inserted.

■ Check all worksheet areas for composition, lines, and layout that may have changed. Use /Move to reposition labels, data, and formulas.

Cautions

▶ Cell addresses in macros do not adjust automatically. Adjust cell addresses in macros to reflect the inserted column(s) or row(s). Range names in macros will remain correct.

▶ Make certain that inserted columns and rows do not pass through databases, print ranges, or a column of macro code. Macros will stop execution if they reach a blank cell. Database and data-entry macros may stop or work incorrectly if they encounter unexpected blank columns or rows in the database or data-entry areas.

▶ Inserting rows and columns uses up conventional memory. Keep this in mind when designing large worksheets.

For more information, see Chapters 4 and 14.

Worksheet Delete Column/Row   /WD

Purpose

Deletes one or more columns or rows from the worksheet.

When you use /WD, the entire column or row and the information and formatting it contains are deleted and cannot be recovered.

Reminders

- Before you delete a column or row, use the End and arrow keys to make sure that distant cells in that column or row do not contain needed data or formulas.

- Place the cell pointer on the first column or row to be deleted before you invoke /WD.

Procedures

1. Type /wd

2. Select one of the following:

Menu Item	*Keystroke*	*Description*
Column	**C**	Deletes column(s) at cell pointer. Remaining columns to the right move left.
Row	**R**	Deletes row(s) at cell pointer. Remaining rows below move up.

3. Delete more than one column by moving the cell pointer right to highlight one cell for each column being deleted. Delete more than one row by moving the cell pointer down to highlight one cell for each row being deleted. Figure W.5 shows the cell pointer highlighting cells B11 to B14 so that these four rows will be deleted.

4. Make certain that the number of highlighted cells equals the number of columns or rows you want deleted.

5. Press Enter. Figure W.6 shows the worksheet after the rows are deleted.

Important Cues

- /Worksheet Delete deletes all the data and formulas in the column or row. To erase a small portion of a worksheet, use /Range Erase.

- Whenever you highlight a series of rows or columns, you can return to a single highlighted row or column by pressing Esc.

Fig. W.5

Specifying rows to be deleted.

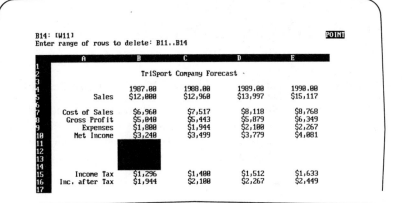

Fig. W.6

The worksheet after rows are deleted.

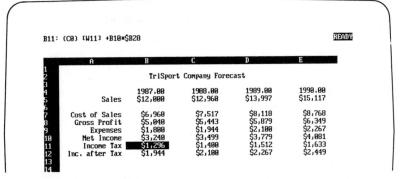

- Formulas, named ranges, and ranges in command prompts are adjusted automatically to the new cell addresses after you delete a column or row.

- Use /Move when you need to reposition a portion of the worksheet and cannot delete a column or row.

Cautions

▶ Formulas that refer to deleted cells have the value ERR.

▶ Deleting a row that passes through an area containing macros can create errors in the macros. Deleting code in the middle of the macro will cause problems, and deleting a blank cell between two macros merges their code.

▶ Deleting a column or row that defines a corner of a command range or range name causes formulas depending on that range to produce ERR. Also, deleting the beginning or ending row in a database or @SUM column causes problems. If you must delete the row or column, delete the corresponding range name, delete the row or column, re-create the range name, and correct the formulas.

Worksheet Column
Set-Width/Reset-Width   /WC

Purpose	Adjusts the column width of an individual column.

Columns wider than 9 characters are needed to display large numbers, to display dates, and to prevent text from being covered by adjacent cell entries. Narrow column widths are useful for short entries, such as (Y/N), and for organizing the display layout.

Reminders

- Make certain that changing the width of a column does not destroy the appearance of displays in another portion of the worksheet.

- Move the cell pointer to the widest entry in the column before you use /WCS.

Procedures

To set a new column width:

1. Type /wc

2. Select **Set-Width**.

3. Enter the new column width by typing the number of characters or by pressing ← or → to shrink or expand the column.

4. Press Enter.

To change the column width to the default width specified under /Worksheet Global Column-Width:

1. Type /wc

2. Select **Reset-Width**.

3. Press Enter.

Important Cues

- Asterisks appear in a cell whose column is too narrow to display numeric or date information.

- Text entries wider than the cell may be partially covered by text or numeric entries in the cell to the right.

- Use /Worksheet Global Column-Width to set the column width for columns that were not set individually with /Worksheet Column.

Caution   Changing a column's width throughout the entire worksheet can alter the appearance of display screens you already have created.

For more information, see Chapter 4.

Worksheet Column Hide/Display   /WC

Purpose   /WCH hides individual columns or a range of columns. Use /WCH to hide columns of information when you prepare confidential financial reports or want to display only results of calculations.

/WCD redisplays a hidden column or a range of hidden columns.

Reminders
- Make certain that hiding the display of a column does not destroy the appearance of displays in another portion of the worksheet.

- Move the cell pointer to the column you want to hide. If you plan to hide a range of columns, position the cell pointer at the upper left corner of the range.

- Move the cell pointer to the column or range of columns you want to redisplay. When displaying a range of previously hidden columns, position the cell pointer at the upper left corner of the range.

Procedures   *To hide a column:*

1. Type /wc

2. Select **Hide**.

3. Specify the column to be hidden by pressing ← or → and then pressing Enter. To hide a range of adjacent columns, specify the range by typing the range address, by entering a range name, or by pressing the period key (.) to anchor the range and moving the pointer to the opposite corner of the range.

4. To hide nonadjacent columns, repeat Steps 1 through 3.

To display a column previously hidden:

1. Type /wc

2. Select **Display**. Hidden columns are marked with an asterisk (∗) beside the column letter.

3. Move the cell pointer to the column you want to redisplay and press Enter. If you want to redisplay a range of columns, specify the range by typing the range address, by entering a range name, or by pressing the period key (.) to anchor the range and moving the pointer to the opposite corner of the range. After you press Enter, the specified columns are displayed.

Important Cues

- Use /WCH to suppress the printing of unnecessary columns.

- /WCH can be used to suppress columns in the current window without affecting the display in other windows. When the windows are cleared, the settings used in the top window of a horizontal split or the left window of a vertical split are kept; the settings used in the bottom or right windows are lost.

- When preparing reports, use /WCH to hide the display of unnecessary data and reduce the number of printed columns.

Cautions

▶ Be sure that other operators who use your worksheet are aware of the hidden columns. Although the values and formulas of hidden columns work properly, the display may be confusing if data appears to be missing.

▶ When columns are hidden on an unprotected worksheet, ranges copied or moved to the hidden area overwrite existing data.

For more information, see Chapter 4.

Worksheet Erase   /WE

Purpose
Erases the entire worksheet and resets all cell formats, label prefixes, and command settings to their original values.

Use this command to erase the worksheet so that you will have a fresh work area.

Reminder
To use the current worksheet again, be sure to save the worksheet before you use /Worksheet Erase.

Procedures
1. Type /we

2. Select **Y** from the following:

Menu Item	Keystroke	Description
Yes	**Y**	Erases the entire worksheet
No	**N**	Avoids erasing the entire worksheet. Use this option if you change your mind or realize that you don't want to erase the whole worksheet.

Important Cues
You don't have to erase a worksheet before you load a new one. The /File Retrieve command automatically erases the current worksheet when the new worksheet is loaded.

Caution
Make certain that you want to erase the entire worksheet. If portions of it can be used in the following worksheet, you may want to use /Range Erase to erase only the unusable portions.

For more information, see Chapter 4 and File Save.

Worksheet Titles   WT

Purpose   Retains the display of column and row headings that would otherwise scroll off the screen.

Reminders
- You can "freeze" cell contents horizontally (rows), vertically (columns), or both ways.

- Move the cell pointer so that the column headings you want frozen on the screen occupy the top row of the spreadsheet. Also move the cell pointer so that the column containing the leftmost row heading will be frozen at the left edge of the screen.

- Move the cell pointer one row below the lowest row to be used as a title, and one column to the right of the columns that contain row headings.

Figure W.7 shows a worksheet with the cell pointer positioned so that rows 1 through 7 and column A will be frozen if **B**oth is chosen from the /**W**ork-sheet **T**itles menu. The currently displayed area from B8 to E14 will still scroll normally.

Fig. W.7

Specifying the range to be frozen.

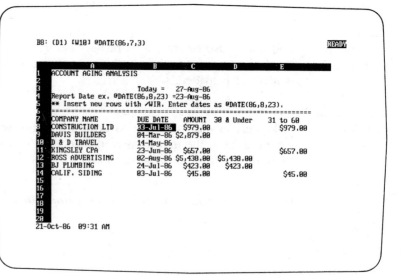

Procedures

1. Type /wt

2. Select one of the following menu items:

Menu Item	Keystroke	Description
Both	**B**	Creates titles from the rows above the cell pointer, and from the columns to the left of the cell pointer
Horizontal	**H**	Creates titles from the rows above the cell pointer
Vertical	**V**	Creates titles from the columns to the left of the cell pointer
Clear	**C**	Removes all frozen title areas so that all worksheet areas scroll

Important Cues

- To return the worksheet to normal, type /wtc

- If you have split the worksheet into two windows with /Worksheet Window, each window can have its own titles.

- Press the Home key to move the cell pointer to the top left corner of the unfrozen area.

- Use the F5 (GoTo) key to move the cell pointer inside the title area. This creates duplicates of the frozen rows and columns. The double appearance can be confusing.

- The cell pointer can enter title areas when you are entering cell addresses in POINT mode.

- /Worksheet Titles can be useful for displaying protected screen areas when /Range Input is active. Position titles so that they display labels and instructions adjacent to the unprotected input range.

- This feature is especially useful for freezing column headings over a database or an accounting spreadsheet. You also can freeze rows of text that describe figures in adjacent cells.

For more information, see Chapter 4.

Worksheet Window   /WW

Purpose

Displays two parts of the worksheet at the same time.

You can choose to split the worksheet horizontally or vertically. The two parts of the worksheet can scroll separately or together, following the same cell pointer movements.

Reminders

Before you use /WW:

• Decide whether you want the worksheet split horizontally or vertically.

• If you want two horizontal windows, move the cell pointer to the top row of what will become the lower window.

• For two vertical windows, move the cell pointer to the column that will become the left edge of the right window.

Figure W.8 shows the cell pointer positioned to create a lower horizontal window with row 21 as the top row. Therefore, on a lower part of the worksheet, the variables can be seen at the same time as the results. Figure W.9 shows the two horizontal windows.

Fig. W.8

Positioning the cell pointer to split the screen horizontally.

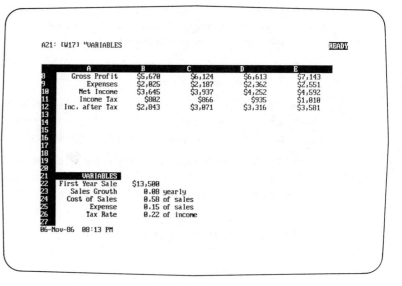

Fig. W.9

The screen split horizontally.

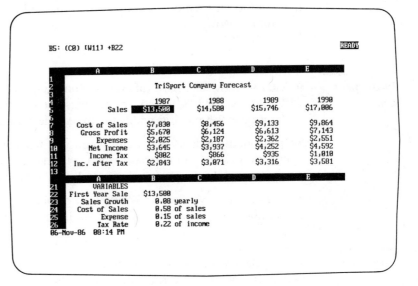

B5: (C0) [W11] +B22   READY

                TriSport Company Forecast

                1987   1988   1989   1990
        Sales $13,500 $14,580 $15,746 $17,006

Cost of Sales $7,830 $8,456 $9,133 $9,864
Gross Profit $5,670 $6,124 $6,613 $7,143
Expenses $2,025 $2,187 $2,362 $2,551
Net Income $3,645 $3,937 $4,252 $4,592
Income Tax $802 $866 $935 $1,010
Inc. after Tax $2,843 $3,071 $3,316 $3,581

VARIABLES
First Year Sale $13,500
Sales Growth   0.08 yearly
Cost of Sales   0.58 of sales
Expense   0.15 of sales
Tax Rate   0.22 of income
06-Nov-86   08:14 PM

Procedures

1. Type /ww

2. Select the desired option(s):

Menu Item	Keystroke	Description
Horizontal	**H**	Splits the worksheet into two horizontal windows at the cell pointer
Vertical	**V**	Splits the worksheet into two vertical windows at the cell pointer
Sync	**S**	Synchronizes two windows so that they move together. Windows are in Sync when they are first opened.
Unsync	**U**	Unsynchronizes two windows so that they can move independently of each other. You can then view simultaneously different rows and columns in the worksheet. A window will move only when it contains the cell pointer.
Clear	**C**	Removes the bottom or right window

3. Repeat Steps 1 and 2 and select Unsync if you want the windows to move independently of each other. You then can simultaneously view different rows and columns in the worksheet.

4. Press the F6 (Window) key to move the cell pointer into the opposite window. Move the cell pointer to position the second window as needed.

Important Cues

■ Each window can have different column widths. When /Worksheet Window Clear is selected, the settings used in the top or left window determine the column width for the single remaining worksheet.

■ Horizontal windows are useful when you work with databases. The criterion range and database column labels can appear in the upper window while the data or extracted data appear in the lower window.

■ You can use /Worksheet Window to display messages, instructions, warnings, help text, etc., without having to leave the worksheet.

Caution

Always clear windows and reposition the screen before you invoke windows in a macro. Macros that split screens may become "confused" if window configuration differs from what the macros "expect."

For more information, see Chapter 4.

Worksheet Status   /WS

Purpose   Displays the current global settings that help you operate the worksheet.

You also can use /WS to check available memory.

Reminder   The screen displays the status of the following information:

Available Memory (Conventional, Expanded)
Math Coprocessor
Recalculation (Method, Order, Iterations)
Circular Reference
Cell Display (Format, Label Prefix, Column Width, Zero
    Suppression)
Global Protection

You can check the worksheet's status whenever a worksheet is displayed.
Figure W.10 shows a typical status screen.

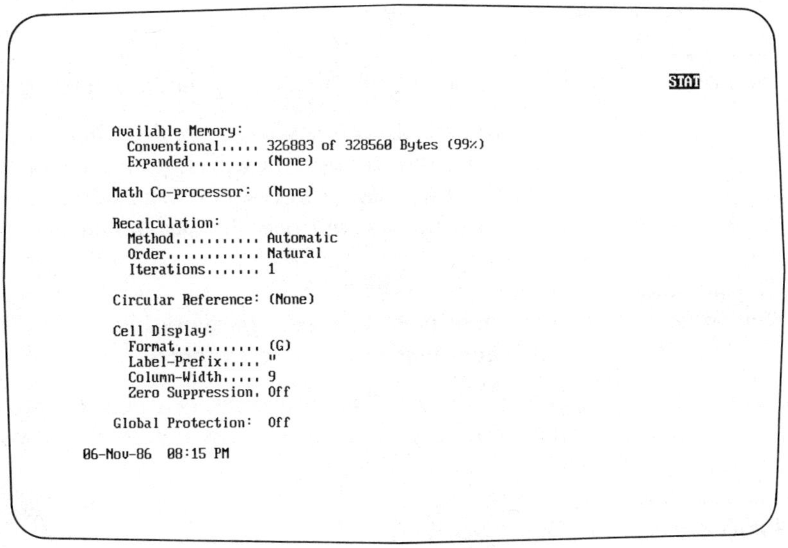

Fig. W.10

A /Worksheet
Status screen.

```
                                                                    STAT

        Available Memory:
          Conventional..... 326883 of 328560 Bytes (99%)
          Expanded......... (None)

        Math Co-processor: (None)

        Recalculation:
          Method........... Automatic
          Order............ Natural
          Iterations....... 1

        Circular Reference: (None)

        Cell Display:
          Format........... (G)
          Label-Prefix..... "
          Column-Width..... 9
          Zero Suppression. Off

        Global Protection: Off

        06-Nov-86  08:15 PM
```

Procedures   1. Type /ws

2. Press any key other than the F1 (Help) key to return to the worksheet.

Important Cues	■ The disk-file size of the saved worksheet cannot be calculated from the amount of memory used.
	■ You can reduce the size of a worksheet by deleting unnecessary formulas, labels, and values. Use **/R**ange **F**ormat **R**eset to reset the numeric format for unused areas; then save the revised worksheet to a file and retrieve a smaller version.
	■ The Circular Reference status displays a single cell within a ring of formulas that depend on each other. The Circular Reference status shows (in this ring) only one cell address at a time.

For more information, see Chapter 4.

Worksheet Page   /WP

Purpose	Manually inserts page breaks in printed worksheets.
	1-2-3 automatically inserts page breaks when printing reaches the bottom margin. For some reports, however, you may want page breaks to occur at designated rows. The **/W**orksheet **P**age command indicates to the printer where manually selected page breaks should occur.
Reminders	● If you will need to reuse the worksheet without page breaks, save the worksheet before you insert them.
	● Before you use /WP, move the cell pointer into the leftmost column of the print range and to one row below where you want the page break.
Procedures	1. Type /wp
	2. Press Enter.
	3. A row is inserted where the page will break, and a double colon (::) appears in the left column. Figure W.11 shows the cell pointer beneath a page-break symbol.

Fig. W.11

Positioning the cell pointer for page-break insertion.

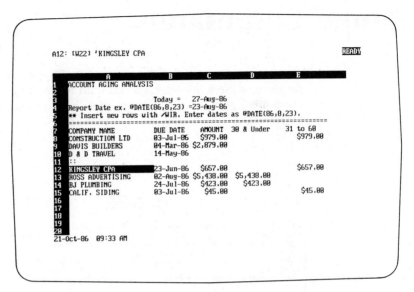

Important Cues

- Use **/W**orksheet **D**elete **R**ow to remove the page break.

- **/W**orksheet **P**age overrides the **/P**rint **F**ile **O**ptions **O**ther **U**nformatted command, which normally suppresses page breaks. If you need to print to disk without page breaks, make sure that you use **/WDR** to remove the page-break markers.

Caution

Do not make entries in the row that contains the page-break marker (::). Entries in this row will not print.

For more information, see Chapter 4.

Range Commands /R

/**Range** commands control the display formats, protection, and manipulation of *portions* of the worksheet. (If you want to affect the *entire* worksheet, such as by inserting an entire column, then look in the /Worksheet command menu.)

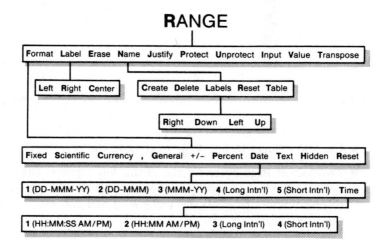

Range Format   /RF

Purpose   Prepares cells so that they display with a specific format for both values (numbers) and formula results.

/**Range** Format formats a cell or range of cells so that numbers appear in a specific format: with fixed decimal places; as currency; with commas only; in scientific notation; or as dates. These formats affect both screen display and printing.

Reminders   • Use /**Worksheet** Global Format to format the majority of the worksheet's cells that will contain numeric data. Use /**Range** Format to reset formats for areas that differ.

• Move the cell pointer to the upper left corner of the range you want to format.

Procedures   1. Type /rf

2. Select a format from the following menu items.

Menu Item	Keystroke	Description
Fixed	F	Fixes the number of decimal places displayed
Scientific	S	Displays large or small numbers, using scientific notation
Currency	C	Displays currency symbols (e.g. $ or £) and commas
,	,	Inserts commas to mark thousands and multiples of thousands
General	G	Displays values with up to 10 decimals or in scientific notation
+/-	+	Creates horizontal bar graphs or time duration graphs on computers that do not have graphics. Each symbol equals one whole number. Positive numbers display as plus (+) symbols; negative numbers, as minus (-) symbols.

Percent	**P**	Displays a decimal number as a whole percentage number with a % sign
Date	**D**	Displays serial-date numbers in the following formats. (Select **Date** to set a Time format.)

Date

1	DD–MMM–YY	12–Jan–51
2	DD–MMM	12–Jan
3	MMM–YY	Jan–51
4	MM/DD/YY	01/12/51
5	MM/DD	01/12

Time

1	HH:MM:SS AM/PM	1:04:34 PM
2	HH:MM AM/PM	1:04 PM
3	HH:MM:SS	13:04:34
4	HH:MM	13:04

Text	**T**	Continues to evaluate formulas as numbers, but displays formulas as text on-screen
Hidden	**H**	Hides contents from the display and printing but still evaluates contents
Reset	**R**	Returns the format to current /Worksheet Global format

3. If 1-2-3 prompts, enter the number of decimal places to be displayed. The full value of a cell is used for calculation. (See the first Caution.)

4. If you select **Date** or **Time**, you must select also a format number to indicate how you want Date or Time to appear.

5. Specify the range by entering the range address, highlighting the range, or using an assigned range name.

6. Verify that the specified range is correct.

7. Press Enter.

Important Cues

- Use /Worksheet Global Format to format new numbers entered throughout the worksheet. Numbers entered in ranges formatted with /Range Format will not be affected.

- /Range Format Hidden is the only format that affects labels. All other /Range Format commands work on values and numeric formulas.

- Dates and times are generated from serial date and time numbers created with @DATE, @DATEVALUE, @TIME, @NOW, and @TIMEVALUE.

- For formats other than General format, asterisks fill the cell when a value is too large to fit the cell's current column width. (With General format, values that are too large are displayed in scientific notation.)

- Use /Worksheet Global Default Other International to display non-USA formats. Select one of these international format options: Punctuation, Currency, Date, or Time.

- Range formats take precedence over Worksheet Global formats.

Cautions

▶ /Range Format rounds only the appearance of the displayed number. It does not round the number used for calculation. This difference can cause displayed numbers to appear to give an incorrect answer to a formula. Enclose numbers, formulas, or cell references in the @ROUND function to ensure that the values in calculations are truly rounded.

▶ Use Fixed decimal format to enter percentage data. Use Percent format to display or print results. Percent format displays a decimal such as .23 as 23%. If Percent format is used for data entry, most users will see 23% and attempt to enter a similar percentage (.24) as 24, producing a grossly incorrect entry of 2400%. If Percent format is used, numeric entries should be made as 24%. The trailing percent sign causes 1-2-3 to divide the value by 100.

*For more information, see **Worksheet Global Format**, **Worksheet Global Default**, and Chapters 5 and 6.*

Range Label

/RL

Purpose   Selects how you want to align text labels in their cells.

Labels narrower than cell width can be aligned to the left, right, or center. To change how numbers appear on-screen, use either /**R**ange Format or /**W**orksheet Global Format.

Reminders   • Move the cell pointer to the upper left corner of the range containing the cells you want to align.

• Use /**W**orksheet Global Label-Prefix to align the majority of labels on the worksheet. After building the worksheet "skeleton" of text, align labels and set column widths with /**R**ange Label and /**W**orksheet Column Set-Width.

Procedures   1. Type /rl

2. Select one of these menu items:

Menu Item	Keystroke	Description
Left	**L**	Aligns labels with cell's left edge
Right	**R**	Aligns labels with cell's right edge
Center	**C**	Centers labels in cell

3. Specify the range by entering the range address, highlighting the range, or using an assigned range name. Figure R.1 shows a highlighted range ready to be aligned to the right or centered.

4. Verify that the specified range is correct.

5. Press Enter.

Important Cues   ▪ The label prefix appears on the status line (the screen's first line, directly before the cell contents).

▪ Alignment works only for text smaller than cell width. Text larger than cell width is left-aligned. Characters wider than cell width "squeeze" out the cell's right edge.

▪ Align labels in a cell by entering one of these label prefixes before typing the label:

Fig. R.1

The highlighted range A5..A12 about to be aligned.

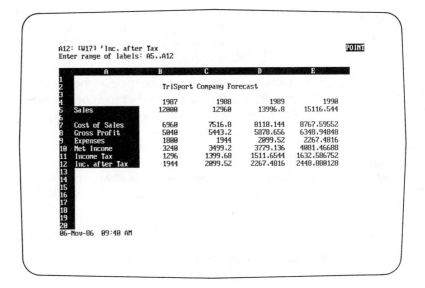

Label Prefix	Function
' (apostrophe)	Aligns label to the left
" (quotation mark)	Aligns label to the right
^ (caret)	Centers label in the cell
\ (backslash)	Repeats character to fill a cell*

* Note that this prefix can't be selected from the menu.

- The worksheet starts with labels left-aligned. Use /**W**orksheet **G**lobal **L**abel-Prefix to set the label prefix used by text entries in areas not specified with /**R**ange **L**abel.

- /**R**ange **L**abel does not affect values (numeric cell entries). Values are always right-aligned.

- Labels beginning with numbers or formula symbols require label prefixes. Enter the label prefix before entering the numbers or symbols. This process is necessary for addresses or part numbers, such as:

Correct	Incorrect
'2207 Cheyenne Dr.	2207 Cheyenne Dr.
"34-567FB	34-567FB

- Use a label prefix to preserve formulas with errors you've not yet identified. For example, if you have a problem with the formula +B5*@PMT(B16B12/12,B14*12), and you don't have time to look for the error (a comma is missing after B16), use an apostrophe label prefix to turn the formula into text. Later, when you have more time, use EDIT mode to remove the apostrophe to change the text back to a formula. Then correct the formula error.

■ Document formulas by inserting a label prefix before each formula and copying the formula as a label to your worksheet documentation area. Later, remove the label prefix from the original formula to restore it to its original, operable form.

Cautions

▶ /Range Label Center will not center labels on the screen or page. You must center the text manually by moving the cell pointer with the text and following these steps:

1. Enter the text if you have not done so already.

2. Determine how many leading spaces are necessary to center the text on-screen.

3. Press the F2 (Edit) key; then press Home. The cursor will be on the label prefix at the beginning of the text.

4. Move the cell pointer right one character and insert spaces in front of the first character to center it.

5. Press Enter.

▶ Macro code text must be labels. If you don't place a label prefix before the macro commands, such as /WGLR, your keystrokes will select menu items.

▶ Numbers or formulas preceded by label prefixes have a value of zero when evaluated by a numeric formula. (In Release 2.0, however, a formula [but not a function] that references a label returns an ERR; Release 2.01 eliminates this bug.) In a database query, you must use text searches to search for these numbers with label prefixes.

*For more information, see **Worksheet Global Label-Prefix, Range Format,** and Chapter 5.*

Range Erase   /RE

Purpose   Erases the contents of a single cell or range of cells.

Reminders
- Use /Worksheet Erase if you want to erase the entire worksheet.

- If you have any doubts about erasing a range of cells, use /File Save to save the worksheet to a file before erasing the range. Erased cells cannot be recovered.

- Move the cell pointer to the upper left corner of the range to be erased.

Procedures
1. Type /re

2. Specify the range to be erased by entering the range address, highlighting the range, or using an assigned range name. Figure R.2 shows a highlighted range to be erased.

Fig. R.2

The highlighted range about to be deleted.

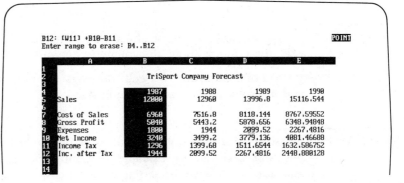

3. Verify that the specified range is correct. If the range is incorrect, press Esc and go back to Step 2.

4. Press Enter.

Important Cues
- Protected cells cannot be erased. To erase protected cells, first remove worksheet protection with /Worksheet Global Protection Disable.

- Erasing data or formulas may produce an ERR display in formulas that depend on the erased data or formulas.

■ Erasing a range does not change the format, label prefix, or protection status assigned to the cells.

Cautions

▶ /Worksheet Delete can be a dangerous command to use to remove a record from a database. You can unintentionally delete a row that looks blank but contains important data off-screen. Use instead /**Range** Erase and sort down empty records.

▶ Be careful not to erase formulas or values hidden with /Worksheet Global Format Hidden or /Range Format Hidden.

*For more information, see **Worksheet Delete**, **Worksheet Erase**, and Chapter 4.*

Range Name   /RN

Purpose

Assigns an alphabetical or alphanumeric name to a cell or a range of cells. (See the Caution about alphanumeric range names.)

Instead of column-and-row cell addresses, use range names to make formulas and macros easy to read and understand.

Reminder

Consider all the possible ways to use range names in your specific 1-2-3 application. Consider, for example, how range names can be used in formulas and macros, or used for setting print ranges, moving the cell pointer to different areas of the worksheet, and setting data ranges for graphs.

Procedures

To create a range name that describes a single cell or range of cells, follow these steps:

1. Move the cell pointer to the cell or upper left corner of the range of cells to be named.

2. Type /rn

3. Select **Create**.

4. When prompted to enter the range name, press the F3 (Name) key to see a full screen display of names already in use. Press Esc to exit the list. If the name you want to use is listed, delete it before you create another range by that name.

5. Type a range name up to 15 characters long. Avoid using symbols other than the underline.

6. Press Enter.

7. Specify the range to be named by entering the range address or highlighting the range.

8. Verify that the range is correct.

9. Press Enter.

To create range names from labels:

1. Move the cell pointer to the upper left corner of the column or row of labels.

2. Type /rn

3. Select **Labels**.

4. Select one of these menu items:

Menu Item	*Keystroke*	*Description*
Right	**R**	Uses the labels to name the cell to the right of each label
Down	**D**	Uses the labels to name the cell below each label
Left	**L**	Uses the labels to name the cell to the left of each label
Up	**U**	Uses the labels to name the cell above each label

5. Specify the range of labels to be named by entering the range address or highlighting the range.

6. Verify that the range encloses only labels.

7. Press Enter.

To delete a range name:

1. Type /rn

2. Select **Delete** to delete a single range name. Select **Reset** to delete all range names.

3. Press Enter. The addresses in formulas of the deleted range names revert to normal cell addresses.

To display the addresses of existing range names:

1. Move the cell pointer to a clear area of the worksheet.

2. Type /rn

3. Select **Table**.

4. Press Enter to create a table of range names and their associated addresses.

Important Cues

■ Use a range name when you enter a function. Instead of entering a function as @SUM(P53..P65), for example, type it as @SUM(EXPENSES).

■ Similarly, use a range name when you respond to a prompt. For example, when the program requests a print range, provide a range name, as in the following:

    Enter print range: JULREPORT

■ To move the cell pointer rapidly to the upper left corner of any range, press the F5 (GoTo) key and then enter the range name or press the F3 (Name) key to display a list of range names. After you have entered the range name or selected a name from the list, press Enter.

■ To print a list of range names, use **/Range Name Table** and press Shift-PrtSc after the list appears.

■ **/Move** moves range names with cells if the entire range is included in the block to be moved.

■ Macro names are range names; therefore, macros must be named using /RNC or /RNL.

Cautions

▶ A range name can be alphanumeric (as in SALES87), but avoid creating a range name that looks like a cell reference (for example, AD19). Such a range name will not function correctly in formulas.

▶ Always delete existing range names before re-creating them in a new location. If you don't delete an original range name, formulas that used the original name may be wrong.

▶ Do not delete columns or rows that form the corner of a named range. Doing so produces an ERR in formulas.

▶ Moving the upper left or lower right corner of a named range shifts the cell addresses that the range name defines.

▶ When two named ranges have the same upper left corner, moving one of the corners will move the address location for both range names. To move a corner of overlapping named ranges, first delete one range name, move the range, and then re-create the deleted range name in its original location.

▶ /**R**ange **N**ame **T**able does not update itself automatically. If you move, copy, or change range names, you must re-create the range name table.

For more information, see Chapter 4.

Range Justify   /RJ

Purpose

Fits text within a desired range by wrapping words to form complete paragraphs.

Use /**R**ange **J**ustify to join and wordwrap automatically any lines of text in adjacent vertical cells to form a paragraph. /**R**ange **J**ustify redistributes words so that text lines are of approximately the same length.

Reminders

● Delete any blank cells or values between vertically adjacent cells you want to join. Blank cells or values stop text from justifying.

● Move the cell pointer to the top of the column of text you want justified. Make sure that the cell pointer is in the first cell containing the text. On the status line, you should see the first words of the text from the first row of the column.

● Remember that other cells are moved to reflect the justification unless you specify a range for /RJ. In figure R.3, a range has been specified in which the text will be reformatted; this keeps the value in B10 from being displaced.

Fig. R.3

The worksheet range marked for justification.

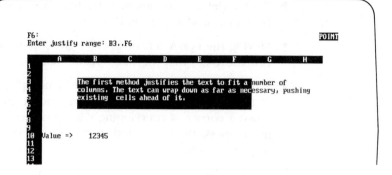

```
F6:                                                                    POINT
Enter justify range: B3..F6

         A      B       C       D       E       F       G       H
1
2
3               The first method justifies the text to fit a number of
4               columns. The text can wrap down as far as necessary, pushing
5               existing  cells ahead of it.
6
7
8
9
10      Value =>      12345
11
12
13
```

Procedures

1. Type /rj

2. Highlight the range in which you want the text to be justified. If you choose not to specify a range for the justification, highlight only the first row of the text column.

3. Press Enter, and the text will be justified. If you specified a range, worksheet cells within the leftmost column of the highlighted range are justified; cells outside the highlighted range are not moved.

Important Cues

- /Range Justify justifies all contiguous text in a column until justification is stopped by nonlabel cell contents (a blank cell, a formula, or a value).

- If you are uncertain about the results of /Range Justify, save your worksheet with /File Save before using /Range Justify.

- Enter long lists of single-word labels as a single text line and justify it down a column. Enter the words with a single space between them, and make certain that the column width is only wide enough to contain the longest word.

- Use /File Import to import text from word processors (ASCII text files only). Once in 1-2-3, the text can be justified with /Range Justify to fit the worksheet.

- Create a simple memo writer by clearing a worksheet of other entries and setting column A's width to 72 characters. Now enter lines of text up to 240 characters, leaving blank cells where you want paragraph marks. To justify the text, move the cell pointer to the first cell in a paragraph. Type /rj and press Enter. Select only the single cell as the justification range. Do the same for the first cell of each paragraph. Use the F2 (Edit) key to make changes.

Cautions

▶ If the specified range is not large enough to hold the justified text, 1-2-3 displays an error message. To solve this problem, enlarge the range or move the text to a new location. If you enlarge the range, you may need to move other cell contents.

▶ Using /**R**ange **J**ustify on protected cells will result in an error. Remove protection with /**W**orksheet **G**lobal **P**rotection **D**isable.

▶ 1-2-3 is not a word processor. /**R**ange **J**ustify is useful for entering long lists of labels or in adjusting paragraphs of edited text, but this capability does not have a word processor's functionality.

*For more information, see **Move, File Import, Worksheet Page,** and Chapter 5.*

Range Unprotect   /RU

Purpose

Allows changes to cells in a protected worksheet.

Use /**R**ange **U**nprotect and /**W**orksheet **G**lobal **P**rotection to protect worksheets from accidental changes. /**R**ange **U**nprotect identifies which cells' contents can be changed when /**W**orksheet **G**lobal **P**rotection is enabled. Cells not identified with /**R**ange **U**nprotect cannot be changed when /**W**orksheet **G**lobal **P**rotection is enabled.

Reminder

Move the cell pointer to the upper left corner of the range you want to identify as unprotected. /**W**orksheet **G**lobal **P**rotection may be enabled or disabled.

Procedures

To identify a cell or a range of cells as unprotected:

1. Type /**r**

2. Select **U**nprotect.

3. Specify the range by entering the range address, highlighting the range, or using an assigned range name.

4. Verify that the range is correct.

5. Press Enter.

6. On some displays, the contents of cells will increase in intensity or change color.

To remove identification from an unprotected range:

1. Type /r

2. Select **Protect.**

3. Specify the range by entering the range address, highlighting the range, or using an assigned range name.

4. Verify that the range is correct.

5. Press Enter.

6. The contents of cells not identified as unprotected will be restored to normal intensity or color, and the U in the status line will disappear.

Important Cues

■ /Range Protect and /Range Unprotect affect data entry only when /Worksheet Global Protection is enabled. The screen display of unprotected contents may be brighter or a different color, depending on your graphics hardware. (See Chapter 4.)

■ Use high-contrast characters in unprotected cells to attract attention to instructions or comments, even when worksheet protection is disabled.

■ Use /Range Input to limit cell-pointer movement to unprotected cells.

■ Use /Worksheet Status to see whether worksheet protection is enabled or disabled.

Caution

Macros that make changes to cell contents will not work correctly if /Worksheet Global Protection is enabled and the macro attempts to change protected cells. Prevent this condition by limiting cell-pointer movement to unprotected cells or by disabling worksheet protection when the macro starts. Macros should enable worksheet protection before they end.

*For more information, see **Worksheet Global Protection, Range Input, Worksheet Status,** and Chapter 4.*

Range Input /RI

Purpose

Restricts cell-pointer movement to unprotected cells.

/Range Input is an excellent way to create fill-in-the-blank worksheets. This prevents inexperienced users from making accidental changes to worksheet labels and formulas.

Reminders

- To use /Range Input effectively, organize your worksheet so that the data-entry cells are together. Figure R.4 shows a worksheet arranged to maximize /Range Input.

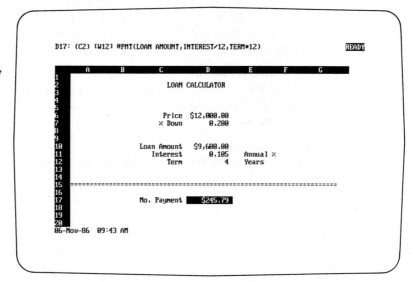

Fig. R.4

Loan Calculator worksheet arranged to maximize /Range Input.

- Before you use /RI, use /Range Unprotect to identify unprotected data entry cells. /Worksheet Global Protection does not have to be enabled.

- Move the cell pointer to one corner of a range that will include the unprotected data-entry cells.

Procedures

1. Type /ri

2. Specify the input range to be displayed. Enter the range address, highlight the range, or use an assigned range name.

3. Verify that the range is correct. If the range is incorrect, press Esc and return to Step 2.

4. Press Enter. The input range's upper left corner is moved to the screen's upper left corner. Cell-pointer movements are restricted to unprotected cells in the designated input range.

5. Make data entries, using normal methods. Press Esc or Enter to exit /Range Input and return to normal cell-pointer movement.

Important Cues

■ /Range Input restricts your key selections to Esc, Enter, Edit, Help, Home, End, ←, →, ↑, or ↓. Use standard alphanumeric keys for data entry and editing.

■ /Range Input is most valuable when used within macros. Within macros, /Range Input can be used to restrict data entry to one worksheet range for one part of the macro and to another worksheet range for another part of the macro.

■ If a macro contains /Range Input, the macro pauses for input until you press Esc or Enter without making an additional entry. When the macro exits /Range Input, the macro continues with the next macro command.

*For more information, see **Range Name, Range Unprotect**, and **Chapter 4**.*

Range Value   /RV

Purpose Converts formulas in a range to their values so that you can copy only the values to a new location.

This command will rapidly convert formula results to unchanging values for database storage.

Reminders
- Check to see that the destination area is large enough to hold the copied values. They will replace existing cell contents.
- Move the cell pointer to the upper left corner of the range containing the formulas.

Procedures
1. Type /rv
2. Specify the source range by entering the range address, highlighting the range, or using an assigned range name.
3. Press Enter.
4. Specify the upper left corner cell of the destination range. Specify this location by typing a cell address or range name, or by moving the cell pointer to this location.
5. Press Enter. The values will appear in the destination range. Values will preserve the numeric formats used in the original formulas.

Important Cues
- /Range Value also copies labels and string formulas and converts string (text) formulas to labels.
- Use /Copy to copy formulas without changing them into values.

Cautions
- ▶ /Range Value overwrites data in the destination (TO) range. Be sure that the destination range is large enough to receive the data without overwriting adjacent cell contents you don't want to alter.
- ▶ If you make the destination range the same as the source range, formulas in the range will be converted to their values, but these values will overwrite and thereby replace the formulas. They are replaced permanently.

*For more information, see **Copy** and Chapter 4.*

Range Transpose   /RT

Purpose

Reorders columns of data into rows of data, or rows of data into columns of data.

/Range Transpose is useful when you want to change data from spreadsheet format (headings on left, data in rows) to database format (headings on top, data in columns), or vice versa.

Reminders

- Make sure that the range to be transposed does not contain formulas. If it contains formulas, use /Range Value to change the formulas into constant values.

- Transpose the new data to a clear worksheet area. The transposed data will overwrite any existing data.

- Move the cell pointer to the upper left corner of the range of cells you want to transpose.

Procedures

1. Type /rt

2. Specify the range to be transposed by entering the range address, highlighting the range, or using an assigned range name.

3. Verify that the range is correct.

4. Press Enter.

5. When 1-2-3 displays the TO: prompt, move the cell pointer to the upper left corner of the destination cells where the transposed data will be copied.

6. Press Enter.

Figure R.5 shows data in A6..B10 transposed to D6..H7.

Fig. R.5

Data in A6..B10 is transposed to D6..H7.

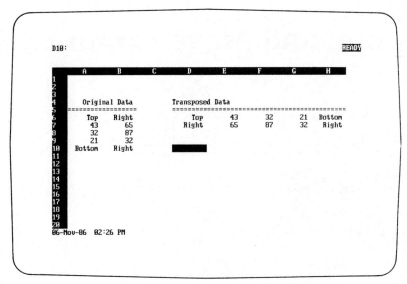

Important Cue

Transposed formulas will usually be incorrect. If the range to be transposed contains formulas, use /Range Value to change the formulas to values, and then transpose the range.

Caution

Do not use the same upper left corner for the source (FROM) and destination (TO) ranges. Not all the data will transpose correctly.

*For more information, see **Range Value** and Chapter 4.*

Copy and Move Commands

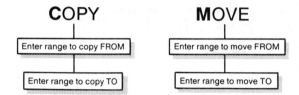

COPY

Enter range to copy FROM

Enter range to copy TO

MOVE

Enter range to move FROM

Enter range to move TO

Copy   /C

Purpose

Copies formulas, values, and labels to new locations.

The cell addresses in copied formulas change to reflect the new location or stay fixed, depending on whether you use relative or absolute cell references.

Reminders

- Make sure that you have enough blank space on the worksheet to receive the cell or range of cells being copied. Copies replace previous cell contents.

- If the receiving cell address is not close to the cell or range of cells being copied, note the address before entering /Copy. Pointing across a long distance to the receiving address can be tedious.

- Before you issue the /Copy command, move the cell pointer to the upper left corner of the range you want copied. If you are copying one cell, put the cell pointer on that cell.

Procedures

1. Type /c

2. The FROM prompt requests the range of the cells to be copied. Highlight a new range, or enter the original range by typing the range name or the range address.

3. Press Enter.

4. At the TO prompt, specify the upper left corner of the worksheet section where you want the duplicate to appear. Move the cell pointer

to the upper left corner position, and press the period key (.) to anchor the first corner. If you want multiple adjacent duplicates, you can highlight additional cells that define the upper left corners of the additional duplicates.

5. Press Enter.

6. Make sure that the copied formulas produce correct answers. If the answers are not correct, the copy procedure probably has adjusted cell addresses that should be fixed.

Important Cues

- /Copy creates duplicates of labels and values. Formulas are adjusted to the new location, depending on whether cell references are relative or absolute.

- You can make single or multiple copies, depending on the range you enter at the TO prompt. Enter the ranges as follows:

Original Range FROM:	Desired Copies	Duplicate Range TO:
One cell	Fill an area	Row, column, or range
Rectangular area	One duplicate	Upper left cell of duplicate, outside original range
Single column	Multiple columns	Adjacent cells across a row, formed from the top cell of each duplicate column
Single row	Multiple rows	Adjacent cells down a column, formed from the left cell in each duplicate row

Cautions

▶ Overlapping FROM and TO ranges (original and duplicate) can cause incorrect results. To avoid them, move the cell pointer off the original cell before anchoring the TO range with a period.

▶ If there is not enough room to receive the copied range, the contents of the existing cells will be covered by the copied data. Use /Move to move existing data on the worksheet, or use /Worksheet Insert to insert blank columns or rows.

*For more information, see **Worksheet Insert Column**, **Worksheet Insert Row**, **Range Value**, **Range Name**, and Chapter 4.*

Move

/M

Purpose

Reorganizes your worksheet by moving blocks of labels, values, or formulas to different locations.

Cell references and range names used in formulas stay the same, which means that formula results do not change.

Reminders

- Make sure that you have enough blank space on the worksheet to receive the cell or range of cells being moved. The moved data will replace previous cell contents.

- Before you issue the /Move command, move the cell pointer to the top left corner of the range to be moved. If you want to move one cell, place the cell pointer on that cell.

Procedures

1. Type /m

2. The FROM prompt requests the range of the cells to be moved. Highlight a new range, or enter the original range by typing the range name or the range address.

3. Press Enter.

4. At the TO prompt, enter the address of the single upper left corner of the range to which the cells will be moved. Enter this cell by typing the cell address, typing a range name, or highlighting the cell with the cell pointer.

5. Press Enter.

Important Cues

- Formulas moved with /Move continue to reference the same cells as before the move. If referenced cells are moved with /Move, all formulas that reference these cells adjust the references to the new location.

- Use /Copy when you want to duplicate a range of cells at a new location while keeping the original range intact.

- Range names move with the moved cells if the named area is completely enclosed.

Cautions

▶ If the worksheet does not have enough room to receive the range of cells being moved, the existing cells will be replaced by the moved data. You can use /Move to move cell contents to make room or add rows and columns with the /Worksheet Insert command.

▶ Moving the anchor cell and/or the diagonally opposite cell of a named range moves the corner(s) of the named range to the new location as well. If you have doubts about what is being moved, save the worksheet, delete the old range name, make the move, and then re-create the range name.

▶ Be careful when moving a named range that has the same upper left corner as another range. Moving one range will change the upper left corner for both named ranges.

For more information, see **Worksheet Insert, Copy, Range Name,** *and* **Chapter 4.**

File Commands /F

File commands are used to save and retrieve worksheets, extract a small worksheet from inside a larger worksheet, combine two worksheets, import ASCII data, and select the drive and directory for storage.

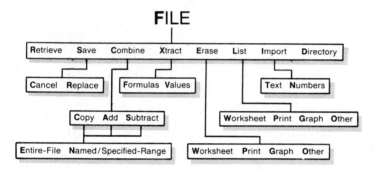

File Retrieve /FR

Purpose   Loads the requested worksheet file from disk.

Reminder   Save the current worksheet with /**File Save** before you begin working on a new one. When a new worksheet is loaded, it replaces the worksheet currently displayed.

Procedures
1. Type /fr

2. Type the file name or use → and possibly ← to move the cell pointer to highlight the file.

3. Press Enter.

Important Cues

■ You can display a listing of file names by pressing the F3 (Name) key in response to the prompt

`Name of file to retrieve:`

Use the arrow keys to move to the desired file name, and then press Enter. To return to the menu without making a selection, press Esc.

■ Retrieve a single file from a different disk drive by typing the drive designation, the path, and the file name, such as

`Name of file to retrieve:` *C:\123\FORECAST\JUNEV3*

In this example, the file JUNEV3 is located on drive C in the FORECAST subdirectory of the 123 directory. You may need to press Esc twice to clear the previous path.

■ Protected worksheets require a password. When you enter a password, be sure to use the same upper- and lowercase letter combination you typed originally.

■ When you start 1-2-3, the worksheet file will load automatically if you save it under the name AUTO123 into the same directory as 123.EXE.

■ To change a drive or directory for the current work session, use the /File **D**irectory command.

■ Use /**W**orksheet **G**lobal **D**efault **D**irectory to change the directory that 1-2-3 uses on startup. Use /WGDU to save the settings to the System disk.

Caution

The retrieved file replaces the worksheet on-screen. Use /File **S**ave to store your current worksheet before you retrieve a new one.

*For more information, see **File Save, File Combine, Worksheet Global Default Directory, File Directory,** and Chapter 7.*

File Save

/FS

Purpose

Saves the current worksheet and settings.

/File Save stores worksheets so that they can be retrieved later.

Reminders

- Remember to save frequently to guard against data loss.

- Name files so that they are easy to remember and group together. If you name related files in a similar way (such as TRENDV1, TRENDV2, and TRENDV3), you can use the DOS wildcards * and ? to copy and erase files.

Procedures

1. Type /fs

2. You can enter the file name for the worksheet by using the default name displayed; by using → and possibly ← to highlight an existing name; by typing a new name; or by entering a new drive designation, path name, and file name.

3. Press Enter.

4. If there is an existing file with the name you have selected, choose one of the following:

Menu Item	Keystroke	Description
Cancel	C	Cancels the save operation
Replace	R	Replaces an existing file with the current file

Important Cues

- Write file names of up to eight characters by using the letters A to Z, the numbers 0 to 9, and the underline character (_) or hyphen (–). Spaces cannot be used.

- Save worksheets with a password; the password must then be entered before the file can be retrieved. To save a file with a password:

  1. Type /fs

  2. Type the file name, press the space bar, and type *P*.

  3. Press Enter.

4. Type a password of up to 15 characters (no spaces). Be sure to remember the upper- and lowercase letter combination. When you retrieve the file, you must enter the password in exactly the same way.

5. Press Enter.

6. After the Verify prompt, type the password again and press Enter.

■ Change a protected file's password by using the backspace key to erase the Password Protected message that is displayed when you use /File Save. Then repeat steps 2 through 6.

■ You can select a file name from the list of file names. When prompted for a name, press Esc to remove the default file name. Press the F3 (Name) key, use the arrow keys to move to the file name you want to replace, and press Enter.

■ Use /File List to display the size and the date of the existing files.

■ Use /File Xtract to save a range of cells from a worksheet.

Cautions

▶ Saving a worksheet to an existing file name replaces the old file. This means that you could accidentally write over necessary files. A safer practice is to save each copy under a different name and delete old versions later, using /File Erase or the DOS ERASE command.

▶ Do not remove your data disk after executing /File Save until the light on your disk drive goes off. Pay no attention to the READY sign. Wait several seconds after the READY sign has disappeared before you remove the disk. If you remove the disk prematurely, information can be lost.

*For more information, see **File Directory, File Erase, File Xtract,** and Chapter 7.*

File Combine   /FC

Purpose   Combines values or formulas from one worksheet with data in another worksheet.

Any part of a saved worksheet can be combined with the current worksheet.

Reminders
- Remember that /File Combine can be used three different ways: to copy the contents from the file worksheet to the current worksheet; to add values from the file worksheet to the current worksheet; and to subtract incoming values from the numeric values in the current worksheet.

- Use /File Import to bring ASCII files into the current worksheet and /Data Parse to organize them. To send your file to an ASCII text file, use /Print File to print the file to disk.

- Before you issue /FC, move the cell pointer to the upper left corner of the range in which the data will be combined.

Procedures   1. Type /fc

2. Select one of the following choices:

Menu Item	Keystroke	Description
Copy	C	Copies incoming cell contents over the cells in the current worksheet. Cells in the current worksheet that correspond to blank incoming cells do not change. Labels and formulas in the current worksheet are replaced.
Add	A	Adds values from cells in the file worksheet to cells containing blanks or values in the current worksheet. Labels and formulas in the current worksheet are not changed.
Subtract	S	Subtracts values from cells in the file worksheet from the corresponding blanks or values in the current worksheet. Labels and formulas in the current worksheet are not changed.

3. Select how much of the saved worksheet file you want to use:

Menu Item	Keystroke	Description
Entire-File	**E**	Combines the entire file worksheet with the current worksheet. Use when the file worksheet has been created with /File **X**tract and contains only raw data.
Named/ Specified-Range	**N**	Combines information from a named portion of the file worksheet into the current worksheet. Use when the file worksheet is a full worksheet that contains information other than the information being combined.

4. If you select Entire-File, choose a file name from the menu by pressing → and possibly ←, by typing the file name, or by pressing F3 to display a list of file names and using the arrow keys. Press Enter. If you select Named/Specified-Range, you are asked to enter the range name (or the coordinates of the range) and the file name.

Important Cues

- If you want to combine, add, or subtract a small portion of the file worksheet, first give that portion a range name. Use /**R**ange **N**ame to name the portion on the file worksheet and save the worksheet back to disk.

- /FCC combines values, labels, and formulas. All cell references, relative and absolute, are adjusted to reflect their new locations on the worksheet.

  Cell references are adjusted according to the upper left corner of the combined data range (the cell pointer location). Combined formulas adjust for the difference between the cell pointer and cell A1 on the current worksheet.

- When creating spreadsheets, you can save time by using /File **X**tract and /File **C**ombine to merge parts of existing spreadsheets to form the new one.

- Use /FCC to copy sections of a macro file to your worksheet so that you don't have to type the macros on every new worksheet. Keep your favorite macros in one worksheet; be sure to give each macro a range name and address that encloses all the macro's code and documentation. You can use /FCC to copy the macro into the new worksheet, but you need to use /**R**ange **N**ame **C**reate or /**R**ange **N**ame **L**abel to rename the macro on the new worksheet.

- When you use /File Combine Add, cells in the incoming file that contain labels or string formulas are not added.

- Use /File Combine Subtract to subtract the values in the incoming worksheet from the values in the current worksheet. When an existing cell is empty, the incoming value is subtracted from zero.

- Create a macro with /File Combine to consolidate worksheets.

Cautions

▶ Data copied into the current worksheet replaces existing data. Blank cells in the incoming worksheet take on the value of the cells in the current worksheet.

▶ Range names are not brought to the new worksheet when a file is combined. This prevents possible conflicts with range names in the current worksheet. After combining files, you must re-create range names with /**Range Name Create** or /**Range Name Label**.

*For more information, see **Range Name Create**, **Range Name Label**, **File Xtract**, and Chapter 7.*

File Xtract   /FX

Purpose

Saves to disk a portion of the current worksheet as a separate worksheet.

You can save the portion as it appears on the worksheet (with formulas) or save only the results of the formulas.

Reminder

Position the cursor at the upper left corner of the range you want to extract.

Procedures

1. Type /fx

2. Choose one of the following:

Menu Item	Keystroke	Description
Formulas	F	Saves as a new worksheet both formulas and cell contents from the current worksheet
Values	V	Saves as a new worksheet formula results and labels

3. Type a file name other than the current worksheet. If you want to overwrite the data in a particular file, select that file name from the menu.

4. Highlight the range of the worksheet to be extracted as a separate file. Enter the range by typing the range address (such as B23..D46), by typing the range name, or by moving the cell pointer to the opposite corner of the range.

5. Press Enter.

Important Cues

■ If you used /FXF to save the portion of a worksheet, the extracted file can function as a normal worksheet.

■ To freeze a worksheet so that formulas and results don't change, extract a file with /File Xtract Values. When you retrieve the file, the formulas are replaced with values. Use this option when you extract Actual data.

■ Use /File Xtract to save memory when a worksheet becomes too large. Separate the worksheet into smaller worksheets that require less memory.

■ Increase worksheet execution speed by breaking large spreadsheets into smaller ones with /File **X**tract **F**ormulas.

Caution

Make sure that the extracted worksheet does not use values or formulas outside the Xtract range.

---

*For more information, see **File Combine** and Chapter 7.*

File Erase   /FE

Purpose

Erases 1-2-3 files from disk.

Use /FE to erase unnecessary files from disk so that you have more available disk space.

Reminders

• Use the DOS ERASE or DEL command to remove a large number of files. From within 1-2-3, select the /**S**ystem command, use the ERASE or DEL command at the DOS prompt, and return to 1-2-3 by typing *exit* and pressing Enter.

• Before you use /FE, use /**F**ile **D**irectory to specify the drive designation and the directory that contains the file(s) you want to erase.

Procedures

1. Type /fe

2. Select the type of file you want to erase:

Menu Item	Keystroke	Description
Worksheet	**W**	Displays worksheet files with .WK1 extensions
Print	**P**	Displays ASCII text files created with /**P**rint or another program. The file extension must be .PRN

Graph	**G**	Displays files created with /Graph, which end with the extension .PIC
Other	**O**	Displays all files in current drive and directory

3. Type the path and the name of the file, or use the arrow keys to highlight the file you want to erase.

4. Press Enter.

5. Verify that you do or do not want to erase the file, by selecting Yes or No from the menu.

Important Cue

You can erase files from different drives or directories either by specifying the drive designation, path, and file name or by changing the settings with **/File Directory**.

For more information, see **File Directory** and **File List.**

File List   /FL

Purpose

Displays all file names of a specific type that are stored on the current drive and directory.

/FL displays the size of the file (in bytes) and the date and time the file was created.

Reminder

Use /File List to select different directories and display the current files.

Procedures

1. Type /fl

2. Select the type of file you want to display:

Menu Item	Keystroke	Description
Worksheet	**W**	Displays worksheet files with .WK1 extensions
Print	**P**	Displays ASCII text files created with /**Print** or another program. The file extension must be .PRN
Graph	**G**	Displays files created with /**Graph**, which end with the extension .PIC
Other	**O**	Displays all files in current drive and directory

3. Use the arrow keys to highlight individual file names. If the list of file names extends off the screen, use the arrow keys, PgDn, or PgUp, to display the file names.

4. Display files from a different directory by moving the cursor to a directory name (such as \BUDGET) and pressing Enter.

5. Press Enter to return to the worksheet.

Important Cues

- Use /FL to check your file listing before you use /**File Erase**.

- 1-2-3 displays the date and time each file was created so that you can find the most recent version of a file. (Date and time values are accurate only if you supply the correct entries at startup. Date and time values can be reset at the DOS prompt with the DATE and TIME commands.)

For more information, see **File Erase, File Directory,** *and* **Chapter** 7.

File Import   /FI

Purpose
Brings ASCII text files from other programs into 1-2-3 worksheets.

Many software programs use ASCII files to exchange data with other programs. Most databases, word processors, and spreadsheets have a method of printing ASCII files to disk.

Reminders
- Remember that /**File Import** can be used two different ways to transfer data into a 1-2-3 worksheet. The first method reads each row of ASCII characters as left-aligned labels in a column; the second method reads into separate cells characters enclosed in quotation marks or numbers surrounded by spaces.

- Be sure you have enough room on the worksheet to receive the imported data; incoming characters will replace the current cell contents. One row in an ASCII file is equal to one row on the worksheet. The number of columns depends on the incoming ASCII data.

- Before you issue /FI, move the cursor to the upper left corner of the range in which you want to import data.

Procedures
1. Type /fi

2. Choose how to import the ASCII file:

Menu Item	*Keystroke*	*Description*
Text	**T**	Makes each row of characters in the ASCII file a left-aligned label in the worksheet. Labels will be in a single column from the cell pointer down.
Numbers	**N**	Enters each row of characters in the ASCII file into a row in the worksheet. Characters within quotation marks are assigned to a cell as a label. Each group of numbers without quotation marks is assigned to a cell as a value. Other characters are ignored.

3. Select or type the name of the ASCII print file. Do not type the .PRN extension.

4. Press Enter.

Important Cues

- ASCII files must have the extension .PRN. If you import a file that does not have the .PRN extension, use the DOS command RENAME to change the extension.

- 1-2-3 cannot import ASCII files that have more than 8,192 rows or more than 240 characters per row. If necessary, you can use a word processor to read, modify, and divide the ASCII files into smaller files before saving them to disk as ASCII files.

- Display ASCII files by using the DOS command TYPE.

- You can print the ASCII file by pressing Ctrl-P before issuing the DOS command TYPE. To disconnect the printer, press Ctrl-P again when printing is complete.

- Some ASCII text files may not be enclosed in quotation marks. Use /File Import Text to bring the file into the worksheet, and /Data Parse to separate the resulting long label into separate cells of data.

Cautions

▶ Incoming data will replace existing cell contents. If you are unsure of the size of the file you are importing, use the DOS command TYPE to review the ASCII file.

▶ Word-processing files contain special control codes that 1-2-3 cannot handle. Be sure to save your word-processing document as an ASCII file before you try to import it into 1-2-3.

For more information, see **Data Parse** *and Chapter 7.*

File Directory   /FD

Purpose   Changes the current disk drive or directory for the current work session.

Reminder   Sketch how your directories and subdirectories are arranged on your hard
                     disk. Include the types of files stored in different directories.

Procedures   1. Type /fd

                     2. If the displayed drive and directory are correct, press Enter. If you want
                        to change the settings, type a new drive letter and directory name; then
                        press Enter.

Important   ■ Access another drive and directory temporarily by selecting /FR or /FS
Cues   and pressing Esc twice to clear the current drive and directory from the
                       command line. Then type the drive designator and directory name,
                       including a final backslash (\ ). You can then either type in a file name
                       or press Enter to see a list of file names on that drive or directory;
                       move the cursor and press Enter to select a name from the list.

                     ■ Access another directory on the same drive by selecting /FR or /FS and
                       pressing the Backspace key as many times as necessary to clear the
                       current directory from the command line. Then type the directory
                       name, including a final backslash (\ ). You can then either type in a file
                       name or press Enter to see a list of file names on that drive or
                       directory; move the cursor and press Enter to select a name from the
                       list.

                     ■ Display file names and directories by selecting /**F**ile **R**etrieve and
                       pressing the F3 (Name) key.

                     ■ You can change 1-2-3's startup drive and directory by using /**W**orksheet
                       Global **D**efault **D**irectory to enter a new drive or directory. Save this
                       new setting to the System disk with /WGDU.

Caution   When specifying drive letters and path names, be sure to enter the correct
                     symbols. The most common mistakes include using a semicolon (;) instead
                     of a colon (:) after the drive designator, using a slash (/) instead of a backslash
                     (\ ) between subdirectory names, and inserting spaces.

                     *For more information, see **Worksheet Global Default Update**, **File List**,*
                     ***File Retrieve**, and **File Save**.*

Print Commands /P

Prints worksheet contents as values or formulas.

Use /PP to send output to the printer, and /PF to send output (as an ASCII file) to disk.

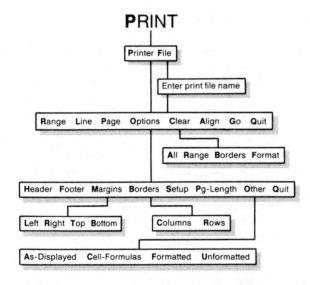

Print Printer /PP

Purpose   Prints worksheet contents (values or formulas) to the printer.

Reminders
- Before you print, check the lower right corner of the screen to see whether the CALC indicator is displayed. If it is, press the Calc key (F9), and wait until the WAIT indicator stops flashing before proceeding with the /Print commands.

- Remember that all /Print menu commands apply when output is printed directly to paper, but some do not apply when output is directed to disk.

- Remember that graphs cannot be printed from the /Print menu. Use the PrintGraph program to print graphs.

- Before you issue /PP, move the cell pointer to the upper left corner of the range to be printed.

Procedures
1. Type /pp

2. Select **Range**.

3. Specify the range to be printed: type the range address, highlight the range, or enter an assigned range name.

4. Verify that the range is correct by pressing the period (.) key four times; then press Enter.

5. Select from the other print options explained in this section.

Important Cues
- You can use 1-2-3's print commands to set formats for your reports and specify the order in which they are printed. Use commands from /Print **Printer/File** Options to control formats for printing.

- Print an ASCII text file to disk by using /**Print** File. Most popular software programs, including word-processing and database programs, can import ASCII text files.

Cautions
▶ Because 1-2-3 keeps track of the number of printed lines, the program's line count may be incorrect if you adjust the paper manually. Adjusting

the page by hand could cause the information to be printed off to one side or could leave blank spaces in the middle of the page.

▶ Printers often retain the last control code specified. To cancel the control code, turn off the printer, wait 15 seconds, and turn the printer back on. You also can correct the problem by inserting a reset printer control code at the beginning of every setup string.

*For more information, see **Print Printer/File**, **Print Printer/File Range**, and Chapter 9.*

Print File   /PF

Purpose Prints worksheet contents as an ASCII text file to disk.

ASCII text files are a common means of transferring data to and from different software packages.

Reminders • Before you print the file, check the lower right corner of the screen to see whether the CALC indicator is displayed. If it is, press the Calc key (F9), and wait until the WAIT indicator stops flashing before proceeding with the /Print commands.

• Before you issue /PF, move the cell pointer to the upper left corner of the range to be printed.

Procedures *To create an ASCII file for use in word processing, follow these steps:*

1. Type /pf

2. Respond to the screen prompt:

    Enter print file name:

    Limit the file name to eight characters with no spaces. 1-2-3 automatically gives the file name a .PRN extension.

3. Select **R**ange.

4. Specify the range to be printed to disk: type the range address, highlight the range, or use an assigned range name.

5. Verify that the range is correct and press Enter.

6. Select **Options Margins**. Set **Top**, **Left**, and **Bottom** margins to zero; set the **Right** margin to 240.

7. Select **/Print Printer/File Options Other Unformatted** to remove headers, footers, and page breaks. (These print options can cause problems when the file is imported by another program.)

To create an ASCII file to be used with a database program, follow these steps:

1. Reset all numbers and dates to **General** format by using **/Range Format General**.

2. Set column widths so that all data is displayed.

3. Type */pf* and specify a file name.

4. Select **Range**.

5. Specify the range to be printed, including only data. Do not include field names or titles. Databases are designed to use data entered in a specific order, which means that including titles and field names in the disk file may disrupt that order. Specify the range by typing the range address, highlighting the range, or using an assigned range name.

6. Verify that the range is correct and press Enter.

7. Select **Options Margins**. Set **Top**, **Left**, and **Bottom** margins to zero; set the **Right** margin to 240.

8. Select **/Print Printer/File Options Other Unformatted** to remove headers, footers, and page breaks.

Important Cues

■ To review an ASCII text file, return to DOS. At the DOS prompt, type the DOS command *TYPE*, a space, the path name, and the name of the ASCII text file you want to review. For example, after the prompt (C>), you could enter

    TYPE C:\123\BUDGET\VARIANCE.PRN

Press Ctrl-S to stop the data from scrolling off the screen. Press the space bar to continue scrolling.

- Make sure that columns are wide enough to display all the data before you print the file to disk. If a column is too narrow, values are changed to asterisks, and labels are truncated.

- Refer to your word processor's documentation for instructions on importing ASCII files.

Cautions

▶ Different database programs accept data in different formats; check to see in what form dates are imported and whether the receiving program accepts blank cells. Be sure to prepare your 1-2-3 file accordingly before printing to an ASCII file. As a general rule, remove numeric formats and align labels to the left before you print the data to disk.

▶ If the right margin setting is too narrow, data may be truncated when the file is printed to disk.

For more information, see **Print Printer, Print Printer/File Range,** *and* **Chapter 9.**

Print Printer/File Range   /PPR or /PFR

Purpose   Defines the area of the worksheet to be printed.

Reminders

- Check the lower right corner of the screen to see whether the CALC indicator is displayed. If it is, press the Calc key (F9), and wait until the WAIT indicator stops flashing before proceeding with the /**Print** commands.

- Remember that graphs cannot be printed from the /**Print** menus. Use the PrintGraph program to print graphs.

- Before you print, move the cell pointer to the upper left corner of the range to be printed.

Procedures   *To define the worksheet area to be printed:*

1. Type */pp* to print directly to paper; */pf* to print to disk. Specify a file name.

2. Select **Range**.

3. Specify the range to be printed: type the range address, highlight the range, or enter an assigned range name.

4. Verify that the range is correct and press Enter.

Important Cues

- /**Print Printer/File Range** "remembers" the last print range used, which means that you can reprint the specified worksheet portion without reentering the range. To change the existing print range, press Esc when 1-2-3 displays the print range. Move the cell pointer to the upper left corner of the area you want to print; type a period (.) to anchor that corner of the print range. Next move the cell pointer to the lower right corner of the print range and press Enter.

- To display the current print range, select /**Range**. The status line displays the current range address, and the specified range is highlighted on the screen. To display each corner of the range, press the period key. Each time you repeat the keystroke, the next corner is displayed.

- The highlighted area must cover all data to be printed. Even if text in a cell extends beyond the cell's right edge, the highlighted range must include all the text.

- Use /**Print Printer/File Options Borders** to print a specified worksheet row or column at the top of every printed page. Use this technique, for example, when you want to print database field names at the top of every page.

- Use /**Worksheet Page** to insert mandatory page breaks in a range.

- After a range has been printed, 1-2-3 does not advance the paper to the next top of form. Instead, 1-2-3 waits for you to print another range. To advance the paper to the next top of form, use /**Print Printer Page**.

- If the print range is wider than the distance between the left and right margins, the remaining characters are printed on the following page (if printed to paper) or in the rows below the data (if printed to disk).

Caution   Data outside the highlighted area will not be printed. For example, if text in
column I spreads across columns J and K, you must include columns J and
K in the print range. Figure P.1 shows in rows 3 to 9 the incorrect way to
highlight text. The unhighlighted text in rows 8 and 9 will not be printed.
All the text highlighted in the figure P.1 is stored in column B. To highlight
correctly this material for printing, use the range B3..G10.

Fig. P.1

*The incorrect way
to highlight text.*

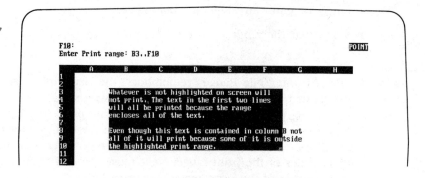

For more information, see **Worksheet Page**, **Print Printer**, **Print File**, and
Chapter 9.

Print Printer/File Line   /PPL or /PFL

Purpose
/Print Printer Line controls printer paper handling from within 1-2-3 by advancing the paper one line. If the printhead is at the bottom of a page, the printhead moves to the top of the next page.

/Print File Line puts a blank line in a .PRN file.

Reminder
Remember that you cannot print graphs from the /Print menu. Use the PrintGraph program to print graphs.

Procedures
1. Select /Print Printer (or File).

2. Select Line to advance the paper one line. Repeat the keystroke (or press Enter) as many times as are necessary to advance the paper to the desired position.

Important Cue
Use this command to insert a blank line between printed ranges.

Caution
You can get paper out of alignment with 1-2-3's internal line count if you change the position of paper in a printer manually (either by turning the platen knob or by pressing the printer's line feed button). Blank lines in the middle of your printed output can signify that the printer and 1-2-3 are out of alignment. To realign the paper and reset 1-2-3, turn off the printer and roll the paper until the top of a page is aligned with the printhead. Then turn on the printer again and use /Print Printer Align to reset 1-2-3.

Print Printer/File Page   /PPP or /PFP

Purpose
/Print **Printer** Page controls paper feed from within 1-2-3 by moving the paper to the bottom of the page for printing any footer, and then by advancing the paper farther until the printhead is at the top of the next page.

/Print **File** Page provides a footer and blank lines for a .PRN file.

Reminders
- Remember that all /Print menu commands apply when output is printed directly to paper, but some do not apply when output is directed to disk.

- Use /**Worksheet** Page to create a page break in a worksheet. When you print the worksheet, a new page will begin at the page break.

Procedures
1. Select /Print **Printer** (or **File**).

2. Select **Page** to print any footer at the bottom of the page, and to position the printhead at the top of the next page.

Important Cue
If the top of form is not in line with the printhead when the paper is advanced, manually move the paper into position and reset 1-2-3 with /**Print Printer Align**.

Cautions
▶ The length of the printed page may not match the length of the paper. Check the paper-length settings with /**Print Printer Options Pg-Length**. This problem occurs also when the page-length setting does not match the number-of-lines-per-inch setting. Use /**Print Printer Options Setup** to change the number of lines per inch to be printed.

▶ The paper in the printer can get out of alignment if you manually advance the paper to the top of the next page. To realign the paper and reset 1-2-3, turn off the printer and roll the paper until the top of a page is aligned with the printhead. Then turn on the printer again and use /**Print Printer Align** to reset 1-2-3.

Print Printer/File
Options Header   /PPOH or /PFOH

Purpose

Prints a header below the top margin on each page.

Use the **Header** option to print page numbers and dates in the heading. Two blank lines are inserted after the print range.

/**Print Printer/File Options Borders** should be used for printing column headings above data.

Reminder

Remember that a header uses the three lines below the top margin.

Procedures

1. Type /*ppo* to print to paper; /*pfo* to print to disk.

2. Select **Header**.

3. Type a header as wide as the margin and paper widths allow. 1-2-3 accepts as the first row on each page a header of up to 240 characters.

4. Press Enter.

Important Cues

■ The date and page number can also be printed automatically in a header. Enter an at sign (@) where you want the date to appear and a number sign (#) where you want the page number. The # causes page numbering to begin with 1 and increase by 1 sequentially.

■ Break the header into as many as three centered segments by entering a vertical bar (|). For example, to print a three-segment header with a system date of October 25, 1987, at page 21, enter:

@|Hill and Dale XeroLandscaping|Page #

The header appears as:

25-Oct-87 Hill and Dale XeroLandscaping Page 21

■ To print a single page with a page number higher than 1, omit the # and specify the page number.

■ Use /**Print Printer/File Options Borders Rows** to select worksheet rows that will be printed above the data on each page. The **Borders** command is especially useful for printing database column headings above the data on each page.

■ Print an extra header line at the top of the first printed page by using a "false" setup string, which consists of the Escape code followed by your text. For EPSON-compatible printers, an example of this string is

    \027"This is a second line."

■ Depending on the first letter in the header, the printer might read the letter as part of the setup string. This could cause the printer to begin printing in a different mode. If, for example, you wanted to type the phrase *Enter new page* after the Escape code, your printer might interpret the E as the code for enhanced mode. To solve this problem, enclose the header in quotation marks.

Caution

Headers longer than margin settings print on the following page.

*For more information, see **Print Printer/File Options Margins**, **Print Printer/File Options Border**, and **Print Printer/File Options Setup**.*

Print Printer/File Options Footer   /PPOF or /PFOF

Purpose

Prints a footer above the bottom margin of each page.

Use **/Print Printer/File Options Footer** to print, for example, a title, department heading, or identifier. Footers can be used to print page numbers and dates automatically.

Reminder

Remember that footers will reduce the size of the printed area reserved for data. Make sure that the page margins are set to allow for footers.

Procedures

1. Type */ppo* to print to paper; */pfo* to print to disk.

2. Select **Footer**.

3. You can type a footer as wide as the margin and paper widths allow. 1-2-3 accepts as the last row on each page a footer of up to 240 characters.

4. Press Enter.

Important Cues

■ The date and page number can be printed automatically in the footer. Enter in the header an at sign (@) where you want the date to appear and a number sign (#) where you want the page number. The # causes page numbering to begin with 1 and increase by 1 sequentially.

■ Break the footer into as many as three centered segments by entering a vertical bar (|). To print a three-segment footer with a system date of October 25, 1987, at page 21, enter:

@|Hill and Dale XeroLandscaping|Page #

The footer appears as:

```
25-Oct-87  Hill and Dale XeroLandscaping   Page 21
```

■ Placing one vertical bar to the left of header data centers the data; no vertical bars left-justifies the data; two vertical bars right-justifies the data. For example, to right-justify the page number you could enter:

||Page #

■ To print a single page with a number higher than 1, omit the # and specify the page number.

Caution

Footers longer than margin settings will be printed on the following page.

*For more information, see **Print Printer/File Options Header**, **Print Printer/File Options Margins**, **Print Printer/File Options Borders**, and **Print Printer/File Options Setup**.*

Print Printer/File
Options Margins
/PPOM or /PFOM

Purpose   Changes the left, right, top, and bottom margins.

Use /PPOM and /PFOM to adjust the appearance of the printed page by chang-ing the size of the printed area.

Reminders
- Determine whether you need to use printer setup strings to change the number of characters per inch or lines per inch printed by the printer.

- Turn the printer off and on to reposition the printhead to the *zero* position. Adjust the paper so that the left edge aligns with the printhead at the zero position. If you always align the paper at this position, printed margins will be consistent.

Procedures
1. Type */ppo* to print to paper; */pfo* to print to disk.

2. Select Margins. Specify margins from these options:

Menu Item	Keystroke	Description
Left	L	Sets from 0 to 240 characters. For printing to disk, set to 0.
Right	R	Sets greater than the left margin but not larger than 240. For printing to disk, set to 240.
Top	T	Sets from 0 to 32 lines. For printing to disk, set to 0.
Bottom	B	Sets from 0 to 32 lines. For printing to disk, set to 0.

Important Cues
- If you change printer setup strings (which can change characters per inch and lines per inch), be sure to change the right, top, and bottom margins. For example, if you use a printer setup string to print in compressed mode on 8-inch paper, reset the right margin from 74 to approximately 130.

- Most printers print at 10 characters per horizontal inch and 6 lines per vertical inch. Standard 8 1/2-by-11-inch paper is 85 characters wide and 66 lines long.

- When you want to print to disk, remember that you should set the left margin to 0 and the right margin to 240. These settings remove blank spaces on the left side of each row. Setting the right margin to 240 ensures that the maximum number of characters per row will be printed to disk.

- Before printing to disk, select /**Print Printer/File Options Other Unformatted** to remove page breaks, headers, and footers. Page breaks, headers, and footers will confuse data transfer to a database. If you are importing the file to a word processor, use the word processor to insert margins, page breaks, headers, and footers.

Caution   If margins are too narrow for the characters in a printed line, the additional characters are printed on the following page. To get a full-width print, use a condensed print setup string.

*For more information, see **Print File** and **Print Printer/File Options Setup**.*

Print Printer/File
Options Borders   /PPOB or /PFOB

Purpose
Prints on every page the rows or columns selected from the worksheet.

Use /PPOB and /PFOB to print database field names as column headings at the top of each printed page.

Reminders
• Before you issue /PPOB or /PFOB, move the cell pointer to the leftmost column or the top row you want to use as a header.

• Remember that in addition to the border rows you select, only the columns included in the print range will be printed.

• Similarly, in addition to the border columns you select, only the rows included in the print range will be printed.

Procedures
1. Type */ppob* to print to paper; */pfob* to print to disk.

2. Select from these menu items:

Menu Item	*Keystroke*	*Description*
Columns	**C**	Prints the selected columns at the left side of each page.
Rows	**R**	Prints the selected rows at the top of each page.

3. Press Esc to remove the current range. Move the cell pointer to the top row of the rows you want to use as a border or to the leftmost column you want to use. Press the period key (.) to anchor the first corner of the border. Then move the cell pointer, highlighting additional rows or columns to be included as borders.

4. Press Enter.

Important Cue
Including borders is useful when you want to print multiple pages. If you want to print sections of a wide worksheet, you can further condense the columns by using /Worksheet Column Hide to hide blank or unnecessary columns.

Cautions

▶ If you include in the print range the rows or columns specified as borders, they will be printed twice.

▶ When you use **/Print Printer/File Options Borders Row** or **Column**, the cell pointer's current location becomes a border automatically. To clear the border selection, use **/Print Printer/File Clear Borders**.

Print Printer
Options Setup   /PPOS

Purpose

Controls from within 1-2-3 the advanced printing features offered by some printers.

Advanced printing features include different character sets, different-sized characters, bold characters, near-letter-quality print, or proportional spacing. Printer control codes entered in setup strings apply to the entire print range.

Reminders

Review these points:

● Your printer manual contains lists of printer setup codes (also known as printer control codes or escape codes). These codes may be shown two ways: as a decimal ASCII number representing a keyboard character, or as the Escape key (ESC) followed by a character.

● 1-2-3 setup strings include decimal number codes (entered as three-digit numbers), preceded by a backslash (\). For example, the EPSON printer control code for condensed print is 15. The 1-2-3 setup string is \015.

● Some codes start with the ESC character, followed by other characters. Because the ESC character cannot be typed in the setup string, the ASCII decimal number for ESC (27) is used instead. For example, the EPSON printer code for emphasized print is

   ESC "E"

In the 1-2-3 setup string, enter ESC "E" as \027E.

- Some printers retain previous control codes. Before sending a new code to the printer, clear the previous codes by turning your printer off and then on. You also can send the printer a *reset code* (\027@ for EPSON-compatible printers). Put the reset code in front of the new code you send. For example, the 1-2-3 printer setup string that resets previous codes and switches to emphasized printing mode is

    \027@\027E

Procedures

1. Type /ppos

2. Enter the setup string. If a setup string has already been entered, press Esc to clear the string. Each string must begin with a backslash (\). Upper- or lowercase letters must be typed as shown in your printer's manual.

3. Press Enter.

Important Cues

■ Setup strings can be up to 39 characters in length. You may be able to create longer setup strings by following these steps:

   1. Enter the first setup string and print only one line of the print range.

   2. Realign the paper to the next top of form.

   3. Clear the previous setup string and enter the remaining setup string. Print the complete print range.

The printer will "remember" the first string and combine it with the second string. Do not use a printer reset code before you enter the second string.

■ If you change character size, change the right margin setting with /**Print Printer/File Options Margin Right**.

■ You cannot combine some character sets or print modes. Your printer manual may list combinations that will work for your printer.

■ Use embedded setup strings in the print range to change printing features by row. Move the cell pointer to the leftmost cell in the print range row where you want the printing to change. Insert a row with /**Worksheet Insert Row**. Type two vertical bars, and then type the appropriate setup string. Note that only one vertical bar will display.

- Don't confuse zero (0) with the letter *o*, or one (1) with the letter *l*. This can be a particularly annoying problem with setup strings because printer manuals can be difficult to read.

- If you get the same several characters of garbage at the top of every printed page, you probably have that garbage in your setup string.

Caution

Some printers retain the most recent printer control code. Clear the last code by turning off the printer for approximately five seconds or by preceding each setup string with the printer reset code. The reset code for EPSON-compatible printers is \027@.

*For more information, see **Print Printer/File Options Margins** and Chapter 9.*

Print Printer/File
Options Pg-Length   /PPOP or /PFOP

Purpose   Specifies the number of lines per page.

The page-length setting and the top- and bottom-margin settings determine the height of the page's printed area. These settings also indicate where the printer should advance the paper to allow for continuous-feed paper perforations.

Reminders   • Check the size of the paper you are using.

• Check whether the setup string you are using changes the number of lines printed per inch.

Procedures   1. Type */ppop* to print to paper; */pfop* to print to disk.

2. Enter the number of lines per page if that number is different from the number shown. Page length can be from 1 to 100 lines.

3. Press Enter.

Important   ■ Most printers print 6 lines per inch unless the ratio is changed with a
Cues   setup string (printer control code). At 6 lines per inch, 11-inch paper has 66 lines, and 14-inch paper has 84 lines.

■ The actual number of printable lines on the default 66-line page is 56. Four lines are used for top and bottom margins, and 6 lines are reserved for the header and footer, regardless of whether you use them.

Caution   To print short page lengths, use /Print Printer/File Options Margins so that the top and bottom margins do not overlap.

*For more information, see **Print Printer/File Options Margins**, **Print Printer/File Options**, and **Print Printer/File Options Setup**.*

Print Printer/File
Options Other   /PPOO or /PFOO

Purpose   Selects how cell contents are printed and whether formatting is used.

Worksheet contents can be printed as displayed on-screen or as formulas. You can print either option with or without formatting features.

Reminders   *Review these points:*

- **As-Displayed** is used with **Formatted** for printing reports and data. This setting is the default setting.

- Use **Cell-Formulas** with **Formatted** to show formulas and cell contents (often used for documentation).

- To print data to disk to be used in a word processor or database, choose **As-Displayed** with **Unformatted**.

- If you are printing to disk (creating an ASCII file to export to a word processor or database), set the left, top, and bottom margins to 0, and the right margin to 240.

Procedures   1. Type */ppoo* to print to paper; */pfoo* to print to disk.

2. Select the type of print from these options:

Menu Item	*Keystroke*	*Description*
As-Displayed	**A**	Prints the range as displayed on-screen. This is the initial setting.
Cell-Formulas	**C**	Prints the contents of each cell on one line of the printout. Contents match information that appears in the control panel: cell address; format; protection status; and cell formula, or value.

3. The **Options** menu will reappear. Select **Other** again and choose the type of formatting from these options:

Menu Item	Keystroke	Description
Formatted	F	Prints with page breaks, headers, and footers. This initial setting is normally used for printing to paper.
Unformatted	U	Prints without page breaks, headers, or footers. This setting is normally used for printing to disk.

4. Select **Quit** to exit **Options**.

Important Cues

- Use Cell-Formulas to print documentation that shows the formulas and cell settings used to create the worksheet. Figure P.2 shows an example of cell listings printed with Cell-Formulas.

Fig. P.2

A sample cell listing printed with Cell-Formulas.

```
O120: [W11] '  --------
P120: [W11] '  --------
Q120: [W11] '  --------
R120: [W11] '  --------
S120: [W11] '  --------
A121: [W9] 'Cash Balance before Borrowings
H121: (,0) [W11] +H118+H119
I121: (,0) [W11] +I118+I119
J121: (,0) [W11] +J118+J119
K121: (,0) [W11] +K118+K119
L121: (,0) [W11] +L118+L119
M121: (,0) [W11] +M118+M119
N121: (,0) [W11] +N118+N119
O121: (,0) [W11] +O118+O119
P121: (,0) [W11] +P118+P119
Q121: (,0) [W11] +Q118+Q119
R121: (,0) [W11] +R118+R119
S121: (,0) [W11] +S118+S119
A122: [W9] 'Minimum Acceptable Cash Balance
```

The following codes may appear in a **Cell-Formulas** listing:

Code	Meaning
PR	Protected cell. Global protection is enabled.
U	Unprotected cell with a /**R**ange **U**nprotect command
F2	Fixed to 2 decimal places with a /**R**ange **F**ormat **F**ixed command
C2	Currency to 2 decimal places with a /**R**ange **F**ormat **C**urrency command
W10	Width of 10 characters

- Include with an archival copy of the formulas a print of the As-Displayed worksheet and a list of range names and associated addresses. /**R**ange **N**ame **T**able will automatically create a range-name address table.

- You normally should select Unformatted for printing to disk. Headers, footers, and page breaks can be added more easily with a word processor than with 1-2-3. Also use Unformatted on files to be imported to databases. Databases expect ASCII-file data in a consistent order, and headers and footers can disrupt that order.

*For more information, see **Print Printer/File Options Margins***.

Print Printer/File Clear   /PPC or /PFC

Purpose

Clears print settings and options—the current print range, borders, headers, and footers—and resets all formats (margins, page length, and Setup strings) to default settings.

Reminders

- The Clear option lets you cancel all or some previous print settings quickly.

- This option is the only way to clear borders after they have been set.

Procedures

1. Select /**Print Printer Clear**.

2. Choose one of the following:

Item	Description
All	Clears all print options and resets all formats and Setup strings
Range	Clears just the print range specification
Borders	Cancels only columns and rows specified as borders
Format	Clears only **Margins**, **Pg-Length**, and **Setup** string formats to their default settings

Important Cues

- The Format option is useful when you make mistakes or want to print one after another reports with different formats.

- Use the /PPC and /PFC commands in macros to cancel prior print settings or to reestablish default settings you have specified. For example, use /Worksheet Global Default Printer menu to create as default settings the ones you use most often for margins, page length, and setup string. Be sure to use /Worksheet Global Default Update to update the configuration file to make these settings the default settings for future sessions. Then when you place a /Print Printer Clear All command at the beginning of a macro (or use the command interactively), the default settings you specify will be entered automatically.

Caution

In 1-2-3, print parameters remain in effect until you give different instructions. If you want to provide a new set of parameters, use /Print Printer Clear All to ensure that you are starting from the default parameters.

Print Printer/File Align   /PPA or /PFA

Purpose

Resets 1-2-3's internal line and page counter.

Reminders

- Use this command only after you have manually aligned the printhead with the top of a sheet of printer paper.

- Check the lower right corner of the screen to see whether the CALC indicator is displayed. If it is, press the Calc key (F9), and the WAIT indicator will appear at the top of the screen. When the WAIT indicator stops flashing, proceed with the /Print command.

- Remember that all /**P**rint menu commands apply when output is printed directly to paper, but some do not apply when output is directed to disk.

Procedures

1. Position the printer paper so that the top of a page is aligned with the printhead.

2. Select /**Print Printer** (or **File**).

3. Select **Align** to synchronize 1-2-3 with the printer.

Cautions

▶ Printed pages may have gaps (blank lines) if you do not use this command.

▶ Because this command resets the page counter, page numbers may be wrong if you use the command before a print session is completed.

Graph Commands /G

/**Graph** commands control the graph's appearance and specify worksheet ranges to be used as graph data.

Store multiple graphs with /**Graph Name** and display them at a later time. To print a graph, use /**Graph Save** to create a .PIC file you can later print with PrintGraph.

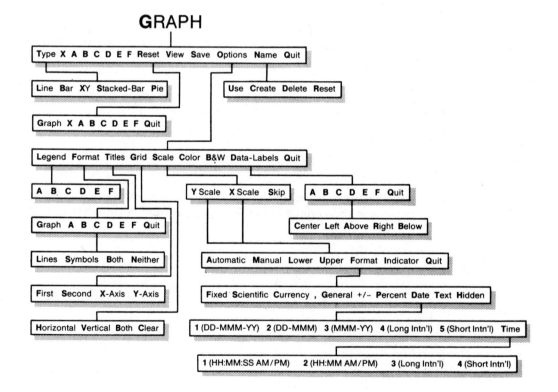

Graph Type   /GT

Purpose   Selects from among the five available types of 1-2-3 graphs: line, bar, XY, stacked-bar, and pie. Each type of graph is best suited for displaying and analyzing specific types of data.

Reminders   • Before you can create a graph, you must have created a worksheet with the same number of cells in each x- and y-axis range, similar to the one in figure G.1. Each *y* data item must be in the same range position as the corresponding *x* value. Figure G.2 shows the bar graph produced from the worksheet displayed in figure G.1.

Fig. G.1

Worksheet with the same number of cells in each x- and y-axis range.

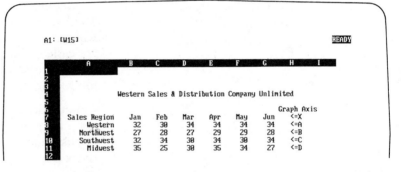

Fig. G.2

Bar graph produced from the worksheet in figure G.1.

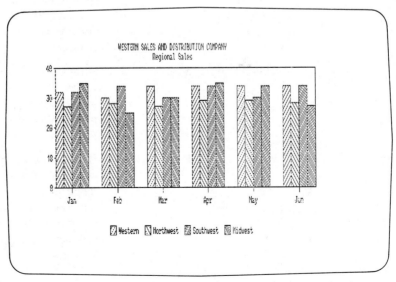

- Remember that except for pie graphs, graphs can have on the y-axis as many as six different series of data. The /Graph menu choices A through F are used to highlight the data series. The pie graph accepts data from only the A range.

Procedures

1. Type /gt

2. Select the type of graph to be displayed from these options:

Menu Item	Keystroke	Description
Line	**L**	Usually depicts a continuous series of data. The change frequently occurs over time. Enter an x-axis label, such as months, in the X-selection range from the /Graph menu.
Bar	**B**	Usually displays discrete data series. The x-axis is often time. Comparative weights between different y values are easier to judge in bar graphs than in line charts. Enter x-axis labels in the X range from the /Graph menu.
XY	**X**	Graphs data-sets of x and y data; good for plotting "clouds" of data. (Unlike line graphs with labels on the x-axis and data on the y-axis, XY graphs have data on both axes.) Each x value can have between one and six y values. Enter x-axis data in the X range of the /Graph menu.
Stacked-Bar	**S**	Shows how proportions change within the whole. Enter x-axis labels in the X range from the /Graph menu. A bar can have as many as six portions.
Pie	**P**	Shows how the whole is divided into component portions. Use only the A range to contain the values of each portion. The X range is used to label the pie wedges. 1-2-3 automatically calculates each portion's percentage from the A values.

3. When you have made your selection, the /Graph menu will reappear.

4. If you have already indicated the data to graph by highlighting the X range and ranges A through F, select View. If you are beginning the graph, see Graph X A B C D E F in this section.

Important Cues

- With 1-2-3 a user can build graphs interactively. After selecting /Graph Type and at least one x- and y-axis range, select View to see the graph as it is currently defined.

- When you save the worksheet to disk, you save also the most recently specified graph type and other graph settings.

- You can shade a pie graph's wedges with eight different shadings. You can even extract wedges from the pie. Use the B range to define the shade of a pie graph wedge and to extract the wedge from the pie. (For an explanation of how to shade the pie graph, see **Graph X A B C D E F** in this section.)

*For more information, see **Graph X A B C D E F** and Chapter 10.*

Graph X A B C D E F   /GX, /GA through /GF

Purpose   Specifies the worksheet ranges containing x-axis and y-axis data or labels.

Reminders   *Review these points:*

- The x-axis is the graph's horizontal (bottom) axis. The y-axis is the graph's vertical (left) axis. The labels or data assigned to the x-axis and the six possible sets of y-axis data (A through F) must have the same number of cells. To ensure that the x-axis and y-axis have an equal number of elements, place all the labels and data on adjacent rows. Figure G.3 shows the x- and y-axis labels and data in rows. Notice that some of the y values are blank, but each range has an equal number of elements.

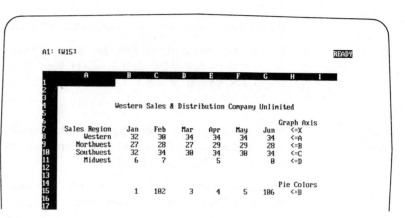

Fig. G.3

Worksheet with some blank y values but an equal number of elements.

- Pie graph ranges are different from those of other graph types. Pie graphs use only the A range for data. The B range contains code numbers to control shading and the extraction of wedges from the pie.

Procedures

To enter x-axis labels and y-axis data, follow these steps:

1. Type /g

2. Select the ranges for x- or y-axis data or labels to be entered from these options:

Menu Item	Description
X	Enters x-axis label range. Creates labels for pie graph wedges and line, bar, and stacked-bar graphs. (X-axis data range for XY graphs.)
A	Enters first y-axis data range. The only data range used by a pie graph.
B	Enters second y-axis data range. Enters pie graph shading values and extraction codes. (For more information, see Important Cues section.)
C to F	Enters third through sixth data ranges

3. Indicate the data range by entering the range address, using a range name, or highlighting the range. If the data range has already been entered, press Esc and enter a new range.

4. Press Enter.

Important Cues

- Ease the task of keeping track of graph data and labels. Put the data and labels in labeled rows, as shown in figure G.3.

- You do not need to change the /Graph menu settings when you change or update the data in the ranges. /Graph remembers all the settings.

- Use /Graph **Reset Graph** to clear all graph settings. Use /Graph **Reset** [X through F] to clear individual ranges and their associated settings.

- 1-2-3 automatically updates graphs when you input new data into the worksheet (for new data or labels in the x- and y-axis ranges). Once you have set the graphs with the /Graph commands, you can view new graphs from the worksheet by pressing Graph (F10). If the computer beeps and no graph appears, you have not defined that graph, or your computer does not have graphics capability.

- Pie graphs do not use the x- and y-axis title options, grids, or scales.

- Pie graphs are limited because they often have too many elements in the A range, causing wedges to be small and labels to overlap. The A range is the only data range needed for pie graphs. Enter wedge labels in the X range, as you would for line graphs.

- Use the B range to enter the numeric codes to control shading or coloring of pie wedges. On color monitors, the eight shades appear as eight different colors. Add 100 to a shading code to extract one or more wedges from the pie.

Caution

If your graph has missing data or the y values do not match the corresponding x positions, check to ensure that the x- and y-axis ranges have the same number of elements. The values in the y ranges (A through F) graph the corresponding x-range cells.

*For more information, see **Graph Type** and Chapter 10.*

/Graph Reset   /GR

Purpose   Cancels all or some of a graph's settings so that you can either create an altogether new graph or exclude from a new graph one or more data ranges from the old graph.

Reminder   The **Graph** option of this command (see the Procedure section) lets you reset all graph parameters quickly.

Procedures   1. Select **/Graph Reset.**

                  2. Choose one of the following:

Menu Item	*Description*
Graph	Resets all graph parameters but does not alter a graph named with **/Graph Name Create.** Use this option if you want to exclude all preceding graph parameters from the new graph.
X	Resets the X range and removes the labels (but not on XY graphs)
A through **F**	Resets a designated range and corresponding labels so that these are not displayed in the new graph
Quit	Returns to the **/Graph** menu

Important   Take advantage of 1-2-3's capability to remember all the parameters of a named
Cue   graph until you use **/Graph Reset.** Use existing parameters of the named graph as a guide for creating a new graph. You may need to suppress only a few settings to create your new graph. After you are satisfied with a **View** of the new graph, use **/Graph Name Create** to save it.

Caution   If you use the name of an existing graph for a new graph, the new graph will replace the first graph, which will be lost.

/Graph View   /GV

Purpose   Displays a graph on the screen.

Reminders
- What is displayed depends on the system hardware and how the system is configured.

- On a nongraphics screen, nothing happens. The computer just beeps. Nevertheless, you can use /Graph Save to save the graph and then print it with the PrintGraph program.

- If your system has a graphics card and either a monochrome display or a color monitor, you can see a graph instead of the worksheet on the screen after you select View. You will have to select /Graph Options Color to see the graph in color.

- If you have a Hercules Graphics Card™ or a COMPAQ® Video Adapter for your monochrome display, a graph will take the place of the worksheet on that screen.

- If 1-2-3 and your system are configured to use two monitors, you can see the worksheet on one screen, and the graph on the other.

Procedures
1. Select View from the /Graph menu when you are ready to see the graph you have created. The graph must be defined before you can view it.

2. Press any key to return to /Graph menu.

3. Select Quit to return to the worksheet and READY mode.

Important Cues
- You can use /Graph View to redraw the graph, but an easier way is to press the F10 (Graph) key in READY mode. F10 is the equivalent of /Graph View but lets you view a graph after a change in the worksheet, without your having to return to the /Graph menu. (The F10 key does not function while a graph menu is visible.) If your system doesn't have two monitors and graphics cards for each, you can use the F10 key to toggle back and forth between the worksheet and the graph. You can therefore use the F10 key to do rapid "what if" analysis with graphics.

- If you want to create a series of graphs and view the series, you must use /Graph Name to name each graph. You can then create easily a macro that will display automatically a whole series of graphs.

- If the screen is blank after you select View, make certain that you have defined the graph adequately, that your system has graphics capability, and that 1-2-3 was installed for your particular graphics device(s). Press any key to return to the /Graph menu. Then select Quit if you want to return to the worksheet.

Graph Save   /GS

Purpose   Saves the graph to be printed later with PrintGraph.

/Graph Save saves a graph version that can be viewed or printed from PrintGraph. You cannot, however, edit graphs saved in PrintGraph.

Use /Graph Name Create and /File Save to save the graph's settings with the worksheet so that you can view multiple graphs.

Reminders   • Select View or press Graph (F10) to review the graph. Ensure that the graph has the correct scaling, labels, and titles.

• Check the screen's lower right corner for a CALC indicator. If CALC appears and the worksheet is still visible, press the Calc key (F9) to update all worksheet values before you save the graph.

• If you need to return to this graph later, use /Graph Name Create to save the graph settings, and then /File Save to save the worksheet to disk.

Procedures   1. Type /g

2. Select Save.

3. Enter a new file name, or use → or ← to highlight a name already on the menu bar. If you choose a name already on the menu bar, the new graph file will overwrite the old graph file.

4. Press Enter.

Important Cues

■ Saved graphs have .PIC file extensions. Other software programs also use .PIC file extensions, but 1-2-3 graph files are rarely compatible with other software.

■ DOS file-name rules apply when you name graph files. Names must be no longer than eight characters (letters, numbers, or underlines [_]). Never use a space or a period in a file name.

■ To save the file to a different drive and directory, change the current directory with /**File Directory**, or enter the drive and directory before the graph name (for example, C:\123\cards\print.pic).

■ Use PrintGraph to view saved graphs before you print them.

Caution

If you need to save graph settings and the worksheet's graph display, name the graph with /**Graph Name Create**, and then use /**File Save** to save the file. /**Graph Save** saves information used only to print the graph. Files saved with /**Graph Save** cannot be edited from the worksheet or from PrintGraph.

---

*For more information, see **Graph Name**, **File Save**, and **Image-Select**.*

Graph Options Legend   /GOL

Purpose   Specifies descriptions to link shadings or colors on the graph to specific
y-axis data ranges.

Legends indicate which line, bar, or point belongs to a specific y-axis data
range.

Y-axis data is entered in ranges A, B, C, D, E, and F. Legend titles for each
range are also assigned by A, B, C, D, E, and F. Figure G.4 shows legends at
the bottom of the bar graph, relating shading patterns to the division names,
Western, NorthWest, SouthWest, and MidWest.

Fig. G.4

*Legends relating
shading patterns to
division names.*

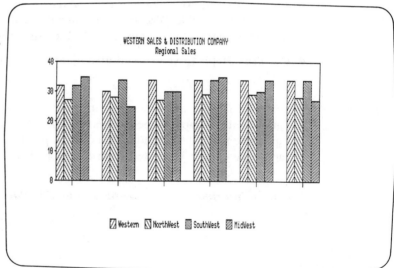

Reminder   As you create a graph, write on paper a list of the legend titles you want to
associate with each data range (ranges A through F). If you have already
created the graph, you can reenter the A-through-F data ranges to see the
associated legend ranges. To reenter these legends, follow the steps outlined
in the following section.

Procedures   1. Type /go

2. Select **Legend**.

3. Select from one of these options the data range for the legend to be created:

Menu Item	Description
A	Creates a legend for y-axis range A
B	Creates a legend for y-axis range B
C	Creates a legend for y-axis range C
D	Creates a legend for y-axis range D
E	Creates a legend for y-axis range E
F	Creates a legend for y-axis range F

4. Enter the text for the legend. 1-2-3 will display the legend along the bottom of the graph. Entering new legends will overwrite previously entered legends. Press Esc to erase the current legend. To keep a legend as it appears, press Enter.

5. Press Enter, and 1-2-3 returns you to the options menu.

6. Select **Quit** to return to the main /Graph menu.

Important Cue

Create changeable legends by entering text in cells. When /Graph Options Legend requests the legend title, you can enter a backslash (\ ) and the cell address or range name of a cell that holds the text. (See the first Caution.)

Cautions

▶ If, by using /Move, **Worksheet** Insert, or **Worksheet** Delete, you relocate a graph's source data, 1-2-3 will not adjust cell addresses that have been used to create legends. Creating legends with range names instead of cell addresses should solve this problem.

▶ If a legend title is too long to fit the allocated space, the legend will push other legends to the right and off the screen. Adjust legend lengths so that they all fit on-screen. If you have several legends, you may have to abbreviate them.

---

*For more information, see **Range Name, Graph X A B C D E F,** and Chapter 10.*

Graph Options Format   /GOF

Purpose   Selects the symbols and lines to present and connect data points.

Some line and XY graphs present information better if the data is linked with data points, or if the data is represented by a series of data points linked with a solid line. Use /Graph Options Format to select the type of data points used for each data range (symbols, lines, or both).

Reminders   *Review these points:*

- Time-related data is usually best represented by a continuous series of related data. Trends and slopes are more obvious when they are represented with lines rather than a cluster of data points.

- Data-point clusters representing multiple readings around different x-axis values are likely candidates for symbols instead of lines. Symbols reflect groupings better. The symbol for each y-axis range is unique so that you can keep data separated.

Procedures   1. Type /go

2. Select the data ranges to be formatted:

Menu Item	Keystroke	Description
Graph	G	Selects a format for the entire graph
A to F	A to F	Selects a format for y-axis data points

3. Select the data point type:

Menu Item	Keystroke	Description
Lines	L	Connects data points with a line.
Symbols	S	Encloses each data point in a symbol. Different ranges have different symbols. Most commonly used with XY graphs.
Both	B	Connects data points with a line and marks the data point.
Neither	N	Selects neither lines nor symbols. Use /Graph Options Data-Labels to "float" labels or data within the graph.

***Important
Cues***

- Figure G.5 is an illustrative worksheet, and figure G.6 shows the corresponding line graph. The A and D data ranges, Western and MidWest, are each plotted with a line. The B and C data ranges, NorthWest and SouthWest, are each plotted with a particular symbol.

Fig. G.5

*Sample worksheet
for the line graph.*

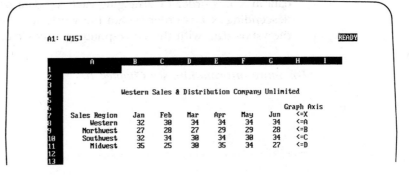

Fig. G.6

*A and C ranges
plotted with lines,
and B and D
ranges plotted with
symbols.*

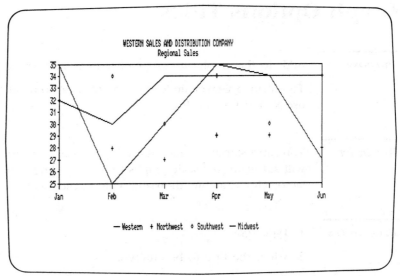

- If you are plotting a regression analysis trend line (**/Data Regression**), set the data points as symbols only and the regression's calculated Y values as a line. This arrangement highlights the trend as a straight line through a swarm of data points.

Cautions

▶ Do not misrepresent data by connecting unrelated data points with lines. If each x,y data pair is an independent event, unrelated by a series, do not connect the data points with a line.

▶ Lines do not connect data points in the left-to-right order in which the points appear on the graph. Lines instead connect the data points in the order in which they are entered in the ranges (first data point entered in the range, second data point entered in the range, etc.). If your xy-line graphs are a confusing jumble of crossed lines, you must sort the data in x-axis order by arranging each x,y data pair in ascending, or descending, x-axis order within the worksheet range. Be sure to move the y-axis data with the corresponding x-axis data.

For more information, see Chapter 10.

Graph Options Titles   /GOT

Purpose
Adds to the graph one or two headings, and to each axis a single title.

To enhance viewer understanding of measurement units used in the graph, use x- and y-axis titles.

Reminder
You must know the measurement units used in the x-axis and y-axis. 1-2-3 will automatically scale graphs to fit accordingly and will display the scaling factor (for example, thousands) along each axis.

Procedures
1. Type /got

2. Select the title to be entered:

Menu Item	*Keystroke*	*Description*
First	**F**	Centers the top heading of a graph
Second	**S**	Centers a second heading of a graph
X-Axis	**X**	Centers a title below the x-axis
Y-Axis	**Y**	Centers a title to the left of the y-axis

3. Type a title up to 39 characters in length. Use cell contents for a title by first entering a backslash (\) and then the cell address. If a title already exists, press Esc to cancel the title, or press Enter to accept it.

4. Press Enter.

Important Cues

In PrintGraph, characters in the first line of a heading are larger than those in other heading lines. The second line and axis titles can be printed in a font or style different from that of the first heading.

Create changeable titles by putting text in cells. When /Graph Options Title requests text, enter a backslash (\) followed by the cell address or range name of the cell holding the text.

Cautions

You can lose titles and headings contained in cell addresses if you move the cells with /Move, /Worksheet Insert, or /Worksheet Delete. Using range names instead of cell addresses will solve this problem.

1-2-3 may display on-screen more characters than PrintGraph can print. This discrepancy is related to the font (character type) used and the number of characters in the title.

Refer to Chapter 10.

Graph Options Grid

/GOG

Purpose

Overlays a grid on a graph to enhance readability.

The grid lines can be horizontal, vertical, or both.

Reminders

- Create a graph to view before you add a grid.
- Know that Grid lines cannot be used with pie graphs.

Procedures

1. Type /gog

2. Select the type of grid:

Menu Item	Keystroke	Description
Horizontal	H	Draws horizontal grid lines over the current graph from each major y-axis division
Vertical	V	Draws vertical grid lines over the current graph from each major x-axis division
Both	B	Draws both horizontal and vertical grid lines
Clear	C	Removes all grid lines

Important Cues

- Select grid lines that run in a direction which will enhance the presentation of data.

- Use grid lines sparingly. Inappropriate grid lines can make some line and XY graphs confusing.

- Use /Graph Options Scale to change the graph's scale, thereby changing the number of grid lines shown on the graph. Note that although this technique changes the number of grid lines, it also magnifies or reduces the graph's proportion.

- Some data-point graphs will be more accurate if you use data labels. Use /Graph Options Data-Labels to create data labels that display precise numbers next to the point on the graph.

For more information, see **Graph Options Scale** *and* **Graph Options Data-Labels.**

Graph Options Scale   /GOS

Purpose

Varies the display along the x and y axes.

Options within this command include:

1. Making changes manually to the upper- or lower-axis end points.

2. Choosing formats for numeric display. (Options are identical to those in /Worksheet Global Format or /Range Format.)

3. Improving display of overlapping x-axis labels by skipping every specified occurrence, such as every second or third label.

Use /Graph Options Scale to manually change the axes end points, thereby expanding or contracting the graph scale. Changing the end points expands or contracts the visible portion of the graph.

Use /Graph Options Scale to format numbers and dates that appear on the axes. These formats are the same as /Range Format options.

Reminder

First create and view the graph. Notice which portions of the graph you want to view and which beginning and ending numbers you should use for the new X-scale or Y-scale. Also notice whether the x-axis labels overlap or seem crowded. You can thin the x-axis tick marks with **/Graph Options Scale Skip**.

Procedures

1. Type /gos

2. Select the axis or skip frequency to be changed from these options:

Menu Item	Keystroke	Description
Y Scale	Y	Changes the y-axis scale or format
X Scale	X	Changes the x-axis scale or format
Skip	S	Changes the frequency with which x-axis indicators display

3. If you select the **Y** Scale or **X** Scale menu items, select the menu item to be scaled from these options:

Menu Item	Keystroke	Description
Automatic	A	Automatically scales the graph to fill the screen—default (normal) selection

Manual	**M**	Overrides automatic scaling with scaling you have selected. Other menu options are available from this selection.
Lower	**L**	Enters the lowest number for axis. Values are rounded.
Upper	**U**	Enters the highest number for axis. Values are rounded.
Format	**F**	Selects the formatting type and decimal display from these options:

	Fixed	+/-
	Scientific	Percent
	Currency	Date
	,	Text
	General	Hidden

| Indicator | **I** | Displays or suppresses the magnitude indicator (thousands, millions, etc.). |
| Quit | **Q** | Leaves this menu. |

4. If you choose Skip, you must enter a number to indicate the frequency intervals at which the x-axis scale tick marks will appear. For example, if you enter the number 25, then the 1st, 26th, and 51st range entries will appear. X-axis tick-mark spacing cannot be controlled from the menu.

Important Cues

- Selecting a scale inside the minimum and maximum data points creates a graph that magnifies an area within the data.

- If data points have grossly different magnitudes, you may not be able to see all the data; some ranges will be too large for the graph, and others will be too small. As an alternative, create multiple graphs, or manually rescale the graph for different data magnitudes.

- If you are comparing graphs, you may find it helpful to manually scale all the graphs the same way, making visual comparisons of size and trends easier.

- In bar graphs, 1-2-3 ensures that zero (the point of origin) always appears on the graph.

■ If y-axis data is greater than 1,000, non-pie graphs automatically convert the numbers to decimals and add the label "Thousands" on the graph's left.

Caution　　You must select Manual for other scale settings to work.

For more information, see **Graph Options Grid** *and Chapter 10.*

Graph Options Color/B&W   /GOC or /GOB

Purpose　　/GOC displays graph data in up to three colors on black if you have a color monitor; print the saved graph in color if supported by your printer.

/GOB displays graph data on a single-color screen (white, amber, or green on black) and prints as displayed.

Reminders　　*Review these points:*

● The default setting assumes that color-capable equipment is not in use.

● Understand that the color assignment for the A through F data series is as follows:

Option	*Color*
A and D	White
B and E	Red
C and F	Blue

Procedures　　*To set the color option:*

1. Type /goc

To restore the B&W option:

1. Type /gob

***Important
Cues***

▶ If you want to see color displayed for a graph with only one data series, specify the B, C, E, or F options to indicate the range. (The pie graph is the only type for which its single, permitted data series must be put in under the A option.)

▶ If you want to view the graph screen display in color but cannot print in color, restore the B&W option before executing /Graph Save.

Caution

In the default B&W setting, the bar and stacked-bar graphs differentiate among data series by displaying slant lines that vary in angle and spacing. If you save a graph in color but print on a noncolor printer, all bars will be solid black, and any corresponding legends will be black. Necessary differentiation among data series will be lost.

For more information, see Chapters 10 and 11.

Graph Options Data-Labels /GOD

Purpose

Labels graph points from data contained in cells.

Graph labels can be numeric values that enhance the graph's accuracy, or text labels that describe specific graph points.

Reminders

• First create the graph. Then view the graph and note future label locations that will correspond to the data they represent. Figure G.7 shows three ranges: the X range, the A range, and A-range labels.

• Enter labels in an order corresponding to the order of the data-entry points they describe. Move to the first cell of the label range—C11 in figure G.7.

• Figure G.8 shows the resulting graph with labels over data points. Note that you do not have to enter a label for every data point.

Fig. G.7

Using X and A ranges to plan the A-range labels.

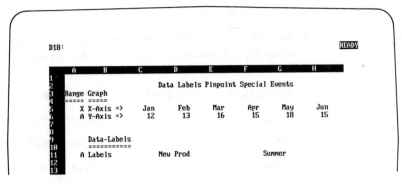

Fig. G.8

The resulting graph with labels over data points.

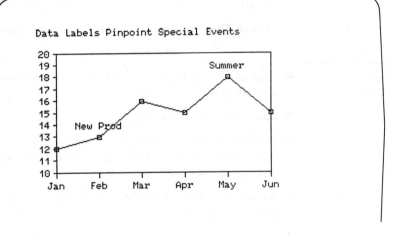

Procedures   *To label graph points using labels or values contained in cells, follow these steps:*

1. Type /god

2. Select the data range for labels to be attached:

Menu Item	Description
A through **F**	Enters the range to be labeled
Quit	Returns to worksheet

3. Specify the range to become labels: enter the range address, highlight the range, or use its range name if one exists. If a range has already been specified, press Esc to erase the range, or press Enter to accept that range as the new range.

4. Press Enter to accept the range of labels.

5. Select the data label location relative to the corresponding data points from the following options. (Note that in figure G.8 the **Above** option has been selected.)

Menu Item	*Keystroke*	*Description*
Center	**C**	Centers a label on a data point
Left	**L**	Aligns a label left of a data point
Above	**A**	Aligns a label above a data point
Right	**R**	Aligns a label right of a data point
Below	**B**	Aligns a label below a data point

6. Choose **Quit**, or return to Step 2 to enter more data labels.

Important Cues

■ Data labels can be values or text. If you use text as data labels, keep the text short to avoid clutter.

■ Data labels do not work with pie graphs.

■ Position "floating" labels anywhere on a graph by associating a set of data labels with data that will be plotted on the graph. To create floating labels, follow these steps:

1. Set up two ranges that have the same number of cell locations and data points on the graph.

2. In one range, enter floating labels in the left-to-right order in which you want them to appear in the graph.

3. In the other range, enter the elevation of the y-axis labels. If the floating labels are to be positioned exactly where you want them, the cells in the elevation and label ranges must parallel actual data points in the x-axis and y-axis.

4. Use **/Graph F** to enter the elevations for the F data range.

5. Use **/Graph Options Data-Labels F** to specify the label range, and press Enter.

6. Press Enter and select **Center** to center the labels on the data points.

7. To keep the F range data from plotting, Use **/Graph Options Format F Neither** (invisible).

For more information, see Chapter 10.

Graph Name   /GN

Purpose   Stores graph settings for later use with the same worksheet.

Because 1-2-3 allows only one graph to be active at a time, use /Graph Name to name graphs and store their settings with the corresponding worksheets. To reproduce a stored graph, recall the graph and graph settings by name.

Reminder   You must create a graph that you can view before you can name it.

Procedures   1. Type /gn

2. Select the activity to name the file from these options:

Menu Item	Keystrokes	Description
Use	U	Retrieves previous graph settings with a saved graph name.
Create	C	Creates a graph name of up to 15 characters for the currently defined graph. Make sure that no graph currently has the same name, because identical names will overwrite graph contents. You are not given a chance to cancel the entry.
Delete	D	Removes the settings and name for the graph name chosen from the menu. Be sure that you have the correct name; you are not given the option to cancel.
Reset	R	Erases all graph names and their settings. You are not given a chance to cancel this command; however, if you have saved your worksheet, you can return to it.

3. Enter the name to create, or choose the name of the graph to be erased. Either type the name or select the name from the menu.

4. Press Enter.

Important Cues

- Using /Graph Name is the only way to store and recall graphs for later use with the same worksheet. /Graph Save saves graphs as .PIC files, which you can later print with PrintGraph.

- Graphs recalled by /Graph Name Use reflect changed data within the graph ranges.

- Create a slide-show effect by naming several graphs and recalling them in succession with a macro that controls /Graph Name Use.

- Remember that graph names can be up to 15 characters in length.

Cautions

▶ You can recall graphs in later work sessions only if you have first saved the graph settings with /Graph Name Create and then saved the worksheet with /File Save. Even in the same work session, you cannot return to a previous graph unless you have saved the graph settings with /Graph Name Create.

Respect the power of /Graph Name Reset. It deletes not only all graph names in the current worksheet, but also all graph parameters. The graph has no "Yes/No" confirmation step; once you press the R for Reset, all graphs are gone.

*For more information, see **File Save**, **File Retrieve**, and Chapter 10.*

PrintGraph Commands

Purpose   Prints graphs that have been saved from the worksheet with /Graph Save. PrintGraph is a supplemental 1-2-3 utility available through the Lotus Access System menu or by typing *pgraph* at the DOS prompt.

PrintGraph Menu Map

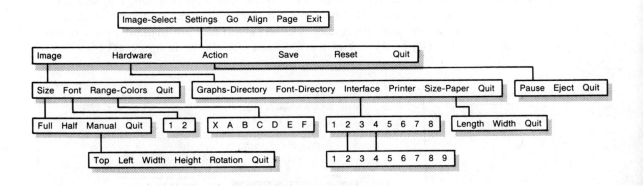

PrintGraph Image-Select   PI

Purpose   Selects .PIC (graph) files to be printed or viewed. Use **PrintGraph Image-**Select to select multiple files that will be printed in sequence.

Reminders   • Use the worksheet to create and save a graph. When you save the graph and its settings to disk from the worksheet, the file name will have a .PIC extension. (For more information on creating and saving graphs, see the Graph section.)

                 • Remember that you can use **PrintGraph Image-Select** to view graphs from within PrintGraph, but you cannot change graphs in PrintGraph. Use PrintGraph only to print previously saved graphs.

                 • Use **PrintGraph Settings Hardware Graphs-Directory** to access the directory in which the .PIC files are located.

Procedures   1. Select **PrintGraph Image-Select** from PrintGraph's menu. You will see a list of the current directory's .PIC files with their respective sizes and creation dates. Previously selected graph files are marked with a number sign (#) to the left of the file names, as shown in figure PG.1.

Fig. PG.1

PrintGraph's list of .PIC files.

```
  Copyright 1986 Lotus Development Corp. All Rights Reserved. Release 2.01  POINT

  Select graphs for output


    PICTURE   DATE     TIME    SIZE
  ----------------------------------        [SPACE] turns mark on and off
  # BILLINGS  08-04-87  15:59    1478       [RETURN] selects marked pictures
    DEXTEMP   08-04-87  16:00    1478       [ESCAPE] exits, ignoring changes
    FIGG4     07-28-87  17:45    9759       [HOME] goes to beginning of list
  # GRWTHLN   08-04-87  16:00    1478       [END] goes to end of list
    INVESTCM  08-04-87  16:00    1478       [UP] and [DOWN] move cursor
    RATIOS    08-04-87  16:01    1478          List will scroll if cursor
    SURVEY    08-04-87  16:01    1478          moved beyond top or bottom
                                            [GRAPH] displays selected picture
```

2. Use ↓ and ↑ to highlight the graph file names. To mark a graph to be printed, highlight the graph and then press the space bar. Selected files will be marked with #. Remove # markings by highlighting the graph file name and again pressing the space bar.

3. To preview the graph on-screen, highlight the file name and press F10 (Graph). Press any key to return to the Image-Select menu.

4. Press Enter to return to the PrintGraph menu. The graphs marked with # will print when you select Go.

5. The selected graph file names will appear on the left side of PrintGraph's main screen. Graphs print in the order selected.

Important Cues

■ If you preview a graph on-screen, it will not look the same as the printed graph or the graph viewed from within the worksheet. PrintGraph's preview graphs use BLOCK1 characters and do not have the same scaling as printed graphs. This preview function serves only as a reminder of which graph belongs to which file name.

■ Previewing graphs from PrintGraph is possible only if you have hardware capable of graphics and those capabilities are installed for 1-2-3.

---

*For more information, see **Graph Save** and **Chapter 11**.*

PrintGraph Settings Image Size PSIS

Purpose

Controls the location of the graph on the printed page, including the graph's size and its rotation.

The Full or Half settings automatically control graph location and rotation.

Reminders

● Remember that settings selected from PrintGraph Settings Image Size control the printed appearance of graphs selected with Image-Select.

● If you want to print more than one graph per page, draw a thumbnail sketch of how the graphs should be arranged on the page and what their size and rotation should be.

Procedures

1. Select **SIS** from PrintGraph's menu.

2. Select the location/rotation of the graph(s) to be printed from these options:

Menu Item	*Keystroke*	*Description*
Full	**F**	Prints large graphs on 8 1/2-by-11-inch paper. Automatically sets rotation to 90 degrees to position the bottom of the graph on the paper's right edge.
Half	**H**	Prints half-sized graphs to fit two graphs per page. Rotation is automatically set to 0 degrees to position the graph upright.
Manual	**M**	Manually sets graph proportions, locations, and rotation.

3. If in Step 2 you selected **Full** or **Half**, skip to Step 5.

4. If in Step 2 you selected **Manual**, enter the proportions, location, and rotation for your graph from these options:

Menu Item	*Keystroke*	*Description*
Top	**T**	Sets the margin in inches at the paper's top.
Left	**L**	Sets the margin between the paper's left edge and the graph.
Width	**W**	Sets the distance across the graph, measured across the direction of the paper feed.
Height	**H**	Sets the graph's height, measured along the direction of the paper feed.
Rotation	**R**	Sets counterclockwise the degrees of rotation. 90 degrees puts the bottom of the graph on the paper's right edge.

5. Press Esc to return to the **Settings Image** menu.

- To print additional graphs on a single page, roll the paper backward to align the paper's serrations with the top of the printer's strike plate. Select **Align** to reset the top of form. Use **Settings Image Size Manual** to adjust graph locations, sizes, and rotations so that graphs will not overlap.

- Any changes to the graph's location, size, or rotation will override any **Full** or **Half** selections you may have made and will shift **Settings Image Size** to **Manual**.

- If you selected **Full** or **Half**, the graph will print automatically with the same proportions as the on-screen graph (a ratio of 1.385 along the x-axis to 1 along the y-axis). If you manually set graph size, you can change these proportions. To maintain on-screen proportions, divide the desired x-axis length by 1.385 to get the appropriate y-axis setting.

- To rotate the graph and maintain on-screen proportions, use the **Height** or **Width** entry-area options to enter the x- and y-axis lengths as calculated in the previous Cue. The options are:

Menu Item	*Rotation*	*Enter Length of*
Height	0	Graph's y-axis
Width		Graph's x-axis
Height	90	Graph's x-axis
Width		Graph's y-axis
Height	180	Graph's y-axis
Width		Graph's x-axis
Height	270	Graph's x-axis
Width		Graph's y-axis

Caution

Graphs rotated at angles other than right angles will be distorted.

For more information, see Chapter 11.

PrintGraph Settings Image Font   PSIF

Purpose

Determines what fonts (print styles) are used for alphanumeric characters in a printed graph. With this command, you can use one font for the title and another for legends, other titles, and scale numbers.

Procedures

1. Select PrintGraph from the 1-2-3 Access System, or type *pgraph* at the DOS prompt. The PrintGraph utility must be in the default disk and directory. The first PrintGraph menu should appear.

2. On this menu see whether the path to the Fonts Directory under HARDWARE SETUP is accurate. If it is not, select Settings Hardware Fonts-Directory to specify the directory in which the .FNT (font) files are located. Press Enter and then Esc to return to the preceding menu selected by Settings.

3. Observe whether the default setting for font 1 and font 2 is BLOCK1. If you do not want to alter the default setting, proceed no further with this command. If you want to change one or both fonts, continue with the following steps.

4. Select Image Font.

5. Choose one of the following:

Menu Item	Description
1	Specifies print style for the top center title
2	Specifies print style for other titles and legends

The screen displays the following list of font options:

```
# BLOCK1
  BOLD
  FORUM
  ITALIC1
  ITALIC2
  LOTUS
  ROMAN1
  ROMAN2
  SCRIPT1
  SCRIPT2
```

The BLOCK1 default setting is preceded by the # marker and is highlighted. (The marker is not visible if you elect to specify font 2 before you choose font 1. See the Cues section.)

A number after a font name is an indication of print darkness. A font ending with 2 has darker print than a font ending with 1. Darker fonts are more evident on high-resolution printers and plotters.

6. To choose a different font, use the down arrow, up arrow, Home, or End keys to point to the font you want.

7. Press the space bar to move the # maker to the desired font. Note that at this point the space bar is a toggle: pressing the space bar repeatedly turns the marker on and off.

8. Press Enter to select the font, or press the Escape key if you want 1-2-3 to ignore your action and to exit from the font menu.

9. Repeat Steps 5 through 8 if you want to select another font.

Important Cues

■ If you first select menu item **1** in Step 5, the font selection you make affects both font 1 and font 2. You can, however, select menu item **2** before you choose **1**. Selecting menu item **2** lets you make font 2 different from font 1. To choose font **2**, simply move the pointer to the desired font and press Enter. Once you have altered font 2, you can make a change to font 1 that will have no affect on font 2 until you end the PrintGraph session or unless you use **Reset** to replace current, unsaved settings with the default settings stored in the PGRAPH.CNF file.

■ For best results with a dot-matrix printer, use the BLOCK fonts and avoid the ITALIC and SCRIPT fonts. If you have a high-density dot-matrix printer, you should be able to use the BOLD, FORUM, and ROMAN fonts with good results.

■ The status screen in the lower portion of the screen should show the selected fonts.

■ Use **PrintGraph Settings Save** to make the **PrintGraph Settings** specifications the default in the PGRAPH.CNF file.

Cautions

▶ If you have a two floppy disk system, do not remove from the system the disk containing the font files while you are using the PrintGraph program.

▶ You cannot specify print style unless the directory that stores the font instructions has been correctly specified.

PrintGraph Settings Image Range-Colors   PSIR

Purpose   Assigns available colors to specified graph ranges for printing.

Reminder   Before you can use Range-Colors, you must select a printer or plotter with PrintGraph Settings Hardware Printer.

Procedures   1. Select PrintGraph from the 1-2-3 Access System menu.

2. Select Settings.

3. If you have not yet designated a printer or plotter, select Hardware Printer. After you make your selection and press Esc, proceed to choose Image Range-Colors.

   Or, if you have already designated a printer or plotter, select Image Range-Colors. The Range Colors menu displays the colors available on your system. Ranges X and A through F will display only black if your system cannot print in color. If your system can print in color, use the right- and left-arrow keys and the Enter key to choose a range and its color.

   The color of range X is the color of the graph itself, including the grid, scale numbers, and x- and y-axis labels. The color for each range from A through F is for each graphed data series and corresponding legend.

4. After you have assigned a color to one range, select another range and assign it a different color. Repeat this process until you have assigned a unique color to each range.

5. Select Quit or press Esc to leave the Range Colors menu.

Caution   Before you can specify range colors, you must have a color-graphics printer or plotter that has been correctly installed. To install your printer or plotter, choose Install from the 1-2-3 Access System menu and follow the instructions for establishing applicable printer or plotter driver sets. Use Settings Hardware Interface and Settings Hardware Printer to specify the current printer or plotter configuration.

PrintGraph Settings Action   **PSA**

Purpose   Causes the printer to pause or stop between graphs.

Procedures   1. Select **PrintGraph** from the 1-2-3 Access System menu.

2. Select **Settings Action**.

3. Select **Pause Yes** to make the printer pause between graphs so that you can choose other print options or change the paper.

   Or select **Eject Yes** to print one graph per page by making the printer advance continous-feed paper automatically to the next page after a graph is printed.

Important Cues

■ If you choose **Pause Yes**, the computer will pause during printing and beep for you to change printer or plotter settings, insert a new sheet of paper, or change plotter pens. To make printing resume, press the space bar.

■ If you elect **Pause No** (the default setting), PrintGraph will print graphs without pausing.

■ If you choose **Eject No**, PrintGraph will print a second graph on a page if the page is long enough. If the page is not long enough, PrintGraph advances the paper to the top of the next page.

■ Use **Settings Hardware Size-Paper** to alter page length.

Cautions

▶ Settings Action Pause affects a printer differently in a network. Printing pauses, but PrintGraph gives no signal at the network device.

▶ Be sure to use Settings Action Pause Yes if your printer does not use continuous-feed paper or have an automatic sheet feeder.

PrintGraph Settings Hardware   PSH

Purpose

Defines for PrintGraph which directories contain graphs and fonts, determines the type(s) of printer(s) to be used and how they connect to the PC, and specifies paper size.

Figure PG.2 shows the PrintGraph menu controlled by **Settings Hardware**. The selections you make from this menu are displayed under the title HARD-WARE SETUP.

Fig. PG.2

The PrintGraph menu showing Settings Hardware.

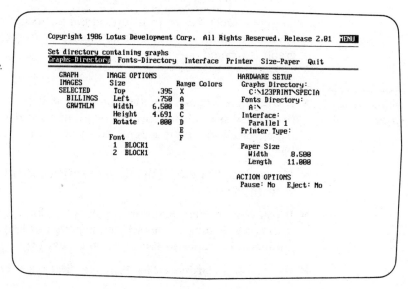

Reminders

- Use 1-2-3's main Install program (described in 1-2-3's Reference Manual) to install the printers and plotters to be used to print or plot graphs. You can install more than one printer and/or plotter at a time. PrintGraph cannot communicate to the printer or plotter until you install the printer or plotter with 1-2-3's main Install program.

- If you are using a printer or plotter connected to a serial port, check the printer's or plotter's manual to find the recommended baud rate (transmission rate).

Procedures   *To change the directory containing the font or graph files, follow these steps:*

1. Select **Settings Hardware** from PrintGraph's menu.

2. Select the directory to be changed from these options:

Menu Item	*Keystroke*	*Description*
Graphs-Directory	**G**	Changes directory where .PIC files are located (for example, C:\123\RESULTS).
Fonts-Directory	**F**	Changes directory where font files are located (for example, C:\123).

To change your PC's interface (hardware connection) used to communicate to the printer or plotter, follow these steps:

1. Select **Settings Hardware** from PrintGraph's menu.

2. Select **Interface**.

3. Select the interface that connects your printer or plotter to your PC from these options:

Setting	*Device*
1	First parallel printer (most printers)
2	First serial printer (most plotters)
3	Second parallel printer
4	Second serial printer
5 through 8	DOS devices: LPT1: through LPT4:

4. If you selected a serial interface (options 2 or 4 in Step 3), enter the baud rate (transmission rate). You can find the recommended baud rate in your printer's or plotter's manual.

To select which printer or plotter installation to use, follow these steps:

1. Select **Settings Hardware** from PrintGraph's menu.

2. Select **Printer**.

3. Use ↓ and ↑ to highlight the printer or plotter installation option to be selected. Some installation options may be listed more than once. If you use a printer or plotter with duplicate installation options, experiment with the duplicate listings because they offer different print intensities and resolution.

4. To select your installation option, use ↓ and ↑ to highlight the option. Press the space bar to mark your choice with a # sign. To remove the # sign, highlight the choice and press the space bar again.

5. Press Enter to return to the Settings Hardware menu.

To select a different page size, follow these steps:

1. Select Settings Hardware from PrintGraph's menu.

2. Select Size-Paper.

3. Enter separately (in inches) the new paper size for Length and Width.

4. Press Enter to return to the Settings Hardware menu.

5. Use the printer's internal control switches (DIP switches) to change the form-length (paper-length) setting. Your printer's manual will describe these miniature switches and their settings.

Important Cue

If Settings Hardware Printer does not list an installation option for your printer, select a similar but earlier printer model from the same manufacturer. Also check with your printer's dealer and Lotus Development Corporation to obtain disks containing additional hardware installation options.

Caution

1-2-3 expects printers to communicate transmitted data with a certain protocol. Most printers and plotters will already be set to send data with this protocol. The following are PrintGraph's transmission settings:

Data bits	8
Stop bits	1 (2 for 110 baud)
Parity	None

For more information, see Chapter 11.

PrintGraph Go, Align, and Page PG, PA, PP

Purpose   Activates the printing process, specifies the printhead position as the top of the page, and advances the paper one page at a time, respectively.

Procedures   1. Check the status area of the PrintGraph screen to verify that the graphs selected have the correct image options, hardware setup, and action options necessary for the current printing.

2. Make sure that the printer has sufficient paper for the print job.

3. Position the printhead to the desired top-of-page position and make sure that the printer is on-line.

4. Select one or more of the following options:

Menu Item	Keystroke	Description
Go	G	Activates the printing operation.
Align	A	Makes the current printhead position the top-of-form position.
Page	P	Advances paper one page when a key is pressed.

Important Cues
- When you use **PA**, PrintGraph inserts a form feed at the end of every page.
- If you want to change the page length specified when the printer was installed, select Install from the Access System menu.

For more information, see Chapter 11.

Data Commands   /D

A database is an organized collection of information. In 1-2-3, a database is stored in a specific area of rows and columns. Each row of the database is called a *record*. Within a row, each column is a *field*. Each field must have a unique label, called the *field name*, entered at the top of the column. 1-2-3 needs this field name to search for specific information.

The 1-2-3 database commands are found if you choose /**Data** from the main menu. The /**Data** commands enable you to perform three functions: database selection and maintenance, data analysis, and data manipulation. The following map shows you how to access each of these commands.

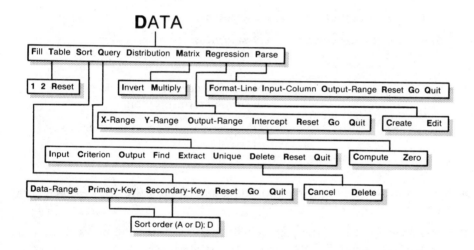

Data Fill   /DF

Purpose   Fills a specified range with a series of equally incremented numbers or dates.

Reminders
- Use /Data Fill to create date or numeric rows or columns, headings for depreciation tables, sensitivity analyses, data tables, or databases.

- Before you issue /DF, move the cell pointer to the upper left corner of the range you want to fill.

Procedures
1. Type /df

2. Define the range to be filled: type the address (such as B23..D46), type a preset range name, or anchor one corner of the range (by typing a period) and move the cell pointer to the opposite corner or opposite end of the range.

3. Press Enter.

4. For the Start value, type the number you want as the beginning number in the filled range, and press Enter. (The default value is 0.)

5. For the Step value, type the positive or negative number by which you want the value to be incremented, and press Enter. (The default value is 1.)

6. Enter a Stop value that is more positive or more negative than the Start value. /DF fills the cells in the range column-by-column from top to bottom and from left to right until the Stop value is encountered or the range is full. (The default value is 8191.)

Important Cues
- If you do not supply a Stop value, 1-2-3 uses the default, which may give you results you don't want. Supply a Stop value if you want 1-2-3 to stop at a particular value before the whole range is filled.

- Use /Data Fill to fill a range of numbers in descending order. Enter a postive or negative Start value and enter a negative Step value. The Stop value must be *less* than the Start value, even if the Stop value is a negative number.

- Formulas or @functions can be used with /Data Fill. For example, to create a range of dates from January 1, 1987, to December 31, 1987, select /**DF**, specify a range (A1..A365), enter the formula @DATE(87,1,1) as the Start value, enter a Step value of 1, and enter the formula @DATE(87,12,31) as the Stop value. Use /**Range Format Date** to display the results in date format.

■ Use /DF to create an index numbering system for database entries. Add blank rows at the end of the database for future entries; insert a column to store the index numbers. Specify this column as the range in the /DF command; enter a Step value of 1. You can then sort the database on any column and return to the original order by sorting on the index column.

■ Use data tables to change the input values in a formula so that you can see how the output changes. If the input values vary by constant amounts, use /**Data Fill** to create an input column or row for the data table.

Cautions

▶ Numbers generated by /**Data Fill** cover previous entries in the cell.

▶ If the Stop value is not large enough, a partial fill occurs. If the Stop value is smaller than the Start value, /**Data Fill** will not even start. Remember that if your increment is negative, the Stop value must be less than the Start value.

For more information, see **Data Table.**

Data Table 1

/DT1

Purpose

Substitutes different values for one variable used in one or many formulas at the top of the data table area.

/DT1 is often used for "what if" or sensitivity analysis.

Reminders

- Remember that /Data Table 1 is used to show how changes in one variable affect the output from one or more formulas.

- Formulas in /DT1 can include @functions.

- If you want to change two variables in a single formula, use /Data Table 2.

- Before executing /DT1, enter data and formulas as though you are solving for a single solution. Figure D.1 shows this in cells B4..C8.

Fig. D.1

Solving for a single solution.

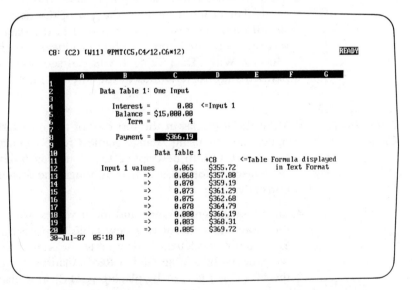

- In the leftmost column of the table, enter the numbers or text that will be used as the replacement for the first variable (Input 1). In the second blank cell in the top row of the data table, type the address of the cell containing the formula. Enter additional formulas to the right on the same row. The upper left corner of the /Data Table 1 area (C11 in fig. D.1) remains blank.

Display the cell addresses of the formulas at the top of the table by using /**R**ange Format **T**ext. You may need to widen the columns if you want to see entire formulas.

Procedures

1. Type /dt1

2. Enter the table range so that it includes the Input 1 values or text in the leftmost column and the formulas in the top row. If a range has been previously specified, press Esc and define the range by typing the address; by typing a range name; or by moving the cell pointer to one corner of the table area, pressing the period (.) key, and moving the cell pointer to the opposite corner.

3. Press Enter.

4. Enter the address for Input 1 by moving the cell pointer to the cell in which the first input values will be substituted. In figure D.1, the values from C12 to C20 will be substituted into C4. Press Enter.

5. 1-2-3 then substitutes an Input 1 value into the designated cell and recalculates each formula at the top of the data table. After each substitution, the results are displayed in the data table. In the figure, the variable input for interest (.080) produces a monthly payment of $366.19. With /**D**ata **T**able **1**, you can see how "sensitive" the monthly payments are to variations in the interest rate.

Important Cues

■ Make the formulas in the top row of the data table area easier to understand by using /**R**ange **N**ame **C**reate to change address locations (such as C4) into descriptive text (such as *Interest*). /**R**ange Format Text displays formulas as text although the formulas still execute correctly.

■ After you designate range and input values, you can change variables in the table and recalculate a new table by pressing the F8 (Table) key. You cannot recalculate a data table the same way you recalculate a worksheet—by setting **G**lobal **R**ecalculation to **A**utomatic, by pressing the F9 (Calc) key, or by placing {CALC} in a macro.

■ If input values vary by a constant amount, create them by using /**D**ata **F**ill.

*For more information, see **Data Fill** and **Chapter 13**.*

Data Table 2   /DT2

Purpose

Substitutes different values for two variables used by one formula.

/DT2 is used often for sensitivity analysis.

Reminders

Review these points:

- /Data Table 2 is used to show how changes in two variables affect the output from one formula.

- Formulas in /Data Table 2 can include @functions.

- If you have to change a single input used by many formulas, use /Data Table 1.

- Before executing /Data Table 2, enter data and formulas as though you were solving for a single solution. Figure D.2 shows this in cells B4..C8.

Fig. D.2

Formulas used to solve one equation.

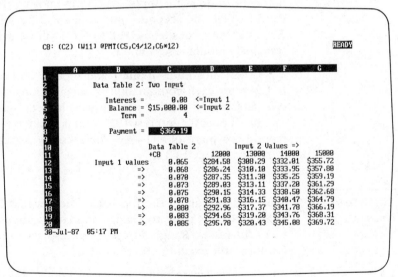

- In the leftmost column of the table, enter the numbers or text that will be used by the first variable, Input 1 (C12..C20 in fig. D.2). In the top row of the table, enter the numbers or text to be used in the second variable, Input 2 (D11..G11). In the blank cell (C11) in the upper left corner of the table, type the address of the cell containing the formula (+C8).

- Make the cell address in the upper left corner of the table visible with /**R**ange Format Text. You may need to widen the columns if you want to see all of the formula.

Procedures

1. Type /dt2

2. Enter the table range so that it includes the Input 1 values in the leftmost column, and the Input 2 values as the top row. If a range has been previously specified, press Esc and define the range by typing the address; by typing an assigned range name; or by moving the cell pointer to one corner of the table area, pressing the period key (.), and moving the cell pointer to the diagonally opposite corner.

3. Press Enter.

4. Enter the address for Input 1 (C4) by moving the cell pointer to the cell in which the first input values will be substituted. In figure D.3, the values from C12 to C20 will be substituted in C4 as the interest amount. Press Enter.

5. Enter the address for Input 2 (C5) by moving the cell pointer to the cell in which the second input values will be substituted. In the example, the values from D11 to G11 will be substituted in C5 as the principal amount. Press Enter.

6. 1-2-3 then substitutes Input 1 and Input 2 and recalculates the formula in C8. After each combination of substitutions, the formula in C8 calculates a new answer and displays it in the grid. In the example, the variable inputs for interest (.075) and balance ($13,000) produce a monthly payment of $314.33. The monthly payment formula (C8) is referenced in cell C11.

Important Cues

- Make the formula in the top left corner easier to understand by using /**R**ange Name Create to change address locations (C4) to descriptive text (*Interest*). /**R**ange Format Text displays formulas as text, but the formulas still execute correctly.

- After you designate range and input values, you can change input values in the input column and row, and recalculate a new table by pressing the F8 (Table) key.

- If input values will be an evenly spaced series of numbers, create them with /**D**ata Fill.

*For more information, see **Data Fill** and Chapter 13.*

Data Sort   /DS

Purpose   Sorts the database in ascending or descending order, according to the entries
               in one or two columns.

Reminders   *Review these points:*

- Sorting can be done on one or two fields (columns). The first sort field
  is called the **Primary-Key**; the second is the **Secondary-Key**. Either key
  can be sorted in ascending or descending order.

- Save a copy of the worksheet with /**File S**ave before sorting. Save to a
  different name to preserve your original file.

- If you have records (rows) in a specific order that you want to return
  to after sorting, insert a column and fill it with index numbers. **Re-sort
  on the index numbers to return to the original order.**

Procedures   1. Type /ds

               2. Highlight the data range to be sorted. It must include every field
                  (column) in the database but does not have to include every record
                  (row). Only records in the specified range will be sorted, however. Do
                  not include the field labels at the top of the database, or the labels will
                  be sorted with the data. Enter the range by typing the address, typing
                  an assigned range name, or anchoring the range at one corner and
                  moving the cell pointer to the opposite corner.

               3. Press Enter.

               4. Move the cell pointer to the column of the database that will be the
                  Primary-Key, and press Enter.

               4. Specify ascending or descending order by entering **A** or **D**.

               5. Select the **Secondary-Key** if you want duplicate copies of the **Primary-
                  Key** sorted. Move the cell pointer to the column of the database that
                  will be the **Secondary-Key**, and press Enter.

               6. Specify ascending or descending order by selecting **A** or **D**.

               7. Select **Go**.

Important Cues

- Select **Quit** to return to READY mode at any time. Select **Reset** to clear previous **Primary-Key**, **Secondary-Key**, and **Data-Range** settings.

- Sort settings are saved with the worksheet. When you enter the **Data-Range**, **Primary-Key**, or **Secondary-Key** options, you can accept the current range setting by pressing Enter.

- During the Install process, you can change the order in which 1-2-3 sorts characters. The three sort precedences are ASCII, Numbers First, and Numbers Last. In ASCII and Numbers First formats, cell contents are sorted as follows:

  > Blank spaces
  > Special characters (!, #, $, etc.)
  > Numeric characters
  > Alpha characters
  > Special compose characters

- In ASCII, uppercase letters are sorted before lowercase; in Numbers First, the case of characters is ignored. Numbers Last is similar to Numbers First except that numeric data is sorted after alpha characters.

Cautions

▶ Do not include blank rows or the data labels at the top of the database when you highlight the **Data-Range**. Blank rows will sort to the top or bottom of the database in ascending or descending order, and the data labels will be sorted into the body of the database.

▶ Formulas in a sorted database may not be accurate because sorting switches rows to new locations. If the addresses do not use absolute and relative addressing correctly, the formulas in sorted records will change. As a rule, use a relative address in a formula when the address refers to a cell in the same row. If the address refers to a cell outside the database, use an absolute address.

▶ If you sort a database without including the full width of records, the sorted portion will be split from the nonsorted portion. Putting the records back together may be nearly impossible. If you saved the worksheet before sorting, you can retrieve the original file.

*For more information, see **Data Fill** and Chapter 13.*

Data Query Input   /DQI

Purpose   Specifies a range of data records to be searched.

Reminders
- You must indicate an input range before you use the Find, Extract, Unique, or Delete options of the /Data Query command.

- The input range can be the entire database or a part of it.

- The input range must include the field names.

Procedures
1. Select /Data Query Input.

2. At the prompt Enter Input range: specify the range of data records you want searched. Either type the range address or move the cell pointer to highlight the range. Be sure to include in the range the field names at the top of the range and any input areas that may be off the screen.

3. If the range specification is acceptable, press Enter.

4. If you want to change the range specification, press Esc to clear the current specification, define or highlight the new range, and press Enter.

5. If you want to proceed to define the criterion range, select Criterion; or if you want to go to READY mode, select Quit to leave the /Data Query command menu.

Important Cue   Redefine the input range if you add one or more rows to the bottom of the range, add one or more columns before or after the range, or delete the first column or the last row or column of the range. A defined input range will be adjusted automatically if you insert or delete rows or columns within the range.

Data Query Criterion   /DQC

Purpose

Specifies which records are to be found in a search.

Reminders

- You must indicate a criterion range before you use the **Find**, **Extract**, **Unique**, or **Delete** options of the /**Data Query** command.

- A criterion range can have as many as 32 fields.

- You do not need to include in the criterion and output ranges all the field names in the database. If you do include all the field names, however, you won't have to alter the criterion range to apply a criterion to a new field.

- The first row of the criterion range must contain field names that *exactly* match the field names of the database.

- The row below the first row of the criterion range contains the search criteria.

- You can use more than one criterion for a search.

- More than one row can contain criteria, but no row in the criterion range should be blank.

- Criteria can be numbers, labels, or formulas. Numbers and labels must be positioned directly below the field name to which they correspond.

- Criteria labels can contain wildcard characters. An asterisk (∗) stands for any group of characters; a question mark (?) represents a single character.

- A tilde (~) before a label excludes that label from a search.

- Criteria can contain logical operators ($<$, $<=$, $>$, $>=$, $<>$).

- You can also use #AND#, #NOT#, or #OR# to create compound logical formulas as criteria.

- Criteria on the same row of the criterion range are treated as if they were linked by #AND# for *every* condition to be met. Criteria on separate rows are treated as if they were linked by #OR# for *any* condition to be met.

Procedures

1. If the worksheet is in READY mode, select /**D**ata **Q**uery **Criterion**. If you have just defined the input range and the /**D**ata **Q**uery command menu is visible, select **Criterion**.

2. At the prompt Enter Criterion range: specify or highlight the range that will contain field names and criteria. The range should contain at least two rows: the first row for field names from the top row of the database you want searched, and the second row for the criteria you specify. Allow two or more rows for criteria if you use them to specify #OR# conditions.

3. If the range specification is acceptable, press Enter.

4. If you want to change the range specification, press Esc to clear the current specification, define or highlight the new range, and press Enter.

Important Cues

- The field names at the top of the criterion range must *exactly* match those of at the top of the database input range. The names can be entered in a different order, but the spelling, upper- and lowercase combinations, and label prefixes must match. The easiest way to create exact criterion range field names is to use /**C**opy.

- Use wildcards in the criteria if you are unsure of spelling or want to find data that may have been misspelled. 1-2-3 will search for only exact matches for the characters in the criterion range.

- You can place the criterion range in the data-entry portion of the worksheet and use a split screen to view the criterion and output ranges simultaneously.

- Database @functions use input and criterion ranges.

Cautions

▶ Including a blank row in the criterion range causes all records to be retrieved (or deleted with /**D**ata **Q**uery **D**elete).

▶ If you alter the number of rows in a defined criterion range, you will need to redefine the range to reflect the change.

Data Query Output   /DQO

Purpose   Assigns a location for the display of records found in a search.

Reminders
- You must indicate an output range before you use the Extract and Unique options of the /Data Query command. The Find and Delete options do not use an output range.

- Like the criterion range, an output range can have as many as 32 fields.

- Locate the output range where it will not overlap the input or criterion ranges. If the output range occupies the same columns as the database or the criterion range, place the output range under these items in the worksheet.

- The first row of the output range must contain field names that match the field names of the input and criterion ranges, but the field names in the output range can be in any order, and the label prefixes and the case of the letters can be different.

- Include in the output range just those field names for which you want a list of records that match criteria.

- You can limit the output range by specifying the size of the (*multiple-row*) range. Or you can ensure that the output range is unlimited in size if you specify the range as the *single* row of field names. That way, the results of the search can be listed in the unlimited area below the field names.

Procedures
1. If the worksheet is in READY mode, select /Data Query Output. If you have just defined the criterion range and the /Data Query command menu is visible, select Output.

2. At the prompt Enter Output range: specify or highlight the range that will contain field names and the results of a search.

3. If the range specification is acceptable, press Enter.

4. If you want to change the range specification, press Esc to clear the current specification, define or highlight the new range, and press Enter.

Caution	If you specify the row of field names as a single-row output range and use /**Data Query Extract**, matching records will be listed below the output range, but any information in the cells in the row-and-column path directly below the output range to the bottom of the worksheet will be erased. If you want to preserve any information in those cells, specify the output range as a multiple-row range. That way, cells below the last row of the output range will be unaffected by any results of a search.

Data Query Find   /DQF

Purpose	Finds records in the database that meet conditions you have set.
	/DQF moves the cell pointer to the first cell of the first record that meets the condition. By pressing ↑ or ↓, you can display previous or succeeding records that meet the criteria. Using /**DQF** can be the best way to access a record in a database quickly.

Reminder	You must define a 1-2-3 database complete with input and criterion ranges.

Procedures	1. Type /dq
	2. Select **Input**.
	3. Move the cell pointer to highlight the input range you want searched. Include in the highlighted range all the field names, records, and fields you want searched. Make sure that you include input areas that may be off the screen. When you have highlighted the correct range, press Enter. If you want to change an existing range, press Esc, highlight a new range, and press Enter.
	4. Select **Criterion**.
	5. Highlight the criterion range. Include only the field names and the rows below the field names that include criteria. Including a blank row in the criterion range causes all records to be retrieved.
	6. Select **Find**.

7. The cell pointer then highlights the first record that meets the criteria. You will hear a beep if no record in the input range meets the criteria. Figure D.3 shows a found record that matches the criteria.

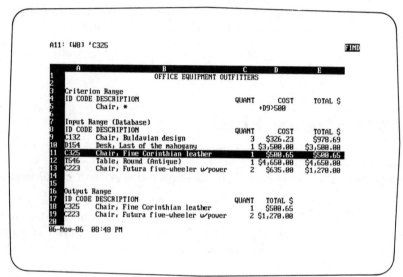

8. Press ↑ or ↓ to find in either direction the next record that meets the criteria. Pressing the Home key or the End key finds in the database the first or last record that meets the criteria.

9. You can edit a record by moving the cell pointer right or left with the arrow keys. When the cell pointer highlights the cell you want to edit, press the F2 (Edit) key. Press Enter when you have finished editing.

10. Return to the /Data Query menu by pressing Enter or Esc when you are not in EDIT mode.

Important Cues

■ After you have entered the /Data Query commands and ranges, you can repeat the operation simply by changing the criteria and pressing the F7 (Query) key.

■ /Data Query Find remembers the last input and criterion range used from the Query menu. You do not have to enter the input and criterion range if they are the same as the previous database command. Check the current ranges by selecting **Input** or **Criterion**; then press Enter to accept the range, or Esc to clear the old range so that you can specify a new one.

■ Use wildcards in the criteria if you are unsure of the spelling or if you want to find data that may have been misspelled. 1-2-3 will find only exact matches for the characters in the criterion range.

■ Before you delete records with /**Data Query Delete**, use /**DQF** to display the records that will be deleted.

Cautions

▶ The field names at the top of the criterion range must match those at the top of the database input range. The names can be entered in a different order, but the spelling and upper- and lowercase combinations must match. The easiest way to create criterion labels is to use /**Copy**.

▶ Make sure that you use /**Range Erase** to erase old criteria from the criterion range. If you enter a space and press Enter to clear a cell, /**Data Query** will try to find a space.

For more information, see Chapter 13.

Data Query Extract   /DQE

Purpose   Copies to a different area of the worksheet any records that meet specified conditions.

Extracts copies of information from a database; matches specific criteria; places output under field names, as shown in figure D.4 starting with row 17.

Fig. D.4

Extracted data in an output range.

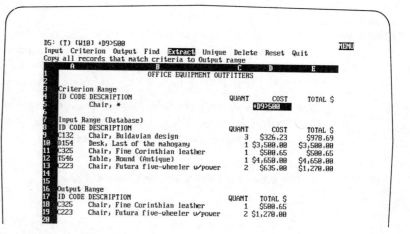

Reminders
- You must define a 1-2-3 database complete with input, output, and criterion ranges. The output range must have field names entered exactly as they appear at the top of each database column.

- Choose an output range in a blank area of the worksheet. You can limit the output range to a specified number of rows, or you can give the output range an unlimited number of rows. Be careful, however, if you choose the "unlimited" method. All cells below the output range are erased, which means that any data below that point will be lost.

Procedures
1. Type /dq

2. Select **Input**.

3. Highlight the database to be used in the search operation. Include in the highlighted range all the field names, records, and fields you want searched. If the existing range is acceptable, press Enter. If you want to

change the existing range, press Esc and highlight a new range. Press Enter after highlighting the input range.

4. Select **C**riterion.

5. Highlight the criterion range. Include only the field names and the rows below the field names that include criteria. Including a blank row causes all records to meet the criteria, and all records will be extracted.

6. Select **O**utput.

7. Highlight the output range. Be sure to highlight the field names as the first row in the output range. Highlight additional rows in the output range depending on whether you want the output range to be limited or unlimited.

8. Select **E**xtract. Records that match the criterion range will be copied to the output range. If there is not enough room in the output range, 1-2-3 will beep, and an error message will appear. To get out of the error, press Esc and create a larger output range, or limit your criteria to a smaller segment of data.

9. Select **Q**uit to return to the worksheet.

Important Cues

■ After entering new criteria in the criterion range, press the F7 (Query) key to repeat the most recent query.

■ **/Data Query Extract** remembers the last input, criterion, and output ranges used from the **Query** menu. You do not have to enter the ranges if they are the same as the previous ranges. Check the current ranges by selecting **Input**, **Criterion**, or **Output**; then press Enter to accept the ranges or Esc to clear the old range so that you can specify a new one.

■ Select the **Reset** command to clear all range settings.

■ Use **/Worksheet Window** to see the input, criterion, and output ranges on one screen. Move the cell pointer between windows by pressing the F6 (Window) key.

■ Use the * and ? wildcards to extract groups of similar records.

■ You can enter the field names in the output range in any order you want; use this feature to reorganize the database field structure or to print selected fields in reports.

■ **/Data Query Unique** works the same way as **/Data Query Extract**, but **/DQU** extracts only unique records that meet the criteria.

Cautions
▶ Field labels in the criterion range must match exactly the field labels in the database.

▶ If you select only the field names as the output range, you are given an unlimited amount of rows for the extracted report, but existing contents below the output field names are erased.

*For more information, see **Data Query Find**, **Data Query Unique**, and Chapter 13.*

Data Query Unique   /DQU

Purpose
Copies to different areas of the worksheet unique records that meet specified conditions.

Reminders
• You must define a 1-2-3 database complete with input, output, and criterion ranges. The output range must have field names entered exactly as they appear at the top of each database column.

• Choose an output range in a blank area of the worksheet. You can limit the output range to a specified number of rows, or you can give the output range an unlimited number of rows. Be careful, however, if you choose the "unlimited" method. All cells below the output range are erased, which means that any data below that point will be lost.

• Make sure that the criteria have been entered correctly in the criterion range.

Procedures
1. Type /dq

2. Select Input.

3. Highlight the database you want to use in the search operation. Include in the highlighted range all the field names, records, and fields you want searched. If the existing range is acceptable, press Enter. If you want to

change the existing range, press Esc and highlight a new range. Press Enter after highlighting the input range.

4. Select **Criterion**.

5. Highlight the criterion range. Include only the field names and the rows below the field names that include criteria. Including a blank row causes all records to meet the criteria, and all records will be retrieved.

6. Select **Output**.

7. Highlight the output range. Highlight the field names as the first row in the output range. You may or may not highlight additional rows in the output range, depending on whether you want the output range to be limited or unlimited.

8. Select **Unique**. Nonduplicate records that match the criterion range will be copied to the output range. If there is not enough room in the output range, 1-2-3 will beep, and an error message will appear. To get out of the error, press Esc and create a larger output range, or limit your criteria to a smaller segment of data.

9. Select **Quit** to return to the worksheet.

Important Cues

■ To extract all records from the database, both duplicate and unique, use **/Data Query Extract**.

■ After entering new criteria in the criterion range or copying new headings into the output range, press the F7 (Query) key to repeat the most recent query.

■ **/Data Query Unique** remembers the last input, criterion, and output ranges used from the **Query** menu. You do not have to enter the ranges if they are the same as the previous ranges. Check the current ranges by selecting **Input**, **Criterion**, or **Output**; then press Enter to accept the ranges, or Esc to clear the old range so that you can specify a new one.

■ Select **Reset** to clear all range settings.

■ Use **/Worksheet Window** to see the input, criterion, and output ranges on one screen. Move the cell pointer between windows with the F6 (Window) key.

■ Make sure that you use **/Range Erase** to remove old criteria. If you enter a space in the criterion range, 1-2-3 will search for records that have a blank space in that field.

Cautions	▶ As with other /Data Query commands, the field names in the criterion range must match the field names in the database.
	▶ If you select only the field names as the output range, you are given an unlimited number of rows for the extracted report, but existing contents below the output field names will be erased.

*For more information, see **Data Query Find**, **Data Query Extract**, and Chapter 13.*

Data Query Delete   /DQD

Purpose	Removes from the input range any records that meet specified conditions.
	Use /DQD to "clean up" your database by removing records that are not current or that have been extracted to another worksheet.

Reminders	• You must define a 1-2-3 database complete with input and criterion ranges.
	• Create a backup file before using /DQD. If data is incorrectly deleted, a copy of the worksheet will be intact.

Procedures	1. Type /dq
	2. Select **Input**.
	3. Highlight the database from which you want to remove records. Include in the highlighted range all the field names, records, and fields you want to delete. If the existing range is acceptable, press Enter. If you want to change the existing range, press Esc and highlight a new range. Press Enter after highlighting the input range.
	4. Select **Criterion**.
	5. Highlight the criterion range.
	6. Select **Delete**.

7. You will be asked whether you want to delete the records. Select **Cancel** to stop the command, or **Delete** to remove the records from the input range.

8. Save the worksheet under a new file name, by using /File Save. Do not save the worksheet to the same file name. Doing so will replace the original database with the database from which records have been deleted.

Important Cues

■ After entering new criteria, press the F7 (Query) key to repeat the most recent query.

■ To check which records will be deleted, select /**Data Query** Find after you have entered the input and criterion ranges. Use ↑ and ↓ to display the records that meet the criteria.

■ Another method of checking the records marked for deletion is to use /**Data Query** Extract to make a copy of the records. Check this copy against the records you want to delete.

■ You do not have to enter the input and criterion ranges if they are the same for the next deletion. Check the current ranges by selecting Input or Criterion; then press Enter to accept the ranges, or Esc to cancel the old range so that you can specify a new one.

■ Create a "rolling" database that stores only current records and removes old records to archive files. Use /DQE to extract old records from the file; save them to another worksheet by using /File Xtract. Then use /**Data Query** Delete to remove the old records from the database file.

Cautions

▶ As with other /**Data Query** commands, the field labels in the criterion range must match the field labels in the database. The labels can appear in a different order, but the spelling and cases must match. The easiest and safest method of creating criterion labels is to use /Copy.

▶ You can inadvertently delete more than you want to with /**Data Query** Delete, particularly if a row in the criterion range is empty when you execute /**DQD**. Make sure that your criterion range is set up correctly before you use this command.

For more information, see **Data Query Find***,* **Data Query Extract***, and Chapter 13.*

Data Distribution   /DD

Purpose

Creates a frequency distribution showing how often specific data occurs in a database.

For example, using data from a local consumer survey, you can have /DD determine how income is distributed. After you set up income brackets as a bin, /DD will show how many peoples' incomes fall within each bin. Figure D.5 shows an example of this distribution. The contents of column E (text values) were entered manually.

Fig. D.5

Example of /Data Distribution.

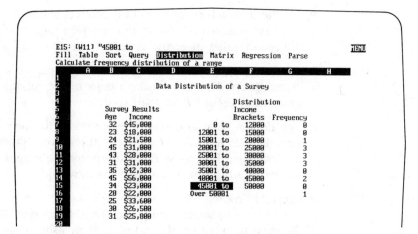

Reminders

- /Data Distribution works only on numeric values.

- Data must be arranged in a column, a row, or a rectangular range. This is called the *value range*.

- You must move the cell pointer to a worksheet portion that has two adjacent blank columns. In the left column, enter the highest value for each entry in the bin range. Enter these *bin values* in ascending order.

Procedures

1. Type /dd

2. Enter the value range, which contains the data being analyzed. If an existing range appears, you can keep it by pressing Enter. To highlight a new range, press Esc and enter a new range by typing the address of the range, typing an assigned range name, or anchoring the cell pointer at the upper left corner of the range and moving the pointer to the

diagonally opposite corner or the opposite end. The value range in the figure is C7..C19.

3. Press Enter.

4. Enter the bin range by typing the range address, typing a preset range name, or anchoring the pointer at the upper left corner of the bin range and moving the pointer to the bottom of the bin range so that all the bin values are highlighted. The bin range in the figure is F7..F15.

5. Press Enter.

6. The frequency distribution will appear in the column to the right of the bin range. In the figure, they appear in G7..G16. Note that the frequency column extends one row beyond the bin range. The last frequency value is the number of values that are greater than the last bin value.

Important Cues

- Use /**D**ata **F**ill to create a bin range with evenly distributed bins.

- You can find distribution patterns of subgroups in your database by first using /**D**ata **Q**uery **E**xtract to create a select database. Use /DD to find distribution in the subgroup.

- You can make data distribution tables easier to read by including a text column at the left of the bin range.

- Use @DCOUNT with /**D**ata **T**able **1** to determine the data distribution for text in a database. Enter the text being counted down the left column of the data table. The input cell is the cell in the criterion range into which you would manually insert text. The @DCOUNT function should be placed in the top row of the data table area.

- Use the /**G**raph commands to create bar and line graphs that display the data distributions.

- Use @DCOUNT if you need to count items that match more than one criterion. (/DD uses the bin as the only criterion.) Insert criteria in the criterion range by using /**D**ata **T**able **1** or /**D**ata **T**able **2**.

Cautions

▶ Text labels and blanks in the values range are evaluated as zero in the value range.

▶ /**D**ata **D**istribution will overwrite any cell contents that previously existed in the frequency column.

For more information, see Chapter 13.

Data Matrix   /DM

Purpose   Multiplies column-and-row matrices of cells.

Inverts columns and rows in square matrices.

Reminder   This is a specialized mathematical command that lets you solve systems of simultaneous linear equations and manipulate the results.

Procedures   *To invert a matrix:*

1. Select /**D**ata **M**atrix.

2. Choose **I**nvert. This lets you invert a nonsingular square matrix of up to 90 rows and columns.

3. Enter the range address or range name of the range you want to invert.

4. Type or highlight an output range to hold the inverted solution matrix. You can indicate or point to only the upper left corner of the output range. You can locate the output range anywhere on the worksheet, including on top of the matrix you are inverting.

5. Press Enter.

To multiply matrices:

1. Select /**D**ata **M**atrix.

2. Choose **M**ultiply. This lets you multiply two rectangular matrices together in accordance with the rules of matrix algebra.

3. Enter the range address or range name of the first range to multiply. The number of columns of the first range must equal the number of rows of the second range. Again, the maximum size of the matrix is 90 rows by 90 columns.

4. Enter the range address or range name of the second range to multiply.

5. Enter an output range to hold the multiplied solution matrix. You can type or point to only the upper left corner of the output range, and then press Enter. The result matrix has the same number of rows as the first matrix, and the same number of columns as the second.

Data Regression   /DR

Purpose

Finds trends in data.

/DR uses multiple-regression analysis to calculate the "best straight line" relating a single dependent Y value to a single independent X value. You can have as many as 16 independent variables for each dependent Y value.

Reminders

- /DR also determines whether one set of values is dependent on another. The measure of this dependency is displayed as R Squared. The closer R Squared is to one, the greater the dependency.

- A completed regression analysis produces the constant and X coefficients so that you can predict new values of Y from a given X. The following equation calculates Y values:

    Y = Constant + Coeff. of X1 * X1 + Coeff. of X2 * X2 + Coeff. of X3 * X3 + . . .

- If there is a single X for each Y, then the formula is the familiar formula for a straight line:

    Y = Constant + Coeff. of X1 * X1

- The Constant term is the location where the best-fit line intersects the y-axis. Figure D.6 shows a worksheet containing sets of X and Y data in the range B5..C10. Plot the X values in C5..C10 against the Y calculated values to see the trend line.

- Enter your sets of X data and Y data in columns that have an equal number of rows. You can have as many rows of data as will fit in memory. The X data must be in matching order with the Y data and must be in adjacent columns. In figure D.6, the X and Y data is in B4..C10.

- The output area must be at least nine rows in length and two columns wider than the number of sets of X values (no less than four columns wide).

Procedures

1. Type /dr

2. Select **X**-Range.

3. Highlight the X range (C5..C10), making sure that the highlighting includes all the rows and columns of X data.

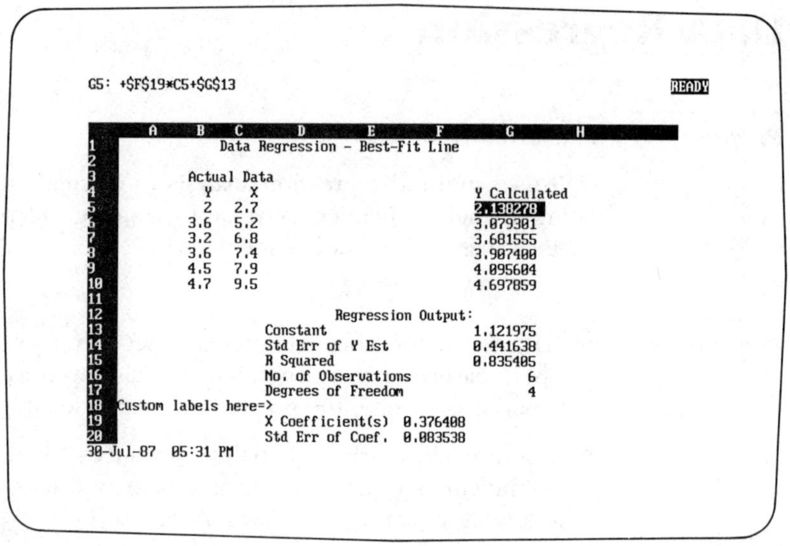

Fig. D.6

The worksheet with single X and Y inputs.

G5: +$F$19*C5+$G$13   READY

```
              A     B     C     D     E     F          G          H
1                         Data Regression - Best-Fit Line
2
3          Actual Data
4            Y     X                              Y Calculated
5            2    2.7                              2.138278
6           3.6   5.2                              3.079301
7           3.2   6.8                              3.681555
8           3.6   7.4                              3.907400
9           4.5   7.9                              4.095604
10          4.7   9.5                              4.697859
11
12                         Regression Output:
13                    Constant              1.121975
14                    Std Err of Y Est      0.441638
15                    R Squared             0.835405
16                    No. of Observations          6
17                    Degrees of Freedom           4
18   Custom labels here=>
19                    X Coefficient(s)  0.376400
20                    Std Err of Coef.  0.083538
   30-Jul-87  05:31 PM
```

4. Select **Y**-Range.

5. Highlight all rows in the Y range (B5..B10).

6. Select **I**ntercept.

7. Select one of the following:

Menu Item	*Keystroke*	*Description*
Compute	**C**	Calculates the best-fit equation; the Y-axis intercept finds its own value
Zero	**Z**	Calculates the best-fit equation but forces the equation to cross the Y-axis at zero when all X values are zero

8. Select **O**utput-Range and enter the cell address of the upper left corner of the output range (D12).

9. Select **G**o to calculate the regression. Figure D.6 shows the ouput in D12..G20.

Important Cues

- You can enter a row of coefficient labels between the Degrees of Freedom row and the X Coefficient(s) rows that will not be overwritten by the output range.

- To create a best-fit straight line from the results of /DR, execute /DR, sort the original X and Y data in ascending order by using X data as the primary sort field (so that the graph will plot correctly), and enter the following formula in the top cell of the calculated Y column:

Ycalc = Xvalue * Coeff. of X1 + Constant

Copy this formula down a column to produce all the calculated Y values for each real X value. Use the /Graph commands to generate an XY graph where the X range for the graph is the real X value. The A graph range is the original Y data, and the B graph range is the calculated Y data.

Caution   /DR produces the warning Cannot Invert Matrix if one set of X values is proportional to another set of X values. They are proportional when one set of X values can be multiplied by a constant to produce the second set of X values.

For more information, see **Graph** *commands and Chapter 13.*

Data Parse   /DP

Purpose   Separates the long labels resulting from /File Import into discrete text and numeric cell entries.

The separated text and numbers are placed in individual cells in a row of an output range.

Reminders   • Import the data with /File Import Text. Each row of text from the file appears as a single cell in a column of labels in the worksheet.

• The long label resulting from /File Import Text may appear to be entries in more than one cell; however, the long label is located in the single cell at the far left.

• Find in the worksheet a clear area to which the parsed data can be copied, and note the cell addresses of the corners. Move the cell pointer to the first cell in the column you want to parse.

- /Data Parse separates the long label by using the rules displayed in the format line. You can edit the format line if you want the data to be separated in a different way.

- If the file you are importing includes numbers surrounded by spaces and text within quotation marks, use /File Import Numbers. This command automatically separates numbers and text in quotation marks into separate cells.

Procedures

1. Type /dp

2. Select Format-Line.

3. Select Create. A format line will be inserted above the current cell pointer. This format line shows 1-2-3's "best guess" at how the data in the cell pointer should be separated.

4. If you want to change the rules displayed by 1-2-3, select Edit from the Format-line menu. Change the format line to include or exclude data, and press Enter.

5. If the imported data is in different formats, such as an uneven number of items or a mixture of field names and numbers, you will need to create additional format lines. Enter these lines at the row where the data format changed. Create additional format lines by selecting Quit and repeating the procedure.

6. Select Input-Column.

7. Highlight the column that contains the data and the format lines. Do not highlight the columns to the right that appear to contain data but do not. Press Enter.

8. Select Output-Range.

9. Move the cell pointer to the upper left corner of the range to receive the parsed data, and press Enter.

10. Select Go.

Important Cues

- Figure D.7 shows two format lines generated automatically by 1-2-3. The first format line is for the field names; the second, for the data. The initial format lines will separate inventory items that have a blank in the name. The asterisk (*) followed by an L shows where 1-2-3 "thinks" that a new field should begin.

Fig. D.7

*Format lines for
/Data Parse.*

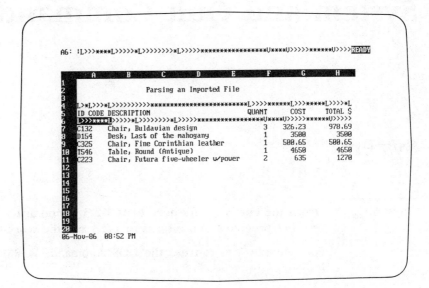

- Use symbols to indicate the first character of a label (L), value (V), date (D), or time (T). You also can choose to skip a character (S), specify additional characters of the same type (>), or add a blank space (*) if the data is longer than the > symbols indicate.

- Editing keys can be used on the format line to change the parsing rules. In addition, you can use ↓, ↑, PgDn, and PgUp keys to scroll the information on-screen. Use this method to see whether the format line has assigned enough space for each piece of data being parsed.

Caution

The output range should be blank. Parsed data covers any information previously in the output range.

---

*For more information, see **File Import** and Chapter 13.*

System and Quit Commands

System   /S

Purpose   Leaves the current worksheet, exits 1-2-3 temporarily, runs DOS commands or other programs, and returns to 1-2-3 and the worksheet.

For example, you can use the DOS commands FORMAT, DIR, COPY, and ERASE.

Reminders
- Be certain that the programs you run from within 1-2-3 can fit in your computer's available memory.
- If you want to run an external DOS command, be sure the command is available in your disk drive or on the Path for a hard disk system.

Procedures
1. Type /s
2. Type the internal DOS commands or program names you want to run.
3. When you have finished running a program, return to DOS.
4. Return to 1-2-3 from the DOS prompt by typing *exit*.

Important Cues
- If COMMAND.COM is not available on disk, the message Cannot invoke DOS appears when you enter **/S**. If this happens, press Esc, insert a disk with the COMMAND.COM file, and retype /s. To return to 1-2-3, you must reinsert the System disk, type *exit*, and press Enter.
- For a complete discussion of the various DOS commands, see *Using PC DOS* or *MS-DOS User's Guide*, 2nd Edition, both published by Que Corporation.

Caution   The operating system file, COMMAND.COM, must be copied onto your 1-2-3 System disk before the /System command will work. On a hard disk, the COMMAND.COM file should be at the root directory (\).

Quit

/Q

Purpose   Leaves 1-2-3 for the current work session and returns to DOS.

Reminder   Make sure that you have saved the current worksheet and graph before exiting 1-2-3.

Procedures 1. Type /q

2. Select **Y** to quit 1-2-3 and return to DOS or the Access System. Any other response will return you to the worksheet.

3. If you started 1-2-3 from the Access System, you will be returned to it. From the Access System menu, choose Exit to leave 1-2-3. If you started 1-2-3 by typing *123*, you will be returned to DOS.

Important Cue   Use COPY or DISKCOPY to create a backup of important files. Be sure to make backup copies regularly, and keep a weekly archival backup copy at a separate location to guard against data loss. In most cases, your computer can be replaced, but your data and worksheets cannot.

Caution   Worksheets that are not saved with /File Save or /File Xtract are lost when you exit 1-2-3.

---

*For more information, see **File Save** and **File Xtract**.*

Installing 1-2-3

Before you run the Install program to install 1-2-3 for your computer system, you need to copy the 1-2-3 disks to your hard disk, if you have one, or to prepare the 1-2-3 disks for use on a two floppy or two microfloppy (PS/2) system. Preparing the disks consists of making backup copies and copying the DOS COMMAND.COM file to the disks you will be using.

The first matter to consider when you prepare to run the Install program is how to tailor 1-2-3 to your particular computer system. There are three different considerations here. First, 1-2-3 has to know what kind of display hardware you have. For example, the way that graphs are displayed on a color monitor is different from the way they are displayed on a single-color monitor (green-on-black, amber-on-black, or gray-on-black).

The second consideration is the printer configuration—for both the text printer and the graphics printer, or plotter. If your text printer is capable of printing graphs or if you have a separate graphics printer or plotter, you will want to configure the printer for 1-2-3 graphics. When you run the Install program, 1-2-3 stores all the installation settings, including the configuration settings for your text and graphics printers, on a file called a driver set. If you have special printing needs and use several printers, you want to configure the printers separately for 1-2-3 by using additional driver sets.

When you know how you want to tailor 1-2-3 for your system, you run the Install program to complete installation.

When you install 1-2-3 on a hard disk system, you have the option of placing the copy-protection information on your hard disk, which makes it easier, but riskier, to start up 1-2-3. This appendix explains the use of the COPYHARD program to install and uninstall the copy-protection information.

Finally, after you have run the Install program and installed 1-2-3 for your system, you will need to prepare data disks for use with 1-2-3.

The 1-2-3 Disks

Lotus delivers 1-2-3 with two different sets of disks: (1) six 5 1\4-inch floppy disks for use on the IBM PC and PC-compatible computers; and (2) four 3 1/2-inch microfloppy disks encased in hard plastic for use on the IBM PS/2 family of computers. The programs contained on the two sets of disks are exactly the same, but the programs are divided among the disks somewhat differently.

The 1-2-3 System disk in both sets of disks contains a hidden copy-protection scheme. Individual files on the System disk can be copied, but you cannot use a "copy" of the System disk to start up the program. When 1-2-3 starts up, the program checks the System disk for the copy-protection scheme. If 1-2-3 can't find the scheme, the program won't run. Lotus provides a Backup System disk in case the System disk is lost or damaged.

Note that in this appendix, for the PS/2 the term *System disk* means *System disk with PrintGraph.*

The 1-2-3 Disks for the IBM PC and PC-Compatible Computers

The 1-2-3 package for the IBM PC and PC-compatibles contains six floppy disks. They are

> System disk
> Backup System disk
> PrintGraph disk
> Utility disk
> Install Library disk
> A View of 1-2-3 disk

The most important of these disks, the System disk, contains all the 1-2-3 operations except one: the commands for printing graphs. Printing graphs requires the use of the separate PrintGraph disk (see Chapter 11).

The Utility disk contains programs for installation and data transfer. With the Install program, you can tailor 1-2-3 to your computer system. The Utility disk also contains a Translate program that you use to transfer data between 1-2-3 and dBASE II, dBASE III, dBASE III Plus, Symphony, Jazz, earlier releases of 1-2-3, and VisiCalc.

The Install Library disk contains the library of drivers that you use with the Install program to set up 1-2-3 for your system. Drivers, briefly, are programs that 1-2-3 uses to control your hardware. For example, different drivers are used to control a color monitor and a black-and-white monitor.

The remaining disk, which contains A View of 1-2-3, presents a brief, on-line demonstration of some of 1-2-3's features. If you are a new user, you should spend a few minutes with this demonstration to become familiar with the program.

Before you can run the Install program to set up 1-2-3 for your system, you must take several steps to prepare your disks. The steps required depend on whether you are going to use 1-2-3 on a computer with a hard disk drive or on a computer with two floppy disk drives. You can now skip to the section "Installing 1-2-3 on a Hard Disk System" or the section "Installing the 1-2-3 Disks for a Two Floppy or a Two Microfloppy Disk System," whichever is appropriate.

The 1-2-3 Disks for the IBM PS/2

The 1-2-3 package for the IBM Personal System/2 family of computers contains four microfloppy disks. They are

System disk with PrintGraph
Backup System disk with PrintGraph
Install disk
View of 1-2-3 with Translate

These four disks contain the same programs as the six floppy disks for use on PCs and PC-compatibles. The programs on the Utility disk and the Install Library disk have been distributed among the System, Install, and View of 1-2-3 disks.

The System disk contains all the 1-2-3 operations, including the commands for printing graphs. You can run 1-2-3 entirely from the System disk. For most PS/2 machines, this is not important because you will probably install 1-2-3 on the hard disk. However, for the Model 30, which may not have a hard disk, this grouping of programs on the System disk helps you avoid annoying disk-swapping.

The Install disk contains the Install program, which you use to tailor 1-2-3 to your computer system. The Install disk also contains the library of drivers that you use with the Install program to set up 1-2-3 for your system. Drivers, briefly, are programs that 1-2-3 uses to control your hardware. For example, different drivers are used to control a color monitor and a black-and-white monitor. This grouping of the Install program and the library of drivers allows you to complete installation from one disk.

The View of 1-2-3 with Translate disk presents a brief, on-line demonstration of some of 1-2-3's features. If you are a new user, you should spend a few minutes with this demonstration to become familiar with the program. This disk also contains the Translate program, which you use to transfer data between 1-2-3 and dBASE II, dBASE III, dBASE III Plus, Symphony, Jazz, earlier releases of 1-2-3, and VisiCalc.

Before you can run the Install program to set up 1-2-3 for your system, you must take several steps to prepare your disks. Because most PS/2 computers have hard disks, the appropriate installation instructions are included in the following section, "Installing 1-2-3 on a Hard Disk System." The steps required to install 1-2-3 for a Model 30, which may have two microfloppy disk drives, are found in the section "Installing the 1-2-3 Disks for a Two Floppy or a Two Microfloppy Disk System."

Copying the 1-2-3 Disks to a Hard Disk

The following steps are required to copy the 1-2-3 disks onto your hard disk so that all the 1-2-3 programs can be started from the hard disk. The instructions in this section are appropriate for the IBM PC, PC-compatibles, and the PS/2.

The following instructions assume that your hard disk is formatted, DOS is installed, and drive C is your default drive.

1. Start your computer; the C> prompt will appear.

2. Create a subdirectory to hold the 1-2-3 files. To create a subdirectory of the current directory (the root directory), use the DOS **Make Directory** command. For example, type *MD \123* to create a subdirectory named 123.

3. Make this subdirectory the current directory. In this case, you type *CD \123*.

4. Starting with the System disk, copy the contents of each 1-2-3 master disk onto the hard disk, following this procedure:

   a. Place, in turn, each master disk in drive A.

   b. Type *copy a:*.*/v* and press Enter. The /v will verify the copy. (DOS recognizes that you want the files copied to the current directory—C:\123.)

   c. When copying is completed, remove the master disk from drive A.

For the IBM PC and PC-compatibles: Do steps 4a through 4c for the PrintGraph disk, the Utility disk, the Install Library disk, and the disk containing A View of 1-2-3.

For the IBM PS/2: Do steps 4a through 4c for the Install disk and the View of 1-2-3 with Translate disk.

Put all the master disks *except* the System disk in a safe place.

Preparing To Install 1-2-3 on a Two Floppy or a Two Microfloppy Disk System

Preparing to install 1-2-3 for a two floppy or a two microfloppy system is a fairly easy procedure and a necessary part of configuring the program to your system. Without this step, the 1-2-3 program will run, but you will not be able to use your printer with 1-2-3 or display graphs on the screen.

If you have a system with two floppy or two microfloppy disk drives, the general procedure for preparing and then using the disks that come with 1-2-3 consists of making backup copies of the 1-2-3 disks and then adding the DOS COMMAND.COM file to the disks you will use to run the 1-2-3 programs. More specifically,

For the IBM PC and PC-compatibles:

1. Make backup copies of the PrintGraph disk, the Utility disk, the Install Library disk, and the disk containing A View of 1-2-3.

2. Add the DOS COMMAND.COM file to the System disk, the Backup System disk, and the copies of the PrintGraph disk, the Utility disk, and the disk containing A View of 1-2-3. (Note: If you use a version of DOS that is 3.2 or higher, COMMAND.COM will not fit on the System or Backup System disk.)

For the IBM PS/2:

1. Make backup copies of the Install disk and the View of 1-2-3 with Translate disk.

2. Add the DOS COMMAND.COM file to the System disk with PrintGraph, the Backup System disk with PrintGraph, and the copies of the Install disk and the View of 1-2-3 with Translate disk.

Making Backup Copies of the 1-2-3 Disks

Lotus provides you with a backup copy of the System disk, but you should make backup copies of the other disks if you work with a two floppy or two microfloppy disk system. You cannot copy the System disk or the Backup

System disk, either one of which must be used to start the program. You frequently will need to use the other 1-2-3 disks as well, however, so it is a good idea to work with backup copies of the master disks and store the masters in a safe place. Should you damage one of the backup disks in any way, you can use the master disk to make a replacement copy.

Before making backup copies, you should become familiar with your computer's disk operating system. For specific explanations of formatting disks and copying files, refer to Que's books *Using PC DOS* or *MS-DOS User's Guide*, 2nd Edition, or check your system's manual. Keep in mind that you can use Release 2 of 1-2-3 with DOS V2.0 or later, but not with DOS V1.0 or V1.1.

Use the following steps to create backup copies of the 1-2-3 disks.

For the IBM PC and PC-compatibles:

1. Format four blank disks, using the DOS FORMAT.COM program.

2. Label the four blank disks as follows:

   Backup Copy: PrintGraph disk
   Backup Copy: Utility disk
   Backup Copy: Install Library disk
   Backup Copy: A View of 1-2-3 disk

3. Copy each 1-2-3 master disk, with the exception of the System disk and the Backup System disk, onto the appropriate formatted blank disk as follows:

   a. With DOS operating, place, in turn, each master 1-2-3 disk in drive A and the formatted blank disk in drive B.

   b. At the A> prompt, type *copy a:*.* b:/v* and press Enter. The /v will verify the copy. (Lotus suggests using the COPY command instead of the DISKCOPY command.)

   c. After all files have been copied from the master disk onto the formatted disk, remove the master disk from drive A and the backup copy from drive B.

   Follow steps 3a through 3c for the PrintGraph Disk, the Utility disk, the Install Library disk, and the disk containing A View of 1-2-3.

For the IBM PS/2:

1. Format two blank disks, using the DOS FORMAT.COM program.

2. Label the two blank disks as follows:

Backup Copy: Install disk

Backup Copy: View of 1-2-3 with Translate disk

3. Copy the Install and the View of 1-2-3 with Translate master disks onto the appropriate formatted blank disk as follows:

   a. With DOS operating, place the master Install disk in drive A and the appropriate formatted blank disk in drive B.

   b. At the A> prompt, type *copy a:*.* b:/v* and press Enter. The /v will verify the copy. (Lotus suggests using the COPY command instead of the DISKCOPY command.)

   c. After all files have been copied from the master disk onto the formatted disk, remove the master disk from drive A and the backup copy from drive B.

   Repeat steps 3a through 3c for the View of 1-2-3 with Translate disk.

Adding COMMAND.COM to the 1-2-3 Disks

For a two floppy or a two microfloppy disk system, Lotus suggests that you copy the COMMAND.COM file from your DOS disk to the System disk and the Backup System disk, and to your copies of the other 1-2-3 disks, except the Install Library disk (the Install disk for PS/2). (Remember that COM-MAND.COM from DOS 3.2 or higher will not fit on the System or Backup System disk.) If you try to exit 1-2-3 when drive A contains a disk that does not hold the COMMAND.COM file, the message Insert disk with COMMAND.COM in drive A and strike any key when ready appears on the screen. By having COMMAND.COM on your 1-2-3 disks, you avoid this problem.

In Release 2.01 of 1-2-3, COMMAND.COM is not required on the Utility disk. You may get an error message indicating insufficient disk space if you attempt to make the copy. If you decide that you want to copy COMMAND.COM onto the Utility disk, first delete an unneeded file, such as the VCWRK.XLT Translate files, from the backup copy of the Utility disk. Then copy COMMAND.COM to the backup.

To copy COMMAND.COM onto each of your 1-2-3 disks, proceed as follows. With the DOS A> prompt on the screen and your DOS disk in drive A:

1. Place the 1-2-3 System disk in drive B. Make sure there is no write-protect tab on the disk.

2. Type the command *copy a:command.com b:/v* and press the Enter key.

3. Remove the disk from drive B.

For the IBM PC and PC-compatibles: Repeat steps 1 through 3 for the Backup System disk and your backup copies of the PrintGraph disk, the Utility disk (unless you have Release 2.01), and the disk containing A View of 1-2-3.

For the IBM PS/2: Repeat steps 1 through 3 for the Backup System disk with PrintGraph and your backup copy of the View of 1-2-3 with Translate disk.

Put all the master disks except the System disk in a safe place.

Installing Driver Programs

Installing driver programs is the next step in tailoring the 1-2-3 disks to your particular system. The drivers are small programs that reside in the driver library on the Install Library disk.

The driver files store information about your computer system, such as information about the display(s), printer(s), and plotter. You can create one or many driver files, depending on your needs. For example, if you want to run 1-2-3 on an IBM Personal Computer that is capable of displaying graphics in color, and also run 1-2-3 on a COMPAQ that displays graphics and text in one color, creating two separate driver files will enable you to run 1-2-3 on either computer whenever you like.

When you make your driver selection, carefully review the options. Whether your system can display graphs and text at the same time and in color depends on a number of factors: the type of monitor(s) you will use; the type of video adapter card(s) (whether it will produce only text or also graphics and color); and the number of colors that are displayed.

Some equipment selections enable you to view text and graphics only at different times on the screen (One Monitor mode). An IBM color monitor with a color/graphics card, for example, will display both graphs and text in color, but not at the same time. On the other hand, some dual-monitor combinations enable you to view color graphs on one screen and text on the other at the same time (Two Monitor mode).

Before you run the Install program, prepare a list of your equipment. When you run Install, you will first need to indicate to 1-2-3 what display hardware you have. For example, a color/graphics card uses graphics control characters to display graphs, but a monochrome adapter displays regular green-on-black text.

Second, you will need to indicate to the program what kind of text printer(s) you have. You can specify more than one printer at installation, and then select the proper one from within 1-2-3.

Third, 1-2-3 will ask you to indicate the graphics printer(s) or plotter(s) you will be using. Again, if you specify several graphics printers during installation, you can later select the appropriate one from within 1-2-3. Note that the same printer can be installed as both the text printer and the graphics printer.

If you do not have a hard disk, keep in mind that multiple drivers take up space on your 1-2-3 disk. If disk space is a problem, keep the list of printers to a minimum, or store your additional driver files on a separate disk. When you want to use another driver, place the system disk containing your usual driver set (123.SET) into drive A: and the disk containing your other drivers into drive B:. At the A> prompt type

Cue:
You can save disk space by storing additional driver sets on a separate disk.

123 B:name

where *name* is the name of the particular driver set you want to use. 1-2-3 will then load onto your computer using the specified driver.

Another installation option you can choose is the sort order, an option that is not affected by the kind of equipment you are using. (Note: to set the sort order, you must select the Advanced Options at the main Installation menu.)

Three data sort options are available:

1. English-like language with numbers first

2. English-like language with numbers last

3. ASCII

The data sort selection regulates whether 1-2-3 sorts database entries beginning with numbers before (selection 1) or after (selection 2) it sorts entries beginning with letters. For example, suppose that you have a database containing inventory codes, some beginning with numbers and some beginning with letters. If you accept the default selection (*numbers first*) for your driver set, 1-2-3 will sort the codes that begin with numbers before those that begin with letters.

The following steps give detailed instructions for installing drivers. Notice that the Install program asks you to provide information for required equipment and any optional equipment you plan to use. The monitor you specify is considered required equipment. If you do not plan to use any optional equipment, you can skip the Install program steps that address optional equipment. For example, if you are not going to use a graphics printer or a plotter, you can skip the 1-2-3 Install program steps for adding these pieces of equipment to the driver set.

Select drivers to run 1-2-3 with your computer system as follows:

Hard Disk Systems

1. Make sure that your current directory is 123 by typing *cd \123* at the DOS C> prompt.

2. Type *install*

3. When the main Install menu appears, select First Time Installation. Then create your driver set by following the step-by-step instructions that appear on your computer screen.

4. If you are creating only one driver set, use the default driver name 123.SET. If you are creating two or more driver sets, you must name each driver. For example, if you have a graphics plotter, you could name your second driver set PLOT.SET.

5. When you exit the Install program, 1-2-3 automatically saves your driver selections for you. If you need to make a change or correction to your existing driver set(s), enter the Install program and select the Change Selected Equipment option; then follow the on-screen instructions.

Two Floppy Disk Systems

1. Insert your Utility disk in drive A, and then type *install*

2. When 1-2-3 prompts you to do so, replace the Utility disk in drive A with the Install Library disk. When the main Install menu appears, select First Time Installation; then create your driver set by following the step-by-step instructions that appear on your screen.

3. If you are creating only one driver set, use the default driver name 123.SET. If you are creating two or more driver sets, you must name each driver. For example, if you have a graphics plotter, you could name your second driver PLOT.SET.

4. Save your driver set(s) on your System, PrintGraph, and A View of 1-2-3 disks by following the on-screen directions. (Note: In Release 2.01, if you try to store additional drivers on your System disk, you may get an error message indicating insufficient disk space. Check your documentation for a way to free up space on the System disk.)

5. If you need to make a change or correction to your existing driver set(s), enter the Install program and select the Change Selected Equipment option; then follow the on-screen instructions.

Two Microfloppy Disk Systems (PS/2 Model 30)

1. Insert your Install disk in drive A, and then type *install*

2. When the main Install menu appears, select First Time Installation; then create your driver set by following the step-by-step instructions that appear on your screen.

3. If you are creating only one driver set, use the default driver name 123.SET. If you are creating two or more driver sets, you must name each driver. For example, if you have a graphics plotter, you could name your second driver PLOT.SET.

4. Save your driver set(s) on your System disk with PrintGraph and the View of 1-2-3 with Translate disk by following the on-screen directions.

5. If you need to make a change or correction to your existing driver set(s), enter the Install program and select the Change Selected Equipment option; then follow the on-screen instructions.

Installing Copy-Protection on the Hard Disk

Normally, you must place the System disk in drive A as a key disk when starting the 1-2-3 program. The System disk is used only to verify that you have a legitimate copy of 1-2-3, and the rest of the 1-2-3 program is read from the hard disk. After 1-2-3 has started up, you can remove the System disk from drive A.

As an alternative, Lotus provides a program (COPYHARD) to write the copy-protection information onto your hard disk. If you use this special program during the Install procedure, you don't have to place the System disk in drive A to start 1-2-3. In fact, you can't use the System disk while the copy protection is installed on the hard disk because the copy protection on the System disk is altered.

If you did not write the copy-protection information onto your hard disk during installation, but later decide to do so, you can access the COPYHARD program by changing to your 123 directory and then typing *copyhard*. You can also access COPYHARD through the Install program; change to the 123 directory, type *install*, and then choose Advanced Options.

To restore the System disk to operation, you must remove the copy-protection information from the hard disk and restore the information onto the System disk. Do this by using the Uninstall option (COPYHARD /U) of the hard disk copy-protect program; change to your 123 directory and type *copyhard /u*. You can also Uninstall COPYHARD by choosing Advanced Options from the Install program.

Think carefully before writing the copy protection onto the hard disk. If something happens to the hard disk, you may lose the copy-protection information.

Do not install the copy protection on your hard disk if you use a tape backup for your hard disk. If you do a file-by-file backup and and then restore the

Warning:
*Do not install copy
protection if you
use tape backup.*

files, you erase all the copy-protection information on the hard disk. If the copy-protection information is lost for any reason, you must use your Backup System disk to run 1-2-3 and seek a replacement for your nonfunctional System disk.

Preparing Data Disks

The final procedure in getting started with 1-2-3 is preparing data disks. For those who are unfamiliar with preparing disks, all disks must be properly formatted using the DOS FORMAT command before they can be used. By using the 1-2-3 /System command, you can access DOS without exiting 1-2-3 (see Chapter 4). Then use the FORMAT command at the DOS system prompt. For more information on how to format disks, see Chris Devoney's *Using PC DOS* or *MS-DOS User's Guide*, 2nd Edition; both books are published by Que Corporation.

Replacing Your 1-2-3 System Disk

As mentioned previously, Lotus provides the Backup System disk in case your master System disk is lost or destroyed. For information on replacing your 1-2-3 System disk, refer to the Customer Assurance Plan that comes with the 1-2-3 disks.

B

Compose Sequences for the Lotus International Character Set

The Lotus International Character Set (LICS) includes characters that you may not find on your keyboard. These special characters include monetary symbols, mathematical symbols and operator signs, and diacritical marks.

To enter a character that is not on your keyboard, you press the Compose key (Alt-F1) and then a series of keystrokes that Lotus calls a *compose sequence*. To create some characters, you can use one of several compose sequences. For example, to enter the character § (the section sign), you press Alt-F1 and then type one of four possible sequences: *SO, so, S0,* or *s0.*

With certain printers, you can even print characters that are not in the Lotus International Character Set. To do this, you use the Compose key with *merge characters.* For example, to create *e* with a ring, follow these steps:

1. Type *e*

2. Press Alt-F1 (Compose)

3. Type *mg**

Although e←* is displayed on the screen, certain printers will print the character correctly, with the ring.

Table B.1 lists the special characters with their LICS codes, a description of each character, and the compose sequence(s) used to create each character.

Although most compose sequences are not order-sensitive, some must be entered in the order shown in the table. (The order-sensitive compose sequences are shown with an asterisk.)

If you use some characters frequently, you can easily create macros to perform the compose sequences for you. You can then store the macros in your macro library and access them as you need them. (See Chapter 14 to learn how to create macros and macro libraries.)

LICS characters can also be generated using the @CHAR function. For example, @CHAR(163) enters the British pound symbol (£) into the worksheet. See Chapter 6 for a complete discussion of the @CHAR function.

LICS Code	Character	Description	Compose Sequence	Fallback Monitor Presentation	Fallback Printer Presentation
193	Á	Uppercase A with acute	A ´	A	A
194	Â	Uppercase A with circumflex	A ^	A	A
195	Ã	Uppercase A with tilde	A ¯	A	A
196	Ä	Uppercase A with umlaut	A "		A
197	Å	Uppercase A with ring	A •		A
198	Æ	Uppercase A with ligature	* A E		AE
199	Ç	Uppercase C with cedilla	C ,		C ⟨BS⟩
200	È	Uppercase E with grave	E `	E	E
201	É	Uppercase E with acute	E ´		E
202	Ê	Uppercase E with circumflex	E ^	E	E
203	Ë	Uppercase E with umlaut	E "	E	E
204	Ì	Uppercase I with grave	I `	I	I
205	Í	Uppercase I with acute	I ´	I	I
206	Î	Uppercase I with circumflex	I ^	I	I
207	Ï	Uppercase I with umlaut	I "	I	I
208	Ð	Uppercase eth (Icelandic)	D –	D	D ⟨BS⟩ –
209	Ñ	Uppercase N with tilde	N ¯		N
210	Ò	Uppercase O with grave	O `	O	O
211	Ó	Uppercase O with acute	O ´	O	O
212	Ô	Uppercase O with circumflex	O ^	O	O
213	Õ	Uppercase O with tilde	O ¯	O	O
214	Ö	Uppercase O with umlaut	O "		O
215	Œ	Uppercase OE diphthong	* O E	O	OE
216	Ø	Uppercase O with slash	O /		O ⟨BS⟩ /
217	Ù	Uppercase U with grave	U `	U	U
218	Ú	Uppercase U with acute	U ´	U	U
219	Û	Uppercase U with circumflex	U ^	U	U
220	Ü	Uppercase U with umlaut	U "		U
221	Ÿ	Uppercase Y with umlaut	Y "	Y	Y
222	Þ	Uppercase thorn (Icelandic)	P –	P	P ⟨BS⟩
223	ß	Lowercase German sharp s	s s		ss
224	à	Lowercase a with grave	a `		a ⟨BS⟩ `
225	á	Lowercase a with acute	a ´		a ⟨BS⟩ ´
226	â	Lowercase a with circumflex	a ^		a ⟨BS⟩ ^
227	ã	Lowercase a with tilde	a ¯	a	a ⟨BS⟩ ¯
228	ä	Lowercase a with umlaut	a "		a ⟨BS⟩ "
229	å	Lowercase a with ring	a •		a
230	æ	Lowercase ae with ligature	a e		ae
231	ç	Lowercase c with cedilla	c ,		c ⟨BS⟩
232	è	Lowercase e with grave	e `		e ⟨BS⟩ `
233	é	Lowercase e with acute	e ´		e ⟨BS⟩ ´
234	ê	Lowercase e with circumflex	e ^		e ⟨BS⟩ ^
235	ë	Lowercase e with umlaut	e "		e ⟨BS⟩ "
236	ì	Lowercase i with grave	i `		i ⟨BS⟩ `
237	í	Lowercase i with acute	i ´		i ⟨BS⟩ ´
238	î	Lowercase i with circumflex	i ^		i ⟨BS⟩ ^
239	ï	Lowercase i with umlaut	i "		i ⟨BS⟩ "
240	ð	Lowercase eth (Icelandic)	d –	d	d ⟨BS⟩ –
241	ñ	Lowercase n with tilde	n ¯		n ⟨BS⟩ ¯
242	ò	Lowercase o with grave	o `		o ⟨BS⟩ `
243	ó	Lowercase o with acute	o ´		o ⟨BS⟩ ´
244	ô	Lowercase o with circumflex	o ^		o ⟨BS⟩ ^
245	õ	Lowercase o with tilde	o ¯	o	o ⟨BS⟩ ¯
246	ö	Lowercase o with umlaut	o "		o ⟨BS⟩ "
247	œ	Lowercase oe with diphthong	* o e	o	oe
248	ø	Lowercase o with slash	o /		o ⟨BS⟩ /
249	ù	Lowercase u with grave	u `		u ⟨BS⟩ `
250	ú	Lowercase u with acute	u ´		u ⟨BS⟩ ´
251	û	Lowercase u with circumflex	u ^		u ⟨BS⟩ ^
252	ü	Lowercase u with umlaut	u "		u ⟨BS⟩ "
253	ÿ	Lowercase y with umlaut	y "		y ⟨BS⟩ "
254	þ	Lowercase thorn (Icelandic)	p –	p	p ⟨BS⟩ –
255					

Do not type •. It indicates that compose sequence is order-sensitive.

LICS Code	Character	Description	Compose Sequence	Fallback Monitor Presentation	Fallback Printer Presentation
129	´	Uppercase acute	* ´ space		
130	ˆ	Uppercase circumflex	* ˆ space		
131	¨	Uppercase umlaut	* " space	"	"
132	˜	Uppercase tilde	* ˜ space		
133					
134					
135					
136					
137					
138					
139					
140					
141					
142					
143					
144	`	Lowercase grave	* space `		
145	´	Lowercase acute	* space ´		
146	ˆ	Lowercase circumflex	* space ˆ		
147	¨	Lowercase umlaut	* space "	"	"
148	˜	Lowercase tilde	space ˜		
149	ı	Lowercase i without dot	i space	i	
150	_	Ordinal indicator	_ space		
151	▲	Begin attribute (display only)	b a		
152	▼	End attribute (display only)	e a		
153	■	Unknown character (display only)			
154	•	Hard space (display only)	space space		
155	←	Merge character (display only)	m g		
156					
157					
158					
159					
160	ƒ	Dutch Guilder	f f		f
161	¡	Inverted exclamation mark	! !		i
162	¢	Cent sign	c¦ C¦ c/ C/		c⟨BS⟩¦
163	£	Pound sign	L= l= L- l-		L⟨BS⟩=
164	"	Low opening double quotes	" ˆ	"	"
165	¥	Yen sign	Y= y= Y- y-		Y⟨BS⟩=
166	Pts	Pesetas sign	* PT pt Pt	Pt	Pt
167	§	Section sign	SO so S0 s0		Sc
168	¤	General currency sign	XO xo X0 x0		O⟨BS⟩X
169	©	Copyright sign	CO co Co c0	c	(c)
170	ª	Feminine Ordinal	a_ A_		a⟨BS⟩_
171	«	Angle quotation mark left	< <		<<
172	Δ	Delta	d d D D		D
173	π	Pi	* PI pi Pi		pi
174	≥	Greater-than-or-equals	* > =		> =
175	÷	Divide sign	: -		/
176	°	Degree sign	ˆ Ø		o(superscripted, if possible)
177	±	Plus/minus sign	+ -		+⟨BS⟩_
178	²	Superscript 2	ˆ 2		2 (superscripted, if possible)
179	³	Superscript 3	ˆ 3	3	3 (superscripted, if possible)
180	„	Low closing double quotes	" v	"	"
181	µ	Micro sign	* / u		u
182	¶	Paragraph sign	¦p ¦P		Pr
183	•	Middle dot	ˆ •		•(superscripted, if possible)
184	™	Trademark sign	* TM Tm tm	T	TM
185	¹	Superscript 1	ˆ 1	1	1 (superscripted, if possible)
186	º	Masculine ordinal	o_ O_		o⟨BS⟩_
187	»	Angle Quotation mark right	> >		>>
188	¼	Fraction one quarter	* 1 4		1/4
189	½	Fraction one half	* 1 2		1/2
190	≤	Less-than-or-equals	* = <		= <
191	¿	Inverted question mark	? ?		?
192	À	Uppercase A with grave	A `	A	A

Do not type *. *It indicates that compose sequence is order-sensitive.*

Index

1-2-3 FUNCTIONS

COMMAND LANGUAGE COMMANDS

A

Using 1-2-3 Just Got Easier—
With 1-2-3 QueCards!

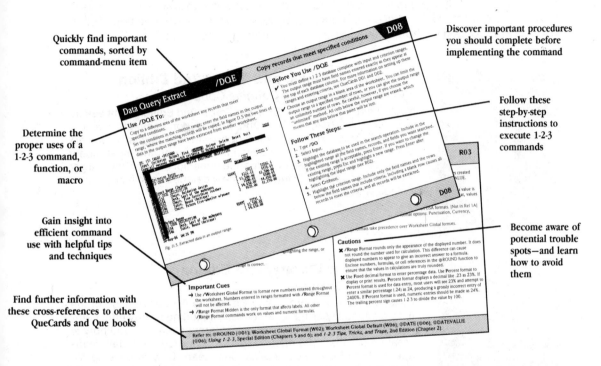

Quickly find important commands, sorted by command-menu item

Discover important procedures you should complete before implementing the command

Determine the proper uses of a 1-2-3 command, function, or macro

Follow these step-by-step instructions to execute 1-2-3 commands

Gain insight into efficient command use with helpful tips and techniques

Become aware of potential trouble spots—and learn how to avoid them

Find further information with these cross-references to other QueCards and Que books

1-2-3 QueCards—the rapid 1-2-3 reference! Each QueCard is a detailed reference to a particular 1-2-3 command, @function, or macro. With QueCards, you can determine instantly how to use a 1-2-3 command—as well as learn helpful hints and tips on avoiding treacherous traps. When you can't remember 1-2-3 commands, you need **1-2-3 Que Cards**!

1-2-3 QueCards—the easy-to-use 1-2-3 reference! QueCards are removable 5″ x 8″ cards, housed in a convenient 3-ring binder. You can use QueCards with the built-in easel or remove the cards and place them next to your computer keyboard. Put hard-to-remember 1-2-3 commands at your fingertips with **1-2-3 QueCards**!

When you want a convenient, comprehensive reference to 1-2-3, you want **1-2-3 QueCards**! Priced at only $21.95, **1-2-3 QueCards** belong next to *your* computer.

Look for **1-2-3 QueCards** at over 7,500 bookstores and computer stores nationwide, or call 1-800-428-5331, ext. 888, to order direct from Que!

Depend on Que
For Your 1-2-3 Solutions!

With Que books, you can start with *Using 1-2-3,* Special Edition, move to *1-2-3 Tips, Tricks, and Traps,* 2nd Edition, step up to *1-2-3 Macro Library,* 2nd Edition, and go on from there. Learn all there is to know about 1-2-3, in an easy-to-follow sequence of clearly written tutorial and reference books. Que backs up the nationwide best-seller, *Using 1-2-3,* Special Edition, with a library of excellent, supporting titles.

1-2-3 Tips, Tricks, and Traps, 2nd Edition
by Dick Andersen and Douglas Cobb

You'll want *1-2-3 Tips, Tricks, and Traps,* 2nd Edition, right beside your copy of *Using 1-2-3,* 2nd Edition, for complete mastery of 1-2-3. This expanded reference, with 500 pages of power-packed tips and tricks, includes information on the most recent enhancements for 1-2-3: expanded memory capability, larger worksheet size, new @functions, new database and macro commands, and much more.

1-2-3 Macro Library, 2nd Edition
by David P. Ewing

Use *1-2-3 Macro Library,* 2nd Edition, to take advantage of the macro capability of 1-2-3, Release 2, including its powerful command language. This easy-to-use reference teaches you how to create more than 100 macros for 1-2-3 spreadsheet, data management, and graphics applications. Learn how to develop file management and print macros, and how to design macros for special applications.

1-2-3 for Business, 2nd Edition
by Douglas Cobb and Leith Anderson

Your copy of *1-2-3 for Business,* 2nd Edition, can make Lotus 1-2-3 the most important management tool you own! This book has been expanded and upgraded to take full advantage of the power of Release 2. A practical business application and model (such as the complete General Ledger) is presented in each chapter, complete with directions on building and using the model. Models can be easily modified or used "as is" for your most immediate needs.

1-2-3 Command Language

by Darien Fenn

1-2-3 Command Language introduces 1-2-3 users to the powerful command language available in Release 2. In teaching you how to program in 1-2-3, this book presents detailed descriptions of the syntax and function of each command and illustrates proper usage of the commands through numerous macro applications. 1-2-3 Command Language helps you learn techniques for developing, testing, debugging, and modifying many complex command language programs.

1-2-3 Business Formula Handbook

by Ron Person

This convenient desktop reference helps you create the formulas you need for building your 1-2-3 models. *1-2-3 Business Formula Handbook* features more than 30 models to show you how to create 1-2-3 formulas for financial analysis, business forecasts, investment analysis, and statistical and survey analyses. Each section explains thoroughly the 1-2-3 model, formulas used, and assumptions. You can easily duplicate each model or modify it for your applications.

Using Lotus HAL

by David Gobel

Lotus HAL, the new companion product for 1-2-3, enables you to use simple words and phrases in place of complicated 1-2-3 commands. *Using Lotus HAL* is the comprehensive guide that shows you how to increase your 1-2-3 productivity with Lotus HAL. This book will teach you easier methods of spreadsheet creation, ways to tailor vocabularies, undocumented Lotus HAL features, shortcuts, and easy-to-create macros. Get the most from 1-2-3 and Lotus HAL with *Using Lotus HAL!*

Using 1-2-3 Workbook and Disk, 2nd Edition

by David P. Ewing

This is a valuable tool for teaching and learning all versions of 1-2-3, including Release 2. This workbook takes students step-by-step through every stage of building a comprehensive 1-2-3 model. Students can advance at their own pace as they learn the basic features and functions of 1-2-3's spreadsheet, database, graphics, and macro capabilities. A bound-in disk contains the workbook models.

More Computer Knowledge from Que

ORDER FROM QUE TODAY

Item	Title	Price	Quantity	Extension
73	1-2-3 QueCards	$21.95		
62	1-2-3 Tips, Tricks, and Traps, 2nd Edition	19.95		
44	1-2-3 Macro Library, 2nd Edition	19.95		
88	1-2-3 For Business, 2nd Edition	19.95		
70	1-2-3 Command Language	19.95		
196	1-2-3 Business Formula Handbook	19.95		
68	dBASE III Plus Handbook, 2nd Edition	21.95		
67	Managing Your Hard Disk	19.95		
56	Using 1-2-3 Workbook and Disk, 2nd Edition	29.95		
94	Using Lotus HAL	19.95		
807	Using PC DOS, 2nd Edition	22.95		
98	Using WordPerfect, 3rd Edition	19.95		

Book Subtotal _____

Shipping & Handling ($2.50 per item) _____

Indiana Residents Add 5% Sales Tax _____

GRAND TOTAL _____

Method of Payment

☐ Check   ☐ VISA   ☐ MasterCard   ☐ American Express

Card Number _____ Exp. Date _____

Cardholder's Name _____

Ship to _____

Address _____

City _____ State _____ ZIP _____

If you can't wait, call **1-800-428-5331** and order TODAY.

All prices subject to change without notice.

Place
Stamp
Here

Que Corporation
P.O. Box 90
Carmel, IN 46032

REGISTRATION CARD

Register your copy of *Using 1-2-3*, Special Edition and receive information about Que's newest products. Complete this registration card and return it to Que Corporation, P.O. Box 90, Carmel, IN 46032.

Name _____ Phone _____

Company _____ Title _____

Address _____

City _____ ST _____ ZIP _____

Please check the appropriate answers:

Where did you buy *Using 1-2-3*, Special Edition?
- ☐ Bookstore (name: _____)
- ☐ Computer store (name: _____)
- ☐ Catalog (name: _____)
- ☐ Direct from Que
- ☐ Other: _____

How many computer books do you buy a year?
- ☐ 1 or less   ☐ 6-10
- ☐ 2-5   ☐ More than 10

How many Que books do you own?
- ☐ 1   ☐ 6-10
- ☐ 2-5   ☐ More than 10

How long have you been using 1-2-3?
- ☐ Less than one year
- ☐ 1-2 years   ☐ 3-5 years

What influenced your purchase of this book? (More than one answer is okay.)
- ☐ Personal recommendation
- ☐ Advertisement   ☐ Que catalog
- ☐ In-store display ☐ Que postcard
- ☐ Price   ☐ Que's reputation

How would you rate the overall content of *Using 1-2-3*, Special Edition?
- ☐ Very good   ☐ Not useful
- ☐ Good   ☐ Poor

How would you rate the *Command Reference Section?*
- ☐ Very good   ☐ Not useful
- ☐ Good   ☐ Poor
COMMENTS: _____

How would you rate the *Troubleshooting Section?*
- ☐ Very good   ☐ Not useful
- ☐ Good   ☐ Poor
COMMENTS: _____

How would you rate the *hands-on practice sessions?*
- ☐ Very good   ☐ Not useful
- ☐ Good   ☐ Poor
COMMENTS: _____

How would you rate the *tear-out command chart?*
- ☐ Very good   ☐ Not useful
- ☐ Good   ☐ Poor
COMMENTS: _____

What do you like *best* about *Using 1-2-3*, Special Edition?

What do you like *least* about *Using 1-2-3*, Special Edition?

How do you use this book?

What other Que products do you own?

What other software do you own?

Please feel free to list any other comments you may have about *Using 1-2-3*, Special Edition.

_____

_____

_____

_____

_____

_____

_____

_____

_____

FOLD HERE

_____

_____

_____

_____

Que Corporation
P.O. Box 90
Carmel, IN 46032

Here's a tiny sample of the kinds of articles you'll read in every issue of *Absolute Reference*:

Discover the incredible power of macros—shortcuts for hundreds of applications and subroutines.

- A macro for formatting text
- Monitoring preset database conditions with a macro
- Three ways to design macro menus
- Building macros with string formulas
- Having fun with the marching macro
- Using the ROWs macro
- Generating a macro for tracking elapsed time

New applications and new solutions—every issue gives you novel ways to harness 1-2-3 and Symphony.

- Creating customized menus for your spreadsheets
- How to use criteria to unlock your spreadsheet program's data management power
- Using spreadsheets to monitor investments
- Improving profits with more effective sales forecasts
- An easy way to calculate year-to-date performance
- Using /**D**ata **F**ill to streamline counting and range filling

Extend your uses—and your command—of spreadsheets.

- Printing spreadsheets sideways can help sell your ideas
- How to add goal-seeking capabilities to your spreadsheet

- Hiding columns to create custom worksheet printouts
- Lay out your spreadsheet for optimum memory management
- Toward an "intelligent" spreadsheet
- A quick way to erase extraneous zeros

Techniques for avoiding pitfalls and repairing the damage when disaster occurs.

- Preventing and trapping errors in your worksheet
- How to create an auditable spreadsheet
- Pinpointing specific errors in your spreadsheets
- Ways to avoid failing formulas
- Catching common debugging and data-entry errors
- Detecting data-entry errors
- Protecting worksheets from accidental (or deliberate) destruction
- Avoiding disaster with the /**S**ystem command

Objective product reviews—we accept *no advertising,* so you can trust our editors' outspoken opinions.

- Metro Desktop Manager
- Freelance Plus
- Informix
- 4Word, InWord, Write-in
- Spreadsheet Analyst
- 101 macros for 1-2-3

Mail this card today for your free evaluation copy or call 1-800-277-7999.

Que Command-Menu Map
for
Lotus® 1-2-3®, Release 2

WHEN IT COMES TO 1-2-3, QUE BOOKS HAVE THE PERFECT SOLUTIONS

PrintGraph Menu Map

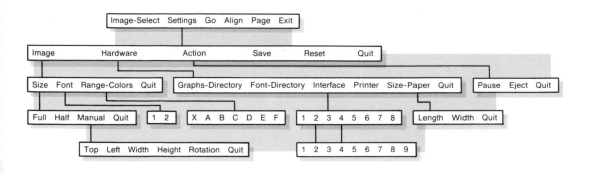

Function Key Operation

Key	Function
Alt-F1 (Compose)	Used with other keys to make International Characters
Alt-F2 (Step)	Shifts 1-2-3 into single-step mode for debugging macros
F1 (Help)	Accesses 1-2-3's on-line help facility
F2 (Edit)	Shifts 1-2-3 into EDIT mode. Allows contents of cells to be altered without retyping entire cell
F3 (Name)	In POINT mode, displays list of range names. Pressed a second time, it switches to full-screen display of range names
F4 (Abs)	Changes relative cell address into absolute or mixed address
F5 (Goto)	Moves cursor to cell coordinates (or range name) provided
F6 (Window)	Moves cursor to other side of split screen
F7 (Query)	Repeats most recent Data Query operation
F8 (Table)	Repeats most recent Data Table operation
F9 (Calc)	Recalculates worksheet
F10 (Graph)	Redraws graph defined by current graph settings

Cursor-Movement Keys

Key	Function
← →	Used to move cursor one column left or right
↑ ↓	Used to position cursor one row up or down
Home	Returns cursor to cell A1. When used with End key (End+Home), positions cursor at active end of worksheet. Also used in EDIT mode to jump to beginning of edit line.
End	When entered before any of the arrow keys, positions cursor in the direction of the arrow key to the cell on the boundary of an empty and filled space. Also used in EDIT mode to jump to end of edit line.
PgUp	Used to move up an entire screen
PgDn	Used to move down an entire screen
Ctrl←	Moves cursor left one screen
Ctrl→	Moves cursor right one screen